TESTIMONIES FOR THE CHURCH

VOLUME THREE

TESTIMONIES
FOR
THE CHURCH

VOLUME THREE

Comprising Testimonies Numbers 21 to 25

by
ELLEN G. WHITE

PACIFIC PRESS® PUBLISHING ASSOCIATION
Nampa, Idaho
Oshawa, Ontario, Canada

Copyright, 1948, by the
Ellen G. White Publications

Printed in United States of America

01 02 03 04 05

CONTENTS

	Page
The Times of Volume Three	3

TESTIMONY 21 (1872)

An Appeal for Burden Bearers	9
Unsanctified Ability	22
Unbalanced Minds	32
Opposing Adventists	36
Intimate Friendship With Worldlings	39
The Cause in New York	48
Relatives in the Church	53
Laborers for God	56
Experience Not Reliable	67
Faithfulness in Home Duties	79
Pride and Vain Thoughts	81
The Work at Battle Creek	85
Peculiar Trials	95
Parables of the Lost	99
The Lost Sheep	99
The Lost Silver	99
The Prodigal Son	100
Labor Among the Churches	104
The Gospel Sower	111
The Wheat and Tares	113
To Wealthy Parents	116

TESTIMONY 22 (1872)

Proper Education	131
Close Confinement at School	135
Physical Decline of the Race	138
Importance of Home Training	141
Physical Labor for Students	148
The Health Reform	161
The Health Institute	165
Danger of Applause	185

Labor for the Erring	186
The Sabbath School	188
Laborers in the Office	190
Love and Duty	195
The Battle Creek Church	197
Missionary Work	202
Effect of Discussions	212
Dangers and Duties of Youth	221
Self-Caring Ministers	227
Inordinate Love of Gain	243

TESTIMONY 23 (1873)

The Laodicean Church	252
Pointed Testimonies in the Church	256
Fighting the Spirit of God	260
Ahab's Case a Warning	262
Achan's Sin and Punishment	263
Duty to Reprove Sin	265
Covetousness Among God's People	269
Confessions Made Too Late	271
Elijah Reproves Ahab	273
The Sacrifice on Mount Carmel	279
Elijah's Humility	287
Elijah in Despondency	288
Moses and Aaron	293
To a Young Minister and His Wife	304
Pioneers in the Cause	311
Daydreaming	329

TESTIMONY 24 (1875)

The Great Rebellion	339
Base Idolatry	339
The Tables of the Law Broken	341
The People Murmur	342
Korah, Dathan, and Abiram	342
Flattery and False Sympathy	345
Character Tested	347

VOL. 3   CONTENTS

   The Rebels Perish 349
   The Rebellion Not Cured 351
   A Lesson for Our Time 353
   Slighted Mercy 355
   Despisers of Reproof 358
Appeal to the Young 362
   Faithful Abraham 368
   Humiliation of Christ 371
Tithes and Offerings 381
Systematic Benevolence 408
Individual Independence 414
   Discussions to Be Avoided 424
   The Authority of the Church 428
Unity in the Church 434
   Self-Confidence a Snare 449
True Refinement in the Ministry 459

TESTIMONY 25 (1875)

Importance of the Work 468
The State of the World 471
The State of the Church 474
Love of the World 477
Presumption 482
Power of Appetite 485
Leadership 492
Calls for Means 510
Duty to the Unfortunate 511
Man's Duty to His Fellow Men 521
   Love and Sympathy at Home 527
   Family Exclusiveness 534
The Sin of Covetousness 544
Industry in the Ministry 551
Parents as Reformers 560
   "Cannot Come Down" 570
Dates of First Publication 575
Scriptural Index 576
General Index 579

THE TIMES OF VOLUME THREE

In 1872, when the first testimony of volume 3 was written, the entire denominational effort of Seventh-day Adventists was in the United States, and largely concentrated in the Central and Northeastern States. There were eighty-six ordained and licensed ministers preaching the message and supervising the work. We owned and operated one publishing house and one small medical institution, both at Battle Creek, Michigan. For a quarter of a century God had led His people as rapidly as they could advance intelligently and in unison, first into a clear understanding of the doctrines taught in the word, then into a sense of their responsibility to publish the message, then to organization of the church, and then to better ways of living. But there were new experiences and great opportunities for advance before the church. The counsels of volume 3 pave the way for these.

Through the preceding twenty-five critical years, Elder James White had been the leader of the new cause. He had started the publishing work, labored tirelessly for church organization, built up the medical work, and had stood at the head in both administrative and editorial lines. He had pioneered the way. With his keen business foresight and his entire devotion to the growing church, he was recognized as *the* leader. This being the case, it was but natural that others should fail to see that they should step in and assume responsibility in the various enterprises of the growing denomination. This volume opens with a discussion of this problem and with an appeal for burden bearers to shoulder the work at the headquarters, relieving James White, who was breaking under the load. Again and again, through the volume, reference is made to the expanding work, the enlarging responsibilities, and the need of younger men to take hold and bear the burdens. The hazards of looking to one man as the great leader were clearly enunciated.

The experiences of this period are akin to that of the eagle teaching its young to fly—first bearing the fledgling upon its back and then leaving it to develop its strength, but with the parent ever near enough to render aid when needed. James White's own failing health, his conviction that others should be stepping in to lift the burdens, and his frequent calls to duty elsewhere, all tended to separate him from the administrative interests at Battle Creek. While Elder and Mrs. White continued to maintain their home midway between the sanitarium and the publishing house in the headquarters city, we find them often in distant parts. In the summers of 1872 and 1873 they spent periods of rest in the mountains of Colorado, and were also for some months in California. A still longer period was spent by them on the West Coast in 1874, at which time Elder White began the publication of the *Signs of the Times*. Thus others were forced to assume responsibilities of leadership at the headquarters, and the work gained strength.

This was a critical period, too, for, during the time when the church was finding its way in the question of leadership and organization, some were inclined to unduly stress individual independence and were in danger of repeating the experience of Korah, Dathan, and Abiram in rebellion against properly constituted authority. Scattered through volume 3 are counsels providing a definite steadying influence through these experiences. Here and there are enumerated in magnificent statements some of the great principles of organization and leadership.

The three-year period of the times of this volume also marked the close of the first decade in the teaching and practice of health reform. Counsel was given to guard against extremes on the one hand and indifference on the other. Again and again, in general articles and personal testimonies, Ellen White pointed to the great principles of temperance and right living, and called the people to advance in their new and helpful health reform experience.

All this was laying the foundation stones for wider expansion. It was in this period that the believers began to get a glimpse of the entire world as the field of labor. It was a staggering view. It presented a challenge. They did not then see the significance of the little church school started in Battle Creek by Goodloe H. Bell, an experienced teacher who had accepted Adventism through his contacts at the sanitarium as a patient. It was in the early summer of 1872 that he began this schoolwork. A little later that year a beginning was made in laying plans for a more advanced school to train workers. In December, as *Testimony* No. 22 reached the hands of our people, they found that it opened with an appeal for such a school and instruction as to how it should be conducted. "Proper Education" is the title of the thirty-page article setting forth the great basic vision on the training of our youth. How could we compass the world with our message unless we had an educated ministry? How could there be an educated ministry unless we had a school? Rising to heed the instruction and meet the challenge set forth so clearly in this volume in pages 131-160, our forefathers established an educational system beginning with Battle Creek College. Its main building was dedicated on January 4, 1875.

Only a few months before this epic occasion, Elder John N. Andrews, one of our leading ministers, was sent to Switzerland to pioneer the heralding of the message in Europe. In the counsels of a few months earlier, Ellen White had written of the need of missionaries "to go to other nations to preach the truth in a guarded, careful manner."—Page 204. With the sailing of Elder Andrews in the autumn of 1874, Seventh-day Adventists began to turn their eyes to other lands.

The timing of the messages of instruction and counsel which have come to us down through the years is interesting. From the year 1859, Seventh-day Adventists had made advancement in assuming their obligations to God as they discerned their stewardship in systematic benevolence; but they did not at the outset perceive the full obligation of the tithe, the tenth of the income. Now in two articles, in the heart of volume 3, the basis of reckoning the tithe obligation was clarified as the messenger of the Lord wrote of a "tenth of the" "income" and of the "nine tenths" which remained. Not until 1879 was this broader concept of systematic benevolence to become a part of denominational policy, but that step which has done so much to assure a steady and much-needed income for a growing work had its roots in these counsels of the two chapters, "Tithes and Offerings" and "Systematic Benevolence," which were published early in 1875. The fuller concept of true stewardship was discerned as we were led to see that the calls for benevolence were designed by God, not merely to raise money, but as a means of developing and perfecting character in the giver.

As might be expected, an aggressive evangelistic program led to conflict with other religious groups, who often challenged us to debate and argument. Ten years earlier Moses Hull, one of our ministers, had lost his way in placing himself on the enemy's ground by such discussions. Now repeated counsels presented guidance as they pointed out the dangers and the small fruitage of such contentious efforts. Volume 3 abounds in such counsels.

So the topics of this volume are varied, ranging from counsel to the wealthy farmer and his uneducated wife to instruction for the minister and the executive. The general articles fill the larger part of this volume. Here and there are found personal messages, published for the benefit of all, because, as Ellen White wrote, so many of them have to do with experiences "which in many respects represent the cases of others."

A few outstanding revelations form the basis of the larger part of this volume. During this period the outstanding visions were less frequent, but more comprehensive. Again and again reference is made to the comprehensive visions of December 10, 1871, and January 3, 1875. The latter is described by James White in a footnote on page 570. The circumstances of the first will be described more fully here: It was at Bordoville, Vermont, that this vision was given. A report of the meeting held at that place, December 9 and 10, was sent to the *Review* by Elder A. C. Bourdeau, in whose house it was held. From it we learn that Mrs. White had labored "especially for the church." At one evening meeting "special testimonies were given to individuals present; and as these were endorsed [by those spoken to], light and freedom broke in." Sunday afternoon two sons of one of the believers and the wife of one of them came to bid Mrs. White good-by. They had been "in a backslidden state." Then Elder Bourdeau gives a vivid picture of what took place:

"At this point, Sister White felt the real burden of their cases, and a special yearning after them for their salvation, and gave them rich instructions. She then kneeled down with them and prayed for them with great earnestness, faith, and tenacity, that they might return unto the Lord. They yielded and prayed, promising to serve the Lord. The Spirit of the Lord drew nearer and nearer. Sister White was free, and soon, unexpectedly to all, she was in vision. She remained in this condition fifteen minutes.

"The news spread, and soon the house was crowded. Sinners trembled, believers wept, and backsliders returned to God. The work was not confined to those present, as we have since learned. Some who had remained at home were powerfully convicted. They saw themselves as they had never done before. The angel of God was shaking the place. The shortness of time, the terrors and nearness of coming judgments and the time of trouble, the worldly-mindedness of the church, their lack of brotherly love, and their state of unreadiness to meet the Lord, were strongly impressed upon the minds of all."—*Review and Herald,* Dec. 26, 1871.

Such were the times of volume 3.

THE TRUSTEES OF THE
ELLEN G. WHITE PUBLICATIONS.

NUMBER TWENTY-ONE

TESTIMONY FOR THE CHURCH

AN APPEAL FOR BURDEN BEARERS

Dear Brethren and Sisters: I feel compelled at this time to fulfill a long-neglected duty.

For years previous to my husband's dangerous and protracted illness he performed more labor than two men should have done in the same time. He saw no time when he could be relieved from the pressure of care and obtain mental and physical rest. Through the testimonies he was warned of his danger. I was shown that he was doing too much brain labor. I will here copy a written testimony, given as far back as August 26, 1855:

"While at Paris, Maine, I was shown that my husband's health was in a critical condition, that his anxiety of mind had been too much for his strength. When the present truth was first published, he put forth great exertion and labored with but little encouragement or help from his brethren. From the first he has taken burdens upon him which were too taxing for his physical strength.

"These burdens, if equally shared, need not have been so wearing. While my husband took much responsibility, some of his brethren in the ministry were not willing to take any. And those who shunned burdens and responsibilities did not realize his burdens, and were not as interested in the advancement of the work and cause of God as they should have been.

My husband felt this lack and laid his shoulder under burdens that were too heavy and which nearly crushed him. As the result of these extra efforts more souls will be saved, but it is these efforts that have told upon his constitution and deprived him of strength. I have been shown that he should in a great measure lay aside his anxiety; God is willing that he should be released from such wearing labor, and that he should spend more time in the study of the Scriptures and in the society of his children, seeking to cultivate their minds.

"I saw that it is not our duty to perplex ourselves with individual trials. Such mental labor endured for others' wrongs should be avoided. My husband can continue to labor with all his energies, as he has done, and as the result go down into the grave, and his labors be lost to the cause of God; or he can now be released, while he has some strength left, and last longer, and his labors be more efficient."

I will now copy from a testimony given in 1859: "In my last vision I was shown that the Lord would have my husband give himself more to the study of the Scriptures, that he may be qualified to labor more effectually in word and doctrine, both in speaking and in writing. I saw that in the past we had exhausted our energies through much anxiety and care to bring the church into a right position. Such wearing labor in various places, bearing the burdens of the church, is not required; for the church should bear their own burdens. Our work is to instruct them in God's word, to urge upon them the necessity of experimental religion, and to define as clearly as possible the correct position in regard to the truth. God would have us raise our voices in the great congregation upon points of present truth which are of vital importance. These should be presented with clearness and with decision, and should also be written out, that the silent messengers may bring them before the people everywhere. A more thorough consecration to the essential work is required on our part; we must be earnest to live in the light of God's countenance. If our minds were less occupied with the trials of the church they would be more free to be exercised upon Bible subjects; and a closer application to Bible truth would accustom the mind to run in that channel, and we would thus be better qualified for the important work devolving upon us.

"I was shown that God did not lay upon us such heavy burdens as we have borne in the past. It is our duty to talk to the church and show them the necessity of working for themselves. They have been carried too much. The reason why we should not be required to take upon ourselves heavy burdens and engage in perplexing labor is that the Lord has work of another character for us to perform. He would not have us exhaust our physical and mental energies, but hold them in reserve, that upon special occasions, whenever help is actually needed, our voices may be heard.

"I saw that important moves would be made, in which our influence would be demanded to lead out; that influences would arise, and errors would occasionally be brought into the church, and that then our influence would be required. But if exhausted by previous labors, we would not possess that calm judgment, discretion, and self-control necessary for the important occasion in which God would have us act a prominent part.

Satan has crippled our efforts by so affecting the church as to call forth from us almost double labor to cut our way through the darkness and unbelief. These efforts to set things in order in the churches have exhausted our strength, and lassitude and debility have followed. I saw that we have a work to do, but the adversary of souls will resist every effort that we attempt to make. The people may be in a state of backsliding, so that God cannot bless them, and this will be disheartening; but we should not be discouraged. We should do our duty in presenting the light, and leave the responsibility with the people."

I will here copy from another testimony, written June 6, 1863: "I was shown that our testimony is still needed in the church, that we should labor to save ourselves trials and cares, and that we should preserve a devotional frame of mind. It is the duty of those in the office to tax their brains more, and of my husband to tax his less. Much time is spent by him upon various matters which confuse and weary his mind, and unfit him for study or for writing, and thus prevent his light from shining in the *Review* as it should.

"My husband's mind should not be crowded and overtaxed. It must have rest, and he must be left free to write and attend to matters which others cannot do. Those engaged in the office could lift from him a great weight of care if they would dedicate themselves to God and feel a deep interest in the work. No selfish feelings should exist among those who labor in the office. It is the work of God in which they are engaged, and they are accountable to Him for their motives and the manner in which this branch of His work is performed. They are required to discipline their minds. Many feel that no blame should be attached to forgetfulness. This is a great mistake. Forgetfulness is sin. It leads to many blunders and to much disorder and many wrongs. Things that should be done ought not to be forgotten. The mind must be tasked; it must be disciplined until it will remember.

"My husband has had much care, and has done many things which others ought to have done, but which he feared to have them do, lest, in their heedlessness, they should make mistakes not easily remedied, and thus involve losses. This has been a great perplexity to his mind. Those who labor in the office should learn. They should study, and practice, and exercise their own brains; for they have this branch of business alone, while my husband has the responsibility of many departments of the work. If a workman makes a failure, he should feel that it rests upon him to repair damages from his own purse, and should not allow the office to suffer loss through his carelessness. He should not cease to bear responsibilities, but should try again, avoiding former mistakes. In this way he will learn to take that care which the word of God ever requires, and then he will do no more than his duty.

"My husband should take time to do those things which his judgment tells him would preserve his health. He has thought that he must throw off the burdens and responsibilities which were upon him, and leave the office, or his mind would become a wreck. I was shown that when the Lord released him from his position, He would give him just as clear evidence of his release as He gave him when He laid the burden of the work upon him. But he has borne too many burdens, and those laboring with him at the office, and also his ministering brethren, have been too willing that he should bear them. They have, as a general thing, stood back from bearing burdens, and have sympathized with those who were murmuring against him, and left him to stand alone while he was bowed down beneath censure, until God has vindicated His own cause. If they had taken their share of the burdens, my husband would have been relieved.

"I saw that God now requires us to take special care of the health He has given us, for our work is not yet done. Our testimony must still be borne, and will have influence. We should preserve our strength to labor in the cause of God when our labor is needed. We should be careful not to take upon ourselves burdens that others can and should bear. We should encourage a cheerful, hopeful, peaceful frame of mind; for our health depends upon our so doing. The work that God requires us to do will not prevent our caring for our health, that we may recover from the effect of overtaxing labor. The more perfect our health, the more perfect will be our labor. When we overtax our strength, and become exhausted, we are liable to take cold, and at such times there is danger of disease assuming a dangerous form. We must not leave the care of ourselves with God, when He has placed that responsibility upon us."

October 25, 1869, while at Adams Center, New York, I was shown that some ministers among us fail to bear all the responsibility that God would have them. This lack throws extra labor upon those who are burden bearers, especially upon my husband. Some ministers fail to move out and venture something in the cause and work of God. Important decisions are to be made; but as mortal man cannot see the end from the beginning, some shrink from venturing and advancing as the providence of God leads. Someone must advance; someone must venture in the fear of God, trusting the result with Him. Those ministers who shun this part of the labor are losing much. They are failing to obtain that experience which God designed they should have to make them strong, efficient men that can be relied upon in any emergency.

Brother A, you shrink from running risks. You are not willing to venture when you cannot see the way perfectly clear. Yet someone must do this very work; someone must walk by faith, or no advance moves will be made, and nothing will be accomplished. A fear that you will make mistakes and mismoves, and then be blamed binds you. You excuse yourself from taking responsibility because you have made some mistakes in the past. But you should move according to your best judgment, trusting the result with God. Someone must do this, and it is a trying position for anyone. One should not bear all this responsibility alone, but with much reflection and earnest prayer, it should be equally shared.

During my husband's affliction, the Lord tested and proved His people to reveal what was in their hearts; and in so doing He showed to them what was undiscovered in themselves that was not according to the Spirit of God. The trying circumstances under which we were placed called out from our brethren that which otherwise would never have been revealed. The Lord proved to His people that the wisdom of man is foolishness, and that unless they possess firm trust and reliance on God, their plans and calculations will prove a failure. We are to learn from all these things. If errors are committed, they should teach and instruct, but not lead to the shunning of burdens and responsibilities. Where much is at stake, and where matters of vital consequence are to be considered, and important questions settled, God's servants should take individual responsibility. They cannot lay off the burden and yet do the will of God. Some ministers are deficient in the qualifications necessary to build up the churches, and they are not willing to wear in the cause of God. They have not a disposition to give themselves wholly to the work, with their interest undivided, their zeal unabated, their patience and perseverance untiring. With these qualifications in lively exercise, the churches would be kept in order, and my husband's labors would not be so heavy. All ministers do not constantly bear in mind that the labor of all must bear the inspection of the judgment, and that every man will be rewarded as his works have been.

Brother A, you have a responsibility to bear in regard to the Health Institute.* You should ponder, you should reflect. Frequently the time that you occupy in reading is the very best time for you to reflect and to study what must be done to set things in order at the Institute and at the office. My husband takes on these burdens because he sees that the work for these institutions must be done by someone. As others will not lead out, he steps into the gap and supplies the deficiency.

God has cautioned and warned my husband in regard to the preservation of his strength. I was shown that he was raised up by the Lord, and that he lives is as a miracle of mercy—not for the purpose of again gathering upon him the burdens under which he once fell, but that the people of God may be benefited by his experience in advancing the general interests of the cause, and in connection with the work the Lord has given me, and the burden He has laid upon me to bear.

Brother A, great care should be exercised by you, especially at Battle Creek. In visiting, your conversation should be upon the most important subjects. Be careful to back up precept by example. This is an important post and will require labor. While you are here, you should take time to ponder the many things which need to be done and which require solemn reflection, careful attention, and most earnest, faithful prayer. You should feel as great an interest in the things relating to

---

*Later known as the Battle Creek Sanitarium.

the cause, to the work at the Health Institute and at the office of publication, as my husband feels; you should feel that the work is yours. You cannot do the work that God has specially qualified my husband to do, neither can he do the work that God has specially qualified you to do. Yet both of you together, united in harmonious labor, you in your office, and my husband in his, can accomplish much.

The work in which we have a common interest is great; and efficient, willing, burden-bearing laborers are few indeed. God will give you strength, my brother, if you will move forward and wait upon Him. He will give my husband and myself strength in our united labor, if we do all to His glory, according to our ability and strength to labor. You should be located where you would have a more favorable opportunity to exercise your gift according to the ability that God has given you. You should lean your whole weight upon God and give Him an opportunity to teach, lead, and impress you. You feel a deep interest in the work and cause of God, and you should look to Him for light and guidance. He will give you light. But, as an ambassador of Christ, you are required to be faithful, to correct wrong in meekness and love, and your efforts will not prove unavailing.

Since my husband has recovered from his feebleness, we have labored earnestly. We have not consulted our own ease or pleasure. We have traveled and labored in camp meetings, and overtaxed our strength, so that it has brought upon us debility, without the advantages of rest. During the year 1870 we attended twelve camp meetings. In a number of these meetings, the burden of labor rested almost wholly upon us. We traveled from Minnesota to Maine, and to Missouri and Kansas.

My husband and I united our efforts to improve the *Health Reformer** and make it an interesting and profitable journal, one that would be desired, not only by our people, but by all classes. This was a severe tax upon him. He also made very important improvements in the *Review* and the

---

*Now called *Good Health*.

Instructor. He accomplished the work which should have been shared by three men. And while all this labor fell upon him in the publishing branch of the work, the business departments at the Health Institute and the Publishing Association required the labor of two men to relieve them of financial embarrassment.

Unfaithful men who had been entrusted with the work at the office and at the Institute, had, through selfishness and a lack of consecration, placed matters in the worst possible condition. There was unsettled business that had to be attended to. My husband stepped into the gap and worked with all his energies. He was wearing. We could see that he was in danger; but we could not see how he could stop, unless the work in the office should cease. Almost every day some new perplexity would arise, some new difficulty caused by the unfaithfulness of the men who had taken charge of the work. His brain was taxed to the utmost. But the worst perplexities are now over, and the work is moving on prosperously.

At the General Conference my husband pleaded to be released from the burdens upon him; but, notwithstanding his pleading, the burden of editing the *Review* and the *Reformer* was placed upon him, with encouragement that men who would take burdens and responsibilities would be encouraged to settle at Battle Creek. But as yet no help has come to lift from him the burdens of the financial work at the office.

My husband is fast wearing. We have attended the four Western camp meetings, and our brethren are urging us to attend the Eastern meetings. But we dare not take additional burdens upon us. When we came from the labor of the Western camp meetings in July, 1871, we found a large amount of business that had been left to accumulate in my husband's absence. We have seen no opportunity for rest yet. My husband must be released from the burdens upon him. There are too many that use his brain instead of using their own. In view of the light which God has been pleased to give us, we plead for you, my brethren, to release my husband. I am not willing to venture the consequences of his going forward and laboring as he has done. He served you faithfully and unselfishly for years, and finally fell under the pressure of the burdens placed upon him. Then his brethren, in whom he had confided, left him. They let him drop into my hands, and forsook him. For nearly two years I was his nurse, his attendant, his physician. I do not wish to pass through the experience a second time. Brethren, will you lift the burdens from us, and allow us to preserve our strength as God would have us, that the cause at large may be benefited by the efforts we may make in His strength? Or will you leave us to become debilitated so that we will become useless to the cause?

The foregoing portion of this appeal was read at the New Hampshire camp meeting, August, 1871.

When we returned from Kansas in the autumn of 1870, Brother B was at home sick with fever. Sister Van Horn, at this very time, was absent from the office in consequence of fever brought upon her by the sudden death of her mother. Brother Smith was also from the office, in Rochester, New York, recovering from a fever. There was a great amount of unfinished work at the office, yet Brother B left his post of duty to gratify his own pleasure. This fact in his experience is a sample of the man. Sacred duties rest lightly upon him.

It was a great breach of the trust reposed in him to pursue the course he did. In what marked contrast with this is the life of Christ, our Pattern! He was the Son of Jehovah, and the Author of our salvation. He labored and suffered for us. He denied Himself, and His whole life was one continued scene of toil and privation. Had He chosen so to do, He could have passed His days in a world of His own creating, in ease and plenty, and claimed for Himself all the pleasures and enjoyment the world could give Him. But He did not consider His own convenience. He lived not to please Himself, but to do good and lavish His blessings upon others.

Brother B was sick with fever. His case was critical. In justice to the cause of God, I feel compelled to state that his sickness was not the result of unwearied devotion to the interests of the office. Imprudent exposure on a trip to Chicago, for his own pleasure, was the cause of his long, tedious, suffering sickness. God did not sustain him in leaving the work, when so many who had filled important positions in the office were absent. At the very time when he should not have excused himself for an hour, he left his post of duty, and God did not sustain him.

There was no period of rest for us, however much we needed it. The *Review,* the *Reformer,* and the *Instructor* must be edited. Many letters had been laid aside until we should return to examine them. Things were in a sad state at the office. Everything needed to be set in order. My husband commenced his labor, and I helped him what I could, but that was but little. He labored unceasingly to straighten out perplexing business matters and to improve the condition of our periodicals. He could not depend upon help from any of his ministering brethren. His head, heart, and hands were full. He was not encouraged by Brethren A and C, when they knew he was standing alone under the burdens at Battle Creek. They did not stay up his hands. They wrote in a most discouraging manner of their poor health, and that they were in such an exhausted condition that they could not be depended on to accomplish any labor. My husband saw that nothing could be hoped for in that direction. Notwithstanding his double labor through the summer, he could not rest. And, irrespective of his weakness, he reined himself up to do the work which others had neglected.

The *Reformer* was about dead. Brother B had urged the extreme positions of Dr. Trall. This had influenced the doctor to come out in the *Reformer* stronger than he otherwise would have done, in discarding milk, sugar, and salt. The position to entirely discontinue the use of these things may be right in its order; but the time had not come to take a general stand upon these points. And those who do take their position, and advocate the entire disuse of milk, butter, and sugar, should have their own tables free from these things. Brother B, even while taking his stand in the *Reformer* with Dr. Trall in regard to the injurious effects of salt, milk, and sugar, did not practice the things he taught. Upon his own table these things were used daily.

Many of our people had lost their interest in the *Reformer,* and letters were daily received with this discouraging request: "Please discontinue my *Reformer.*" Letters were received from the West, where the country is new and fruit scarce, inquiring: "How do the friends of health reform live at Battle Creek? Do they dispense with salt entirely? If so, we cannot at present adopt the health reform. We can get but little fruit, and we have left off the use of meat, tea, coffee, and tobacco; but we must have something to sustain life."

We had spent some time in the West, and knew the scarcity of fruit, and we sympathized with our brethren who were conscientiously seeking to be in harmony with the body of Sabbathkeeping Adventists. They were becoming discouraged, and some were backsliding upon the health reform, fearing that at Battle Creek they were radical and fanatical. We could not raise an interest anywhere in the West to obtain subscribers for the *Health Reformer.* We saw that the writers in the *Reformer* were going away from the people and leaving them behind. If we take positions that conscientious Christians, who are indeed reformers, cannot adopt, how can we expect to benefit that class whom we can reach only from a health standpoint?

We must go no faster than we can take those with us whose consciences and intellects are convinced of the truths we advocate. We must meet the people where they are. Some of us have been many years in arriving at our present position in health reform. It is slow work to obtain a reform in diet. We have powerful appetites to meet; for the world is given to gluttony. If we should allow the people as much time as we have required to come up to the present advanced state in reform, we would be very patient with them, and allow them to advance step by step, as we have done, until their feet are firmly established upon the health reform platform. But we should be very cautious not to advance too fast, lest we be obliged to retrace our steps. In reforms we would better come one step short of the mark than to go one step beyond it. And if there is error at all, let it be on the side next to the people.

Above all things, we should not with our pens advocate positions that we do not put to a practical test in our own families, upon our own tables. This is dissimulation, a species of hypocrisy. In Michigan we can get along better without salt, sugar, and milk than can many who are situated in the Far West or in the far East, where there is a scarcity of fruit. But there are very few families in Battle Creek who do not use these articles upon their tables. We know that a free use of these things is positively injurious to health, and, in many cases, we think that if they were not used at all, a much better state of health would be enjoyed. But at present our burden is not upon these things. The people are so far behind that we see it is all they can bear to have us draw the line upon their injurious indulgences and stimulating narcotics. We bear positive testimony against tobacco, spirituous liquors, snuff, tea, coffee, flesh meats, butter, spices, rich cakes, mince pies, a large amount of salt, and all exciting substances used as articles of food.

If we come to persons who have not been enlightened in regard to health reform, and present our strongest positions at first, there is danger of their becoming discouraged as they see how much they have to give up, so that they will make no effort to reform. We must lead the people along patiently and gradually, remembering the hole of the pit whence we were digged.

UNSANCTIFIED ABILITY

I have been shown that Brother B has serious defects in his character, which disqualify him for being closely connected with the work of God where important responsibilities are to be borne. He has sufficient mental ability, but the heart, the affections, have not been sanctified to God; therefore he cannot be relied upon as qualified for so important a work as the publication of the truth in the office at Battle Creek. A mistake or a neglect of duty in this work affects the cause of God at large. Brother B has not seen his failings, therefore he does not reform.

It is by small things that our characters are formed to habits of integrity. You, my brother, have been disposed to undervalue the importance of the little incidents of everyday life. This is a great mistake. Nothing with which we have to do is really small. Every action is of some account, either on the side of right or on the side of wrong. It is only by exercising principle in small transactions of ordinary life that we are tested and our characters formed. In the varied circumstances of life we are tested and proved, and thereby we acquire power to stand the greater and more important tests that we are called to endure, and are qualified to still more important positions. The mind must be trained through daily tests to habits of fidelity, to a sense of the claims of right and duty above inclination and pleasure. Minds thus trained do not waver between right and wrong, as the reed trembles in the wind; but as soon as matters come before them, they discern at once that principle is involved, and they instinctively choose the right without long debating the matter. They are loyal because they have trained themselves in habits of faithfulness and truth. By being faithful in that which is least, they acquire strength, and it becomes easy for them to be faithful in greater matters.

Brother B's education has not been such as to strengthen

UNSANCTIFIED ABILITY

those high moral qualities that would enable him to stand alone in the strength of God in defense of truth, amid the severest opposition, firm as a rock to principle, true to moral character, unmoved by human praise or censure or rewards, preferring death rather than a violated conscience. Such integrity is needed in the office of publication, where solemn, sacred truths are going forth, upon which the world is to be tested.

The work of God calls for men of high moral powers to engage in its promulgation. Men are wanted whose hearts are nerved with holy fervor, men of strong purpose who are not easily moved, who can lay down every selfish interest and give all for the cross and the crown. The cause of present truth is suffering for men who are loyal to a sense of right and duty, whose moral integrity is firm, and whose energy is equal to the opening providence of God. Such qualifications as these are of more value than untold wealth invested in the work and cause of God. Energy, moral integrity, and strong purpose for the right are qualities that cannot be supplied with any amount of gold. Men possessing these qualifications will have influence everywhere. Their lives will be more powerful than lofty eloquence. God calls for men of heart, men of mind, men of moral integrity, whom He can make the depositaries of His truth, and who will correctly represent its sacred principles in their daily life.

In some respects Brother B has ability that but few have. If his heart were sanctified to the work he could fill an important position in the office with acceptance to God. He needs to be converted and to humble himself as a little child, and seek pure, heart religion, in order for his influence in the office, or in the cause of God anywhere, to be what it ought to be. As his influence has been, it has injured all connected with the office, but more especially the young. His position as foreman gave him influence. He did not conduct himself conscientiously in the fear of God. He favored particular ones more than others. He neglected those who, for their faithfulness and ability, deserved special encouragement, and he brought distress and perplexity upon those in who he should have had a special interest. Those who link their affections and interest to one or two, and favor them to the disadvantage of others, should not retain their position in the office for a day. This unsanctified partiality for special ones who may please the fancy, to the neglect of others who are conscientious and God-fearing, and in His sight of more value, is offensive to God. That which God values we should value. The ornament of a meek and quiet spirit He regards of higher value than external beauty, outward adornment, riches, or worldly honor.

The true followers of Christ will not choose intimate friendship with those whose characters have serious defects, and whose example as a whole it would not be safe to follow, while it is their privilege to associate with persons who observe a conscientious regard for duty in business, and in religion. Those who lack principle and devotion generally exert a more positive influence to mold the minds of their intimate friends than is exerted by those who seem well balanced and able to control and influence the defective in character, those lacking spirituality and devotion.

Brother B's influence, if unsanctified, endangers the souls of those who follow his example. His ready tact and ingenuity are admired, and lead those connected with him to give him credit for qualifications that he does not possess. At the office he was reckless of his time. If this had affected himself only, it would have been a small matter; but his position as foreman gave him influence. His example before those in the office, especially the apprentices, was not circumspect and conscientious. If, with his ingenious talent, Brother B possessed a high sense of moral obligation, his services would be invaluable to the office. If his principles had been such that nothing could have moved him from the straight line of duty, that no inducement which could have been presented would have purchased his consent to a wrong action, his influence would have molded others; but his desires for pleasure allured him from his post of duty. If he had stood in the strength of God, unmoved by censure or flattery, steady to principle, faithful to his convictions of truth and justice, he would have been a superior man and would have won a commanding influence everywhere. Brother B lacks frugality and economy. He lacks the tact which would enable him to adapt himself to the opening providence of God and make him a minuteman. He loves human praise. He is swayed by circumstances, and is subject to temptation, and his integrity cannot be relied upon.

Brother B's religious experience was not sound. He moved from impulse, not from principle. His heart was not right with God, and he did not have the fear of God and His glory before him. He acted very much like a man engaged in common business; he had but very little sense of the sacredness of the work in which he was engaged. He had not practiced self-denial and economy, therefore he had no experience in this. At times he labored earnestly and manifested a good interest in the work. Then again he would be careless of his time and spend precious moments in unimportant conversation, hindering others from doing their duty and setting them an example of recklessness and unfaithfulness. The work of God is sacred and calls for men of lofty integrity. Men are wanted whose sense of justice, even in the smallest matters, will not allow them to make an entry of their time that is not minute and correct—men who will realize that they are handling means that belongs to God, and who would not unjustly appropriate one cent to their own use; men who will be just as faithful and exact, careful and diligent, in their labor, in the absence of their employer as in his presence, proving by their faithfulness that they are not merely men pleasers, eye-servants, but are conscientious, faithful, true workmen, doing right, not for human praise, but because they love and choose the right from a high sense of their obligation to God.

Parents are not thorough in the education of their children. They do not see the necessity of molding their minds by discipline. They give them a superficial education, manifesting greater care for the ornamental than for that solid education which would so develop and direct the faculties as to bring out the energies of the soul, and cause the powers of mind to expand and strengthen by exercise. The faculties of the mind need cultivation, that they may be exercised to the glory of God. Careful attention should be given to the culture of the intellect, that the various organs of the mind may have equal strength by being brought into exercise, each in its distinctive office. If parents allow their children to follow the bent of their own minds, their own inclination and pleasure, to the neglect of duty, their characters will be formed after this pattern, and they will not be competent for any responsible position in life. The desires and inclinations of the young should be restrained, their weak points of character strengthened, and their overstrong tendencies repressed.

If one faculty is suffered to remain dormant, or is turned out of its proper course, the purpose of God is not carried out. All the faculties should be well developed. Care should be given to each, for each has a bearing upon the others, and all must be exercised in order that the mind be properly balanced. If one or two organs are cultivated and kept in continual use because it is the choice of your children to put the strength of the mind in one direction to the neglect of other mental powers, they will come to maturity with unbalanced minds and inharmonious characters. They will be apt and strong in one direction, but greatly deficient in other directions just as important. They will not be competent men and women. Their deficiencies will be marked, and will mar the entire character.

Brother B has cultivated an almost ungovernable propensity for sight-seeing and trips of pleasure. Time and means are wasted to gratify his desire for pleasure excursions. His selfish love of pleasure leads to the neglect of sacred duties. Brother B loves to preach, but he has never taken up this work feeling the woe upon him if he preach not the gospel. He has frequently left work in the office which demanded his care, to comply with calls from some of his brethren in other churches. If he had felt the solemnity of the work of God for this time, and gone forth making God his trust, practicing self-denial, and lifting the cross of Christ, he would have accomplished good. But he frequently had so little realization of the holiness of the work, that he would improve the opportunity of visiting other churches in making the occasion a scene of self-gratification, in short, a pleasure trip. What a contrast between his course and that pursued by the apostles, who went forth burdened with the word of life, and in the demonstration of the Spirit preached Christ crucified! They pointed out the living way through self-denial and the cross. They had fellowship with their Saviour in His sufferings, and their greatest desire was to know Christ Jesus, and Him crucified. They considered not their own convenience, nor counted their lives dear unto themselves. They lived not to enjoy, but to do good, and to save souls for whom Christ died.

Brother B can present arguments upon doctrinal points, but the practical lessons of sanctification, self-denial, and the cross, he has not experienced in himself. He can speak to the ear, but not having felt the sanctifying influence of these truths upon his heart, nor practiced them in his life, he fails to urge the truth home upon the conscience with a deep sense of its importance and solemnity in view of the judgment, when every case must be decided. Brother B has not trained his mind, and his deportment out of meeting has not been exemplary. The burden of the work has not seemed to rest upon him, but he has been trifling and boyish, and by his example has lowered the standard of religion. Sacred and common things have been placed on a level.

Brother B has not been willing to endure the cross; he has not been willing to follow Christ from the manger to the judgment hall and Calvary. He has brought upon himself sore affliction by seeking his own pleasure. He has yet to learn that his own strength is weakness and his wisdom is folly. If he had felt that he was engaged in the work of God, and that he was indebted to One who had given him time and talents, and who required that they be improved to His glory,—had he stood faithfully at his post,—he would not have suffered that long, tedious sickness. His exposure upon that pleasure trip caused him months of suffering and would have caused his death had it not been for the earnest, effectual prayer of faith put up in his behalf by those who felt that he was not prepared to die. Had he died at that time his case would have been far worse than that of the unenlightened sinner. But God mercifully heard the prayers of His people and gave him a new lease of life, that he might have opportunity to repent of his unfaithfulness and to redeem the time. His example had influenced many in Battle Creek in the wrong direction.

Brother B came up from his sickness, but how little did he or his family feel humbled under the hand of God. The work of the Spirit of God, and wisdom from Him, are not manifested that we may be happy and satisfied with ourselves, but that our souls may be renewed in knowledge and true holiness. How much better would it have been for this brother if his affliction had prompted to faithful searching of heart, to discover the imperfections in his character, that he might put them away, and with humble spirit come forth from the furnace as gold purified, reflecting the image of Christ.

The sickness that he had brought upon himself, the church helped him bear. His watchers were provided, and his expenses were in a great measure borne by the church; yet neither he nor his family appreciated this generosity and tenderness on the part of the church. They felt that they deserved all that was done for them. As Brother B came up from his sickness, he felt wrong toward my husband because he disapproved his course, which was so censurable. He united with others to injure my husband's influence, and since he has left the office he has not felt right. He would poorly stand the test of being proved by God.

Brother B has not yet learned the lesson that he will have to learn if he is saved at last—to deny self, and resist his desire for pleasure. He will have to be brought over the ground again and tried still more closely, because he failed to endure the trials of the past. He has displeased God in justifying self. He has but little experience in the fellowship of the sufferings of Christ. He loves display and does not economize his means. The Lord knows. He weighs the inward feelings and intentions of the heart. He understands man. He tests our fidelity. He requires that we should love and serve Him with the whole mind, and heart, and strength. The lovers of pleasure may put on a form of godliness that involves some self-denial even, and they may sacrifice time and money, and yet self not be subdued, and the will not be brought into subjection to the will of God.

The influence of the D girls was very bad in Battle Creek. They had not been trained. Their mother had neglected her sacred duty and had not restrained her children. She had not brought them up in the fear and admonition of the Lord. They had been indulged and shielded from bearing responsibilities until they had no relish for the plain, homely duties of life. The mother had educated the daughters to think much of dress, but the inward adorning was not exalted before them. These young girls were vain and proud. Their minds were impure; their conversation was corrupting; and yet there was a class in Battle Creek who would associate with this stamp of minds, and they could not associate with them without coming down to their level. These girls were not dealt as severely with as the case demanded. They love the society of young men, and the young men are the theme of their meditation and of their conversation. They have corrupted manners, and are headstrong and self-confident.

The entire family love display. The mother is not a prudent, dignified woman. She is not qualified to bring up children. To dress her children to make a show is of greater consequence to her than the inward adorning. She has not disciplined herself. Her will has not been brought into conformity to the will of God. Her heart is not right with God.

She is a stranger to the operation of His Spirit upon the heart, bringing the desires and affections into conformity to the obedience of Christ. She does not possess ennobling qualities of mind and does not discern sacred things. She has let her children do as they pleased. The fearful experience that she has had with two of her elder children has not made the deep impression on her mind that the circumstances demanded. She has educated her children to love dress, vanity, and folly. She has not disciplined her two younger girls. A D, under a proper influence, would be a worthy young man; but he has much to learn. He follows inclination rather than duty. He loves to follow his own will and pleasure, and has not a correct knowledge of the duties devolving upon a Christian. Self-gratification, and his own inclination, he would gladly interpret to be duty. Self-gratification he has not overcome. He has a work to do to clear his spiritual vision, that he may understand what it is to be sanctified to God, and learn the high claims of God upon him. The serious defects in his education have affected his life.

If, with his good qualifications, Brother B were well balanced and a faithful foreman of the office, his labor would be of great value to the office, and he could earn double wages. But for the past years, considering his deficiency, with his unconsecrated influence, the office could better afford to do without him, even if his services could be had for nothing. Brother and Sister B have not learned the lesson of economy. The gratification of the taste, and the desire for pleasure and display, have had an overpowering influence upon them. Small wages would be of more advantage to them than large, for they would use all as they pass along, were it ever so much. They would enjoy as they go, and then when affliction draws upon them, would be wholly unprepared. Twenty dollars a week would be laid out about the same as twelve. Had Brother and Sister B been economical managers, denying themselves, they could ere this have had a home of their own, and besides this have had means to draw upon in case of adversity. But they will not economize as others have done, upon whom they have sometimes been dependent. If they neglect to learn these lessons, their characters will not be found perfect in the day of God.

Brother B has been the object of the great love and condescension of Christ, and yet he has never felt that he could imitate the great Exemplar. He claims, and all his life has sought after, a better portion in this life than was given our Lord. He has never felt the depths of ignorance and sin from which Christ has proposed to lift him and to link him to His divine nature.

It is a fearful thing to minister in sacred things when the heart and hands are not holy. To be a co-worker with Christ involves fearful responsibilities; to stand as His representative is no small matter. The fearful realities of the judgment will test every man's work. The apostle said, "We preach not ourselves, but Christ Jesus the Lord;" "for God, who commanded the light to shine out of darkness, hath shined in our hearts, to give the light of the knowledge of the glory of God in the face of Jesus Christ." The sufficiency of the apostle was not in himself, but in the gracious influence of the Spirit of Christ, which filled his soul and brought every thought into subjection to the obedience of Christ. The power of truth attending the word preached will be a savor of life unto life or of death unto death. Ministers are required to be living examples of the mind and spirit of Christ, living epistles, known and read of all men. I tremble when I consider that there are some ministers, even among Seventh-day Adventists, who are not sanctified by the truths which they preach. Nothing less than the quick and powerful Spirit of God working in the hearts of His messengers to give the knowledge of the glory of God, can gain for them the victory.

Brother B's preaching has not been marked by the sanction of God's Spirit. He can talk fluently and make a point plain, but his preaching has lacked spirituality. His appeals have not touched the heart with a new tenderness. There has been an array of words, but the hearts of his hearers have not been quickened and melted with a sense of a Saviour's love. Sinners have not been convicted and drawn to Christ by a sense that "Jesus of Nazareth passeth by." Sinners should have a clear impression given them of the nearness and willingness of Christ to give them present salvation. A Saviour should be presented before the people, while the heart of the speaker should be subdued and imbued with His Spirit. The very tones of the voice, the look, the words, should possess an irresistible power to move hearts and control minds. Jesus should be found in the heart of the minister. If Jesus is in the words and in the tones of the voice, if they are mellow with His tender love, it will prove a blessing of more value than all the riches, pleasures, and glories of the earth; for such blessings will not come and go without accomplishing a work. Convictions will be deepened, impressions will be made, and the question will be raised: "What shall I do to be saved?"

UNBALANCED MINDS

God has committed to each of us sacred trusts, for which He holds us accountable. It is His purpose that we so educate the mind as to be able to exercise the talents He has given us in such a manner as to accomplish the greatest good and reflect the glory to the Giver. We are indebted to God for all the qualities of the mind. These powers can be cultivated, and so discreetly directed and controlled as to accomplish the purpose for which they were given. It is duty to so educate the mind as to bring out the energies of the soul and develop every faculty. When all the faculties are in exercise, the intellect will be strengthened, and the purpose for which they were given will be accomplished.

Many are not doing the greatest amount of good because they exercise the intellect in one direction and neglect to give careful attention to those things for which they think they are not adapted. Some faculties that are weak are thus allowed to lie dormant because the work that should call them into exercise, and consequently give them strength, is not pleasant. All the powers of the mind should be exercised, all the faculties cultivated. Perception, judgment, memory, and all the reasoning powers should have equal strength in order that minds may be well balanced.

If certain faculties are used to the neglect of others, the design of God is not fully carried out in us; for all the faculties have a bearing and are dependent, in a great measure, upon one another. One cannot be effectually used without the operation of all, that the balance may be carefully preserved. If all the attention and strength are given to one, while others lie dormant, the development is strong in that one and will lead to extremes, because all the powers have not been cultivated. Some minds are dwarfed and not properly balanced. All minds are not naturally constituted alike. We have varied minds; some are strong upon certain points and very weak upon others. These deficiencies, so apparent, need not and should not exist. If those who possess them would strengthen the weak points in their character by cultivation and exercise they would become strong.

It is agreeable, but not most profitable, to exercise those faculties which are naturally the strongest, while we neglect those that are weak, but which need to be strengthened. The feeblest faculties should have careful attention, that all the powers of the intellect may be nicely balanced and all do their part like well-regulated machinery. We are dependent upon God for the preservation of all our faculties. Christians are under obligation to Him to so train the mind that all the faculties may be strengthened and more fully developed. If we neglect to do this, they will never accomplish the purpose for which they were designed. We have no right to neglect any one of the powers that God has given us. We see monomaniacs all over the country. They are frequently sane upon every subject but one. The reason of this is that one organ of the mind was specially exercised while the others were permitted to lie dormant. The one that was in constant use became worn and diseased, and the man became a wreck. God was not glorified by his pursuing this course. Had he exercised all the organs equally, all would have had a healthy development; all the labor would not have been thrown upon one, therefore no one would have broken down.

Ministers should be guarded, lest they thwart the purposes of God by plans of their own. They are in danger of narrowing down the work of God, and confining their labor to certain localities, and not cultivating a special interest for the work of God in all its various departments. There are some who concentrate their minds upon one subject to the exclusion of others which may be of equal importance. They are one-idea men. All the strength of their being is concentrated on the subject upon which the mind is exercised for the time. Every other consideration is lost sight of. This one favorite theme is the burden of their thoughts and the theme of their conversation. All the evidence which has a bearing upon that subject is eagerly seized and appropriated, and dwelt upon at so great length that minds are wearied in following them.

Time is frequently lost in explaining points which are really unimportant, and which would be taken for granted without producing proof; for they are self-evident. But the real, vital points should be made as plain and forcible as language and proof can make them. The power to concentrate the mind upon one subject to the exclusion of all others is well in a degree; but the constant exercise of this faculty wears upon those organs that are called into use to do this work; it throws too great a tax upon them, and the result is a failure to accomplish the greatest amount of good. The principal wear comes upon one set of organs, while the others lie dormant. The mind cannot thus be healthfully exercised, and, in consequence, life is shortened.

All the faculties should bear a part of the labor, working harmoniously, balancing one another. Those who put the whole strength of their mind into one subject are greatly deficient on other points, for the reason that the faculties are not equally cultivated. The subject before them enchains their attention, and they are led on and on, and go deeper and deeper into the matter. They see knowledge and light as they become interested and absorbed. But there are very few minds that can follow them unless they have given the subject the same depth of thought. There is danger of such men plowing, and planting the seed of truth so deep that the tender, precious blade will never find the surface.

Much hard labor is often expended that is not called for and that will never be appreciated. If those who have large concentrativeness cultivate this faculty to the neglect of others, they cannot have well-proportioned minds. They are like machinery in which only one set of wheels works at a time. While some wheels are rusting from inaction, others are wearing from constant use. Men who cultivate one or two faculties, and do not exercise all equally, cannot accomplish one half the good in the world that God designed they should. They are one-sided men; only half of the power that God has given them is put to use, while the other half is rusting with inaction.

If this class of minds have a special work, requiring thought, they should not exercise all their powers upon that one thing, to the exclusion of every other interest. While they make the subject before them their principal business, other branches of the work should have a portion of their time. This would be much better for themselves and for the cause generally. One branch of the work should not have exclusive attention to the neglect of all others. In their writings some need to be constantly guarded, that they do not make points blind that are plain, by covering them up with many arguments which will not be of lively interest to the reader. If they linger tediously upon points, giving every particular which suggests itself to the mind, their labor is nearly lost. The interest of the reader will not be deep enough to pursue the subject to its close. The most essential points of truth may be made indistinct by giving attention to every minute point. Much ground is covered; but the work upon which so much labor is expended is not calculated to do the greatest amount of good, by awakening a general interest.

In this age, when pleasing fables are drifting upon the surface and attracting the mind, truth presented in an easy style, backed up with a few strong proofs, is better than to search and bring forth an overwhelming array of evidence; for the point then does not stand so distinct in many minds as before the objections and evidences were brought before them. With many, assertions will go further than long arguments. They take many things for granted. Proof does not help the case in the minds of such.

OPPOSING ADVENTISTS

Our most bitter opponents are found among the first-day Adventists. They do not engage in the warfare honorably. They will pursue any course, however unreasonable and inconsistent, to cover up the truth and try to make it appear that the law of God is of no force. They flatter themselves that the end will justify the means. Men of their own number, in whom they had not confidence, will commence a tirade against the Sabbath of the fourth commandment, and they will give publicity to their statements, however untrue, unjust, and even ridiculous, if they can make them bear against the truth which they hate.

We should not be moved or disconcerted by this unjust warfare from unreasonable men. Those who receive, and are pleased with, what these men speak and write against the truth are not the ones who would be convinced of the truth or who would honor the cause of God if they should accept it. Time and strength can be better employed than to dwell at length upon the quibbles of our opponents who deal in slander and misrepresentations. While precious time is employed in following the crooks and turns of dishonest opponents, the people who are open to conviction are dying for want of knowledge. A train of senseless quibbles of Satan's own invention is brought before minds, while the people are crying for food, for meat in due season.

It takes those who have trained their minds to war against the truth to manufacture quibbles. And we are not wise to take them from their hands, and pass them out to thousands who would never have thought of them had we not published them to the world. This is what our opponents want to have done; they want to be brought to notice and to have us publish for them. This is especially true of some. This is their main object in writing out their falsehoods and in misrepresenting the truth and the characters of those who love and advocate the truth. They will die out more speedily to be left unnoticed, to have their errors and falsehoods treated with silent contempt. They do not want to be let alone. Opposition is the element that they love. If it were not for this, they would have but little influence.

The first-day Adventists as a class are the most difficult to reach. They generally reject the truth, as did the Jews. We should, as far as possible, go forward as though there were not such a people in existence. They are the elements of confusion, and immoralities exist among them to a fearful extent. It would be the greatest calamity to have many of their number embrace the truth. They would have to unlearn everything and learn anew, or they would cause us great trouble. There are occasions where their glaring misrepresentations will have to be met. When this is the case it should be done promptly and briefly, and we should then pass on to our work. The plan of Christ's teaching should be ours. He was plain and simple, striking directly at the root of the matter, and the minds of all were met.

It is not the best policy to be so very explicit and say all upon a point that can be said, when a few arguments will cover the ground and be sufficient for all practical purposes to convince or silence opponents. You may remove every prop today and close the mouths of objectors so that they can say nothing, and tomorrow they will go over the same ground again. Thus it will be, over and over, because they do not love the light and will not come to the light, lest their darkness and error should be removed from them. It is a better plan to keep a reserve of arguments than to pour out a depth of knowledge upon a subject which would be taken for granted without labored argument. Christ's ministry lasted only three years, and a great work was done in that short period. In these last days there is a great work to be done in a short time. While many are getting ready to do something, souls will perish for the light and knowledge.

If men who are engaged in presenting and defending the truth of the Bible undertake to investigate and show the fallacy and inconsistency of men who dishonestly turn the truth of God into a lie, Satan will stir up opponents enough to keep their pens constantly employed, while other branches of the work will be left to suffer.

We must have more of the spirit of those men who were engaged in building the walls of Jerusalem. We are doing a great work, and we cannot come down. If Satan sees that he can keep men answering the objections of opponents, and thus keep their voices silent, and hinder them from doing the most important work for the present time, his object is accomplished.

The *Sabbath History* has been kept from the people too long. They need this precious work even if they do not have it in all its perfection. It never can be prepared in a manner to fully silence unreasonable opponents, who are unstable and who wrest the Scriptures unto their own destruction. This is a busy world. Men and women who engage in the business of life have not time to meditate, or even to read the word of God enough to understand all its important truths. Long, labored arguments will interest but a few; for the people have to read as they run. You can no more remove the objections to the Sabbath commandment from the minds of first-day Adventists than could the Saviour of the world, by His great power and miracles, convince the Jews that He was the Messiah, after they had once set themselves to reject Him. Like the obstinate, unbelieving Jews, they have chosen darkness rather than light, and should an angel direct from the courts of heaven speak to them, they would say it was Satan.

The world needs labor now. Calls are coming in from every direction like the Macedonian cry: "Come over and help us." Plain, pointed arguments, standing out as mileposts, will do more toward convincing minds generally than will a large array of arguments which cover a great deal of ground, but which none but investigating minds will have interest to follow. The *Sabbath History* should be given to the people. While one edition is circulating, and the people are being benefited by it, greater improvements may be made, until everything possible has been done to bring it to perfection. Our success will be in reaching common minds. Those who have talent and position are so exalted above the simplicity of the work, and so well satisfied with themselves, that they feel no need of the truth. They are exactly where the Jews were, self-righteous, self-sufficient. They are whole and have no need of a physician.

INTIMATE FRIENDSHIP WITH WORLDLINGS

December 10, 1871, I was shown, Brother E, that you and your sisters were in a very dangerous condition; and that which makes your position the more dangerous is that you do not realize your true state. I saw you enveloped in darkness. This darkness has not settled upon you suddenly. You commenced to enter the mist of darkness gradually, and almost imperceptibly, until the darkness is as light to you, yet the cloud is becoming more dense every day. Now and then I saw a gleaming of light separating the darkness from you; then again it would close about you, firmer and more dense than before.

Your singing schools have ever been a snare to you. Neither you nor your sisters have a depth of experience that will enable you to be brought in contact with the influences you meet in your singing schools, without being affected. It would take stronger minds, with greater decision of character than you three possess, to be brought into the society you are and not be affected. Listen to the words of Christ: "Ye are the light of the world. A city that is set on an hill cannot be hid. Neither do men light a candle, and put it under a bushel, but on a candlestick; and it giveth light unto all that are in the house. Let your light so shine before men, that they may see your good works, and glorify your Father which is in heaven." Have your example and influence been of that positive character that has impressed and convicted your associates? I think not. You have been injured. Darkness has settled upon you and dimmed your light so that it has not burned with that luster to dispel the darkness about others. You have been separating further and further from God.

You, my brother, have but a faint sense of what you have been doing. You have been standing directly in the way of your sisters' advancement in the divine life. They, more especially F, have been entangled with the bewitching, satanic wiles of spiritualism, and if she rids herself of this unholy slime of Satan, which has perverted her sense of eternal things, she will have to make mighty effort. It will be but a hairbreadth escape. You have been blinded, deceived, and enchanted yourself. You do not see yourself. You are all very weak when you might be strong in the precious, saving truth, strengthened, established, and settled upon the Rock Christ Jesus. I feel deeply. I tremble for you. I see temptations on every hand, and you with so little power to resist them.

Brother E, I was shown that you are infatuated; you are deceived as to your motives and the real purposes of your heart. I saw you in the society of Brother G's daughter. She has never yielded her heart to Christ. I was shown her affected and convicted. But your course was not of that character to deepen conviction, or to give her the impression that there was special importance attached to these matters. You profess to hold sacred the salvation of the soul, and the present truth. She does not respect the Sabbath from principle. She loves the vanity of the world and enjoys the pride and amusements of life. But you have been departing so gradually from God, and from the light, that you do not see the separation which the truth necessarily brings between those who love God and those who are lovers of pleasure more than lovers of God. I saw that you were attracted to her society. Religious meetings and sacred duties were of minor importance, while the presence of a mere child, who has no knowledge of the truth or of heavenly things, fascinated you. You have overlooked self-denial and the cross, which lie directly in the pathway of every disciple of Christ.

I was shown that if you had been walking in the light you would have taken your position decidedly for the truth. Your example would have shown that you considered the truth you profess of that importance that your affections and heart could go only where the image of Christ was discernible. Christ now says to you: Which will you have, Me or the world? Your decision is to be made here. Will you follow the promptings of an unsanctified heart, turn away from self-denial for Christ's sake, and step over the cross without lifting it? Or will you lift that cross, heavy though it may be, and make some sacrifice for the truth's sake? May God help you to see where you are, that you may place a true estimate upon eternal things. You now have so little spiritual eyesight that the holy and sacred are placed upon a level with the common. You have responsibilities. Your influence affects your sisters to a great extent. Your only safety is in separation from the world.

I was shown you, my brother, taking the young with you to scenes of amusement at the time of a religious interest, and also engaging in singing schools with worldlings who are all darkness and who have evil angels all around them. How does your feeble, dim light appear amid this darkness and temptation? Angels of God do not attend you upon these occasions. You are left to go in your own strength. Satan is well pleased with your position; for he can make you more efficient in his service than if you did not profess to be a Christian keeping all the commandments of God. The True Witness addresses the Laodicean church: "I know thy works, that thou art neither cold nor hot: I would thou wert cold or hot. So then because thou art lukewarm, and neither cold nor hot, I will spew thee out of my mouth. Because thou sayest, I am rich, and increased with goods, and have need of nothing and knowest not that thou art wretched, and miserable, and poor, and blind, and naked. I counsel thee to buy of Me gold tried in the fire, that thou mayest be rich; and white raiment, that thou mayest be clothed, and that the shame of thy nakedness do not appear; and anoint thine eyes with eyesalve, that thou mayest see. As many as I love, I rebuke and chasten: be zealous therefore, and repent."

You are blinded and infatuated. You have felt strong when you were weakness itself. You can be strong in the Mighty One. You can be an instrument of righteousness if you are willing to suffer for Christ's sake. You and your sisters may redeem the time if you will, but it will cost an effort. Your younger sister is linked to one who is not worthy of her affections. There are serious defects in his character. He does not have reverence for sacred and holy things; his heart has not been changed by the Spirit of God. He is selfish, boastful, and loves pleasure more than duty. He has no experience in self-denial and humiliation.

In forming friendship, great caution should be exercised lest an intimacy be contracted with one whose example it would not be safe to imitate, for the effect of such an intimacy is to lead away from God, from devotion, and the love of the truth. It is positively dangerous for you to be intimate with friends who have not a religious experience. If either of you, or all three of you, follow the leadings of God's Spirit, or value your soul's salvation, you will not choose as your particular and intimate friends those who do not maintain a serious regard for religious things, and who do not live under its practical influence. Eternal considerations should come first with you. Nothing can have a more subtle and positively dangerous influence upon the mind, and serve more effectually to banish serious impressions and the convictions of the Spirit of God, than to associate with those who are vain and careless, and whose conversation is upon the world and vanity. The more engaging these persons may be in other respects, the more dangerous is their influence as companions, because they throw around an irreligious life so many pleasing attractions.

God has claims upon all three of you which you cannot lightly throw aside. Jesus has bought you with the price of His own blood. "Ye are not your own, for ye are bought with a price: therefore glorify God in your body, and in your spirit, which are God's." Have you no sacrifice to make for God? Great responsibilities stand before you each in everyday life. Your record is daily passing up to God. Great dangers lie hidden in your pathway. If I could, I would take you in my arms and bear you safely over them; but this I am not permitted to do. You are in the most critical period of your life history. If you arouse the energies of the soul and direct them to securing things of eternal interest, and if you make everything subordinate to this, you will make a success of perfecting Christian character. You may all engage in the spiritual warfare against besetting sins, and you may, through Christ, come off victors. But it will be no child's play. It will be a stern warfare, involving self-denial and cross bearing. The danger is that you will not fully realize your backslidings and your perilous condition. Unless you view life as it is, cast aside the brilliant fancies of imagination, and come down to the sober lessons of experience, you will awake when it is too late. You will then realize the terrible mistake you have made.

Your education has not been of that kind to form solid, substantial characters, therefore you have to obtain now the education which you should have had years ago. Your mother was too fond of you. A mother cannot love her children too well, but she may love unwisely and allow her affection to blind her to their best interests. You have had an indulgent, tender mother. She has shielded her children too much. Her life has been nearly crushed out by the burdens which her children should have taken, and which they could have borne better than she.

The lack of firmness and self-denial in your characters is a serious drawback in obtaining a genuine religious experience that will not be sliding sand. Firmness and integrity of purpose should be cultivated. These qualities are positively necessary to a successful Christian life. If you have integrity of soul you will not be swayed from the right. No motive will be sufficient to move you from the straight line of duty; you will be loyal and true to God. The pleadings of affection and love, the yearnings of friendship, will not move you to turn aside from truth and duty; you will not sacrifice duty to inclination.

If you, my brother, are allured to unite your life interest with a young, inexperienced girl, who is really deficient in education in the common, practical daily duties of life, you make a mistake; but this deficiency is small compared with her ignorance in regard to her duty to God. She has not been destitute of light; she has had religious privileges, and yet she has not felt her wretched sinfulness without Christ. If, in your infatuation, you can repeatedly turn from the prayer meeting, where God meets with His people, in order to enjoy the society of one who has no love for God and who sees no attractions in the religious life, how can you expect God to prosper such a union? Be not in haste. Early marriages should not be encouraged. If either young women or young men have no respect for the claims of God, if they fail to heed the claims which bind them to religion, there will be danger that they will not properly regard the claims of the husband or of the wife. The habit of frequently being in the society of the one of your choice, and that, too, at the sacrifice of religious privileges and of your hours of prayer, is dangerous; you sustain a loss that you cannot afford. The habit of sitting up late at night is customary; but it is not pleasing to God, even if you are both Christians. These untimely hours injure health, unfit the mind for the next day's duties, and have an appearance of evil. My brother, I hope you will have self-respect enough to shun this form of courtship. If you have an eye single to the glory of God you will move with deliberate caution. You will not suffer lovesick sentimentalism to so blind your vision that you cannot discern the high claims that God has upon you as a Christian.

Dear youth, I address myself to you three. Let it be your aim to glorify God and attain His moral likeness. Invite the Spirit of God to mold your characters. Now is your golden opportunity to wash your robes of character and make them white in the blood of the Lamb. I regard this as the turning point in the destiny of each of you. Which will you choose, says Christ, Me or the world? God calls for an unconditional surrender of the heart and affections to Him. If you love friends, brothers or sisters, father or mother, houses or lands, more than Me, says Christ, you are not worthy of Me. Religion lays the soul under the greatest obligation to her claims, to walk by her principles. As the mysterious magnet points to the north, so do the claims of religion point to the glory of God. You are bound by your baptismal vows to honor your Creator and to resolutely deny self and crucify your affections and lusts, and bring even your thoughts into obedience to the will of Christ.

Avoid running into temptation. When temptations surround you, and you cannot control the circumstances which expose you to them, then you may claim the promise of God and with confidence and conscious power exclaim: "I can do all things through Christ which strengtheneth me." There is strength for you all in God. But you will never feel your need of that strength which alone is able to save you, unless you feel your weakness and sinfulness. Jesus, your precious Saviour, now calls you to take your position firmly upon the platform of eternal truth. If you suffer with Him, He will crown you with glory in His everlasting kingdom. If you are willing to sacrifice all for Him, then He will be your Saviour. But if you choose your own way you will follow on in darkness until it is too late to secure the eternal reward.

What have you been willing to suffer for the truth's sake? You have a very short period in which to cultivate the noble traits of your characters. You have all been, to some extent, dissatisfied and unhappy. You have had many complaints to make. You have talked unbelief and have censured others. Especially is this true of F and H. Your hearts have been filled with pride, and even with bitterness at times. Your closets have been neglected, and you have not loved the exercises of religious duties. If you had been persevering in your efforts to grow up into Christ, your living Head, you would now be strong, and competent to bless others with your influence. If you had cultivated a steady, uniform, unwavering energy you would now be strong to resist temptation. But these precious qualities can only be gained through a surrender of the soul to the claims of religion. Then the motives will be high, and the intellect and affections will be balanced by noble principles. God will work with us if we will only engage in healthy action. We must feel the necessity of uniting our human efforts and zealous action with divine power. We can stand forth in God, strong to conquer. You, Brother E, have greatly failed in energy of purpose to do and to endure.

What a great mistake is made in the education of children and youth, in favoring, indulging, and petting them. They become selfish and inefficient, and lack energy in the little things of life. They are not trained to acquire strength of character by the performance of everyday duties, lowly though they may be. You neglect to do willingly and cheerfully that which lies directly before you to do, and which someone must do. There is a great desire with all of us to find a larger, more exalted work.

No one is qualified for great and important work unless he has been faithful in the performance of little duties. It is by degrees that the character is formed and that the soul is trained to put forth effort and energy proportionate to the task which is to be accomplished. If we are creatures of circumstance, we shall surely fail of perfecting Christian characters. You must master circumstances, and not allow circumstances to master you. You can find energy at the cross of Christ. You can now grow by degrees, and conquer difficulties, and overcome force of habit. You need to be stimulated by the lifegiving force of Jesus. You should be attracted to Christ and clothed with His divine beauty and excellence. Brother G's daughter has an education to gain; she is no more competent for the duties and difficulties of life as a wife than a schoolgirl ten years old.

Religion should dictate and guide you in all your pursuits, and should hold absolute control over your affections. If you yield yourselves unreservedly into the hands of Christ, making His power your strength, then will your moral vision be clear to discern quality of character that you may not be deceived by appearances and make great mistakes in your friendship. Your moral power must be keen and sensitive, that it may bear severe tests and not be marred. Your integrity of soul should be so firm that vanity, display, or flattery will not move you.

Oh, it is a great thing to be right with God, the soul in harmony with its Maker, so that, amid the contagion of evil example, which by its deceitful appearance would lure the soul from duty, angels may be sent to your rescue! But bear in mind, if you invite temptation, you will not have divine aid to keep you from being overcome. The three worthies endured the fiery furnace, for Jesus walked with them into the fiery flame. If they had, of themselves, walked into the fire, they would have been consumed. Thus will it be with you. If you do not walk deliberately into temptation, God will sustain you when the temptation comes.

THE CAUSE IN NEW YORK

While in Vermont, December 10, 1871, I was shown some things in regard to New York. The cause in that state seemed to be in a deplorable condition. There were but few laborers, and these were not as efficient as their profession of faith in the sacred truths for this time demanded them to be. There are those in the state who minister in word and doctrine, who are not thorough workmen. Although they believe the theory of the truth, and have been preaching for years, they will never be competent laborers until they work upon a different plan. They have spent much time among the churches, when they are not qualified to benefit them. They themselves are not consecrated to God. They need the spirit of endurance to suffer for Christ's sake, "to drink of the cup," and "be baptized with the baptism," before they are prepared to help others. Unselfish, devoted workmen are needed, to bring things up in New York to the Bible standard. These men have not been in the line of their duty in traveling among the churches. If God has called them to His work, it is to save sinners. They should prove themselves by going out into new fields, that they may know for themselves whether God has committed to them the work of saving souls.

Had Brethren Taylor, Saunders, Cottrell, Whitney, and Brother and Sister Lindsay labored in new fields, they would now be far in advance of what they are. Meeting the opposition of opponents would drive them to their Bibles for arguments to sustain their position, and this would increase their knowledge of the Scriptures and would give them a consciousness of their ability in God to meet opposition in any form. Those who are content to go over and over the same ground among the churches will be deficient in the experience they should have. They will be weak—not strong to will and do and suffer for the truth's sake. They will be inefficient workmen.

Those who have the cause of God at heart and feel love for precious souls for whom Christ died, will not seek their own ease or pleasure. They will do as Christ has done. They will go forth "to seek and to save that which was lost." He said: "I came not to call the righteous, but sinners to repentance."

If ministers in New York wish to help the church, they can do so in no better way than to go out into new fields and labor to bring souls into the truth. When the church see that the ministers are all aglow with the spirit of the work, that they feel deeply the force of the truth, and are seeking to bring others to the knowledge of it, it will put new life and vigor into them. Their hearts will be stirred to do what they can to aid in the work. There is not a class of people in the world who are more willing to sacrifice of their means to advance the cause than are Seventh-day Adventists. If the ministers do not utterly discourage them by their indolence and inefficiency, and by their lack of spirituality, they will generally respond to any appeal that may be made that commends itself to their judgment and consciences. But they want to see fruit. And it is right that the brethren in New York should demand fruit of their ministers. What have they done? What are they doing?

Ministers in New York should have been far in advance of what they are. But they have not engaged in that kind of labor which called forth earnest effort and strong opposition. Had they done so they would have been driven to their Bibles and to prayer in order to be able to answer their opponents, and in the exercise of their talents would have doubled them. There are ministers in New York who have been preaching for years, but who cannot be depended upon to give a course of lectures. They are dwarfed. They have not exercised their minds in the study of the word and in meeting opposition, so that they might become strong in God. Had they, like faithful soldiers of the cross of Christ, gone forth "without the camp," depending upon God and their own energies, rather than leaning so heavily upon their brethren, they would have obtained an experience, and would now be qualified to engage in the work wherever their help is most needed. If the ministers generally in New York had left the churches to labor for themselves, and had not stood in their way, both churches and ministers would now be further advanced in spirituality and in the knowledge of the truth.

Many of our brethren and sisters in New York have been backsliding upon health reform. There is but a small number of genuine health reformers in the state. Light and spiritual understanding have been given to the brethren in New York. But the truth that has reached the understanding, the light that has shone upon the soul, which has not been appreciated and cherished, will witness against them in the day of God. Truth has been given to save those who would believe and obey. Their condemnation is not because they did not have the light, but because they had the light and did not walk in it.

God has furnished man with abundant means for the gratification of natural appetite. He has spread before him, in the products of the earth, a bountiful variety of food that is palatable to the taste and nutritious to the system. Of these our benevolent heavenly Father says that we may "freely eat." We may enjoy the fruits, the vegetables, the grains, without doing violence to the laws of our being. These articles, prepared in the most simple and natural manner, will nourish the body, and preserve its natural vigor without the use of flesh meats.

God created man a little lower than the angels and bestowed upon him attributes that will, if properly used, make him a blessing to the world and cause him to reflect the glory to the Giver. But although made in the image of God, man has, through intemperance, violated principle and God's law in his physical nature. Intemperance of any kind benumbs the perceptive organs and so weakens the brain-nerve power that eternal things are not appreciated, but placed upon a level with the common. The higher powers of the mind designed for elevated purposes, are brought into slavery to the baser passions. If our physical habits are not right, our mental and moral powers cannot be strong; for great sympathy exists between the physical and the moral. The apostle Peter understood this and raised his voice of warning to his brethren: "Dearly beloved, I beseech you as strangers and pilgrims, abstain from fleshly lusts, which war against the soul."

There is but little moral power in the professed Christian world. Wrong habits have been indulged, and physical and moral laws have been disregarded, until the general standard of virtue and piety is exceedingly low. Habits which lower the standard of physical health enfeeble mental and moral strength. The indulgence of unnatural appetites and passions has a controlling influence upon the nerves of the brain. The animal organs are strengthened, while the moral are depressed. It is impossible for an intemperate man to be a Christian, for his higher powers are brought into slavery to the passions.

Those who have had the light upon the subjects of eating and dressing with simplicity in obedience to physical and moral laws, and who turn from the light which points out their duty, will shun duty in other things. If they blunt their consciences to avoid the cross which they will have to take up to be in harmony with natural law, they will, in order to shun reproach, violate the Ten Commandments. There is a decided unwillingness with some to endure the cross and despise the shame. Some will be laughed out of their principles. Conformity to the world is gaining ground among God's people, who profess to be pilgrims and strangers, waiting and watching for the Lord's appearing. There are many among professed Sabbathkeepers in New York who are more firmly wedded to worldly fashions and lusts than they are to healthy bodies, sound minds, or sanctified hearts.

God is testing and proving individuals in New York. He has permitted some to have a measure of prosperity, to develop what is in their hearts. Pride and love of the world have separated them from God. The principles of truth are virtually sacrificed, while they profess to love the truth. Christians should wake up and act. Their influence is telling upon, and molding, the opinions and habits of others. They will have to bear the weighty responsibility of deciding by their influence the destiny of souls.

The Lord, by close and pointed truths for these last days, is cleaving out a people from the world and purifying them unto Himself. Pride and unhealthful fashions, the love of display, the love of approbation—all must be left with the world if we would be renewed in knowledge after the image of Him who created us. "For the grace of God that bringeth salvation hath appeared to all men, teaching us that, denying ungodliness and worldly lusts, we should live soberly, righteously, and godly, in this present world; looking for that blessed hope, and the glorious appearing of the great God and our Saviour Jesus Christ; who gave Himself for us, that He might redeem us from all iniquity, and purify unto Himself a peculiar people, zealous of good works."

The church in _____ need sifting. A thorough conversion is necessary before they can be in working order. Selfishness, pride, envy, malice, evil surmising, backbiting, gossiping, and tattling have been cherished among them, until the Spirit of God has but little to do with them. While some who profess to know God remain in their present state, their prayers are an abomination in His sight. They do not sustain their faith by their works, and it would have been better for some never to have professed the truth than to have dishonored their profession as they have. While they profess to be servants of Christ, they are servants of the enemy of righteousness; and their works testify of them that they are not acquainted with God and that their hearts are not in obedience to the will of Christ. They make child's play of religion; they act like pettish children.

The children of God, the world over, are one great brotherhood. Our Saviour has clearly defined the spirit and principles which should govern the actions of those who, by their consistent, holy lives, distinguish themselves from the world.

Love for one another, and supreme love to their heavenly Father, should be exemplified in their conversation and works. The present condition of many of the children of God is like that of a family of ungrateful and quarrelsome children.

There is danger of even ministers in New York being of that class who are ever learning and never able to come to the knowledge of the truth. They do not practice what they learn. They are hearers, but not doers. These ministers need an experience in the truth that will enable them to comprehend the elevated character of the work.

We are living in a most solemn, important time of this earth's history. We are amid the perils of the last days. Important and fearful events are before us. How necessary that all who do fear God and love His law should humble themselves before Him, and be afflicted and mourn, and confess the sins that have separated God from His people. That which should excite the greatest alarm, is that we do not feel or understand our condition, our low estate, and that we are satisfied to remain as we are. We should flee to the word of God and to prayer, individually seeking the Lord earnestly, that we may find Him. We should make this our first business.

The members of the church are responsible for the talents committed to their trust, and it is impossible for Christians to meet their responsibilities unless they occupy that elevated position that is in accordance with the sacred truths which they profess. The light that shines upon our pathway makes us responsible to let that light shine forth to others in such a manner that they will glorify God.

RELATIVES IN THE CHURCH

The advancement of the church in _____ in spiritual things is not in proportion to the light which has shone upon their pathway. God has committed to each talents to be improved by putting them out to the exchangers, that when the Master comes He may receive His own with usury. The church at _____ is largely composed of valuable material, but its members fail to reach the high standard which it is their privilege to attain

The working material in the church is found mostly in branches of three families which are connected by marriage. There is more talent in the church, and more material to make good workmen, than can be employed to advantage in that locality. The entire church are not growing in spirituality. They are not favorably situated to develop strength by calling into exercise the talents that God has given them. There is not room for all to work. One gets in the way of another. There is a lack of spiritual strength. If this church were less a family church each would feel individual responsibility.

If the talent and influence of several of its members should be exercised in other churches, where they would be drawn out to help where help is really needed, they would be obtaining an experience of the highest value in spiritual things, and by thus bearing responsibilities and burdens in the work of God would be a blessing to others. While engaged in helping others, they would be following the example of Christ. He came not to be ministered unto, but to minister to others. He pleased not Himself. He made Himself of no reputation, but took upon Himself the form of a servant, and spent His life in doing good. He could have spent His days on earth in ease and plenty, and have appropriated to Himself the enjoyments of this life. But He lived not to enjoy, He lived to do good and to save others from suffering, and His example is for us to follow.

If consecrated to God, Brethren I and J could bear greater responsibilities than they have borne. They have thought that they would be prompt to respond to any call that should be made for means, and that this was the principal burden that they had to bear in the cause of God. But God requires more of them than this. If they had trained their minds to a more critical study of the word of God, that they might have become laborers in His cause, and had worked for the salvation of sinners as earnestly as they have to obtain the things of this life, they would have developed strength and wisdom to engage in the work of God where laborers are greatly needed.

These brethren, by remaining in a family community, are being dwarfed in mental and spiritual strength. It is not the best policy for children of one, two, or three families that are connected by marriage, to settle within a few miles of one another. The influence is not good on the parties. The business of one is the business of all. The perplexities and troubles which every family must experience more or less, and which, as far as possible, should be confined within the limits of the family circle, are extended to family connections, and have a bearing upon the religious meetings. There are matters which should not be known to a third person, however friendly and closely connected he may be. Individuals and families should bear them. But the close relationship of several families, brought into constant intercourse, has a tendency to break down the dignity which should be maintained in every family. In performing the delicate duty of reproving and admonishing, there will be danger of injuring feelings, unless it be done with the greatest tenderness and care. The best models of character are liable to errors and mistakes, and great care should be exercised that too much is not made of little things.

Such family and church relationship as exists in _____ is very pleasant to the natural feelings, but it is not the best, all things considered, for the development of symmetrical Christian characters. The close relationship and the familiar associations with one another, while united in church capacity, render the influence feeble. That dignity, that high regard, confidence, and love that make a prosperous church is not preserved. All parties would be much happier to be separated and to visit occasionally, and their influence upon one another would be tenfold greater.

United as these families are by marriage, and mingling as they do in one another's society, each is awake to the faults and errors of the others, and feels in duty bound to correct them; and because these relatives are really dear to one another, they are grieved over little things that they would not notice in those not so closely connected. Keen sufferings of mind are endured, because feelings will arise with some that they have not been treated impartially and with all that consideration which they deserved. Petty jealousies sometimes arise, and molehills become mountains. These little misunderstandings and petty variances cause more severe suffering of mind than do trials that come from other sources.

These things make these truly conscientious, noble-minded men and women feeble to endure, and they are not developing the character they might were they differently situated. They are dwarfed in mental and spiritual growth, which threatens to destroy their usefulness. Their labors and interests are confined mostly to themselves. Their influence is narrowed down when it should be widening and becoming more general, that they may, by being placed in a variety of circumstances, bring into exercise the powers which God has given them, in such a manner as shall contribute most to His glory. All the faculties of the mind are capable of high improvement. The energies of the soul need to be aroused and brought into action for the glory of God.

LABORERS FOR GOD

God calls for missionaries. There are men of ability in the church at _____ who will grow in capacity and power as they exercise their talents in the work and cause of God. If these brethren will educate themselves to make the cause of God their first interest, and will sacrifice their pleasure and inclination for the truth's sake, the blessing of God will rest upon them. These brethren, who love the truth, and who have been for years rejoicing because of increasing light upon the Scriptures, should let their light shine forth to those who are in darkness. God will be to them wisdom and power, and will glorify Himself in working with and by those who wholly follow Him. "If *any man* serve Me, him will My Father honor." The wisdom and power of God will be given to the willing and faithful.

The brethren in _____ have been willing to give of their means for the various enterprises, but they have withheld themselves. They have not said: Here am I, Lord; send me. It is not the strength of human instruments, but the power and wisdom of Him who employs them and works with them that makes men successful in doing the work that is necessary to be done. By offering our goods to the Possessor of heaven and earth while we withhold ourselves we cannot meet His approbation nor secure His blessing. There must be in the hearts of the brethren and sisters in _____ a principle to lay all, even themselves, upon the altar of God.

Men are needed in Battle Creek who can and will take burdens and bear responsibilities. The call has been given time and again, but hardly a response has been made. Some would have answered the call if their worldly interests would have been advanced by so doing. But as there was no prospect of increasing their means by coming to Battle Creek, they could see no duty to come. "To obey is better than sacrifice." And without obedience and unselfish love, the richest offerings are too meager to be presented to the Possessor of all things.

God calls upon the brethren and sisters in _____ to arise and come up to the help of the Lord, to the help of the Lord against the mighty. The reason why there is so little strength among those who profess the truth is that they do not exercise the ability that God has given them. Very many have wrapped their talent in a napkin and hid it in the earth. It is by using the talents that they increase. God will test and prove His people.

Brother and Sister I have been faithful burden bearers in the cause of God, and now their children should not stand back and let the burdens rest so heavily upon them. It is time that the powers of the less-worn minds of the children should be exercised and they work more especially in the Master's vineyard.

Some of the brethren and sisters in New York have felt anxious that Brother and Sister K, especially Sister K, should be encouraged to labor among the churches. But this is the wrong place for them to prove themselves. If God has indeed laid upon them the burden of labor, it is not for the churches; for these are generally in advance of them. There is a world before Brother and Sister K, a world lying in wickedness. Their field is a large one. They have plenty of room to try their gifts and test their calling without entering into other men's labors and building upon a foundation that they have not laid. Brother and Sister K have been very slow to obtain an experience in self-denial. They have been slow to adopt the health reform in all its branches. The churches are in advance of them in the denial of appetite. Therefore they cannot be a benefit to the churches in this direction, but rather a hindrance.

Brother K has not been a blessing to the church in _____, but a great burden. He has stood directly in the way of their advancement. He has not been in a condition to help when and where they needed help the most. He has not correctly represented our faith; his conversation and life have not been unto holiness. He has been far behind, and has not been ready or willing to discern the leadings of God's providence. He has stood in the way of sinners; he has not been in such a position that his influence would recommend our faith to unbelievers.

His example has been a hindrance to the church and to his unbelieving neighbors. If Brother K had been wholly consecrated to God, his works would have been fruitful, productive of much good. But that which more especially distinguishes God's people from the popular religious bodies is not their profession alone, but their exemplary characters and their principles of unselfish love. The powerful, purifying influence of the Spirit of God upon the heart, carried out in words and works, separates them from the world and designates them as God's peculiar people. The character and disposition of Christ's followers will be like their Master's. He is the pattern, the holy and perfect example given for Christians to imitate. His true followers will love their brethren and be in harmony with them. They will love their neighbors as Christ has given them example and will make any sacrifice if they can by so doing persuade souls to leave their sins and be converted to the truth.

The truth, deeply rooted in the hearts of believers, will spring up and bear fruit unto righteousness. Their words and works are the channels through which the pure principles of truth and holiness are conveyed to the world. Especial blessings and privileges are for those who love the truth and walk according to the light they have received. If they neglect to do this, their light will become darkness. When the people of God become self-sufficient, the Lord leaves them to their own wisdom. Mercy and truth are promised to the humble in heart, the obedient and faithful.

Brother K has stood in the way of his children. If he had been consecrated to God, having his heart in the work, and living out the truth he professed, he would have felt the importance of commanding his household after him, as did faithful Abraham.

The lack of harmony and love between the two brothers K is a reproach to the cause of God. Both are at fault. Both have a work to do in subduing self and cultivating the Christian graces. God is dishonored by the dissensions, and I do not go too far when I say hatred, that exist between these two natural brothers. Brother A K is greatly at fault. He has cherished feelings that have not been in accordance with the will of God. He knows the peculiarities of his brother, B K, that he has a fretful, unhappy temperament. Frequently he cannot see good when it lies directly in his path. He sees only evil and becomes discouraged very easily. Satan magnifies a molehill into a mountain before him. All things considered, Brother B K has in many things pursued a less censurable course than his brother, because it has been less injurious to the cause of present truth.

These natural brothers must be fully reconciled to each other before they can lift the reproach from the cause of God that their disunion has caused. "In this the children of God are manifest, and the children of the devil: whosoever doeth not righteousness is not of God, neither he that loveth not his brother." "He that saith he is in the light, and hateth his brother, is in darkness even until now." Those who labor for God should be clean vessels, sanctified to the Master's use. "Be ye clean, that bear the vessels of the Lord." "If a man say, I love God, and hateth his brother, he is a liar: for he that loveth not his brother whom he hath seen, how can he love God whom he hath not seen? And this commandment have we from Him, That he who loveth God love his brother also."

The ambassadors of Christ have a responsible and sacred work before them. They are savors of life unto life, or of death unto death. Their influence decides the destiny of souls for whom Christ died. Brother and Sister K both lack experience. Their lives have not been unto holiness. They have not had a deep and thorough knowledge of the divine will. They have not been steadily advancing onward and upward in the divine life, so that their experience could be of value to the church. Their course has burdened the church not a little.

Sister K's past life has not been of such a character that her experience could be a blessing to others. She has not lived up to her convictions of duty. Her conscience has been violated too many times. She has been a pleasure seeker and has given her life to vanity, frivolity, and fashion, in face of the light of truth which has shone upon her pathway. She knew the way, but neglected to walk in it. The Lord gave Sister K a testimony of warning and reproof. She believed the testimony and separated herself from that class who were lovers of pleasure more than lovers of God. Then, as she viewed her past life, so full of neglects and wrongs, she gave up to unbelief and stolid gloom. Despair spread its dark wings over her. Her marriage to Brother K changed the order of things somewhat, but at times since she has been very gloomy and desponding.

Sister K has a good knowledge of the prophecies and can trace them and speak upon them very readily. Some of the brethren and sisters have been anxious to urge Brother and

Sister K to go out as active laborers. But there is danger of their working from a wrong standpoint. Sister K's educational advantages have been superior to those of many by whom she is surrounded. As she has labored publicly, she has depended upon her own strength more than upon the Spirit of God. She has had a spirit of lofty independence and has thought that she was qualified to teach rather than be taught. With her lack of experience in spiritual things she is unprepared to labor among the churches. She has not the discernment and spiritual strength necessary to build them up. If she and her husband engage in this work at all, they should commence by exerting a good influence in the church at _____. Their labor should be bestowed where the work most needs to be done.

There is work to be done in new fields. Sinners who never have heard the warning message need to be warned. Here Brother and Sister K have ample room to work and prove their calling. No one should hinder them in their efforts in new fields. There are sinners to save in every direction. But some ministers are inclined to go over and over the same ground among the churches, when their labors cannot help them, and their time is wasted.

We wish that all the Lord's servants were laborers. The work of warning souls should not be confined to ministers alone, but brethren who have the truth in their hearts, and who have exerted a good influence at home, should feel that a responsibility rests upon them to devote a part of their time to going out among their neighbors and into adjoining towns to be missionaries for God. They should carry our publications and engage in conversation and, in the spirit of Christ, pray with and for those whom they visit. This is the work that will arouse a spirit of investigation and reformation.

For years the Lord has been calling the attention of His people to health reform. This is one of the great branches of the work of preparation for the coming of the Son of man. John the Baptist went forth in the spirit and power of Elijah to prepare the way of the Lord and to turn the people to the wisdom of the just. He was a representative of those living in these last days to whom God has entrusted sacred truths to present before the people to prepare the way for the second appearing of Christ. John was a reformer. The angel Gabriel, direct from heaven, gave a discourse upon health reform to the father and mother of John. He said that he should not drink wine or strong drink, and that he should be filled with the Holy Ghost from his birth.

John separated himself from friends and from the luxuries of life. The simplicity of his dress, a garment woven of camel's hair, was a standing rebuke to the extravagance and display of the Jewish priests, and of the people generally. His diet, purely vegetable, of locusts and wild honey, was a rebuke to the indulgence of appetite and the gluttony that everywhere prevailed. The prophet Malachi declares: "Behold, I will send you Elijah the prophet before the coming of the great and dreadful day of the Lord: and he shall turn the heart of the fathers to the children, and the heart of the children to their fathers." Here the prophet describes the character of the work. Those who are to prepare the way for the second coming of Christ are represented by faithful Elijah, as John came in the spirit of Elijah to prepare the way for Christ's first advent. The great subject of reform is to be agitated, and the public mind is to be stirred. Temperance in all things is to be connected with the message, to turn the people of God from their idolatry, their gluttony, and their extravagance in dress and other things.

The self-denial, humility, and temperance required of the righteous, whom God especially leads and blesses, is to be presented to the people in contrast to the extravagant, health-destroying habits of those who live in this degenerate age. God has shown that health reform is as closely connected with the third angel's message as the hand is with the body. There is nowhere to be found so great a cause of physical and moral degeneracy as a neglect of this important subject. Those who indulge appetite and passion, and close their eyes to the light for fear they will see sinful indulgences which they are unwilling to forsake, are guilty before God. Whoever turns from the light in one instance hardens his heart to disregard the light upon other matters. Whoever violates moral obligations in the matter of eating and dressing prepares the way to violate the claims of God in regard to eternal interests. Our bodies are not our own. God has claims upon us to take care of the habitation He has given us, that we may present our bodies to Him a living sacrifice, holy and acceptable. Our bodies belong to Him who made them, and we are in duty bound to become intelligent in regard to the best means of preserving them from decay. If we enfeeble the body by self-gratification, by indulging the appetite, and by dressing in accordance with health-destroying fashions, in order to be in harmony with the world, we become enemies of God.

Brother and Sister K have not appreciated the light upon health reform. They have not seen a place for it in connection with the third message. Providence has been leading the people of God out from the extravagant habits of the world, away from the indulgence of appetite and passion, to take their stand upon the platform of self-denial and temperance in all things. The people whom God is leading will be peculiar. They will not be like the world. But if they follow the leadings of God they will accomplish His purposes, and will yield their will to His will. Christ will dwell in the heart. The temple of God will be holy. Your body, says the apostle, is the temple of the Holy Ghost. God does not require His children to deny themselves to the injury of physical strength. He requires them to obey natural law, to preserve physical health. Nature's path is the road He marks out, and it is broad enough for any Christian. God has, with a lavish hand, provided us with rich and varied bounties for our sustenance and enjoyment. But in order for us to enjoy the natural appetite, which will preserve health and prolong life, He restricts the appetite. He says: Beware; restrain, deny, unnatural appetite. If we create a perverted appetite, we violate the laws of our being and assume the responsibility of abusing our bodies and of bringing disease upon ourselves.

The spirit and power of Elijah have been stirring hearts to reform and directing them to the wisdom of the just. Brother and Sister K have not been converted to the health reform, notwithstanding the amount of evidence that God has given upon the subject. Self-denial is essential to genuine religion. Those who have not learned to deny themselves are destitute of vital, practical godliness. We cannot expect anything else than that the claims of religion will come in contact with the natural affections and worldly interests. There is work for everyone in the vineyard of the Lord. None should be idle. Angels of God are all astir, ascending to heaven and descending to earth again with messages of mercy and warning. These heavenly messengers are moving upon minds and hearts. There are men and women everywhere whose hearts are susceptible of being inspired with the truth. If those who have a knowledge of the truth would now work in unison with the Spirit of God, we would see a great work accomplished.

New fields are open in which all can test their calling by experimental effort in bringing souls out from darkness and error, and establishing them upon the platform of eternal truth. If Brother and Sister K feel that God has called them to engage in His work, they have enough to do to call sinners to repentance; but in order for God to work in and through them, they need a thorough conversion. The work of fitting a people in these last days for the coming of Christ, is a most sacred, solemn work, and calls for devoted, unselfish laborers. Those who have humility, faith, energy, perseverance, and decision will find plenty to do in their Master's vineyard. There are responsible duties to be performed, which require earnestness and the exertion of all their energies. It is willing service that God accepts. If the truth we profess is of such infinite importance as to decide the destiny of souls, how careful should we be in its presentation.

"The path of the just is as the shining light, that shineth more and more unto the perfect day." Brother and Sister K, had you walked in the light as it shone upon your pathway, had you been drawing nearer to God, steadfastly believing the truth and walking humbly before God in the light He has given, you would now have an experience that would be of inestimable value. Had you improved the talents lent you of God, you would have shone as lights in the world. But light becomes darkness to all those who will not walk in it. In order to be accepted and blessed of God as our fathers were, we must, like them, be faithful. We must improve our light as the ancient, faithful prophets improved theirs. God requires of us according to the grace that He has bestowed upon us, and He will not accept less than He claims. All His righteous demands must be fully met. In order for us to discharge our responsibilities, we must stand on that elevated ground which the order and advancement of holy, sacred truth has prepared for us.

Brother L fails to realize the sanctifying influence of the truth of God upon the heart. He is not as patient, humble, and forbearing as he should be. He is easily stirred; self arises, and he says and does many things without due reflection. He does not at all times exert a saving influence. If he were imbued with the Spirit of Christ, he could with one hand take hold of the Mighty One, while with the hand of faith and love he would reach the poor sinner. Brother L needs the powerful influence of divine love; for this will renew and refine the heart, sanctify the life, and elevate and ennoble the entire man. Then his words and works will savor of heaven rather than of his own spirit.

If the words of eternal life are sown in the heart, fruit will be produced unto righteousness and peace. A spirit of self-sufficiency and self-importance must be overcome by you, my dear brother. You should cultivate a spirit that is willing to be instructed and counseled. Whatever others may say or do, you should say: What is that to me? Christ has bidden me follow Him. You should cultivate a spirit of meekness. You need an experience in genuine godliness, and unless you have this, you cannot engage in the work of God understandingly.

Your spirit must soften and be subdued by being brought into obedience to the will of Christ. You should at all times maintain the lowly dignity of a follower of Jesus. Our deportment, our words and actions, preach to others. We are living epistles, known and read of all men.

You should be careful not to preach the truth from strife or contention, for if you do you will most assuredly turn the battle against yourself and be found advancing the cause of the enemy rather than the truth of God. Every time that you engage in a contest it should be from a sense of duty. If you make God your strength and subdue yourself, and let the truth bear away the victory, the devices of Satan and his fiery darts will fall upon himself, and you will be strengthened, kept from error, and guarded from every false way. You need to cultivate caution and not rush on in your own strength. The work is important and sacred, and you need great wisdom. You should counsel with your brethren who have had experience in the work. But, above everything else, you should obtain a thorough knowledge of your own weakness and dangers, and should strengthen the weak points in your character, that you may not make shipwreck of faith.

We are living amid the perils of the last days, and if we have a spirit of self-sufficiency and independence we shall be exposed to the wiles of Satan and be overcome. Self-importance must be put away from you, and you be hid in God, depending alone upon Him for strength. The churches do not need your labor. If you are consecrated to God, you can labor in new fields, and God will work with you. Purity of heart and life God will accept. Anything short of this, He will not regard. We must suffer with Christ if we would reign with Him.

Brother M could have accomplished good if he had, years ago, given all for Christ. He has not been sanctified through the truth; his heart has not been right with God. He has hid his talent in the earth. What will he who has put his talents to a wrong use say when the Master shall require him to give account of his stewardship? Brother M has not been an honor to the cause of God. It is dangerous to contend with the providence of God and to be dissatisfied with almost everything, as though there had been a special arrangement of circumstances to tempt and destroy. The work of pruning and purifying to fit us for heaven is a great work and will cost us much suffering and trial, because our wills are not subjected to the will of Christ. We must go through the furnace till the fires have consumed the dross and we are purified and reflect the divine image. Those who follow their inclinations and are governed by appearances are not good judges of what God is doing. They are filled with discontent. They see failure where there is indeed triumph, a great loss where there is gain; and, like Jacob, they are ready to exclaim, "All these things are against me," when the very things whereof they complain are all working together for their good.

No cross, no crown. How can one be strong in the Lord without trials? To have strength we must have exercise. To have strong faith, we must be placed in circumstances where our faith will be exercised. The apostle Paul, just before his martyrdom, exhorted Timothy: "Be thou partaker of the afflictions of the gospel according to the power of God." It is through much tribulation that we are to enter the kingdom of God. Our Saviour was tried in every possible way, and yet He triumphed in God continually. It is our privilege to be strong in the strength of God under all circumstances and to glory in the cross of Christ.

EXPERIENCE NOT RELIABLE

Dear Sister N: In the view given me December 10, 1871, I saw that some things had been great hindrances to your recovery of health. Your peculiar traits of character have prevented you from receiving the good you might have received, and from improving in health as you might have improved.

You have a special routine to go through and you will not be turned aside from it. You have your ideas, which you carry out, when frequently they are not in harmony with physical law, but simply with your judgment.

You have a strong mind and set will, and you think you understand your own case better than others can, because you trace your feelings. You are guided by your feelings and are governed by your experience. You have tried this and that plan to your entire satisfaction, and have decided that your judgment was the best to follow in your own case. But what has been your standard? Answer: *Your feelings.* Now, my sister, what have your feelings to do with the real facts in the case? But very little. Feelings are a poor criterion, especially when under the control of a strong imagination and firm will. You have a very determined mind, and your course is mapped out before you; but you do not view your case from a correct standpoint. Your judgment is not safe to be relied upon when it relates to your own case.

I was shown that you had made some improvement, but not as much, as fast, or as thorough, as you might, because you take your case into your own hands. For this reason, and that you might feel it your duty to be guided by the judgment of the more experienced, I wished you to come to the Health Institute. The physicians of the Health Institute understand disease, its causes and proper treatment, better than you can; and if you will yield your set ideas willingly, and abide by their judgment, there is hope of your recovery. But if you refuse to do this, I see no hope of your becoming what you might be with proper treatment.

As I have before stated, you, my sister, rely upon experience. Your experience decides you to pursue a certain course. But that which many term experience is not experience at all; it is simply habit, or mere indulgence, blindly and frequently ignorantly followed, with a firm, set determination, and without intelligent thought or inquiry relative to the laws at work in the accomplishment of the result.

Real experience is a variety of careful experiments made with the mind freed from prejudice and uncontrolled by previously established opinions and habits. The results are marked with careful solicitude and an anxious desire to learn, to improve, and to reform on every habit that is not in harmony with physical and moral laws. The idea of others' gainsaying what you have learned by experience seems to you to be folly and even cruelty itself. But there are more errors received and firmly retained from false ideas of experience than from any other cause, for the reason that what is generally termed experience is not experience at all; because there has never been a fair trial by actual experiment and thorough investigation, with a knowledge of the principle involved in the action.

Your experience was shown to me as not reliable, because opposed to natural law. It is in conflict with the unchangeable principles of nature. Superstition, my dear sister, arising from a diseased imagination, arrays you in conflict with science and principle. Which shall be yielded? Your strong prejudices and very set ideas in regard to what course is best to be pursued relative to yourself have long held you from good. I have understood your case for years, but have felt incompetent to present the matter in so clear a manner that you could see and comprehend it, and put to a practical use the light given you.

There are many invalids today who will ever remain so because they cannot be convinced that their experience is not reliable. The brain is the capital of the body, the seat of all the nervous forces and of mental action. The nerves proceeding from the brain control the body. By the brain nerves, mental impressions are conveyed to all the nerves of the body as by telegraph wires; and they control the vital action of every part of the system. All the organs of motion are governed by the communications they receive from the brain.

If your mind is impressed and fixed that a bath will injure you, the mental impression is communicated to all the nerves of the body. The nerves control the circulation of the blood;

therefore the blood is, through the impression of the mind, confined to the blood vessels, and the good effects of the bath are lost. All this is because the blood is prevented by the mind and will from flowing readily, and from coming to the surface to stimulate, arouse, and promote the circulation. For instance, you are impressed that if you bathe you will become chilly. The brain sends this intelligence to the nerves of the body, and the blood vessels, held in obedience to your will, cannot perform their office and cause a reaction after the bath. There is no reason in science or philosophy why an occasional bath, taken with studious care, should do you anything but real good. Especially is this the case where there is but little exercise to keep the muscles in action and to aid the circulation of the blood through the system. Bathing frees the skin from the accumulation of impurities which are constantly collecting, and keeps the skin moist and supple, thereby increasing and equalizing the circulation.

Persons in health should on no account neglect bathing. They should by all means bathe as often as twice a week. Those who are not in health have impurities of the blood, and the skin is not in a healthy condition. The multitude of pores, or little mouths, through which the body breathes become clogged and filled with waste matter. The skin needs to be carefully and thoroughly cleansed, that the pores may do their work in freeing the body from impurities; therefore feeble persons who are diseased surely need the advantages and blessings of bathing as often as twice a week, and frequently even more than this is positively necessary. Whether a person is sick or well, respiration is more free and easy if bathing is practiced. By it the muscles become more flexible, the mind and body are alike invigorated, the intellect is made brighter, and every faculty becomes livelier. The bath is a soother of the nerves. It promotes general perspiration, quickens the circulation, overcomes obstructions in the system, and acts beneficially on the kidneys and urinary organs. Bathing helps the bowels, stomach, and liver, giving energy and new life to each. It also promotes digestion, and instead of the system's being weakened it is strengthened. Instead of increasing the liability to cold, a bath, properly taken, fortifies against cold because the circulation is improved and the uterine organs, which are more or less congested, are relieved; for the blood is brought to the surface, and a more easy and regular flow of the blood through all the blood vessels is obtained.

Experience is said to be the best teacher. Genuine experience is indeed superior to book knowledge. But habits and customs gird men and women as with iron bands, and they are generally justified by experience, according to the common understanding of the term. Very many have abused precious experience. They have clung to their injurious habits, which are decidedly enfeebling to physical, mental, and moral health; and when you seek to instruct them, they sanction their course by referring to their experience. But true experience is in harmony with natural law and science.

Here is where we have met the greatest difficulties in religious matters. The plainest facts may be presented, the clearest truths, sustained by the word of God, may be brought before the mind; but the ear and heart are closed, and the all-convincing argument is: "my experience." Some will say: "The Lord has blessed me in believing and doing as I have; therefore I cannot be in error." "My experience" is clung to, and the most elevating, sanctifying truths of the Bible are rejected for what they are pleased to style experience. Many of the grossest habits are cherished under the plea of experience. Many fail to reach that physical, intellectual, and moral improvement which it is their privilege and duty to attain, because they will contend for the reliability and safety of their experience, although that misjudged experience is opposed to the plainest revealed facts. Men and women whose wrong habits have destroyed their constitution and health will be found recommending their experience as safe for others to follow, when it is this very experience that has robbed them of vitality and health. Many examples might be given to show

how men and women have been deceived by relying upon their experience.

The Lord made man upright in the beginning. He was created with a perfectly balanced mind, the size and strength of all its organs being perfectly developed. Adam was a perfect type of man. Every quality of mind was well proportioned, each having a distinctive office, and yet all dependent one upon another for the full and proper use of any one of them. Adam and Eve were permitted to eat of all the trees in the garden, save one. The Lord said to the holy pair: In the day that ye eat of the tree of knowledge of good and evil, ye shall surely die. Eve was beguiled by the serpent to believe that God would not do as He said He would. "Ye shall not surely die," said the serpent. Eve ate and imagined that she felt the sensations of a new and more exalted life. She bore the fruit to her husband, and that which had an overpowering influence upon him was her experience. The serpent had said that she should not die, and she felt no ill effects from the fruit, nothing which could be interpreted to mean death but, just as the serpent had said, a pleasurable sensation which she imagined was as the angels felt. Her experience stood arrayed against the positive command of Jehovah, and Adam permitted himself to be seduced by the experience of his wife. Thus it is with the religious world generally. God's express commands are transgressed, and because "sentence against an evil work is not executed speedily, therefore the heart of the sons of men is fully set in them to do evil."

In the face of the most positive commands of God, men and women will follow their own inclinations and then dare to pray over the matter, to prevail upon God to consent to allow them to go contrary to His expressed will. The Lord is not pleased with such prayers. Satan comes to the side of such persons, as he did to Eve in Eden, and impresses them, and they have an exercise of mind, and this they relate as a most wonderful experience which the Lord has given them. A true experience will be in perfect harmony with natural and divine law. False experience will array itself against science and the principles of Jehovah. The religious world is covered with a pall of moral darkness. Superstition and bigotry control the minds of men and women, and blind their judgment so that they do not discern their duty to their fellow men and their duty to yield unquestioned obedience to the will of God.

Balaam inquired of God if he might curse Israel, because in so doing he had the promise of great reward. And God said, "Thou shalt not go;" but he was urged by the messengers, and greater inducements were presented. Balaam had been shown the will of the Lord in this matter, but he was so eager for the reward that he ventured to ask God the second time. The Lord permitted Balaam to go. Then he had a wonderful experience, but who would wish to be guided by such an experience? There are those who would understand their duty clearly if it were in harmony with their natural inclinations. Circumstances and reason may clearly indicate their duty; but when against their natural inclination, these evidences are frequently set aside. Then these persons will presume to go to God to learn their duty. But God will not be trifled with. He will permit such persons to follow the desires of their own hearts. Psalm 81:11, 12: "But My people would not hearken to My voice." "So I gave them up unto their own hearts' lust: and they walked in their own counsels."

Those who desire to follow a course which pleases their fancy are in danger of being left to follow their own inclinations, supposing them to be the leadings of God's Spirit. The duty of some is indicated sufficiently clear by circumstances and facts; but, through the solicitations of friends, in harmony with their own inclinations, they swerve from the path of duty and pass over the clear evidences in the case; then, with apparent conscientiousness, they pray long and earnestly for light. They have earnest feeling in the matter, and they interpret this to be the Spirit of God. But they are deceived. This course grieves the Spirit of God. They had light and in the very reason of things should have understood their duty; but a few pleasing inducements balance their minds in the wrong direction, and they urge these before the Lord and press their case, and the Lord allows them to have their own way. They have so strong an inclination to follow their own course that He permits them to do so and to suffer the results. These imagine that they have a wonderful experience.

My dear sister, firmness is a strong and controlling influence in your mind. You have acquired strength to stand up and brace against opposition, and carry through difficult and perplexing enterprises. You do not love contention. You are highly sensitive and feel deeply. You are strictly conscientious, and your judgment must be convinced before you will yield to the opinions of others. Had your physical health been unimpaired, you would have made an eminently useful woman. You have long been diseased, and this has affected your imagination so that your thoughts have been concentrated upon yourself, and the imagination has affected the body. Your habits have not been good in many respects. Your food has not been of the right quantity or quality. You have eaten too largely and of a poor quality of food which could not be converted into good blood. You have educated the stomach to this kind of diet. This, your judgment has taught you, was the best, because you realized the least disturbance from it. But this was not a correct experience. Your stomach was not receiving that vigor that it should from your food. Taken in a liquid state your food would not give healthful vigor or tone to the system. But when you change this habit, and eat more solids and less liquids, your stomach will feel disturbed. Notwithstanding this you should not yield the point; you should educate your stomach to bear a more solid diet. You have worn too great an amount of clothing and have debilitated the skin by so doing. You have not given your body a chance to breathe. The pores of the skin, or little mouths through which the body breathes, have become closed, and the system has been filled with impurities.

Your habit of riding out in the open air and sunshine has been very beneficial. Your life out of doors has sustained you so that you have the measure of physical strength that you now enjoy. But you have neglected other exercise which was even more essential than this. You have depended upon your carriage to go even a short distance. You have thought that if you walked even a little way it would injure you, and you have felt weary in doing so. But in this your experience is not reliable.

The same power of motion which you exercise in getting in and out of a carriage, and in going up and down stairs, could just as well be exercised in walking and in performing the ordinary and necessary duties of life. You have been very helpless in regard to domestic duties. You have not felt that you could have the care of your husband's clothes or of his food. Now, my sister, this inability exists more in your imagination than in your inability to perform. You think it will weary and tax you to do this and that; and it does. But you have strength that if put to a practical and economical use would accomplish much good and make you far more useful and happy. You have so great a dread of becoming helpless that you do not exercise the strength with which the Lord has blessed you. In many things you have helped your husband. At the same time you have taxed his patience and strength. When he has thought that you could change some of your habits and improve, you have felt that he did not understand your case. Your friends have felt that you might be more useful in your home and not so helpless. This has grieved you. You thought they did not understand. Some have unwisely pressed their opinion of your case upon you, and this, too, has grieved you. You have felt that God, in answer to prayer, would help you, and you have many times been helped in this way. But you have not gained that physical strength which it was your privilege to enjoy, because you have not performed your part. You have not worked in full union with the Spirit of God.

The Lord has given you a work to do which He does not propose to do for you. You should move out from principle, in harmony with natural law, irrespective of feeling. You should begin to act upon the light that God has given you. You may not be able to do this all at once, but you can do much by moving out gradually in faith, believing that God will be your helper, that He will strengthen you. You could exercise in walking and in performing duties requiring light labor in your family, and not be so dependent upon others. The consciousness that you can do will give you increased strength. If your hands were more employed and your brain less exercised in planning for others, your physical and mental strength would increase. Your brain is not idle, but there is not corresponding labor on the part of the other organs of the body. Exercise, to be of decided advantage to you, should be systematized and brought to bear upon the debilitated organs that they may become strengthened by use. The movement cure is a great advantage to a class of patients who are too feeble to exercise. But for all who are sick to rely upon it, making it their dependence, while they neglect to exercise their muscles themselves, is a great mistake.

Thousands are sick and dying around us who might get well and live if they would; but their imagination holds them. They fear that they will be made worse if they labor or exercise, when this is just the change they need to make them well. Without this they never can improve. They should exercise the power of the will, rise above their aches and debility, engage in useful employment, and forget that they have aching backs, sides, lungs, and heads. Neglecting to exercise the entire body, or a portion of it, will bring on morbid conditions. Inaction of any of the organs of the body will be followed by a decrease in size and strength of the muscles, and will cause the blood to flow sluggishly through the blood vessels.

If there are duties to be done in your domestic life, you do not think it possible that you could do them, but you depend upon others. Sometimes it is exceedingly inconvenient for you to obtain the help you need. You frequently expend double the strength required to perform the task, in planning and searching for someone to do the work for you. If you would only bring your mind to do these little acts and family duties yourself, you would be blessed and strengthened in it, and your influence in the cause of God would be far greater. God made Adam and Eve in Paradise, and surrounded them with everything that was useful and lovely. He planted for them a beautiful garden. No herb nor flower nor tree was wanting which might be for use or ornament. The Creator of man knew that the workmanship of His hands could not be happy without employment. Paradise delighted their souls, but this was not enough; they must have labor to call into exercise the wonderful organs of the body. The Lord had made the organs for use. Had happiness consisted in doing nothing, man, in his state of holy innocence, would have been left unemployed. But He who formed man knew what would be for his best happiness, and He no sooner made him than He gave him his appointed work. In order to be happy, he must labor.

God has given us all something to do. In the discharge of the various duties which we are to perform, which lie in our pathway, our lives will be made useful, and we shall be blessed. Not only will the organs of the body be strengthened by exercise, but the mind also will acquire strength and knowledge through the action of those organs. The exercise of one muscle, while others are left with nothing to do, will not strengthen the inactive ones any more than the continual exercise of one of the organs of the mind will develop and strengthen the organs not brought into use. Each faculty of the mind and each muscle has its distinctive office, and all require to be exercised in order to become properly developed and retain healthful vigor. Each organ and muscle has its work to do in the living organism. Every wheel in the machinery must be a living, active, working wheel. Nature's fine and wonderful works need to be kept in active motion in order to accomplish the object for which they were designed. Each faculty has a bearing upon the others, and all need to be exercised in order to be properly developed. If one muscle of the body is exercised more than another, the one used will become much the larger, and will destroy the harmony and beauty of the development of the system. A variety of exercise will call into use all the muscles of the body.

Those who are feeble and indolent should not yield to their inclination to be inactive, thus depriving themselves of air and sunlight, but should practice exercising out of doors in walking or working in the garden. They will become very much fatigued, but this will not injure them. You, my sister, will experience weariness, yet it will not hurt you; your rest will be sweeter after it. Inaction weakens the organs that are not exercised. And when these organs are used, pain and weariness are experienced, because the muscles have become feeble. It is not good policy to give up the use of certain muscles because pain is felt when they are exercised. The pain is frequently caused by the effort of nature to give life and vigor to those parts that have become partially lifeless through inaction. The motion of these long-disused muscles will cause pain, because nature is awakening them to life.

Walking, in all cases where it is possible, is the best remedy for diseased bodies, because in this exercise all the organs of the body are brought into use. Many who depend upon the movement cure could accomplish more for themselves by muscular exercise than the movements can do for them. In some cases want of exercise causes the bowels and muscles to become enfeebled and shrunken, and these organs that have become enfeebled for want of use will be strengthened by exercise. There is no exercise that can take the place of walking. By it the circulation of the blood is greatly improved.

The active use of the limbs will be of the greatest advantage to you, Sister N. You have had many notions, and have been very sanguine, which has been to your injury. While you fear to trust yourself in the hands of the physicians, and think that you understand your case better than they do, you cannot be benefited, but only harmed, by their treatment of your case. Unless physicians can obtain the confidence of their patients, they can never help them. If you prescribe for yourself, and think you know what treatment you should have, better than the physicians do, you cannot be benefited. You must yield your will and ideas, and not rein yourself up to resist their judgment and advice in your case.

May the Lord help you, my sister, to have not only faith but corresponding works.

FAITHFULNESS IN HOME DUTIES

Dear Sister O: I think you are not happy. In seeking for some great work to do, you overlook present duties lying directly in your path. You are not happy, because you are looking above the little everyday duties of life for some higher and greater work to do. You are restless, uneasy, and dissatisfied. You love to dictate better than you love to perform. You love better to tell others what to do than with ready cheerfulness to take hold and do yourself.

You could have made your father's home more happy had you studied your inclination less and the happiness of others more. When engaged in the common, ordinary duties of life you fail to put your heart into your labor. Your mind is reaching forward and beyond to a work more agreeable, higher, or more honorable. Somebody must do these very things that you take no pleasure in and even dislike. These plain, simple duties, if done with willingness and faithfulness, will give you an education which it is necessary for you to obtain in order to have a love for household duties. Here is an experience that is highly essential for you to gain, but you do not love it. You murmur at your lot, thus making those around you unhappy and meeting with a great loss yourself. You may never be called to do a work which will bring you before the public. But all the work we do that is necessary to be done, be it washing dishes, setting tables, waiting upon the sick, cooking, or washing, is of moral importance; and until you can cheerfully and happily take up these duties you are not fitted for greater and higher duties. The humble tasks before us are to be taken up by someone; and those who do them should feel that they are doing a necessary and honorable work, and that in their mission, humble though it may be, they are doing the work of God just as surely as was Gabriel when sent to the prophets. All are working in their order in their respective spheres. Woman in her home, doing the simple duties of life that must be done, can and should exhibit faithfulness, obedience, and love as sincere as angels in their sphere. Conformity to the will of God makes any work honorable that must be done.

What you need is love and affection. Your character needs to be molded. Your worrying must be laid aside, and in place of this you must cherish gentleness and love. Deny self. We were not created angels, but lower than the angels; yet our work is important. We are not in heaven, but upon the earth. When we are in heaven, then we shall be qualified to do the lofty and elevating work of heaven. It is here in this world that we must be tested and proved. We should be armed for conflict and for duty.

The highest duty that devolves upon youth is in their own homes, blessing father and mother, brothers and sisters, by affection and true interest. Here they can show self-denial and self-forgetfulness in caring and doing for others. Never will woman be degraded by this work. It is the most sacred, elevated office that she can fill. What an influence a sister may have over brothers! If she is right she may determine the character of her brothers. Her prayers, her gentleness, and her affection may do much in a household. My sister, these noble qualities can never be communicated to other minds unless they first exist in your own. That contentment of mind, that affection, gentleness, and sunniness of temper which will reach every heart, will reflect upon you what your heart gives forth to others. If Christ does not reign in the heart, there will be discontent and moral deformity. Selfishness will require of others that which we are unwilling to give them. If Christ is not in the heart, the character will be unlovely.

It is not a great work and great battles alone which try the soul and demand courage. Everyday life brings its perplexities, trials, and discouragements. It is the humble work which frequently draws upon the patience and the fortitude. Self-reliance and resolution will be necessary to meet and conquer all difficulties. Secure the Lord to stand with you, in every place to be your consolation and comfort. A meek and quiet spirit you much need, and without it you cannot have happiness. May God help you, my sister, to seek meekness and righteousness. It is the Spirit of God that you need. If you are willing to be anything or nothing, God will help and strengthen and bless you. But if you neglect the little duties you will never be entrusted with greater.

PRIDE AND VAIN THOUGHTS

Dear Children P and Q: You are deceived in regard to yourselves. You are not Christians. To be true Christians is to be Christlike. You are far from the mark in this respect; but I hope that you will not be deceived until it is too late for you to form characters for heaven.

Your example has not been good. You have not come to the point to obey the words of Christ: "If any man will come after Me, let him deny himself, and take up his cross, and follow Me." Here are lessons that you have not learned. The denial of self has not been a part of your education. You have neglected to study the words of life. "Search the scriptures," said the heavenly Teacher. He knew that this was necessary for all in order for them to become Christ's true followers. You love to read storybooks, but do not find the word of God interesting. You should restrict your reading to the word of God and to books that are of a spiritual and useful character. In so doing you will close a door against temptation, and you will be blessed.

Had you improved the light that has been given in Battle Creek, you would now be far in advance of what you are in the divine life. Both of you are vain and proud. You have not felt that you must give an account of your stewardship. You are accountable to God for all your privileges and for all the means which pass through your hands. You have sought your own pleasure and selfish gratification at the expense of conscience and the approval of God. You do not act like servants of Christ, who are responsible to the Saviour who has bought you with His own precious blood. "Know ye not, that to whom ye yield yourselves servants to obey; his servants ye are to whom ye obey; whether of sin unto death, or of obedience unto righteousness? But God be thanked, that ye were the servants of sin, but ye have obeyed from the heart that form of doctrine which was delivered you. Being then made free from sin, ye became the servants of righteousness."

You are professedly the servants of Christ. Do you then yield to Him ready and willing obedience? Do you earnestly inquire how you shall best please Him who has called you to be soldiers of the cross of Christ? Do you both lift the cross and glory in it? Answer these questions to God. All your acts, however secret you may think they have been, are open to your heavenly Father. Nothing is hidden, nothing covered. All your acts and the motives which prompt them are open to His sight. He has full knowledge of all your words and thoughts. It is your duty to control your thoughts. You will have to war against a vain imagination. You may think that there can be no sin in permitting your thoughts to run as they naturally would without restraint. But this is not so. You are responsible to God for the indulgence of vain thoughts; for from vain imaginations arises the committal of sins, the actual doing of those things upon which the mind has dwelt. Govern your thoughts, and it will then be much easier to govern your actions. Your thoughts need to be sanctified. Paul writes to the Corinthians: "Casting down imaginations, and every high thing that exalteth itself against the knowledge of God, and bringing into captivity every thought to the obedience of Christ." When you come into this position, the work of consecration will be better understood by you both. Your thoughts will be pure, chaste, and elevated; your actions pure and sinless. Your bodies will be preserved in sanctification and honor, that you may present them "a living sacrifice, holy, acceptable unto God, which is your reasonable service." You are required to deny self in little as well as in greater things. You should make an entire surrender to God; you are not approved of Him in your present state.

You have had an unsanctified influence over the youth in _____. Your love of show leads to an expenditure of means which is wrong. You do not realize the claims that the Lord has upon you. You have not become acquainted with the sweet results of self-denial. Its fruits are sacred. To serve yourselves and to please yourselves has been the order of your lives. To spend your means to gratify pride has been your practice. Oh, how much better it would have been for you to have restrained your desires and made some sacrifice for the truth of God, and by thus denying the lust of the eye, the lust of the flesh, and the pride of life have had something to put into the treasury of God! Instead of purchasing frivolous things, put your little into the bank of heaven, that when the Master comes you may receive both principal and interest.

Have you both studied how much you could do to honor your Redeemer upon the earth? Oh, no! You have been pleased to honor yourselves and to receive honor of others, but to study to show yourselves approved of God has not been the burden of your lives. Religion, pure and undefiled, with its strong principles, would prove to you an anchor. In order to answer life's great ends you must avoid the example of those who are seeking for their own pleasure and enjoyment, and who have not the fear of God before them. God has made provisions for you that are ample. He has provided that if you comply with the conditions laid down in His word, and separate from the world, you may receive strength from Him to repress every debasing influence and to develop that which is noble, good, and elevating. Christ will be in you "a well of water springing up into everlasting life." The will, the intellect, and every emotion, when controlled by religion, have a transforming power.

"Whether therefore ye eat, or drink, or whatsoever ye do, do all to the glory of God." Here is a principle which lies at the foundation of every act, thought, and motive; the consecration of the entire being, both physical and mental, to the control of the Spirit of God. The unsanctified will and passions must be crucified. This may be regarded as a close and severe work. Yet it must be done, or you will hear the terrible sentence from the mouth of Jesus: "Depart." You can do all things through Christ, who strengtheneth you. You are of that age when the will, the appetite, and the passions clamor for indulgence. God has implanted these in your nature for high and holy purposes. It is not necessary that they should become a curse to you by being debased. They will become this only when you refuse to submit to the control of reason and conscience. Restrain, deny, are words and works with which you are not familiar by experience. Temptations have swayed you. Unsanctified minds fail to receive that strength and comfort that God has provided for them. They are restless and possess a strong desire for something new, something to gratify, to please and excite the mind; and this is called pleasure. Satan has alluring charms to engage the interest and excite the imagination of the youth in particular, that he may fasten them in his snare. You are building upon the sand. You need to cry earnestly: "O Lord, my inmost soul convert." You can have an influence for good over other young people, or you can have an influence for evil.

May the God of peace sanctify you wholly, soul, body, and spirit.

THE WORK AT BATTLE CREEK

In a vision given me at Bordoville, Vermont, December 10, 1871, I was shown that the position of my husband has been a very difficult one. A pressure of care and labor has been upon him. His brethren in the ministry have not had these burdens to bear, and they have not appreciated his labors. The constant pressure upon him has taxed him mentally and physically. I was shown that his relation to the people of God was similar, in some respects, to that of Moses to Israel. There were murmurers against Moses, when in adverse circumstances, and there have been murmurers against him.

There has been no one in the ranks of Sabbathkeepers who would do as my husband has done. He has devoted his interest almost entirely to the building up of the cause of God, regardless of his own personal interests and at the sacrifice of social enjoyment with his family. In his devotion to the cause he has frequently endangered his health and life. He has been so much pressed with the burden of this work that he has not had suitable time for study, meditation, and prayer. God has not required him to be in this position, even for the interest and progress of the publishing work at Battle Creek. There are other branches of the work, other interests of the cause, that have been neglected through his devotion to this one. God has given us both a testimony which will reach hearts. He has opened before me many channels of light, not only for my benefit, but for the benefit of His people at large. He has also given my husband great light upon Bible subjects, not for himself alone, but for others. I saw that these things should be written and talked out, and that new light would continue to shine upon the word.

I saw that we could accomplish tenfold more to build up the cause by laboring among the people of God, bearing a varied testimony to meet the wants of the cause in different places and under different circumstances, than we could to remain at Battle Creek. Our gifts are needed in the same field in writing and in speaking. While my husband is overburdened, as he has been, with an accumulation of cares and financial matters, his mind cannot be as fruitful in the word as it otherwise would be. And he is liable to be assailed by the enemy; for he is in a position where there is a constant pressure, and men and women will be tempted, as were the Israelites, to complain and murmur against him who stands in the most responsible position in the cause and work of God.

While standing under these burdens that no one else would venture to take, my husband has sometimes, under the pressure of care, spoken without due consideration and with apparent severity. He has sometimes censured those in the office because they did not take care. And when needless mistakes have occurred, he has felt that indignation for the cause of God was justifiable in him. This course has not always been attended with the best results. It has sometimes resulted in a neglect on the part of those reproved to do the very things they should have done; for they feared they would not do them right; and would then be blamed for it. Just as far as this has been the case, the burden has fallen heavier upon my husband.

The better way would have been for him to be away from the office more than he has been, and leave the work with others to do. And if, after patient and fair trial, they proved themselves unfaithful, or not capacitated for the work, they should have been discharged, and left to engage in business where their blunders and mistakes would affect their own personal interests and not the cause of God.

There were those who stood at the head of the business of the Publishing Association who were, to say the very least, unfaithful. And had those in particular who were associated with them as trustees been aware and their eyes not blinded and their sensibilities not paralyzed, these men would have been separated from the work long before they were.

When my husband recovered from his long and severe sickness, he took hold of the work confused and embarrassed as it was left by unfaithful men. He labored with all the resolution and strength of mind and body that he possessed to bring the work up and to redeem it from the disgraceful perplexity into which it had been brought by those who had their own interests prominent and who did not feel that it was a sacred work in which they were engaged. God's hand has been reached out in judgment over these unfaithful ones. Their course and the result should prove a warning to others not to do as they have done.

The experience of my husband during the period of his sickness was unfortunate for him. He had worked in this cause with interest and devotion as no other man had done. He had ventured and taken advance positions as Providence had led, regardless of censure or praise. He had stood alone and battled through physical and mental sufferings, not regarding his own interests, while those whom God designed should stand by his side left him when he most needed their help. He had not only been left to battle and struggle without their help and sympathy, but frequently he had to meet their opposition and murmurings—murmurings against one who was doing tenfold more than any of them to build up the cause of God. All these things have had their influence; they have molded the mind that was once free from suspicion, trustful, and confiding, and caused him to lose confidence in his brethren. Those who have acted a part in bringing about this work will, in a great degree, be responsible for the result. God would have led them if they had earnestly and devotedly served Him.

I was shown that my husband had given his brethren unmistakable evidences of his interest in, and devotion to, the work of God. After he had spent years of his life in privation and unceasing toil to establish the publishing interests upon a sure basis he gave away to the people of God that which was his own and which he could just as well have kept and received the profits from had he chosen so to do. By this act he showed the people that he was not seeking to advantage himself, but to promote the cause of God.

When sickness came upon my husband, many acted in the same unfeeling manner toward him that the Pharisees did toward the unfortunate and oppressed. The Pharisees would tell the suffering ones that their afflictions were on account of their sins, and that the judgments of God had come upon them. By so doing they would increase their weight of suffering. When my husband fell under his weight of care, there were those who were merciless.

When he began to recover, so that in his feebleness and poverty he commenced to labor some, he asked those who then stood at the head of matters at the office for 40 per cent discount on a one-hundred dollar order for books. He was willing to pay sixty dollars for the books which he knew cost the Association only fifty dollars. He asked this special discount in view of his past labors and sacrifices in favor of the publishing department, but was denied this small favor. He was coolly told that they could give him but 25 per cent discount. My husband thought this very hard, yet he tried to bear it in a Christian manner. God in heaven marked the unjust decision, and from that time took the case in His own hands, and has returned the blessings removed, as He did to faithful Job. From the time of that heartless decision, He has been working for His servant, and has raised him above his former health of body, clearness and strength of mind, and freedom of spirit. And since that time my husband has had the pleasure of passing out with his own hands thousands of dollars worth of our publications without price. God will not utterly forget nor forever forsake those who have been faithful, even if they sometimes commit errors.

My husband has had a zeal for God and for the truth, and at times this zeal has led him to overlabor to the injury of physical and mental strength. But the Lord has not regarded this as so great a sin as the neglect and unfaithfulness of His servants in reproving wrongs. Those who praised the unfaithful and flattered the unconsecrated were sharers in their sin of neglect and unfaithfulness.

God has selected my husband and given him special qualifications, natural ability, and an experience to lead out His people in the advance work. But there have been murmurers among Sabbathkeeping Adventists as there were among ancient Israel, and these jealous, suspicious ones, by their suggestions and insinuations, have given occasion to the enemies of our faith to distrust my husband's honesty. These jealous ones of the same faith have placed matters before unbelievers in a false light, and the impressions made stand in the way of many embracing the truth. They regard my husband as a schemer, a selfish, avaricious man, and they are afraid of him and of the truth held by us as a people.

When the appetite of ancient Israel was restricted, or when any close requirement was brought to bear upon them, they reflected upon Moses, that he was arbitrary, that he wished to rule them, and to be altogether a prince over them, when he was only an instrument in God's hand to bring His people into a position of submission and obedience to God's voice.

Modern Israel have murmured and become jealous of my husband because he has pleaded for the cause of God. He has encouraged liberality, he has rebuked those who loved this world, and has censured selfishness. He has pleaded for donations to the cause of God and, to encourage liberality in his brethren, has led off by liberal donations himself; but by many murmuring, jealous ones even this has been interpreted that he wished to be personally benefited by the means of his brethren and that he had enriched himself at the expense of the cause of God; when the facts in the case are that God has entrusted means in his hands to raise him above want so that he need not be dependent upon the mercies of a changeable, murmuring, jealous people. Because we have not selfishly studied our own interest, but have cared for the widow and the fatherless, God has in His providence worked in our behalf and blessed us with prosperity and an abundance.

Moses sacrificed a prospective kingdom, a life of worldly honor and luxury in kingly courts, choosing rather to suffer affliction with the people of God than to enjoy the pleasures of sin for a season, for he esteemed the reproach of Christ greater riches than all the treasures of Egypt. Had we chosen a life of ease and freedom from labor and care we might have done so. But this was not our choice. We chose active labor in the cause of God, an itinerant life, with all its hardships, privations, and exposure, to a life of indolence. We have not lived for ourselves, to please ourselves, but we have tried to live for God, to please and glorify Him. We have not made it an object to labor for property; but God has fulfilled His promise in giving us a hundredfold in this life. He may prove us by removing it from us. If so, we pray for submission to humbly bear the test.

While He has committed to our trust talents of money and influence, we will try to invest them in His cause, that should fires consume and adversity diminish, we can have the pleasure of knowing that some of our treasure is where fires cannot consume or adversity sweep away. The cause of God is a sure bank that can never fail, and the investment of our time, our interest, and our means in it is a treasure in the heavens that faileth not.

I was shown that my husband has had threefold the care he should have had. He has felt tried that Brethren R and S did not help him bear his responsibilities, and has felt grieved because they did not help him in the business matters in connection with the Institute and the Publishing Association. There has been a continual advancement in the work of publishing ever since the unfaithful were separated from it. And as the work increased, there should have been men to share the responsibilities; but some who could have done this had no desire, because it would not increase their possessions as much as some more lucrative business.

There is not that talent in our office that there should be. The work demands the choicest and most select persons to engage in it. With the present state of things in the office my husband will still feel the pressure that he has felt, but which he should no longer bear. It is only by a miracle of God's mercy that he has stood under the burden so long. But there are now many things to be considered. By his persevering care and devotion to the work he has shown what may be done in the publishing department. Men with unselfish interests combined with sanctified judgment may make the work at the office a success. My husband has so long borne the burden alone that it has told fearfully upon his strength, and there is a positive necessity for a change. He must be relieved from care to a great degree, and yet he can work in the cause of God in speaking and writing.

When we returned from Kansas in the autumn of 1870, both of us should have had a period of rest. Weeks of freedom from care were necessary to bring up our exhausted energies. But when we found the important post at Battle Creek nearly deserted, we felt compelled to take hold of the work with double energies, and labored beyond our strength. I was shown that my husband should stand there no longer unless there are men who will feel the wants of the cause and bear the burdens of the work, while he shall simply act as a counselor. He must lay the burden down, for God has an important work for him to do in writing and speaking the truth. Our influence in laboring in the wide field will tell more for the upbuilding of the cause of God. There is a great amount of prejudice in many minds. False statements have placed us in a wrong position before the people, and this stands in the way of many embracing the truth. If they are made to believe that those who occupy responsible positions in the work at Battle Creek are designing and fanatical they conclude that the entire work is wrong and that our views of Bible truth must be incorrect, and they fear to investigate and receive the truth. But we are not to go forth to call the people to look to us; we are not generally to speak of ourselves and vindicate our characters; but we are to speak the truth, exalt the truth, speak of Jesus, exalt Jesus, and this, attended by the power of God, will remove prejudice and disarm opposition.

Brethren R and S love to write; so does my husband. And

God has let His light shine upon His word, and has led him into a field of rich thought that would be a blessing to the people of God at large. While he has borne a triple burden, some of his ministering brethren have let the responsibility drop heavily upon him, consoling themselves with the thought that God had placed Brother White at the head of the work and qualified him for it, and that the Lord had not fitted them for the position; therefore they have not taken the responsibility and borne the burdens which they might have borne.

There should be men who would feel the same interest that my husband has felt. There never has been a more important period in the history of Seventh-day Adventists than the present. Instead of the publishing work diminishing, the demand for our publications is greatly increasing. There will be more to do instead of less. My husband has been murmured against so much, he has contended with jealousy and falsehood so long, and has seen so little faithfulness in men, that he has become suspicious of almost everyone, even of his own brethren in the ministry. The ministering brethren have felt this, and for fear that they should not move wisely, in many instances have not moved at all. But the time has come when these men must labor unitedly to lift the burdens. The ministering brethren lack faith and confidence in God. They believe the truth, and in the fear of God they should unite their efforts, and bear the burdens of this work which God has laid upon them.

If, after one has done the best he can in his judgment, another thinks he can see where he could have improved the matter, he should kindly and patiently give the brother the benefit of his judgment, but should not censure him nor question his integrity of purpose any sooner than he himself would wish to be suspected or unjustly censured. If the brother who feels the cause of God at heart sees that, in his earnest efforts to do, he has made a failure, he will feel deeply over the matter; for he will be inclined to distrust himself and to lose confidence in his own judgment. Nothing will so weaken his courage and godlike manhood as to realize his mistakes in the work that God has appointed him to do, a work which he loves better than his life. How unjust, then, for his brethren who discover his errors to keep pressing the thorn deeper and deeper into his heart, to make him feel more intensely, when with every thrust they are weakening his faith and courage, and his confidence in himself to work successfully in the upbuilding of the cause of God.

Frequently the truth and facts are to be plainly spoken to the erring, to make them see and feel their error that they may reform. But this should ever be done with pitying tenderness, not with harshness or severity, but considering one's own weakness, lest he also be tempted. When the one at fault sees and acknowledges his error, then, instead of grieving him, and seeking to make him feel more deeply, comfort should be given. In the sermon of Christ upon the mount He said: "Judge not, that ye be not judged. For with what judgment ye judge, ye shall be judged: and with what measure ye mete, it shall be measured to you again." Our Saviour reproved for rash judgment. "Why beholdest thou the mote that is in thy brother's eye; . . . and, behold, a beam is in thine own eye?" It is frequently the case that while one is quick to discern the errors of his brethren, he may be in greater faults himself, but be blind to them.

All who are followers of Christ should deal with one another exactly as we wish the Lord to deal with us in our errors and weaknesses, for we are all erring and need His pity and forgiveness. Jesus consented to take human nature, that He might know how to pity, and how to plead with His Father in behalf of sinful, erring mortals. He volunteered to become man's Advocate, and He humiliated Himself to become acquainted with the temptations wherewith man was beset, that He might succor those who should be tempted, and be a tender and faithful high priest.

Frequently there is necessity for plainly rebuking sin and reproving wrong. But ministers who are working for the salvation of their fellow men should not be pitiless toward the errors of one another, nor make prominent the defects in their organizations. They should not expose or reprove their weaknesses. They should inquire if such a course, pursued by another toward themselves, would bring about the desired effect; would it increase their love for, and confidence in, the one who thus made prominent their mistakes? Especially should the mistakes of ministers who are engaged in the work of God be kept within as small a circle as possible, for there are many weak ones who will take advantage if they are aware that those who minister in word and doctrine have weaknesses like other men. And it is a most cruel thing for the faults of a minister to be exposed to unbelievers, if that minister is counted worthy to labor in the future for the salvation of souls. No good can come of this exposure, but only harm. The Lord frowns upon this course, for it is undermining the confidence of the people in those whom He accepts to carry forward His work. The character of every fellow laborer should be jealously guarded by brother ministers. Saith God: "Touch not Mine anointed, and do My prophets no harm." Love and confidence should be cherished. A lack of this love and confidence in one minister for another does not increase the happiness of the one thus deficient, but as he makes his brother unhappy he is unhappy himself. There is greater power in love than was ever found in censure. Love will meet its way through barriers, while censure will close up every avenue of the soul.

My husband must have a change. Losses may occur at the office of publication for want of his long experience, but the loss of money cannot bear any comparison to the health and life of God's servant. The income of means may not be as large for want of economical managers, but if my husband should fail again, it would dishearten his brethren and weaken their hands. Means cannot come in as an equivalent.

There is much to be done. Missionaries should be in the field who are willing, if need be, to go to foreign countries to present the truth before those who sit in darkness. But there is little disposition among young men to consecrate themselves to God and to devote their talents to His service. They are too willing to shun responsibilities and burdens. They are not obtaining the experience in burden bearing or the knowledge of the Scriptures that they should have to fit them for the work that God would accept at their hands. It is the duty of all to see how much they can do for the Master who has died for them. But many are seeking to do just as little as possible and are cherishing the faint hope of getting into heaven at last. It is their privilege to have stars in their crown because of souls saved through their instrumentality. But alas! indolence and spiritual sloth prevail everywhere. Selfishness and pride occupy a large place in their hearts, and there is but little room for heavenly things.

In the prayer that Christ taught His disciples was the request: Forgive us our trespasses as we forgive those who trespass against us. We cannot repeat this prayer from the heart and dare to be unforgiving, for we ask the Lord to forgive our trespasses against Him in the same manner that we forgive those who trespass against us. But few realize the true import of this prayer. If those who are unforgiving did comprehend the depth of its meaning they would not dare to repeat it and ask God to deal with them as they deal with their fellow mortals. And yet this spirit of hardness and lack of forgiveness exists even among brethren to a fearful extent. Brother is exacting with brother.

PECULIAR TRIALS

The position that my husband has so long occupied in the cause and work of God has been one of peculiar trials. His adaptation to business and his clear foresight have led his ministering brethren to drop responsibilities upon him which they should have borne themselves. This has made his burdens very great. And while his brethren have not taken their share of the burdens, they have lost a valuable experience which it was their privilege to obtain had they exercised their minds in the direction of caretaking, of seeing and feeling what must be done for the upbuilding of the cause.

Great trials have been brought upon my husband by his ministering brethren's not standing by him when he most needed their help. The disappointment he has repeatedly felt when those whom he depended upon failed him in times of greatest need has nearly destroyed his power to hope and believe in the constancy of his ministering brethren. His spirits have been so wounded that he has felt justified in being grieved, and he has allowed his mind to dwell upon discouragements. This channel of darkness God would have him close, for he is in danger of making shipwreck here. When his mind becomes depressed, it is natural for him to bring up the past and dwell upon his past sufferings; and unreconciliation takes hold upon his spirits, that God has suffered him to be so beset with trials unnecessarily brought upon him.

The Spirit of God has been grieved because he has not fully committed his ways to God and trusted himself entirely in His hands, not allowing his mind to run in the channel of doubt and unbelief in regard to the integrity of his brethren. In talking doubts and discouragements he has not remedied the evil but has weakened his own powers and given Satan advantage to annoy and distress him. He has erred in talking out his discouragements and dwelling upon the unpleasant features of his experience. In thus talking he scatters darkness but not light. He has at times laid a weight of discouragement upon his brethren, which did not bring to him the least help, but only weakened their hands. He should make it a rule not to talk unbelief or discouragement, or dwell upon his grievances. His brethren generally have loved and pitied him, and have excused this in him, knowing the pressure of care upon him, and his devotion to the cause of God.

My husband has labored untiringly to bring the publishing interest up to its present state of prosperity. I saw that he had had more sympathy and love from his brethren than he has thought he had. They eagerly search the paper to find something from his pen. If there is a tone of cheerfulness in his writings, if he speaks encouragingly, their hearts are lightened, and some even weep with tender feelings of joy. But if gloom and sadness are expressed, the countenances of his brethren and sisters, as they read, grow sad, and the spirit which characterizes his writings is reflected upon them.

The Lord is seeking to teach my husband to have a spirit of forgiveness, and forgetfulness of the dark passages in his experience. The remembrance of the unpleasant past only saddens the present, and he lives over again the unpleasant portion of his life's history. In so doing he is clinging to the darkness and is pressing the thorn deeper into his spirit. This is my husband's infirmity, and it is displeasing to God. This brings darkness and not light. He may feel apparent relief for the time in expressing his feelings; but it only makes more acute the sense of how great his sufferings and trials have been, until the whole becomes magnified in his imagination, and the errors of his brethren, who have aided in bringing these trials upon him, look so grievous that their wrongs seem to him past endurance.

My husband has cherished this darkness so long by living over the unhappy past that he has but little power to control his mind when dwelling upon these things. Circumstances and events which once he would not have minded, magnify before him into grievous wrongs on the part of his brethren. He has become so sensitive to the wrongs under which he has suffered that it is necessary that he should be as little as possible in the vicinity of Battle Creek, where many of the unpleasant circumstances occurred. God will heal his wounded spirit, if he will let Him. But in doing this, he will have to bury the past. He should not talk of it, or write of it.

It is positively displeasing to God for my husband to recount his difficulties and his peculiar grievances of the past. If he had looked upon these things in the light that they were not done to him, but to the Lord, whose instrument he is, then he would have received a great reward. But he has taken the murmurings of his brethren as though done to himself and has felt called upon to make all understand the wrong and wickedness of thus complaining of him when he did not deserve their censure and abuse.

Had my husband felt that he could leave this matter all with the Lord, and that their murmurings and their neglect were against the Master instead of the servant in the Master's service, he would not have felt so aggrieved, and it would not have hurt him. He should have left it with the Lord, whose servant he is, to fight his battles for him and vindicate his cause. Then he would have finally received a precious reward for all his sufferings for Christ's sake.

I saw that my husband should not dwell upon the painful facts in our experience. Neither should he write his grievances, but keep as far from them as he can. The Lord will heal the wounds of the past if he will turn his attention away from them. "For our light affliction, which is but for a moment, worketh for us a far more exceeding and eternal weight of glory; while we look not at the things which are seen, but at the things which are not seen: for the things which are seen are temporal; but the things which are not seen are eternal." When confessions are made by his brethren who have been wrong, he should accept the confessions and generously, nobly, seek to encourage those who have been deceived by the enemy. He should cultivate a forgiving spirit and should not dwell upon the mistakes and errors of others, for in so doing he not only weakens his own soul, but tortures the minds of his brethren who have erred, when they may have done all that they can do by confession to correct their past errors. If God sees it necessary that any portion of their past course should be presented before them, that they may understand how to shun errors in future, He will do this work; but my husband should not trust himself to do it, for it awakens past scenes of suffering that the Lord would have him forget.

PARABLES OF THE LOST

THE LOST SHEEP

I was referred to the parable of the lost sheep. The ninety and nine sheep are left in the wilderness, and search is instituted for the one that has strayed. When the lost sheep is found, the shepherd elevates it to his shoulder and returns with rejoicing. He does not return murmuring and censuring the poor lost sheep for having made him so much trouble, but his return with the burden of the sheep is with rejoicing.

And a still greater demonstration of joy is demanded. Friends and neighbors are called to rejoice with the finder, "for I have found my sheep which was lost." The finding was the theme of rejoicing; the straying was not dwelt upon; for the joy of finding overbalanced the sorrow of the loss and the care, the perplexity and the peril, incurred in searching for the lost sheep and restoring it to safety. "I say unto you, that likewise joy shall be in heaven over one sinner that repenteth, more than over ninety and nine just persons, which need no repentance."

THE LOST SILVER

The lost piece of silver is designed to represent the erring, straying sinner. The carefulness of the woman to find the lost silver is to teach the followers of Christ a lesson in regard to their duty to the erring ones who are straying from the path of right. The woman lighted the candle to increase her light, and then swept the house, and sought diligently till she found it.

Here is clearly defined the duty of Christians toward those who need help because of their straying from God. The erring ones are not to be left in darkness and error, but every available means is to be used to bring them again to the light. The candle is lighted; and, with earnest prayer for heavenly light to meet the cases of those enshrouded in darkness and unbelief, the word of God is searched for clear points of truth, that Christians may be so fortified with arguments from the word of God, with its reproofs, threatenings, and encouragements that the erring ones may be reached. Indifference or neglect will meet the frown of God.

When the woman found the silver, she called her friends and her neighbors together, saying: "Rejoice with me; for I have found the piece which I had lost. Likewise, I say unto you, there is joy in the presence of the angels of God over one sinner that repenteth." If the angels of God rejoice over the erring who see and confess their wrongs and return to the fellowship of their brethren, how much more should the followers of Christ, who are themselves erring, and who every day need the forgiveness of God and of their brethren, feel joy over the return of a brother or a sister who has been deceived by the sophistry of Satan and has taken a wrong course and suffered because of it.

Instead of holding the erring off, their brethren should meet them where they are. Instead of finding fault with them because they are in the dark, they should light their own lamp by obtaining more divine grace and a clearer knowledge of the Scriptures, that they may dispel the darkness of those in error by the light that they bring to them. And when they succeed, and the erring feel their error and submit to follow the light, they should be received gladly, and not with a spirit of murmuring or an effort to impress upon them their exceeding sinfulness, which had called forth extra exertion, anxiety, and wearisome labor. If the pure angels of God hail the event with joy, how much more should their brethren rejoice, who have themselves needed sympathy, love, and help when they have erred and in their darkness have not known how to help themselves.

THE PRODIGAL SON

My attention was called to the parable of the prodigal son. He made a request that his father should give him his portion of the estate. He desired to separate his interest from that of his father, and to manage his share as best suited his own inclination. His father complied with the request, and the son selfishly withdrew from his father, that he might not be troubled with his counsel or reproofs.

The son thought he should be happy when he could use his portion according to his own pleasure, without being annoyed by advice or restraint. He did not wish to be troubled with mutual obligation. If he shared his father's estate, his father had claims upon him as a son. But he did not feel under any obligation to his generous father, and he braced his selfish, rebellious spirit with the thought that a portion of his father's property belonged to him. He requested his share, when rightfully he could claim nothing and should have had nothing.

After his selfish heart had received the treasure, of which he was so undeserving, he went his way at a distance from his father, that he might even forget that he had a father. He despised restraint and was fully determined to have pleasure in any way and manner that he chose. After he had, by his sinful indulgences, spent all that his father had given him, the land was visited by a famine, and he felt pinching want. He then began to regret his sinful course of extravagant pleasure, for he was destitute and needed the means that he had squandered. He was obliged to come down from his life of sinful indulgence to the low business of feeding swine.

After he had come as low as he could he thought of the kindness and love of his father. He then felt the need of a father. He had brought upon himself his position of friendlessness and want. His own disobedience and sin had resulted in his separating himself from his father. He thought of the privileges and bounties that the hired servants of his father's house freely enjoyed, while he who had alienated himself from his father's house was perishing with hunger. Humiliated through adversity, he decided to return to his father by humble confession. He was a beggar, destitute of comfortable or even decent clothing. He was wretched in consequence of privation and was emaciated with hunger.

While the son was at a distance from his home, his father

saw the wanderer, and his first thought was of that rebellious son who had left him years before to follow a course of unrestrained sin. The paternal feeling was stirred. Notwithstanding all the marks of his degradation the father discerned his own image. He did not wait for his son to come all the distance to him, but hastened to meet him. He did not reproach his son, but with the tenderest pity and compassion, that, in consequence of his course of sin, he had brought upon himself so much suffering, the father hastened to give him proofs of his love and tokens of his forgiveness.

Although his son was emaciated and his countenance plainly indicated the dissolute life he had passed, although he was clothed with beggar's rags and his naked feet were soiled with the dust of travel, the father's tenderest pity was excited as the son fell prostrate in humility before him. He did not stand back upon his dignity; he was not exacting. He did not array before his son his past course of wrong and sin, to make him feel how low he had sunk. He lifted him up and kissed him. He took the rebellious son to his breast and wrapped his own rich robe about the nearly naked form. He took him to his heart with such warmth, and evinced such pity, that if the son had ever doubted the goodness and love of his father, he could do so no longer. If he had a sense of his sin when he decided to return to his father's house, he had a much deeper sense of his ungrateful course when he was thus received. His heart, before subdued, was now broken because he had grieved that father's love.

The penitent, trembling son, who had greatly feared that he would be disowned, was unprepared for such a reception. He knew he did not deserve it, and he thus acknowledged his sin in leaving his father: "I have sinned against heaven, and in thy sight, and am no more worthy to be called thy son." He begged only to be accounted as a hired servant. But the father requested his servants to pay him special tokens of respect and to clothe him as if he had ever been his own obedient son.

The father made the return of his son an occasion of special rejoicing. The elder son in the field knew not that his brother had returned, but he heard the general demonstrations of joy and inquired of the servants what it all meant. It was explained that his brother, whom they had thought dead, had returned, and that his father had killed the fatted calf for him because he had received him again as from the dead.

The brother was then angry and would not go in to see or receive his brother. His indignation was stirred that his unfaithful brother, who had left his father and thrown the heavy responsibility upon him of fulfilling the duties which should have been shared by both, should now be received with such honor. This brother had pursued a course of wicked-profligacy, wasting the means his father had given him, until he was reduced to want, while his brother at home had been faithfully performing the duties of a son; and now this profligate comes to his father's house and is received with respect and honor beyond anything that he himself had ever received.

The father entreated his elder son to go and receive his brother with gladness because he was lost and is found; he was dead in sin and iniquity, but is alive again; he has come to his moral senses and abhors his course of sin. But his elder son pleads: "Lo, these many years do I serve thee, neither transgressed I at any time thy commandment: and yet thou never gavest me a kid, that I might make merry with my friends: but as soon as this thy son was come, which hath devoured thy living with harlots, thou hast killed for him the fatted calf."

He assured his son that he was ever with him, and that all he had was his, but that it was right that they should show this demonstration of joy, for "thy brother was dead, and is alive again; and was lost, and is found." The fact that the lost is found, the dead is alive again, overbears all other considerations with the father.

This parable was given by Christ to represent the manner in which our heavenly Father receives the erring and repenting. The father is the one sinned against; yet he, in the compassion of his soul, full of pity and forgiveness, meets the prodigal and shows his great joy that his son, whom he believed to be dead to all filial affection, has become sensible of his great sin and neglect, and has come back to his father, appreciating his love and acknowledging his claims. He knows that the son who has pursued a course of sin and now repents needs his pity and his love. This son has suffered; he has felt his need, and he comes to his father as the only one who can supply this great need.

The return of the prodigal son was a source of the greatest joy. The complaints of the elder brother were natural, but not right. Yet this is frequently the course that brother pursues toward brother. There is too much effort to make those in error feel where they have erred, and to keep reminding them of their mistakes. Those who have erred need pity, they need help, they need sympathy. They suffer in their feelings, and are frequently desponding and discouraged. Above everything else, they need free forgiveness.

LABOR AMONG THE CHURCHES

In the work done for the church at Battle Creek in the spring of 1870, there was not all that dependence upon God that the important occasion demanded. Brethren R and S did not make God their trust, and move in His strength and with His grace, as fully as they should.

When Brother S thinks a person is wrong, he is frequently too severe. He fails to exercise that compassion and consideration that he would have shown toward himself under like circumstances. He is also in great danger of misjudging and erring in dealing with minds. It is the nicest and most critical work ever given to mortals, to deal with minds. Those who engage in this work should have clear discernment and good powers of discrimination. True independence of mind is an element entirely different from rashness. That quality of independence which leads to a cautious, prayerful, deliberate opinion should not be easily yielded, not until the evidence is sufficiently strong to make it certain that we are wrong. This independence will keep the mind calm and unchangeable amid the multitudinous errors which prevail, and will lead those in responsible positions to look carefully at the evidence on every side, and not be swayed by the influence of others, or by the surroundings, to form conclusions without intelligent, thorough knowledge of all the circumstances.

The investigation of cases in Battle Creek was very much after the order in which a lawyer criticizes a witness, and there was a decided absence of the Spirit of God. There were a few united in this work who were active and zealous. Some were self-righteous and self-sufficient, and their testimonies were relied upon, and their influence swayed the judgment of Brethren R and S. Because of some trivial deficiency, Sisters T and U were not received as members of the church. Brethren R and S should have had judgment and discrimination to see that these objections were not of sufficient weight to keep these sisters out of the church. Both of them had been long in the faith and had been true to the observance of the Sabbath for eighteen or twenty years.

Sister V, who brought up these things, should have urged against herself more weighty reasons why she should not have become a member of the church. Was she without sin? Were all her ways perfect before God? Was she perfect in patience, self-denial, gentleness, forbearance, and calmness of temper? If she were without the weaknesses of common women, then she could cast the first stone. Those sisters who were left out of the church were worthy of a place in it; they were beloved of God. But they were dealt with unwisely, without sufficient cause. There were others whose cases were handled with no more heavenly wisdom and without even sound judgment. Brother S's judgment and power of discrimination have been perverted for very many years through the influence of his wife, who has been a most effective medium of Satan. If he had possessed the genuine quality of independence he would have had proper self-respect and with becoming dignity would have built up his own house. When he has started upon a course designed to command respect in his family he has generally carried the matter too far and has been severe and has talked harshly and overbearingly. Becoming conscious of this after a time, he would then go to the opposite extreme and come down from his independence.

In this state of mind he would receive reports from his wife, give up his judgment, and be easily deceived by her intrigues. She would sometimes feign to be a great sufferer and would relate what privations she had endured and what neglect from her brethren, in the absence of her husband. Her prevarications and cunning artifices to abuse the mind of her husband have been great. Brother S has not fully received the light which the Lord has given him in times past in regard to his wife or he would not have been deceived by her as he has been. He has been brought into bondage many times by her spirit because his own heart and life have not been fully consecrated to God. His feelings kindled against his brethren, and he oppressed them. Self has not been crucified. He should seek earnestly to bring all his thoughts and feelings into subjection to the obedience of Christ. Faith and self-denial would have been Brother S's strong helpers. If he had girded on the whole armor of God and chosen no other defense than that which the Spirit of God and the power of truth gives him, he would have been strong in the strength of God.

But Brother S is weak in many things. If God required him to expose and condemn a neighbor, to reprove and correct a brother, or to resist and destroy his enemies, it would be to him a comparatively natural and easy work. But a warfare against self, subduing the desires and affections of his own heart, and searching out and controlling the secret motives of the heart, is a more difficult warfare. How unwilling is he to be faithful in such a contest as this! The warfare against self is the greatest battle that was ever fought. The yielding of self, surrendering all to the will of God and being clothed with humility, possessing that love that is pure, peaceable, and easy to be entreated, full of gentleness and good fruits, is not an easy attainment. And yet it is his privilege and his duty to be a perfect overcomer here. The soul must submit to God before it can be renewed in knowledge and true holiness. The holy life and character of Christ is a faithful example. His confidence in His heavenly Father was unlimited. His obedience and submission were unreserved and perfect. He came not to be ministered unto, but to minister to others. He came not to do His own will, but the will of Him that sent Him. In all things He submitted Himself to Him that judgeth righteously. From the lips of the Saviour of the world were heard these words: "I can of Mine own self do nothing."

He became poor, and made Himself of no reputation. He was hungry and frequently thirsty, and many times weary in His labors; but He had not where to lay His head. When the cold, damp shades of night gathered about Him, the earth was frequently His bed. Yet He blessed those who hated Him. What a life! what an experience! Can we, the professed followers of Christ, cheerfully endure privation and suffering as did our Lord, without murmuring? Can we drink of the cup and be baptized with the baptism? If so, we may share with Him His glory in His heavenly kingdom. If not, we shall have no part with Him.

Brother S has an experience to gain, without which his work will do positive injury. He is affected too much by what others tell him of the erring; he is apt to decide according to the impressions made upon his mind, and he deals with severity, when a milder course would be far better. He does not bear in mind his own weakness, and how hard it is for him to have his course questioned, even when he is wrong. When he decides that a brother or sister is wrong he is inclined to carry the matter through and press his censure, although in doing so he hurts his own soul and endangers the souls of others.

Brother S should shun church trials and should have nothing to do in settling difficulties, if he can possibly avoid it. He has a valuable gift, which is needed in the work of God. But he should separate himself from influences which draw upon his sympathies, confuse his judgment, and lead him to move unwisely. This should not and need not be. He exercises too little faith in God. He dwells too much upon his bodily infirmities and strengthens unbelief by dwelling upon poor feelings. God has strength and wisdom in store for those who seek for it earnestly, in faith believing.

I was shown that Brother S is a strong man upon some points, while upon others he is as weak as a child. His course in dealing with the erring has had a scattering influence. He has confidence in his ability to labor in setting things in order where he thinks it is needed, but he does not view the matter aright. He weaves into his labors his own spirit, and he does not discriminate, but often deals without tenderness. There is such a thing as overdoing the matter in performing strict duty to individuals. "And of some have compassion, making a difference: and others save with fear, pulling them out of the fire; hating even the garment spotted by the flesh."

Duty, stern duty, has a twin sister, which is kindness. If duty and kindness are blended, decided advantage will be gained; but if duty is separated from kindness, if tender love is not mingled with duty, there will be a failure, and much harm will be the result. Men and women will not be driven, but many can be won by kindness and love. Brother S has held aloft the gospel whip, and his own words have frequently been the snap to that whip. This has not had an influence to spur others to greater zeal and to provoke them to good works, but it has aroused their combativeness to repel his severity.

If Brother S had walked in the light, he would not have made so many serious failures. "If any man walk in the day, he stumbleth not, because he seeth the light of this world. But if a man walk in the night, he stumbleth, because there is no light in him." The path of obedience is the path of safety. "He that walketh uprightly walketh surely." Walk in the light, and "then shalt thou walk in thy way safely, and thy foot shall not stumble." Those who do not walk in the light will have a sickly, stunted religion. Brother S should feel the importance of walking in the light, however crucifying to self. It is earnest effort, prompted by love for souls, which strengthens the heart and develops the graces.

My brother, you are naturally independent and self-sufficient. You estimate your ability to do, more highly than it will bear. You pray for the Lord to humble you and fit you for His work, and when He answers your prayer and puts you under the course of discipline necessary for the accomplishment of the object, you frequently give way to doubts and despondency, and think you have reason for discouragement. When Brother W has cautioned and held you back from engaging in church difficulties, you have frequently felt that he was restraining you.

I was shown your labors in Iowa. There was a decided failure to gather with Christ. You distracted, confused, and scattered the poor sheep. You had a zeal, but it was not according to knowledge. Your labors were not in love, but in sternness and severity. You were exacting and overbearing. You did not strengthen the sick and bind up the lame. Your injudicious harshness pushed some out of the fold who can never be reached and brought back. Words fitly spoken are like apples of gold in pictures of silver. Words unfitly spoken are the reverse. Your influence will be like desolating hail.

You have felt restless under restraint when Brother W has cautioned, advised, and reproved you. You have thought that if you could be free and act yourself, you could do a good and great work. But your wife's influence has greatly injured your usefulness. You have not ruled well your own house; you have failed to command your household after you. You have thought that you understood how to manage your home matters. But how have you been deceived! You have too often followed the promptings of your own spirit, which has resulted in perplexities and discouragements, and these have clouded your discernment and weakened you spiritually so that your labors have been marked with great imperfection.

The labors of Brethren R and S in _____ were premature. These brethren had their past experience with its mistakes before them, which should have been sufficient to guard them from engaging in a work that they were not qualified to perform. There was enough that needed to be done. It was a hard place in which to raise up a church. Opposing influences surrounded them. Every move made should have been with due caution and prayerful consideration.

These two brethren had been warned and reproved repeatedly for moving injudiciously, and they should not have taken the responsibilities upon themselves that they did. Oh, how much better would it have been for the cause of God in _____ had they been laboring in new fields! Satan's seat is in _____, as well as in other wicked cities, and he is a wily foe to contend with. There were disorderly elements among the Sabbathkeepers in _____ that were hindrances to the cause. But there is a proper time to speak and act, a golden opportunity which will show the best results of labor put forth.

If things had been left to more fully develop before they were touched, there would have been a separation of the disorderly, unconsecrated ones, and there would not have been an opposition party. This should ever be saved if possible. The church might better suffer much annoyance, and exercise the more patience, than to get in a hurry, drive matters, and provoke a combative spirit. Those who really loved the truth for the truth's sake should have pursued their course with the glory of God in view and let the light of truth shine out before all.

They might expect that the elements of confusion and dissatisfaction among them would make them trouble. Satan would not remain quiet and see a company raised up in _____ to vindicate truth and to dispel sophistry and error. His ire would be kindled, and he would institute a war against those who keep the commandments of God and have the testimony of Jesus. But this should not have made the faithful believers impatient or discouraged. These things should have had an influence to make the true believer more guarded, watchful, and prayerful—more tender, pitiful, and loving to those who were making so great a mistake in regard to eternal things. As Christ has borne, and continues to bear, with our errors, our ingratitude, and our feeble love, so should we bear with those who test and try our patience. Shall the followers of the self-denying, self-sacrificing Jesus be unlike their Lord? Christians should have hearts of kindness and forbearance.

THE GOSPEL SOWER

The parable of the gospel sower, which Christ presented before His hearers, contains a lesson that we should study. Those who preach present truth and scatter the good seed will realize the same results as the gospel sower. All classes will be affected more or less by the presentation of pointed and convincing truth. Some will be wayside hearers. They will be affected by the truths spoken; but they have not cultivated the normal powers, they have followed inclination rather than duty, and evil habits have hardened their hearts until they have become like the hard, beaten road. These may profess to believe the truth; but they will have no just sense of its sacred, elevated character. They do not separate from the friendship of the lovers of pleasure and corrupt society; but they place themselves where they are constantly tempted, and may well be represented by the unfenced field. They invite the temptations of the enemy and finally lose the regard they seemed to have for the truth when the good seed was dropped into their hearts.

Some are stony-ground hearers. They readily receive anything new and exciting. The word of truth they receive with joy. They talk earnestly, with ardor and zeal in reference to their faith and hope, and may even administer reproof to those of long experience for some apparent deficiency or for their lack of enthusiasm. But when they are tested and proved by the heat of trial and temptation, when the pruning knife of God is applied, that they may bring forth fruit unto perfection, their zeal dies, their voices are silent. No longer do they boast in the strength and power of truth.

This class are controlled by feeling. They have not depth and stability of character. Principle does not reach down deep, underlying the springs of action. They have in word exalted the truth, but are not doers of it. The seed of truth has not rooted down below the surface. The heart has not been renewed by the transforming influence of the Spirit of God. And when the truth calls for working men and women, when sacrifices have to be made for the truth's sake, they are somewhere else; and when trials and persecution come, they fall away because they have no depth of earth. The truth, plain, pointed, and close, is brought to bear upon the heart and reveals the deformity of character. Some will not bear this test, but frequently close their eyes to their imperfections; although their consciences tell them that the words spoken by the messengers of God, which bear so closely upon their Christian characters, are truth, yet they will not listen to the voice. They are offended because of the word and yield the truth rather than submit to be sanctified through it. They flatter themselves that they may get to heaven an easier way.

Still another class is represented in the parable. Men and women who listen to the word are convinced of the truth and accept it without seeing the sinfulness of their hearts. The love of the world holds a large place in their affections. In deal they love to get the best of the bargain. They prevaricate, and by deception and fraud gain means which will ever prove as a thorn to them; for it will overbalance their good purposes and intentions. The good seed sown in their hearts is choked. Frequently they are so full of care and anxiety, fearing that they will not gain means, or that they will lose what they have gained, that they make their temporal matters primary. They do not nourish the good seed. They do not attend meetings where their hearts can be strengthened by religious privileges. They fear that they will meet with some loss in temporal things. The deceitfulness of riches leads them to flatter themselves that it is duty to toil and gain all they can, that they may help the cause of God; and yet the more they increase their earthly riches the less are their hearts inclined to part with their treasure, until their hearts are fully turned from the truth they loved. The good seed is choked because overgrown with unnecessary worldly cares and needless anxiety—with love for the worldly pleasures and honors which riches give.

THE WHEAT AND TARES

In another parable which Jesus presented to His disciples, He likened the kingdom of heaven to a field wherein a man sowed good seed, but in which while he was sleeping, the enemy sowed tares. The question was asked the householder: "Didst not thou sow good seed in thy field? from whence then hath it tares? He said unto them, An enemy hath done this. The servants said unto him, Wilt thou then that we go and gather them up? But he said, Nay, lest while ye gather up the tares, ye root up also the wheat with them. Let both grow together until the harvest: and in the time of harvest I will say to the reapers, Gather ye together first the tares, and bind them in bundles to burn them: but gather the wheat into my barn." If faithfulness and vigilance had been preserved, if there had been no sleeping or negligence upon the part of any, the enemy would not have had so favorable an opportunity to sow tares among the wheat. Satan never sleeps. He is watching, and he improves every opportunity to set his agents to scatter error, which finds good soil in many unsanctified hearts.

The sincere believers of truth are made sad, and their trials and sorrows greatly increased, by the elements among them which annoy, dishearten, and discourage them in their efforts. But the Lord would teach His servants a lesson of great carefulness in all their moves. "Let both grow together." Do not forcibly pull up the tares, lest in rooting them up the precious blades will become loosened. Both ministers and church members should be very cautious, lest they get a zeal not according to knowledge. There is danger of doing too much to cure difficulties in the church, which, if let alone, will frequently work their own cure. It is bad policy to take hold of matters in any church prematurely. We shall have to exercise the greatest care, patience, and self-control to bear these things and not go to work in our own spirit to set them in order.

The work done in _____ was premature and caused an untimely separation in that little church. If the servants of God could have felt the force of our Saviour's lesson in the parable of the wheat and tares, they would not have undertaken the work they did. Before steps are taken which will give even those who are utterly unworthy the least occasion to complain of being separated from the church, the matter should always be made a subject of the most careful consideration and earnest prayer. Steps were taken in _____ which created an opposition party. Some were wayside hearers, others were stony-ground hearers, and still others were of that class who received the truth while the heart had a growth of thorns which choked the good seed—these would never have perfected Christian characters. But there were a few who might have been nourished and strengthened, and have become settled and established in the truth. But the positions taken by Brethren R and S brought a premature crisis, and then there was a lack of wisdom and judgment in managing the faction.

If persons are as deserving of being separated from the church as Satan was of being cast out of heaven, they will have sympathizers. There is always a class who are more influenced by individuals than they are by the Spirit of God and sound principles; and, in their unconsecrated state, these are ever ready to take sides with the wrong and give their pity and sympathy to the very ones who least deserve it. These sympathizers have a powerful influence with others; things are seen in a perverted light, great harm is done, and many souls are ruined. Satan in his rebellion took a third part of the angels. They turned from the Father and from His Son, and united with the instigator of rebellion. With these facts before us we should move with the greatest caution. What can we expect but trial and perplexity in our connection with men and women of peculiar minds? We must bear this and avoid the necessity of rooting up the tares, lest the wheat be rooted up also.

"In the world ye shall have tribulation," says Christ; but in Me ye shall have peace. The trials to which Christians are subjected in sorrow, adversity, and reproach are the means appointed of God to separate the chaff from the wheat. Our pride, selfishness, evil passions, and love of worldly pleasure must all be overcome; therefore God sends us afflictions to test and prove us, and show us that these evils exist in our characters. We must overcome through His strength and grace, that we may be partakers of the divine nature, having escaped the corruption that is in the world through lust. "For our light affliction," says Paul, "which is but for a moment, worketh for us a far more exceeding and eternal weight of glory; while we look not at the things which are seen, but at the things which are not seen: for the things which are seen are temporal; but the things which are not seen are eternal." Afflictions, crosses, temptations, adversity, and our varied trials are God's workmen to refine us, sanctify us, and fit us for the heavenly garner.

The harm done to the cause of truth by premature moves can never be fully repaired. The cause of God in _____ has not advanced as it might, and will not stand in as favorable a light before the people as before this work was done. There are frequently persons among us whose influence seems to be but a cipher on the right side. Their lives seem to be useless; but let them become rebellious and combative, and they become zealous workmen for Satan. This work is more in accordance with the feelings of the natural heart. There is great need of self-examination and secret prayer. God has promised wisdom to those who ask Him. Missionary labor is frequently entered upon by those unprepared for the work. Outward zeal is cultivated, while secret prayer is neglected. When this is the case, much harm is done, for these laborers seek to regulate the consciences of others by their own rule. Self-control is much needed. Hasty words stir up strife. Brother S is in danger of indulging a spirit of sharp criticism. This does not become ministers of righteousness.

Brother S, you have much to learn. You have been inclined to charge your failures and your discouragements to Brother W, but close investigation of your motives and of your course of action would reveal other causes which exist in yourself for these discouragements. Following the inclinations of your own natural heart brings you into bondage. The severe, torturing spirit in which you sometimes indulge cuts off your influence. My brother, you have a work to do for yourself which no other person can do for you. Each must give an account of himself to God. He has given us His law as a mirror into which we may look and discover the defects in our characters. We are not to look into this mirror for the purpose of seeing our neighbor's faults reflected, of watching to see if he comes up to the standard, but to see the defects in ourselves, that we may remove them. Knowledge is not all that we need; we must follow the light. We are not left to choose for ourselves and to obey that which is agreeable to us and to disobey when it best suits our convenience. Obedience is better than sacrifice.

TO WEALTHY PARENTS

At the camp meeting in Vermont, in 1870, I felt urged by the Spirit of God to bear a plain testimony relative to the duty of aged and wealthy parents in the disposition of their property. I had been shown that some men who are shrewd, prudent, and sharp in regard to the transaction of business generally, men who are distinguished for promptness and thoroughness, manifest a want of foresight and promptness in regard to a proper disposal of their property while they are living. They know not how soon their probation may close; yet they pass on from year to year with their business unsettled, and frequently their lives finally close without their having the use of their reason. Or they may die suddenly, without a moment's warning, and their property be disposed of in a manner that they would not have approved. These are guilty of negligence; they are unfaithful stewards.

Christians who believe the present truth should manifest wisdom and foresight. They should not neglect the disposition of their means, expecting a favorable opportunity to adjust their business during a long illness. They should have their business in such a shape that, were they called at any hour to leave it, and should they have no voice in its arrangement, it might be settled as they would have had it were they alive. Many families have been dishonestly robbed of all their property and have been subjected to poverty because the work that might have been well done in an hour had been neglected. Those who make their wills should not spare pains or expense to obtain legal advice and to have them drawn up in a manner to stand the test.

I saw that those who profess to believe the truth should show their faith by their works. They should, with the unrighteous mammon, make friends, that they may finally be received into everlasting habitations. God has made men stewards of means. He has placed in their hands the money with which to carry forward the great work for the salvation of souls for whom Christ left His home, His riches, His glory, and became poor that He might, by His own humiliation and sacrifice, bring many sons and daughters of Adam to God. In His providence the Lord has ordained that the work in His vineyard should be sustained by the means entrusted to the hands of His stewards. A neglect on their part to answer the calls of the cause of God in carrying forward His work shows them to be unfaithful and slothful servants.

I had been shown some things in reference to the cause in Vermont, but more especially at Bordoville and vicinity. The following is from *Testimony for the Church,* No. 20:

"There is a work to be accomplished for many who live at Bordoville. I saw that the enemy was busily at work to carry his points. Men to whom God has entrusted talents of means have shifted upon their children the responsibility which Heaven has appointed them of being stewards for God. Instead of rendering to God the things that are His, they claim that all they have is their own, as though by their own might and power and wisdom they had obtained their possessions."

"Some place their means beyond their control by putting it into the hands of their children. Their secret motive is to place themselves in a position where they will not feel responsible to give of their property to spread the truth. These love in word, but not in deed and in truth. They do not realize that it is the Lord's money they are handling, not their own."

"Parents should have great fear in entrusting children with the talents of means that God has placed in their hands, unless they have the surest evidence that their children have greater interest in, love for, and devotion to, the cause of God than they themselves possess, and that these children will be more earnest and zealous in forwarding the work of God, and more benevolent in carrying forward the various enterprises connected with it which call for means. But many place their means in the hands of their children, thus throwing upon them the responsibility of their own stewardship, because Satan prompts them to do it. In so doing they effectually place that means in the enemy's ranks. Satan works the matter to suit his own purpose and keeps from the cause of God the means which it needs, that it may be abundantly sustained."

"Many who have made a high profession of faith are deficient in good works. If they should show their faith by their works they could exert a powerful influence on the side of truth. But they do not improve upon the talents of means lent them of God. Those who think to ease their consciences by willing their property to their children, or by withholding from God's cause and suffering it to pass into the hands of unbelieving, reckless children for them to squander or hoard up and worship, will have to render an account to God; they are unfaithful stewards of their Lord's money. They allow Satan to outgeneral them through these children, whose minds are under his control. Satan's purposes are accomplished in many ways, while the stewards of God seem stupefied and paralyzed; they do not realize their great responsibility and the reckoning which must shortly come."

I was shown that the probation of some in the vicinity of _____ was soon to close, and that it was important that their work be finished to God's acceptance, that in the final settlement they might hear the "Well done" from the Master. I was also shown the inconsistency of those who profess to believe the truth withholding their means from the cause of God, that they may leave it for their children. Many fathers and mothers are poor in the midst of abundance. They abridge, in a degree, their own personal comforts and frequently deny themselves of those things that are necessary for the enjoyment of life and health, while they have ample means at their command. They feel forbidden, as it were, to appropriate their means for their own comfort or for charitable purposes. They have one object before them, and that is to save property to leave for their children. This idea is so prominent, so interwoven with all their actions, that their children learn to look forward to the time when this property will be theirs. They depend upon it, and this prospect has an important but not a favorable influence upon their characters. Some become spendthrifts, others become selfish and avaricious, and still others grow indolent and reckless. Many do not cultivate habits of economy; they do not seek to become self-reliant. They are aimless, and have but little stability of character. The impressions received in childhood and youth are wrought in the texture of character and become the principle of action in mature life.

Those who have become acquainted with the principles of the truth should closely follow the word of God as their guide. They should render to God the things that are God's. I was shown that several in Vermont were making a great mistake in regard to appropriating the means that God had entrusted to their keeping. They were overlooking the claims of God upon all that they have. Their eyes were blinded by the enemy of righteousness, and they were taking a course which would result disastrously for themselves and their dear children.

Children were influencing their parents to leave their property in their hands for them to appropriate according to their judgment. With the light of God's word, so plain and clear in reference to the money lent to stewards, and with the warnings and reproofs which God has given through the *Testimonies* in regard to the disposition of means—if, with all this light before them, children either directly or indirectly influence their parents to divide their property while living, or to will it mainly to the children to come into their hands after the death of their parents, they take upon themselves fearful responsibilities. Children of aged parents who profess to believe the truth should, in the fear of God, advise and entreat their parents to be true to their profession of faith, and take a course in regard to their means which God can approve. Parents should lay up for themselves treasures in heaven by appropriating their means themselves to the advancement of the cause of God. They should not rob themselves of heavenly treasure by leaving a surplus of means to those who have enough; for by so doing they not only deprive themselves of the precious privilege of laying up a treasure in the heavens that faileth not, but they rob the treasury of God.

I stated at the camp meeting that when property is willed principally to children, while none is appropriated to the cause of God, or, if any, a meager pittance unworthy to be mentioned, this property would frequently prove a curse to the children who inherit it. It would be a source of temptation and would open a door through which they would be in danger of falling into many dangerous and hurtful lusts.

Parents should exercise the right that God has given them. He entrusted to them the talents He would have them use to His glory. The children were not to become responsible for the talents of the father. While they have sound minds and good judgment, parents should, with prayerful consideration, and with the help of proper counselors who have experience in the truth and a knowledge of the divine will, make disposition of their property. If they have children who are afflicted or are struggling in poverty, and who will make a judicious use of means, they should be considered. But if they have unbelieving children who have abundance of this world, and who are serving the world, they commit a sin against the Master, who has made them His stewards, by placing means in their hands merely because they are their children. God's claims are not to be lightly regarded.

And it should be distinctly understood that because parents have made their will, this will not prevent them from giving means to the cause of God while they live. This they should do. They should have the satisfaction here, and the reward hereafter, of disposing of their surplus means while they live. They should do their part to advance the cause of God. They should use the means lent them by the Master to carry on the work which needs to be done in His vineyard.

The love of money lies at the root of nearly all the crimes committed in the world. Fathers who selfishly retain their means to enrich their children, and who do not see the wants of the cause of God and relieve them, make a terrible mistake. The children whom they think to bless with their means are cursed with it.

Money left to children frequently becomes a root of bitterness. They often quarrel over the property left them and in case of a will, are seldom all satisfied with the disposition made by the father. And instead of the means left exciting gratitude and reverence for his memory, it creates dissatisfaction, murmuring, envy, and disrespect. Brothers and sisters who were at peace with one another are sometimes made at variance, and family dissensions are often the result of inherited means. Riches are desirable only as a means of supplying present wants and of doing good to others. But inherited riches oftener become a snare to the possessor than a blessing. Parents should not seek to have their children encounter the temptations to which they expose them in leaving them means which they themselves have made no effort to earn.

I was shown that some children professing to believe the truth would, in an indirect manner, influence the father to keep his means for his children instead of appropriating it to the cause of God while he lives. Those who have influenced their father to shift his stewardship upon them little know what they are doing. They are gathering upon themselves double responsibility, that of balancing the father's mind so that he did not fulfill the purpose of God in the disposition of the means lent him of God to be used to His glory, and the additional responsibility of becoming stewards of means that should have been put out to the exchangers by the father, that the Master could have received His own with usury.

Many parents make a great mistake in placing their property out of their hands into the hands of their children while they are themselves responsible for the use or abuse of the talent lent them of God. Neither parents nor children are made happier by this transfer of property. And the parents, if they live a few years even, generally regret this action on their part. Parental love in their children is not increased by this course. The children do not feel increased gratitude and obligation to their parents for their liberality. A curse seems to lay at the root of the matter, which only crops out in selfishness on the part of the children and unhappiness and miserable feelings of cramped dependence on the part of the parents.

If parents, while they live, would assist their children to help themselves, it would be better than to leave them a large amount at death. Children who are left to rely principally upon their own exertions make better men and women, and are better fitted for practical life than those children who have depended upon their father's estate. The children left to depend upon their own resources generally prize their abilities, improve their privileges, and cultivate and direct their faculties to accomplish a purpose in life. They frequently develop characters of industry, frugality, and moral worth, which lie at the foundation of success in the Christian life. Those children for whom parents do the most, frequently feel under the least obligation toward them. The errors of which we have spoken have existed in _____ . Parents have shifted their stewardship upon their children.

At the camp meeting at _____, 1870, I appealed to those who had means to use that means in the cause of God as His faithful stewards, and not leave this work for their children. It is a work which God has left them to do, and when the Master calls them to account, they can, as faithful stewards, render to Him that which He has lent them, both principal and interest.

Brethren X, Y, Z were presented before me. These men were making a mistake in regard to the appropriation of their means. Some of their children were influencing them in this work, and were gathering upon their souls responsibilities that they were ill-prepared to bear. They were opening a door and inviting the enemy to come in with his temptations to harass and destroy them. The two younger sons of Brother X were in great danger. They were associating with individuals of a stamp of character which would not elevate, but would debase them. The subtle influence of these associations was gaining an imperceptible influence over these young men. The conversation and deportment of evil companions were of that character to separate them from the influence of their sisters and their sisters' husbands. While speaking upon this subject at the camp meeting I felt deeply. I knew the persons were before me whom I had seen in vision. I urged upon those who heard me the necessity of thorough consecration to God. I called no names, for I was not permitted to do this.

I was to dwell upon principles, appeal to the hearts and consciences, and give those who professed to love God and keep His commandments an opportunity to develop character. God would send them warnings and admonitions, and if they really desired to do His will they had an opportunity. Light was given, and then we were to wait and see if they would come to the light.

I left the camp meeting with a burden of anxiety upon my mind in reference to the persons whose danger I had been shown. In a few months news reached us of Brother Y's death. His property was left to his children. Last December we had an appointment to hold meetings in Vermont. My husband was indisposed and could not go. In order to save too great a disappointment, I consented to go to Vermont in company with Sister Hall. I spoke to the people with some freedom, but our conference meetings were not free. I knew that the Spirit of the Lord could not have a free course until confessions were made and there was a breaking of heart before God. I could not keep silent. The Spirit of the Lord was upon me, and I related briefly the substance of what I have written. I called the names of some present who were standing in the way of the work of God.

The result of leaving property to children by will, and also of parents' shifting the responsibility of their stewardship upon their children while the parents were living, had been verified before them. Covetousness had led Brother Y's sons to pursue a wrong course. This was especially true of one of his sons. I labored faithfully, relating the things which I had seen in reference to the church, especially to the sons of Brother Y. One of these brothers, himself a father, was corrupt in heart and life, a reproach to the precious cause of present truth; his low standard of morals was corrupting to the youth.

The Spirit of the Lord came into the meetings, and humble confessions were made by some, accompanied by tears. After the meeting I had an interview with the younger sons of Brother X. I pleaded with them, and entreated them for their souls' sake to turn square about, break away from the company of those who were leading them on to ruin, and seek for the things which make for their peace. While pleading for these young men, my heart was drawn out after them, and I longed to see them submit to God. I prayed for them, and urged them to pray for themselves. We were gaining the victory; they were yielding. The voice of each was heard in humble, penitential prayer, and I felt that indeed the peace of God rested upon us. Angels seemed to be all around us, and I was shut up in a vision of God's glory. The state of the cause at _____ was again shown me. I saw that some had backslidden far from God. The youth were in a state of backsliding.

I was shown that the two younger sons of Brother X were naturally goodhearted, conscientious young men, but that Satan had blinded their perception. Their companions were not all of that class which would strengthen and improve their morals or increase their understanding and love for the truth and heavenly things. "One sinner destroyeth much good." The ridicule and corrupt conversation of these companions had had its effect to dispel serious and religious impressions.

It is wrong for Christians to associate with those whose morals are loose. An intimate, daily intercourse which occupies time without contributing in any degree to the strength of the intellect or morals is dangerous. If the moral atmosphere surrounding persons is not pure and sanctified, but is tainted with corruption, those who breathe this atmosphere will find that it operates almost insensibly upon the intellect and heart to poison and to ruin. It is dangerous to be conversant with those whose minds naturally take a low level. Gradually and imperceptibly those who are naturally conscientious and love purity will come to the same level and partake of and sympathize with the imbecility and moral barrenness with which they are so constantly brought in contact.

It was important that the associations of these young men should change. "Evil communications corrupt good manners." Satan has worked through agents to ruin these young men. Nothing can more effectually prevent or banish serious impressions and good desires than association with vain, careless, and corrupt-minded persons. Whatever attractions such persons may possess by their wit, sarcasm, and fun, the fact that they treat religion with levity and indifference is sufficient reason why they should not be associated with. The more engaging they are in other respects, the more should their influence be dreaded as companions, because they throw around an irreligious life so many dangerous attractions.

These young men should choose for their associates those who love the purity of truth, whose morals are untainted, and whose habits are pure. They must comply with the conditions laid down in the word of God, if they would indeed become sons of God, members of the royal family, children of the heavenly King. "Come out from among them, and be ye separate, saith the Lord, and touch not the unclean thing; and I will receive you." God loves these young men, and if they will follow the leadings of His Spirit, and walk in His counsel, He will be their strength.

God has given Brother A Y good abilities, quick perceptions, and a good understanding of His word. If his heart were sanctified, he could have an influence for good with his brothers, as well as his neighbors and those with whom he associates. But the love of money has taken so firm a hold of his soul, and has been so interwoven with all the transactions of life, that he has become conformed to the world instead of being transformed by the renewing of the mind. His powers have been perverted and debased by sordid love of gain, which has made him selfish, penurious, and overbearing. Had his qualities been put into active use in his Master's service, rather than used to serve his own selfish interests, had his object and aim been to do good and glorify God, the qualities of mind that God had given him would impart to his character an energy, humility, and efficiency which could not fail to command respect and would give him an influence over all with whom he associated.

I was shown that the property left by the father had indeed been a root of bitterness to his children. Their peace and happiness, and their confidence in one another, had been greatly disturbed by it. Brother A Y did not need his father's property. He had enough talents to handle that God had entrusted to his management. If he made a right disposition of that which he had, he would at least be among that number who were faithful in that which is least. The addition of the stewardship of his father's property, which he had covetously desired, was a heavier responsibility than he could well manage.

For several years the love of money has been rooting out the love of humanity and the love of God. And as the means of his father were within his reach, he desired to retain all that was possible in his own hands. He pursued a selfish course toward his brothers because he had the advantage and could do so. His brothers have not had right feelings. They have felt bitter toward him. He has in deal advantaged himself to the disadvantage of others until his course has reproached the cause of God. He has lost command of himself. His greatest object has been gain, selfish gain. The love of money in the heart was the root of all this evil. I was shown that had he turned his powers to labor in the vineyard of the Lord he would have done much good, but these qualifications perverted can do a great deal of harm.

The brothers B have not had the help they ought to have had. A B has labored to great disadvantage. He has taken too many burdens upon him, which has crippled his labors so that he has not increased in spiritual strength and courage as he should. The church, who have the light of truth, and should be strong in God to will and do, and to sacrifice, if need be, for the truth's sake, have been like weak children. They have required the time and labor of Brother A B to settle difficulties which should never have existed. And when these difficulties have arisen because of selfishness and unsanctified hearts, they could have been put away in an hour, had there been humility and a spirit of confession.

The brothers B make a mistake in remaining at _____ .

They should change their location and not see this place oftener than a few times in the year. They would have greater freedom in bearing their testimony. These brethren have not felt freedom in speaking out truth and facts as they have existed. If they had lived elsewhere, they would have been more free from burdens, and their testimony would have had tenfold more weight when they did visit this church. While Brother A B has been weighed down with petty church trials and kept at _____, he should have been laboring abroad. He has served tables until his mind has become clouded, and he does not comprehend the force and power of the truth. He has not been awake to the real wants of the cause of God. He has been losing spirituality and courage. The work of keeping up systematic benevolence has been neglected. Some of the brethren, whose whole interest was once in the advancement of the cause of God, have been growing selfish and penurious instead of becoming more self-sacrificing and their love for the truth and devotion to it increasing. They have been growing less devotional and more like the world. Father C is one of this number. He needs a new conversion. Brother C has been favored with superior privileges, and if these are not improved, condemnation and darkness will follow equal to the light he has had, for the nonimprovement of the talents lent of God for him to improve.

The brethren in Vermont have grieved the Spirit of God in allowing their love for the truth and their interest in the work of God to decline.

Brother D B overtaxed his strength last season while laboring in new fields with the tent without suitable help. God does not require this brother, or any of His servants, to injure their health by exposure and taxing labor. The brethren at _____ should have felt an interest that would have been shown by their works. They could have secured help if they had been awake to the interest of the cause of God and felt the worth of souls. While Brother D B felt a deep sense of the work of God and the value of souls, which called for continual effort, a large church at _____ by their petty difficulties held Brother A B from helping his brother. These brothers should come up with renewed courage, shake themselves from the trials and discouragements which have held them at _____ and crippled their testimony, and should claim strength from the Mighty One. They should have borne a plain, free testimony to Brother X and Y, and urged the truth home, and done what they could to have these men make a proper distribution of their property. Brother A B, in taking so many burdens, is lessening his mental and physical strength.

If Brother C had been walking in the light for a few years past, he would have felt the value of souls. Had he been cultivating a love for the truth he might have been qualified to teach the truth to others. He might have helped Brother D B in his work with the tent. He might at least have taken the burdens of the church at home. If he had had love for his brethren, and been sanctified through the truth, he could have been a peacemaker instead of a stirrer-up of strife, which, united with other difficulties, called Brother A B from his brother's side at a most important time and resulted in Brother D B's laboring far beyond his strength. And yet, after Brother D B had done all that he could, the work was not accomplished that might have been had there been the interest there should have been in _____ to supply help when it was so much needed. A fearful responsibility rests upon that church for their neglect of duty.

I was shown that Brother X's course in dividing his property among his children was shifting the responsibility upon them which he should not have laid off. He now sees that the result of this course has brought to him no increase of affection from his children. They have not felt under obligation to their parents for what they have done for them. These children were young and inexperienced. They were not qualified to bear the responsibility laid upon them. Their hearts were unconsecrated, and true friends were looked upon by them as designing enemies, while those who would separate very friends were accepted. These agents of Satan were continually suggesting false ideas to the minds of these young men, and the hearts of brothers and sisters, father and mother, were at variance.

Father X made a mistake. Had he confided more in his daughters' husbands, who loved the truth in sincerity, and had he been more willing to be helped by the advice of these men of experience, great mistakes might have been prevented. But this is the way the enemy generally succeeds in managing matters in regard to the appropriation of means.

These cases mentioned were designed of God to be developed that all might see the effect of the deceitfulness of riches upon the heart. The result in these cases, which is apparent to all, should prove a warning to fathers and mothers and to ambitious children. The word of God defines covetousness as idolatry. It is impossible for men and women to keep the law of God and love money. The heart's affections should be placed upon heavenly things. Our treasure should be laid up in heaven, for where our treasure is, there will our heart be also.

NUMBER TWENTY-TWO

TESTIMONY FOR THE CHURCH

PROPER EDUCATION

It is the nicest work ever assumed by men and women to deal with youthful minds. The greatest care should be taken in the education of youth to so vary the manner of instruction as to call forth the high and noble powers of the mind. Parents and schoolteachers are certainly disqualified to properly educate children if they have not first learned the lesson of self-control, patience, forbearance, gentleness, and love. What an important position for parents, guardians, and teachers! There are very few who realize the most essential wants of the mind and how to direct the developing intellect, the growing thoughts and feelings of youth.

There is a time for training children and a time for educating youth, and it is essential that in school both of these be combined in a great degree. Children may be trained for the service of sin or for the service of righteousness. The early education of youth shapes their characters both in their secular and in their religious life. Solomon says: "Train up a child in the way he should go: and when he is old, he will not depart from it." This language is positive. The training which Solomon enjoins is to direct, educate, and develop. In order for parents and teachers to do this work, they must themselves understand "the way" the child should go. This embraces more than merely having a knowledge of books. It takes in everything that is good, virtuous, righteous, and holy.

It comprehends the practice of temperance, godliness, brotherly kindness, and love to God and to one another. In order to attain this object, the physical, mental, moral, and religious education of children must have attention.

The education of children, at home or at school, should not be like the training of dumb animals; for children have an intelligent will, which should be directed to control all their powers. Dumb animals need to be trained, for they have not reason and intellect. But the human mind must be taught self-control. It must be educated to rule the human being, while animals are controlled by a master and are trained to be submissive to him. The master is mind, judgment, and will for his beast. A child may be so trained as to have, like the beast, no will of his own. Even his individuality may be merged in the one who superintends his training; his will, to all intents and purposes, is subject to the will of the teacher.

Children who are thus educated will ever be deficient in moral energy and individual responsibility. They have not been taught to move from reason and principle; their wills have been controlled by another, and the mind has not been called out, that it might expand and strengthen by exercise. They have not been directed and disciplined with respect to their peculiar constitutions and capabilities of mind, to put forth their strongest powers when required. Teachers should not stop here, but should give special attention to the cultivation of the weaker faculties, that all the powers may be brought into exercise, and carried forward from one degree of strength to another, that the mind may attain due proportions.

There are many families of children who appear to be well trained while under the training discipline; but when the system which has held them to set rules is broken up, they seem to be incapable of thinking, acting, or deciding for themselves. These children have been so long under iron rule, not allowed to think and act for themselves in those things in which it was highly proper that they should, that they have no confidence in themselves to move out upon their own judgment, having an opinion of their own. And when they go out from their parents to act for themselves, they are easily led by others' judgment in the wrong direction. They have not stability of character. They have not been thrown upon their own judgment as fast and as far as practicable, and therefore their minds have not been properly developed and strengthened. They have so long been absolutely controlled by their parents that they rely wholly upon them; their parents are mind and judgment for them.

On the other hand, the young should not be left to think and act independently of the judgment of their parents and teachers. Children should be taught to respect experienced judgment and to be guided by their parents and teachers. They should be so educated that their minds will be united with the minds of their parents and teachers, and so instructed that they can see the propriety of heeding their counsel. Then when they go forth from the guiding hand of their parents and teachers, their characters will not be like the reed trembling in the wind.

The severe training of youth, without properly directing them to think and act for themselves as their own capacity and turn of mind will allow, that by this means they may have growth of thought, feelings of self-respect, and confidence in their own ability to perform, will ever produce a class who are weak in mental and moral power. And when they stand in the world to act for themselves they will reveal the fact that they were trained like the animals, and not educated. Their wills, instead of being guided, were forced into subjection by the harsh discipline of parents and teachers.

Those parents and teachers who boast of having complete control of the minds and wills of the children under their care would cease their boastings could they trace out the future lives of the children who are thus brought into subjection by force or through fear. These are almost wholly unprepared to share in the stern responsibilities of life. When these youth are no longer under their parents and teachers, and are compelled to think and act for themselves, they are almost sure to take a wrong course and yield to the power of temptation. They do not make this life a success, and the same deficiencies are seen in their religious life. Could the instructors of children and youth have the future result of their mistaken discipline mapped out before them, they would change their plan of education. That class of teachers who are gratified that they have almost complete control of the wills of their scholars are not the most successful teachers, although the appearance for the time being may be flattering.

God never designed that one human mind should be under the complete control of another. And those who make efforts to have the individuality of their pupils merged in themselves, and to be mind, will, and conscience for them, assume fearful responsibilities. These scholars may, upon certain occasions, appear like well-drilled soldiers. But when the restraint is removed, there will be seen a want of independent action from firm principle existing in them. Those who make it their object to so educate their pupils that they may see and feel that the power lies in themselves to make men and women of firm principle, qualified for any position in life, are the most useful and permanently successful teachers. Their work may not show to the very best advantage to careless observers, and their labors may not be valued as highly as are those of the teacher who holds the minds and wills of his scholars by absolute authority; but the future lives of the pupils will show the fruits of the better plan of education.

There is danger of both parents and teachers commanding and dictating too much, while they fail to come sufficiently into social relation with their children or scholars. They often hold themselves too much reserved, and exercise their authority in a cold, unsympathizing manner which cannot win the hearts of their children and pupils. If they would gather the children close to them, and show that they love them, and would manifest an interest in all their efforts and even in their sports, sometimes even being a child among children, they would make the children very happy and would gain their love and win their confidence. And the children would sooner respect and love the authority of their parents and teachers.

The habits and principles of a teacher should be considered of even greater importance than his literary qualifications. If he is a sincere Christian he will feel the necessity of having an equal interest in the physical, mental, moral, and spiritual education of his scholars. In order to exert the right influence, he should have perfect control over himself, and his own heart should be richly imbued with love for his pupils, which will be seen in his looks, words, and acts. He should have firmness of character, and then he can mold the minds of his pupils as well as instruct them in the sciences. The early education of youth generally shapes their characters for life. Those who deal with the young should be very careful to call out the qualities of the mind, that they may better know how to direct its powers so that they may be exercised to the very best account.

CLOSE CONFINEMENT AT SCHOOL

The system of education carried out for generations back has been destructive to health and even life itself. Many young children have passed five hours each day in schoolrooms not properly ventilated, nor sufficiently large for the healthful accommodation of the scholars. The air of such rooms soon becomes poison to the lungs that inhale it. Little children, whose limbs and muscles are not strong, and whose brains are undeveloped, have been kept confined indoors to their injury. Many have but a slight hold on life to begin with. Confinement in school from day to day makes them nervous and diseased. Their bodies are dwarfed because of the exhausted condition of the nervous system. And if the lamp of life goes out, the parents and teachers do not consider that they had any direct influence in quenching the vital spark. When standing by the graves of the children, the afflicted parents look upon their bereavement as a special dispensation of

Providence, when, by inexcusable ignorance, their own course has destroyed the lives of their children. To then charge their death to Providence is blasphemy. God wanted the little ones to live and be disciplined, that they might have beautiful characters and glorify Him in this world and praise Him in the better world.

Parents and teachers, in taking the responsibility of training these children, do not feel their accountability before God to become acquainted with the physical organism, that they may treat the bodies of their children and pupils in a manner to preserve life and health. Thousands of children die because of the ignorance of parents and teachers. Mothers will spend hours over needless work upon their own dresses and those of their children to fit them for display, and will then plead that they cannot find time to read up and obtain the information necessary to take care of the health of their children. They think it less trouble to trust their bodies to the doctors. In order to be in accordance with fashion and custom, many parents have sacrificed the health and lives of their children.

To become acquainted with the wonderful human organism, the bones, muscles, stomach, liver, bowels, heart, and pores of the skin, and to understand the dependence of one organ upon another for the healthful action of all, is a study in which most mothers take no interest. They know nothing of the influence of the body upon the mind and of the mind upon the body. The mind, which allies finite to the infinite, they do not seem to understand. Every organ of the body was made to be servant to the mind. The mind is the capital of the body. Children are allowed to eat flesh meats, spices, butter, cheese, pork, rich pastry, and condiments generally. They are also allowed to eat irregularly and between meals of unhealthful food. These things do their work of deranging the stomach, exciting the nerves to unnatural action, and enfeebling the intellect. Parents do not realize that they are sowing the seed which will bring forth disease and death.

Many children have been ruined for life by urging the intellect and neglecting to strengthen the physical powers. Many have died in childhood because of the course pursued by injudicious parents and schoolteachers in forcing their young intellects, by flattery or fear, when they were too young to see the inside of a schoolroom. Their minds have been taxed with lessons when they should not have been called out, but kept back until the physical constitution was strong enough to endure mental effort. Small children should be left as free as lambs to run out of doors, to be free and happy, and should be allowed the most favorable opportunities to lay the foundation for sound constitutions.

Parents should be the only teachers of their children until they have reached eight or ten years of age. As fast as their minds can comprehend it, the parents should open before them God's great book of nature. The mother should have less love for the artificial in her house and in the preparation of her dress for display, and should find time to cultivate, in herself and in her children, a love for the beautiful buds and opening flowers. By calling the attention of her children to their different colors and variety of forms, she can make them acquainted with God, who made all the beautiful things which attract and delight them. She can lead their minds up to their Creator and awaken in their young hearts a love for their heavenly Father, who has manifested so great love for them. Parents can associate God with all His created works. The only schoolroom for children from eight to ten years of age should be in the open air amid the opening flowers and nature's beautiful scenery. And their only textbook should be the treasures of nature. These lessons, imprinted upon the minds of young children amid the pleasant, attractive scenes of nature, will not be soon forgotten.

In order for children and youth to have health, cheerfulness, vivacity, and well-developed muscles and brains, they should be much in the open air and have well-regulated employment and amusement. Children and youth who are kept at school and confined to books, cannot have sound physical constitutions. The exercise of the brain in study, without corresponding physical exercise, has a tendency to attract the blood to the brain, and the circulation of the blood through the system becomes unbalanced. The brain has too much blood and the extremities too little. There should be rules regulating their studies to certain hours, and then a portion of their time should be spent in physical labor. And if their habits of eating, dressing, and sleeping are in accordance with physical law, they can obtain an education without sacrificing physical and mental health.

PHYSICAL DECLINE OF THE RACE

The book of Genesis gives quite a definite account of social and individual life, and yet we have no record of an infant's being born blind, deaf, crippled, deformed, or imbecile. There is not an instance upon record of a natural death in infancy, childhood, or early manhood. There is no account of men and women dying of disease. Obituary notices in the book of Genesis run thus: "And all the days that Adam lived were nine hundred and thirty years: and he died." "And all the days of Seth were nine hundred and twelve years: and he died." Concerning others, the record states: He lived to a good old age; and he died. It was so rare for a son to die before the father that such an occurrence was considered worthy of record: "And Haran died before his father Terah." Haran was a father of children before his death.

God endowed man with so great vital force that he has withstood the accumulation of disease brought upon the race in consequence of perverted habits and has continued for six thousand years. This fact of itself is enough to evidence to us the strength and electrical energy that God gave to man at his creation. It took more than two thousand years of crime and indulgence of base passions to bring bodily disease upon the race to any great extent. If Adam, at his creation, had not been endowed with twenty times as much vital force as men now have, the race, with their present habits of living in violation of natural law, would have become extinct. At the time of Christ's first advent the race had degenerated so rapidly that an accumulation of disease pressed upon that generation, bringing in a tide of woe and a weight of misery inexpressible.

The wretched condition of the world at the present time has been presented before me. Since Adam's fall the race has been degenerating. Some of the reasons for the present deplorable condition of men and women, formed in the image of God, were shown me. And a sense of how much must be done to arrest, even in a degree, the physical, mental, and moral decay, caused my heart to be sick and faint. God did not create the race in its present feeble condition. This state of things is not the work of Providence, but the work of man; it has been brought about by wrong habits and abuses, by violating the laws that God has made to govern man's existence. Through the temptation to indulge appetite, Adam and Eve first fell from their high, holy, and happy estate. And it is through the same temptation that the race have become enfeebled. They have permitted appetite and passion to take the throne, and to bring into subjection reason and intellect.

The violation of physical law, and the consequence, human suffering, have so long prevailed that men and women look upon the present state of sickness, suffering, debility, and premature death as the appointed lot of humanity. Man came from the hand of his Creator perfect and beautiful in form, and so filled with vital force that it was more than a thousand years before his corrupt appetite and passions, and general violations of physical law, were sensibly felt upon the race. More recent generations have felt the pressure of infirmity and disease still more rapidly and heavily with every generation. The vital forces have been greatly weakened by the indulgence of appetite and lustful passion.

The patriarchs from Adam to Noah, with but few exceptions, lived nearly a thousand years. Since the days of Noah the length of life has been tapering. Those suffering with disease were brought to Christ from every city, town, and village for Him to heal; for they were afflicted with all manner of diseases. And disease has been steadily on the increase through successive generations since that period. Because of the continued violation of the laws of life, mortality has increased to a fearful extent. The years of man have been shortened, so that the present generation pass to the grave, even before the age at which the generations that lived the first few thousand years after the creation came upon the stage of action.

Disease has been transmitted from parents to children, from generation to generation. Infants in the cradle are miserably afflicted because of the sins of their parents, which have lessened their vital force. Their wrong habits of eating and dressing, and their general dissipation, are transmitted as an inheritance to their children. Many are born insane, deformed, blind, deaf, and a very large class are deficient in intellect. The strange absence of principle which characterizes this generation, and which is shown in their disregard of the laws of life and health, is astonishing. Ignorance prevails upon this subject, while light is shining all around them. With the majority, their principal anxiety is, What shall I eat? what shall I drink? and wherewithal shall I be clothed? Notwithstanding all that is said and written in regard to how we should treat our bodies, appetite is the great law which governs men and women generally.

The moral powers are weakened because men and women will not live in obedience to the laws of health and make this great subject a personal duty. Parents bequeath to their offspring their own perverted habits, and loathsome diseases corrupt the blood and enervate the brain. The majority of men and women remain in ignorance of the laws of their being, and indulge appetite and passion at the expense of intellect and morals, and seem willing to remain in ignorance of the result of their violation of nature's laws. They indulge the depraved appetite in the use of slow poisons which corrupt the blood and undermine the nervous forces, and in consequence bring upon themselves sickness and death. Their friends call the result of this course the dispensation of Providence. In this they insult Heaven. They rebelled against the laws of nature and suffered the punishment for thus abusing her laws. Suffering and mortality now prevail everywhere, especially among children. How great is the contrast between this generation and those who lived during the first two thousand years!

IMPORTANCE OF HOME TRAINING

I inquired if this tide of woe could not be prevented and something be done to save the youth of this generation from the ruin which threatens them. I was shown that one great cause of the existing deplorable state of things is that parents do not feel under obligation to bring up their children to conform to physical law. Mothers love their children with an idolatrous love and indulge their appetite when they know that it will injure their health and thereby bring upon them disease and unhappiness. This cruel kindness is manifested to a great extent in the present generation. The desires of children are gratified at the expense of health and happy tempers because it is easier for the mother, for the time being, to gratify them than to withhold that for which they clamor.

Thus mothers are sowing the seed that will spring up and bear fruit. The children are not educated to deny their appetites and restrict their desires. And they become selfish, exacting, disobedient, unthankful, and unholy. Mothers who are doing this work will reap with bitterness the fruit of the seed they have sown. They have sinned against Heaven and against their children, and God will hold them accountable.

Had education for generations back been conducted upon altogether a different plan, the youth of this generation would not now be so depraved and worthless. The managers and teachers of schools should have been those who understood physiology and who had an interest, not only to educate the youth in the sciences, but to teach them how to preserve health so that they might use their knowledge to the best account after they had obtained it. There should have been connected with the schools, establishments for carrying on various branches of labor, that the students might have employment and the necessary exercise out of school hours.

The students' employment and amusements should have been regulated with reference to physical law and should have been adapted to preserve to them the healthy tone of all the powers of body and mind. Then a practical knowledge of business could have been obtained while their literary education was being gained. Students at school should have had their moral sensibilities aroused to see and feel that society has claims upon them and that they should live in obedience to natural law so that they can, by their existence and influence, by precept and example, be an advantage and blessing to society. It should be impressed upon the youth that all have an influence that is constantly telling upon society to improve and elevate or to lower and debase. The first study of the young should be to know themselves and how to keep their bodies in health.

Many parents keep their children at school nearly the year round. These children go through the routine of study mechanically, but do not retain that which they learn. Many of these constant students seem almost destitute of intellectual life. The monotony of continual study wearies the mind, and they take but little interest in their lessons; and to many the application to books becomes painful. They have not an inward love of thought and an ambition to acquire knowledge. They do not encourage in themselves habits of reflection and investigation.

Children are in great need of proper education in order that they may be of use in the world. But any effort that exalts intellectual culture above moral training is misdirected. Instructing, cultivating, polishing, and refining youth and children should be the main burden with both parents and teachers. Close reasoners and logical thinkers are few for the reason that false influences have checked the development of the intellect. The supposition of parents and teachers that continual study would strengthen the intellect has proved erroneous, for in many cases it has had the opposite effect.

In the early education of children many parents and teachers fail to understand that the greatest attention needs to be given to the physical constitution, that a healthy condition of body and brain may be secured. It has been the custom to encourage children to attend school when they are mere babies, needing a mother's care. When of a delicate age they are frequently crowded into ill-ventilated schoolrooms, where they sit in wrong positions upon poorly constructed benches, and as the result the young and tender frames of some have become deformed.

The disposition and habits of youth will be very likely to be manifested in mature manhood. You may bend a young tree into almost any shape that you choose, and if it remains and grows as you have bent it, it will be a deformed tree and will ever tell of the injury and abuse received at your hand. You may, after years of growth, try to straighten the tree, but all your efforts will prove unavailing. It will ever be a crooked tree. This is the case with the minds of youth. They should be carefully and tenderly trained in childhood. They may be trained in the right direction or in the wrong, and in their future lives they will pursue the course in which they were directed in youth. The habits formed in youth will grow with the growth and strengthen with the strength, and will generally be the same in afterlife, only continually growing stronger.

We are living in an age when almost everything is superficial. There is but little stability and firmness of character, because the training and education of children from their cradle is superficial. Their characters are built upon sliding sand. Self-denial and self-control have not been molded into their characters. They have been petted and indulged until they are spoiled for practical life. The love of pleasure controls minds, and children are flattered and indulged to their ruin. Children should be so trained and educated that they will expect temptations and calculate to meet difficulties and dangers. They should be taught to have control over themselves and to nobly overcome difficulties; and if they do not willfully rush into danger and needlessly place themselves in the way of temptation; if they shun evil influences and vicious society, and then are unavoidably compelled to be in dangerous company, they will have strength of character to stand for the right and preserve principle, and will come forth in the strength of God with their morals untainted. If youth who have been properly educated make God their trust, their moral powers will stand the most powerful test.

But few parents realize that their children are what their example and discipline have made them, and that they are responsible for the characters their children develop. If the hearts of Christian parents were in obedience to the will of Christ, they would obey the injunction of the heavenly Teacher: "But seek ye first the kingdom of God, and His righteousness, and all these things shall be added unto you." If those who profess to be followers of Christ would only do this, they would give, not only to their children, but to the unbelieving world, examples that would rightly represent the religion of the Bible.

If Christian parents lived in obedience to the requirements of the divine Teacher, they would preserve simplicity in eating and dressing, and would live more in accordance with natural law. They would not then devote so much time to artificial life, in making for themselves cares and burdens that Christ has not laid upon them, but that He has positively bid them shun. If the kingdom of God and His righteousness were the first and all-important consideration with parents, but little precious time would be lost in needless outward ornamentation while the minds of their children are almost entirely neglected. The precious time devoted by many parents to dressing their children for display in their scenes of amusement would better, far better, be spent in cultivating their own minds in order that they may be competent to properly instruct their children. It is not essential to the salvation or happiness of these parents that they use the precious probationary time that God has lent them, in dressing, visiting, and gossiping.

Many parents plead that they have so much to do that they have no time to improve their minds, to educate their children for practical life, or to teach them how they may become lambs of Christ's fold. Not until the final settlement, when the cases of all will be decided, and the acts of our entire lives will be laid open to our view in the presence of God and the Lamb and all the holy angels, will parents realize the almost infinite value of their misspent time. Very many will then see that their wrong course has determined the destiny of their children. Not only have they failed to secure for themselves the words of commendation from the King of glory, "Well done, thou good and faithful servant: . . . enter thou into the joy of thy Lord," but they hear pronounced upon their children the terrible denunciation, "Depart!" This separates their children forever from the joys and glories of heaven, and from the presence of Christ. And they themselves also receive the denunciation: Depart, "thou wicked and slothful servant." Jesus will never say "Well done" to those who have not earned the "Well done" by their faithful lives of self-denial and self-sacrifice to do others good and to promote His glory. Those who live principally to please themselves instead of to do others good will meet with infinite loss.

If parents could be aroused to a sense of the fearful responsibility which rests upon them in the work of educating their children, more of their time would be devoted to prayer and less to needless display. They would reflect and study and pray earnestly to God for wisdom and divine aid to so train their children that they may develop characters that God will approve. Their anxiety would not be to know how they can educate their children so that they will be praised and honored of the world, but how they can educate them to form beautiful characters that God can approve.

Much study and earnest prayer for heavenly wisdom are needed to know how to deal with youthful minds, for very much depends upon the direction parents give to the minds and wills of their children. To balance their minds in the right direction and at the right time is a most important work, for their eternal destiny may depend on the decisions made at some critical moment. How important, then, that the minds of parents be as free as possible from perplexing, wearing care in temporal things, that they may think and act with calm consideration, wisdom, and love, and make the salvation of the souls of their children the first and highest consideration! The great object which parents should seek to attain for their dear children should be the inward adorning. Parents cannot afford to allow visitors and strangers to claim their attention, and by robbing them of time, which is life's great capital, make it impossible for them to give their children each day that patient instruction which they must have to give right direction to their developing minds.

This lifetime is too short to be squandered in vain and trifling diversion, in unprofitable visiting, in needless dressing for display, or in exciting amusements. We cannot afford to squander the time given us of God in which to bless others and in which to lay up for ourselves a treasure in heaven. We have none too much time for the discharge of necessary duties. We should give time to the culture of our own hearts and minds in order that we may be qualified for our lifework. By neglecting these essential duties and conforming to the habits and customs of fashionable, worldly society, we do ourselves and our children a great wrong.

Mothers who have youthful minds to train and the characters of children to form should not seek the excitement of the world in order to be cheerful and happy. They have an important lifework, and they and theirs cannot afford to spend time in an unprofitable manner. Time is one of the important talents which God has entrusted to us and for which He will call us to account. A waste of time is a waste of intellect. The powers of the mind are susceptible of high cultivation. It is the duty of mothers to cultivate their minds and keep their hearts pure. They should improve every means within their reach for their intellectual and moral improvement, that they may be qualified to improve the minds of their children. Those who indulge their disposition to be in company will soon feel restless unless visiting or entertaining visitors. Such have not the power of adaptation to circumstances. The necessary, sacred home duties seem commonplace and uninteresting to them. They have no love for self-examination or self-discipline. The mind hungers for the varying, exciting scenes of worldly life; children are neglected for the indulgence of inclination; and the recording angel writes: "Unprofitable servants." God designs that our minds should not be purposeless, but should accomplish good in this life.

If parents would feel that it is a solemn duty enjoined upon them of God to educate their children for usefulness in this life; if they would adorn the inner temple of the souls of their sons and daughters for the immortal life, we should see a great change in society for the better. There would not then be manifest so great indifference to practical godliness, and it would not be so difficult to arouse the moral sensibilities of children to understand the claims that God has upon them. But parents become more and more careless in the education of their children in the useful branches. Many parents allow their children to form wrong habits and to follow their own inclination, and fail to impress upon their minds the danger of their doing this and the necessity of their being controlled by principle.

Children frequently begin a piece of work with enthusiasm, but, becoming perplexed or wearied with it, they wish to change and take hold of something new. Thus they may take hold of several things, meet with a little discouragement, and give them up; and so they pass from one thing to another, perfecting nothing. Parents should not allow the love of change to control their children. They should not be so much engaged with other things that they will have no time to patiently discipline the developing minds. A few words of encouragement, or a little help at the right time, may carry them over their trouble and discouragement, and the satisfaction they will derive from seeing the task completed that they undertook will stimulate them to greater exertion.

Many children, for want of words of encouragement and a little assistance in their efforts, become disheartened and change from one thing to another. And they carry this sad defect with them in mature life. They fail to make a success of anything they engage in, for they have not been taught to persevere under discouraging circumstances. Thus the entire lifetime of many proves a failure, because they did not have correct discipline when young. The education received in childhood and youth affects their entire business career in mature life, and their religious experience bears a corresponding stamp.

PHYSICAL LABOR FOR STUDENTS

With the present plan of education a door of temptation is opened to the youth. Although they generally have too many hours of study, they have many hours without anything to do. These leisure hours are frequently spent in a reckless manner. The knowledge of bad habits is communicated from one to another, and vice is greatly increased. Very many young men who have been religiously instructed at home, and who go out to the schools comparatively innocent and virtuous, become corrupt by associating with vicious companions. They lose self-respect and sacrifice noble principles. Then they are prepared to pursue the downward path, for they have so abused their consciences that sin does not appear so exceeding sinful. These evils, which exist in the schools that are conducted according to the present plan, might be remedied in a great degree if study and labor could be combined. The same evils exist in the higher schools, only in a greater degree; for many of the youth have educated themselves in vice, and their consciences are seared.

Many parents overrate the stability and good qualities of their children. They do not seem to consider that they will be exposed to the deceptive influences of vicious youth. Parents have their fears as they send them some distance away to school, but flatter themselves that, as they have had good examples and religious instruction, they will be true to principle in their high-school life. Many parents have but a faint idea to what extent licentiousness exists in these institutions of learning. In many cases the parents have labored hard and suffered many privations for the cherished object of having their children obtain a finished education. And after all their efforts, many have the bitter experience of receiving their children from their course of studies with dissolute habits and ruined constitutions. And frequently they are disrespectful to their parents, unthankful, and unholy. These abused parents, who are thus rewarded by ungrateful children, lament that they sent their children from them to be exposed to temptations and come back to them physical, mental, and moral wrecks. With disappointed hopes and almost broken hearts they see their children, of whom they had high hopes, follow in a course of vice and drag out a miserable existence.

But there are those of firm principles who answer the expectation of parents and teachers. They go through the course of schooling with clear consciences and come forth with good constitutions and morals unstained by corrupting influences. But the number is few.

Some students put their whole being into their studies and concentrate their mind upon the object of obtaining an education. They work the brain, but allow the physical powers to remain inactive. The brain is overworked, and the muscles become weak because they are not exercised. When these students graduate, it is evident that they have obtained their education at the expense of life. They have studied day and night, year after year, keeping their minds continually upon the stretch, while they have failed to sufficiently exercise their muscles. They sacrifice all for a knowledge of the sciences, and pass to their graves.

Young ladies frequently give themselves up to study to the neglect of other branches of education even more essential for practical life than the study of books. And after having obtained their education, they are often invalids for life. They neglected their health by remaining too much indoors, deprived of the pure air of heaven and of the God-given sunlight. These young ladies might have come from their schools in health, had they combined with their studies household labor and exercise in the open air.

Health is a great treasure. It is the richest possession mortals can have. Wealth, honor, or learning is dearly purchased, if it be at the loss of the vigor of health. None of these attainments can secure happiness, if health is wanting. It is a terrible sin to abuse the health that God has given us; for every abuse of health enfeebles us for life and makes us losers, even if we gain any amount of education.

In many cases parents who are wealthy do not feel the importance of giving their children an education in the practical duties of life as well as in the sciences. They do not see the necessity, for the good of their children's minds and morals, and for their future usefulness, of giving them a thorough understanding of useful labor. This is due their children, that, should misfortune come, they could stand forth in noble independence, knowing how to use their hands. If they have a capital of strength they cannot be poor, even if they have not a dollar. Many who in youth were in affluent circumstances may be robbed of all their riches and be left with parents and brothers and sisters dependent upon them for sustenance. Then how important that every youth be educated to labor, that they may be prepared for any emergency! Riches are indeed a curse when their possessors let them stand in the way of their sons and daughters' obtaining a knowledge of useful labor, that they may be qualified for practical life.

Those who are not compelled to labor, frequently do not

have sufficient active exercise for physical health. Young men, for want of having their minds and hands employed in active labor, acquire habits of indolence and frequently obtain what is most to be dreaded, a street education—lounging about stores, smoking, drinking, and playing cards.

Young ladies will read novels, excusing themselves from active labor because they are in delicate health. Their feebleness is the result of their lack of exercising the muscles God has given them. They may think they are too feeble to do housework, but will work at crochet and tatting, and preserve the delicate paleness of their hands and faces, while their care-burdened mothers toil hard to wash and iron their garments. These ladies are not Christians, for they transgress the fifth commandment. They do not honor their parents. But the mother is the one who is most to blame. She has indulged her daughters and excused them from bearing their share of household duties, until work has become distasteful to them, and they love and enjoy delicate idleness. They eat, and sleep, and read novels, and talk of the fashions, while their lives are useless.

Poverty, in many cases, is a blessing; for it prevents youth and children from being ruined by inaction. The physical as well as the mental powers should be cultivated and properly developed. The first and constant care of parents should be to see that their children have firm constitutions, that they may be sound men and women. It is impossible to attain this object without physical exercise. For their own physical health and moral good, children should be taught to work, even if there is no necessity so far as want is concerned. If they would have pure and virtuous characters they must have the discipline of well-regulated labor, which will bring into exercise all the muscles. The satisfaction that children will have in being useful, and in denying themselves to help others, will be the most healthful pleasure they ever enjoyed. Why should the wealthy rob themselves and their dear children of this great blessing?

Parents, inaction is the greatest curse that ever came upon

youth. Your daughters should not be allowed to lie in bed late in the morning, sleeping away the precious hours lent them of God to be used for the best purpose and for which they will have to give an account to Him. The mother does her daughters great injury by bearing the burdens that they should share with her for their own present and future good. The course that many parents pursue in allowing their children to be indolent and to gratify their desire for reading romance is unfitting them for real life. Novel and storybook reading are the greatest evils in which youth can indulge. Novel and love-story readers always fail to make good, practical mothers. They are air-castle builders, living in an unreal, an imaginary world. They become sentimental and have sick fancies. Their artificial life spoils them for anything useful. They are dwarfed in intellect, although they they flatter themselves that they are superior in mind and manners. Exercise in household labor is of the greatest advantage to young girls.

Physical labor will not prevent the cultivation of the intellect. Far from it. The advantages gained by physical labor will balance a person and prevent the mind from being overworked. The toil will come upon the muscles and relieve the wearied brain. There are many listless, useless girls who consider it unladylike to engage in active labor. But their characters are too transparent to deceive sensible persons in regard to their real worthlessness. They simper and giggle, and are all affectation. They appear as though they could not speak their words fairly and squarely, but torture all they say with lisping and simpering. Are these ladies? They were not born fools, but were educated such. It does not require a frail, helpless, overdressed, simpering thing to make a lady. A sound body is required for a sound intellect. Physical soundness and a practical knowledge of all the necessary household duties will never be hindrances to a well-developed intellect; both are highly important for a lady.

All the powers of the mind should be called into use and developed in order for men and women to have well-balanced minds. The world is full of one-sided men and women who have become such because one set of their faculties was cultivated while others were dwarfed from inaction. The education of most youth is a failure. They overstudy, while they neglect that which pertains to practical business life. Men and women become parents without considering their responsibilities, and their offspring sink lower in the scale of human deficiency than they themselves. Thus the race is fast degenerating. The constant application to study, as the schools are now conducted, is unfitting youth for practical life. The human mind will have action. If it is not active in the right direction, it will be active in the wrong. In order to preserve the balance of the mind, labor and study should be united in the schools.

Provision should have been made in past generations for education upon a larger scale. In connection with the schools should have been agricultural and manufacturing establishments. There should also have been teachers of household labor. And a portion of the time each day should have been devoted to labor, that the physical and mental powers might be equally exercised. If schools had been established upon the plan we have mentioned, there would not now be so many unbalanced minds.

God prepared for Adam and Eve a beautiful garden. He provided for them everything that their wants required. He planted for them fruit-bearing trees of every variety. With a liberal hand He surrounded them with His bounties. The trees for usefulness and beauty, and the lovely flowers which sprang up spontaneously and flourished in rich profusion around them, were to know nothing of decay. Adam and Eve were rich indeed. They possessed Eden. Adam was lord in his beautiful domain. None can question the fact that he was rich. But God knew that Adam could not be happy unless he had employment. Therefore He gave him something to do; he was to dress the garden.

If men and women of this degenerate age have a large amount of earthly treasure, which, in comparison with that

Paradise of beauty and wealth given the lordly Adam, is very insignificant, they feel themselves above labor and educate their children to look upon it as degrading. Such rich parents, by precept and example, instruct their children that money makes the gentleman and the lady. But our idea of the gentleman and the lady is measured by the intellect and the moral worth. God estimates not by dress. The exhortation of the inspired apostle Peter is: "Whose adorning let it not be that outward adorning of plaiting the hair, and of wearing of gold, or of putting on of apparel; but let it be the hidden man of the heart, in that which is not corruptible, even the ornament of a meek and quiet spirit, which is in the sight of God of great price." A meek and quiet spirit is exalted above worldly honor or riches.

The Lord illustrates how He estimates the worldly wealthy who lift up their souls unto vanity because of their earthly possessions, by the rich man who tore down his barns and built greater, that he might have room to bestow his goods. Forgetful of God, he failed to acknowledge whence all his possessions came. No grateful thanks ascended to his gracious Benefactor. He congratulated himself thus: "Soul, thou hast much goods laid up for many years; take thine ease, eat, drink, and be merry." The Master, who had entrusted to him earthly riches with which to bless his fellow men and glorify his Maker, was justly angry at his ingratitude and said: "Thou fool, this night thy soul shall be required of thee: then whose shall those things be, which thou hast provided? So is he that layeth up treasure for himself, and is not rich toward God." Here we have an illustration of how the infinite God estimates man. An extensive fortune, or any degree of wealth, will not secure the favor of God. All these bounties and blessings come from Him to prove, test, and develop the character of man.

Men may have boundless wealth; yet if they are not rich toward God, if they have no interest to secure to themselves the heavenly treasure and divine wisdom, they are counted fools by their Creator, and we leave them just where God leaves them. Labor is a blessing. It is impossible for us to enjoy health without labor. All the faculties should be called into use that they may be properly developed and that men and women may have well-balanced minds. If the young had been given a thorough education in the different branches of labor, if they had been taught labor as well as the sciences, their education would have been of greater advantage to them.

A constant strain upon the brain while the muscles are inactive, enfeebles the nerves, and students have an almost uncontrollable desire for change and exciting amusements. And when they are released, after being confined to study several hours each day, they are nearly wild. Many have never been controlled at home. They have been left to follow inclination, and they think that the restraint of the hours of study is a severe tax upon them; and since they do not have anything to do after study hours, Satan suggests sport and mischief for a change. Their influence over other students is demoralizing. Those students who have had the benefits of religious teaching at home, and who are ignorant of the vices of society, frequently become the best acquainted with those whose minds have been cast in an inferior mold, and whose advantages for mental culture and religious training have been very limited. And they are in danger, by mingling in the society of this class and by breathing an atmosphere that is not elevating but that tends to lower and degrade the morals, of sinking to the same low level as their companions. It is the delight of a large class of students, in their unemployed hours, to have a high time. And very many of those who leave their homes innocent and pure become corrupted by their associations at school.

I have been led to inquire: Must all that is valuable in our youth be sacrificed in order that they may obtain a school education? Had there been agricultural and manufacturing establishments connected with our schools, and had competent teachers been employed to educate the youth in the different branches of study and labor, devoting a portion of each day to mental improvement and a portion to physical labor, there would now be a more elevated class of youth to come upon the stage of action to have influence in molding society. Many of the youth who would graduate at such institutions would come forth with stability of character. They would have perseverance, fortitude, and courage to surmount obstacles, and such principles that they would not be swayed by a wrong influence, however popular. There should have been experienced teachers to give lessons to young ladies in the cooking department. Young girls should have been instructed to manufacture wearing apparel, to cut, make, and mend garments, and thus become educated for the practical duties of life.

For young men there should be establishments where they could learn different trades which would bring into exercise their muscles as well as their mental powers. If the youth can have but a one-sided education, which is of the greater consequence, a knowledge of the sciences,—with all the disadvantages to health and life,—or a knowledge of labor for practical life? We unhesitatingly answer: The latter. If one must be neglected, let it be the study of books.

There are very many girls who have married and have families who have but little practical knowledge of the duties devolving upon a wife and mother. They can read, and play upon an instrument of music; but they cannot cook. They cannot make good bread, which is very essential to the health of the family. They cannot cut and make garments, for they never learned how. They considered these things unessential, and in their married life they are as dependent upon someone to do these things for them as are their own little children. It is this inexcusable ignorance in regard to the most needful duties of life which makes very many unhappy families.

The impression that work is degrading to fashionable life has laid thousands in the grave who might have lived. Those who perform only manual labor frequently work to excess without giving themselves periods of rest; while the intellectual class overwork the brain and suffer for want of the healthful vigor the physical labor gives. If the intellectual would to some extent share the burden of the laboring class and thus strengthen the muscles, the laboring class might do less and devote a portion of their time to mental and moral culture. Those of sedentary and literary habits should take physical exercise, even if they have no need to labor so far as means are concerned. Health should be a sufficient inducement to lead them to unite physical with mental labor.

Moral, intellectual, and physical culture should be combined in order to have well-developed, well-balanced men and women. Some are qualified to exercise greater intellectual strength than others, while others are inclined to love and enjoy physical labor. Both of these classes should seek to improve where they are deficient, that they may present to God their entire being, a living sacrifice, holy and acceptable to Him, which is their reasonable service. The habits and customs of fashionable society should not gauge their course of action. The inspired apostle Paul adds: "And be not conformed to this world: but be ye transformed by the renewing of your mind, that ye may prove what is that good, and acceptable, and perfect, will of God."

The minds of thinking men labor too hard. They frequently use their mental powers prodigally, while there is another class whose highest aim in life is physical labor. The latter class do not exercise the mind. Their muscles are exercised while their brains are robbed of intellectual strength, just as the minds of thinking men are worked while their bodies are robbed of strength and vigor by their neglect to exercise the muscles. Those who are content to devote their lives to physical labor and leave others to do the thinking for them, while they simply carry out what other brains have planned, will have strength of muscle but feeble intellects. Their influence for good is small in comparison to what it might be if they would use their brains as well as their muscles. This class fall more readily if attacked by disease; the system is vitalized by the electrical force of the brain to resist disease.

Men who have good physical powers should educate themselves to think as well as to act, and not depend upon others to be brains for them. It is a popular error with a large class to regard work as degrading. Therefore young men are very anxious to educate themselves to become teachers, clerks, merchants, lawyers, and to occupy almost any position that does not require physical labor. Young women regard housework as demeaning. And although the physical exercise required to perform household labor, if not too severe, is calculated to promote health, yet they will seek for an education that will fit them to become teachers or clerks, or will learn some trade which will confine them indoors to sedentary employment. The bloom of health fades from their cheeks, and disease fastens upon them, because they are robbed of physical exercise and their habits are perverted generally. All this because it is fashionable! They enjoy delicate life, which is feebleness and decay.

True, there is some excuse for young women not choosing housework for employment, because those who hire kitchen girls generally treat them as servants. Frequently their employers do not respect them and treat them as though they were unworthy to be members of their families. They do not give them the privileges they do the seamstress, the copyist, and the teacher of music. But there can be no employment more important than that of housework. To cook well, to present healthful food upon the table in an inviting manner requires intelligence and experience. The one who prepares the food that is to be placed in our stomachs, to be converted into blood to nourish the system, occupies a most important and elevated position. The position of copyist, dressmaker, or music teacher cannot equal in importance that of the cook.

The foregoing is a statement of what might have been done by a proper system of education. Time is too short now to accomplish that which might have been done in past generations, but we can do much, even in these last days, to correct the existing evils in the education of youth. And because time is short, we should be in earnest and work zealously to give the young that education which is consistent with our faith. We are reformers. We desire that our children should study to the best advantage. In order to do this, employment should be given them which will call the muscles into exercise. Daily, systematic labor should constitute a part of the education of the youth, even at this late period. Much can now be gained by connecting labor with schools. In following this plan the students will realize elasticity of spirit and vigor of thought, and will be able to accomplish more mental labor in a given time than they could by study alone. And they can leave school with their constitutions unimpaired and with strength and courage to persevere in any position in which the providence of God may place them.

Because time is short, we should work with diligence and double energy. Our children may never enter college, but they can obtain an education in those essential branches which they can turn to a practical use and which will give culture to the mind and bring its powers into use. Very many youth who have gone through a college course have not obtained that true education that they can put to practical use. They may have the name of having a collegiate education, but in reality they are only educated dunces.

There are many young men whose services God would accept if they would consecrate themselves to Him unreservedly. If they would exercise those powers of the mind in the service of God which they use in serving themselves and in acquiring property they would make earnest, persevering, successful laborers in the vineyard of the Lord. Many of our young men should turn their attention to the study of the Scriptures, that God may use them in His cause. But they do not become as intelligent in spiritual knowledge as in temporal things; therefore they fail to do the work of God which they could do with acceptance. There are but few to warn sinners and win souls to Christ, when there should be many. Our young men generally are wise in worldly matters, but not intelligent in regard to the things of the kingdom of God. They might turn their minds in a heavenly, divine channel and walk in the light, going on from one degree of light and strength to another until they could turn sinners to Christ and point the unbelieving and desponding to a bright track heavenward. And when the warfare is ended, they might be welcomed to the joy of their Lord.

Young men should not enter upon the work of explaining the Scriptures and lecturing upon the prophecies when they do not have a knowledge of the important Bible truths they try to explain to others. They may be deficient in the common branches of education and therefore fail to do the amount of good they could do if they had had the advantages of a good school. Ignorance will not increase the humility or spirituality of any professed follower of Christ. The truths of the divine word can be best appreciated by an intellectual Christian. Christ can be best glorified by those who serve Him intelligently. The great object of education is to enable us to use the powers which God has given us in such a manner as will best represent the religion of the Bible and promote the glory of God.

We are indebted to Him who gave us existence, for all the talents which have been entrusted to us; and it is a duty we owe to our Creator to cultivate and improve upon the talents He has committed to our trust. Education will discipline the mind, develop its powers, and understandingly direct them, that we may be useful in advancing the glory of God. We need a school where those who are just entering the ministry may be taught at least the common branches of education and where they may also learn more perfectly the truths of God's word for this time. In connection with these schools, lectures should be given upon the prophecies. Those who really have good abilities such as God will accept to labor in His vineyard would be very much benefited by only a few months' instruction at such a school.

THE HEALTH REFORM

December 10, 1871, I was again shown that the health reform is one branch of the great work which is to fit a people for the coming of the Lord. It is as closely connected with the third angel's message as the hand is with the body. The law of Ten Commandments has been lightly regarded by man, but the Lord would not come to punish the transgressors of that law without first sending them a message of warning. The third angel proclaims that message. Had men ever been obedient to the law of Ten Commandments, carrying out in their lives the principles of those precepts, the curse of disease now flooding the world would not be.

Men and women cannot violate natural law by indulging depraved appetite and lustful passions, and not violate the law of God. Therefore He has permitted the light of health reform to shine upon us, that we may see our sin in violating the laws which He has established in our being. All our enjoyment or suffering may be traced to obedience or transgression of natural law. Our gracious heavenly Father sees the deplorable condition of men who, some knowingly but many ignorantly, are living in violation of the laws that He has established. And in love and pity to the race, He causes the light to shine upon health reform. He publishes His law and the penalty that will follow the transgression of it, that all may learn and be careful to live in harmony with natural law. He proclaims His law so distinctly and makes it so prominent that it is like a city set on a hill. All accountable beings can understand it if they will. Idiots will not be responsible. To make plain natural law, and urge the obedience of it, is the work that accompanies the third angel's message to prepare a people for the coming of the Lord.

Adam and Eve fell through intemperate appetite. Christ came and withstood the fiercest temptation of Satan and, in behalf of the race, overcame appetite, showing that man may overcome. As Adam fell through appetite and lost blissful

Eden, the children of Adam may, through Christ, overcome appetite and through temperance in all things regain Eden.

Ignorance is no excuse now for the transgression of law. The light shines clearly, and none need be ignorant, for the great God Himself is man's instructor. All are bound by the most sacred obligations to God to heed the sound philosophy and genuine experience which He is now giving them in reference to health reform. He designs that the great subject of health reform shall be agitated and the public mind deeply stirred to investigate; for it is impossible for men and women with all their sinful, health-destroying, brain-enervating habits, to discern sacred truth, through which they are to be sanctified, refined, elevated, and made fit for the society of heavenly angels in the kingdom of glory.

The inhabitants of the Noachian world were destroyed because they were corrupted through the indulgence of perverted appetite. Sodom and Gomorrah were destroyed through the gratification of unnatural appetite, which so benumbed the intellect that they could not discern the difference between the sacred claims of God and the clamor of appetite. The latter enslaved them, and they became so ferocious and bold in their detestable abominations that God would not tolerate them upon the earth. God ascribes the wickedness of Babylon to her gluttony and drunkenness.

The apostle Paul exhorts the church: "I beseech you therefore, brethren, by the mercies of God, that ye present your bodies a living sacrifice, holy, acceptable unto God, which is your reasonable service." Men, then, can make their bodies unholy by sinful indulgences. If unholy, they are unfitted to be spiritual worshipers and are not worthy of heaven. If man will cherish the light that God in mercy gives him upon health reform, he may be sanctified through the truth and fitted for immortality. But if he disregards that light and lives in violation of natural law he must pay the penalty.

God created man perfect and holy. But man fell from his holy estate because he transgressed God's law. Since the Fall there has been a rapid increase of disease, suffering, and death. Yet notwithstanding man has insulted his Creator, God's love is still extended to the race; and He permits light to shine that man may see that in order to live a perfect life he must live in harmony with those natural laws which govern his being. Therefore it is of the greatest importance that he know how to live so that his powers of body and mind may be exercised to the glory of God.

It is impossible for man to present his body a living sacrifice, holy, and acceptable to God, while, because it is customary for the world to do so, he is indulging in habits that are lessening physical, mental, and moral vigor. The apostle adds: "And be not conformed to this world: but be ye transformed by the renewing of your mind, that ye may prove what is that good, and acceptable, and perfect, will of God." Jesus, seated upon the Mount of Olives, gave instruction to His disciples concerning the signs which should precede His coming. He said: "But as the days of Noah were, so shall also the coming of the Son of man be. For as in the days that were before the Flood they were eating and drinking, marrying and giving in marriage, until the day that Noah entered into the ark, and knew not until the Flood came, and took them all away; so shall also the coming of the Son of man be."

The same sins exist in our day which brought the wrath of God upon the world in the days of Noah. Men and women now carry their eating and drinking to gluttony and drunkenness. This prevailing sin, the indulgence of perverted appetite, inflamed the passions of men in the days of Noah and led to general corruption, until their violence and crimes reached to heaven, and God washed the earth of its moral pollution by a flood.

The same sins of gluttony and drunkenness benumbed the moral sensibilities of the inhabitants of Sodom so that crimes seemed to be the delight of the men and women of that wicked city. Christ thus warns the world: "Likewise also as it was in the days of Lot; they did eat, they drank, they bought, they sold, they planted, they builded; but the same day that Lot went out of Sodom it rained fire and brimstone from heaven, and destroyed them all. Even thus shall it be in the day when the Son of man is revealed."

Christ has here left us a most important lesson. He does not in His teaching encourage indolence. His example was the opposite of this. Christ was an earnest worker. His life was one of self-denial, diligence, perseverance, industry, and economy. He would lay before us the danger of making eating and drinking paramount. He reveals the result of giving up to indulgence of appetite. The moral powers are enfeebled so that sin does not appear sinful. Crimes are winked at, and base passions control the mind until general corruption roots out good principles and impulses, and God is blasphemed. All this is the result of eating and drinking to excess. This is the very condition of things which He declares will exist at His second coming.

Will men and women be warned? Will they cherish the light, or will they become slaves to appetite and base passions? Christ presents to us something higher to toil for than merely what we shall eat, and what we shall drink, and wherewithal we shall be clothed. Eating, drinking, and dressing are carried to such excess that they become crimes, and are among the marked sins of the last days, and constitute a sign of Christ's soon coming. Time, money, and strength, which are the Lord's, but which He has entrusted to us, are wasted in needless superfluities of dress and luxuries for the perverted appetite, which lessen vitality and bring suffering and decay. It is impossible to present our bodies a living sacrifice to God when they are filled with corruption and disease by our own sinful indulgence.

Knowledge must be gained in regard to how to eat and drink and dress so as to preserve health. Sickness is caused by violating the laws of health; it is the result of violating nature's law. Our first duty, one which we owe to God, to ourselves, and to our fellow men, is to obey the laws of God, which include the laws of health. If we are sick we impose a weary tax upon our friends and unfit ourselves for discharging our duties to our families and to our neighbors. And when premature death is the result of our violation of nature's law, we bring sorrow and suffering to others; we deprive our neighbors of the help we ought to render them in living; we rob our families of the comfort and help we might render them, and rob God of the service He claims of us to advance His glory. Then, are we not, in the worst sense, transgressors of God's law?

But God is all-pitiful, gracious, and tender, and when light comes to show who have injured their health by sinful indulgences, and they are convinced of sin, and repent and seek pardon, He accepts the poor offering rendered to Him, and receives them. Oh, what tender mercy that He does not refuse the remnant of the abused life of the suffering, repenting sinner! In His gracious mercy He saves these souls as by fire. But what an inferior, pitiful sacrifice, at best, to offer to a pure and holy God! Noble faculties have been paralyzed by wrong habits of sinful indulgence. The aspirations are perverted, and the soul and body defaced.

THE HEALTH INSTITUTE

The great work of reform must go forward. The Health Institute has been established at Battle Creek to relieve the afflicted, to disseminate light, to awaken the spirit of inquiry, and to advance reform. This institution is conducted upon principles which are different from those of any other hygienic institution in the land. Money is not the great object with its friends and conductors. They conduct it from a conscientious, religious standpoint, aiming to carry out the principles of Bible hygiene. Most institutions of the kind are established upon different principles and are conservative, making it their object to meet the popular class halfway and to so shape their course that they will receive the greatest patronage and the most money.

The Health Institute at Battle Creek is established upon firm religious principles. Its conductors acknowledge God as the real proprietor. Physicians and helpers look to Him for guidance, and aim to move conscientiously, in His fear. For this reason it stands upon a sure basis. When feeble, suffering invalids learn in regard to the principles of the directors, superintendent, physicians, and helpers at the Institute that they have the fear of God before them, they will feel safer there than at popular institutions.

If those connected with the Health Institute at Battle Creek should descend from the pure, exalted principles of Bible truth to imitate the theories and practices of those at the head of other institutions, where only the diseases of invalids are treated, and that merely for money, the conductors not working from a high, religious standpoint, God's special blessing would not rest upon the Institute. This institution is designed of God to be one of the greatest aids in preparing a people to be perfect before God. In order to attain to this perfection, men and women must have physical and mental strength to appreciate the elevated truths of God's word and be brought into a position where they will discern the imperfections in their moral characters. They should be in earnest to reform, that they may have friendship with God. The religion of Christ is not to be placed in the background and its holy principles laid down to meet the approval of any class, however popular. If the standard of truth and holiness is lowered, the design of God will not then be carried out in this institution.

But our peculiar faith should not be discussed with patients. Their minds should not be unnecessarily excited upon subjects wherein we differ, unless they themselves desire it; and then great caution should be observed not to agitate the mind by urging upon them our peculiar faith. The Health Institute is not the place to be forward to enter into discussion upon points of our faith wherein we differ with the religious world generally. Prayer meetings are held at the Institute in which all may take part if they choose, but there is an abundance to dwell upon in regard to Bible religion without touching objectionable points of difference. Silent influence will do more than open controversy.

In exhortation in the prayer meetings some Sabbathkeepers have felt that they must bring in the Sabbath and the third angel's message or they could not have freedom. This is characteristic of narrow minds. Patients not acquainted with our faith do not know what is meant by the third angel's message. The introduction of these terms without a clear explanation of them does only harm. We must meet the people where they are, and yet we need not sacrifice one principle of the truth. The prayer meeting will prove a blessing to patients, helpers, and physicians. Brief and interesting seasons of prayer and social worship will increase the confidence of patients in their physicians and helpers. The helpers should not be deprived of these meetings by work unless it is positively necessary. They need them and should enjoy them.

By thus establishing regular meetings the patients gain confidence in the Institute and feel more at home. And thus the way is prepared for the seed of truth to take root in some hearts. These meetings especially interest some who profess to be Christians and make a favorable impression upon those who do not. Mutual confidence is increased in one another, and prejudice is weakened and in many cases entirely removed. Then there is an anxiety to attend the Sabbath meeting. There, in the house of God, is the place to speak our denominational sentiments. There the minister can dwell with clearness upon the essential points of present truth and with the spirit of Christ, in love and tenderness, urge home upon all the necessity of obedience to all the requirements of God, and let the truth convict hearts.

I was shown that a larger work could be accomplished if there were gentlemen physicians of the right stamp of mind who had proper culture and a thorough understanding of every part of the work devolving on a physician. The physicians should have a large stock of patience, forbearance, kind-liness, and pity; for they need these qualifications in dealing with suffering invalids, who are diseased in body, and many of whom are diseased both in body and in mind. It is not an easy matter to obtain the right class of men and women, those who are fitted for the place and who will work harmoniously, zealously, and unselfishly for the benefit of suffering invalids. Men are wanted at the Institute who will have the fear of God before them and who can minister to sick minds and keep prominent the health reform from a religious standpoint.

Those who engage in this work should be consecrated to God and not make it their only object to treat the body merely to cure disease, thus working from the popular physician's standpoint, but to be spiritual fathers, to minister to diseased minds, and point the sin-sick soul to the never-failing remedy, the Saviour who died for them. Those who are reduced by disease are sufferers in more than one sense. They can endure bodily pain far better than they can bear mental suffering. Many carry a violated conscience and can be reached only by the principles of Bible religion.

When the poor, suffering paralytic was brought to the Saviour, the urgency of the case seemed not to admit of a moment's delay, for already dissolution was doing its work upon the body. When those who bore him upon his bed saw that they could not come directly into the presence of Christ, they at once tore open the roof and let down the bed whereon the sick of the palsy lay. Our Saviour saw and understood his condition perfectly. He also knew that this wretched man had a sickness of the soul far more aggravating than bodily suffering. He knew that the greatest burden he had borne for months was on account of sins. The crowd of people waited with a most breathless silence to see how Christ would treat this case, apparently so hopeless, and were astonished to hear the words which fell from His lips: "Son be of good cheer; thy sins be forgiven thee."

These were the most precious words that could fall upon

THE HEALTH INSTITUTE

the ear of that sick sufferer, for the burden of sin had lain so heavily upon him that he could not find the least relief. Christ lifts the burden that so heavily oppressed him: *"Be of good cheer;"* I, your Saviour, came to forgive sins. How quickly the pallid countenance of the sufferer changes! Hope takes the place of dark despair, and peace and joy take the place of distressing doubt and stolid gloom. The mind being restored to peace and happiness, the suffering body can now be reached. Next comes from the divine lips: "Thy sins be forgiven thee;" "arise; and walk." In the effort to obey the will, those lifeless, bloodless arms are quickened; a healthful current of blood flows through the veins; the leaden color of his flesh disappears, and the ruddy glow of health takes its place. The limbs that for long years have refused to obey the will are now quickened to life, and the healed paralytic grasps his bed and walks through the crowd to his home, glorifying God.

This case is for our instruction. Physicians who would be successful in the treatment of disease should know how to minister to a diseased mind. They can have a powerful influence for good if they make God their trust. Some invalids need to be relieved of pain before the mind can be reached. After relief has come to the body, the physician can frequently the more successfully appeal to the conscience, and the heart will be more susceptible to the influences of the truth. There is danger of those connected with the Health Institute losing sight of the object for which such an institution was established by Seventh-day Adventists, and working from the worlding's standpoint, patterning after other institutions.

The Health Institute was not established among us for the purpose of obtaining money, although money is very necessary to carry forward the institution successfully. Economy should be exercised by all in the expenditure of means, that money be not used needlessly. But there should be sufficient means to invest in all necessary conveniences which will make the work of helpers, and especially of physicians, as easy as possible.

And the directors of the Institute should avail themselves of every facility which will aid in the successful treatment of patients.

Patients should be treated with the greatest sympathy and tenderness. And yet the physicians should be firm and not allow themselves, in their treatment of the sick, to be dictated to by patients. Firmness on the part of the physicians is necessary for the good of the patients. But firmness should be mingled with respectful courtesy. No physician or helper should contend with a patient, or use harsh, irritating words, or even words not the most kindly, however provoking the patient may be.

One of the great objects of our Health Institute is to direct sin-sick souls to the Great Physician, the true healing Fountain, and call their attention to the necessity of reform from a religious standpoint, that they no longer violate the law of God by sinful indulgences. If the moral sensibilities of invalids can be aroused and they see that they are sinning against their Creator by bringing sickness upon themselves and by the indulgence of appetite and debasing passions, when they leave the Health Institute they will not leave their principles behind, but will take them with them and be genuine health reformers at home. If the moral sensibilities are aroused, patients will have a determination to carry out their convictions of conscience; and if they see the truth they will obey it. They will have true, noble independence to practice the truths to which they assent. And if the mind is at peace with God, the bodily conditions will be more favorable.

The greatest responsibility rests upon the church at Battle Creek to live and walk in the light, and to preserve their simplicity and separation from the world, that their influence may tell with convincing power upon strangers to the truth who attend our meetings. If the church at Battle Creek is a lifeless body, filled with pride, exalted above the simplicity of true godliness, and leaning to the world, its influence will be to scatter from Christ and to make the most solemn and essential truths of the Bible of no force. The members of this church have opportunities to be benefited by lectures from the physicians of the Health Institute. They can obtain information upon the great subject of health reform if they desire it. But the church at Battle Creek, who make great profession of the truth, are far behind other churches who have not been blessed with the advantages they have had. The neglect of the church to live up to the light which they have had upon health reform is a discouragement to the physicians and to the friends of the Health Institute. If the church would manifest a greater interest in the reforms which God Himself has brought to them to fit them for His coming, their influence would be tenfold what it now is.

Many who profess to believe the *Testimonies* live in neglect of the light given. The dress reform is treated by some with great indifference and by others with contempt, because there is a cross attached to it. For this cross I thank God. It is just what we need to distinguish and separate God's commandment-keeping people from the world. The dress reform answers to us as did the ribbon of blue to ancient Israel. The proud, and those who have no love for sacred truth, which will separate them from the world, will show it by their works. God in His providence has given us the light upon health reform, that we may understand it in all its bearings, follow the light it brings, and by rightly relating ourselves to life have health that we may glorify God and be a blessing to others.

The church in general at Battle Creek have not sustained the Institute by their example. They have not honored the light of health reform by carrying it out in their families. The sickness that has visited many families in Battle Creek need not have been if they had followed the light God has given them. Like ancient Israel they have disregarded the light and could see no more necessity of restricting their appetite than did ancient Israel. The children of Israel would have flesh meats and said, as many now say: We shall die without meat. God gave rebellious Israel flesh, but His curse was with it. Thousands of them died while the meat they desired was between their teeth. We have the example of ancient Israel and the warning for us not to do as they did. Their history of unbelief and rebellion is left on record as a special warning that we should not follow their example of murmuring at God's requirements. How can we pass on so indifferently, choosing our own course, following the sight of our own eyes, and departing further and further from God, as did the Hebrews? God cannot do great things for His people because of their hardness of heart and sinful unbelief.

God is no respecter of persons; but in every generation they that fear the Lord and work righteousness are accepted of Him; while those who are murmuring, unbelieving, and rebellious will not have His favor nor the blessings promised to those who love the truth and walk in it. Those who have the light and do not follow it, but disregard the requirements of God, will find that their blessings will be changed into curses and their mercies into judgments. God would have us learn humility and obedience as we read the history of ancient Israel, who were His chosen and peculiar people, but who brought their own destruction by following their own ways.

The religion of the Bible is not detrimental to the health of the body or of the mind. The influence of the Spirit of God is the very best medicine that can be received by a sick man or woman. Heaven is all health, and the more deeply the heavenly influences are realized the more sure will be the recovery of the believing invalid. At some other health institutions they encourage amusements, plays, and dancing to get up an excitement, but are fearful as to the result of a religious interest. Dr. Jackson's theory in this respect is not only erroneous but dangerous. Yet he has talked this in such a manner that, were his instructions heeded, patients would be led to think that their recovery depended upon their having as few thoughts of God and heaven as possible. It is true that there are persons with ill-balanced minds who imagine themselves to be very religious and who impose upon themselves fasting and prayer to the injury of their health. These souls suffer themselves to be deceived. God has not required this of them. They have a pharisaical righteousness, which springs, not from Christ, but from themselves. They trust to their own good works for salvation and are seeking to buy heaven by meritorious works of their own instead of relying, as every sinner should, alone upon the merits of a crucified and risen Saviour. Christ and true godliness, today and forever, will be health to the body and strength to the soul.

The cloud which has rested upon our Health Institute is lifting, and the blessing of God has attended the efforts made to place it upon a right basis and to correct the errors of those who through unfaithfulness brought great embarrassment upon it and discouragement upon its friends everywhere

Those who have assigned to the charitable uses of the Institute the interest, or dividend, of their stock, have done a noble thing, which will meet its reward. All those who have not made an assignment, who are able to do so, should, at their first opportunity, assign all or a part, as most of the stockholders have done. And as the growing interest and usefulness of this institution demand it, all, especially those who have not done so, should continue to take stock in it.

I saw that there was a large amount of surplus means among our people, a portion of which should be put into the Health Institute. I also saw that there are many worthy poor among our people who are sick and suffering, and who have been looking toward the Institute for help, but who are not able to pay the regular prices for board, treatment, etc. The Institute has struggled hard with debts the last three years and could not treat patients to any considerable extent without full pay. It would please God for all our people who are able to do so to take stock liberally in the Institute to place it in a condition where it can help God's humble, worthy poor. In connection with this I saw that Christ identities Himself with suffering humanity, and that what we have the privilege of doing for even the least of His children, whom He calls His brethren, we do to the Son of God.

"Then shall the King say unto them on His right hand, Come, ye blessed of My Father, inherit the kingdom prepared for you from the foundation of the world: for I was an hungered, and ye gave Me meat: I was thirsty, and ye gave Me drink: I was a stranger, and ye took Me in: naked, and ye clothed Me: I was sick, and ye visited Me: I was in prison, and ye came unto Me. Then shall the righteous answer Him, saying, Lord, when saw we Thee an hungered, and fed thee? or thirsty, and gave Thee drink? When saw we Thee a stranger, and took Thee in? or naked, and clothed Thee? Or when saw we Thee sick, or in prison, and came unto Thee? And the King shall answer and say unto them, Verily I say unto you, Inasmuch as ye have done it unto one of the least of these My brethren, ye have done it unto Me. Then shall He say also unto them on the left hand, Depart from Me, ye cursed, into everlasting fire, prepared for the devil and his angels: for I was anhungered, and ye gave Me no meat: I was thirsty, and ye gave Me no drink: I was a stranger, and ye took Me not in: naked, and ye clothed Me not: sick, and in prison, and ye visited Me not. Then shall they also answer Him, saying, Lord, when saw we Thee anhungered, or athirst, or a stranger, or naked, or sick, or in prison, and did not minister unto Thee? Then shall He answer them, saying, Verily I say unto you, Inasmuch as ye did it not to one of the least of these, ye did it not to Me. And these shall go away into everlasting punishment: but the righteous into life eternal."

To raise the Health Institute from its low state in the autumn of 1869 to its present prosperous, hopeful condition has demanded sacrifices and exertions of which its friends abroad know but little. Then it had a debt of thirteen thousand dollars and had but eight paying patients. And what was worse still, the course of former managers had been such as to so far discourage its friends that they had no heart to furnish means to lift the debt or to recommend the sick to patronize the Institute. It was at this discouraging point that my husband decided in his mind that the Institute property must be sold to pay the debts, and the balance, after the payment of debts, be refunded to stockholders in proportion to the amount of stock each held. But one morning, in prayer at the family altar, the Spirit of God came upon him as he was praying for divine guidance in matters pertaining to the Institute, and he exclaimed, while bowed upon his knees: "The Lord will vindicate every word He has spoken through vision relative to the Health Institute, and it will be raised from its low estate and prosper gloriously."

From that point of time we took hold of the work in earnest and have labored side by side for the Institute to counteract the influence of selfish men who had brought embarrassment upon it. We have given of our means, thus setting an example to others. We have encouraged economy and industry on the part of all connected with the Institute and have urged that physicians and helpers work hard for small pay until the institute should again be fully established in the confidence of our people. We have borne a plain testimony against the manifestation of selfishness in anyone connected with the Institute and have counseled and reproved wrongs. We knew that the Health Institute would not succeed unless the blessing of the Lord rested upon it. If His blessing attended it, the friends of the cause would have confidence that it was the work of God and would feel safe to donate means to make it a living enterprise, that it might be able to accomplish the design of God.

The physicians and some of the helpers went to work earnestly. They worked hard under great discouragements. Drs. Ginley, Chamberlain, and Lamson worked with earnestness and energy, for small pay, to build up this sinking institution. And, thank God, the original debt has been removed, and large additions for the accommodation of patients have been made and paid for. The circulation of the *Health Reformer,* which lies at the very foundation of the success of the Institute, has been doubled, and it has become a live journal. Confidence in the Institute has been fully restored in the minds of most of our people, and there have been as many patients at the Institute, nearly the year round, as could well be accommodated and properly treated by our physicians.

It is a matter of deep regret that the first managers of the Institute should take a course to nearly overwhelm it in debt and discouragement. But the financial losses which stockholders have felt and regretted have been small in comparison to the labor, perplexity, and care which my husband and I have borne without pay, and which physicians and helpers have borne for small wages. We have taken stock in the Institute to the amount of fifteen hundred dollars, which is "assigned," but which is a small consideration compared with the wear we have suffered in consequence of former reckless managers. But as the Institute now stands higher in reputation and patronage than ever before, and as the property is worth more than all the money that has been invested, and as former errors have been corrected, those who have lost their confidence have no excuse for cherishing feelings of prejudice. And if they still manifest a lack of interest, it will be because they choose to cherish prejudice rather than to be led by reason.

In the providence of God, Brother A has given his interest and energies to the Health Institute. He has had an unselfish interest to advance the interests of the Institute and has not spared or favored himself. If he depends on God and makes Him his strength and counselor he can be a blessing to physicians, helpers, and patients. He has linked his interest to everything connected with the Institute and has been a blessing to others in cheerfully bearing burdens which were neither few nor light. He has blessed others, and these blessings will again be reflected upon him.

But Brother A is in danger of taking upon himself burdens which others can and should bear. He should not wear himself out in doing those things which others, whose time is less valuable, can do. He should act as a director and superintendent. He should preserve his strength, that with his experienced judgment he can direct others what to do. This is necessary in order for him to maintain a position of influence in the Institute. His experience in managing with wisdom and economy is valuable. But he is in danger of separating his interest too much from his family, of becoming too much absorbed in the Institute, and of taking too many burdens upon himself, as my husband has done. My husband's interest for the Health Institute, the Publishing Association, and the cause generally was so great that he broke down and has been compelled to retire from the work for a time, when, had he done less for these institutions and divided his interest with his family, he would not have had a constant strain in one direction, and would have preserved his strength to continue his labors uninterruptedly. Brother A is the man for the place. But he should not do as my husband has done, even if matters are not in as prosperous a condition as if he devoted his entire energies to them. God does not require either my husband or Brother A to deprive himself of social family enjoyment, to divorce himself from home and family, even for the interest of these important institutions.

During the past three or four years several have had an interest for the Health Institute and have made efforts to place it in a better condition. But some have lacked discernment and experience. As long as Brother A acts an unselfish part and clings to God, He will be his helper and his counselor.

The physicians of the Health Institute should not feel compelled to do work that helpers can do. They should not serve in the bathroom or in the movement room, expending their vitality in doing what others might do. There should be no lack of helpers to nurse the sick and to watch with the feeble ones who need watchers. The physicians should reserve their strength for the successful performance of their professional duties. They should tell others what to do. If there is a want of those whom they can trust to do these things, suitable persons should be employed and properly instructed, and suitably remunerated for their services.

None should be employed as laborers but those who will work unselfishly in the interest of the Institute, and such should be well paid for their services. There should be a sufficient force, especially during the sickly season of summer, so that none need to overwork. The Health Institute has overcome its embarrassments; and physicians and helpers should not be compelled to labor as hard, and suffer such privations, as when it was so heavily embarrassed in consequence of unfaithful men, who managed it almost into the ground.

I was shown that the physicians at our Institute should be men and women of faith and spirituality. They should make God their trust. There are many who come to the Institute who have, by their own sinful indulgence, brought upon themselves disease of almost every type. This class do not deserve the sympathy that they frequently require. And it is painful to the physicians to devote time and strength to this class, who are debased physically, mentally, and morally. But there is a class who have, through ignorance, lived in violation of nature's laws. They have worked intemperately and have eaten intemperately, because it was the custom to do so. Some have suffered many things from many physicians, but have not been made better, but decidedly worse. At length they are torn from business, from society, and from their families; and as their last resort they come to the Health Institute with some faint hope that they may find relief. This class need sympathy. They should be treated with the greatest tenderness, and care should be taken to make clear to their understanding the laws of their being, that they may, by ceasing to violate them, and by governing themselves, avoid suffering and disease, the penalty of nature's violated law.

Dr. B is not the best adapted to fill a position as physician at the Institute. He sees men and women ruined in constitution, who are weak in mental and moral power, and he thinks it time lost to treat such cases. This may be so in many cases.

But he should not become discouraged and disgusted with sick and suffering patients. He should not lose his pity, sympathy, and patience, and feel that his life is poorly employed when doing for those who can never appreciate the labor they receive, and who will not use their strength, if they regain it, to bless society, but will pursue the same course of self-gratification that they did in losing health. Dr. B should not become weary or discouraged. He should remember Christ, who came in direct contact with suffering humanity. Although, in many cases, the afflicted had brought disease upon themselves by their sinful course in violating natural law, Jesus pitied their weakness, and when they came to Him with disease the most loathsome, He did not stand aloof for fear of contamination; He touched them and bade disease give back.

"And as He entered into a certain village, there met Him ten men that were lepers, which stood afar off: and they lifted up their voices, and said, Jesus, Master, have mercy on us. And when He saw them, He said unto them, Go show yourselves unto the priests. And it came to pass, that, as they went, they were cleansed. And one of them, when he saw that he was healed, turned back, and with a loud voice glorified God, and fell down on his face at His feet, giving Him thanks: and he was a Samaritan. And Jesus answering said, Were there not ten cleansed? but where are the nine? There are not found that returned to give glory to God, save this stranger. And He said unto him, Arise, go thy way: thy faith hath made thee whole."

Here is a lesson for us all. These lepers were so corrupted by disease that they had been restricted from society lest they should contaminate others. Their limits had been prescribed by the authorities. Jesus comes within their sight, and in their great suffering they cry unto Him who alone has power to relieve them. Jesus bids them show themselves to the priests. They have faith to start on their way, believing in the power of Christ to heal them. As they go on their way they realize that the horrible disease has left them. But only one has feelings of gratitude, only one feels his deep indebtedness to Christ for this great work wrought for him. This one returns praising God, and in the greatest humiliation falls at the feet of Christ, acknowledging with thankfulness the work wrought for him. And this man was a stranger; the other nine were Jews.

For the sake of this one man, who would make a right use of the blessing of health, Jesus healed the whole ten. The nine passed on without appreciating the work done, and rendered no grateful thanks to Jesus for doing the work.

Thus will the physicians of the Health Institute have their efforts treated. But if, in their labor to help suffering humanity, one out of twenty makes a right use of the benefits received and appreciates their efforts in his behalf, the physicians should feel grateful and satisfied. If one life out of ten is saved, and one soul out of one hundred is saved in the kingdom of God, all connected with the Institute will be amply repaid for all their efforts. All their anxiety and care will not be wholly lost. If the King of glory, the Majesty of heaven, worked for suffering humanity, and so few appreciated His divine aid, the physicians and helpers at the Institute should blush to complain if their feeble efforts are not appreciated by all and seem to be thrown away on some.

I was shown that the nine who did not return to give glory to God correctly represent some Sabbathkeepers who come to the Health Institute as patients. They receive much attention and should realize the anxiety and discouragements of the physicians, and should be the last to cause them unnecessary care and burdens. Yet I regret to say that frequently the patients who are most difficult to manage at the Health Institute are those of our faith. They are more free to make complaints than are any other class. Worldlings, and professed Christians of other denominations, appreciate the efforts made for their recovery more than many Sabbathkeepers do. And when they return to their homes they exert an influence more in favor of the Health Institute than do Sabbathkeepers. And some of those who are so free to question, and to complain of the management at the Institute, are those who have been treated at reduced prices.

This has been very discouraging to physicians and helpers; but they should remember Christ, their great Pattern, and not become weary in well-doing. If one among a large number is grateful and exerts a right influence, they should thank God and take courage. That one may be a stranger, and the inquiry may arise: Where are the nine? Why do not all Sabbathkeepers give their interest and support in favor of the Health Institute? Some Sabbathkeepers have so little interest that, while receiving attention at the Institute free of charge, they will speak disparagingly to patients of the means employed for the recovery of the sick. I wish such to consider their course. The Lord regards them as He did the nine lepers who returned not to give Him glory. Strangers do their duty and appreciate the efforts made for their recovery, while these cast an influence against those who have tried to do them good.

Dr. B needs to cultivate courtesy and kindness lest he shall unnecessarily injure the feelings of the patients. He is frank and openhearted, conscientious, sincere, and ardent. He has a good understanding of disease, but he should have a more thorough knowledge of how to treat the sick. With this knowledge he needs self-culture, refinement of manners, and to be more select in his words and illustrations in his parlor talks.

Dr. B is highly sensitive and naturally of a quick, impulsive temper. He moves too much upon the spur of the moment. He has made efforts to correct his hasty spirit and to overcome his deficiencies, but he has a still greater effort to make. If he sees things moving wrong he is in too great haste to tell the ones in error what he thinks, and he does not always use the most appropriate words for the occasion. He sometimes so offends patients that they hate him and leave the Institute with hard feelings, to the detriment of both themselves and the Institute. It seldom does any good to talk in a censuring manner to patients who are diseased in body and mind.

But few who have moved in the society of the world, and who view things from a worldling's standpoint, are prepared to have a statement of facts in regard to themselves presented before them. The truth even is not to be spoken at all times. There is a fit time and opportunity to speak when words will not offend. The physicians should not be overworked and their nervous systems prostrated, for this condition of body will not be favorable to calm minds, steady nerves, and a cheerful, happy spirit. Dr. B has been confined too steadily to the Institute. He should have had change. He should go out of Battle Creek occasionally and rest and visit, not always making professional visits, but visiting where he can be free and where his mind will not be anxious about the sick.

The privilege of getting away from the Health Institute should occasionally be accorded to all the physicians, especially to those who bear burdens and responsibilities. If there is such a scarcity of help that this cannot be done, more help should be secured. To have physicians overworked, and thus disqualified to perform the duties of their profession, is a thing to be dreaded. It should be prevented if possible, for its influence is against the interests of the Institute. The physicians should keep well. They must not get sick by overlabor or by any imprudence on their part.

I was shown that Dr. B is too easily discouraged. There will ever be things arising to annoy, perplex, and try the patience of physicians and helpers. They must be prepared for this and not become excited or unbalanced. They must be calm and kind whatever may occur. They are exerting an influence which will be reflected by the patients in other states and which will be reflected again upon the Health Institute for good or for evil. They should ever consider that they are dealing with men and women of diseased minds, who frequently view things in a perverted light and yet are confident that they understand matters perfectly. Physicians should understand that a soft answer turneth away wrath. Policy must be used in an institution where the sick are treated, in order to successfully control diseased minds and benefit the sick. If physicians can remain calm amid a tempest of inconsiderate, passionate words, if they can rule their own spirits when provoked and abused, they are indeed conquerors. "He that ruleth his spirit [is better] than he that taketh a city." To subdue self, and bring the passions under the control of the will, is the greatest conquest that men and women can achieve.

Dr. B is not blind to his peculiar temperament. He sees his failings, and when he feels the pressure upon him he is disposed to beat a retreat and turn his back upon the battlefield. But he will gain nothing by pursuing this course. He is situated where his surroundings and the pressure of circumstances are developing the strong points in his character, points from which the roughness needs to be removed, that he may become refined and elevated. For him to flee from the contest will not remove the defects in his character. Should he run away from the Institute, he would not in so doing remove or overcome the defects in his character. He has a work before him to overcome these defects if he would be among the number who are to stand without fault before the throne of God, having come up through great tribulation, and having washed their robes of character and made them white in the blood of the Lamb. The provision has been made for us to wash. The fountain has been prepared at infinite expense, and the burden of washing rests upon us, who are imperfect before God. The Lord does not propose to remove these spots of defilement without our doing anything on our part. We must wash our robes in the blood of the Lamb. We may lay hold of the merits of the blood of Christ by faith, and through His grace and power we may have strength to overcome our errors, our sins, our imperfections of character, and come off victorious, having washed our robes in the blood of the Lamb.

Dr. B should seek to add daily to his stock of knowledge and to cultivate courteousness and refinement of manners. In his parlor talks he is too apt to come down to a low level; they do not have an influence to elevate. He should bear in mind that he is associated with all classes of minds and that the impressions he gives will be extended to other states and will be reflected upon the Institute. To deal with men and women whose minds as well as bodies are diseased is a nice work. Great wisdom is needed by the physicians at the Institute in order to cure the body through the mind. But few realize the power that the mind has over the body. A great deal of the sickness which afflicts humanity has its origin in the mind and can only be cured by restoring the mind to health. There are very many more than we imagine who are sick mentally. Heart sickness makes many dyspeptics, for mental trouble has a paralyzing influence upon the digestive organs.

In order to reach this class of patients, the physician must have discernment, patience, kindness, and love. A sore, sick heart, a discouraged mind, needs mild treatment, and it is through tender sympathy that this class of minds can be healed. The physicians should first gain their confidence, and then point them to the all-healing Physician. If their minds can be directed to the Burden Bearer, and they can have faith that He will have an interest in them, the cure of their diseased bodies and minds will be sure.

Other health institutions are looking with a jealous eye upon the Health Institute at Battle Creek. They work from the world's standpoint, while the managers of the Health Institute work from a religious standpoint, acknowledging God as their proprietor. They do not labor selfishly for means alone, but for the sake of Christ and humanity. They are seeking to benefit suffering humanity, to heal the diseased mind as well as the suffering body, by directing invalids to Christ, the sinner's Friend. They do not leave religion out of the question, but make God their trust and dependence. The sick are directed to Jesus. After the physicians have done what they can in behalf of the sick, they ask God to work with their efforts and restore the suffering invalids to health. This He has done in some cases in answer to the prayer of faith. And this He will continue to do if they are faithful and put their trust in Him. The Health Institute will be a success, for God sustains it. And if His blessing attends the Institute, it will prosper and will be the means of doing a great amount of good. Other institutions are aware that a high standard of moral and religious influence exists at our Institute. They see that its conductors are not actuated by selfish, worldly principles, and they are jealous in regard to its commanding and leading influence.

DANGER OF APPLAUSE

I have been shown that great caution should be used, even when it is necessary to lift a burden of oppression from men and women, lest they lean to their own wisdom and fail to make God their only dependence. It is not safe to speak in praise of persons or to exalt the ability of a minister of Christ. In the day of God, very many will be weighed in the balance and found wanting because of exaltation. I would warn my brethren and sisters never to flatter persons because of their ability, for they cannot bear it. Self is easily exalted, and, in consequence, persons lose their balance. I say again to my brethren and sisters: If you would have your souls clean from the blood of all men, never flatter, never praise the efforts of poor mortals; for it may prove their ruin. It is unsafe, by our words and actions, to exalt a brother or sister, however apparently humble may be his or her deportment. If they really possess the meek and lowly spirit which God so highly esteems, help them to retain it. This will not be done by censuring them nor by neglecting to properly appreciate their true worth. But there are few who can bear praise without being injured.

Some ministers of ability who are now preaching present truth, love approbation. Applause stimulates them, as the glass of wine does the inebriate. Place these ministers where they have a small congregation which promises no special excitement and which provokes no decided opposition, and they will lose their interest and zeal, and appear as languid in the work as the inebriate when he is deprived of his dram. These men will fail to make real, practical laborers until they learn to labor without the excitement of applause.

LABOR FOR THE ERRING

Brethren C and D failed in some respects in their management of church matters at Battle Creek. They moved too much in their own spirit and did not make God their whole dependence. They failed of doing their duty by not leading the church to God, the Fountain of living waters, at which they could supply their want and satisfy their soul hunger. The renewing, sanctifying influence of the Holy Spirit, which would give peace and hope to the troubled conscience, and restore health and happiness to the soul, was not made of the highest importance. The good object they had in view was not attained. These brethren had too much of a spirit of cold criticism in the examination of individuals who presented themselves for church membership. The spirit of weeping with those who weep and rejoicing with those who rejoice was not in the hearts of these ministering brethren as it should have been.

Christ identified Himself with the necessities of His people. Their needs and their sufferings were His. He says: "I was anhungered, and ye gave Me meat: I was thirsty, and ye gave Me drink: I was a stranger, and ye took Me in: naked, and ye clothed Me: I was sick, and ye visited Me: I was in prison, and ye came unto Me." God's servants should have hearts of tender affection and sincere love for the followers of Christ. They should manifest that deep interest that Christ brings to view in the care of the shepherd for the lost sheep;

they should follow the example given by Christ and exercise the same compassion and gentleness, and the same tender, pitying love that He has exercised toward us.

The great moral powers of the soul are faith, hope, and love. If these are inactive, a minister may be ever so earnest and zealous, but his labor will not be accepted of God and cannot be productive of good to the church. A minister of Christ who bears the solemn message from God to the people should ever deal justly, love mercy, and walk humbly before God. The spirit of Christ in the heart will incline every power of the soul to nourish and protect the sheep of His pasture, like a faithful, true shepherd. Love is the golden chain which binds believing hearts to one another in willing bonds of friendship, tenderness, and faithful constancy, and which binds the soul to God. There is a decided lack of love, compassion, and pitying tenderness among brethren. The ministers of Christ are too cold and heartless. Their hearts are not all aglow with tender compassion and earnest love. The purest and most elevated devotion to God is that which is manifested in the most earnest desires and efforts to win souls to Christ. The reason ministers who preach present truth are not more successful is that they are deficient, greatly deficient, in faith, hope, and love. There are toils and conflicts, self-denials and secret heart trials, for us all to meet and bear. There will be sorrow and tears for our sins; there will be constant struggles and watchings, mingled with remorse and shame because of our deficiencies.

Let not the ministers of the cross of our dear Saviour forget their experience in these things; but let them ever bear in mind that they are but men, liable to err, and possessing like passions with their brethren, and that if they help their brethren they must be persevering in their efforts to do them good, having their hearts filled with pity and love. They must come to the hearts of their brethren and help them where they are weak and need help the most. Those who labor in word and doctrine should break their own hard, proud, unbelieving hearts if they would witness the same in their brethren. Christ has done all for us because we were helpless; we were bound in chains of darkness, sin, and despair, and could therefore do nothing for ourselves. It is through the exercise of faith, hope, and love that we come nearer and nearer to the standard of perfect holiness. Our brethren feel the same pitying need of help that we have felt. We should not burden them with unnecessary censure, but should let the love of Christ constrain us to be very compassionate and tender, that we can weep over the erring and those who have backslidden from God. The soul is of infinite value. Its worth can be estimated only by the price paid to ransom it. Calvary! Calvary! Calvary! will explain the true value of the soul.

THE SABBATH SCHOOL

Vital godliness is a principle to be cultivated. The power of God can accomplish for us that which all the systems in the world cannot effect. The perfection of Christian character depends wholly upon the grace and strength found alone in God. Without the power of grace upon the heart, assisting our efforts and sanctifying our labors, we shall fail of saving our own souls and of saving the souls of others. System and order are highly essential, but none should receive the impression that these will do the work without the grace and power of God operating upon the mind and heart. Heart and flesh would fail in the round of ceremonies, and in the carrying out of our plans, without the power of God to inspire and give courage to perform.

The Sabbath school at Battle Creek was made the one great theme of interest with Brother E. It absorbed the minds of the young, while other religious duties were neglected. Frequently, after the Sabbath school was closed, the superintendent, a number of the teachers, and quite a number of scholars would return home to rest. They felt that their burden for the day was ended and that they had no further duty. When the bell sounded forth the hour for public service, and the people left their homes for the house of worship, they would meet a large portion of the school passing to their homes. And however important the meeting, the interest of a large share of the Sabbath school could not be awakened to take any pleasure in the instruction given by the minister upon important Bible subjects. While many of the children did not attend public service, some that remained were not advantaged by the word spoken; for they felt that it was a wearisome tax.

There should be discipline and order in our Sabbath schools. Children who attend these schools should prize the privileges they enjoy and should be required to observe the regulations of the school. And even greater care should be taken by the parents to see that their children have their Scripture lessons than is taken to see that their day school lessons are prepared. Their Scripture lessons should be learned more perfectly than their lessons in the common schools. If parents and children see no necessity for this interest, then the children might better remain at home; for the Sabbath school will fail to prove a blessing to them. Parents and children should work in harmony with superintendent and teachers, thus giving evidence that they appreciate the labor put forth for them. Parents should take special interest in the religious education of their children, that they may have a more thorough knowledge of the Scriptures.

There are many children who plead a lack of time as a reason why their Sabbath school lessons are not learned, but there are few who could not find time to learn their lessons if they had an interest in them. Some devote time to amusement and sight-seeing; others to the needless trimming of their dresses for display, thus cultivating pride and vanity. The precious hours thus prodigally spent are God's time, for which they must render an account to Him. The hours spent in needless ornamentation or in amusements and idle conversation will, with every work, be brought into judgment.

LABORERS IN THE OFFICE

Those in the office who profess to believe the truth should show the power of the truth in their lives and prove that they are working onward and upward from the basis of principle. They should be molding their lives and characters after the perfect Model. If all could look with a discerning eye into the tremendous realities of eternity, what a horror of condemnation would seize some in the office who now pass on with seeming indifference, although separated from eternal scenes by a very small space. Many warnings have been given, and urged home with intense feeling and earnest prayers, every one of which is faithfully registered in heaven, to balance the account of each in the day of final investigation. The unwearying love of Christ has followed those engaged in His work in the office. God has followed them with blessings and entreaties, yet hating the sins and unfaithfulness that cling to them as the leprosy. The deep and solemn truths to which those in the office have had the privilege of listening should take hold upon their sympathies and lead them to a high appreciation of the light that God has given them. If they will walk in the light, it will beautify and ennoble their lives with heaven's own adornment, purity and true goodness.

A way is opened before everyone in the office to engage from the heart directly in the work of Christ and the salvation of souls. Christ left heaven and the bosom of His Father to come to a friendless, lost world to save those who would be saved. He exiled Himself from His Father and exchanged the pure companionship of angels for that of fallen humanity, all polluted with sin. With grief and amazement, Christ witnesses the coldness, the indifference and neglect, with which His professed followers in the office treat the light and the messages of warning and of love He has given them. Christ has provided the bread and water of life for all who hunger and thirst.

The Lord requires all in the office to labor from high motives. In His own life, Christ has given them an example. All should labor with interest, devotion, and faith for the salvation of souls. If all in the office will labor with unselfish purposes, discerning the sacredness of the work, the blessing of God will rest upon them. If all had cheerfully and gladly taken up their several burdens, the wear and perplexity would not have come so heavily upon my husband.

How few earnest prayers have been sent up to God in faith for those who worked in the office who were not fully in the truth! Who has felt the worth of the soul for whom Christ died? Who have been laborers in the vineyard of the Lord? I saw that angels were grieved with the trifling frivolities of the professed followers of Christ who were handling sacred things in the office. Some have no more sense of the sacredness of the work than if they were engaged in common labor. God now calls for the fruitless cumberers of the ground to consecrate themselves to Him and center their affections and hopes in Him.

The Lord would have all connected with the office become caretakers and burden bearers. If they are pleasure seekers, if they do not practice self-denial, they are not fit for a place in the office. The workers at the office should feel when they enter it that it is a sacred place, a place where the work of God is being done in the publication of a truth which will decide the destiny of souls. This is not felt or realized as it should be. There is conversation in the typesetting department which diverts the mind from the work. The office is no place for visiting, for a courting spirit, or for amusement or selfishness. All should feel that they are doing work for God. He who sifts all motives and reads all hearts is proving, and trying, and sifting His people, especially those who have light and knowledge, and who are engaged in His sacred work. God is a searcher of hearts and a trier of the reins, and will accept nothing less than entire devotion to the work and consecration to Himself. All in the office should take up their daily duties as if in the presence of God. They should not be satisfied with doing just enough to pass along, and receive their wages; but all should work in any place where they can help the most. In Brother White's absence there are some faithful ones; there are others who are eyeservants. If all in the office who profess to be followers of Christ had been faithful in the performance of duty in the office, there would have been a great change for the better. Young men and young women have been too much engrossed in each other's society, talking, jesting, and joking, and angels of God have been driven from the office.

Marcus Lichtenstein was a God-fearing youth; but he saw so little true religious principle in those in the church and those working in the office that he was perplexed, distressed, disgusted. He stumbled over the lack of conscientiousness in keeping the Sabbath manifested by some who yet professed to be commandment keepers. Marcus had an exalted regard for the work in the office; but the vanity, the trifling, and the lack of principle stumbled him. God had raised him up and in His providence connected him with His work in the office. But there is so little known of the mind and will of God by some who work in the office that they looked upon this great work of the conversion of Marcus from Judaism as of no great importance. His worth was not appreciated. He was frequently pained with the deportment of F and of others in the office; and when he attempted to reprove them, his words were received with contempt that he should venture to instruct them. His defective language was an occasion of jest and amusement with some.

Marcus felt deeply over the case of F, but he could not see how he could help him. Marcus never would have left the office if the young men had been true to their profession. If he makes shipwreck of faith, his blood will surely be found on the skirts of the young who profess Christ, but who, by their works, their words, and their deportment, state plainly that they are not of Christ, but of the world. This deplorable state of neglect, of indifference and unfaithfulness, must cease; a thorough and permanent change must take place in the office, or those who have had so much light and so great privileges should be dismissed and others take their places, even if they be unbelievers. It is a fearful thing to be self-deceived. Said the angel, pointing to those in the office: "Except your righteousness shall exceed the righteousness of the scribes and Pharisees, ye shall in no case enter into the kingdom of heaven." A profession is not enough. There must be a work inwrought in the soul and carried out in the life.

The love of Christ reaches to the very depths of earthly misery and woe, or it would not meet the case of the veriest sinner. It also reaches to the throne of the Eternal, or man could not be lifted from his degraded condition, and our necessities would not be met, our desires would not be satisfied. Christ has led the way from earth to heaven. He forms the connecting link between the two worlds. He brings the love and condescension of God to man, and brings man up through His merits to meet the reconciliation of God. Christ is the way, the truth, and the life. It is hard work to follow on, step by step, painfully and slowly, onward and upward, in the path of purity and holiness. But Christ has made ample provision to impart new vigor and divine strength at every advance step in the divine life. This is the knowledge and experience that the hands in the office all want, and must have, or they daily bring reproach upon the cause of Christ.

Brother G is making a mistake in his life. He puts too high an estimate upon himself. He has not commenced to build in a right way to make a success of life. He is building at the top, but the foundation is not laid right. The foundation must be laid underground, and then the building can go up. He needs a discipline and experience in the everyday duties of life which the sciences will not give; all his education will not give him physical exercise to become inured to the hardships of life.

From what has been shown me, there should be a careful selection of help in the office. The young and untried and unconsecrated should not be placed there, for they are exposed to temptations and have not fixed characters. Those who have formed their characters, who have fixed principles, and who have the truth of God in the heart will not be a constant source of care and anxiety, but rather helps and blessings. The office of publication is amply able to make arrangements to secure good helpers, those who have ability and principle. And the church, in their turn, should not seek to advantage themselves one penny from those who come to the office to labor and learn their trade. There are positions where some can earn better wages than at the office, but they can never find a position more important, more honorable, or more exalted than the work of God in the office. Those who labor faithfully and unselfishly will be rewarded. For them there is a crown of glory prepared, compared with which all earthly honors and pleasures are as the small dust of the balance. Especially will those be blessed who have been faithful to God in watching over the spiritual welfare of others in the office. Pecuniary and temporal interests, in comparison with this, sink into insignificance. In one scale is gold dust; in the other, a human soul of such value that honor, riches, and glory have been sacrificed by the Son of God to ransom it from the bondage of sin and hopeless despair. The soul is of infinite value and demands the utmost attention. Every man who fears God in that office should put away childish and vain things, and, with true moral courage, stand erect in the dignity of his manhood, shunning low familiarity, yet binding heart to heart in the bond of Christian interest and love. Hearts yearn for sympathy and love, and are as much refreshed and strengthened by them as flowers are by showers and sunshine.

The Bible should be read every day. A life of religion, of devotion to God, is the best shield for the young who are exposed to temptation in their associations while acquiring an education. The word of God will give the correct standard of right and wrong, and of moral principle. A fixed principle of truth is the only safeguard for youth. Strong purposes and a resolute will close many an open door to temptation and to influences that are unfavorable to the maintenance of Christian character. A weak, irresolute spirit indulged in boyhood and youth will make a life of constant toil and struggle because decision and firm principle are wanting. Such will ever be trammeled in making a success of this life, and they will be in danger of losing the better life. It will be safe to be earnest for the right. The first consideration should be to honor God, and the second, to be faithful to humanity, performing the duties which each day brings, meeting its trials and bearing its burdens with firmness and a resolute heart. Earnest and untiring effort, united with strong purpose and entire trust in God, will help in every emergency, will qualify for a useful life in this world, and give a fitness for the immortal life.

LOVE AND DUTY

Love has a twin sister, which is duty. Love and duty stand side by side. Love exercised while duty is neglected will make children headstrong, willful, perverse, selfish, and disobedient. If stern duty is left to stand alone without love to soften and win, it will have a similar result. Duty and love must be blended in order that children may be properly disciplined.

Anciently, directions were given to the priests: "And they shall teach My people the difference between the holy and profane, and cause them to discern between the unclean and the clean. And in controversy they shall stand in judgment; and they shall judge it according to My judgments." "When I say unto the wicked, O wicked man, thou shalt surely die; if thou dost not speak to warn the wicked from his way, that wicked man shall die in his iniquity; but his blood will I require at thine hand. Nevertheless, if thou warn the wicked of his way to turn from it; if he do not turn from his way, he shall die in his iniquity; but thou hast delivered thy soul."

Here the duty of God's servants is made plain. They cannot be excused from the faithful discharge of their duty to reprove sins and wrongs in the people of God, although it may be a disagreeable task and may not be received by the one who is at fault. But in most cases the one reproved would accept the warning and heed reproof were it not that others stand in the way. They come in as sympathizers and pity the one reproved and feel that they must stand in his defense. They do not see that the Lord is displeased with the wrongdoer, because the cause of God has been wounded and His name reproached. Souls have been turned aside from the truth and have made shipwreck of faith as the result of the wrong course pursued by the one in fault; but the servant of God whose discernment is clouded and whose judgment is swayed by wrong influences would as soon take his position with the offender whose influence has done much harm, as with the reprover of wrong and of sin, and in so doing he virtually says to the sinner: "Do not be troubled, do not be cast down; you are about right after all." These say to the sinner: "It shall be well with thee."

God requires His servants to walk in the light and not cover their eyes that they may not discern the working of Satan. They should be prepared to warn and reprove those who are in danger through his subtlety. Satan is working on the right hand and on the left to obtain vantage ground. He rests not. He is persevering. He is vigilant and crafty to take advantage of every circumstance and turn it to his account in his warfare against the truth and the interests of the kingdom of God. It is a lamentable fact that God's servants are not half as much awake to the wiles of Satan as they should be. And instead of resisting the devil that he may flee from them, many are inclined to make a compromise with the powers of darkness.

THE BATTLE CREEK CHURCH

There are serious objections to having the school located at Battle Creek. The church is large, and there are quite a number of youth connected with it. If the influence which one member has over another in so large a church were of an elevating character, leading to purity and consecration to God, then the youth coming to Battle Creek would have greater advantages than if the school were located elsewhere. But if the influences at Battle Creek shall be in the future what they have been for several years past, I would warn parents to keep their children from Battle Creek. There are but few in that large church who have an influence that will steadily draw souls to Christ; while there are many who will, by their example, lead the youth away from God to the love of the world.

With many of the church at Battle Creek there is a great lack of feeling their responsibility. Those who have practical religion will retain their identity of character under any circumstances. They will not be like the reed trembling in the wind. Those situated at a distance feel that they would be highly favored could they have the privilege of living in Battle Creek, among a strong church, where their children could be benefited by the Sabbath school and meetings. Some of our brethren and sisters in times past have made sacrifices to have their children live there. But they have been disappointed in almost every case. There were but few in the church to manifest an unselfish interest for these youth. The church generally stood as pharisaical strangers, aloof from those who needed their help the most. Some of the youth connected with the church, who were professedly serving God, but loving pleasure and the world more, were ready to make the acquaintance of youthful strangers who came among them, and to exert a strong influence over them to lead them to the world instead of nearer to God. When these return home, they are further from the truth than when they came to Battle Creek.

Men and women are wanted at the heart of the work who will be nursing fathers and mothers in Israel, who will have hearts that can take in more than merely me and mine. They should have hearts that will glow with love for the dear youth, whether they are members of their own families or children of their neighbors. They are members of God's great family, for whom Christ had so great an interest that He made every sacrifice that it was possible for Him to make to save them. He left His glory, His majesty, His kingly throne and robes of royalty, and became poor, that through His poverty the children of men might be made rich. He finally poured out His soul unto death that He might save the race from hopeless misery. This is the example of disinterested benevolence that Christ has given us to pattern after.

In the special providence of God many youth and also those of mature age have been thrown into the arms of the Battle Creek church for them to bless with the great light God has given them, and that, through their disinterested efforts, they might have the precious privilege of bringing them to Christ and to the truth. Christ commissions His angels to minister unto those who are brought under the influence of the truth, to soften their hearts and make them susceptible of the influences of His truth. While God and His angels are doing their work, those who profess to be followers of Christ seem to be coolly indifferent. They do not work in unison with Christ and holy angels. Although they profess to be servants of God they are serving their own interest and loving their own pleasure, and souls are perishing around them. These souls can truly say: "No man careth for my soul." The church have neglected to improve the privileges and blessings within their reach, and through their neglect of duty have lost golden opportunities of winning souls to Christ.

Unbelievers have lived among them for months, and they have made no special efforts to save them. How can the Master regard such servants? The unbelieving would have responded to efforts made in their behalf if the brethren and sisters had lived up to their exalted profession. If they had been seeking an opportunity to work for the interest of their Master, to advance His cause, they would have manifested kindness and love for them, they would have sought opportunities to pray with and for them, and would have felt a solemn responsibility resting upon them to show their faith by their works, by precept and example. Through their instrumentality these souls might have been saved to be as stars in the crown of their rejoicing. But, in many cases, the golden opportunity has passed never to return. The souls that were in the valley of decision have taken their position in the ranks of the enemy and become enemies of God and the truth. And the record of the unfaithfulness of the professed followers of Jesus has gone up to heaven.

I was shown that if the youth at Battle Creek were true to their profession, they might exert a strong influence for good over their fellow youth. But a large share of the youth at Battle Creek need a Christian experience. They know not God by experimental knowledge. They have not individually a personal experience in the Christian life, and they must perish with the unbelieving unless they obtain this experience. The youth of this class follow inclination rather than duty. Some do not seek to be governed by principle. They do not agonize to enter in at the strait gate, trembling with fear lest they will not be able. They are confident, boastful, proud, disobedient, unthankful, and unholy. Just such a class as this lead souls in the broad road to ruin. If Christ is not in them, they cannot exemplify Him in their lives and characters.

The church at Battle Creek have had great light. As a people they have been peculiarly favored of God. They have not been left in ignorance in regard to the will of God concerning them. They might be far in advance of what they now are, if they had walked in the light. They are not that separate, peculiar, and holy people that their faith demands, and that God recognizes and acknowledges as children of the light. They are not as obedient and devotional as their exalted position and sacred obligation as children walking in the light require them to be. The most solemn message of mercy ever given to the world has been entrusted to them. The Lord has made that church the depositaries of His commandments in a sense that no other church is. God did not show them His special favor in trusting to them His sacred truth that they alone might be benefited by the light given, but that the light reflected upon them from heaven should shine forth to others and be reflected again to God by those who receive the truth glorifying Him. Many in Battle Creek will have a fearful account to give in the day of God for this sinful neglect of duty.

Many of those who profess to believe the truth in Battle Creek contradict their faith by their works. They are as unbelieving, and as far from fulfilling the requirements of God and from coming up to their profession of faith, as was the Jewish church at the time of Christ's first advent. Should Christ make His appearance among them, reproving and rebuking selfishness, pride, and love of the friendship of the world, as He did at His first advent, but few would recognize Him as the Lord of glory. The picture He would present before them of their neglect of duty they would not receive, but would tell Him to His face: "You are entirely mistaken; we have done this good and great thing, and performed this and that wonderful work, and we are entitled to be highly exalted for our good works."

The Jews did not go into darkness all at once. It was a gradual work, until they could not discern the gift of God in sending His Son. The church at Battle Creek have had superior advantages, and they will be judged by the light and privileges they have had. Their deficiencies, their unbelief, their hardness of heart, and their neglect to cherish and follow the light are not less than those of the favored Jews, who refused the blessings they might have accepted, and crucified the Son of God. The Jews are now an astonishment and reproach to the world.

The church at Battle Creek are like Capernaum, which Christ represents as being exalted unto heaven by the light and privileges that had been given them. If the light and privileges with which they had been blessed had been given to Sodom and Gomorrah, they might have stood unto this day. If the light and knowledge which the church in Battle Creek have received had been given the nations who sit in darkness, they might have been far in advance of that church.

The Laodicean church really believed, and enjoyed the blessings of the gospel, and thought they were rich in the favor of God, when the True Witness called them poor, naked, blind, and miserable. This is the case with the church at Battle Creek and with a large share of those who profess to be God's commandment-keeping people. The Lord seeth not as man seeth. His thoughts and ways are not as our ways.

The words and law of God, written in the soul, and exhibited in a consecrated, holy life, have a powerful influence to convict the world. Covetousness which is idolatry, and envy, and love of the world, will be rooted from the habits of those who are obedient to Christ, and it will be their pleasure to deal justly, to love mercy, and to walk humbly before God. Oh, how much is comprised in this, walking humbly before God! The law of God, if written in the heart, will bring the mind and will into subjection to the obedience of Christ.

Our faith is peculiar. Many who profess to be living under the sound of the last message of mercy are not separated in their affections from the world. They bow down before the friendship of the world and sacrifice light and principle to secure its favor. The apostle describes the favored people of God in these words: "But ye are a chosen generation, a royal priesthood, an holy nation, a peculiar people; that ye should show forth the praises of Him who hath called you out of darkness into His marvelous light."

MISSIONARY WORK

December 10, 1871, I was shown that God would accomplish a great work through the truth if devoted, self-sacrificing men would give themselves unreservedly to the work of presenting it to those in darkness. Those who have a knowledge of the precious truth and who are consecrated to God should avail themselves of every opportunity where there is an opening to press in the truth. Angels of God are moving on the hearts and consciences of the people of other nations, and honest souls are troubled as they witness the signs of the times in the unsettled state of the nations. The inquiry arises in their hearts. What will be the end of all these things? While God and angels are at work to impress hearts, the servants of Christ seem to be asleep. But few are working in unison with the heavenly messengers. All men and women who are Christians in every sense of the word should be workers in the vineyard of the Lord. They should be wide-awake, zealously laboring for the salvation of their fellow men, and should imitate the example that the Saviour of the world has given them in His life of self-denial, sacrifice, and faithful, earnest labor.

There has been but little of the missionary spirit among Sabbathkeeping Adventists. If ministers and people were sufficiently aroused, they would not rest thus indifferently while God has honored them by making them the depositaries of His law by printing it in their minds and writing it upon their hearts. These truths of vital importance are to test the world; and yet in our own country there are cities, villages, and towns that have never heard the warning message. Young men who feel stirred by the appeals that have been made for help in this great work of advancing the cause of God make some advance moves, but do not get the burden of the work upon them sufficiently to accomplish what they might. They are willing to do a small work which does not require special effort. Therefore they do not learn to place their whole dependence upon

God and by living faith draw from the great Fountain and Source of light and strength in order that their efforts may prove wholly successful.

Those who think that they have a work to do for the Master should not commence their efforts among the churches; they should go out into new fields and prove their gifts. In this way they can test themselves and settle the matter to their own satisfaction, whether God has indeed chosen them for this work. They will feel the necessity of studying the word of God and praying earnestly for heavenly wisdom and divine aid. By meeting with opponents who bring up objections to the important points of our faith, they will be brought where they will obtain a most valuable experience. They will feel their weakness and be driven to the word of God and to prayer. In this exercise of their gifts they will be learning and improving and gaining confidence, courage, and faith, and will eventually have a valuable experience.

The Brethren H commenced right in this work. In their labor they did not go among the churches, but went out into new fields. They commenced humble. They were little in their own eyes and felt the necessity of their whole dependence being in God. These brothers, especially A H, are now in great danger of becoming self-sufficient. When he has discussed with opponents, the truth has obtained the victory, and he has begun to feel strong in himself. As soon as he gets above the simplicity of the work, his labors will not benefit the precious cause of God. He should not encourage a love for discussions, but should avoid them whenever he can. These contests with the powers of darkness in debate seldom result the best for the advancement of present truth.

If young men who commence to labor in this cause would have the missionary spirit, they would give evidence that God has indeed called them to the work. But when they do not go out into new places, but are content to go from church to church, they give evidence that the burden of the work is not upon them. The ideas of our young preachers are not broad enough. Their zeal is too feeble. Were the young men awake and devoted to the Lord, they would be diligent every moment of their time and would seek to qualify themselves to become laborers in the missionary field rather than to become combatants.

Young men should be qualifying themselves by becoming familiar with other languages, that God may use them as mediums to communicate His saving truth to those of other nations. These young men may obtain a knowledge of other languages even while engaged in laboring for sinners. If they are economical of their time they can be improving their minds and qualifying themselves for more extended usefulness. If young women who have borne but little responsibility would devote themselves to God, they could qualify themselves for usefulness by studying and becoming familiar with other languages. They could devote themselves to the work of translating.

Our publications should be printed in other languages, that foreign nations may be reached. Much can be done through the medium of the press, but still more can be accomplished if the influence of the labors of the living preacher goes with our publications. Missionaries are needed to go to other nations to preach the truth in a guarded, careful manner. The cause of present truth can be greatly extended by personal effort. The contact of individual mind with individual mind will do more to remove prejudice, if the labor is discreet, than our publications alone can do. Those who engage in this work should not consult their ease or inclination; neither should they have love for popularity or display.

When the churches see young men possessing zeal to qualify themselves to extend their labors to cities, villages, and towns that have never been aroused to the truth, and missionaries volunteering to go to other nations to carry the truth to them, the churches will be encouraged and strengthened far more than to themselves receive the labors of inexperienced young men. As they see their ministers' hearts all aglow with love and zeal for the truth, and with a desire to save souls, the churches will arouse themselves. These generally have the gifts and power within themselves to bless and strengthen themselves, and to gather the sheep and lambs into the fold. They need to be thrown upon their own resources, that all the gifts that are lying dormant may thus be called into active service.

As churches are established, it should be set before them that it is even from among them that men must be taken to carry the truth to others and raise new churches; therefore they must all work, and cultivate to the utmost the talents that God has given them, and be training their minds to engage in the service of their Master. If these messengers are pure in heart and life, if their example is what it should be, their labors will be highly successful; for they have a most powerful truth, one that is clear and connected, and that has convincing arguments in its favor. They have God on their side and the angels of God to work with their efforts.

The reason there has been so little accomplished by those who preach the truth is not wholly because the truth they bear is unpopular, but because the men who bear the message are not sanctified by the truths they preach. The Saviour withdraws His smiles, and the inspiration of His Spirit is not upon them. The presence and power of God to convict the sinner and cleanse from all unrighteousness is not manifest. Sudden destruction is right upon the people, and yet they are not fearfully alarmed. Unconsecrated ministers make the work very hard for those who follow after them and who have the burden and spirit of the work upon them.

The Lord has moved upon men of other tongues and has brought them under the influence of the truth, that they might be qualified to labor in His cause. He has brought them within reach of the office of publication, that its managers might avail themselves of their services if they were awake to the wants of the cause. Publications are needed in other languages to raise an interest and the spirit of inquiry among other nations.

In a most remarkable manner the Lord wrought upon the heart of Marcus Lichtenstein and directed the course of this young man to Battle Creek, that he might there be brought under the influence of the truth and be converted; that he might obtain an experience and be united to the office of publication. His education in the Jewish religion would have qualified him to prepare publications. His knowledge of Hebrew would have been a help to the office in the preparation of publications through which access could be gained to a class that otherwise could not be reached. It was no inferior gift that God gave to the office in Marcus. His deportment and conscientiousness were in accordance with the principles of the wonderful truths he was beginning to see and appreciate.

But the influence of some in the office grieved and discouraged Marcus. Those young men who did not esteem him as he deserved, and whose Christian life was a contradiction to their profession, were the means that Satan used to separate from the office the gift which God had given to it. He went away perplexed, grieved, discouraged. Those who had had years of experience, and who should have had the love of Christ in their hearts, were so far separated from God by selfishness, pride, and their own folly that they could not discern the special work of God in connecting Marcus with the office.

If those who are connected with the office had been awake and not spiritually paralyzed, Brother I would long ago have been connected with the office and might now be prepared to do a good work which much needs to be done. He should have been engaged in teaching young men and women, that they might now be qualified to become workers in missionary fields.

Those engaged in the work have been about two thirds dead because of yielding to wrong influences. They have been where God could not impress them by His Holy Spirit. And, oh, how my heart aches as I see that so much time has passed, and that the great work that might have been done is left undone because those in important positions have not walked in the light! Satan has stood prepared to sympathize with the men in holy office and to tell them that God does not require of them as much zeal and unselfish, devoted interest as Brother White expects; and they settle down carelessly in Satan's easy chair, and the ever-vigilant, persevering foe binds them in chains of darkness while they think that they are all right. Satan works on their right hand and on their left, and all around them; and they know it not. They call darkness light, and light darkness.

If those in the office of publication are indeed engaged in the sacred work of giving the last solemn message of warning to the world, how careful should they be to carry out in their lives the principles of the truth they are handling. They should have pure hearts and clean hands.

Our people connected with the office have not been awake to improve the privileges within their reach and to secure all the talent and influence that God has provided for them. With nearly all connected with the office there is a very great failure to realize the importance and sacredness of the work. Pride and selfishness exist to a very great degree, and angels of God are not attracted to the office as they would be if hearts there were pure and in communion with God. Those laboring in the office have not had a vivid sense that the truths that they were handling were of heavenly origin, designed to accomplish a certain and special work, as did the preaching of Noah before the Flood. As the preaching of Noah warned, tested, and proved the inhabitants of the world before the flood of waters destroyed them from off the face of the earth, so the truth of God for these last days is doing a similar work of warning, testing, and proving the world. The publications which go forth from the office bear the signet of the Eternal. They are being scattered all through the land and are deciding the destiny of souls. Men are now greatly needed who can translate and prepare our publications in other languages so that the message of warning may go to all nations and test them by the light of the truth, that men and women, as they see the light, may turn from transgression to obedience of the law of God.

Every opportunity should be improved to extend the truth to other nations. This will be attended with considerable expense, but expense should in no case hinder the performance of this work. Means are of value only as they are used to advance the interest of the kingdom of God. The Lord has lent men means for this very purpose, to use in sending the truth to their fellow men. There is a great amount of surplus means in the ranks of Seventh-day Adventists. And the selfish withholding of it from the cause of God is blinding their eyes to the importance of the work of God, making it impossible for them to discern the solemnity of the times in which we live, or the value of eternal riches. They do not view Calvary in the right light, and therefore cannot appreciate the worth of the soul for which Christ paid such an infinite price.

Men will invest means in that which they value the most and which they think will bring them the greatest profits. When men will run great risks and invest much in worldly enterprises, but are unwilling to venture or invest much in the cause of God to send the truth to their fellow men, they evidence that they value their earthly treasure just as much more highly than the heavenly as their works show.

If men would lay their earthly treasure upon the altar of God, and would work as zealously to secure the heavenly treasure as they did to gain the earthly, they would invest means cheerfully and gladly wherever they could see an opportunity to do good and aid the cause of their Master. Christ has given them unmistakable evidence of His love and fidelity to them, and has entrusted them with means to test and prove their fidelity to Him. He left heaven, His riches and glory, and for their sakes became poor, that they through His poverty might be made rich. After thus condescending to save man, Christ requires no less of him than that he should deny himself and use the means He has lent him in saving his fellow men, and by so doing give evidence of his love for his Redeemer and show that he values the salvation brought to him by such an infinite sacrifice.

Now is the time to use means for God. Now is the time to be rich in good works, laying up in store for ourselves a good foundation against the time to come, that we may lay hold on eternal life. One soul saved in the kingdom of God is of more value than all earthly riches. We are answerable to God for the souls of those with whom we are brought in contact, and the closer our connections with our fellow men the greater our responsibility. We are one great brotherhood, and the welfare of our fellow men should be our great interest. We have not one moment to lose. If we have been careless in this matter, it is high time we were now in earnest to redeem the time, lest the blood of souls be found on our garments. As children of God, none of us are excused from taking a part in the great work of Christ in the salvation of our fellow men.

It will be a difficult work to overcome prejudice and to convince the unbelieving that our efforts to help them are disinterested. But this should not hinder our labor. There is no precept in the word of God that tells us to do good to those only who appreciate and respond to our efforts, and to benefit those only who will thank us for it. God has sent us to work in His vineyard. It is our business to do all we can. "In the morning sow thy seed, and in the evening withhold not thine hand: for thou knowest not whether shall prosper, either this or that." We have too little faith. We limit the Holy One of Israel. We should be grateful that God condescends to use any of us as His instruments. For every earnest prayer put up in faith for anything, answers will be returned. They may not come just as we have expected; but they will come, not perhaps as we have devised, but at the very time when we most need them. But, oh, how sinful is our unbelief! "If ye abide in Me, and My words abide in you, ye shall ask what ye will, and it shall be done unto you."

Young men who are engaged in this work should not trust too much to their own abilities. They are inexperienced and should seek to learn wisdom from those who have had long experience in the work and who have had opportunities to study character.

Instead of our ministering brethren laboring among the churches, God designs that we should spread abroad and our missionary labor be extended over as much ground as we can possibly occupy to advantage, going in every direction to raise up new companies. We should ever leave upon the minds of new disciples an impression of the importance of our mission. As able men are converted to the truth, they should not require laborers to keep their flagging faith alive; but these men should be impressed with the necessity of laboring in the vineyard. As long as churches rely upon laborers from abroad to strengthen and encourage their faith, they will not become strong in themselves. They should be instructed that their strength will increase in proportion to their personal efforts. The more closely the New Testament plan is followed in missionary labor, the more successful will be the efforts put forth.

We should work as did our divine Teacher, sowing the seeds of truth with care, anxiety, and self-denial. We must have the mind of Christ if we would not become weary in well-doing. His was a life of continual sacrifice for others' good. We must follow His example. We must sow the seed of truth and trust in God to quicken it to life. The precious seed may lie dormant for some time, when the grace of God may convict the heart and the seed sown be awakened to life and spring up and bear fruit to the glory of God. Missionaries in this great work are wanted to labor unselfishly, earnestly, and perseveringly as co-workers with Christ and the heavenly angels in the salvation of their fellow men.

Especially should our ministers beware of indolence and pride, which are apt to grow out of a consciousness that we have the truth and strong arguments which our opponents cannot meet; and while the truths which we handle are mighty to the pulling down of the strongholds of the powers of darkness, there is danger of neglecting personal piety, purity of heart, and entire consecration to God. There is danger of their feeling that they are rich and increased with goods, while they lack the essential qualifications of Christians. They may be wretched, poor, blind, miserable, and naked. They do not feel the necessity of living in obedience to Christ every day and every hour. Spiritual pride eats out the vitals of religion. In order to preserve humility, it would be well to remember how we appear in the sight of a holy God, who reads every secret of the soul, and how we should appear in the sight of our fellow men if they all knew us as well as God knows us. For this reason, to humble us, we are directed to confess our faults, and improve this opportunity to subdue our pride.

Ministers should not neglect physical exercise. They should seek to make themselves useful and to be a help where they are dependent upon the hospitalities of others. They should not allow others to wait upon them, but should rather lighten the burdens of those who, having so great a respect for the gospel ministry, would put themselves to great inconvenience to do for them that which they should do for themselves. The poor health of some of our ministers is because of their neglect of physical exercise in useful labor.

As the matter has resulted, I was shown that it would have been better had the Brethren J done what they could in the preparation of tracts to be circulated among the French. If these works were not prepared in all their perfection, they might better have been circulated, that the French people might have had an opportunity to search the evidences of our faith. There are great risks in delay. The French should have had books setting forth the reasons of our faith. The Brethren J were not prepared to do justice to these works, for they needed to be spiritualized and enlivened themselves or the books prepared would bear the stamp of their minds. They needed to be corrected, lest their preaching and writing should be tedious. They needed to educate themselves to come at once to the point and make the essential features of our faith stand forth clearly before the people. The work has been hindered by Satan, and much has been lost because these works were not prepared when they should have been. These brethren can do much good if they are fully devoted to the work and if they will follow the light that God has given them.

EFFECT OF DISCUSSIONS

December 10, 1871, I was shown the dangers of Brother K. His influence upon the cause of God is not what it should be or what it might be. He seems to be in blindness as to the result of his course; he does not discern what kind of wake he leaves behind him. He does not labor in a manner that God can accept. I saw that he was in as great peril as was Moses Hull before he left the truth. He trusted in himself. He thought he was of so great value to the cause of truth that the cause could not spare him. Brother K has felt very much the same. He relies too much on his own strength and wisdom. If he could see his weakness as God sees it he would never flatter himself or feel in the least to triumph. And unless he makes God his dependence and strength he will make shipwreck of faith as surely as did Moses Hull.

He does not in his labors draw strength from God. He depends upon an excitement to arouse his ambition. In laboring with a few, where there is no special excitement to stimulate, he loses his courage. When the labor goes hard and he is not borne up by this special excitement, he does not then cling the firmer to God and become more earnest to press through the darkness and gain the victory. Brother K, you frequently become childish, weak, and inefficient at the very time when you should be strongest. This should evidence to you that your zeal and animation are not always from the right source.

I was shown that here is the danger of young ministers who engage in discussion. They turn their minds to the study of the word to gather the sharp things, and they become sarcastic and, in their efforts to meet an opponent, too frequently leave God out of the question. The excitement of debate lessens their interest in meetings where this special excitement does not exist. Those who engage in debates are not the most successful laborers and the best adapted to build up the cause. By some, discussion is coveted, and they prefer this kind of labor above any other. They do not study the Bible with humility of mind, that they may know how to attain the love of God; as Paul says: "That Christ may dwell in your hearts by faith; that ye, being rooted and grounded in love, may be able to comprehend with all saints what is the breadth, and length, and depth, and height; and to know the love of Christ, which passeth knowledge, that ye might be filled with all the fullness of God."

Young preachers should avoid discussions, for they do not increase spirituality or humbleness of mind. In some cases it may be necessary to meet a proud boaster against the truth of God in open debate; but generally these discussions, either oral or written, result in more harm than good. After a discussion the greater responsibility rests upon the minister to keep up the interest. He should beware of the reaction which is liable to take place after a religious excitement, and not yield to discouragement himself.

Men who will not admit the claims of God's law, which are so very plain, will generally take a lawless course; for they have so long taken sides with the great rebel in warring against the law of God, which is the foundation of His government in heaven and earth, that they are trained in this labor. In their warfare they will not open their eyes or consciences to light. They close their eyes, lest they shall become enlightened. Their case is as hopeless as was that of the Jews who would not see the light which Christ brought to them. The wonderful evidences which He gave them of His Messiahship in the miracles that He performed, in healing the sick, raising the dead, and doing the works which no other man had done or could do, instead of melting and subduing their hearts, and overcoming their wicked prejudices, inspired them with satanic hatred and fury such as Satan possessed when he was thrust out of heaven. The greater light and evidence they had, the greater was their hatred. They were determined to extinguish the light by putting Christ to death.

The haters of God's law, which is the foundation of His government in heaven and earth, occupy the same ground as did the unbelieving Jews. Their defiant power will follow those who keep the commandments of God, and any amount of light will be rejected by them. Their consciences have so long been violated, and their hearts have grown so hard by their choosing darkness rather than light, that they feel that it is a virtue in them, in order to gain their object, to bear false witness or stoop to almost any course of equivocation or deception, as did the Jews in their rejection of Christ. They reason that the end justifies the means. They virtually crucify the law of the Father, as the Jews crucified Christ.

Our work should be to embrace every opportunity to present the truth in its purity and simplicity where there is any desire or interest to hear the reasons of our faith. Those who have dwelt mostly upon the prophecies and the theoretical points of our faith should without delay become Bible students upon practical subjects. They should take a deeper draft at the fountain of divine truth. They should carefully study the life of Christ and His lessons of practical godliness, given for the benefit of all and to be the rule of right living for all who should believe on His name. They should be imbued with the spirit of their great Exemplar and have a high sense of the sacred life of a follower of Christ.

Christ met the case of every class in the subjects and manner of His teaching. He dined and lodged with the rich and the poor, and made Himself familiar with the interests and occupations of men, that He might gain access to their hearts. The learned and the most intellectual were gratified and charmed with His discourses, and yet they were so plain and simple as to be comprehended by the humblest minds. Christ availed Himself of every opportunity to give instruction to the people upon those heavenly doctrines and precepts which should be incorporated into their lives and which would distinguish them from all other religionists because of their holy, elevated character. These lessons of divine instruction are not brought to bear upon men's consciences as they should be. These sermons of Christ furnish ministers believing present truth with discourses which will be appropriate on almost any occasion. Here is a field of study for the Bible student, in which he cannot be interested without having the spirit of the heavenly Teacher in his own heart. Here are subjects which Christ presented to all classes. Thousands of people of every stamp of character and every grade of society were attracted and charmed with the matter brought before them.

Some ministers who have been long in the work of preaching present truth have made great failures in their labors. They have educated themselves as combatants. They have studied out argumentative subjects for the object of discussion, and these subjects which they have prepared they love to use. The truth of God is plain, clear, and conclusive. It is harmonious and, in contrast with error, shines with clearness and beauty. Its consistency commends it to the judgment of every heart that is not filled with prejudice. Our preachers present the arguments upon the truth, which have been made ready for them, and, if there are no hindrances, the truth bears away the victory. But I was shown that in many cases the poor instrument takes the credit of the victory gained, and the people, who are more earthly than spiritual, praise and honor the instrument, while the truth of God is not exalted by the victory it gained.

Those who love to engage in discussion generally lose their spirituality. They do not trust in God as they should. They have the theory of the truth prepared to whip an opponent. The feelings of their own unsanctified hearts have prepared many sharp, close things to use as a snap to their whip to irritate and provoke their opponent. The spirit of Christ has no part in this. While furnished with conclusive arguments, the debater soon thinks that he is strong enough to triumph over his opponent, and God is left out of the matter. Some of our ministers have made discussion their principal business. When in the midst of the excitement raised by discussion, they seem nerved up and feel strong and talk strong; and in the excitement many things pass with the people as all right, which in themselves are decidedly wrong and a shame to him who was guilty of uttering words so unbecoming a Christian minister.

These things have a bad influence on ministers who are handling sacred, elevated truths, truths which are to prove as a savor of life unto life, or of death unto death, to those who hear them. Generally the influence of discussions upon our ministers is to make them self-sufficient and exalted in their own estimation. This is not all. Those who love to debate are unfitted for being pastors to the flock. They have trained their minds to meet opponents and to say sarcastic things, and they cannot come down to meet hearts that are sorrowing and need comforting. They have also dwelt so much upon the argumentative that they have neglected the practical subjects that the flock of God need. They have but little knowledge of the sermons of Christ, which enter into the everyday life of the Christian, and they have but little disposition to study them. They have risen above the simplicity of the work. When they were little in their own eyes, God helped them; angels of God ministered unto them and made their labors highly successful in convincing men and women of the truth. But in the training of their minds for discussion they frequently become coarse and rough. They lose the interest and tender sympathy which should ever attend the efforts of a shepherd of Christ.

Debating ministers are generally disqualified to help the flock where they most need help. Having neglected practical religion in their own hearts and lives, they cannot teach it to the flock. Unless there is an excitement, they do not know how to labor; they seem shorn of their strength. If they try to speak, they do not seem to know how to present a subject that is proper for the occasion. When they should present a subject which will feed the flock of God, and which will reach and melt hearts, they go back to some of the old stereotyped matter and go through the arranged arguments, which are dry and uninteresting. Thus, instead of light and life, they bring darkness to the flock and also to their own souls.

Some of our ministers fail to cultivate spirituality, but encourage a show of zeal and a certain activity which rests upon an uncertain foundation. Ministers of calm contemplation, of thought and devotion, of conscience and faith combined with activity and zeal, are wanted in this age. The two qualities, thought and devotion, activity and zeal, should go together.

Debating ministers are the most unreliable among us, because they cannot be depended upon when the work goes hard. Bring them into a place where there is but little interest, and they manifest a want of courage, zeal, and real interest. They depend as much upon being enlivened and invigorated by the excitement created by debate or opposition as does the inebriate upon his dram. These ministers need to be converted anew. They need to drink deep of the unceasing streams which proceed from the eternal Rock.

The eternal welfare of sinners regulated the conduct of Jesus. He went about doing good. Benevolence was the life of His soul. He not only did good to all who came to Him soliciting His mercy, but He perseveringly sought them out. He was never elated with applause or dejected by censure or disappointment. When He met with the greatest opposition and the most cruel treatment He was of good courage. The most important discourse that Inspiration has given us, Christ preached to only one listener. As He sat upon the well to rest, for He was weary, a Samaritan woman came to draw water; He saw an opportunity to reach her mind, and through her to reach the minds of the Samaritans, who were in great darkness and error. Although weary, He presented the truths of His spiritual kingdom, which charmed the heathen woman and filled her with admiration for Christ. She went forth publishing the news: "Come, see a man which told me all things that ever I did: is not this the Christ?" This woman's testimony converted many to a belief in Christ. Through her report many came to hear Him for themselves and believed because of His own word.

However small may be the number of interested listeners,

if the heart is reached and the understanding convinced, they can, like the Samaritan woman, carry a report which will raise the interest of hundreds to investigate for themselves. While laboring in places to create an interest, there will be many discouragements; but if at first there seems to be but little interest, it is no evidence that you have mistaken your duty and place of labor. If the interest steadily increases, and the people move understandingly, not from impulse, but from principle, the interest is much more healthy and durable than it is where a great excitement and interest are created suddenly, and the feelings are excited by listening to a debate, a sharp contest on both sides of the question, for and against the truth. Fierce opposition is thus created, positions are taken, and rapid decisions made. A feverish state of things is the result. Calm consideration and judgment are wanting. Let this excitement subside, or let reaction take place by indiscreet management, and the interest can never be raised again. The feelings and sympathies of the people were stirred; but their consciences were not convicted, their hearts were not broken and humbled before God.

In the presentation of unpopular truth, which involves a heavy cross, preachers should be careful that every word is as God would have it. Their words should never cut. They should present the truth in humility, with the deepest love for souls and an earnest desire for their salvation, and let the truth cut. They should not defy ministers of other denominations and seek to provoke a debate. They should not stand in a position like that of Goliath when he defied the armies of Israel. Israel did not defy Goliath, but Goliath made his proud boasts against God and His people. The defying, the boasting, and the railing must come from the opposers of truth, who act the Goliath. But none of this spirit should be seen in those whom God has sent forth to proclaim the last message of warning to a doomed world.

Goliath trusted in his armor. He terrified the armies of Israel by his defiant, savage boastings, while he made a most imposing display of his armor, which was his strength. David, in his humility and zeal for God and his people, proposed to meet this boaster. Saul consented and had his own kingly armor placed upon David. But he would not consent to wear it. He laid off the king's armor, for he had not proved it. He had proved God and, in trusting in Him, had gained special victories. To put on Saul's armor would give the impression that he was a warrior, when he was only little David who tended the sheep. He did not mean that any credit be given to the armor of Saul, for his trust was in the Lord God of Israel. He selected a few pebbles from the brook, and with his sling and staff, his only weapons, he went forth in the name of the God of Israel to meet the armed warrior.

Goliath disdained David, for his appearance was that of a mere youth untaught in the tactics of warfare. Goliath railed upon David and cursed him by his gods. He felt that it was an insult upon his dignity to have a mere stripling, without so much as an armor, come to meet him. He made his boast of what he would do to him. David did not become irritated because he was looked upon as so inferior, neither did he tremble at his terrible threats, but replied: "Thou comest to me with a sword, and with a spear, and with a shield: but I come to thee in the name of the Lord of hosts, the God of the armies of Israel, whom thou hast defied." David tells Goliath that in the name of the Lord he will do to him the very things that Goliath had threatened to do to David. "And all this assembly shall know that the Lord saveth not with sword and spear: for the battle is the Lord's, and He will give you into our hands."

Our ministers should not defy and provoke discussion. Let the defying be on the side of the opposers of God's truth. I was shown that Brother K and other ministers have acted too much the part of Goliath. And then after they have dared and provoked discussion they have trusted in their prepared arguments, as Saul wanted David to trust in his armor. They have not, like humble David, trusted in the God of Israel, and made Him their strength. They have gone forth confident and boastful, like Goliath, magnifying themselves and not hiding behind Jesus. They knew the truth was strong, and therefore have not humbled their hearts and in faith trusted in God to give the truth the victory. They have become elated and lost their balance, and frequently the discussions have not been successful, and the result has been an injury to their own souls and to the souls of others.

I was shown that some of our young ministers are getting a passion for debating, and that, unless they see their danger, this will prove a snare to them. I was shown that Brother L is in great danger. He is training his mind in the wrong direction. He is in danger of getting above the simplicity of the work. When he gets on Saul's armor, if, like David, he has wisdom to lay it off because he has not proved it, he may recover himself before he goes too far. These young preachers should study the practical teachings of Christ as well as the theoretical and learn of Jesus, that they may have His grace, His meekness, His humility and lowliness of mind. If they, like David, are brought into a position where God's cause really calls for them to meet a defier of Israel, and if they go forth in the strength of God, relying wholly upon Him, He will carry them through and cause His truth to triumph gloriously. Christ has given us an example. "Yet Michael the Archangel, when contending with the devil He disputed about the body of Moses, durst not bring against him a railing accusation, but said, The Lord rebuke thee."

As soon as a preacher comes down from the position a minister should ever occupy, and descends to the comical to create a laugh over his opponent, or when he is sarcastic and sharp, and rails upon him, he does that which the Saviour of the world did not dare to do; for he places himself upon the enemy's ground. Ministers who contend with opposers of the truth of God do not have to meet men merely, but Satan and his host of evil angels. Satan watches for a chance to get the advantage of ministers who are advocating the truth, and when they cease to put their entire trust in God, and their words are not in the spirit and love of Christ, the angels of God cannot strengthen and enlighten them. They leave them to their own strength, and evil angels press in their darkness; for this reason the opponents of the truth sometimes seem to have the advantage, and the discussion does more harm than real good.

God's servants should come nearer to Him. Brethren K, L, M, and N should be seeking to cultivate personal piety, rather than to encourage a love of debate. They should be seeking to become shepherds to the flock, rather than to be fitting themselves to create an excitement by swaying the feelings of the people. These brethren are in danger of depending more upon their popularity and their success with the people as smart debaters than upon being humble, faithful laborers and meek, devoted followers of Christ, co-workers with Him.

DANGERS AND DUTIES OF YOUTH

ADDRESSED TO TWO YOUNG MEN

Last December I was shown the dangers and temptations of youth. The two younger sons of Father O need to be converted. They need to die daily to self. Paul, the faithful apostle, had a fresh experience daily. He says: "I die daily." This is exactly the experience that these young men need. They are in danger of overlooking present duty and of neglecting the education that is essential for practical life. They regard education in books as the all-important matter to be attended to in order to make life a success.

These young men have duties at home which they overlook. They have not learned to take up the duties and bear the home responsibilities which it is their duty to bear. They have a faithful, practical mother, who has borne many burdens which her children should not have suffered her to bear. In this they have failed to honor their mother. They have not shared the burdens of their father as was their duty, and have neglected to honor him as they should. They follow inclination rather than duty. They have pursued a selfish course in their lives, in shunning burdens and toil, and have failed to obtain a valuable experience which they cannot afford to be deprived of if they would make life a success. They have not felt the importance of being faithful in little things, nor have they felt under obligation to their parents to be true, thorough, and faithful in the humble, lowly duties of life which lie directly in their pathway. They look above the common branches of knowledge, so very necessary for practical life.

If these young men would be a blessing anywhere, it should be at home. If they yield to inclination, instead of being guided by the cautious decision of sober reason, sound judgment, and enlightened conscience, they cannot be a blessing to society or to their father's family, and their prospects in this world and in the better world may be endangered. Many youth receive the impression that their early life is not designed for caretaking, but to be frittered away in idle sport, in jesting, in joking, and in foolish indulgences. While engaged in folly and indulgence of the senses, some think of nothing but the momentary gratification connected with it. Their desire for amusement, their love for society and for chatting and laughing, increases by indulgence, and they lose all relish for the sober realities of life, and home duties seem uninteresting. There is not enough change to meet their minds, and they become restless, peevish, and irritable. These young men should feel it a duty to make home happy and cheerful. They should bring sunshine into the dwelling, rather than a shadow by needless repining and unhappy discontent.

These young men should remember that they are responsible for all the privileges they have enjoyed, that they are accountable for the improvement of their time and must render an exact account for the improvement of their abilities. They may inquire: Shall we have no amusement or recreation? Shall we work, work, work, without variation? Any amusement in which they can engage asking the blessing of

God upon it in faith will not be dangerous. But any amusement which disqualifies them for secret prayer, for devotion at the altar of prayer, or for taking part in the prayer meeting is not safe, but dangerous. A change from physical labor that has taxed the strength severely may be very necessary for a time, that they may again engage in labor, putting forth exertion with greater success. But entire rest may not be necessary, or even be attended with the best results so far as their physical strength is concerned. They need not, even when weary with one kind of labor, trifle away their precious moments. They may then seek to do something not so exhausting, but which will be a blessing to their mother and sisters. In lightening their cares by taking upon themselves the roughest burdens they have to bear, they can find that amusement which springs from principle and which will yield them true happiness, and their time will not be spent in trifling or in selfish indulgence. Their time may be ever employed to advantage, and they be constantly refreshed with variation, and yet be redeeming the time, so that every moment will tell with good account to some one.

You have thought that it was of the highest importance to obtain an education in the sciences. There is no virtue in ignorance, and knowledge will not necessarily dwarf Christiain growth; but if you seek for it from principle, having the right object before you and feeling your obligation to God to use your faculties to do good to others and promote His glory, knowledge will aid you to accomplish this end; it will help you to bring into exercise the powers which God has given you, and to employ them in His service.

But, young men, if you gain ever so much knowledge and yet fail to put that knowledge to a practical use you fail of your object. If, in obtaining an education, you become so absorbed in your studies that you neglect prayer and religious privileges, and become careless and indifferent to the welfare of your souls, if you cease to learn in the school of Christ, you are selling your birthright for a mess of pottage. The object for which you are obtaining an education should not be lost sight of for a moment. It should be to so develop and direct your faculties that you may be more useful and bless others to the extent of your ability. If by obtaining knowledge you increase your love of yourselves, and your inclination to excuse yourselves from bearing responsibilities, you are better without an education. If you love and idolize books, and allow them to get between you and your duties, so that you feel a reluctance to leave your studies and your reading to do essential labor that someone must do, you should restrain your desire to study and cultivate a love for doing those things in which you now take no interest. He that is faithful in that which is least will also be faithful in greater things.

You need to cultivate love and affection for your parents and for your brothers and sisters. "Be kindly affectioned one to another with brotherly love; in honor preferring one another; not slothful in business; fervent in spirit; serving the Lord; rejoicing in hope; patient in tribulation; continuing instant in prayer; distributing to the necessity of saints; given to hospitality." Young men, you cannot afford to sacrifice your eternal interests for your school studies. Your teachers may stimulate you by applause, and you may be deceived by the sophistry of Satan. You may be led on step by step to seek to excel and to obtain the approbation of your teachers, but your knowledge in the divine life, in experimental religion, will grow less and less. Your names will stand registered before the holy, exalted angels and before the Creator of the universe and Christ, the Majesty of heaven, in a very poor light. Opposite them will be a record of sins, of mistakes, failures, neglects, and such ignorance in spiritual knowledge that the Father and His Son, Jesus our Advocate, and ministering angels will be ashamed to own you as children of God.

In attending school you are exposed to a variety of temptations to which you would not be exposed at home in your father's house, under the watchcare of God-fearing parents. If while at home you prayed by yourselves twice or three times a day for grace to escape the corruptions that are in the world through lust, you need to pray as much more earnestly and constantly when at school, exposed to temptations and the contaminating influences which prevail in schools in this degenerate age, as your surroundings are more unfavorable to the formation of Christian character.

These young men have not sufficient strength of Christian character; especially is this the case with A O. He is not settled, rooted, and grounded in the truth. His hold of God has been so slight that he has not been receiving strength and light from above, but has been gathering darkness to his own soul. He has heard unbelief talked so much and has taken so little practical interest in the truth that he is not prepared to give a reason of his hope. He is unstable like a reed trembling in the wind. He is kind at heart, yet loves fun, idleness, and the company of his young friends. He has indulged this inclination to the sacrifice of his soul's interest. It is important, my brother, that you avoid mingling too much in the society of irreligious youth. The culture of your mind and heart, in connection with the practical duties of life, requires that a large share of your time be spent in the society of those whose conversation and faith will increase your faith and love for the truth.

You have tried to throw off the restraint that the belief of the truth imposes, but you have not dared to be very bold in your unbelief. Too often the levities of the world, and the society of those from whom self-communion and religion are excluded, have been your choice, and you have been, to all intents and purposes, reckoned with that class who bring the truth into contempt. You are not strong enough in faith or purpose to be in such society. In order to kill time you have indulged in a spirit of trifling which has done positive injury to you by blunting your conscience. You love approbation. If you gain this in an honorable way, it is not so sinful; but you are in danger of deceiving yourself and others; you need to be guarded on this point and see that you earn all the approval you receive. If you are approved because of your sound principles and moral worth, this is your gain. But if you are petted and courted and flattered because you can make bright speeches and apt remarks, and because you are cheerful, lively, and witty, and not because of intellectual and moral worth, you will be looked upon by sensible, godly men and women as an object of pity rather than envy. You should be guarded against flattery. Whoever is foolish enough to flatter you cannot be your true friend. Your true friends will caution, entreat, and warn you, and reprove your faults.

You have opened your mind to dark unbelief. Close it in the fear of God. Seek for the evidences, the pillars, of our faith and lay hold upon them with firm grasp. You need this confidence in present truth, for it will prove an anchor to you. It will impart to your character an energy, efficiency, and noble dignity that will command respect. Encourage habits of industry. You are seriously lacking here. Both you and your brother have brilliant ideas of success, but remember that in God is your only hope. Your prospects may at times look flattering to you, but anticipations which exalt you above simple, humble home duties, and above religious duties, will prove a failure. You, my dear young friends, need to humble your hearts before God and be obtaining a rich and valuable experience in the Christian life by following on to know the Lord and blessing others by daily lives of spotless purity, of noble integrity, of thoroughness in the performance of Christian duty and the duties of practical life. You have duties to do at home; you have responsibilities to bear which you have not yet lifted.

That which ye sow ye shall also reap. These young men are now sowing the seed. Every act of their lives, every word spoken, is a seed for good or evil. As is the seed, so will be the crop. If they indulge hasty, lustful, perverted passions or give up to the gratification of appetite or the inclination of their unsanctified hearts; if they foster pride or wrong principles and cherish habits of unfaithfulness or dissipation, they will reap a plentiful harvest of remorse, shame, and despair.

Angels of God are seeking to lead these young men to cry unto the Lord in sincerity: "Be Thou the guide of my youth." Angels are inviting and seeking to draw them from the snares of Satan. Heaven may be theirs if they will seek to obtain it. A crown of immortal glory will be theirs if they will give all for heaven.

SELF-CARING MINISTERS

Brother R, your influence has not been of that character which would do honor to the cause of present truth. Had you been sanctified by the truth you preach to others, you would have been of ten times more advantage to the cause of God than you have been. You have relied so much upon creating a sensation that without this you have but little courage. These great excitements and sensational interests are your strength and glory and success as a laborer, but these are not pleasing to God. Your labors in this direction are seldom what you flatter yourself that they are.

Close investigation reveals the fact that there are but very few sheaves to be gathered after these specially exciting meetings. Yet, from all the experience of the past, you have not learned to change your manner of labor. You have been slow to learn how to shape your future labors in such a manner as to shun the errors of the past. The reason of this has been, that, like the inebriate, you love the stimulus of these sensational meetings; you long for them as the drunkard longs for a glass of liquor to arouse his flagging energies. These debates, which create an excitement, are mistaken for zeal for God and love for the truth. You have been almost destitute of the Spirit of God to work with your efforts. If you had God with you in all your moves, and if you felt a burden for souls and had the wisdom to skillfully manage these exciting seasons to press souls into the kingdom of Christ, you could see fruits of your labors, and God would be glorified. Your soul should be all aglow with the spirit of the truth you present to others. After you have labored to convict souls of the claims that the law of God has upon them, teaching them repentance toward God and faith in Christ, then your work is but just begun. You too frequently excuse yourself from completing the work and leave a heavy burden for others to take up in finishing the work that you ought to have done. You say that you are not qualified to finish up the work. Then the sooner you qualify yourself to bear the burdens of a shepherd, or pastor, of the flock, the better.

As a true shepherd you should discipline yourself to deal with minds and to give to each of the flock of God his portion of meat in due season. You should be careful and study to have a store of practical subjects that you have investigated and that you can enter into the spirit of and present in a plain, forcible manner to the people at the right time and place as they may need. You have not been thoroughly furnished from the word of Inspiration unto all good works. When the flock have needed spiritual food, you have frequently presented some argumentative subject that was no more appropriate for the occasion than an oration upon national affairs. If you would task yourself and educate your mind to a knowledge of the subjects with which the word of God has amply furnished you, you could build up the cause of God by feeding the flock with food which would be proper and which would give spiritual health and strength as their wants require.

You have yet to learn the work of a true shepherd. When you understand this, the cause and work of God will rest upon you with such weight that you will not be inclined to jest and joke, and engage in light and frivolous conversation. A minister of Christ who has a proper burden of the work and a high sense of the exalted character and sacredness of his mission will not be inclined to be light and trifling with the lambs of the flock.

A true shepherd will have an interest in all that relates to the welfare of the flock, feeding, guiding, and defending them.

He will carry himself with great wisdom and will manifest a tender consideration for all, being courteous and compassionate to all, especially to the tempted, the afflicted, and the desponding. Instead of giving this class the sympathy that their particular cases have demanded and that their infirmities have required, you, my brother, have shunned this class, while you have drawn largely upon others for sympathy. "Even as the Son of man came not to be ministered unto, but to minister, and to give His life a ransom for many." "Verily, verily, I say unto you, The servant is not greater than his lord; neither he that is sent greater than he that sent him." "But made Himself of no reputation, and took upon Him the form of a servant, and was made in the likeness of men." "We then that are strong ought to bear the infirmities of the weak, and not to please ourselves. Let every one of us please his neighbor for his good to edification. For even Christ pleased not Himself; but, as it is written, The reproaches of them that reproached Thee fell on Me."

It is not the work of a gospel minister to lord it over God's heritage, but in lowliness of mind, with gentleness and long forbearance, to exhort, reprove, rebuke, with all long-suffering and doctrine. How will the foregoing scriptures compare with your past life? You have been cultivating a selfish disposition nearly all your life. You married a woman of a strong, set will. Her natural disposition was supremely selfish. You were both lovers of self, and uniting your interests did not help the case of either, but increased the peril of both. Neither of you were conscientious, and neither had the fear of God before you in a high sense. Love of self, self-gratification, has been the ruling principle. Both of you have had so little consecration to God that you could not benefit each other. You have each wanted your own way; each has wanted to be petted and praised and waited upon.

The Lord saw your dangers and time and again sent you warnings through the *Testimonies* that your eternal interests were endangered unless you overcame your love of self, and conformed your will to the will of God. Had you heeded the admonitions and warnings from the Lord, had you turned square about, made an entire change, your wife would not now be in the snare of the enemy, left of God to believe the strong delusions of Satan. Had you followed the light that God has given, you would now be a strong and efficient laborer in the cause of God, qualified to accomplish tenfold more than you are now competent to do. You have become weak because you have failed to cherish the light. You have been able but a small part of the time to discern the voice of the True Shepherd from that of a stranger. Your neglect to walk in the light has brought darkness upon you, and your conscience by being often violated, has become benumbed.

Your wife did not believe and follow the light that the Lord in mercy sent her. She despised reproof, and herself closed the door through which the voice of the Lord was heard to counsel and warn her. Satan was pleased, and there was nothing to hinder him from insinuating himself into her confidence, and, by his pleasing, flattering deceptions, leading her captive at his will.

The Lord gave you a testimony that your wife was a hindrance to you in your labors and that you should not have her accompany you unless you had the most positive evidence that she was a converted woman, transformed by the renewing of her mind. You then felt that you had an excuse to plead for a home; you made this testimony your excuse and worked accordingly, although you had no need of a home of your own. Your wife had duties to do to her parents which she had neglected all her life. If she had taken up this long-neglected duty with a cheerful spirit she would not now be left captive to Satan to do his will and to corrupt her heart and soul in his service.

Your want of a home was imaginary, like many of your supposed wants. You obtained the home that your selfishness desired, and you could leave your wife comfortably situated. But God was preparing a final test for her. The affliction of her mother was of a nature which would have aroused sympathy in her heart if it had not been thoroughly seared, calloused by selfishness. But this providence of God failed to arouse the filial love of the daughter for her suffering mother. She had no home cares to stand in her way, no children to share her love and care, and her attention was devoted to her poor self.

The burden of care that her father had to bear was too much for his age and strength, and he was prostrated with keen sufferings. Surely then if the daughter had a sensitive spot in her heart, she could not help feeling and arousing to a sense of her duty to share the burdens of her sister and her sister's husband. But she revealed by her indifference, and by shunning all the care and burden that she well could, that her heart was well-nigh as unimpressible as a stone.

To be close by her parents and yet be so indifferent would tell against her. She communicated the state of things to her husband. Brother R was as selfish as his wife, and he sent an urgent request for her to come to him. How did angels of God, the tender, pitying, loving, ministering angels look upon this act? The daughter left strangers to do those tender offices that she should have cheerfully shared with her burdened sister. Angels looked with astonishment and grief upon the scene and turned from this selfish woman. Evil angels took the places of these, and she was led captive by Satan at his will. She was a medium of Satan and so proved to be a great hindrance to her husband; his labors were of but little account.

The cause of God would have stood higher in _____ if that last effort had not been made, for the work was not completed. An interest was raised. but was left to sink where it could never be raised again. I ask you, Brother R, to compare the scriptures previously quoted relative to the work and ministry of Christ with your course of conduct through your labors as a gospel minister, but more especially in the instance I have mentioned, where duty was too plain for any mistake if the conscience and affections had not become paralyzed by a long course of continued idolatry of self.

Because of your leaving your parents in their suffering when they needed help, the church was obliged to take this burden and to watch with the suffering members of Christ's body. In this heartless neglect you brought the frown of God upon yourselves. God does not lightly pass by such things. They are recorded by the angels. God cannot prosper those who go directly contrary to the plainest duty specified in His word, the duty of children to their parents. Children who feel under no more obligation to their earthly parents than you have done, but can so easily step out from the responsibilities upon them, will not have due respect for their heavenly Father; they will not reverence or respect the claims that God has upon them. If they disrespect and dishonor their earthly parents they will not respect and love their Creator. In neglecting her parents, your wife transgressed the fifth precept of the Decalogue: "Honor thy father and thy mother: that thy days may be long upon the land which the Lord thy God giveth thee." This is the first commandment with promise. Those who disrespect or dishonor their parents need not expect that the blessing of God will attend them. Our parents have claims upon us that we cannot throw off or lightly regard. But children who have not been trained and controlled in childhood, and who have been permitted to make themselves the objects of their care, selfishly seeking their own ease and avoiding burdens, become heartless and do not respect the claims of their parents, who watched over them in their infancy.

Brother R, you have been selfish in these things yourself and greatly deficient in duty. You have required attention and care, but you have not given the same in return. You have been selfish and exacting, and have frequently been unreasonable and given your wife occasion for trial. Both of you have been unconsecrated and astonishingly selfish. You have made but little sacrifice for the truth's sake. You, as well as your wife, have avoided burdens, and have occupied a position to be waited upon rather than to try to be as little burden as possible.

Ministers of Christ should feel it a duty binding upon them, if they receive the hospitalities of their brethren or friends, to leave a blessing with the family by seeking to encourage and strengthen its members. They should not neglect the duties of a pastor, as they visit from house to house. They should become familiar with every member of the family, that they may understand the spiritual condition of all, and vary their manner of labor to meet the case of each. When a minister bearing the solemn message of warning to the world receives the hospitable courtesies of friends and brethren, and neglects the duties of a shepherd of the flock and is careless in his example and deportment, engaging with the young in trifling conversation, in jesting and joking, and in relating humorous anecdotes to create laughter, he is unworthy of being a gospel minister and needs to be converted before he should be entrusted with the care of the sheep and lambs. Ministers who are neglectful of the duties devolving on a faithful pastor give evidence that they are not sanctified by the truths they present to others and should not be sustained as laborers in the vineyard of the Lord till they have a high sense of the sacredness of the work of a minister of Christ.

When there are only evening meetings to attend, there is much time that can be used to great advantage in visiting from house to house, meeting the people where they are. And if ministers of Christ have the graces of the Spirit, if they imitate the great Exemplar, they will find access to hearts and will win souls to Christ. Some ministers bearing the last message of mercy are too distant. They do not improve the opportunities that they have of gaining the confidence of unbelievers, by their exemplary deportment, their unselfish interest for the good of others, their kindness, forbearance, humbleness of mind, and their respectful courtesy. These fruits of the Spirit will exert a far greater influence than will the preaching in the desk without individual effort in families. But the preaching of pointed, testing truths to the people, and corresponding individual efforts from house to house to back up pulpit effort, will greatly extend the influence for good, and souls will be converted to the truth.

Some of our ministers carry too light responsibilities, they shun individual care and burdens; for this reason they do not feel that need of help from God that they would if they lifted the burdens that the work of God and our faith require them to lift. When burdens in this cause have to be borne, and when those who bear them are brought into strait places, they will feel the need of living near to God, that they may have confidence to commit their ways to Him and in faith claim that help which He alone can give. They will then be daily obtaining an experience in faith and trust, which is of the highest value to gospel ministers. Their work is more solemn and sacred than ministers generally realize. They should carry with them a sanctified influence. God requires that those who minister in sacred things should be men who feel jealous for His cause. The burden of their work should be the salvation of souls. Brother R, you have not felt as the prophet Joel describes: "Let the priests, the ministers of the Lord, weep between the porch and the altar, and let them say, Spare Thy people, O Lord, and give not Thine heritage to reproach." "They that sow in tears shall reap in joy. He that goeth forth and weepeth, bearing precious seed, shall doubtless come again with rejoicing, bringing his sheaves with him."

Brother R, I was shown in what marked contrast with the requirements of God's word your course of labor has been. You have been careless in your words and in your deportment. The sheep have had the burden to care for the shepherd, to warn, reprove, exhort, and weep over the reckless course of their shepherd, who, by accepting his office, acknowledges that he is mouthpiece for God. Yet he cares far more for himself than he does for the poor sheep. You have not felt a burden for souls. You have not gone forth to your labors weeping and praying for souls that sinners might be converted. Had you done this you would be sowing seed which would spring up after many days and bear fruit to the glory of God. When there is no work that you can do by the fireside in conversation and prayer with families, you should then show industry and economy of time, and train yourself to bear responsibilities by useful employment.

You and your wife might have saved yourselves many ill turns and been more cheerful and happy had you sought your ease less and combined physical labor with your study. Your muscles were made for use, not to be inactive. God gave to Adam and Eve in Eden all that their wants required; yet their heavenly Father knew that they needed employment in order to retain their happiness. If you, Brother R, would exercise your muscles in laboring with your hands some portion of each day, combining labor with study, your mind would be better balanced, your thoughts would be of a purer and more elevated character, and your sleep would be more natural and healthful. Your head would be less confused and stupid because of a congested brain. Your thoughts upon sacred truth would be clearer, and your moral powers more vigorous. You do not love labor; but it is for your good to have more physical exercise daily; for it will quicken the sluggish blood to healthful activity, and will carry you above discontent and infirmities.

You should not neglect diligent study, but should pray for light from God that He would open to your understanding the treasures of His word, that you may be thoroughly furnished unto all good works. You will never be in a position where it is not necessary for you to watch and pray earnestly in order to overcome your besetments. You will need to be guarded continually to keep self out of sight. You have encouraged a habit of making yourself very prominent, dwelling upon your family difficulties and your poor health. In short, yourself has been the theme of your conversation and has come in between you and your Saviour. You should forget self and hide behind Jesus. Let the dear Saviour be magnified, but lose sight of self. When you see and feel your weakness you will not see that there is anything in yourself worthy of notice or remark. The people have not only been wearied, but disgusted, with your preliminaries before you present your subject. Every time that you speak to the people and mention your family trials you lower yourself in their estimation and suggest suspicions that you are not all right.

You have the example of ministers who have exalted themselves and who have coveted praise from the people. They were petted and flattered by the indiscreet until they became exalted and self-sufficient, and, trusting in their own wisdom, made shipwreck of faith. They thought that they were so popular that they could take almost any course and yet retain their popularity. Here has been your presumption. When the deportment of a minister of Christ gives gossiping tongues facts as subject matter to discuss and his morality is seriously questioned, he should not call this jealousy or slander. You should be cautious how you encourage a habitual train of thought from which habits are formed that will prove your ruin. Mark those whose course you should abhor, and then forbear to take the first step in the direction they have traveled.

You have been self-sufficient and so blinded and deluded by Satan that you could not discern your weakness and many errors. "But the fruit of the Spirit is love, joy, peace, longsuffering, gentleness, goodness, faith, meekness, temperance: against such there is no law. And they that are Christ's have crucified the flesh with the affections and lusts. If we live in the Spirit, let us also walk in the Spirit. Let us not be desirous of vainglory, provoking one another, envying one another."

I was shown fields of labor. Towns, cities, and villages everywhere should hear the message of warning; for all will be tested and proved by the message of present truth. A great work is to be done, but the laborers who enter these fields should be men of sound judgment who know how to deal with minds. They should be men of patience, kindness, and courtesy who have the fear of God before them.

You frequently gain the confidence of the people; but if, by careless deportment or some injudicious move, by severity or an overbearing spirit, you then lose their confidence, more harm will result to the cause of God than if no effort had been made. Great injury has been done to the cause of God by ministers moving from impulse. Some are easily stirred and frequently become irritated; and, if abused, they retaliate. This is just what Satan exults to have them do. The enemies of truth triumph over this weakness in a minister of Christ, for it is a reproach to the cause of present truth. Those who show this weakness of character do not rightly represent the truth or the ministers of our faith. The indiscretion of one minister throws a cloud of suspicion upon all and makes the labors of those who follow after him exceedingly difficult.

Brother R, when you go out to engage in labor in a new field you love to dwell upon the argumentative, because you have educated your mind for this kind of labor. But your labors have not been one tenth as valuable as they would have been had you qualified yourself by practical experience to give the people discourses upon practical subjects. You need to become a learner in the school of Christ, that you may experience practical godliness. When you have the saving power of truth in your own soul you cannot forbear feeding the flock of God with the same practical truths which have made your own heart joyful in God. The practical and the doctrinal should be combined in order to impress hearts with the importance of yielding to the claims of truth after the understanding has been convinced by the weight of evidence. The servants of Christ should imitate the example of the Master in the manner of their labor. They should constantly keep before the people, in the best manner to be comprehended by them, the necessity of practical godliness, and should bring them, as did our Saviour in His teachings, to see the necessity of religious principle and righteousness in everyday life. The people are not fed by the ministers of popular churches, and souls are starving for food that will nourish and give spiritual life.

Your life has not been marked with humbleness of mind and meekness of deportment. You love God in word, but not in deed and in truth. Your dignity is easily hurt. Ministers should first feel the sanctifying influence of the truth upon their own hearts and in their own lives, and then their pulpit efforts will be enforced by their example out of the desk. Ministers need to be softened and sanctified themselves before God can in a special manner work with their efforts.

You have let slip the golden opportunity of gathering a harvest of souls because it was impossible for God to work with your efforts, for your heart was not right with Him. Your spirit was not pure before Him who is the embodiment of purity and holiness. If you regard iniquity in your heart, the Lord will not hear your prayer. Our God is a jealous God. He knoweth the thoughts and the imaginations and devices of the heart. You have followed your own judgment and made a sad failure when you might have had success. There is too much at stake in these efforts, to do the work negligently or recklessly. Souls are being tested upon important, eternal truth, and what you may say or do will have an influence to balance them in deciding either for or against the truth. When you should have been in humility before God, pleading for Him to work with your efforts, feeling the weight of the cause and the value of souls, you have chosen the society of young ladies, regardless of the sacred work of God and of your office as a minister of the gospel of Christ. You were standing between the living and the dead; yet you engaged in light and frivolous conversation, in jesting and joking.

How can ministering angels be round about you, shedding light upon you and imparting strength to you? When you should be seeking to find ways and means to enlighten the minds of those in error and darkness you are pleasing yourself and are too selfish to engage in a work for which you have no inclination or love. If our position is criticized by those who are investigating, you have but little patience with them. You frequently give them a short, severe reply, as though they had no business to search closely, but must take all that is presented as truth, without investigating for themselves. In your ministerial labors you have turned many souls away from the truth by your manner of treating them. You are not always impatient and unapproachable; when you feel like it you will take time to answer questions candidly; but frequently you are uncourteous and exacting, and are pettish and irritable like a child.

A concealed golden wedge and a Babylonish garment troubled the entire camp of Israel. The frown of God was brought upon the people because of the sin of one man. Thousands were slain upon the field of battle because God would not bless and prosper a people among whom there was even one sinner, one who had transgressed His word. This sinner was not in holy office, yet a jealous God could not go forth to battle with the armies of Israel while these concealed sins were in the camp.

Notwithstanding the apostle's warning is before us to "abstain from all appearance of evil," some persist in pursuing a course unbecoming Christians. God requires His people to be holy, to keep themselves separate from the works of darkness, to be pure in heart and life, and unspotted from the world. The children of God, by faith in Christ, are His chosen people; and when they stand upon the holy ground of Bible truth they will be saved from fellowship with the unfruitful works of darkness.

Brother R, you have stood directly in the way of the work of God and have brought great darkness and discouragement upon His cause. You have been blinded by Satan; you have worked for sympathy and have obtained it. Had you stood in the light you could have discerned the power of Satan at work to deceive and destroy you. The children of God do not eat and drink to please the appetite, but to preserve life and strength to do their Master's will. They clothe themselves for health, not for display or to keep pace with changing fashion. The desire of the eye and the pride of life are banished from their wardrobes and from their houses, from principle. They move from godly sincerity, and their conversation is elevated and heavenly.

God is very pitiful, for He understands our weaknesses and

our temptations; and when we come to Him with broken hearts and contrite spirits, He accepts our repentance, and promises that, as we take hold of His strength to make peace with Him, we shall make peace with Him. Oh, what gratitude, what joy, should we feel that God is merciful!

You have failed to rely upon the strength of God. You have dwelt upon yourself and made yourself the theme of thought and conversation. Your trials have been magnified to yourself and others, and your mind has been diverted from the truth, from the Pattern which we are required to copy, to weak Brother R.

When out of the desk you should have felt the worth of souls and been seeking opportunities to present the truth to individuals, but you have not felt the responsibility devolving upon a gospel minister. Jesus and righteousness have not been your themes, and many opportunities have been lost that, if improved, might have decided more than a score of souls to give all for Christ and the truth. But the burden you would not lift. The pastoral labor involved a cross, and you would not engage in it.

I saw angels of God watching the impressions you make and the fruits you bear out of meeting, and your general influence upon believers and unbelievers. I saw these angels veil their faces in sadness and in sorrow turn reluctantly from you. Frequently you were engaged in matters of minor consequence, and when you had efforts to make which required the vigor of all your energies, clear thought, and earnest prayer, you followed your own pleasure and inclination, and trusted to your own strength and wisdom to meet, not men alone, but principalities and powers, Satan and his angels. This was doing the work of God negligently and placing the truth and cause of God in jeopardy, periling the salvation of souls.

An entire change must take place in you before you can be entrusted with the work of God. You should consider your life a solemn reality and that it is no idle dream. As a watchman upon the walls of Zion, you are answerable for the souls of the people. You should settle into God. You move without due consideration, from impulse rather than from principle. You have not felt the positive necessity of training your mind, nor of crucifying in yourself the old man with the affections and lusts. You need to be balanced by the weight of God's Spirit, and all your movements regulated by it. You are now uncertain in all you undertake. You do and undo; you build up and then tear down; you kindle an interest and then from lack of consecration and divine wisdom you quench it. You have not been strengthened, established, and settled. You have had but little faith; you have not lived a life of prayer. You need so much to link your life with God, and then you will not sow to the flesh and reap corruption in the end.

Jesting, joking, and worldly conversation belong to the world. Christians who have the peace of God in their hearts will be cheerful and happy without indulging in lightness or frivolity. While watching unto prayer they will have a serenity and peace which will elevate them above all superfluities. The mystery of godliness, opened to the mind of the minister of Christ, will raise him above earthly and sensual enjoyments. He will be a partaker of the divine nature, having escaped the corruption that is in the world through lust. The communication opened between God and his soul will make him fruitful in the knowledge of God's will and open before him treasures of practical subjects that he can present to the people, which will not cause levity or the semblance of a smile, but will solemnize the mind, touch the heart, and arouse the moral sensibilities to the sacred claims that God has upon the affections and life. Those who labor in word and doctrine should be men of God, pure in heart and life.

You are in the greatest danger of bringing reproach upon the cause of God. Satan knows your weakness. His angels communicate your weak points to those who are deceived by his lying wonders, and they are already counting you as one of their number. Satan exults to have you pursue an unwise course because you place yourself upon his ground and give him advantage over you. He well knows that the indiscretion of men who advocate the law of God will turn souls from the truth. You have not taken upon your soul the burden of the work and labored carefully and earnestly in private to favorably impress minds in regard to the truth. You too frequently become impatient, irritable, and childish, and make yourself enemies by your abrupt manners. Unless you are on your guard, you prejudice souls against the truth. Unless you are a transformed man, and will carry out in your life the principles of the sacred truths you present in the desk, your labors will amount to but little.

A weight of responsibility rests upon you. It is the watchman's duty to be ever at his post, watching for souls as one that must give an account. If your mind is diverted from the great work and filled with unholy thoughts; if selfish plans and projects rob of sleep, and in consequence the mental and physical strength is lessened, you sin against your own soul and against God. Your discernment is blunted, and sacred things are placed upon a level with the common. God is dishonored, His cause reproached, and the good work you might have done had you made God your trust is marred. Had you preserved the vigor of your powers to put the strength of your brain and entire being into the important work of God without reserve, you would have realized a much greater work, and it would have been more perfectly done.

Your labors have been defective. A master workman engages his men to do for him a very nice and valuable job which requires study and much careful thought. As they agree to do the work they know that, in order to accomplish the task aright, all their faculties need to be aroused and in the very best condition to put forth their best efforts. But one man of the company is ruled by perverse appetite. He loves strong drink. Day after day he gratifies his desire for stimulus, and, while under the influence of this stimulus, the brain is clouded, the nerves are weakened, and his hands are unsteady. He continues his labor day after day and nearly ruins the job entrusted to him. That man forfeits his wages and does almost irreparable injury to his employer. Through his unfaithfulness he loses the confidence of his master as well as of his fellow workmen. He was entrusted with a great responsibility, and in accepting that trust he acknowledged that he was competent to do the work according to the directions given by his employer. But through his own love of self the appetite was indulged and the consequences risked.

Your case, Brother R, is similar to this. But the accountability of a minister of Christ, who is to warn the world of a coming judgment, is as much more important than that of the common workman as eternal things are of more consequence than temporal. If the minister of the gospel yields to his inclination rather than to be guided by duty, if he indulges self at the expense of spiritual strength, and as the result moves indiscreetly, souls will rise up in the judgment to condemn him for his unfaithfulness. The blood of souls will be found on his garments. It may seem to the unconsecrated minister a small thing to be fitful, impulsive, and unconsecrated; to build up, and then to tear down; to dishearten, distress, and discourage the very souls that have been converted by the truth he has presented. It is a sad thing to lose the confidence of the very ones whom he has been laboring to save. But the result of an unwise course pursued by the minister will never be fully understood until the minister sees as God seeth.

INORDINATE LOVE OF GAIN

Brother S, I was shown, December 10, 1871, that there are serious defects in your character, which, unless seen and overcome, will prove your ruin; and you will not only be weighed in the balances of the sanctuary, and found wanting yourself, but your influence will determine the destiny of others. You are either gathering with Christ or scattering abroad.

I was shown that you have a deeply rooted love for the

world. The love of money is the root of all evil. You flatter yourself that you are about right, when you are not. God seeth not as man seeth. He looks at the heart. His ways are not our ways, nor His thoughts our thoughts. Your great care and anxiety is to acquire means. This absorbing passion has been increasing upon you until it is overbalancing your love of the truth. Your soul is being corrupted through the love of money. Your love for the truth and for its advancement is very weak. Your earthly treasures claim and hold your affections.

You have a knowledge of the truth; you are not ignorant of the claims of Scripture; you know your Master's will, for He has plainly revealed it. But your heart is not inclined to follow the light which shines upon your pathway. You have a large measure of self-conceit. Your love for self is greater than your love for the cause of present truth. Your self-confidence and your self-sufficiency will certainly prove your ruin unless you can see your weakness and errors, and reform. You are arbitrary. You have a set will of your own to maintain, and although the opinions of others may be correct, and your judgment wrong, yet you are not the man to yield. You hold firmly to your advanced opinion, irrespective of the judgment of others. I wish you could see the danger of continuing the course you have been pursuing. If your eyes could be enlightened by the Spirit of God, you would see these things clearly.

Your wife loves the truth, and she is a practical woman, a woman of principle. But you do not appreciate her value. She has worked hard for the common good of the family, but you have not given her your confidence. You have not counseled with her as was your duty. You keep your matters very much to yourself; you do not love to open your heart to your wife and let her know your exercises of mind and your real faith and feelings. You are secretive. Your wife does not hold the honored place in your family that she deserves and that she is capable of filling.

You feel that your wife should not interfere with your plans and arrangements, and you too frequently set your will and plans of operation in opposition to hers. You act as though her identity should be merged in yours. You are not satisfied to have her act as though she had an individuality, an identity of her own. God holds her accountable for her individuality. You cannot save her, and she cannot save you. She has a conscience of her own by which she must be guided. You are too willing to be conscience for her and sometimes for your children. God has higher claims upon your wife than you can have. She must form a character for herself, and she is accountable to God for the character she develops.

You have a character to form, and you are accountable to God for the character that you develop. You have a controlling influence and possess a dictatorial spirit, which is not in accordance with the will of God. You must cease to be so exacting. You have prided yourself upon your fine taste and organization. You have nice ideas, but you have not carried this exact and fine perception into your character and into your deportment. You have failed to perfect a symmetrical character. You have good ideas of order and arrangement, but all these nice qualities of the mind have become blunted by being perverted. You have not complied with the conditions laid down in the word of God for becoming a son of God. All the promises of God are upon conditions. "Come out from among them; and be ye separate, saith the Lord, and touch not the unclean thing, and I will receive you, and will be a Father unto you, and ye shall be My sons and daughters, saith the Lord Almighty. Having therefore these promises, dearly beloved, let us cleanse ourselves from all filthiness of the flesh and spirit, perfecting holiness in the fear of God." This experience you have yet to obtain. You love to get into the company of unbelievers and hear them talk, and talk yourself. Jesus cannot be glorified with your conversation, and if you had had the spirit of Jesus you could not have been so much in the society of those who had no love for the truth of God.

You have felt that there were hindrances to your children's becoming Christians, and have felt that others were to blame. But do not deceive yourself in regard to this matter. Your influence as a father has been sufficient, if there were nothing else to hinder, to stand in their way. Your example and your conversation have been of such a character that your children could not believe that your course was consistent with your profession. Your conversation with unbelievers has been of such a low order, and so light, so filled with jesting and joking, that your influence could never elevate them. Your deal with others has not always been strictly honest. You have not loved God with all your heart, mind, and strength, and your neighbor as yourself. If in your power, you would advantage yourself at your neighbor's disadvantage. Every dollar which comes to you in this manner will carry with it a curse which you will feel sooner or later. God marks every act of injustice, be it done to believer or unbeliever, and He will not pass it over. Your acquisitive disposition is a snare to you. Your deal with your fellow men cannot endure the test of the judgment.

Your Christian character is spotted with avarice. These spots will have to be removed, or you will lose eternal life. We each have a work to do for the Master; we each have talents to improve. The humblest and poorest of the disciples of Jesus can be a blessing to others. They may not realize that they are doing any special good but, by their unconscious influence, they may start waves of blessing which will widen and deepen, and the happy result of their words and consistent deportment they may never know until the final distribution of rewards. They do not feel or know that they are doing anything great. They are not required to weary themselves with anxieties about success. They have only to go forward, not with many words and vain glorying and boasting, but quietly, faithfully doing the work which God's providence has assigned them, and they will not lose their reward. Thus will it be in your case. The memorial of your life will be written in the book of records; and, if you are finally an overcomer, there will be souls saved through your efforts, by your self-denial, your good words and consistent Christian life. And when the rewards are finally distributed to all as their works have been, redeemed souls will call you blessed, and the Master will say: "Well done, good and faithful servant," "enter thou into the joy of thy Lord."

The world is indeed full of hurry, and of pride, selfishness, avarice, and violence; and it may seem to us that it is a waste of time and breath to be ever in season and out of season, and on all occasions to hold ourselves in readiness to speak words that are gentle, pure, elevating, chaste, and holy, in the face of the whirlwind of confusion, bustle, and strife. And yet words fitly spoken, coming from sanctified hearts and lips, and sustained by a godly, consistent Christian deportment, will be as apples of gold in pictures of silver. You have been as one of the vain talkers and have appeared as one of the world. You have sometimes been careless in your words and reckless in your conversation and have lowered yourself as a Christian in the opinion of unbelievers. You have sometimes spoken of the truth; but your words have not borne that serious, anxious interest that would affect the heart. They have been accompanied with light, trivial remarks that would lead those with whom you converse to decide that your faith is not genuine and that you do not believe the truths you profess. Words in favor of the truth, spoken in the calm self-possession of a right purpose and from a pure heart, will do much to disarm opposition and win souls. But a harsh, selfish, denunciatory spirit will only drive further from the truth and awaken a spirit of opposition.

You are not to wait for great occasions, or to expect extraordinary abilities, before you work in earnest for God. You need not have a thought of what the world will think of you. If your intercourse with them and your godly conversation are a living testimony to them of the purity and sincerity of your faith, and they are convinced that you desire to benefit them, your words will not be wholly lost upon them, but will be productive of good.

A servant of Christ, in any department of the Christian service, will by precept and by example have a saving influence upon others. The good seed sown may lie some time in a cold, worldly, selfish heart without evidencing that it has taken root; but frequently the Spirit of God operates upon that heart and waters it with the dew of heaven, and the long-hidden seed springs up and finally bears fruit to the glory of God. We know not in our lifework which shall prosper, this or that. These are not questions for us poor mortals to settle. We are to do our work, leaving the result with God. If you were in darkness and ignorance, you would not be as guilty. But you have had great light, you have heard much truth; but you are not a doer of the word.

Christ's life is the pattern for us all. His example of self-denial, self-sacrifice, and disinterested benevolence is for us to follow. His entire life is an infinite demonstration of His great love and condescension to save sinful man. "Love one another, as I have loved you," says Christ. How will our life of self-denial, sacrifice, and benevolence bear comparison with the life of Christ? "Ye are," says Christ, addressing His disciples, "the light of the world." "Ye are the salt of the earth." If this is our privilege and also our duty, and we are bodies of darkness and of unbelief, what a fearful responsibility we assume! We may be channels of light or of darkness. If we have neglected to improve the light that God had given us, and have failed to advance in knowledge and true holiness as the light has directed the way, we are guilty and in darkness according to the light and truth we have neglected to improve. In these days of iniquity and peril the characters and works of professed Christians will not generally bear the test nor endure the exposure when examined by the light that now shines upon them. There is no concord between Christ and Belial; there is no communion between light and darkness. How, then, can the spirit of Christ and the spirit of the world be in harmony? The Lord our God is a jealous God. He requires the sincere affection and unreserved confidence of those who profess to love Him. Says the psalmist: "If I regard iniquity in my heart, the Lord will not hear me."

You have stood directly in the way of the salvation of your children. You lay their indifference to religious things to other causes than the true. Your example is a stumbling block to them. They know by your fruits, by your words and works, that you do not believe in the near coming of Christ. Some of them do not hesitate to make sport of the idea of the near coming of Christ and of the shortness of time. They take great satisfaction when you drive a sharp bargain. They think that father is keen in a trade and that nobody can get the better of him, and they are following in your footsteps. Faith without works is dead, being alone. Money has given you power, and you have used that power to take advantage of the necessities of others. Your speculations in business life have not been honest, you have not been just with your fellow men. By your trades you have sacrificed your reputation as a Christian and as an honest man. By fair trading, means did not come into your possession fast enough to satisfy your thirst for gain, and you have frequently made the poor man's burdens heavier by taking advantage of his necessity to increase your property. Look carefully, Brother S. You are making fearful losses for earthly gain. You are losing manly integrity and heavenly virtue, in the hour of temptation. Is this gain or loss? Are you richer or poorer for all such increase? To you it is a fearful loss, for it takes just so much from the treasure you might have been accumulating in heaven.

Every opportunity to help a brother in need, or to aid the cause of God in the spread of the truth, is a pearl that you can send beforehand and deposit in the bank of heaven for safekeeping. God is testing and proving you. He has been giving His blessings to you with a lavish hand and is now watching to see what use you are making of them, to see if you will help those who need help and if you will feel the worth of souls and do what you can with the means that He has entrusted to you. Every such opportunity improved adds to your heavenly treasure. But love of self has led you to prefer earthly possessions even at the sacrifice of the heavenly. You choose the treasures that moth and rust corrupt rather than those which are as enduring as eternity. It is your privilege to exercise tender compassion and to bless others; but your eyes are so blinded by the god of this world that you cannot discern this precious gem—the blessing to be received by doing good, by being rich in good works, ready to distribute, willing to communicate, laying up for yourself a good foundation against the time to come, that you may lay hold on eternal life. You are imperiling your soul by neglecting to avail yourself of precious opportunities to secure the heavenly treasure. Are you really richer for your penuriousness, for your close managing? God is proving you, and it is for you to determine whether you will come out gold or valueless dross. Should your probation close tonight, how would your life record stand? Not a dollar of what you have gained could you take with you. The curse of every unjust act would attend you. Your sharpness in trade, when viewed in the mirror that God will present before you, will not lead to self-congratulation. Covetousness is idolatry.

Your only hope is to humble your heart before God. "For what shall it profit a man, if he shall gain the whole world, and lose his own soul? or what shall a man give in exchange for his soul?" I entreat of you: Do not close your eyes to your danger. Do not be blind to the higher interests of the soul, to the blessed and glorious prospects for the better life. The anxious, burdened seekers for worldly gain are blind and insane. They turn from the immortal, imperishable treasure, to this world. The glitter and tinsel of this world captivate their senses, and eternal things are not valued. They labor for that which satisfieth not and spend their money for that which is not bread, when Jesus offers them peace and hope and infinite blessings, for a life of obedience. All the treasures of the earth would not be rich enough to buy these precious gifts. Yet many are insane and turn from the heavenly inducement.

Christ will keep the names of all who count no sacrifice too costly to be offered to Him upon the altar of faith and love. He sacrificed all for fallen humanity. The names of the obedient, self-sacrificing, and faithful will be engraved upon the palms of His hands; they will not be spewed from His mouth, but be taken in His lips, and He will specially plead in their behalf before the Father. When the selfish and proud are forgotten, they will be remembered; their names will be immortalized. In order to be happy ourselves, we must live to make others happy. It is well for us to yield our possessions, our talents, and our affections in grateful devotion to Christ, and in that way find happiness here and immortal glory hereafter.

The long night of watching, of toil and hardship, is nearly past. Christ is soon to come. Get ready. The angels of God are seeking to attract you from yourself and from earthly things. Let them not labor in vain. Faith, living faith, is what you need; faith that works by love and purifies the soul. Remember Calvary and the awful, the infinite sacrifice there made for man. Jesus now invites you to come to Him just as you are and make Him your strength and everlasting Friend.

NUMBER TWENTY-THREE

TESTIMONY FOR THE CHURCH

THE LAODICEAN CHURCH

The message to the church of the Laodiceans is a startling denunciation, and is applicable to the people of God at the present time.

"And unto the angel of the church of the Laodiceans write: These things saith the Amen, the faithful and true Witness, the beginning of the creation of God; I know thy works, that thou art neither cold nor hot: I would thou wert cold or hot. So then because thou art lukewarm, and neither cold nor hot, I will spew thee out of My mouth. Because thou sayest, I am rich, and increased with goods, and have need of nothing; and knowest not that thou art wretched, and miserable, and poor, and blind, and naked."

The Lord here shows us that the message to be borne to His people by ministers whom He has called to warn the people is not a peace-and-safety message. It is not merely theoretical, but practical in every particular. The people of God are represented in the message to the Laodiceans as in a position of carnal security. They are at ease, believing themselves to be in an exalted condition of spiritual attainments. "Because thou sayest, I am rich, and increased with goods, and have need of nothing; and knowest not that thou art wretched, and miserable, and poor, and blind, and naked."

What greater deception can come upon human minds than

a confidence that they are right when they are all wrong! The message of the True Witness finds the people of God in a sad deception, yet honest in that deception. They know not that their condition is deplorable in the sight of God. While those addressed are flattering themselves that they are in an exalted spiritual condition, the message of the True Witness breaks their security by the startling denunciation of their true condition of spiritual blindness, poverty, and wretchedness. The testimony, so cutting and severe, cannot be a mistake, for it is the True Witness who speaks, and His testimony must be correct.

It is difficult for those who feel secure in their attainments, and who believe themselves to be rich in spiritual knowledge, to receive the message which declares that they are deceived and in need of every spiritual grace. The unsanctified heart is "deceitful above all things, and desperately wicked." I was shown that many are flattering themselves that they are good Christians, who have not a ray of light from Jesus. They have not a living experience for themselves in the divine life. They need a deep and thorough work of self-abasement before God before they will feel their true need of earnest, persevering effort to secure the precious graces of the Spirit.

God leads His people on step by step. The Christian life is a constant battle and a march. There is no rest from the warfare. It is by constant, unceasing effort that we maintain the victory over the temptations of Satan. As a people we are triumphing in the clearness and strength of the truth. We are fully sustained in our positions by an overwhelming amount of plain Scriptural testimony. But we are very much wanting in Bible humility, patience, faith, love, self-denial, watchfulness, and the spirit of sacrifice. We need to cultivate Bible holiness. Sin prevails among the people of God. The plain message of rebuke to the Laodiceans is not received. Many cling to their doubts and their darling sins while they are in so great a deception as to talk and feel that they are in need of nothing. They think the testimony of the Spirit of God in reproof is uncalled for or that it does not mean them. Such are in the greatest need of the grace of God and spiritual discernment that they may discover their deficiency in spiritual knowledge. They lack almost every qualification necessary to perfect Christian character. They have not a practical knowledge of Bible truth, which leads to lowliness of life and a conformity of their will to the will of Christ. They are not living in obedience to all God's requirements.

It is not enough to merely profess to believe the truth. All the soldiers of the cross of Christ virtually obligate themselves to enter the crusade against the adversary of souls, to condemn wrong and sustain righteousness. But the message of the True Witness reveals the fact that a terrible deception is upon our people, which makes it necessary to come to them with warnings, to break their spiritual slumber, and arouse them to decided action.

In my last vision I was shown that even this decided message of the True Witness had not accomplished the design of God. The people slumber on in their sins. They continue to declare themselves rich and having need of nothing. Many inquire: Why are all these reproofs given? Why do the *Testimonies* continually charge us with backsliding and with grievous sins? We love the truth; we are prospering; we are in no need of these testimonies of warning and reproof. But let these murmurers see their hearts and compare their lives with the practical teachings of the Bible, let them humble their souls before God, let the grace of God illuminate the darkness, and the scales will fall from their eyes, and they will realize their true spiritual poverty and wretchedness. They will feel the necessity of buying gold, which is pure faith and love; white raiment, which is a spotless character made pure in the blood of their dear Redeemer; and eyesalve, which is the grace of God and which will give clear discernment of spiritual things and detect sin. These attainments are more precious than the gold of Ophir.

I have been shown that the greatest reason why the people of God are now found in this state of spiritual blindness is that they will not receive correction. Many have despised the reproofs and warnings given them. The True Witness condemns the lukewarm condition of the people of God, which gives Satan great power over them in this waiting, watching time. The selfish, the proud, and the lovers of sin are ever assailed with doubts. Satan has ability to suggest doubts and to devise objections to the pointed testimony that God sends, and many think it a virtue, a mark of intelligence in them, to be unbelieving and to question and quibble. Those who desire to doubt will have plenty of room. God does not propose to remove all occasion for unbelief. He gives evidence, which must be carefully investigated with a humble mind and a teachable spirit, and all should decide from the weight of evidence.

Eternal life is of infinite value and will cost us all that we have. I was shown that we do not place a proper estimate upon eternal things. Everything worth possessing, even in this world, must be secured by effort, and sometimes by most painful sacrifice. And this is merely to obtain a perishable treasure. Shall we be less willing to endure conflict and toil, and to make earnest efforts and great sacrifices, to obtain a treasure which is of infinite value, and a life which will measure with that of the Infinite? Can heaven cost us too much?

Faith and love are golden treasures, elements that are greatly wanting among God's people. I have been shown that unbelief in the testimonies of warning, encouragement, and reproof is shutting away the light from God's people. Unbelief is closing their eyes so that they are ignorant of their true condition. The True Witness thus describes their blindness: "And knowest not that thou art wretched, and miserable, and poor, and blind, and naked."

Faith in the soon coming of Christ is waning. "My Lord delayeth His coming" is not only said in the heart, but expressed in words and most decidedly in works. Stupidity in this watching time is sealing the senses of God's people as to the signs of the times. The terrible iniquity which abounds calls for the greatest diligence and for the living testimony, to keep sin out of the church. Faith has been decreasing to a fearful degree, and it is only by exercise that it can increase.

In the rise of the third angel's message those who engaged in the work of God had something to venture; they had sacrifices to make. They started this work in poverty and suffered the greatest deprivations and reproach. They met determined opposition, which drove them to God in their necessity and kept their faith alive. Our present plan of systematic benevolence amply sustains our ministers, and there is no want and no call for the exercise of faith as to a support. Those who start out now to preach the truth have nothing to venture. They have no risks to run, no special sacrifices to make. The system of truth is made ready to their hand, and publications are provided for them, vindicating the truths they advance.

Some young men start out with no real sense of the exalted character of the work. They have no privations, hardships, or severe conflicts to meet, which would call for the exercise of faith. They do not cultivate practical self-denial and cherish a spirit of sacrifice. Some are becoming proud and lifted up, and have no real burden of the work upon them. The True Witness speaks to these ministers: "Be zealous therefore, and repent." Some of them are so lifted up in pride that they are really a hindrance and a curse to the precious cause of God. They do not exert a saving influence upon others. These men need to be thoroughly converted to God themselves and sanctified by the truths they present to others.

POINTED TESTIMONIES IN THE CHURCH

Very many feel impatient and jealous because they are frequently disturbed with warnings and reproofs which keep their sins before them. Says the True Witness: "I know thy works." The motives, the purposes, the unbelief, the suspicions and jealousies may be hid from men, but not from Christ.

THE LAODICEAN CHURCH

The True Witness comes as a counselor: "I counsel thee to buy of Me gold tried in the fire, that thou mayest be rich; and white raiment, that thou mayest be clothed, and that the shame of thy nakedness do not appear; and anoint thine eyes with eyesalve, that thou mayest see. As many as I love, I rebuke and chasten; be zealous therefore, and repent. Behold, I stand at the door, and knock: if any man hear My voice, and open the door, I will come in to him, and will sup with him, and he with Me. To him that overcometh will I grant to sit with Me in My throne, even as I also overcame, and am set down with My Father in His throne."

Those who are reproved by the Spirit of God should not rise up against the humble instrument. It is God, and not an erring mortal, who has spoken to save them from ruin. Those who despise the warning will be left in blindness to become self-deceived. But those who heed it, and zealously go about the work of separating their sins from them in order to have the needed graces, will be opening the door of their hearts that the dear Saviour may come in and dwell with them. This class you will ever find in perfect harmony with the testimony of the Spirit of God.

Ministers who are preaching present truth should not neglect the solemn message to the Laodiceans. The testimony of the True Witness is not a smooth message. The Lord does not say to them, You are about right; you have borne chastisement and reproof that you never deserved; you have been unnecessarily discouraged by severity; you are not guilty of the wrongs and sins for which you have been reproved.

The True Witness declares that when you suppose you are really in a good condition of prosperity you are in need of everything. It is not enough for ministers to present theoretical subjects; they should also present those subjects which are practical. They need to study the practical lessons that Christ gave His disciples and make a close application of the same to their own souls and to the people. Because Christ bears this rebuking testimony, shall we suppose that He is destitute of tender love to His people? Oh, no! He who died to redeem man from death, loves with a divine love, and those whom He loves He rebukes. "As many as I love, I rebuke and chasten." But many will not receive the message that Heaven in mercy sends them. They cannot endure to be told of their neglect of duty and of their wrongs, their selfishness, their pride and love of the world.

I was shown that God has laid upon my husband and me a special work, to bear a plain testimony to His people, and to cry aloud and spare not, to show the people their transgressions and the house of Israel their sins. But there is a class who will not receive the message of reproof, and they raise their hands to shield those whom God would reprove and correct. These are ever found sympathizing with those whom God would make to feel their true poverty.

The word of the Lord, spoken through His servants, is received by many with questionings and fears. And many will defer their obedience to the warning and reproofs given, waiting till every shadow of uncertainty is removed from their minds. The unbelief that demands perfect knowledge will never yield to the evidence that God is pleased to give. He requires of His people faith that rests upon the weight of evidence, not upon perfect knowledge. Those followers of Christ who accept the light that God sends them must obey the voice of God speaking to them when there are many other voices crying out against it. It requires discernment to distinguish the voice of God.

Those who will not act when the Lord calls upon them, but who wait for more certain evidence and more favorable opportunities, will walk in darkness, for the light will be withdrawn. The evidence given one day, if rejected, may never be repeated.

Many are tempted in regard to our work and are calling it in question. Some, in their tempted condition, charge the difficulties and perplexities of the people of God to the testimonies of reproof that we have given them. They think the trouble is with the ones who bear the message of warning, who point out the sins of the people and correct their errors. Many are deceived by the adversary of souls. They think that the labors of Brother and Sister White would be acceptable if they were not continually condemning wrong and reproving sin. I was shown that God has laid this work upon us, and when we are hindered from meeting with His people and from bearing our testimony and counteracting the surmisings and jealousies of the unconsecrated, then Satan presses in his temptations very strongly. Those who have been ever on the questioning, doubting side feel at liberty to suggest their doubts and to insinuate their unbelief. Some have sanctimonious and apparently conscientious and very pious doubts, which they cautiously drop, but which have tenfold more power to strengthen those who are wrong, and to lessen our influence and weaken the confidence of God's people in our work, than if they came out more frankly. These poor souls, I saw, were deceived by Satan. They flatter themselves that they are all right, that they are in favor with God and are rich in spiritual discernment, when they are poor, blind, and wretched. They are doing the work of Satan, but think they have a zeal for God.

Some will not receive the testimony that God has given us to bear, flattering themselves that we may be deceived and that they may be right. They think that the people of God are not in need of plain dealing and of reproof, but that God is with them. These tempted ones, whose souls have ever been at war with the faithful reproving of sin, would cry: Speak unto us smooth things. What disposition will these make of the message of the True Witness to the Laodiceans? There can be no deception here. This message must be borne to a lukewarm church by God's servants. It must arouse His people from their security and dangerous deception in regard to their real standing before God. This testimony, if received, will arouse to action and lead to self-abasement and confession of sins. The True Witness says: "I know thy works, that thou art neither cold nor hot." And again, "As many as I love, I rebuke and chasten: be zealous therefore, and repent." Then comes the promise: "Behold, I stand at the door, and knock: if any man hear My voice, and open the door, I will come in to him, and will sup with him, and he with Me." "To him that overcometh will I grant to sit with Me in My throne, even as I also overcame, and am set down with My Father in His throne."

The people of God must see their wrongs and arouse to zealous repentance and a putting away of those sins which have brought them into such a deplorable condition of poverty, blindness, wretchedness, and fearful deception. I was shown that the pointed testimony must live in the church. This alone will answer to the message to the Laodiceans. Wrongs must be reproved, sin must be called sin, and iniquity must be met promptly and decidedly, and put away from us as a people.

FIGHTING THE SPIRIT OF GOD

Those who have a spirit of opposition to the work that for twenty-six years we have been pressed by the Spirit of God to do, and who would break down our testimony, I saw are not fighting against us, but against God, who has laid upon us the burden of a work that He has not given to others. Those who question and quibble, and think it a virtue to doubt, and who would discourage; those who have been the means of making our work hard and of weakening our faith, hope, and courage have been the ones to surmise evil, to insinuate suspicious charges, and to watch with jealousy for occasion against us. They take it for granted that because we have human weaknesses it is a positive evidence that we are wrong and that they are right. If they can find a semblance of anything that they can use to injure us they do it with a spirit of triumph and are ready to denounce our work of reproving wrong and condemning sin as a harsh, dictatorial spirit.

But while we do not accept their version of our case as the reason for our afflictions, while we maintain that God has appointed us to a more trying work than He has others, we acknowledge with humility of soul and with repentance that our faith and courage have been severely tried and that we have sometimes failed to trust wholly in Him who has appointed us our work. When we gather courage again, after sore disappointment and trials, we deeply regret that we ever distrusted God, gave way to human weaknesses, and permitted discouragement to cloud our faith and lessen our confidence in God. I have been shown that God's ancient servants suffered disappointments and discouragements as well as we poor mortals. We were in good company; nevertheless this did not excuse us.

As my husband has stood by my side to sustain me in my work and has borne a plain testimony in unison with the work of the Spirit of God, many have felt that it was he personally who was injuring them, when it was the Lord who laid upon him the burden and who was, through His servant, reproving them and seeking to bring them where they would repent of their wrongs and have the favor of God.

Those whom God has chosen for an important work have ever been received with distrust and suspicion. Anciently, when Elijah was sent with a message from God to the people, they did not heed the warning. They thought him unnecessarily severe. They even thought that he must have lost his senses because he denounced them, the favored people of God, as sinners and their crimes as so aggravated that the judgments of God would awaken against them. Satan and his host have ever been arrayed against those who bear the message of warning and who reprove sins. The unconsecrated will also be united with the adversary of souls to make the work of God's faithful servants as hard as possible.

If my husband has been pressed beyond measure and has become discouraged and desponding, if we have at times seen nothing desirable in life that we should choose it, this is nothing strange or new. Elijah, one of God's great and mighty prophets, as he fled for his life from the rage of the infuriated Jezebel, a fugitive, weary and travel-worn, desired to die rather than to live. His bitter disappointment in regard to Israel's faithfulness had crushed his spirits, and he felt that he could no longer put confidence in man. In the day of Job's affliction and darkness, he utters these words: "Let the day perish wherein I was born."

Those who are not accustomed to feel to the very depths, who have not stood under burdens as a cart beneath sheaves, and who have never had their interest identified so closely with the cause and work of God that it seems to be a part of their very being and dearer to them than life, cannot appreciate the feelings of my husband any more than Israel could appreciate the feelings of Elijah. We deeply regret being disheartened, whatever the circumstances may have been.

AHAB'S CASE A WARNING

Under the perverted rule of Ahab, Israel departed from God and corrupted their ways before Him. "And Ahab the son of Omri did evil in the sight of the Lord above all that were before him. And it came to pass, as if it had been a light thing for him to walk in the sins of Jeroboam the son of Nebat, that he took to wife Jezebel the daughter of Ethbaal king of the Zidonians, and went and served Baal, and worshiped him. And he reared up an altar for Baal in the house of Baal, which he had built in Samaria. And Ahab made a grove; and Ahab did more to provoke the Lord God of Israel to anger than all the kings of Israel that were before him."

Ahab was weak in moral power. He did not have a high sense of sacred things; he was selfish and unprincipled. His union by marriage with a woman of decided character and positive temperament, who was devoted to idolatry, made them both special agents of Satan to lead the people of God into idolatry and terrible apostasy. The determined spirit of Jezebel molded the character of Ahab. His selfish nature was incapable of appreciating the mercies of God to His people and his obligation to God as the guardian and leader of Israel. The fear of God was daily growing less in Israel. The blasphemous tokens of their blind idolatry were to be seen among the Israel of God. There were none who dared to expose their lives by openly standing forth in opposition to the prevailing blasphemous idolatry. The altars of Baal, and the priests of Baal who sacrificed to the sun, moon, and stars, were conspicuous everywhere. They had consecrated temples and groves wherein the work of men's hands was placed to be worshiped. The benefits which God gave to this people called forth from them no gratitude to the Giver. All the bounties of heaven,—the running brooks, the streams of living waters, the gentle dew, the showers of rain which refreshed the earth and caused their fields to bring forth abundantly,—these they ascribed to the favor of their gods.

Elijah's faithful soul was grieved. His indignation was aroused, and he was jealous for the glory of God. He saw that Israel was plunged into fearful apostasy. And when he called to mind the great things that God had wrought for them, he was overwhelmed with grief and amazement. But all this was forgotten by the majority of the people. He went before the Lord, and, with his soul wrung with anguish, pleaded for Him to save His people if it must be by judgements. He pleaded with God to withhold from His ungrateful people dew and rain, the treasures of heaven, that apostate Israel might look in vain to their gods, their idols of gold, wood, and stone, the sun, moon, and stars, to water and enrich the earth, and cause it to bring forth plentifully. The Lord told Elijah that He had heard his prayer and would withhold dew and rain from His people until they should turn unto Him with repentance.

ACHAN'S SIN AND PUNISHMENT

God had specially guarded His people against mingling with the idolatrous nations around them, lest their hearts should be deceived by the attractive groves and shrines, temples and altars which were arranged in the most expensive, alluring manner to pervert the senses so that God would be supplanted in the minds of the people.

The city of Jericho was devoted to the most extravagant idolatry. The inhabitants were very wealthy, but all the riches that God had given them they counted as the gift of their gods. They had gold and silver in abundance; but, like the people before the Flood, they were corrupt and blasphemous, and insulted and provoked the God of heaven by their wicked works. God's judgments were awakened against Jericho. It was a stronghold. But the Captain of the Lord's host Himself came from heaven to lead the armies of heaven in an attack upon the city. Angels of God laid hold of the massive walls and brought them to the ground. God had said that the city of Jericho should be accursed and that all should perish except Rahab and her household. These should be saved because of the favor that Rahab showed the messengers of the Lord. The word of the Lord to the people was: "And ye, in anywise keep yourselves from the accursed thing, lest ye make yourselves accursed, when ye take of the accursed thing, and make the camp of Israel a curse, and trouble it." "And Joshua adjured them at that time, saying, Cursed be the man before the Lord, that riseth up and buildeth this city Jericho: he shall lay the foundation thereof in his first-born, and in his youngest son shall he set up the gates of it."

God was very particular in regard to Jericho, lest the people should be charmed with the things that the inhabitants had worshiped and their hearts be diverted from God. He guarded His people by most positive commands; yet notwithstanding the solemn injunction from God by the mouth of Joshua, Achan ventured to transgress. His covetousness led him to take of the treasures that God had forbidden him to touch because the curse of God was upon them. And because of this man's sin the Israel of God were as weak as water before their enemies.

Joshua and the elders of Israel were in great affliction. They lay before the ark of God in most abject humility because the Lord was wroth with His people. They prayed and wept before God. The Lord spoke to Joshua: "Get thee up; wherefore liest thou thus upon thy face? Israel hath sinned, and they have also transgressed My covenant which I commanded them: for they have even taken of the accursed thing, and have also stolen, and dissembled also, and they have put it even among their own stuff. Therefore the children of Israel could not stand before their enemies, but turned their backs before their enemies, because they were accursed: neither will I be with you any more, except ye destroy the accursed from among you."

DUTY TO REPROVE SIN

I have been shown that God here illustrates how He regards sin among those who profess to be His commandment-keeping people. Those whom He has specially honored with witnessing the remarkable exhibitions of His power, as did ancient Israel, and who will even then venture to disregard His express directions, will be subjects of His wrath. He would teach His people that disobedience and sin are exceedingly offensive to Him and are not to be lightly regarded. He shows us that when His people are found in sin they should at once take decided measures to put that sin from them, that His frown may not rest upon them all. But if the sins of the people are passed over by those in responsible positions, His frown will be upon them, and the people of God, as a body, will be held responsible for those sins. In His dealings with His people in the past the Lord shows the necessity of purifying the church from wrongs. One sinner may diffuse darkness that will exclude the light of God from the entire congregation. When the people realize that darkness is settling upon them, and they do not know the cause, they should seek God earnestly, in great humility and self-abasement, until the wrongs which grieve His Spirit are searched out and put away.

The prejudice which has arisen against us because we have reproved the wrongs that God has shown me existed, and the cry that has been raised of harshness and severity, are unjust. God bids us speak, and we will not be silent. If wrongs are apparent among His people, and if the servants of God pass on indifferent to them, they virtually sustain and justify the sinner, and are alike guilty and will just as surely receive the displeasure of God; for they will be made responsible for the sins of the guilty. In vision I have been pointed to many instances where the displeasure of God has been incurred by a neglect on the part of His servants to deal with the wrongs and sins existing among them. Those who have excused these wrongs have been thought by the people to be very amiable and lovely in disposition, simply because they shunned to discharge a plain Scriptural duty. The task was not agreeable to their feelings; therefore they avoided it.

The spirit of hatred which has existed with some because the wrongs among God's people have been reproved has brought blindness and a fearful deception upon their own souls, making it impossible for them to discriminate between right and wrong. They have put out their own spiritual eyesight. They may witness wrongs, but they do not feel as did Joshua and humble themselves because the danger of souls is felt by them.

The true people of God, who have the spirit of the work of the Lord and the salvation of souls at heart, will ever view sin in its real, sinful character. They will always be on the side of faithful and plain dealing with sins which easily beset the people of God. Especially in the closing work for the church, in the sealing time of the one hundred and forty-four thousand who are to stand without fault before the throne of God, will they feel most deeply the wrongs of God's professed people. This is forcibly set forth by the prophet's illustration of the last work under the figure of the men each having a slaughter weapon in his hand. One man among them was clothed with linen, with a writer's inkhorn by his side. "And the Lord said unto him, Go through the midst of the city, through the midst of Jerusalem, and set a mark upon the foreheads of the men that sigh and that cry for all the abominations that be done in the midst thereof."

THE LAODICEAN CHURCH

Who are standing in the counsel of God at this time? Is it those who virtually excuse wrongs among the professed people of God and who murmur in their hearts, if not openly, against those who would reprove sin? Is it those who take their stand against them and sympathize with those who commit wrong? No, indeed! Unless they repent, and leave the work of Satan in oppressing those who have the burden of the work and in holding up the hands of sinners in Zion, they will never receive the mark of God's sealing approval. They will fall in the general destruction of the wicked, represented by the work of the five men bearing slaughter weapons. Mark this point with care: Those who receive the pure mark of truth, wrought in them by the power of the Holy Ghost, represented by a mark by the man in linen, are those "that sigh and that cry for all the abominations that be done" in the church. Their love for purity and the honor and glory of God is such, and they have so clear a view of the exceeding sinfulness of sin, that they are represented as being in agony, even sighing and crying. Read the ninth chapter of Ezekiel.

But the general slaughter of all those who do not thus see the wide contrast between sin and righteousness, and do not feel as those do who stand in the counsel of God and receive the mark, is described in the order to the five men with slaughter weapons: "Go ye after him through the city, and smite: let not your eye spare, neither have ye pity: slay utterly old and young, both maids, and little children, and women: but come not near any man upon whom is the mark; and begin at My sanctuary."

In the case of Achan's sin God said to Joshua: "Neither will I be with you any more, except ye destroy the accursed from among you." How does this instance compare with the course pursued by those who will not raise their voice against sin and wrong, but whose sympathies are ever found with those who trouble the camp of Israel with their sins? Said God to Joshua: "Thou canst not stand before thine enemies, until ye take away the accursed thing from among you." He pronounced the punishment which would follow the transgression of His covenant.

Joshua then began a diligent search to find out the guilty one. He took Israel by their tribes, then by their families, and next individually; and Achan was designated as the guilty one. But that the matter might be plain to all Israel, that there should be no occasion given them to murmur and to say that the guiltless was made to suffer, Joshua used policy. He knew Achan was the transgressor and that he had concealed his sin and provoked God against His people. Joshua discreetly induced Achan to make confession of his sin, that God's honor and justice might be vindicated before Israel. "And Joshua said unto Achan, My son, give, I pray thee, glory to the Lord God of Israel, and make confession unto Him; and tell me now what thou hast done; hide it not from me.

"And Achan answered Joshua, and said, Indeed I have sinned against the Lord God of Israel, and thus and thus have I done: When I saw among the spoils a goodly Babylonish garment, and two hundred shekels of silver, and a wedge of gold of fifty shekels weight, then I coveted them, and took them; and, behold, they are hid in the earth in the midst of my tent, and the silver under it. So Joshua sent messengers, and they ran unto the tent; and, behold, it was hid in his tent, and the silver under it. And they took them out of the midst of the tent, and brought them unto Joshua, and unto all the children of Israel, and laid them out before the Lord. And Joshua, and all Israel with him, took Achan the son of Zerah, and the silver, and the garment, and the wedge of gold, and his sons, and his daughters, and his oxen, and his asses, and his sheep, and his tent, and all that he had: and they brought them unto the Valley of Achor. And Joshua said, Why hast thou troubled us? the Lord shall trouble thee this day. And all Israel stoned him with stones, and burned them with fire, after they had stoned them with stones."

The Lord told Joshua that Achan had not only taken the things which He had positively charged them not to take, lest they be accursed, but he had stolen and had also dissembled. The Lord said that Jericho and all its spoils should be consumed, except the gold and silver, which were to be reserved for the treasury of the Lord. The victory of taking Jericho was not obtained through warfare or the exposure of the people. The Captain of the Lord's host had led the armies of heaven. The battle was the Lord's; it was He who fought the battle. The children of Israel did not strike a blow. The victory and glory were the Lord's, and the spoils were His. He directed all to be consumed except the gold and silver, which He reserved for His treasury. Achan understood well the reserve made and that the treasures of gold and silver which he coveted were the Lord's. He stole from God's treasury for his own benefit.

COVETOUSNESS AMONG GOD'S PEOPLE

I saw that many who profess to be keeping the commandments of God are appropriating to their own use the means which the Lord has entrusted to them and which should come into His treasury. They rob God in tithes and in offerings. They dissemble and withhold from Him to their own hurt. They bring leanness and poverty upon themselves and darkness upon the church because of their covetousness, their dissembling, and their robbing God in tithes and in offerings.

I saw that many souls will sink in darkness because of their covetousness. The plain, straight testimony must live in the church, or the curse of God will rest upon His people as surely as it did upon ancient Israel because of their sins. God holds His people, as a body, responsible for the sins existing in individuals among them. If the leaders of the church neglect to diligently search out the sins which bring the displeasure of God upon the body, they become responsible for these sins. But to deal with minds is the nicest work in which men ever engaged. All are not fitted to correct the erring. They have not wisdom to deal justly, while loving mercy. They are not inclined to see the necessity of mingling love and tender compassion with faithful reproofs. Some are ever needlessly severe, and do not feel the necessity of the injunction of the apostle: "And of some have compassion, making a difference: and others save with fear, pulling them out of the fire."

There are many who do not have the discretion of Joshua and who have no special duty to search out wrongs and to deal promptly with the sins existing among them. Let not such hinder those who have the burden of this work upon them; let them not stand in the way of those who have this duty to do. Some make it a point to question and doubt and find fault because others do the work that God has not laid upon them. These stand directly in the way to hinder those upon whom God has laid the burden of reproving and correcting prevailing sins in order that His frown may be turned away from His people. Should a case like Achan's be among us, there are many who would accuse those who might act the part of Joshua in searching out the wrong, of having a wicked, fault-finding spirit. God is not to be trifled with and His warnings disregarded with impunity by a perverse people.

I was shown that the manner of Achan's confession was similar to the confessions that some among us have made and will make. They hide their wrongs and refuse to make a voluntary confession until God searches them out, and then they acknowledge their sins. A few persons pass on in a course of wrong until they become hardened. They may even know that the church is burdened, as Achan knew that Israel were made weak before their enemies because of his guilt. Yet their consciences do not condemn them. They will not relieve the church by humbling their proud, rebellious hearts before God and putting away their wrongs. God's displeasure is upon His people, and He will not manifest His power in the midst of them while sins exist among them and are fostered by those in responsible positions.

Those who work in the fear of God to rid the church of hindrances and to correct grievous wrongs, that the people of God may see the necessity of abhorring sin and may prosper in purity, and that the name of God may be glorified, will ever meet with resisting influences from the unconsecrated. Zephaniah thus describes the true state of this class and the terrible judgments that will come upon them.

"And it shall come to pass at that time, that I will search Jerusalem with candles, and punish the men that are settled on their lees: that say in their heart, The Lord will not do good, neither will He do evil." "The great day of the Lord is near, it is near, and hasteth greatly, even the voice of the day of the Lord: the mighty man shall cry there bitterly. That day is a day of wrath, a day of trouble and distress, a day of wasteness and desolation, a day of darkness and gloominess, a day of clouds and thick darkness, a day of the trumpet and alarm against the fenced cities, and against the high towers. And I will bring distress upon men, that they shall walk like blind men, because they have sinned against the Lord and their blood shall be poured out as dust, and their flesh as the dung. Neither their silver nor their gold shall be able to deliver them in the day of the Lord's wrath; but the whole land shall be devoured by the fire of His jealousy: for He shall make even a speedy riddance of all them that dwell in the land."

CONFESSIONS MADE TOO LATE

When a crisis finally comes, as it surely will, and God speaks in behalf of His people, those who have sinned, those who have been a cloud of darkness and who have stood directly in the way of God's working for His people, may become alarmed at the length they have gone in murmuring and in bringing discouragement upon the cause; and, like Achan, becoming terrified, they may acknowledge that they have sinned. But their confessions are too late and are not of the right kind to benefit themselves, although they may relieve the cause of God. Such do not make their confessions because of a conviction of their true state and a sense of how displeasing their course has been to God. God may give this class another test, another proving, and let them show that they are no better prepared to stand free from all rebellion and sin than before their confessions were made. They are inclined to be ever on the side of wrong. And when the call is made for those who will be on the Lord's side to make a decided move to vindicate the right, they will manifest their true position. Those who have been nearly all their lives controlled by a spirit as foreign to the Spirit of God as was Achan's will be very passive when the time comes for decided action on the part of all. They will not claim to be on either side. The power of Satan has so long held them that they seem blinded and have no inclination to stand in defense of right. If they do not take a determined course on the wrong side, it is not because they have a clear sense of the right, but because they dare not.

God will not be trifled with. It is in the time of conflict that the true colors should be flung to the breeze. It is then that the standard-bearers need to be firm and let their true position be known. It is then that the skill of every true soldier for the right is tested. Shirkers can never wear the laurels of victory. Those who are true and loyal will not conceal the fact, but will put heart and might into the work, and venture their all in the struggle, let the battle turn as it will. God is a sin-hating God. And those who encourage the sinner, saying, It is well with thee, God will curse.

Confessions of sin made at the right time to relieve the people of God will be accepted of Him. But there are those among us who will make confessions, as did Achan, too late to save themselves. God may prove them and give them another trial for the sake of evidencing to His people that they will not endure one test, one proving of God. They are not in harmony with right. They despise the straight testimony that reaches the heart, and would rejoice to see everyone silenced who gives reproof.

ELIJAH REPROVES AHAB

The people of Israel had gradually lost their fear and reverence for God until His word through Joshua had no weight with them. "In his [Ahab's] days did Hiel the Bethelite build Jericho: he laid the foundation thereof in Abiram his firstborn, and set up the gates thereof in his youngest son Segub, according to the word of the Lord, which he spake by Joshua the son of Nun."

While Israel was apostatizing, Elijah remained a loyal and true prophet of God. His faithful soul was greatly distressed as he saw that unbelief and infidelity were fast separating the children of Israel from God, and he prayed that God would save His people. He entreated that the Lord would not wholly cast away His sinning people, but that He would by judgments if necessary arouse them to repentance and not permit them to go to still greater lengths in sin and thus provoke Him to destroy them as a nation.

The message of the Lord came to Elijah to go to Ahab with the denunciations of His judgments because of the sins of Israel. Elijah traveled day and night until he reached the palace of Ahab. He solicited no admission, and waited not to be formally announced. All unexpectedly to Ahab, Elijah stands before the astonished king of Samaria in the coarse garments usually worn by the prophets. He makes no apology for his abrupt appearance, without invitation; but, raising his hands to heaven, he solemnly affirms by the living God, who made the heavens and the earth, the judgments which would come upon Israel: "There shall not be dew nor rain these years, but according to my word."

This startling denunciation of God's judgments because of the sins of Israel fell like a thunderbolt upon the apostate king. He seemed to be paralyzed with amazement and terror; and before he could recover from his astonishment, Elijah, without waiting to see the effect of his message, disappeared as suddenly as he came. His work was to speak the word of woe from God, and he instantly withdrew. His word had locked up the treasures of heaven, and his word was the only key which could open them again.

The Lord knew that there was no safety for His servant among the children of Israel. He would not trust him with apostate Israel, but sent him to find an asylum among a heathen nation. He directed him to a woman who was a widow and who was in such poverty that she could barely sustain life with the most meager fare. A heathen woman living up to the best light she had was in a more acceptable state with God than the widows of Israel, who had been blessed with special privileges and great light, and yet did not live according to the light which God had given them. As the Hebrews had rejected light, they were left in darkness, and God would not trust His servant among His people, who had provoked His divine anger.

Now there is an opportunity for apostate Ahab and pagan Jezebel to test the power of their gods and to prove the word of Elijah false. Jezebel's prophets are numbered by hundreds. Against them all stands Elijah, alone. His word has locked heaven. If Baal can give dew and rain, and cause vegetation to flourish; if he can cause the brooks and streams to flow on as usual, independent of the treasures of heaven in the showers of rain, then let the king of Israel worship him and the people say that he is God.

Elijah was a man subject to like passions as ourselves. His mission to Ahab, and the terrible denunciation to him of the judgments of God, required courage and faith. On his way to Samaria the perpetually flowing streams, the hills covered with verdure, the forests of stately, flourishing trees,—everything his eye rested upon flourishing in beauty and glory,—would naturally suggest unbelief. How can all these things in nature, now so flourishing, be burned with drought? How can these streams that water the land and that have never been known to cease their flow, become dry? But Elijah did not cherish unbelief. He went forth on his mission at the peril of his life. He fully believed that God would humble His apostate people and that through the visitation of His judgments He would bring them to humiliation and repentance. He ventured everything in the mission before him.

When Ahab recovers in a degree from his astonishment at the words of Elijah, the prophet is gone. He makes diligent inquiry for him, but no one has seen him or can give any information respecting him. Ahab informs Jezebel of the word of woe that Elijah has uttered in his presence, and her hatred against the prophet is expressed to the priests of Baal. They unite with her in denouncing and cursing the prophet of Jehovah. The news of the prophet's denunciations spread throughout the land, arousing the fears of some and the wrath of many.

After a few months the earth, unrefreshed by dew or rain, becomes dry, and vegetation withers. The streams that have never been known to cease their flow, decrease, and the brooks dry up. Jezebel's prophets offer sacrifices to their gods and call upon them night and day to refresh the earth by dew and rain. But the incantations and deceptions formerly practiced by them to deceive the people do not answer the purpose now. The priests have done everything to appease the anger of their gods; with a perseverance and zeal worthy of a better cause have they lingered around their pagan altars, while the flames of sacrifice burn on all the high places, and the fearful cries and entreaties of the priests of Baal are heard night after night through doomed Samaria. But the clouds do not appear in the heavens to cut off the burning rays of the sun. The word of Elijah stands firm, and nothing that Baal's priests can do will change it.

An entire year passes, and another commences, and yet there is no rain. The earth is parched as though a fire had passed over it. The flourishing fields are as the scorching desert. The air becomes dry and suffocating, and the dust storm blinds the eyes and nearly stops the breath. The groves of Baal are leafless, and the forest trees give no shade, but appear as skeletons. Hunger and thirst are telling upon man and beast with fearful mortality.

All this evidence of God's justice and judgment does not awaken Israel to repentance. Jezebel is filled with insane madness. She will not bend nor yield to the God of heaven. Baal's prophets, Ahab, Jezebel, and nearly the whole of Israel, charge their calamity upon Elijah. Ahab has sent to every kingdom and nation in search of the strange prophet and has required an oath of the kingdoms and nations of Israel that they know nothing in regard to him. Elijah had locked heaven with his word and had taken the key with him, and he could not be found.

Jezebel then decides that as she cannot make Elijah feel her murderous power, she will be revenged by destroying the prophets of God in Israel. No one who professed to be a prophet of God shall live. This determined, infuriated woman executes her work of madness by slaying the Lord's prophets. Baal's priests and nearly all Israel are so far deluded that they think that if the prophets of God were slain, the calamity under which they are suffering would be averted.

But the second year passes, and the pitiless heavens give no rain. Drought and famine are doing their sad work, and yet the apostate Israelites do not humble their proud, sinful hearts before God; but they murmur and complain against the prophet of God who brought this dreadful state of things upon them. Fathers and mothers see their children perish, with no power to relieve them. And yet the people are in such terrible darkness that they cannot see that the justice of God is awakened against them because of their sins and that this terrible calamity is sent in mercy to them to save them from fully denying and forsaking the God of their fathers.

It cost Israel suffering and great affliction to be brought to that repentance that was necessary in order to recover their lost faith and a clear sense of their responsibility to God. Their apostasy was more dreadful than drought or famine. Elijah waited and prayed in faith through the long years of drought and famine that the hearts of Israel, through their affliction, might be turned from their idolatry to allegiance to God. But notwithstanding all their sufferings, they stood firm in their idolatry and looked upon the prophet of God as the cause of their calamity. And if they could have had Elijah in their power they would have delivered him to Jezebel, that she might satisfy her revenge by taking his life. Because Elijah dared to utter the word of woe which God bade him, he made himself the object of their hatred. They could not see God's hand in the judgments under which they were suffering because of their sins, but charged them to the man Elijah. They abhorred not the sins which had brought them under the chastening rod, but hated the faithful prophet, God's instrument to denounce their sins and calamity.

"And it came to pass after many days, that the word of the Lord came to Elijah in the third year, saying, Go, show thyself unto Ahab; and I will send rain upon the earth." Elijah hesitates not to start on his perilous journey. For three years he had been hated, and hunted from city to city by the mandate of the king, and the whole nation have given their oath that he cannot be found. And now, by the word of God, he is to present himself before Ahab.

During the apostasy of all Israel, and while his master is a worshiper of Baal, the governor of Ahab's house has proved faithful to God. At the risk of his own life he has preserved the prophets of God by hiding them by fifties in a cave and feeding them. While the servant of Ahab is searching throughout the kingdom for springs and brooks of water, Elijah presents himself before him. Obadiah reverenced the prophet of God, but as Elijah sends him with a message to the king, he is greatly terrified. He sees danger and death to himself and also to Elijah. He pleads earnestly that his life may not be sacrificed; but Elijah assures him with an oath that he will see Ahab that day. The prophet will not go to Ahab but as one of God's messengers, to command respect, and he sends a message by Obadiah: "Behold Elijah is here." If Ahab wants to see Elijah, he now has the opportunity to come to him. Elijah will not go to Ahab.

With astonishment mingled with terror the king hears the message that Elijah whom he fears and hates, is coming to meet him. He has long sought for the prophet that he might destroy him, and he knows that Elijah would not expose his life to come to him unless guarded or with some terrible denunciation. He remembers the withered arm of Jeroboam and decides that it is not safe to lift up his hand against the messenger of God. And with fear and trembling, and with a large retinue and an imposing display of armies, he hastens to meet Elijah. And as he meets face to face the man whom he has so long sought, he dares not harm him. The king, so passionate, and so filled with hatred against Elijah, seems to be powerless and unmanned in his presence. As he meets the prophet he cannot refrain from speaking the language of his heart: "Art thou he that troubleth Israel?" Elijah, indignant, and jealous for the honor and glory of God, answers the charge of Ahab with boldness: "I have not troubled Israel; but thou, and thy father's house, in that ye have forsaken the commandments of the Lord."

The prophet, as God's messenger, had reproved the sins of the people, denouncing upon them the judgments of God because of their wickedness. And now, standing alone in conscious innocence, firm in his integrity, surrounded by the train of armed men, Elijah shows no timidity, neither does he show the least reverence to the king. The man whom God has talked with, and who has a clear sense of how God regards man in his sinful depravity, has no apology to make to Ahab nor homage to give him. As God's messenger, Elijah now commands and Ahab at once obeys as though Elijah were monarch and he the subject.

THE SACRIFICE ON MOUNT CARMEL

Elijah demands a convocation at Carmel of all Israel and also of all the prophets of Baal. The awful solemnity in the looks of the prophet gives him the appearance of one standing in the presence of the Lord God of Israel. The condition of Israel in their apostasy demands a firm demeanor, stern speech, and commanding authority. God prepares the message to fit the time and occasion. Sometimes He puts His Spirit upon His messengers to sound an alarm day and night, as did His messenger John: "Prepare ye the way of the Lord." Then, again, men of action are needed who will not be swerved from duty, but whose energy will arouse and demand, "Who is on the Lord's side?" let him come over with us. God will have a fitting message to meet His people in their varied conditions.

Swift messengers are sent throughout the kingdom with the message from Elijah. Representatives are sent from cities, towns, villages, and families. All seem in haste to answer the call, as though some wonderful miracle is to be performed. According to Elijah's command, Ahab gathers the prophets of Baal at Carmel. The heart of Israel's apostate leader is overawed, and he tremblingly follows the direction of the stern prophet of God.

The people assemble upon Mount Carmel, a place of beauty when the dew and rain fall upon it causing it to flourish; but now its beauty is languishing under the curse of God. Upon this mount, which was the excellency of groves and flowers, Baal's prophets had erected altars for their pagan worship. This mountain was conspicuous; it overlooked the surrounding countries and was in sight of a large portion of the kingdom. As God had been signally dishonored by the idolatrous worship carried on here, Elijah chose this as the most conspicuous place for the display of God's power and to vindicate His honor.

Jezebel's prophets, eight hundred and fifty in number, like

a regiment of soldiers prepared for battle, march out in a body with instrumental music and imposing display. But there is trembling in their hearts as they consider that at the word of this prophet of Jehovah the land of Israel has been destitute of dew and rain three years. They feel that some fearful crisis is at hand. They had trusted in their gods, but could not unsay the words of Elijah and prove him false. Their gods were indifferent to their frantic cries, prayers, and sacrifices.

Elijah, early in the morning, stands upon Mount Carmel, surrounded by apostate Israel and the prophets of Baal. A lone man in that vast multitude, he stands undaunted. He whom the whole kingdom has charged with its weight of woe is before them, unterrified and unattended by visible armies and imposing display. He stands, clad in his coarse garment, with awful solemnity in his countenance, as though fully aware of his sacred commission as the servant of God to execute His commands. Elijah fastens his eyes upon the highest ridge of mountains where had stood the altar of Jehovah when the mountain was covered with flourishing trees and flowers. The blight of God is now upon it; all the desolation of Israel is in full view of the neglected, torn-down altar of Jehovah, and in sight are the altars of Baal. Ahab stands at the head of the priests of Baal, and all wait in anxious, fearful expectation for the words of Elijah.

In the full light of the sun, surrounded by thousands,—men of war, prophets of Baal, and the monarch of Israel,—stands the defenseless man, Elijah, apparently alone, yet not alone. The most powerful host of heaven surrounds him. Angels who excel in strength have come from heaven to shield the faithful and righteous prophet. With stern and commanding voice Elijah cries: "How long halt ye between two opinions? if the Lord be God, follow Him: but if Baal, then follow him. And the people answered him not a word." Not one in that vast assembly dared utter one word for God and show his loyalty to Jehovah.

What astonishing deception and fearful blindness had, like

a dark cloud, covered Israel! This blindness and apostasy had not closed about them suddenly; it had come upon them gradually as they had not heeded the word of reproof and warning which the Lord had sent to them because of their pride and their sins. And now, in this fearful crisis, in the presence of the idolatrous priests and the apostate king, they remained neutral. If God abhors one sin above another, of which His people are guilty, it is doing nothing in case of an emergency. Indifference and neutrality in a religious crisis is regarded of God as a grievous crime and equal to the very worst type of hostility against God.

All Israel is silent. Again the voice of Elijah is heard addressing them: "I, even I only, remain a prophet of the Lord; but Baal's prophets are four hundred and fifty men. Let them therefore give us two bullocks; and let them choose one bullock for themselves, and cut it in pieces, and lay it on wood, and put no fire under: and I will dress the other bullock, and lay it on wood, and put no fire under: and call ye on the name of your gods, and I will call on the name of the Lord: and the God that answereth by fire, let Him be God. And all the people answered and said, It is well spoken. And Elijah said unto the prophets of Baal, Choose you one bullock for yourselves, and dress it first; for ye are many; and call on the name of your gods, but put no fire under. And they took the bullock which was given them, and they dressed it, and called on the name of Baal from morning even until noon, saying, O Baal, hear us. But there was no voice, nor any that answered. And they leaped upon the altar which was made."

The proposition of Elijah is reasonable. The people dare not evade it, and they find courage to answer: The word is good. The prophets of Baal dare not dissent or evade the matter. God has directed this trial and has prepared confusion for the authors of idolatry and a signal triumph for His name. The priests of Baal dare not do otherwise than accept the conditions. With terror and guiltiness in their hearts, while outwardly bold and defiant, they rear their altar, lay on the wood and the victim, and then begin their incantations, their chanting and bawling, characteristics of pagan worship. Their shrill cries re-echo through forests and mountains: "O Baal, hear us." The priests gather in an army about their altars, and with leaping, and writhing, and screaming, and stamping, and with unnatural gestures, and tearing their hair, and cutting their flesh, they manifest apparent sincerity.

The morning passes and noon comes, and yet there is no move of their gods in pity to Baal's priests, the deluded worshipers of idols. No voice answers their frantic cries. The priests are continually devising how, by deception, they can kindle a fire upon the altars and give the glory to Baal. But the firm eye of Elijah watches every motion. Eight hundred voices become hoarse. Their garments are covered with blood, and yet their frantic excitement does not abate. Their pleadings are mingled with cursings to their sun-god that he does not send fire for their altars. Elijah stands by, watching with eagle eye lest any deception should be practiced; for he knows that if, by any device, they could kindle their altar fire, he would be torn in pieces upon the spot. He wishes to show the people the folly of their doubting and halting between two opinions when they have the wonderful works of God's majestic power in their behalf and innumerable evidences of His infinite mercies and loving-kindness toward them.

"And it came to pass at noon, that Elijah mocked them, and said, Cry aloud: for he is a god; either he is talking, or he is pursuing, or he is in a journey, or peradventure he sleepeth, and must be awaked. And they cried aloud, and cut themselves after their manner with knives and lancets, till the blood gushed out upon them. And it came to pass, when midday was past, and they prophesied until the time of the offering of the evening sacrifice, that there was neither voice, nor any to answer, nor any that regarded."

How gladly would Satan, who fell like lightning from heaven, come to the help of those whom he has deceived, whose minds he has controlled, and who are fully devoted to his service. Gladly would he send the lightning and kindle their sacrifices; but Jehovah has set Satan's bounds. He has restrained his power, and all his devices cannot convey one spark to Baal's altars. Evening draws on. The prophets of Baal are weary, faint, and confused. One suggests one thing, and one another, until they cease their efforts. Their shrieks and curses no longer resound over Mount Carmel. With weakness and despair they retire from the contest.

The people have witnessed the terrible demonstrations of the unreasonable, frantic priests. They have beheld their leaping upon the altar as though they would grasp the burning rays from the sun to serve their altars. They have become tired of the exhibitions of demonism, of pagan idolatry; and they feel earnest and anxious to hear what Elijah will speak.

Elijah's turn has now come. "And Elijah said unto all the people, Come near unto me. And all the people came near unto him. And he repaired the altar of the Lord that was broken down. And Elijah took twelve stones, according to the number of the tribes of the sons of Jacob, unto whom the word of the Lord came, saying, Israel shall be thy name: and with the stones he built an altar in the name of the Lord: and he made a trench about the altar, as great as would contain two measures of seed. And he put the wood in order, and cut the bullock in pieces, and laid him on the wood, and said, Fill four barrels with water, and pour it on the burnt sacrifice, and on the wood. And he said, Do it the second time. And they did it the second time. And he said, Do it the third time. And they did it the third time. And the water ran round about the altar; and he filled the trench also with water. And it came to pass at the time of the offering of the evening sacrifice, that Elijah the prophet came near, and said, Lord God of Abraham, Isaac, and of Israel, let it be known this day that Thou art God in Israel, and that I am Thy servant, and that I have done all these things at Thy word. Hear me, O Lord, hear me, that this people may know that Thou art the Lord God, and that Thou hast turned their heart back again. Then the fire of the

Lord fell, and consumed the burnt sacrifice, and the wood, and the stones, and the dust, and licked up the water that was in the trench. And when all the people saw it, they fell on their faces: and they said, The Lord, He is the God; the Lord, He is the God."

Elijah at the hour of evening sacrifice repairs the altar of God which the apostasy of Israel has allowed the priests of Baal to tear down. He does not call upon one of the people to aid him in his laborious work. The altars of Baal are all prepared; but he turns to the broken-down altar of God, which is more sacred and precious to him in its unsightly ruins than all the magnificent altars of Baal.

Elijah respects the Lord's covenant with His people, although they have apostatized. With calmness and solemnity he repairs the broken-down altar with twelve stones, according to the number of the twelve tribes of Israel. The disappointed priests of Baal, wearied with their vain, frenzied efforts, are sitting or lying prostrate on the ground, waiting to see what Elijah will do. They are filled with fear and hatred toward the prophet for proposing a test which has exposed their weakness and the inefficiency of their gods.

The people of Israel stand spellbound, pale, anxious, and almost breathless with awe, while Elijah calls upon Jehovah, the Creator of the heavens and the earth. The people have witnessed the fanatical, unreasonable frenzy of the prophets of Baal. In contrast they are now privileged to witness the calm, awe-inspiring deportment of Elijah. He reminds the people of their degeneracy, which has awakened the wrath of God against them, and then calls upon them to humble their hearts and turn to the God of their fathers, that His curse may be removed from them. Ahab and his idolatrous priests are looking on with amazement mingled with terror. They await the result with anxious, solemn silence.

After the victim is laid upon the altar, he commands the people to flood the sacrifice and the altar with water, and to fill the trench round about the altar. He then reverentially bows before the unseen God, raises his hands toward heaven, and offers a calm and simple prayer, unattended with violent gestures or contortions of the body. No shrieks resound over Carmel's height. A solemn silence, which is oppressive to the priests of Baal, rests upon all. In his prayer, Elijah makes use of no extravagant expressions. He prays to Jehovah as though He were nigh, witnessing the whole scene, and hearing his sincere, fervent, yet simple prayer. Baal's priests have screamed, and foamed, and leaped, and prayed, very long—from morning until near evening. Elijah's prayer is very short, earnest, reverential, and sincere. No sooner is that prayer uttered than flames of fire descend from heaven in a distinct manner, like a brilliant flash of lightning, kindling the wood for sacrifice and consuming the victim, licking up the water in the trench and consuming even the stones of the altar. The brilliancy of the blaze illumes the mountain and is painful to the eyes of the multitude. The people of the kingdom of Israel not gathered upon the mount are watching with interest those there assembled. As the fire descends, they witness it and are amazed at the sight. It resembles the pillar of fire at the Red Sea, which by night separated the children of Israel from the Egyptian host.

The people upon the mountain prostrate themselves in terror and awe before the unseen God. They cannot look upon the bright consuming fire sent from heaven. They fear that they will be consumed in their apostasy and sins, and cry out with one voice, which resounds over the mountain and echoes to the plains below with terrible distinctness: "The Lord, He is the God; the Lord, He is the God." Israel is at last aroused and undeceived. They see their sin and how greatly they have dishonored God. Their anger is aroused against the prophets of Baal. With terror, Ahab and Baal's priests witness the wonderful exhibition of Jehovah's power. Again the voice of Elijah is heard in startling words of command to the people: "Take the prophets of Baal; let not one of them escape." The people are ready to obey his word. They seize the false prophets who have deluded them, and bring them to the brook Kishon, and there, with his own hand, Elijah slays these idolatrous priests.

The judgments of God having been executed upon the false priests, the people having confessed their sins and acknowledged their fathers' God, the withering curse of God is now to be withdrawn, and He is to renew His blessings unto His people and again refresh the earth with dew and rain.

Elijah addresses Ahab: "Get thee up, eat and drink; for there is a sound of abundance of rain." While Ahab went up to feast, Elijah went up from the fearful sacrifice to the top of Mount Carmel to pray. His work of slaying the pagan priests had not unfitted him for the solemn exercise of prayer. He had performed the will of God. After he had, as God's instrument, done what he could to remove the cause of Israel's apostasy by slaying the idolatrous priests, he could do no more. He then intercedes in behalf of sinning, apostate Israel. In the most painful position, his face bowed between his knees, he most earnestly supplicates God to send rain. Six times in succession he sends his servant to see if there is any visible token that God has heard his prayer. He does not become impatient and faithless because the Lord does not immediately give the token that his prayer is heard. He continues in earnest prayer, sending his servant seven times to see if God has granted any signal. His servant returns the sixth time from his outlook toward the sea with the discouraging report that there is no sign of clouds forming in the brassy heavens. The seventh time he informs Elijah that there is a small cloud to be seen, about the size of a man's hand. This is enough to satisfy the faith of Elijah. He does not wait for the heavens to gather blackness, to make the matter sure. In that small, rising cloud his faith hears the sound of abundance of rain. His works are in accordance with his faith. He sends a message to Ahab by his servant: "Prepare thy chariot, and get thee down, that the rain stop thee not."

ELIJAH'S HUMILITY

Here Elijah ventured something upon his faith. He did not wait for sight. "And it came to pass in the meanwhile, that the heaven was black with clouds and wind, and there was a great rain. And Ahab rode, and went to Jezreel. And the hand of the Lord was on Elijah; and he girded up his loins, and ran before Ahab to the entrance of Jezreel."

Elijah had passed through great excitement and labor during the day; but the Spirit of the Lord came upon him because he had been obedient and had done His will in executing the idolatrous priests. Some will be ready to say: What a hard, cruel man Elijah must have been! And anyone who defends the honor of God at any risk will bring censure and condemnation upon himself from a large class.

The rain began to descend. It was night, and the blinding rain prevented Ahab from seeing his course. Elijah, nerved by the Spirit and power of God, girded his coarse garment about him and ran before the chariot of Ahab, guiding his course to the entrance of the city. The prophet of God had humiliated Ahab before his people. He had slain his idolatrous priests, and now he wished to show to Israel that he acknowledged Ahab as his king. As an act of special homage he guided his chariot, running before it to the entrance of the gate of the city.

Here is a lesson for young men who profess to be servants of God, bearing His message, who are exalted in their own estimation. They can trace nothing remarkable in their experience, as could Elijah, yet they feel above performing duties which to them appear menial. They will not come down from their ministerial dignity to do needful service, fearing that they will be doing the work of a servant. All such should learn from the example of Elijah. His word locked the treasures of heaven, the dew and rain, from the earth three years. His word alone was the key to unlock heaven and bring showers of rain. He was honored of God as he offered his simple prayer in the presence of the king and the thousands of Israel, in answer to which fire flashed from heaven and kindled the fire upon the altar of sacrifice. His hand executed the judgment of God in slaying eight hundred and fifty priests of Baal; and yet, after the exhausting toil and most signal triumph of the day, he who could bring clouds and rain and fire from heaven was willing to perform the service of a menial and run before the chariot of Ahab in the darkness and in the wind and rain to serve the sovereign whom he had not feared to rebuke to his face because of his sins and crimes. The king passed within the gates. Elijah wrapped himself in his mantle and lay upon the bare earth.

ELIJAH IN DESPONDENCY

After Elijah had shown such undaunted courage in a contest between life and death, after he had triumphed over the king, the priests, and the people, we would naturally suppose that he would never give way to despondency or be awed into timidity.

After his first appearance to Ahab, denouncing upon him the judgments of God because of his and Israel's apostasy, God directed his course from Jezebel's power to a place of safety in the mountains, by the brook Cherith. There He honored Elijah by sending food to him morning and evening by an angel of heaven. Then, as the brook became dry, He sent him to the widow of Sarepta, and wrought a miracle daily to keep the widow's family and Elijah in food. After he had been blessed with evidences of such love and care from God, we would suppose that Elijah would never distrust Him. But the apostle tells us that he was a man of like passions as we, and subject, as we are, to temptations.

Ahab related to his wife the wonderful events of the day and the marvelous exhibitions of the power of God showing that Jehovah, the Creator of the heavens and the earth, was God; also that Elijah had slain the prophets of Baal. At this,

Jezebel, who was hardened in sin, became infuriated. Bold, defiant, and determined in her idolatry, she declared to Ahab that Elijah should not live.

That night a messenger aroused the weary prophet and delivered the word of Jezebel, given in the name of her pagan gods, that she would, in the presence of Israel, do to Elijah as he had done to the priests of Baal. Elijah should have met this threat and oath of Jezebel with an appeal for protection to the God of heaven, who had commissioned him to do the work he had done. He should have told the messenger that the God in whom he trusted would be his protector against the hatred and threats of Jezebel. But the faith and courage of Elijah seem to forsake him. He starts up from his slumbers bewildered. The rain is pouring from the heavens, and darkness is on every side. He loses sight of God and flees for his life as though the avenger of blood were close behind him. He leaves his servant behind him on the way, and in the morning he is far from the habitations of men, upon a dreary desert alone.

"And when he saw that, he arose, and went for his life, and came to Beersheba, which belongeth to Judah, and left his servant there. But he himself went a day's journey into the wilderness, and came and sat down under a juniper tree: and he requested for himself that he might die; and said, It is enough; now, O Lord, take away my life; for I am not better than my fathers. And as he lay and slept under a juniper tree, behold then an angel touched him, and said unto him, Arise and eat. And he looked, and, behold, there was a cake baken on the coals, and a cruse of water at his head. And he did eat and drink, and laid him down again. And the angel of the Lord came again the second time, and touched him, and said, Arise and eat; because the journey is too great for thee. And he arose, and did eat and drink, and went in the strength of that meat forty days and forty nights unto Horeb the mount of God. And he came thither unto a cave, and lodged there; and, behold, the word of the Lord came to him, and He said unto him, What doest thou here, Elijah?"

Elijah should have trusted in God, who had warned him when to flee and where to find an asylum from the hatred of Jezebel, secure from the diligent search of Ahab. The Lord had not warned him at this time to flee. He had not waited for the Lord to speak to him. He moved rashly. Had he waited with faith and patience, God would have shielded His servant and would have given him another signal victory in Israel by sending His judgments upon Jezebel.

Weary and prostrate, Elijah sits down to rest. He is discouraged and feels like murmuring. He says. "Now, O Lord, take away my life; for I am not better than my fathers." He feels that life is no more desirable. He expected after the signal display of God's power in the presence of Israel that they would be true and faithful to God. He expected that Jezebel would no longer have influence over the mind of Ahab and that there would be a general revolution in the kingdom of Israel. And when the threatening message from Jezebel was delivered to him, he forgot that God was the same all-powerful and pitiful God that He was when he prayed to Him for fire from heaven, and it came, and for rain, and it came. God had granted every request; yet Elijah is a fugitive far from the homes of men, and he wishes never to look upon man again.

How did God look upon His suffering servant? Did He forsake him because despondency and despair had seized him? Oh, no. Elijah was prostrated with discouragement. All day had he toiled without food. When he guided the chariot of Ahab, running before it to the gate of the city, he was strong of courage. He had high hopes that Israel as a nation would return to their allegiance to God and be reinstated in His favor. But the reaction which frequently follows elevation of faith and marked and glorious success, was pressing upon Elijah. He was exalted to Pisgah's top, to be humiliated to the lowliest valley in faith and feeling. But God's eye was still upon His servant. He loved him no less when he felt brokenhearted and forsaken of God and man than when, in answer to his prayer, fire flashed from heaven illuminating Carmel.

Those who have not borne weighty responsibilities, or who have not been accustomed to feel very deeply, cannot understand the feelings of Elijah and are not prepared to give him the tender sympathy he deserves. God knows and can read the heart's sore anguish under temptation and sore conflict.

As Elijah sleeps under the juniper tree, a soft touch and pleasant voice arouse him. He starts at once in his terror, as if to flee, as though the enemy who was in pursuit of his life had indeed found him. But in the pitying face of love bending over him he sees, not the face of an enemy, but of a friend. An angel has been sent with food from heaven to sustain the faithful servant of God. His voice says to Elijah: "Arise and eat." After Elijah had partaken of the refreshment prepared for him, he again slumbered. A second time the angel of God ministers to the wants of Elijah. He touches the weary, exhausted man, and in pitying tenderness says to him: "Arise and eat; because the journey is too great for thee." Elijah was strengthened and pursued his journey to Horeb. He was in a wilderness. At night he lodged in a cave for protection from the wild beasts.

Here God, through one of His angels, met with Elijah, and inquired of him: "What doest thou here, Elijah?" I sent you to the brook Cherith, I sent you to the widow of Sarepta, I sent you to Samaria with a message to Ahab, but who sent you this long journey into the wilderness? And what errand have you here? Elijah mourns out the bitterness of his soul to the Lord: "And he said, I have been very jealous for the Lord God of hosts: for the children of Israel have forsaken Thy covenant, thrown down Thine altars, and slain Thy prophets with the sword; and I, even I only, am left; and they seek my life, to take it away. And he said, Go forth, and stand upon the mount before the Lord. And, behold, the Lord passed by, and a great and strong wind rent the mountains, and brake in pieces the rocks before the Lord; but the Lord was not in the wind: and after the wind an earthquake; but the Lord was not in the earthquake: and after the earthquake a fire; but the Lord was not in the fire: and after the fire a still small voice. And it was so, when Elijah heard it, that he wrapped his face in his mantle, and went out, and stood in the entering in of the cave. And, behold, there came a voice unto him, and said, What doest thou here, Elijah? And he said, I have been very jealous for the Lord God of hosts: because the children of Israel have forsaken Thy covenant, thrown down Thine altars, and slain Thy prophets with the sword; and I, even I only, am left; and they seek my life, to take it away."

Then the Lord manifests Himself to Elijah, showing him that quiet trust and firm reliance upon God will ever find Him a present help in time of need.

I have been shown that my husband has erred in giving way to despondency and distrust of God. Time and again has God revealed Himself to him by remarkable evidences of His care, love, and power. But when he has seen that his interest and jealousy for God and His cause have not been understood or appreciated, he has at times given way to discouragement and to despair. God has given my husband and me a special and important work to do in His cause, to reprove and counsel His people. When we see our reproofs slighted and are repaid with hatred instead of sympathy, then we have frequently let go our faith and trust in the God of Israel; and, like Elijah, we have yielded to despondency and despair. Here has been the great error in the life of my husband—his becoming discouraged because his brethren have brought trials upon him instead of helping him. And when his brethren see, in the sadness and despondency of my husband, the effect of their unbelief and lack of sympathy, some are prepared to triumph over him and take advantage of his discouraged state, and feel that, after all, God cannot be with Brother White or he would not manifest weakness in this direction. I refer such to the work of Elijah and to his despondency and discouragements. Elijah, although a prophet of God, was a man subject to like passions as we are. We have the frailties of mortal feelings to contend with. But if we trust in God,

He will never leave nor forsake us. Under all circumstances we may have firm trust in God, that He will never leave nor forsake us while we preserve our integrity.

My husband may take courage in his affliction, that he has a pitying heavenly Father who reads the motives and understands the purposes of the soul. Those who stand in the front of the conflict, and who are reined up by the Spirit of God to do a special work for Him, will frequently feel a reaction when the pressure is removed, and despondency may sometimes press them hard and shake the most heroic faith and weaken the most steadfast minds. God understands all our weaknesses. He can pity and love when the hearts of men may be as hard as flint. To wait patiently and trust in God when everything looks dark is the lesson that my husband must learn more fully. God will not fail him in his integrity

MOSES AND AARON

Upon Mount Hor Aaron died and was buried. Moses, Aaron's brother, and Eleazar, his son, accompanied him to the mount. The painful duty was laid upon Moses to remove from his brother Aaron the sacerdotal robes and place them upon Eleazar, for God had said that he should succeed Aaron in the priesthood. Moses and Eleazar witnessed the death of Aaron, and Moses buried him in the mount. This scene upon Mount Hor carries our minds back to some of the most striking events in the life of Aaron.

Aaron was a man of amiable disposition, whom God selected to stand with Moses and speak for him; in short, to be mouthpiece for Moses. God might have chosen Aaron as leader; but He who is acquainted with hearts, who understands character, knew that Aaron was yielding and lacked moral courage to stand in defense of the right under all circumstances, irrespective of consequences. Aaron's desire to have the good will of the people sometimes led him to commit great wrongs. He too frequently yielded to their entreaties, and in so doing dishonored God. The same lack of firmness for the right in his family resulted in the death of two of his sons. Aaron was eminent for piety and usefulness, but he neglected to discipline his family. Rather than perform the task of requiring respect and reverence of his sons, he allowed them to follow their inclinations. He did not discipline them in self-denial, but yielded to their wishes. They were not disciplined to respect and reverence parental authority. The father was the proper ruler of his own family as long as he lived. His authority was not to cease, even after his children were grown up and had families of their own. God Himself was the monarch of the nation, and from the people He claimed obedience and honor.

The order and prosperity of the kingdom depended upon the good order of the church. And the prosperity, harmony, and order of the church depended upon the good order and thorough discipline of families. God punishes the unfaithfulness of parents, to whom He has entrusted the duty of maintaining the principles of parental government, which lie at the foundation of church discipline and the prosperity of the nation. One undisciplined child has frequently marred the peace and harmony of a church, and incited a nation to murmuring and rebellion. In a most solemn manner the Lord has enjoined upon children their duty to affectionately respect and honor their parents. And on the other hand He requires parents to train up their children and with unceasing diligence to educate them with regard to the claims of His law and to instruct them in the knowledge and fear of God. These injunctions which God laid upon the Jews with so much solemnity, rest with equal weight upon Christian parents. Those who neglect the light and instruction which God has given in His word in regard to training their children and commanding their households after them, will have a fearful account to settle. Aaron's criminal neglect to command the respect and reverence of his sons resulted in their death.

God distinguished Aaron by choosing him and his male posterity for the priesthood. His sons ministered in the sacred office. Nadab and Abihu failed to reverence the command of God to offer sacred fire upon their censers with the incense before Him. God had forbidden them, upon pain of death, to present the common fire before Him with the incense.

But here is seen the result of loose discipline. As these sons of Aaron had not been educated to respect and reverence the commands of their father, as they disregarded parental authority, they did not realize the necessity of explicitly following the requirements of God. When indulging their appetite for wine and while under its exciting stimulus, their reason was clouded, and they could not discern the difference between the sacred and the common. Contrary to God's express direction, they dishonored Him by offering common instead of sacred fire. God visited them with His wrath; fire went forth from His presence and destroyed them.

Aaron bore his severe affliction with patience and humble submission. Sorrow and keen agony wrung his soul. He was convicted of his neglect of duty. He was priest of the most high God, to make atonement for the sins of the people. He was priest of his household, yet he had been inclined to pass over the folly of his children. He had neglected his duty to train and educate them to obedience, self-denial, and reverence for parental authority. Through feelings of misplaced indulgence, he failed to mold their characters with high reverence for eternal things. Aaron did not see, any more than many Christian parents now see, that his misplaced love and the indulgence of his children in wrong was preparing them for the certain displeasure of God and for His wrath to break forth upon them to their destruction. While Aaron neglected to exercise his authority, the justice of God awakened against them. Aaron had to learn that his gentle remonstrance, without a firm exercise of parental restraint, and his imprudent tenderness toward his sons were cruelty in the extreme. God took the work of justice into His own hands and destroyed the sons of Aaron.

When God called for Moses to come up into the mount, it was six days before he was received into the cloud, into the immediate presence of God. The top of the mountain was all aglow with the glory of God. And yet even while the children of Israel had this glory in their very sight, unbelief was so natural to them that they began to murmur with discontent because Moses was absent. While the glory of God signified His sacred presence upon the mountain, and their leader was in close converse with God, they should have been sanctifying themselves by close searching of heart, humiliation, and godly fear. God had left Aaron and Hur to take the place of Moses. In his absence the people were to consult and advise with these men of God's appointment.

Here Aaron's deficiency as a leader or governor of Israel is seen. The people beset him to make them gods to go before them into Egypt. Here was an opportunity for Aaron to show his faith and unwavering confidence in God, and with firmness and decision to meet the proposition of the people. But his natural desire to please and to yield to the people led him to sacrifice the honor of God. He requested them to bring their ornaments to him, and he wrought out for them a golden calf and proclaimed before the people: "These be thy gods, O Israel, which brought thee up out of the land of Egypt." And to this senseless god he made an altar and proclaimed on the morrow a feast to the Lord. All restraint seemed to be removed from the people. They offered burnt offerings to the golden calf, and a spirit of levity took possession of them. They indulged in shameful rioting and drunkenness; they ate, they drank, and rose up to play.

A few weeks only had passed since they had made a solemn covenant with God to obey His voice. They had listened to the words of God's law, spoken in awful grandeur from Sinai's mount, amid thunderings and lightnings and earthquakes. They had heard the declaration from the lips of God Himself: "I am the Lord thy God, which have brought thee out of the land of Egypt, out of the house of bondage. Thou shalt have no other gods before Me. Thou shalt not make unto thee any graven image, or any likeness of anything that is in heaven above, or that is in the earth beneath, or that is in the water under the earth: thou shalt not bow down thyself to them, nor serve them: for I the Lord thy God am a jealous God, visiting the iniquity of the fathers upon the children unto the third and fourth generation of them that hate Me; and showing mercy unto thousands of them that love Me, and keep My commandments."

Aaron and also his sons had been exalted by being called into the mount to there witness the glory of God. "And they saw the God of Israel: and there was under His feet as it were a paved work of a sapphire stone, and as it were the body of heaven in His clearness."

God had appointed Nadab and Abihu to a most sacred work, therefore He honored them in a most wonderful manner. He gave them a view of His excellent glory, that the scenes they should witness in the mount would abide with them and the better qualify them to minister in His service and render to Him that exalted honor and reverence before the people which would give them clearer conceptions of His character and awaken in them due obedience and reverence for all His requirements.

Before Moses left his people for the mount, he read to them the words of the covenant that God had made with them, and they with one voice answered: "All that the Lord hath said will we do, and be obedient." How great must have been the sin of Aaron, how aggravated in the sight of God!

While Moses was receiving the law of God in the mount, the Lord informed him of the sin of rebellious Israel and requested him to let them go, that He might destroy them. But Moses pleaded before God for the people. Although Moses was the meekest man that lived, yet when the interests of the people over whom God had appointed him as leader were at stake, he lost his natural timidity and with singular persistency and wonderful boldness pleaded with God for Israel. He would not consent that God should destroy His people, although God promised that in their destruction He would exalt Moses and raise up a better people than Israel.

Moses prevailed. God granted his earnest petition not to blot out His people. Moses took the tables of the covenant, the law of Ten Commandments, and descended from the mount. The boisterous, drunken revelry of the children of Israel reached his ears long before he came to the camp. When he saw their idolatry, and that they had broken in a most marked manner the words of the covenant, he became overwhelmed with grief and indignation at their base idolatry. Confusion and shame on their account took possession of him, and he there threw down the tables and broke them. As they had broken their covenant with God, Moses, in breaking the tables, signified to them that so also God had broken His covenant with them. The tables whereupon was written the law of God were broken.

Aaron, with his amiable disposition, so very mild and pleasing, sought to conciliate Moses, as though no very great sin had been committed by the people, over which he should feel thus deeply. Moses asked in anger: "What did this people unto thee, that thou hast brought so great a sin upon them? And Aaron said, Let not the anger of my lord wax hot: thou knowest the people, that they are set on mischief. For they said unto me, Make us gods, which shall go before us: for as for this Moses, the man that brought us up out of the land of Egypt, we wot not what is become of him. And I said unto them, Whosoever hath any gold, let them break it off. So they gave it me: then I cast it into the fire, and there came out this calf." Aaron would have Moses think that some wonderful miracle had transformed their golden ornaments into the shape of a calf. He did not relate to Moses that he, with other workmen, had wrought out this image.

Aaron had thought that Moses had been too unyielding to the wishes of the people. He thought that if Moses had been less firm, less decided at times, and that if he had made a compromise with the people and gratified their wishes, he would have had less trouble, and there would have been more peace and harmony in the camp of Israel. He, therefore, had been trying this new policy. He carried out his natural temperament by yielding to the wishes of the people, to save dissatisfaction and preserve their good will, and thereby prevent a rebellion, which he thought would certainly come if he did not yield to their wishes. But had Aaron stood unwaveringly for God; had he met the intimation of the people for him to make them gods to go before them to Egypt with the just indignation and horror that their proposition deserved; had he cited them to the terrors of Sinai, where God had spoken His law in such glory and majesty; had he reminded them of their solemn covenant with God to obey all that He should command them; had he told them that he would not, at the sacrifice of his life, yield to their entreaties, he would have had influence with the people to prevent a terrible apostasy. But when, in the absence of Moses, his influence was required to be used in the right direction, when he should have stood as firm and unyielding as did Moses, to prevent the people from pursuing a course of sin, his influence was exerted on the wrong side. He was powerless to make his influence felt in vindication of God's honor in keeping His holy law. But on the wrong side he swayed a powerful influence. He directed, and the people obeyed.

When Aaron took the first step in the wrong direction, the spirit which had actuated the people imbued him, and he took the lead and directed as a general, and the people were singularly obedient. Here Aaron gave decided sanction to the most aggravated sins, because it was less difficult than to stand in vindication of the right. When he swerved from his integrity in giving sanction to the people in their sins he seemed inspired with a decision, earnestness, and zeal new to him. His timidity seemed suddenly to disappear. With a zeal that he had never manifested in standing in defense of the honor of God against wrong he seized the instruments to work out the gold into the image of a calf. He ordered an altar to be built, and, with assurance worthy of a better cause, he proclaimed to the people that on the morrow there would be a feast to the Lord. The trumpeters took the word from the mouth of Aaron and sounded the proclamation from company to company of the armies of Israel.

Aaron's calm assurance in a wrong course gave him greater influence with the people than Moses could have had in leading them in a right course and in subduing their rebellion. What terrible spiritual blindness had come upon Aaron that he should put light for darkness and darkness for light! What presumption in him to proclaim a feast to the Lord over their idolatrous worship of a golden image! Here is seen the power that Satan has over minds that are not fully controlled by the Spirit of God. Satan had set up his banner in the midst of Israel, and it was exalted as the banner of God.

"These," said Aaron without hesitation or shame, "be thy gods, O Israel, which brought thee up out of the land of Egypt." Aaron influenced the children of Israel to go to greater lengths in idolatry than had entered their minds. They were no longer troubled lest the burning glory like flaming fire upon the mount had consumed their leader. They thought they had a general who just suited them, and they were ready to do anything that he suggested. They sacrificed to their golden god; they offered peace offerings, and gave themselves up to pleasure, rioting, and drunkenness. They were then decided in their own minds that it was not because they were wrong that they had so much trouble in the wilderness; but the difficulty, after all, was with their leader. He was not the right kind of man. He was too unyielding and kept their sins continually before them, warning, reproving, and threatening them with God's displeasure. A new order of things had come, and they were pleased with Aaron and pleased with themselves. They thought: If Moses had only been as amiable and mild as Aaron, what peace and harmony would have prevailed in the camp of Israel! They cared not now whether Moses ever came down from the mount or not.

When Moses saw the idolatry of Israel and his indignation

was so aroused at their shameful forgetfulness of God that he threw down the tables of stone and broke them, Aaron stood meekly by, bearing the censure of Moses with commendable patience. The people were charmed with Aaron's lovely spirit and were disgusted with the rashness of Moses. But God seeth not as man sees. He condemned not the ardor and indignation of Moses against the base apostasy of Israel.

The true general then takes his position for God. He has come direct from the presence of the Lord, where he pleaded with Him to turn away His wrath from His erring people. Now he has another work to do, as God's minister, to vindicate His honor before the people, and let them see that sin is sin, and righteousness is righteousness. He has a work to do to counteract the terrible influence of Aaron. "Then Moses stood in the gate of the camp, and said, Who is on the Lord's side? let him come unto me. And all the sons of Levi gathered themselves together unto him. And he said unto them, Thus saith the Lord God of Israel, put *every man* his sword by his side, and go in and out from gate to gate throughout the camp, and slay every man his brother, and every man his companion, and every man his neighbor. And the children of Levi did according to the word of Moses: and there fell of the people that day about three thousand men. For Moses had said, Consecrate yourselves today to the Lord, even every man upon his son, and upon his brother, that He may bestow upon you a blessing this day."

Here Moses defines genuine consecration as obedience to God, to stand in vindication of the right and to show a readiness to carry out the purpose of God in the most unpleasant duties, showing that the claims of God are higher than the claims of friends or the lives of the nearest relatives. The sons of Levi consecrated themselves to God to execute His justice against crime and sin.

Aaron and Moses both sinned in not giving glory and honor to God at the waters of Meribah. They were both wearied and provoked with the continual complaining of Israel, and, at a time when God was to mercifully display His glory to the people, to soften and subdue their hearts and lead them to repentance, Moses and Aaron claimed the power of opening the rock for them. "Hear now, ye rebels; must we fetch you water out of this rock?" Here was a golden opportunity to sanctify the Lord in the midst of them, to show them the long-suffering of God and His tender pity for them. They had murmured against Moses and Aaron because they could not find water. Moses and Aaron took these murmurings as a great trial and dishonor to themselves, forgetting that it was God whom the people were grieving. It was God whom they were sinning against and dishonoring, not those who were appointed of God to carry out His purpose. They were insulting their best Friend in charging their calamities upon Moses and Aaron; they were murmuring at God's providence.

This sin of these noble leaders was great. Their lives might have been illustrious to the close. They had been greatly exalted and honored; yet God does not excuse sin in those in exalted positions any sooner than He does in those in more humble positions. Many professed Christians look upon men who do not reprove and condemn wrong, as men of piety and Christians indeed, while they think that those who stand boldly in defense of the right, and will not yield their integrity to unconsecrated influences, lack piety and a Christian spirit.

Those who stand in defense of the honor of God and maintain the purity of truth at any cost will have manifold trials, as did our Saviour in the wilderness of temptation. While those who have yielding temperaments, who have not courage to condemn wrong, but keep silent when their influence is needed to stand in defense of the right against any pressure, may avoid many heartaches and escape many perplexities, they will also lose a very rich reward, if not their own souls. Those who are in harmony with God, and who through faith in Him receive strength to resist wrong and stand in defense of the right, will always have severe conflicts and will frequently have to stand almost alone. But precious victories will be theirs while they make God their dependence. His grace will be their strength. Their moral sensibility will be keen and clear, and their moral powers will be able to withstand wrong influences. Their integrity, like that of Moses, will be of the purest character.

The mild and yielding spirit of Aaron, and his desire to please the people, blinded his eyes to their sins and to the enormity of the crime that he was sanctioning. His course in giving influence to wrong and sin in Israel cost the lives of three thousand men. In what contrast with this is the course of Moses. After he had evidenced to the people that they could not trifle with God with impunity; after he had shown them the just displeasure of God because of their sins, by giving the terrible decree to slay friends or relatives who persisted in their apostasy; after the work of justice to turn away the wrath of God, irrespective of their feelings of sympathy for loved friends and relatives who continued obstinate in their rebellion—after this, Moses was prepared for another work. He proved who was the true friend of God and the friend of the people.

"And it came to pass on the morrow, that Moses said unto the people, Ye have sinned a great sin: and now I will go up unto the Lord; peradventure I shall make an atonement for your sin. And Moses returned unto the Lord and said, Oh, this people have sinned a great sin, and have made them gods of gold. Yet now, if Thou wilt forgive their sin—; and if not, blot me, I pray Thee, out of Thy book which Thou has written. And the Lord said unto Moses, Whosoever hath sinned against Me, him will I blot out of My book. Therefore now go, lead the people unto the place of which I have spoken unto thee: behold, Mine Angel shall go before thee: nevertheless in the day when I visit I will visit their sin upon them. And the Lord plagued the people, because they made the calf, which Aaron made."

Moses supplicated God in behalf of sinning Israel. He did not try to lessen their sin before God; he did not excuse them in their sin. He frankly acknowledged that they had sinned a great sin and had made them gods of gold. Then he loses his timidity, and the interest of Israel is so closely interwoven with his life that he comes with boldness to God and prays for Him to forgive His people. If their sin, he pleads, is so great that God cannot forgive them, if their names must be blotted from His book, he prays the Lord to blot out his name also. When the Lord renewed His promise to Moses, that His Angel should go before him in leading the people to the Promised Land, Moses knew that his request was granted. But the Lord assured Moses that if He was provoked to visit the people for their transgressions, He would surely punish them for this grievous sin also. But if they were henceforth obedient, He would blot this great sin out of His book.

TO A YOUNG MINISTER AND HIS WIFE

Dear Brother and Sister A: For some months I have felt that it was time to write to you some things which the Lord was pleased to show me in regard to you several years ago. Your cases were shown me in connection with those of others who had a work to do for themselves in order to be fitted for the work of presenting the truth. I was shown that you were both deficient in essential qualifications and that if these are not obtained your usefulness and the salvation of your own souls will be endangered. You have some faults in your characters which it is very important that you should correct. If you neglect to take hold of the work resolutely and in earnest, these wrongs will increase upon you and will greatly cripple your influence in the cause and work of God, and will finally result in your being separated from the work of preaching the truth, which you love so well.

In the vision given me for B, I was shown that he had a very unfortunate stamp of character. He had not been disciplined, and his temper had not been subdued. He had been permitted to have his own head and to do very much as he pleased. He was greatly deficient in reverence for God and man. He had a strong, unsubmissive spirit and but a very faint idea of proper gratitude to those who were doing their utmost for him. He was extremely selfish.

I was shown that independence, a firm, set, unyielding will, a lack of reverence and due respect for others, selfishness and too great self-confidence, mark the character of Sister A. If she does not watch closely and overcome these defects in her character she will surely fail of sitting with Christ in His throne.

In regard to Brother A, I was shown that many of the things mentioned in the testimony to B applied to you. I was pointed back to your past life. I saw that from a child you have been self-confident, headstrong, and self-willed, and have followed your own mind. You have an independent spirit, and it has been very difficult for you to yield to anyone. When it was your duty to yield your way and your wishes to others, you would carry matters out in your own rash way. You have felt that you were fully competent to think and act for yourself independently. The truth of God has been accepted and loved by you and has done much for you, but it has not wrought all that transformation necessary for the perfection of Christian character. When you first started out to labor in the cause of God you felt more humble and were willing to be advised and counseled. But as you began to be successful in a degree, your self-confidence increased, and you were less humble and became more independent.

As you looked at the work of Brother and Sister White you thought that you could see where you could have done better than they. Feelings have been cherished in your heart against them. You were naturally skeptical, infidel, in your feelings. As you have seen their work, and heard the reproofs given to those who were wrong, you have questioned how you would bear such plain testimony. You decided that you could not receive it, and began to brace yourself against the manner of their laboring, and thus opened a door in your heart for suspicion, doubt, and jealousy of them and their work.

You became prejudiced in your feelings against their labor. You watched, and listened, and gathered up all you could, and surmised much. Because God had given you a measure of success, you began to place your short experience and labors upon a level with Brother White's labors. You flattered yourself that, were you in his place, you could do very much better than he. You began to grow large in your own eyes. You thought your knowledge far more extensive and valuable than it was. Had you had one-hundredth part of the experience in real labor, care, perplexity, and burden bearing in this cause that Brother White has had, you would be better able to understand his work and be better prepared to sympathize with him in his labors, rather than to murmur and be suspicious and jealous of him.

In regard to your own post of labor you should be very jealous of yourself lest you fail to do your work to God's acceptance, and lest you fail to honor the cause of truth in your labors. You should, in humiliation of soul, feel: "Who is sufficient for these things?" The reason why both of you are so ready to question and surmise in regard to Brother White's work is because you know so little about it. So few real burdens have ever pressed upon your souls, so little real anguish for the cause of God has touched your hearts, so little perplexity and real distress have you borne for others, that you are no more prepared to appreciate his work than is a ten-year-old boy the care, anxiety, and wearisome toil of his burdened father. The boy may pass along joyous in spirit because he has not the experience of the burdened, careworn father. He may wonder at the fears and anxieties of the father, which look needless to him; but when years of experience shall be added to his life, when he takes hold of and bears its real burdens, then he may look back to his father's life and understand that which was mysterious to him in his boyhood; for bitter experience has given him knowledge.

I was shown that you are in danger of getting above the

simplicity of the work and of placing yourself upon the pinnacle. You feel that you need no reproof and counsel, and the language of your heart is: "I am capable of judging, discriminating, and determining between right and wrong. I will not have my rights infringed upon. No one shall dictate to me. I am capable of forming my own plans of action. I am as good as anybody. God is with me and gives me success in my efforts. Who has authority to interfere with me?" These words I heard you utter, as your case was passing before me in vision, not to any person, but as if in conversation with yourself. My attending angel repeated these words, as he pointed to you both: "Except ye be converted, and become as little children, ye shall not enter into the kingdom of heaven. Whosoever shall humble himself as this little child, the same is greatest in the kingdom of heaven."

I saw that the strength of the children of God is in their humility. When they are little in their own eyes, Jesus will be to them their strength and their righteousness, and God will prosper their labors. I was shown that God would prove Brother A. He would give him a measure of prosperity; and if he would bear the test, if he would turn the blessings of God to good account, not taking honor to himself and not becoming lifted up, selfish, and self-confident, the Lord would continue His blessings for the sake of His cause and for His own glory.

I saw, Brother A, that you were in the greatest danger of becoming lifted up, self-righteous, self-sufficient, and feeling that you are rich and in need of nothing. Unless you guard yourself upon these points, the Lord will allow you to go on until you make your weakness apparent to all. You will be brought into positions where you will be sorely tempted if others do not regard you in as exalted a light as you estimate yourself and your ability. I was shown that you were poorly prepared to bear much prosperity and a great amount of success. A thorough conversion alone will do the work necessary to be done in your case.

I have been shown that both of you are naturally selfish. You are in constant danger, unless guarded, of thinking and acting in reference to yourselves. You will lay your plans for your own accommodation, without taking into account how much you may inconvenience others. You are inclined to carry out your ideas and plans without regarding the plans and respecting the views or feelings of others. Both of you should cultivate reverence and respect for others.

Brother A, you have considered that your work was of too great importance for you to come down to engage in household duties. You have not a love for these requirements. You neglected them in your younger days. But these small duties which you neglect are essential to the formation of a well-developed character.

I have been shown that our ministers generally are deficient in making themselves useful in the families where they are entertained. Some devote their minds to study because they love this employment. They do not feel that it is a duty which God enjoins upon ministers to make themselves a blessing in the families which they visit, but many give their minds to books and shut themselves away from the family and do not converse with them upon the subjects of truth. The religious interests in the family are scarcely mentioned. This is all wrong. Ministers who have not the burden and care of the publishing interest upon them, and who have not the perplexities and numerous cares of all the churches, should not feel that their labor is excessively hard. They should feel the deepest interest in the families they visit; they should not feel that they are to be petted and waited upon while they give nothing in return. There is an obligation resting upon Christian families to entertain the ministers of Christ, and there is also a duty resting upon ministers who receive the hospitality of Christian friends to feel under mutual obligation to bear their own burdens as far as possible and not be a tax to their friends. Many ministers entertain the idea that they must be especially favored and waited upon, and they are frequently injured and their usefulness crippled by being treated as pets.

Brother and Sister A, while among your brethren you have too frequently made it a practice to make arrangements agreeable to yourselves and to take a course to gather attention to yourselves, without considering the convenience or inconvenience of others. You are in danger of making yourselves a center. You have received the attention and consideration of others when, for the good of your own souls as well as for the benefit of others, you should have devoted more attention to those you visited. Such a course would have given you far greater influence, and you would have been blessed in winning more souls to the truth.

Brother A, you have ability to present the truth to others. You have an investigative mind, but there are serious defects in your character, which I have mentioned and which must be overcome. You neglect many of the little courtesies of life because you think so much of yourself that you do not realize that these little attentions are required of you. God would not have you burden others while you neglect to see and do the things that someone must do. It does not detract from the dignity of a gospel minister to bring in wood and water when needed or to exercise by doing necessary work in the family where he is entertained. In not seeing these little important duties and improving the opportunity to do them, he deprives himself of real blessings and also deprives others of the good that it is their privilege to receive from him.

Some of our ministers do not have an amount of physical exercise proportionate to the taxation of the mind. As the result they are suffering from debility. There is no good reason why the health of ministers who have to perform only the ordinary duties devolving upon the minister should fail. Their minds are not constantly burdened with perplexing cares and heavy responsibilities in regard to the important institutions among us. I saw that there is no real reason why they should fail in this important period of the cause and work if they will pay due regard to the light that God has given them in regard to how to labor and how to exercise, and will give proper attention to their diet.

Some of our ministers eat very heartily and then do not exercise sufficiently to work off the waste matter which accumulates in the system. They will eat and then spend most of their time sitting down, reading, studying, or writing, when a share of their time should be devoted to systematic physical labor. Our preachers will certainly break down in health unless they are more careful not to overload the stomach by too great a quantity of even healthful food. I saw that you, Brother and Sister A, were both in danger on this point. Overeating prevents the free flow of thought and words, and that intensity of feeling which is so necessary in order to impress the truth upon the heart of the hearer. The indulgence of appetite beclouds and fetters the mind, and blunts the holy emotions of the soul. The mental and moral powers of some of our preachers are enfeebled by improper eating and lack of physical exercise. Those who crave great quantities of food should not indulge their appetite, but should practice self-denial and retain the blessings of active muscles and unoppressed brains. Overeating stupefies the entire being by diverting the energies from the other organs to do the work of the stomach.

The failure of our ministers to exercise all the organs of the body proportionately causes some organs to become worn, while others are weak from inaction. If wear is left to come almost exclusively upon one organ or set of muscles, the one most used must become overwearied and greatly weakened. Each faculty of the mind, and each muscle, has its distinctive office, and all are required to be equally exercised in order to become properly developed and to retain healthful vigor. Each organ has its work to do in the living organism. Every wheel in the machinery must be a living, active, working wheel. All the faculties have a bearing upon one another, and all need to be exercised in order to be properly developed.

Brother and Sister A, neither of you enjoy physical, domestic labor. Both of you need to cultivate a love for the practical duties of life. This education is necessary for your health and will increase your usefulness. You think too much of what you eat. You should not touch those things which will give a poor quality of blood; both of you have scrofula.

Brother A, your love for reading and your dislike for physical taxation, while talking and exercising your throat, make you liable to disease of the throat and lungs. You should be guarded and should not speak hurriedly, rattling off what you have to say as though you had a lesson to repeat. You should not let the labor come upon the upper portion of the vocal organs, for this will constantly wear and irritate them, and will lay the foundation for disease. The action should come upon the abdominal muscles. The lungs and throat should be the channel, but should not do all the work.

I was shown that the manner in which you and your wife eat will bring disease, which, when once fastened upon you, will not be easily overcome. You may both bear up for years and not show any special signs of breaking, but cause will be followed by the sure results. God will not work a miracle for either of you to preserve your health and life. You must eat and study and work understandingly, following enlightened conscience. Our preachers should all be sincere, genuine health reformers, not merely adopting the reforms because others do, but from principle, in obedience to the word of God. God has given us great light upon the health reform, which He requires us all to respect. He does not send light to be rejected or disregarded by His people without their suffering the consequences.

PIONEERS IN THE CAUSE

I was shown that neither of you really know yourselves. If God should let the enemy loose upon you, as He did upon His servant Job, He would not find in you that spirit of steadfast integrity that He found in Job, but a spirit of murmuring and of unbelief. Had you been situated at Battle Creek during my husband's illness, at the time of the trial of our brethren and sisters there, when Satan had special power upon them, both of you would have drunk deep of their spirit of jealousy and faultfinding. You would have been among the number, as zealous as the rest, to make a diseased, careworn man, a paralytic, an offender for a word.

You are inclined to offset your deficiencies by magnifying and dwelling upon the wrongs you suppose exist in Brother and Sister White; and had you an opportunity, as those had in Battle Creek, you would venture to go to greater lengths than did some of them in their wicked crusade against us, for you have less faith and less reverence than some of them had, and would be less inclined to respect our work and our calling.

I was shown that, notwithstanding you have before you the sad experience and example of others who have become disaffected and have murmured and been faultfinding and jealous of us, you would fail to be warned by their example, and God would test your fidelity and reveal the secrets of your hearts. Your distrust, suspicions, and jealousies would be revealed, and your weaknesses exposed, that you might see them and understand yourselves, if you would.

I saw you listening to the conversation of men and women, and saw that you were only too pleased to gather up their views and impressions that were detrimental to our labors. Some found fault with one thing, and some with another, as did the murmurers among the children of Israel when Moses was their leader. Some were censuring our course, saying that we were not as conservative as we ought to be; we did not seek to please the people as we might; we talked too plainly; we reproved too sharply. Some were talking in regard to Sister White's dress, picking at straws. Others were expressing dissatisfaction with the course that Brother White pursued, and remarks were passing from one to another, questioning their course and finding fault. An angel stood before these persons, unseen by them, busily writing their words in the book which is to be opened to the view of God and angels.

Some are eagerly watching for something to condemn in

Brother and Sister White, who have grown gray in their service in the cause of God. Some express their views that the testimony of Sister White cannot be reliable. This is all that many unconsecrated ones want. The testimonies of reproof have checked their vanity and pride; but if they dared, they would go to almost any length in fashion and pride. God will give all such an opportunity to prove themselves and to develop their true characters.

Some years ago I saw that we would yet have to meet the same spirit which rose at Paris, Maine, and which has never been thoroughly cured. It has slumbered, but it is not dead. From time to time this spirit of determined murmuring and rebellion has cropped out in different individuals who have at some time been leavened with this wicked spirit which has followed us for years. Sister A, this spirit has been cherished by you to some extent, and has had an influence to mold your views and feelings. Sanctimonious infidelity has been gradually growing in the mind of C, and it is not now easy, even for her, to get rid of it. This same determined spirit which held D and others in Maine in a fanatical delusion so long, against every influence to lead them to the truth, has had a powerful, deceptive influence over E's mind in _____, and the same influence has affected you. You were of that calm, determined, unyielding temperament that the enemy could affect, and the same results, only in a greater degree, will attend your influence, if wrong, as attended that of Sister E.

Feelings of suspicion, jealousy, and unbelief have for years been gaining power upon your mind. You have a hatred for reproof. You are very sensitive, and your sympathies arise at once for anyone who is reproved. This is not a sanctified feeling, and is not prompted by the Spirit of God. Brother and Sister A, I was shown that when this spirit of faultfinding and murmuring should be developed in you, when it should be manifested and the leaven of dissatisfaction, jealousy, and unbelief which has cursed the life of E and her husband should appear, we would have a work to do to meet it decidedly and give that spirit no quarter; and that, until this should be developed, I should keep silent, for there was a time to speak and a time to keep silent. I saw that, should apparent prosperity attend the labors of Brother A, unless he was a thoroughly converted man he would be in danger of losing his soul. He does not have becoming respect for the position and labors of others; he considers himself second to none.

I was shown that temptations will continually increase in regard to the labors of Brother and Sister White. Our work is a peculiar work, it is different in character from that of any others who labor in the field. God does not call ministers who have only to labor in word and doctrine to do our work, neither does He call us to do only their work. We each have, in some respects, a distinct work. God has been pleased to open to me the secrets of the inner life and the hidden sins of His people. The unpleasant duty has been laid upon me to reprove wrongs and to reveal hidden sins. When I have been compelled by the Spirit of God to reprove sins that others did not know existed, it has stirred up the natural feelings in the hearts of the unsanctified. While some have humbled their hearts before God, and with repentance and confession have forsaken their sins, others have felt a spirit of hatred rise in their hearts. Their pride has been hurt when their course has been reproved. They entertain the thought that it is Sister White who is hurting them, instead of feeling grateful to God that He has in mercy spoken to them through His humble instrument, to show them their dangers and their sins, that they may put them away before it shall be too late for wrongs to be righted.

Some are ready to inquire: Who told Sister White these things? They have even put the question to me: Did anyone tell you these things? I could answer them: Yes; yes, the angel of God has spoken to me. But what they mean is: Have the brethren and sisters been exposing their faults? For the future, I shall not belittle the testimonies that God has given me, to make explanations to try to satisfy such narrow minds, but shall treat all such questions as an insult to the Spirit of God. God has seen fit to thrust me into positions in which He has not placed any other one in our ranks. He has laid upon me burdens of reproof that He has not given to any other one. My husband has stood by my side to sustain the testimonies and to give his voice in union with the testimony of reproof. He has been compelled to take a decided stand to press back the unbelief and rebellion which has been bold and defiant, and which would break down any testimony that I might bear, because the ones reproved were cut and felt deeply over the reproof given. This is exactly as God designed. He meant that they should feel. It was necessary that they should feel before their proud hearts would yield up their sins and they would cleanse their hearts and lives from all iniquity.

In every advance move that God has led us to make, in every step gained by God's people, there have been ready tools of Satan among us, to stand back and suggest doubts and unbelief, and to throw obstacles in our way, to weaken our faith and courage. We have had to stand like warriors, ready to press and fight our way through the opposition raised. This has made our work tenfold harder than it otherwise would have been. We have had to stand as firm and unyielding as a rock. This firmness has been interpreted to be hardheartedness and willfulness. God never designed that we should swerve, first to the right and then to the left, to gratify the minds of unconsecrated brethren. He designed that our course should be straightforward. One and another have come to us, professing to have a great burden for us to have us go this way or that, contrary to the light that God has given us. What if we had followed these false lights and fanatical impressions? Surely our people should not then put confidence in us. We have had to set our faces as flints for the right and then press on to work and duty.

Some among us have been ever ready to carry matters to extremes, to overreach the mark. They seem to be without an anchor. Such have greatly injured the cause of truth. There are others who seem never to have a position where they can stand firmly and surely, ready to battle if need be when God calls for faithful soldiers to be found at the post of duty. There are those who will not make a charge upon the enemy when required of God to do so. They will do nothing until others have fought the battle and gained the victory for them, and then they are ready to share the spoils. How much can God count upon such soldiers? They are accounted as cowards in His cause.

This class, I saw, gained no experience for themselves in regard to warfare against sin and Satan. They were more inclined to fight against the faithful soldiers of Christ than against Satan and his host. Had they girded on the armor and pressed into the battle, they would have gained a valuable experience which it was their privilege to have. But they had no courage to contend for the right, to venture something in the warfare, and to learn how to attack Satan and take his strongholds. Some have no idea of running any risk or venturing anything themselves. But somebody must venture; someone must run risks in this cause. Those who will not venture and expose themselves to censure will stand all prepared to watch those who do bear responsibilities, and will be ready, if there is a semblance of chance, to find fault with them and injure them if they can. This has been the experience of Brother and Sister White in their labors. Satan and his host have been arrayed against them, but these were not all; when those who should have stood by them in the warfare have seen them overburdened and pressed beyond measure, they have stood prepared to join Satan in his work to discourage and weaken them, and, if possible, drive them from the field.

Brother and Sister A, I have been shown that as you have traveled you have been looked up to and highly esteemed, and treated with greater respect and deference than was for your good. It is not natural for you to treat with like respect those who have borne the burdens which God has laid upon them in His cause and work. Both of you love your ease. You are not inclined to be turned out of your course or to inconvenience yourselves. You desire to have things bend to your convenience. You have large self-esteem and exalted opinions of your acquirements. You have not had the perplexing cares and burdens to bear, and the important decisions to make which involved the interests of God's cause, that have fallen to the lot of my husband. God has made him a counselor to His people, to advise and counsel such young men as yourself, as children in the truth. And when you take that humble position which a true sense of your real state will lead you to take, you will be willing to be counseled. It is because of the few responsibilities you have borne that you do not understand why Brother White should feel more deeply than you. There is just this difference between you and him in this matter. He has invested thirty of the best years of his life to the cause of God, while you have had but few years of experience and have had comparatively nothing of the hardships to meet that he has had.

After those who led out in this work have labored hard to prepare the truth and bring the work up ready to your hand, you embrace it and go out to labor, presenting the precious arguments which others, with inexpressible anxiety, have searched out for you. While you are amply provided for in point of means, your weekly wages sure, leaving you no reason for care or anxiety in this direction, these pioneers of the cause suffered deprivations of every kind. They had no assurance of anything. They were dependent upon God and upon the few truehearted ones who received their labors. While you have sympathizing brethren to sustain you and fully appreciate your labors, the first laborers in this work had but very few to stand by them. All could be counted in a few minutes. We knew what it was to go hungry for want of food and to suffer with cold for the want of suitable clothing. We have traveled all night by private conveyance to visit the brethren, because we had no means with which to defray the expenses of hotel fare. We traveled miles on foot, time and again, because we had no money to hire a carriage. Oh, how precious was the truth to us! how valuable souls purchased by the blood of Christ!

We have no complaints to make of our sufferings in those days of close want and perplexity, which made the exercise of faith necessary. They were the happiest days of our lives. There we learned the simplicity of faith. There, while in affliction we tested and proved the Lord. He was our consolation. He was to us like the shadow of a great rock in a weary land. It is unfortunate for you, my brother, and for our young ministers generally, that you and they have not had a similar experience in privation, in trial, and in need; for such an experience would be worth to you more than houses or lands, gold or silver.

When we refer to our past experience of excessive labor and want, and of laboring with our hands to support ourselves and to publish the truth at the very commencement of the work, some of our young preachers of but few years' experience in the work seem to be annoyed and charge us with boasting of our own works. The reason of this is that their own lives have been so free from wearing care, want, and self-sacrifice that they know not how to sympathize with us, and the contrast is not agreeable to their feelings. To have presented before them the experience of others which is in such wide contrast with their own course does not make their labors appear in so favorable a light as they would have them.

When we commenced this work we were both in feeble health. My husband was a dyspeptic; yet three times a day, in faith, we made our supplications to God for strength. My husband went into the hayfield with his scythe, and, in the strength that God gave him in answer to our earliest prayers, he there earned, by mowing, means with which to purchase us neat, plain clothing and to pay our fare to a distant state to present the truth to our brethren.

We have a right to refer to the past, as did the apostle Paul.

"And when I was present with you, and wanted, I was chargeable to no man: for that which was lacking to me the brethren which came from Macedonia supplied: and in all things I have kept myself from being burdensome unto you, and so will I keep myself. As the truth of Christ is in me, no man shall stop me of this boasting in the regions of Achaia." In referring to our past experience, we are carrying out the exhortation of the apostle to the Hebrews: "But call to remembrance the former days, in which, after ye were illuminated, ye endured a great fight of afflictions; partly, whilst ye were made a gazingstock both by reproaches and afflictions; and partly, whilst ye became companions of them that were so used."

Our lives are interwoven with the cause of God. We have no separate interest aside from this work. And when we see the advancement that the cause has made from a very small beginning, coming up slowly yet surely to strength and prosperity; as we see the success of the cause in which we have toiled, and suffered, and nearly sacrificed our lives, who shall prevent or forbid our boasting in God? Our experience in this cause is valuable to us. We have invested everything in it.

Moses was the meekest man that lived; yet, because of the murmurings of the children of Israel, he was repeatedly compelled to bring up their course of sin after leaving Egypt and to vindicate his course as their leader. Just before leaving Israel, when he was about to die, he rehearsed before them their course of rebellion and murmuring since they had left Egypt, and how his interest and love for them had led him to plead with God in their behalf. He related to them how he had earnestly entreated of the Lord to let him pass over Jordan into the Promised Land; "but the Lord was wroth with me for your sakes, and would not hear me." Moses presented before them their sins, and said to them: "Ye have been rebellious against the Lord from the day that I knew you." He related to them how many times he had pleaded with God and humbled his soul in anguish because of their sins.

It was the design of God that Moses should frequently remind Israel of their transgressions and rebellion, that they might humble their hearts before God in view of their sins. The Lord would not have them forget the errors and sins which had provoked His anger against them. The rehearsal of their transgressions, and of the mercies and goodness of God to them, which they had not appreciated, was not agreeable to their feelings. Nevertheless, God directed that this should be done.

I have been shown that young men like you, who have had but a few years of imperfect experience in the cause of present truth, are not the ones whom God will trust to bear weighty responsibilities and to lead out in this work. Such should manifest a delicacy in taking positions which will conflict with the judgment and opinions of those of mature experience, whose lives have been interwoven with the cause of God nearly as many years as you have lived and who have had an active part in this work from its small beginning. God will not select men of but little experience and considerable self-confidence to lead out in this sacred, important work. There is much at stake here. Men who have had but little experience in the sufferings, trials, opposition, and privations that have been endured to bring the work up to its present condition of prosperity should be very jealous of themselves.

Young men who now engage in the work of preaching the truth should cultivate modesty and humility. They should be careful how they become exalted, lest they be overthrown. They will be accountable for the clear light of truth which now shines upon them. I saw that God is displeased with the disposition that some have to murmur against those who have fought the heaviest battles for them and who endured so much in the commencement of the message, when the work went hard.

The experienced laborers, those who toiled under the weight and the oppressive burdens when there were but few to help bear them, God regards; and He has a jealous care for those who have proved faithful. He is displeased with those who are ready to find fault with and reproach those servants of God who have grown gray in building up the cause of present truth. Your reproaches and your murmurings, young men, will surely stand against you in the day of God. As long as God has not laid heavy responsibilities upon you, do not get out of your place and rely upon your own independent judgment and assume responsibilities for which you are not fitted.

Dear brother and sister, you need to cultivate watchfulness and humility, and to be diligent in prayer. The more closely you live to God, the more clearly will you discern your weaknesses and your dangers. A practical view of the law of God, a clear discernment of the atonement of Christ, will give you a knowledge of yourselves and will show you wherein you fail to perfect Christian character. In short, you both need a daily experience in God's will concerning you. When you see your great spiritual lack you will realize the fact that human depravity, specified in the word of God, is true in your experience. You are both pharisaical, and are in danger of remaining voluntarily and fearfully in the dark in regard to your dangers and your true standing before God.

You both need to learn the duties which devolve upon you in the various circumstances and relations of life. You have neglected your duties to both God and man. Self-knowledge you need so much. The ignorance of your own hearts leads you to overlook the necessity of a daily, living experience in the divine life. In a degree you overlook the necessity of having a divine influence constantly with you. This is positively necessary in doing the work of God. If you neglect this, and pass on in self-confidence and self-sufficiency, you will be left to make very great blunders. You need constantly to cherish lowliness of mind and a spirit of dependence. He who feels his own weakness will look higher than himself and will feel the need of constant strength from above. The grace of God will lead him to exercise and cherish a spirit of constant gratitude. He who is best acquainted with his own weakness will know that it is the matchless grace of God alone that will triumph over the rebellion of the heart.

You need to become acquainted with the weak as well as the strong points in your characters, that you may be constantly guarded lest you engage in enterprises, and assume responsibilities, for which God has never designed you. You should not compare your actions and measure your lives by any human standard, but with the rule of duty revealed in the Bible. You have a work to do for yourselves, Brother and Sister A, that you have not dreamed was necessary. For years you have been cherishing temptations and jealousies in regard to us and our work. This is not pleasing to God. You may think that you believe the testimonies that God has given, but unbelief in regard to their being of God is gaining ground with you.

Your labors, Brother A, would be more effectual in the conversion of souls to the truth if you dwelt upon the practical as well as the theoretical, having the living, practical elements in your own heart and carrying them out in your own life. You need to have a firmer hold from above. You are too dependent upon your surroundings. If you have a large congregation, you are elevated, and you desire to address them. But sometimes your congregations diminish, your spirits sink, and you have but little courage to labor. Surely something is wanting. Your hold is not firm enough upon God. Some of the most important truths in the teachings of Christ were preached by Him to one Samaritan woman who came to draw water as He, being weary, sat upon the well to rest. The fountain of living waters was within Him. The fountain of living waters must be in us, springing up to refresh those who are brought under our influence.

Christ sought for men wherever He could find them—in the public streets, in private houses, in the synagogues, by the seaside. He toiled all day, preaching to the multitude and healing the sick that were brought to Him; and frequently, after He had dismissed the people that they might return to their homes to rest and sleep, He spent the entire night in prayer, to come forth and renew His labors in the morning. O brother and sister, you do not know anything in reality of self-denial and self-sacrifice for Christ and for the truth's sake. You must depend more fully upon God and less upon your own abilities. You need to hide in God.

You are inclined, Brother A, to be severe in reproof and to form your own conclusions in regard to individuals, especially if their course has crossed your track; and, according to your views of the case, you sometimes deal with them in an unsparing manner. You have not been a tenderhearted, pitiful, courteous man, as was your Exemplar. You need to soften your spirit, to be more courteous and kind, and to have greater disinterested benevolence. You need to bring your soul into closer communion with God by earnest prayer mixed with living faith. Every prayer offered in faith lifts the suppliant above discouraging doubts and human passions. Prayer gives strength to renew the conflict with the powers of darkness, to bear trials patiently, and to endure hardness as good soldiers of Christ.

While you take counsel with your doubts and fears, or try to solve everything that you cannot see clearly before you have faith, your perplexities will only increase and deepen. If you come to God, feeling helpless and dependent, as you really are, and in humble, trusting prayer make your wants known to Him whose knowledge is infinite, who sees everything in creation and who governs everything by His will and word, He can and will attend to your cry, and will let light shine into your heart and all around you; for through sincere prayer your soul is brought into connection with the mind of the Infinite. You may have no remarkable evidence at the time that the face of your Redeemer is bending over you in compassion and love, but this is even so. You may not feel His visible touch, but His hand is upon you in love and pitying tenderness.

God loves both of you and wants to save you with an abundant salvation. But it must not be in your way, but in God's own appointed way. You must comply with the conditions laid down in the Scriptures of truth, and God will as surely fulfill on His part as His throne is sure. Because the admonitions that God sends to His people are humiliating to human nature, you must not, my brother, rise up against these reproofs and warnings. You need to die daily, to experience a daily crucifixion to self.

According to the light that God has given me in vision, wickedness and deception are increasing among God's people who profess to keep His commandments. Spiritual discernment to see sin as it exists, and then to put it out of the camp, is decreasing among God's people; and spiritual blindness is fast coming upon them. The straight testimony must be revived, and it will separate those from Israel who have ever been at war with the means that God has ordained to keep corruptions out of the church. Wrongs must be called wrongs. Grievous sins must be called by their right name. All of God's people should come nearer to Him and wash their robes of character in the blood of the Lamb. Then will they see sin in the true light and will realize how offensive it is in the sight of God.

It seemed a small matter to our first parents, when tempted, to transgress the command of God in one small act and eat of a tree that was beautiful to the eye and pleasant to the taste. To the transgressors this was but a small act, but it destroyed their allegiance to God and opened a flood of woe and guilt which has deluged the world. Who can know, in the moment of temptation, the terrible consequences which will result from one wrong, hasty step! Our only safety is to be shielded by the grace of God every moment, and not put out our own spiritual eyesight so that we will call evil, good, and good, evil. Without hesitation or argument, we must close and guard the avenues of the soul against evil.

It will cost us an effort to secure eternal life. It is only by long and persevering effort, sore discipline, and stern conflict that we shall be overcomers. But if we patiently and determinedly, in the name of the Conqueror who overcame in our behalf in the wilderness of temptation, overcome as He overcame, we shall have the eternal reward. Our efforts, our self-denial, our perseverance, must be proportionate to the infinite value of the object of which we are in pursuit.

You must not allow your sympathies for yourselves to shield you and others in wrong because you see nothing in outward appearances to condemn. God sees; He can read the motives and purposes of the soul. I entreat you in the name of our Master, who has called us and appointed us our work, to keep your hands off and leave us to do the work that God has laid upon us. Keep your words of sympathy and pity for those who really deserve them, those who are pressed by the Spirit of God to show His people their transgressions and the house of Israel their sins. Error and sin in these last days are embraced more readily than truth and righteousness. The soldiers of the cross of Christ are now required to gird on the Christian armor and to press back the moral darkness that is flooding the world.

God will give both of you precious victories if you surrender yourselves wholly to Him and let His grace subdue your proud hearts. Your self-righteousness will avail nothing with God. Nothing should be done by fits and starts or in a spirit of rashness. Wrongs cannot be righted, nor reformations in character made, by a few feeble, intermittent efforts. Sanctification is not a work of a day or a year, but of a lifetime. Without continual efforts and constant activity, there can be no advancement in the divine life, no attainment of the victor's crown. We are doing up work for the judgment, and it is unsafe to work in our own wisdom and trust to our own judgment. With the spirit of self-confidence that you now possess, neither of you could be happy in heaven; for there all, even the exalted angels, are subordinate. You have yet to learn subordination and submission. Both of you must be transformed by the grace of God.

Sister A, I saw that you should be careful that you do not open a door of temptation to your husband that you cannot close at will. It is easier to invite the enemy into your hearts than to dismiss him after he has the ground. Your pride is easily hurt, and you need to come closer to God, and seek with earnestness for grace, divine grace, to endure hardness as a good soldier of Christ Jesus. God will be your helper if you choose Him for your strength. Both of you should encourage greater devotion to God. The only way to watch humbly is to watch prayerfully. Do not for a moment think that you may sit down and enjoy yourselves, and study your own pleasure and convenience. The life of Christ is our example. He was a man of sorrows and acquainted with grief; He was wounded, He was bruised. You are too well satisfied with your position. You have need of constant watchfulness, lest Satan beguile you through his subtlety, corrupt your minds, and lead you into inconsistencies and gross darkness. Your watchfulness should be characterized by a spirit of humble dependence upon God. It should not be carried on with a proud, self-reliant spirit, but with a deep sense of your personal weakness and a childlike trust in the promises of God.

It is now an easy and pleasant task to preach the truth of the third angel's message, in comparison with what it was when the message first started, when the numbers were few and we were looked upon as fanatics. Those who bore the responsibility of the work in the rise and early progress of the message knew what conflict, distress, and soul anguish were. Night and day the burden was heavy upon them. They thought not of rest or convenience even when they were pressed with suffering and disease. The shortness of time called for activity, and the laborers were few.

Frequently, when brought into strait places, the entire night has been spent in earnest, agonizing prayer with tears for help from God and for light to shine upon His word. When the light has come and the clouds have been driven back, what joy and grateful happiness have rested upon the anxious, earnest seekers! Our gratitude to God was as complete as had been our earnest, hungering cry for light. Some nights we could not sleep because our hearts were overflowing with love and gratitude to God.

Men who now go forth to preach the truth have things made ready to their hand. They cannot now experience such privations as the laborers in present truth have endured before them. The truth has been brought out, link after link, till it forms a clear, connected chain. To bring the truth out in such clearness and harmony has required careful research. Opposition, the most bitter and determined, drove the servants of God to the Lord and to their Bibles. Precious indeed to them was the light which came from God.

I have been shown that the reason why some cannot discern the right is because they have so long cherished the enemy, who has worked side by side with them while they have not discerned his power. It sometimes seems hard to wait patiently till God's time comes to vindicate the right. But I have been shown that if we become impatient we lose a rich reward. As faithful husbandmen in God's great field, we must sow with tears and be patient and hopeful. We must meet troubles and sorrows. Temptations and wearisome toil will afflict the soul, but we must patiently wait in faith to reap with joy. In the final victory God will have no use for those persons who are nowhere to be found in time of peril and danger, when the strength, courage, and influence of all are required to make a charge upon the enemy. Those who stand like faithful soldiers to battle against wrong, and to vindicate the right, warring against principalities and powers, against the rulers of the darkness of this world, against spiritual wickedness in high places, will each receive the commendation from the Master: "Well done, thou *good* and *faithful* servant: . . . enter thou into the joy of thy Lord."

Never was there greater need of faithful warnings and reproofs, and close, straight dealing, than at this very time. Satan has come down with great power, knowing that his time is short. He is flooding the world with pleasing fables, and the people of God love to have smooth things spoken to them. Sin and iniquity are not abhorred. I was shown that God's people must make more firm, determined efforts to press back the incoming darkness. The close work of the Spirit of God is needed now as never before. Stupidity must be shaken off. We must arouse from the lethargy that will prove our destruction unless we resist it. Satan has a powerful, controlling influence upon minds. Preachers and people are in danger of being found upon the side of the powers of darkness. There is no such thing now as a neutral position. We are all decidedly for the right or decidedly with the wrong. Said Christ: "He that is not with Me is against Me, and he that gathereth not with Me scattereth abroad."

There are ever to be found those who will sympathize with those who are wrong. Satan had sympathizers in heaven, and took large numbers of the angels with him. God and Christ and heavenly angels were on one side, and Satan on the other. Notwithstanding the infinite power and majesty of God and Christ, angels became disaffected. The insinuations of Satan took effect, and they really came to believe that the Father and the Son were their enemies and that Satan was their benefactor. Satan has the same power and the same control over minds now, only it has increased a hundredfold by exercise and experience. Men and women today are deceived, blinded by his insinuations and devices, and know it not. By giving place to doubts and unbelief in regard to the work of God, and by cherishing feelings of distrust and cruel jealousies, they are preparing themselves for complete deception. They rise up with bitter feelings against the ones who dare to speak of their errors and reprove their sins.

Those who have in the fear of God ventured out to faithfully meet error and sin, calling sin by its right name, have discharged a disagreeable duty with much suffering of feelings to themselves; but they get the sympathy of but few and suffer the neglect of many. The sympathizers are on the wrong side, and they carry out the purposes of Satan to defeat the design of God.

Reproofs always hurt human nature. Many are the souls that have been destroyed by the unwise sympathy of their brethren; for, because the brethren sympathized with them, they thought they must indeed have been abused, and that the reprover was all wrong and had a bad spirit. The only hope for sinners in Zion is to fully see and confess their wrongs, and put them away. Those who step in to destroy the edge of sharp reproof that God sends, saying that the reprover was partly wrong and the reproved was not just right, please the enemy. Any way that Satan can devise to make the reproofs of none effect will accomplish his design. Some will lay blame upon the one whom God has sent with a message of warning, saying, He is too severe; and in so doing they become responsible for the soul of the sinner whom God desired to save, and to whom, because He loved him, He sent correction, that he might humble his soul before God and put his sins from him. These false sympathizers will have an account to settle with the Master by-and-by for their work of death.

There are many who profess to believe the truth who are blind to their own danger. They cherish iniquity in their hearts and practice it in their lives. Their friends cannot read their hearts, and frequently think that such are all right.

Black Hawk, Colorado, Aug. 12, 1873.

DAYDREAMING

Dear Sister E: I have been shown that you need a thorough conversion. You have accepted the truth, but have not received the blessings that the truth brings, because you have not experienced its transforming power. You are in danger of losing both worlds unless you have a more thorough work of grace in your heart and unless your will is brought into conformity to the mind and will of Christ.

You are not now on the right track to obtain that peace

and happiness which the true, humble, cross-bearing believer is sure to receive. You have the stamp of your father's character. You have a selfish disposition; you do not realize this, but it is true. Your principal thoughts are for yourself, to please yourself, to do those things which will be most agreeable to yourself, without reference to the happiness of those around you. You are making a mistake in searching for happiness. If you find it, it will be in the performance of duty and the forgetfulness of self. While your thoughts are so much upon yourself, you cannot be happy.

You neglect to cheerfully engage in the work which God has left you to do. You overlook the common, simple duties lying directly in your pathway, and your mind wanders off to some greater work, which you imagine will be more congenial to your taste, and which will supply the lack in your life, the barrenness in your soul. You will surely be disappointed here. The work which God has left you to do is to take up the common, everyday duties which are right around you and do the plain, homely duties of life cheerfully, not mechanically, but having your heart in what you do, performing with your heart, as well as with your hands, the simple duties which lie before you.

You do not study to make others happy; your eyes are not open, trying to discern what little things you can do, what little attentions in the daily courtesies of life you can show to your parents and the members of the household. You have felt too much that it was a virtue to shut yourself away from the family, and brood over your unhappy thoughts and unhappy experience, gathering thorns, and taking satisfaction in wounding yourself with them. You indulge in a dreamy habit, which must be broken up. You leave duties undone. Work which you ought to do to relieve others you neglect for the pleasure of indulging your own unhappy musings. You do not know yourself. Up to duty! Arouse yourself and take up your neglected duty. Redeem the past by future faithfulness. Take hold of the work before you, and, in the faithful performance of duty, you will forget yourself and will not have time to muse and become gloomy, and feel disagreeable and unhappy.

You have almost everything to learn in the Christian experience. You are not improving as fast as you might, and as you must, if you ever obtain eternal life. You are now forming a character for heaven or one which will debar you from heaven. You have had your mind and thoughts so engrossed in yourself that you have not realized what you must do in order to become a true follower of the meek and lowly Jesus. You have neglected your home duties. You have been a cloud and a shadow in the family, when it was your privilege to shed light and be a blessing to the dear ones around you. You have been pettish, fretful, and unhappy when there was, in reality nothing to make you so. You have not been awake to see what you might do to lift the burdens from your mother and to bless your parents in every way possible. You have looked to your parents and sisters to help you to be happy and to minister to you, to do for you, while your thoughts have been centered upon yourself. You have not had the grace of God in your heart, while you have deceived yourself in thinking that you were really advanced in the knowledge of the divine will.

You have been ready to engage in conversation with those not of our faith, when it was impossible for you to present an intelligent reason of our faith before them. In this you do not rightly represent the truth and do much more injury to the cause of truth than you do good. If you should talk less in vindication of our faith and study your Bible more and let your deportment be of that character which would testify that the influence of the truth was good upon your heart and life, you would do far more good than by mere talk, while you lack faithfulness in so many things.

If you are careful to follow the example of our self-denying, self-sacrificing Redeemer, who was ever seeking to do good and to bless others, but not to find ease and pleasure, and enjoyment for Himself, you will then bless others with your influence. In our mingling in society, in families or in whatever relations of life we are placed, either limited or extended, there are many ways wherein we may acknowledge our Lord and many ways wherein we may deny Him. We may deny Him in our words, by speaking evil of others, by foolish talking, jesting and joking, by idle or unkind words, or by prevaricating, speaking contrary to truth. In our words we may confess that Christ is not in us. In our character we may deny Him by loving our ease, by shunning the duties and burdens of life which someone must bear if we do not, and by loving sinful pleasure. We may also deny Christ by pride of dress and conformity to the world, or by uncourteous behavior. We may deny Him by loving our own opinions and by seeking to maintain and justify self. We may also deny Him in allowing the mind to run in the channel of lovesick sentimentalism and to brood over our supposed hard lot and trials.

No one can truly confess Christ before the world unless the mind and spirit of Christ live in him. It is impossible to communicate that which we have not. The conversation and the deportment should be a real and visible expression of grace and truth within. If the heart is sanctified, submissive, and humble, the fruits will be seen outwardly and will be a most effectual confession of Christ. Words and profession are not enough. You, my sister, must have something more than this. You are deceiving yourself. Your spirit, your character, and your actions do not show a spirit of meekness, self-denial, and charity. Words and profession may express much humility and love; but if the conduct is not regulated daily by the grace of God, you are not a partaker of the heavenly gift, you have not forsaken all for Christ, you have not surrendered your own will and pleasure to become His disciple.

You commit sin and deny your Saviour by dwelling on gloomy things, by gathering trials to yourself, and by borrowing troubles. You bring the troubles of tomorrow into today, and embitter your own heart, and bring burdens and a cloud upon those around you, by manufacturing trials. The precious probationary time that God has given you in which to do good and become rich in good works you are very unwise to employ in thinking unhappy thoughts and in airy castle-building. You suffer your imagination to run upon subjects that will bring you no relief or happiness. Your daydreaming stands directly in the way of your obtaining a sound, healthy, intelligent experience in the things of God and a moral fitness for the better life.

The truth of God received into the heart is able to make you wise unto salvation. In believing and obeying it you will receive grace sufficient for the duties and trials of today. Grace for tomorrow you do not need. You should feel that you have only to do with today. Overcome for today; deny self for today; watch and pray for today; obtain victories in God for today. Our circumstances and surroundings, the changes daily transpiring around us, and the written word of God which discerns and proves all things—these are sufficient to teach us our duty and just what we ought to do, day by day. Instead of suffering your mind to run in a channel of thought from which you will derive no benefit, you should be searching the Scriptures daily and doing those duties in daily life which may now be irksome to you, but which must be done by someone.

The beauties of nature have a tongue that speaks to our senses without ceasing. The open heart can be impressed with the love and glory of God as seen in the works of His hand. The listening ear can hear and understand the communications of God through the works of nature. There is a lesson in the sunbeam and in the various objects in nature that God has presented to our view. The green fields, the lofty trees, the buds and flowers, the passing cloud, the falling rain, the babbling brook, the sun, moon, and stars in the heavens, all invite our attention and meditation, and bid us become acquainted with God, who made them all. The lessons to be learned from the various objects of the natural world are these: They are obedient to the will of their Creator; they never deny God, never refuse obedience to any intimation of His will. Fallen beings alone refuse to yield full obedience to their Maker. Their words and works are at variance with God and opposed to the principles of His government.

Your thoughts are not elevated. There is enough in the natural world to lead you to love and adore your Creator. There is food for thought without shutting yourself away to feed on disappointed hopes and perverted imaginings. Do not be ready to talk with unbelievers and to enter into argument with those who oppose the truth, for you are not furnished with Scripture knowledge to do this. You have neglected to study your Bible. You can best recommend the truth by the meekness of your life and the faithful discharge of your daily duties. If you are conscientiously strict to do your part, and are faithful and earnest to see what you can and should do for those for whom you labor, you will then better represent the truth. The best way in which you can recommend the truth is, not by argument, not by talk, but by living it daily, by leading a consistent, modest, humble life as a disciple of Christ.

It is a sad thing to be discontented with our surroundings or with the circumstances which have placed us where our duties seem humble and unimportant. Private and humble duties are distasteful to you; you are restless, uneasy, and dissatisfied. All this springs from selfishness. You think more of yourself than others think of you. You love yourself better than you love your parents, sisters, and brother, and better than you love God. You desire more congenial labor, for which you think you will be better fitted. You are not willing to work and wait in the humble sphere of action where God has placed you, until He proves and tests you, and you demonstrate your ability and fitness for a higher position. "Blessed are the meek: for they shall inherit the earth." The spirit of meekness is not a spirit of discontent, but it is directly the opposite.

Those professed Christians who are constantly whining and complaining, and who seem to think happiness and a cheerful countenance a sin, have not the genuine article of religion. Those who look upon nature's beautiful scenery as they would upon a dead picture, who choose to look upon dead leaves rather than to gather the beautiful living flowers, who take a mournful pleasure in all that is melancholy in the language spoken to them by the natural world, who see no beauty in valleys clothed with living green and grand mountain heights clothed with verdure, who close their senses to the joyful voice which speaks to them in nature and which is sweet and musical to the listening ear—these are not in Christ. They are not walking in the light, but are gathering to themselves darkness and gloom, when they could just as well have brightness and the blessing of the Sun of Righteousness arising in their hearts with healing in His beams.

My young sister, you are living an imaginary life. You cannot detect or realize a blessing in anything. You imagine troubles and trials which do not exist; you exaggerate little annoyances into grievous trials. This is not the meekness which Christ blessed. It is an unsanctified, rebellious, unfilial discontent. Meekness is a precious grace, willing to suffer silently, willing to endure trials. Meekness is patient and labors to be happy under all circumstances. Meekness is always thankful and makes its own songs of happiness, making melody in the heart to God. Meekness will suffer disappointment and wrong, and will not retaliate. Meekness is not to be silent and sulky. A morose temper is the opposite of meekness; for this only wounds and gives pain to others, and takes no pleasure to itself.

You have but just entered the school of Christ. You have almost everything yet to learn. You do not now dress extravagantly, but you have pride of appearance. You desire to dress with less simplicity. You think considerably more of dress than you should. Christ invites you: "Come unto Me, all ye that labor and are heavy-laden, and I will give you rest. Take My yoke upon you, and learn of Me; for I am meek and lowly in heart: and ye shall find rest unto your souls. For My yoke is easy, and My burden is light." Submit your neck to the yoke which Christ imposes and you will find in this submission the very happiness that you have tried to gain to yourself in your own way by following your own course.

You may be cheerful if you will bring even your thoughts into subjection to the will of Christ. You should make no delay, but closely search your own heart and die to self daily. You may inquire: How can I master my own actions and control my inward emotions? Many who profess not the love of God do control their spirit to a considerable extent without the aid of the special grace of God. They cultivate self-control. This is indeed a rebuke to those who know that from God they may obtain strength and grace, and yet do not exhibit the graces of the Spirit. Christ is our model. He was meek and lowly. Learn of Him, and imitate His example. The Son of God was faultless. We must aim at this perfection and overcome as He overcame, if we would have a seat at His right hand.

You have peculiarities of character which need to be sternly disciplined and resolutely controlled before you can with any safety enter the marriage relation. Therefore marriage should be put from your mind until you overcome the defects in your character, for you would not make a happy wife. You have neglected to educate yourself for systematic household labor. You have not seen the necessity of acquiring habits of industry. The habit of enjoying useful labor, once formed, will never be lost. You are then prepared to be placed in any circumstance in life, and you will be fitted for the position. You will learn to love activity. If you enjoy useful labor, your mind will be occupied with your employment, and you will not find time to indulge in dreamy fancies.

Knowledge of useful labor will impart to your restless and dissatisfied mind energy, efficiency, and a becoming, modest dignity, which will command respect. You know but very little of yourself; you know not the deceptions of your own heart. The heart is deceitful above all things and desperately wicked. Search your heart carefully, and take time for meditation and prayer. Unless you see the defects in your character and with genuine sincerity correct your errors, you cannot be a disciple of Christ.

You love to think and talk about young men. You interpret their civilities as a special regard for yourself. You flatter yourself that you are more highly esteemed than you really are. Your conversation should be upon subjects that will profit, that will refine and elevate. You are not, my dear child, cultivating habits of frankness and sincerity. Your heart is not right. Your influence is not good upon the young, for you have not the mind of Christ; yet you flatter yourself that you have made great advancement in the Christian life.

A reformation must commence in your father's family. You bear the stamp of your father's character. You should endeavor to shun his errors and his extremes. If you are truly a disciple of Christ you will see important work to do at your home. Every family may be a perpetual school. The elder sisters can exert a strong influence upon the younger members of the family. The younger, witnessing the example of the older, will be led more by the principle of imitation than by oft-repeated precepts. The eldest daughter should ever feel it a Christian duty devolving upon her to aid the mother in bearing her many toilsome burdens. Hours are worse than lost that are spent in bed, in sleep, or in gloomy musings, while the shoulders of some in the family are bowed to carry the heavy, toilsome load.

The elder daughters may assist in the education of the younger members of the family. Here is an excellent opportunity for you, kindly, diligently, and having the fear of the Lord before you, to teach those less advanced than yourself. You may gain the affections of those you try to help. You may here have one of the best of schools in which to exercise the Christian graces. You do not love children. In fact, you do not love anything which requires steady, earnest, persevering effort. You do not love steady application. You love change and variety, and are constantly seeking to find something that will please yourself and give you happiness. You need self-education, and you can obtain this better now than at any future time. You have almost every change to make in your life, and may God help you to take hold of the work without delay. Only the pure, the good, and the holy will dwell with Christ when He cometh into His kingdom.

You cannot obtain heaven without earnest, persevering effort. As viewed in the light of heaven, your life hitherto has been aimless and nearly useless. You now have opportunity to redeem the time and to wash your robe of character in the blood of the Lamb. God will help you if you feel your need of His help. Your righteousness is of no value with God. It is only through the merits of Christ that you will be victor at last. And if you can be among those who shall be saved with an everlasting salvation, heaven will be cheap enough.

NUMBER TWENTY-FOUR

TESTIMONY FOR THE CHURCH

THE GREAT REBELLION

Korah, Dathan, and Abiram rebelled against Moses and Aaron, and so against the Lord. The Lord had placed special responsibilities upon Moses and Aaron in selecting them for the priesthood and in conferring upon them the dignity and authority of leading the congregation of Israel. Moses was afflicted by the continual rebellion of the Hebrews. As God's appointed, visible leader, he had been connected with the Israelites through seasons of peril, and had borne with their discontent, their jealousies, and their murmurings, without retaliation and without seeking to be released from his trying position.

When the Hebrews were brought into scenes of danger or where their appetite was restricted, instead of trusting in God, who had done wondrous things for them, they murmured against Moses. The Son of God, although invisible to the congregation, was the leader of the Israelites. His presence went before them and conducted all their travels, while Moses was their visible leader, receiving his directions from the Angel, who was Christ.

BASE IDOLATRY

In the absence of Moses the congregation demanded of Aaron to make them gods to go before them and lead them back into Egypt. This was an insult to their chief leader, the Son of the infinite God. Only a few weeks before, they had stood trembling with awe and terror before the mount, listening to the words of the Lord: "Thou shalt have no other gods before Me." The glory which sanctified the mount when the voice was heard which shook the mountain to its foundation, still hovered over it in sight of the congregation; but the Hebrews turned away their eyes and asked for other gods. Moses, their visible leader, was in converse with God in the mount. They forgot the promise and the warning of God: "Behold I send an Angel before thee, to keep thee in the way, and to bring thee into the place which I have prepared. Beware of Him, and obey His voice, provoke Him not; for He will not pardon your transgressions: for My name is in Him."

The Hebrews were cruelly unbelieving and basely ungrateful in their impious request: "Make us gods, which shall go before us." If Moses was absent, the presence of the Lord remained; they were not forsaken. The manna continued to fall, and they were fed by a divine hand morning and evening. The cloudy pillar by day and the pillar of fire by night signified the presence of God, which was a living memorial before them. The divine presence was not dependent upon the presence of Moses. But at the very time that he was pleading with the Lord in the mount in their behalf, they were rushing into shameful errors, into transgression of the law so recently given in grandeur.

Here we see the weakness of Aaron. Had he stood with true moral courage and in boldness rebuked the leaders in this shameful request, his timely words would have saved that terrible apostasy. But his desire to be popular with the congregation, and his fear of incurring their displeasure, led him to cowardly sacrifice the allegiance of the Hebrews in that decisive moment. He raised an altar, made a graven image, and proclaimed a day in which to consecrate that image as an object of worship and to proclaim before all Israel: These be the gods which led you out of Egypt. While the top of the mount is still illuminated with the glory of God, he calmly witnesses the merriment and dancing to this senseless image; and Moses is sent down from the mount by the Lord to rebuke the people. But Moses would not consent to leave the mount until his pleadings in behalf of Israel were heard and his request that God would pardon them was granted.

THE TABLES OF THE LAW BROKEN

Moses came from the mount with the precious record in his hands, a pledge of God to man on condition of obedience. Moses was the meekest man upon the earth, but when he viewed the apostasy of Israel he was angry and jealous for the glory of God. In his indignation he cast to the ground the precious pledge of God, which was more dear to him than life. He saw the law broken by the Hebrews, and in his zeal for God, to deface the idol that they were worshiping, he sacrificed the tables of stone. Aaron stood by, calmly, patiently bearing the severe censure of Moses. All this might have been prevented by a word from Aaron at the right time. True, noble decision for the right in the hour of Israel's peril would have balanced their minds in the right direction.

Does God condemn Moses? No, no; the great goodness of God pardons the rashness and zeal of Moses, because it was all on account of his fidelity and his disappointment and grief at the sight of his eyes in the evidence of Israel's apostasy. The man who might have saved the Hebrews in the hour of their peril is calm. He does not show indignation because of the sins of the people, neither does he reproach himself and manifest remorse under the sense of his wrongs; but he seeks to justify his course in a grievous sin. He makes the people accountable for his weakness in yielding to their requests. He was unwilling to bear the murmuring of Israel and to stand under the pressure of their clamors and unreasonable wishes, as Moses had done. He entered into the spirit and feelings of the people without remonstrance, and then sought to make them responsible.

The congregation of Israel thought Aaron a much more pleasant leader than Moses. He was not so unyielding. They thought that Moses showed a very bad spirit, and their sympathies were with Aaron, whom Moses so severely censured. But God pardoned the indiscretion of honest zeal in Moses, while He held Aaron accountable for his sinful weakness and lack of integrity under a pressure of circumstances. In order to save himself, Aaron sacrificed thousands of the Israelites. The Hebrews felt the punishment of God for this act of apostasy, but in a short time they were again full of discontent and rebellion.

THE PEOPLE MURMUR

When the armies of Israel prospered, they took all the glory to themselves; but when they were tested and proved by hunger or warfare they charged all their hardships to Moses. The power of God which was manifested in a remarkable manner in their deliverance from Egypt, and seen from time to time all through their journeyings, should have inspired them with faith and forever closed their mouths from one expression of ingratitude. But the least apprehension of want, the least fear of danger from any cause, overbalanced the benefits in their favor and caused them to overlook the blessings received in their times of greatest danger. The experience they passed through in the matter of worshiping the golden calf should have made so deep an impression upon their minds as never to be effaced. But although the marks of God's displeasure were fresh before them in their broken ranks and missing numbers because of their repeated offenses against the Angel who was leading them, they did not take these lessons to heart and by faithful obedience redeem their past failure; and again they were overcome by the temptations of Satan.

The best efforts of the meekest man upon the earth could not quell their insubordination. The unselfish interest of Moses was rewarded with jealousy, suspicion, and calumny. His humble shepherd's life was far more peaceful and happy than his present position as pastor of that vast congregation of turbulent spirits. Their unreasonable jealousies were more difficult to manage than the fierce wolves of the wilderness.

But Moses dared not choose his own course and do as best pleased himself. He had left the shepherd's crook at God's command and in its place had received a rod of power. He dared not lay down this scepter and resign his position till God should dismiss him.

It is Satan's work to tempt minds. He will insinuate his wily suggestions and stir up doubting, questioning, unbelief, and distrust of the words and acts of the one who stands under responsibilities and who is seeking to carry out the mind of God in his labors. It is the special purpose of Satan to pour upon and around the servants of God's choice, troubles, perplexities, and opposition, so that they will be hindered in their work and, if possible, discouraged. Jealousies, strife, and evil surmising will counteract, in a great measure, the very best efforts that God's servants, appointed to a special work, may be able to put forth.

Satan's plan is to drive them from the post of duty by working through agents. All whom he can excite to distrust and suspicion he will use as his instruments. The position of Moses in carrying the burdens that he bore for the Israel of God was not appreciated. There is in the nature of man, when not under the direct influence of the Spirit of God, a disposition to envy, jealousy, and cruel distrust, which, if not subdued, will lead to a desire to undermine and tear down others, while selfish spirits will seek to build themselves up upon their ruins.

KORAH, DATHAN, AND ABIRAM

By God's appointment these men had been entrusted with special honors. They had been of that number who, with the seventy elders, went up with Moses into the mount and beheld the glory of God. They saw the glorious light which covered the divine form of Christ. The bottom of this cloud was in appearance like the "paved work of a sapphire stone, and as it were the body of heaven in his clearness." These men were in the presence of the glory of the Lord and did eat and drink without being destroyed by the purity and unsurpassed glory that was reflected upon them. But a change had come. A temptation, slight at first, had been harbored; and as it was encouraged it had strengthened until the imagination was controlled by the power of Satan. These men upon the most frivolous pretense ventured upon their work of disaffection. At first they hinted and expressed doubts, which took so readily with many minds that they ventured still further. And being more and more confirmed in their suspicions by a word from one and another, each expressing what he thought of certain things which had come under his notice, these deluded souls really came to believe that they had a zeal for the Lord in the matter and that they would not be excusable unless they carried out to the full their purpose of making Moses see and feel the preposterous position he occupied toward Israel. A little leaven of distrust and of dissension, envy, and jealousy was leavening the camp of Israel.

Korah, Dathan, and Abiram first commenced their cruel work upon the men to whom God had entrusted sacred responsibilities. They were successful in alienating two hundred and fifty princes who were famous in the congregation, men of renown. With these strong and influential men on their side, they felt sure of making a radical change in the order of things. They thought they could transform the government of Israel and greatly improve it from its present administration.

Korah was not satisfied with his position. He was connected with the service of the tabernacle, yet he desired to be exalted to the priesthood. God had established Moses as chief governor, and the priesthood was given to Aaron and his sons. Korah determined to compel Moses to change the order of things, that he might be raised to the dignity of the priesthood. To be more sure of accomplishing his purpose, he drew Dathan and Abiram, descendants of Reuben, into his rebellion. These reasoned that, being descendants of the eldest son of Jacob, the chief authority, which Moses usurped, belonged to them; and, with Korah, they were resolved to obtain the office of the priesthood. These three became very zealous in an evil work and influenced two hundred and fifty men of renown, who were also determined to have a share in the priesthood and the government, to join them.

God had honored the Levites to do service in the tabernacle because they took no part in making and worshiping the golden calf and because of their faithfulness in executing the order of God upon the idolaters. To the Levites was also assigned the office of erecting the tabernacle and encamping around about it, while the hosts of Israel pitched their tents at a distance from it. And when they journeyed, the Levites took down the tabernacle and bore it and the ark and all the sacred articles of furniture. Because God thus honored the Levites, they became ambitious for still higher office, that they might obtain greater influence with the congregation. "And they gathered themselves together against Moses and against Aaron, and said unto them, Ye take too much upon you, seeing all the congregation are holy, every one of them, and the Lord is among them: wherefore then lift ye up yourselves above the congregation of the Lord?"

FLATTERY AND FALSE SYMPATHY

There is nothing which will please the people better than to be praised and flattered when they are in darkness and wrong, and deserve reproof. Korah gained the ears of the people, and next their sympathies, by representing Moses as an overbearing leader. He said that he was too harsh, too exacting, too dictatorial, and that he reproved the people as though they were sinners when they were a holy people, sanctified to the Lord, and the Lord was among them. Korah rehearsed the incidents in their experience in their travels through the wilderness, where they had been brought into strait places, and where many of them had died because of murmuring and disobedience, and with their perverted senses they thought they saw very clearly that all their trouble might have been saved if Moses had pursued a different course. He was too unyielding, too exacting, and they decided that all their disasters in the wilderness were chargeable to him.

Korah, the leading spirit, professed great wisdom in discerning the true reason for their trials and afflictions.

In this work of disaffection there was greater harmony and union of views and feelings among these discordant elements than had ever been known to exist before. Korah's success in gaining the larger part of the congregation of Israel on his side led him to feel confident that he was wise and correct in judgment, and that Moses was indeed usurping authority that threatened the prosperity and salvation of Israel. He claimed that God had opened the matter to him and laid upon him the burden of changing the government of Israel just before it was too late. He stated that the congregation were not at fault; they were righteous; that this great cry about the murmuring of the congregation bringing upon them the wrath of God was all a mistake; and that the people only wanted to have their rights; they wanted individual independence.

As a sense of the self-sacrificing patience of Moses would force itself upon their memories, and as his disinterested efforts in their behalf while they were in the bondage of slavery would come before them, their consciences would be somewhat disturbed. Some were not wholly with Korah in his views of Moses and sought to speak in his behalf. Korah, Dathan, and Abiram must assign some reason before the people why Moses had from the first shown so great an interest for the congregation of Israel. Their selfish minds, which had been debased as Satan's instruments, suggested that they had at last found out the object of the apparent interest of Moses. He had designed to keep them wandering in the wilderness until they all, or nearly all, should perish and he should come into possession of their property.

Korah, Dathan, and Abiram, and the two hundred and fifty princes who had joined them, first became jealous, then envious, and next rebellious. They had talked in regard to the position of Moses as ruler of the people until they imagined that it was a very enviable position which any of them could fill as well as he. And they gave themselves up to discontent until they really deceived themselves and thought that Moses and Aaron had placed themselves in the position which they occupied in Israel. They said that Moses and Aaron exalted themselves above the congregation of the Lord in taking upon them the priesthood and the government, and that this office should not be conferred on their house alone. They said that it was sufficient for them if they were on a level with their brethren; for they were no more holy than the people, who were equally favored with God's peculiar presence and protection.

CHARACTER TESTED

As Moses listened to the words of Korah, he was filled with anguish and fell upon his face before the people. "And he spake unto Korah and unto all his company, saying, Even tomorrow the Lord will show who are His, and who is holy; and will cause him to come near unto Him: even him whom He hath chosen will He cause to come near unto Him. This do; take you censers, Korah, and all his company; and put fire therein, and put incense in them before the Lord tomorrow: and it shall be that the man whom the Lord doth choose, he shall be holy. Ye take too much upon you, ye sons of Levi. And Moses said unto Korah, Hear, I pray you, ye sons of Levi: seemeth it but a small thing unto you, that the God of Israel hath separated you from the congregation of Israel, to bring you near to Himself to do the service of the tabernacle of the Lord, and to stand before the congregation to minister unto them? And He hath brought thee near to Him, and all thy brethren the sons of Levi with thee: and seek ye the priesthood also? For which cause both thou and all thy company are gathered together against the Lord: and what is Aaron, that ye murmur against him?" Moses told them that Aaron had assumed no office of himself, that God had placed him in the sacred office.

Dathan and Abiram said: "Is it a small thing that thou hast brought us up out of a land that floweth with milk and honey, to kill us in the wilderness, except thou make thyself altogether a prince over us? Moreover thou hast not brought us into a land that floweth with milk and honey, or given us inheritance of fields and vineyards: wilt thou put out the eyes of these men? we will not come up."

They accused Moses of being the cause of their not entering the Promised Land. They said that God had not dealt with them thus, and that He had not said that they should die in the wilderness, and they would never believe that He had said so; it was Moses who had said this, not the Lord; and it was all arranged by Moses never to bring them to the land of Canaan. They spoke of his leading them from a land that flowed with milk and honey. In their blind rebellion they forgot their sufferings in Egypt and the desolating plagues brought upon the land. And they now accuse Moses of bringing them from a good land to kill them in the wilderness, that he might be made rich with their possessions. They inquire of Moses, in an insolent manner, if he thought that none of all the host of Israel were wise enough to understand his motives and discover his imposture, or if he thought they would all submit to have him lead them about like blind men as he pleased, sometimes toward Canaan, then back again toward the Red Sea and Egypt. These words they spoke before the congregation, and they utterly refused any longer to acknowledge the authority of Moses and Aaron.

Moses was greatly moved at these unjust accusations. He appealed to God before the people whether he had ever acted arbitrarily, and implored Him to be his judge. The people in general were disaffected and influenced by the misrepresentations of Korah. "And Moses said unto Korah, Be thou and all thy company before the Lord, thou, and they, and Aaron, tomorrow: and take every man his censer, and put incense in them, and bring ye before the Lord every man his censer, two hundred and fifty censers; thou also, and Aaron, each of you his censer. And they took every man his censer, and put fire in them, and laid incense thereon, and stood in the door of the tabernacle of the congregation with Moses and Aaron."

Korah and his company who in their self-confidence aspired to the priesthood even took the censers and stood in the door of the tabernacle with Moses. Korah had cherished his envy and rebellion until he was self-deceived, and he really thought that the congregation were a very righteous people and that Moses was a tyrannical ruler, continually dwelling upon the necessity of the congregation's being holy, when there was no need of it, for they were holy.

These rebellious ones had flattered the people in general to believe that they were right and that all their troubles arose from Moses, their ruler, who was continually reminding them of their sins. The people thought that if Korah could lead them and encourage them by dwelling upon their righteous acts instead of reminding them of their failures, they would have a very peaceful, prosperous journey, and he would without doubt lead them, not back and forward in the wilderness, but into the Promised Land. They said that it was Moses who had told them that they could not go into the land, and that the Lord had not thus said.

THE REBELS PERISH

Korah, in his exalted self-confidence, gathered all the congregation of Israel against Moses and Aaron, "unto the door of the tabernacle of the congregation: and the glory of the Lord appeared unto all the congregation. And the Lord spake unto Moses and unto Aaron, saying, Separate yourselves from among this congregation, that I may consume them in a moment. And they fell upon their faces, and said, O God, the God of the spirits of all flesh, shall one man sin, and wilt Thou be wroth with all the congregation?

"And the Lord spake unto Moses, saying, Speak unto the congregation, saying, Get you up from about the tabernacle of Korah, Dathan, and Abiram. And Moses rose up and went unto Dathan and Abiram; and the elders of Israel followed him. And he spake unto the congregation, saying, Depart, I pray you, from the tents of these wicked men, and touch nothing of theirs, lest ye be consumed in all their sins. So they gat up from the tabernacle of Korah, Dathan, and Abiram, on every side: and Dathan and Abiram came out, and stood in the door of their tents, and their wives, and their sons, and their little children. And Moses said, Hereby ye shall know that the Lord hath sent me to do all these works; for I have not done them of mine own mind. If these men die the common death of all men, or if they be visited after the visitation of all men, then the Lord hath not sent me. But if the Lord make a new thing, and the earth open her mouth, and swallow them up, with all that appertain unto them, and they go down quick into the pit; then ye shall understand that these men have provoked the Lord." As Moses ceased speaking, the earth opened, and their tents, and all that pertained unto them, were swallowed up. They went down alive into the pit, the earth closed over them, and they perished from among the congregation.

As the children of Israel heard the cry of the perishing ones, they fled a great distance from them. They knew that they were in a measure guilty, for they had received the accusations against Moses and Aaron, and they were afraid that they would also perish with them. But the judgment of God was not yet finished. A fire came from the cloud of glory and consumed the two hundred and fifty men that offered incense. These were princes; that is, men generally of good judgment and of influence in the congregation, men of renown. They were highly esteemed, and their judgment had often been sought in difficult matters. But they were affected by a wrong influence, and became envious, jealous, and rebellious. They perished not with Korah, Dathan, and Abiram because they were not the first in rebellion. They were first to see the end of the leaders in the rebellion, and have an opportunity to repent of their crime. But they were not reconciled to the destruction of those wicked men, and the wrath of God came upon them and destroyed them also.

"And the Lord spake unto Moses, saying, Speak unto Eleazar the son of Aaron the priest, that he take up the censers out of the burning, and scatter thou the fire yonder; for they are hallowed. The censers of these sinners against their own souls, let them make them broad plates for a covering of the altar: for they offered them before the Lord, therefore they are hallowed: and they shall be a sign unto the children of Israel."

THE REBELLION NOT CURED

After this terrible exhibition of God's judgment the people returned to their tents. They were terrified, but not humbled. They had been deeply influenced by the spirit of rebellion and had been flattered by Korah and his company to believe that they were a very good people and that they had been wronged and abused by Moses. Their minds were so thoroughly imbued with the spirit of those who had perished that it was difficult to free themselves from their blind prejudice. If they should admit that Korah and his company were all wicked and Moses righteous, then they would be compelled to receive as the word of God that which they were unwilling to believe, that they should certainly all die in the wilderness. They were not willing to submit to this and tried to believe that it was all an imposture, that Moses had deceived them. The men who had perished had spoken pleasant words to them and had manifested special interest and love for them, and they thought Moses a designing man. They decided that they could not be wrong; that, after all, those men who had perished were good men, and Moses had by some means been the cause of their destruction.

Satan can lead deceived souls to great lengths. He can pervert their judgment, their sight, and their hearing. It was so in the case of the Israelites. "But on the morrow all the congregation of the children of Israel murmured against Moses and against Aaron, saying, Ye have killed the people of the Lord." The people were disappointed that the matter resulted as it did in favor of Moses and Aaron. The appearance of Korah and his company, all impiously exercising the priests' office with their censers, struck the people with admiration. They did not see that these men were offering a daring affront to the divine Majesty. When they were destroyed, the people were terrified; but after a short time all came in a tumultuous manner to Moses and Aaron, and charged them with the blood of those who had perished by the hand of God.

"And it came to pass, when the congregation was gathered against Moses and against Aaron, that they looked toward the tabernacle of the congregation: and, behold, the cloud covered it, and the glory of the Lord appeared. And Moses and Aaron came before the tabernacle of the congregation. And the Lord spake unto Moses, saying, Get you up from among this congregation, that I may consume them as in a moment. And they fell upon their faces." Notwithstanding the rebellion of Israel and their cruel conduct to Moses, he still manifested for them the same interest as before. Falling upon his face before the Lord, he implored Him to spare the people. While thus praying for the Lord to pardon the sins of His people, Moses requested Aaron to make an atonement for their sin while he remained before the Lord, that his prayers might ascend with the incense and be acceptable to God, and that all the congregation might not perish in their rebellion.

"And Moses said unto Aaron, Take a censer, and put fire therein from off the altar, and put on incense, and go quickly unto the congregation, and make an atonement for them: for there is wrath gone out from the Lord; the plague is begun. And Aaron took as Moses commanded, and ran into the midst of the congregation, and, behold, the plague was begun among the people and he put on incense, and made an atonement for the people. And he stood between the dead and the living; and the plague was stayed. Now they that died in the plague were fourteen thousand and seven hundred, beside them that died about the matter of Korah. And Aaron returned unto Moses unto the door of the tabernacle of the congregation: and the plague was stayed."

A LESSON FOR OUR TIME

In the case of Korah, Dathan, and Abiram we have a lesson of warning lest we follow their example. "Neither let us tempt Christ, as some of them also tempted, and were destroyed of serpents. Neither murmur ye, as some of them also murmured, and were destroyed of the destroyer. Now all these things happened unto them for ensamples: and they are written for our admonition, upon whom the ends of the world are come."

We have evidence in God's word of the liability of His people to be greatly deceived. There are many instances where what may seem to be a sincere zeal for the honor of God has its origin in leaving the soul unguarded for the enemy to tempt and to impress the mind with a perverted sense of the real state of things. And we may expect just such things in these last days, for Satan is just as busy now as he was in the congregation of Israel. The cruelty and strength of prejudice are not understood. After the congregation had the evidence before their sight of the destruction of these leaders in rebellion, the power of suspicion and distrust which had been let into their souls was not removed. They saw the ground open and the leaders of rebellion go down into the bowels of the earth. This fearful exhibition surely ought to have cured them and led them to the deepest repentance for their abuse of Moses.

Here God gave all Israel an opportunity to see and to feel the sinfulness of their course, which should have led them to repentance and confession. He gave the deceived ones overwhelming evidence that they were sinners and that His servant Moses was right. They had an opportunity to pass one night in reflection upon the fearful visitation of Heaven which they had witnessed. But reason was perverted. Korah had instigated the rebellion, and two hundred and fifty princes had joined him in spreading the disaffection. All the congregation were, to a greater or less degree, affected with the prevailing jealousy, surmisings and hatred against Moses, which had brought the displeasure of God in a fearfully marked manner. Yet our gracious God shows Himself a God of justice and mercy. He made a distinction between the instigators—the leaders in the rebellion—and those who had been deceived or led by them. He pitied the ignorance and folly of those who had been deceived.

God spoke to Moses to bid the congregation leave the tents of the men whom they had chosen in the place of Moses. The very men whose destruction they premeditated were the instruments in the hands of God of saving their lives upon that occasion. Said Moses: "Get you up from about the tabernacle of Korah." They also were in alarming danger of being destroyed in their sins by the wrath of God, for they were sharers in the crimes of the men to whom they had given their sympathy and with whom they had associated.

If while Moses was trying the test before the congregation of Israel, those who had started the rebellion had repented and sought the forgiveness of God and of His injured servant, the vengeance of God would even then have been stayed. But there in their tents boldly stood Korah, the instigator of the rebellion, and his sympathizers, as if in defiance of God's wrath, as though God had never wrought through His servant Moses. And much less did these rebellious ones act as though they had been so recently honored of God by being brought with Moses almost directly into His presence, and beholding His unsurpassed glory. These men saw Moses come down from the mount after he had received the second tables of stone and while his face was so resplendent with the glory of God that the people would not approach him, but fled from him. He called to them, but they seemed terrified. He presented the tables of stone and said: I pleaded in your behalf and have turned the wrath of God from you. I urged that, if God must forsake and destroy His congregation, my name might also be blotted from His book. Lo, He has answered me, and these tables of stone that I hold in my hand are the pledge given me of His reconciliation with His people.

The people perceive that it is the voice of Moses; that, although he is transformed and glorified, he is Moses yet. They tell him that they cannot look into his face, for the radiant light in his countenance is exceedingly painful to them. His face is like the sun; they cannot look upon it. When Moses finds out the difficulty, he covers his face with a veil. He does not plead that the light and glory upon his face is the reflection of God's glory that He placed upon him, and that the people must bear it; but he covers his glory. The sinfulness of the people make it painful to behold his glorified face. So will it be when the saints of God are glorified just previous to the second appearing of our Lord. The wicked will retire and shrink away from the sight, for the glory in the countenances of the saints will pain them. But all this glory upon Moses, all this divine stamp seen upon God's humble servant, is forgotten.

SLIGHTED MERCY

The Hebrews had an opportunity to reflect upon the scene that they had witnessed in the visitation of God's wrath upon the most prominent ones in this great rebellion. The goodness and mercy of God were displayed in not completely exterminating this ungrateful people when His wrath was kindled against the most responsible ones. He gave the congregation who had permitted themselves to be deceived, space for repentance. The fact that the Lord, their invisible Leader, showed so much long-suffering and mercy in this instance is distinctly recorded as evidence of His willingness to forgive the most grievous offenders when they have a sense of their sin and return unto Him with repentance and humiliation. The congregation had been arrested in their presumptuous course by the display of the Lord's vengeance; but they were not convinced that they were great sinners against Him, deserving His wrath for their rebellious course.

It is hardly possible for men to offer a greater insult to God than to despise and reject the instrumentalities that He has appointed to lead them. They had not only done this, but had purposed to put both Moses and Aaron to death. These men fled from the tents of Korah, Dathan, and Abiram through fear of destruction; but their rebellion was not cured. They were not in grief and despair because of their guilt. They felt not the effect of an awakened, convicted conscience because they had abused their most precious privileges and sinned against light and knowledge. We may here learn precious lessons of the long-suffering of Jesus, the Angel who went before the Hebrews in the wilderness.

Their invisible Leader would save them from a disgraceful destruction. Forgiveness lingers for them. It is possible for them to find pardon if they will even now repent. The vengeance of God has now come near to them and appealed to them to repent. A special, irresistible interference from heaven has arrested their presumptuous rebellion. If they now respond to the interposition of God's providence they may be saved. But the repentance and humiliation of the congregation must be proportionate to their transgression. The revelation of the signal power of God has placed them beyond uncertainty. They may have a knowledge of the true position and holy calling of Moses and Aaron if they will accept it. But their neglect to regard the evidences that God had given them was fatal. They did not realize the importance of immediate action on their part to seek pardon of God for their grievous sins.

That night of probation to the Hebrews was not passed by them in confessing and repenting of their sins, but in devising some way to resist the evidences which showed them to be the greatest of sinners. They still cherished their jealous hatred of the men of God's appointment and strengthened themselves in their mad course of resisting the authority of Moses and Aaron. Satan was at hand to pervert the judgment and lead them blindfolded to destruction. Their minds had been most thoroughly poisoned with disaffection, and they had the matter fixed beyond a question in their minds that Moses and Aaron were wicked men, and that they were responsible for the death of Korah, Dathan, and Abiram, who they thought would have been the saviors of the Hebrews by bringing in a better order of things, where praise would take the place of reproof, and peace the place of anxiety and conflict.

The day before, all Israel had fled in alarm at the cry of the doomed sinners who went down into the pit; for they said: "Lest the earth swallow us up also." "But on the morrow all the congregation of the children of Israel murmured against Moses and against Aaron, saying, Ye have killed the people of the Lord." In their indignation they were prepared to lay violent hands upon the men of God's appointment, who they believed had done a great wrong in killing those who were good and holy.

But the Lord's presence is manifested in His glory over the tabernacle, and rebellious Israel are arrested in their mad, presumptuous course. The voice of the Lord from His terrible glory now speaks to Moses and Aaron in the same words which they were the day before commanded to address to the congregation of Israel: "Get you up from among this congregation, that I may consume them as in a moment."

Here we find a striking exhibition of the blindness that will compass human minds that turn from light and evidence. Here we see the strength of settled rebellion, and how difficult it is to be subdued. Surely the Hebrews had had the most convincing evidence in the destruction of the men who had deceived them; but they still stood forth boldly and defiantly, and accused Moses and Aaron of killing good and holy men. "For rebellion is as the sin of witchcraft, and stubbornness is as iniquity and idolatry."

Moses did not feel the guilt of sin and did not hasten away at the word of the Lord and leave the congregation to perish, as the Hebrews had fled from the tents of Korah, Dathan, and Abiram the day before. Moses lingered; for he could not consent to give up all that vast multitude to perish, although he knew that they deserved the vengeance of God for their persistent rebellion. He prostrated himself before God because the people felt no necessity for humiliation; he mediated for them because they felt no need of interceding in their own behalf.

Moses here typifies Christ. At this critical time Moses manifested the True Shepherd's interest for the flock of His care. He pleaded that the wrath of an offended God might not utterly destroy the people of His choice. And by his intercession he held back the arm of vengeance, that a full end was not made of disobedient, rebellious Israel. He directed Aaron what course to pursue in that terrible crisis when the wrath of God had gone forth and the plague had begun. Aaron stood with his censer, waving it before the Lord, while the intercessions of Moses ascended with the smoke of the incense. Moses dared not cease his entreaties. He took hold of the strength of the Angel, as did Jacob in his wrestling, and like Jacob he prevailed. Aaron was standing between the living and the dead when the gracious answer came: I have heard thy prayer, I will not consume utterly. The very men whom the congregation despised and would have put to death were the ones to plead in their behalf that the avenging sword of God might be sheathed and sinful Israel spared.

DESPISERS OF REPROOF

The apostle Paul plainly states that the experience of the Israelites in their travels has been recorded for the benefit of those living in this age of the world, those upon whom the ends of the world are come. We do not consider that our dangers are any less than those of the Hebrews, but greater. There will be temptations to jealousies and murmurings, and there will be outspoken rebellion, as are recorded of ancient Israel. There will ever be a spirit to rise up against the reproof of sins and wrongs. But shall the voice of reproof be hushed because of this? If so, we shall be in no better situation than are the various denominations in our land who are afraid to touch the errors and prevailing sins of the people.

Those whom God has set apart as ministers of righteousness have solemn responsibilities laid upon them to reprove the sins of the people. Paul commanded Titus: "These things speak, and exhort, and rebuke with all authority. Let no man despise thee." There are ever those who will despise the one who dares to reprove sin; but there are times when reproof must be given. Paul directs Titus to rebuke a certain class sharply, that they may be sound in the faith. Men and women who, with their different organizations, are brought together in church capacity have peculiarities and faults. As these are developed, they will require reproof. If those who are placed in important positions never reproved, never rebuked, there would soon be a demoralized condition of things that would greatly dishonor God. But how shall the reproof be given? Let the apostle answer: "With all long-suffering and doctrine." Principle should be brought to bear upon the one who needs reproof, but never should the wrongs of God's people be passed by indifferently.

There will be men and women who despise reproof and whose feelings will ever rise up against it. It is not pleasant to be told of our wrongs. In almost every case where reproof is necessary, there will be some who entirely overlook the fact that the Spirit of the Lord has been grieved and His cause reproached. These will pity those who deserved reproof, because personal feelings have been hurt. All this unsanctified sympathy places the sympathizers where they are sharers in the guilt of the one reproved. In nine cases out of ten if the one reproved had been left under a sense of his wrongs, he might have been helped to see them and thereby have been reformed. But meddlesome, unsanctified sympathizers place altogether a wrong construction upon the motives of the reprover and the nature of the reproof given, and by sympathizing with the one reproved lead him to feel that he has been really abused; and his feelings rise up in rebellion against the one who has only done his duty. Those who faithfully discharge their unpleasant duties under a sense of their accountability to God will receive His blessing. God requires His servants to be always in earnest to do His will. In the apostle's charge to Timothy he exhorts him to "preach the word; be instant in season, out of season; reprove, rebuke, exhort with all long-suffering and doctrine."

The Hebrews were not willing to submit to the directions and restrictions of the Lord. They simply wanted their own way, to follow the leadings of their own mind, and be controlled by their own judgment. Could they have been left free to do this, no complaints would have been made of Moses; but they were restless under restraint.

God would have His people disciplined and brought into harmony of action, that they may see eye to eye and be of the same mind and of the same judgment. In order to bring about this state of things, there is much to be done. The carnal heart must be subdued and transformed. God designs that there shall ever be a living testimony in the church. It will be necessary to reprove and exhort, and some will need to be rebuked sharply, as the case demands. We hear the plea: "Oh, I am so sensitive, I cannot bear the least reflection!" If these persons would state the case correctly, they would say: "I am so self-willed, so self-sufficient, so proud-spirited, that I will not be dictated to; I will not be reproved. I claim the right of individual judgment; I have a right to believe and talk as I please." The Lord would not have us yield up our individuality. But what man is a proper judge of how far this matter of individual independence should be carried?

Peter exhorts his brethren: "Likewise, ye younger, submit yourselves unto the elder. Yea, all of you be subject one to another, and be clothed with humility: for God resisteth the proud, and giveth grace to the humble." The apostle Paul also exhorts his Philippian brethren to unity and humility: "If there be therefore any consolation in Christ, if any comfort of love, if any fellowship of the Spirit, if any bowels and mercies, fulfill ye my joy, that ye be like-minded, having the same love, being of one accord, of one mind. Let nothing be done through strife or vainglory; but in lowliness of mind let each esteem other better than themselves. Look not every man on his own things, but every man also on the things of others. Let this mind be in you, which was also in Christ Jesus." Again Paul exhorts his brethren: "Let love be without dissimulation. Abhor that which is evil; cleave to that which is good. Be kindly affectioned one to another with brotherly love; in honor preferring one another." In writing to the Ephesians he says: "Submitting yourselves one to another in the fear of God."

The history of the Israelites presents before us the great danger of deception. Many do not have a sense of the sinfulness of their own natures nor of the grace of forgiveness. They are in nature's darkness, subject to temptations and to great deception. They are far from God; yet they take great satisfaction in their lives, when their conduct is abhorred of God. This class will ever be at war with the leadings of the Spirit of God, especially with reproof. They do not wish to be disturbed. Occasionally they have selfish fears and good purposes, and sometimes anxious thoughts and convictions; but they have not a depth of experience, because they are not riveted to the eternal Rock. This class never see the necessity of the plain testimony. Sin does not appear so exceedingly sinful to them for the very reason that they are not walking in the light as Christ is in the light.

There is still another class who have had great light and special conviction, and a genuine experience in the workings of the Spirit of God; but the manifold temptations of Satan have overcome them. They do not appreciate the light that God has given them. They do not heed the warnings and reproofs from the Spirit of God. They are under condemnation. They will ever be at variance with the straight testimony because it condemns them.

God designs that His people shall be a unit, that they shall see eye to eye and be of the same mind and of the same judgment. This cannot be accomplished without a clear, pointed living testimony in the church. The prayer of Christ was that His disciples might be one as He was one with His Father. "Neither pray I for these alone, but for them also which shall believe on Me through their word; that they all may be one; as Thou, Father, art in Me, and I in Thee, that they also may be one in Us: that the world may believe that Thou hast sent Me. And the glory which Thou gavest Me I have given them; that they may be one, even as We are one: I in them, and Thou in Me, that they may be made perfect in one; and that the world may know that Thou hast sent Me, and hast loved them, as Thou hast loved Me."

APPEAL TO THE YOUNG

Dear Youth: From time to time the Lord has given me testimonies of warning for you. He has given you encouragement if you would yield your hearts' best and holiest affections to Him. As these warnings revive distinctly before me, I feel a sense of your danger that I know you do not feel. The school located in Battle Creek brings together many young people of different mental organizations. If these youth are not consecrated to God and obedient to His will, and do not walk humbly in the way of His commandments, the location of a school in Battle Creek will prove a means of great discouragement to the church. This school may be made a blessing or a curse. I entreat you who have named the name of Christ to depart from all iniquity and develop characters that God can approve.

I inquire: Do you believe that the testimonies of reproof which have been given you are of God? If you really believe that the voice of God has spoken to you, pointing out your dangers, do you heed the counsels given? Do you keep these testimonies of warning fresh in your minds by reading them often with prayerful hearts? The Lord has spoken to you, children and youth, again and again, but you have been slow to heed the warnings given. If you have not rebelliously braced your hearts against the views that God has given of your characters and your dangers, and against the course marked out for you to pursue, some of you have been inattentive in regard to the things required of you that you might gain spiritual strength and be a blessing in the school, in the church, and to all with whom you associate.

Young men and women, you are accountable to God for the light that He has given you. This light and these warnings, if not heeded, will rise up in the judgment against you. Your dangers have been plainly stated; you have been cautioned and guarded on every side, hedged in with warnings. In the house of God you have listened to the most solemn, heart-searching truths presented by the servants of God in demonstration of the Spirit. What weight do these solemn appeals have upon your hearts? What influence do they have upon your characters? You will be held responsible for every one of these appeals and warnings. They will rise up in the judgment to condemn those who pursue a life of vanity, levity, and pride.

Dear young friends, that which you sow, you will also reap. Now is the sowing time for you. What will the harvest be? What are you sowing? Every word you utter, every act you perform, is a seed which will bear good or evil fruit and will result in joy or sorrow to the sower. As is the seed sown, so will be the crop. God has given you great light and many privileges. After this light has been given, after your dangers have been plainly presented before you, the responsibility becomes yours. The manner in which you treat the light that God gives you will turn the scale for happiness or woe. You are shaping your destinies for yourselves.

You all have an influence for good or for evil on the minds and characters of others. And just the influence which you exert is written in the book of records in heaven. An angel is attending you and taking record of your words and actions. When you rise in the morning, do you feel your helplessness and your need of strength from God? and do you humbly, heartily make known your wants to your heavenly Father? If so, angels mark your prayers, and if these prayers have not gone forth out of feigned lips, when you are in danger of unconsciously doing wrong and exerting an influence which will lead others to do wrong, your guardian angel will be by your side, prompting you to a better course, choosing your words for you, and influencing your actions.

If you feel in no danger, and if you offer no prayer for help and strength to resist temptations, you will be sure to go astray; your neglect of duty will be marked in the book of God in heaven, and you will be found wanting in the trying day. There are some around you who have been religiously instructed, and some who have been indulged, petted, flattered, and praised until they have been literally spoiled for practical life. I am speaking in regard to persons that I know. Their characters are so warped by indulgence, flattery, and indolence that they are useless for this life. And if useless so far as this life is concerned, what may we hope for that life where all is purity and holiness, and where all have harmonious characters? I have prayed for these persons; I have addressed them personally. I could see the influence that they would exert over other minds in leading them to vanity, love of dress, and carelessness in regard to their eternal interests. The only hope for this class is for them to take heed to their ways, humble their proud, vain hearts before God, make confession of their sins, and be converted.

Vanity in dress as well as the love of amusement is a great temptation for the youth. God has sacred claims upon us all. He claims the whole heart, the whole soul, the whole affections. The answer which is sometimes made to this statement is: "Oh, I do not profess to be a Christian!" What if you do not? Has not God the same claims upon you that He has upon the one who professes to be His child? Because you are bold in your careless disregard of sacred things, is your sin of neglect and rebellion passed over by the Lord? Every day that you disregard the claims of God, every opportunity of offered mercy that you slight, is charged to your account and will swell the list of sins against you in the day when the accounts of every soul will be investigated. I address you, young men and women, professors or nonprofessors: God calls for your affections, for your cheerful obedience and devotion to Him. You now have a short time of probation, and you may improve this opportunity to make an unconditional surrender to God.

Obedience and submission to God's requirements are the conditions given by the inspired apostle by which we become children of God, members of the royal family. Every child and youth, every man and woman, has Jesus rescued by His own blood from the abyss of ruin to which Satan was compelling them to go. Because sinners will not accept of the salvation freely offered them, are they released from their obligations? Their choosing to remain in sin and bold transgression does not lessen their guilt. Jesus paid a price for them, and they belong to Him. They are His property; and if they will not yield obedience to Him who has given His life for them, but devote their time and strength and talents to the service of Satan, they are earning their wages, which is death. Immortal glory and eternal life is the reward that our Redeemer offers to those who will be obedient to Him. He has made it possible for them to perfect Christian character through His name and to overcome on their own account as He overcame in their behalf. He has given them an example in His own life, showing them how they may overcome. "The wages of sin is death; but the gift of God is eternal life through Jesus Christ our Lord."

The claims of God are equally binding upon all. Those who choose to neglect the great salvation offered to them freely, who choose to serve themselves and remain enemies of God, enemies of the self-sacrificing Redeemer, are earning their wages. They are sowing to the flesh and will of the flesh reap corruption.

Those who have put on Christ by baptism, by this act showing their separation from the world and that they have covenanted to walk in newness of life, should not set up idols in their hearts. Those who have once rejoiced in the evidence of sins forgiven, who have tasted a Saviour's love and who then persist in uniting with the foes of Christ, rejecting the perfect righteousness that Jesus offers them and choosing the ways that He has condemned, will be more severely judged than the heathen who have never had the light and have never known God or His law. Those who refuse to follow the light which God has given them, choosing the amusements, vanities, and follies of the world, and refusing to conform their conduct to the just and holy requirements of God's law, are guilty of the most aggravating sins in the sight of God. Their guilt and their wages will be proportionate to the light and privileges which they have had.

We see the world absorbed in their own amusements. The first and highest thoughts of the larger portion, especially of women, are of display. Love of dress and pleasure is wrecking the happiness of thousands. And some of those who profess to love and keep the commandments of God ape this class as near as they possibly can and retain the Christian name. Some of the young are so eager for display that they are even willing to give up the Christian name if they can only follow out their inclination for vanity of dress and love of pleasure. Self-denial in dress is a part of our Christian duty. To dress plainly, abstaining from display of jewelry and ornaments of every kind, is in keeping with our faith. Are we of the number who see the folly of worldlings in indulging in extravagance of dress as well as in love of amusements? If so, we should be of that class who shun everything that gives sanction to this spirit which takes possession of the minds and hearts of those who live for this world only and who have no thought or care for the next.

Christian youth, I have seen in some of you a love for dress and display which has pained me. In some who have been well instructed, who have had religious privileges from their babyhood, and who have put on Christ by baptism, thus professing to be dead to the world, I have seen a vanity in dress and a levity in conduct that have grieved the dear Saviour and have been a reproach to the cause of God. I have marked with pain your religious declension and your disposition to trim and ornament your apparel. Some have been so unfortunate as to come into possession of gold chains or pins, or both, and have shown bad taste in exhibiting them, making them conspicuous to attract attention. I can but associate these characters with the vain peacock, that displays his gorgeous feathers for admiration. It is all this poor bird has to attract attention, for his voice and form are anything but attractive.

The young may endeavor to excel in seeking for the ornament of a meek and quiet spirit, a jewel of inestimable value that may be worn with heavenly grace. This adorning will possess attractions for many in this world, and will be esteemed of great price by the heavenly angels, and above all by our heavenly Father, and will fit the wearers to be welcome guests in the heavenly courts.

The youth have faculties that, with proper cultivation, would qualify them for almost any position of trust. If they had made it their object in obtaining an education to so exercise and develop the powers that God has given them that they might be useful and prove a blessing to others, their minds would not be dwarfed to an inferior standard. They would show depth of thought and firmness of principle, and would command influence and respect. They might have an elevating influence upon others, which would lead souls to see and acknowledge the power of an intelligent Christian life. Those who have greater care to ornament their persons for display than to educate the mind and exercise their powers for the greatest usefulness, that they may glorify God, do not realize their accountability to God. They will be inclined to be superficial in all they undertake and will narrow their usefulness and dwarf their intellect.

I feel deeply pained at heart for the fathers and mothers of these youth, as well as for the children. There has been a lack in the training of these children which leaves a heavy responsibility somewhere. Parents who have petted and indulged their children instead of from principle judiciously restraining them, can see the characters they have formed. As the training has been, so the character inclines.

FAITHFUL ABRAHAM

My mind goes back to faithful Abraham, who, in obedience to the divine command given him in a night vision at Beersheba, pursues his journey with Isaac by his side. He sees before him the mountain which God had told him He would signalize as the one upon which he was to sacrifice. He removes the wood from the shoulder of his servant and lays it upon Isaac, the one to be offered. He girds up his soul with firmness and agonizing sternness, ready for the work which God requires him to do. With a breaking heart and unnerved hand, he takes the fire, while Isaac inquires: Father, here is the fire and the wood; but where is the offering? But, oh, Abraham cannot tell him now! Father and son build the altar, and the terrible moment comes for Abraham to make known to Isaac that which has agonized his soul all that long journey, that Isaac himself is the victim. Isaac is not a lad; he is a full-grown young man. He could have refused to submit to his father's design had he chosen to do so. He does not accuse his father of insanity, nor does he even seek to change his purpose. He submits. He believes in the love of his father and that he would not make this terrible sacrifice of his only son if God had not bidden him do so. Isaac is bound by the trembling, loving hands of his pitying father because God has said it. The son submits to the sacrifice because he believes in the integrity of his father. But when everything is ready, when the faith of the father and the submission of the son are fully tested, the angel of God stays the uplifted hand of Abraham that is about to slay his son and tells him that it is enough. "Now I know that thou fearest God, seeing thou hast not withheld thy son, thine only son from Me."

This act of faith in Abraham is recorded for our benefit. It teaches us the great lesson of confidence in the requirements of God, however close and cutting they may be; and it teaches children perfect submission to their parents and to God. By Abraham's obedience we are taught that nothing is too precious for us to give to God.

Isaac was a figure of the Son of God, who was offered a sacrifice for the sins of the world. God would impress upon Abraham the gospel of salvation to man. In order to do this, and make the truth a reality to him as well as to test his faith, He required him to slay his darling Isaac. All the sorrow and agony that Abraham endured through that dark and fearful trial were for the purpose of deeply impressing upon his understanding the plan of redemption for fallen man. He was made to understand in his own experience how unutterable was the self-denial of the infinite God in giving His own Son to die to rescue man from utter ruin. To Abraham no mental torture could be equal to that which he endured in obeying the divine command to sacrifice his son.

God gave His Son to a life of humiliation, self-denial, poverty, toil, reproach, and to the agonizing death of crucifixion. But there was no angel to bear the joyful message: "It is enough; You need not die, My well-beloved Son." Legions of angels were sorrowfully waiting, hoping that, as in the case of Isaac, God would at the last moment prevent His shameful death. But angels were not permitted to bear any such message to God's dear Son. The humiliation in the judgment hall and on the way to Calvary went on. He was mocked, derided, and spit upon. He endured the jeers, taunts, and revilings of those who hated Him, until upon the cross He bowed His head and died.

Could God give us any greater proof of His love than in thus giving His Son to pass through this scene of suffering? And as the gift of God to man was a free gift, His love infinite, so His claims upon our confidence, our obedience, our whole heart, and the wealth of our affections are correspondingly infinite. He requires all that it is possible for man to give. The submission on our part must be proportionate to the gift of God; it must be complete and wanting in nothing. We are all debtors to God. He has claims upon us that we cannot meet without giving ourselves a full and willing sacrifice. He claims prompt and willing obedience, and nothing short of this will He accept. We have opportunity now to secure the love and favor of God. This year may be the last year in the lives of some who read this. Are there any among the youth who read this appeal who would choose the pleasures of the world before that peace which Christ gives the earnest seeker and the cheerful doer of His will?

God is weighing our characters, our conduct, and our motives in the balances of the sanctuary. It will be a fearful thing to be pronounced wanting in love and obedience by our Redeemer, who died upon the cross to draw our hearts unto Him. God has bestowed upon us great and precious gifts. He has given us light and a knowledge of His will, so that we need not err or walk in darkness. To be weighed in the balance and found wanting in the day of final settlement and rewards will be a fearful thing, a terrible mistake which can never be corrected. Young friends, shall the book of God be searched in vain for your names?

God has appointed you a work to do for Him which will make you colaborers with Him. All around you there are souls to save. There are those whom you can encourage and bless by your earnest efforts. You may turn souls from sin to righteousness. When you have a sense of your accountability to God you will feel the need of faithfulness in prayer and faithfulness in watching against the temptations of Satan. You will, if you are indeed Christians, feel more like mourning over the moral darkness in the world than indulging in levity and pride of dress. You will be among those who are sighing and crying for the abominations that are done in the land. You will resist the temptations of Satan to indulge in vanity and in trimmings and ornaments for display. The mind is narrowed and the intellect dwarfed that can be gratified with these frivolous things to the neglect of high responsibilities.

The youth in our day may be workers with Christ if they will; and in working, their faith will strengthen and their knowledge of the divine will will increase. Every true purpose and every act of right doing will be recorded in the book of life. I wish I could arouse the youth to see and feel the sinfulness of living for their own gratification and dwarfing their intellects to the cheap, vain things of this life. If they would elevate their thoughts and words above the frivolous attractions of this world and make it their aim to glorify God, His peace, which passeth all understanding, would be theirs.

HUMILIATION OF CHRIST

Did not our Exemplar tread a hard, self-denying, self-sacrificing, humble path on our account in order to save us? He encountered difficulties, experienced disappointments, and suffered reproach and affliction in His work of saving us. And shall we refuse to follow where the King of glory has led the way? Shall we complain of hardship and trial in the work of overcoming on our own account, when we remember the sufferings of our Redeemer in the wilderness of temptation, in the Garden of Gethsemane, and on Calvary? All these were endured to show us the way and to bring us the divine help that we must have or perish. If the youth would win eternal life, they need not expect that they can follow their own inclinations. The prize will cost them something, yes, everything. They can now have Jesus or the world. How many dear youth will suffer privation, weariness, toil, and anxiety in order to serve themselves and gain an object in this life! They do not think of complaining of the hardships and difficulties they encounter in order to serve their own interest. Why, then, should they shrink from conflict, self-denial, or any sacrifice in order to obtain eternal life?

Christ came from the courts of glory to this sin-polluted world and humbled Himself to humanity. He identified Himself with our weaknesses and was tempted in all points like as we are. Christ perfected a righteous character here upon the earth, not on His own account, for His character was pure and spotless, but for fallen man. His character He offers to man if he will accept it. The sinner, through repentance of his sins, faith in Christ, and obedience to the perfect law of God, has the righteousness of Christ imputed to him; it becomes his righteousness, and his name is recorded in the Lamb's book of life. He becomes a child of God, a member of the royal family.

Jesus paid an infinite price to redeem the world, and the race was given into His hands; they became His property. He sacrificed His honor, His riches, and His glorious home in the royal courts and became the son of Joseph and Mary. Joseph was one of the humblest of day laborers. Jesus also worked; he lived a life of hardship and toil. When His ministry commenced, after His baptism. He endured an agonizing fast of nearly six weeks. It was not merely the gnawing pangs of hunger which made His sufferings inexpressibly severe, but it was the guilt of the sins of the world which pressed so heavily upon Him. He who knew no sin was made sin for us. With this terrible weight of guilt upon Him because of our sins He withstood the fearful test upon appetite, and upon love of the world and of honor, and pride of display which leads to presumption. Christ endured these three great leading temptations and overcame in behalf of man, working out for him a righteous character, because He knew man could not do this of himself. He knew that upon these three points Satan was to assail the race. He had overcome Adam, and he designed to carry forward his work till he completed the ruin of man. Christ entered the field in man's behalf to conquer Satan for him because He saw that man could not overcome on his own account. Christ prepared the way for the ransom of man by His own life of suffering, self-denial, and self-sacrifice, and by His humiliation and final death. He brought help to man that he might, by following Christ's example, overcome on his own account, as Christ has overcome for him.

"What? know ye not that your body is the temple of the Holy Ghost which is in you, which ye have of God, and ye are not your own? for ye are bought with a price: therefore glorify God in your body, and in your spirit, which are God's." "Know ye not that ye are the temple of God, and that the Spirit of God dwelleth in you? If any man defile the temple of God, him shall God destroy; for the temple of God is holy, which temple ye are." "Be ye not unequally yoked together with unbelievers: for what fellowship hath righteousness with unrighteousness? and what communion hath light with darkness? and what concord hath Christ with Belial? or what part hath he that believeth with an infidel? and what agreement hath the temple of God with idols? for ye are the temple of the living God; as God hath said, I will dwell in them, and walk in them; and I will be their God, and they shall be My people. Wherefore come out from among them; and be ye separate, saith the Lord, and touch not the unclean thing; and I will receive you, and will be a Father unto you, and ye shall be My sons and daughters, saith the Lord Almighty."

How graciously and tenderly our heavenly Father deals with His children! He preserves them from a thousand dangers to them unseen and guards them from the subtle arts of Satan, lest they should be destroyed. Because the protecting care of God through His angels is not seen by our dull vision, we do not try to contemplate and appreciate the ever-watchful interest that our kind and benevolent Creator has in the work of His hands; and we are not grateful for the multitude of mercies that He daily bestows upon us.

The young are ignorant of the many dangers to which they are daily exposed. They can never fully know them all; but if they are watchful and prayerful, God will keep their consciences sensitive and their perceptions clear, that they may discern the workings of the enemy and be fortified against his attacks. But many of the young have so long followed their own inclinations that duty is a meaningless word to them. They do not realize the high and holy duties which they may have to do for the benefit of others and for the glory of God; and they utterly neglect to perform them.

If the youth could only awake to deeply feel their need of strength from God to resist the temptations of Satan, precious victories would be theirs, and they would obtain a valuable experience in the Christian warfare. How few of the young think of the exhortation of the inspired apostle Peter: "Be sober, be vigilant; because your adversary the devil, as a roaring lion, walketh about, seeking whom he may devour: whom resist steadfast in the faith." In the vision given to John he saw the power of Satan over men and exclaimed: "Woe to the inhabiters of the earth and of the sea! for the devil is come down unto you, having great wrath, because he knoweth that he hath but a short time."

The only safety for the young is in unceasing watchfulness and humble prayer. They need not flatter themselves that they can be Christians without these. Satan conceals his temptations and his devices under a cover of light, as when he approached Christ in the wilderness. He was then in appearance as one of the heavenly angels. The adversary of our souls will approach us as a heavenly guest, and the apostle recommends sobriety and vigilance as our only safety. The young who indulge in carelessness and levity, and who neglect Christian duties, are continually falling under the temptations of the enemy, instead of overcoming as Christ overcame.

The service of Christ is not drudgery to the fully consecrated soul. Obedience to our Saviour does not detract from our happiness and true pleasure in this life, but it has a refining, elevating power upon our characters. The daily study of the precious words of life found in the Bible strengthens the intellect and furnishes a knowledge of the grand and glorious works of God in nature. Through the study of the Scriptures we obtain a correct knowledge of how to live so as to enjoy the greatest amount of unalloyed happiness. The Bible student is also furnished with Scripture arguments so that he can meet the doubts of unbelievers and remove them by the clear light of truth. Those who have searched the Scriptures may ever be fortified against the temptations of Satan; they may be thoroughly furnished to all good works and prepared to give to every man that asketh them a reason of the hope that is in them.

The impression is too frequently left upon minds that religion is degrading and that it is a condescension for sinners to accept of the Bible standard as their rule of life. They think that its requirements are unrefined, and that, in accepting it, they must relinquish all their tastes for, and enjoyment of, that which is beautiful, and instead must accept of humiliation and degradation. Satan never fastens a greater deception upon minds than this. The pure religion of Jesus requires of its followers the simplicity of natural beauty and the polish of natural refinement and elevated purity, rather than the artificial and false.

While pure religion is looked upon as exacting in its demands and, with the young especially, is unfavorably contrasted with the false glitter and tinsel of the world, the Bible requirements are regarded as humiliating, self-denying tests, which take from them all the enjoyment of life. But the religion of the Bible ever has a tendency to elevate and refine. And had the professed followers of Christ carried out the principles of pure religion in their lives, the religion of Christ would be acceptable to more refined minds. The religion of the Bible has nothing in it which would jar upon the finest feelings. It is, in all its precepts and requirements, as pure as the character of God and as elevated as His throne.

The Redeemer of the world has warned us against the pride of life, but not against its grace and natural beauty. He pointed to all the glowing beauty of the flowers of the field and to the lily reposing in its spotless purity upon the bosom of the lake and said: "Consider the lilies of the field, how they grow; they toil not, neither do they spin: and yet I say unto you, That even Solomon in all his glory was not arrayed like one of these." Here He shows that notwithstanding persons may have great care, and may toil with weariness to make themselves objects of admiration by their outward decorations, all their artificial adornments, which they value so highly, will not bear comparison with the simple flowers of the field for natural loveliness. Even these simple flowers, with God's adornment, would outvie in loveliness the gorgeous apparel of Solomon. "Even Solomon in all his glory was not arrayed like one of these."

Here is an important lesson for every follower of Christ. The Redeemer of the world speaks to the youth. Will you listen to His words of heavenly instruction? He presents before you themes for thought that will ennoble, elevate, refine, and purify, but which will never degrade or dwarf the intellect. His voice is speaking to you: "Ye are the light of the world. A city that is set on an hill cannot be hid." "Let your light so shine before men, that they may see your good works, and glorify your Father which is in heaven." If the light of God be in you, it will shine forth to others. It can never be concealed.

Dear youth, a disposition in you to dress according to the fashion, and to wear lace and gold and artificials for display, will not recommend to others your religion or the truth that you profess. People of discernment will look upon your attempts to beautify the external as proof of weak minds and proud hearts. Simple, plain, unpretending dress will be a recommendation to my youthful sisters. In no better way can you let your light shine to others than in your simplicity of dress and deportment. You may show to all that, in comparison with eternal things, you place a proper estimate upon the things of this life.

Now is your golden opportunity to form pure and holy characters for heaven. You cannot afford to devote these precious moments to trimming and ruffling and beautifying the external to the neglect of the inward adorning. "Whose adorning let it not be that outward adorning of plaiting the hair, and of wearing of gold, or of putting on of apparel; but let it be the hidden man of the heart, in that which is not corruptible, even the ornament of a meek and quiet spirit, which is in the sight of God of great price."

God, who created everything lovely and beautiful that the eye rests upon, is a lover of the beautiful. He shows you how He estimates true beauty. The ornament of a meek and quiet spirit is in His sight of *great price*. Shall we not seek earnestly to gain that which God estimates as more valuable than costly dress or pearls or gold? The inward adorning, the grace of meekness, a spirit in harmony with the heavenly angels, will not lessen true dignity of character or make us less lovely here in this world.

Religion, pure and undefiled, ennobles its possessor. You will ever find with the true Christian a marked cheerfulness, a holy, happy confidence in God, a submission to His providences, that is refreshing to the soul. By the Christian, God's love and benevolence can be seen in every bounty he receives. The beauties in nature are a theme for contemplation. In studying the natural loveliness surrounding us, the mind is carried up through nature to the Author of all that is lovely. All the works of God are speaking to our senses, magnifying His power, exalting His wisdom. Every created thing has in it charms which interest the child of God and mold his taste to regard these precious evidences of God's love above the work of human skill.

The prophet, in words of glowing fervor, magnifies God in His created works: "When I consider Thy heavens, the work of Thy fingers, the moon and the stars, which Thou hast ordained; what is man, that Thou art mindful of him? and the son of man, that Thou visitest him?" "O Lord our Lord, how excellent is Thy name in all the earth! I will praise thee, O Lord, with my whole heart; I will show forth all Thy marvelous works."

It is absence of religion that makes the path of so many professors of religion shadowy. There are those who may pass for Christians but who are unworthy the name. They have not Christian characters. When their Christianity is put to the test, its falsity is too evident. True religion is seen in the daily deportment. The life of the Christian is characterized by earnest, unselfish working to do others good and to glorify God. His path is not dark and gloomy. An inspired writer has said: "But the path of the just is as the shining light, that shineth more and more unto the perfect day. The way of the wicked is as darkness: they know not at what they stumble."

And shall the young live vain and thoughtless lives of fashion and frivolity, dwarfing their intellect to the matter of dress and consuming their time in sensual pleasure? When they are all unready, God may say to them: "This night your folly shall end." He may permit mortal sickness to come upon those who have borne no fruit to His glory. While facing the realities of eternity, they may begin to realize the value of time and of the life they have lost. They may then have some sense of the worth of the soul. They see that their lives have not glorified God in lighting the path of others to heaven. They have lived to glorify self. And when racked with pain and with anguish of soul they cannot have clear conceptions of eternal things. They may review their past lives, and in their remorse may each cry out: "I have done nothing for Jesus, who has done everything for me. My life has been a terrible failure."

While you pray, dear youth, that you may not be led into temptation, remember that your work does not end with the prayer. You must then answer your own prayer as far as possible by resisting temptation, and leave that which you cannot do for yourselves for Jesus to do for you. You cannot be too guarded in your words and in your deportment, lest you invite the enemy to tempt you. Many of our youth, by their careless disregard of the warnings and reproofs given them, open the door wide for Satan to enter. With God's word for our guide and Jesus as our heavenly Teacher we need not be ignorant of His requirements or of Satan's devices and be overcome by his temptations. It will be no unpleasant task to be obedient to the will of God when we yield ourselves fully to be directed by His Spirit.

Now is the time to work. If we are children of God, as long as we live in the world He will give us our work. We can never say that we have nothing to do so long as there remains a work undone. I wish that all the young could see, as I have seen, the work that they can do and that God will hold them responsible for neglecting. The greatest work that was ever accomplished in the world was done by Him who was a man of sorrows and acquainted with grief. A frivolous-minded person will never accomplish good.

The spiritual weakness of many young men and women in this age is deplorable because they could be powerful agents for good if they were consecrated to God. I mourn greatly the lack of stability with the young. This we should all deplore. There seems to be a lack of power to do right, a lack of earnest effort to obey the calls of duty rather than those of inclination. There seems to be with some but little strength to resist temptation. The reason why they are dwarfs in spiritual things is because they do not by exercise grow spiritually strong. They stand still when they should be going forward. Every step in the life of faith and duty is a step toward heaven. I want greatly to hear of a reformation in many respects such as the young have never heretofore realized. Every inducement that Satan can invent is pressed upon them to make them indifferent and careless in regard to eternal things. I suggest that special efforts be made by the youth to help one another to live faithful to their baptismal vows and that they pledge themselves solemnly before God to withdraw their affections from dress and display.

I would remind the youth who ornament their persons and wear feathers upon their hats that, because of their sins, our Saviour's head wore the shameful crown of thorns. When you devote precious time to trimming your apparel, remember that the King of glory wore a plain, seamless coat. You who weary yourselves in decorating your persons, please bear in mind that Jesus was often weary from incessant toil and self-denial and self-sacrifice to bless the suffering and needy. He spent whole nights in prayer upon the lonely mountains, not because of His weakness and His necessities, but because He saw, He felt, the weakness of your natures to resist the temptations of the enemy upon the very points where you are now overcome. He knew that you would be indifferent in regard to your dangers and would not feel your need of prayer. It was on our account that He poured out His prayers to His Father with strong cries and tears. It was to save us from the very pride and love of vanity and pleasure which we now indulge, and which crowds out the love of Jesus, that those tears were shed and that our Saviour's visage was marred with sorrow and anguish more than any of the sons of men.

Will you, young friends, arise and shake off this dreadful indifference and stupor which has conformed you to the world? Will you heed the voice of warning which tells you that destruction lies in the path of those who are at ease in this hour of danger? God's patience will not always wait for you, poor, trifling souls. He who holds our destinies in His hands will not always be trifled with. Jesus declares to us that there is a greater sin than that which caused the destruction of Sodom and Gomorrah. It is the sin of those who have the great light of truth in these days and who are not moved to repentance. It is the sin of rejecting the light of the most solemn message of mercy to the world. It is the sin of those who see Jesus in the wilderness of temptation, bowed down as with mortal agony because of the sins of the world, and yet are not moved to thorough repentance. He fasted nearly six weeks to overcome, in behalf of men, the indulgence of appetite and vanity, and the desire for display and worldly honor. He has shown them how they may overcome on their own account as He overcame; but it is not pleasant to their natures to endure conflict and reproach, derision and shame, for His dear sake. It is not agreeable to deny self and to be ever seeking to do good to others. It is not pleasant to overcome as Christ overcame, so they turn from the pattern which is plainly given them to copy and refuse to imitate the example that the Saviour came from the heavenly courts to leave them.

It shall be more tolerable for Sodom and Gomorrah in the day of judgment than for those who have had the privileges and the great light which shines in our day, but who have neglected to follow the light and to give their hearts fully to God.

TITHES AND OFFERINGS

The mission of the church of Christ is to save perishing sinners. It is to make known the love of God to men and to win them to Christ by the efficacy of that love. The truth for this time must be carried into the dark corners of the earth, and this work may begin at home. The followers of Christ should not live selfish lives; but, imbued with the Spirit of Christ, they should work in harmony with Him.

There are causes for the present coldness and unbelief. The love of the world and the cares of life separate the soul from God. The water of life must be in us, and flowing out from us, springing up into everlasting life. We must work out what God works in. If the Christian would enjoy the light of life, he must increase his efforts to bring others to the knowledge of the truth. His life must be characterized by exertion and sacrifices to do others good; and then there will be no complaints of lack of enjoyment.

Angels are ever engaged in working for the happiness of others. This is their joy. That which selfish hearts would consider humiliating service, ministering to those who are wretched and in every way inferior in character and rank, is the work of the pure, sinless angels in the royal courts of heaven. The spirit of Christ's self-sacrificing love is the spirit which pervades heaven and is the very essence of its bliss.

Those who feel no special pleasure in seeking to be a blessing to others, in working, even at a sacrifice, to do them good, cannot have the spirit of Christ or of heaven; for they have no union with the work of heavenly angels and cannot participate in the bliss that imparts elevated joy to them. Christ has said: "Joy shall be in heaven over one sinner that repenteth, more than over ninety and nine just persons, which need no repentance." If the joy of angels is to see sinners repent, will it not be the joy of sinners, saved by the blood of Christ, to see others repent and turn to Christ through their instrumentality? In working in harmony with Christ and the holy angels we shall experience a joy that cannot be realized aside from this work.

The principle of the cross of Christ brings all who believe under heavy obligations to deny self, to impart light to others, and to give of their means to extend the light. If they are in connection with heaven they will be engaged in the work in harmony with the angels.

The principle of worldlings is to get all they can of the perishable things of this life. Selfish love of gain is the ruling principle in their lives. But the purest joy is not found in riches nor where covetousness is always craving, but where contentment reigns and where self-sacrificing love is the ruling principle. There are thousands who are passing their lives in indulgence and whose hearts are filled with repining. They are victims of selfishness and discontent in the vain effort to satisfy their minds with indulgence. But unhappiness is stamped upon their very countenances, and behind them is a desert, because their course is not fruitful in good works.

In proportion as the love of Christ fills our hearts and controls our lives, covetousness, selfishness, and love of ease will be overcome, and it will be our pleasure to do the will of Christ, whose servants we claim to be. Our happiness will then be proportionate to our unselfish works, prompted by the love of Christ.

Divine wisdom has appointed, in the plan of salvation, the law of action and reaction, making the work of beneficence, in all its branches, twice blessed. He that gives to the needy blesses others, and is blessed himself in a still greater degree. God could have reached His object in saving sinners without the aid of man; but He knew that man could not be happy without acting a part in the great work in which he would be cultivating self-denial and benevolence.

That man might not lose the blessed results of benevolence, our Redeemer formed the plan of enlisting him as His co-worker. By a chain of circumstances which would call forth his charities, He bestows upon man the best means of cultivating benevolence and keeps him habitually giving to help the poor and to advance His cause. He sends His poor as the representatives of Himself. By their necessities a ruined world are drawing forth from us talents of means and of influence to present to them the truth, of which they are in perishing need. And as we heed these calls by labor and by acts of benevolence we are assimilated to the image of Him who for our sakes became poor. In bestowing we bless others, and thus accumulate true riches.

There has been a great lack of Christian benevolence in the church. Those who were the best able to do for the advancement of the cause of God have done but little. God has mercifully brought a class to the knowledge of the truth, that they might appreciate its priceless value in comparison with earthly treasures. Jesus has said to these: "Follow Me." He is testing them with an invitation to the supper which He has prepared. He is watching to see what characters they will develop, whether their own selfish interests will be considered of greater value than eternal riches. Many of these dear brethren are now by their actions framing the excuses mentioned in the following parable:

"Then said He unto him, A certain man made a great supper, and bade many: and sent his servant at suppertime to say to them that were bidden, Come; for all things are now ready. And they all with one consent began to make excuse. The first said unto him, I have bought a piece of ground, and I must needs go and see it: I pray thee have me excused. And another said, I have bought five yoke of oxen, and I go to prove them: I pray thee have me excused. And another said, I have married a wife, and therefore I cannot come. So that servant came, and showed his lord these things. Then the master of the house being angry said to his servant, Go out quickly into the streets and lanes of the city, and bring in hither the poor, and the maimed, and the halt, and the blind."

This parable correctly represents the condition of many professing to believe the present truth. The Lord has sent them an invitation to come to the supper which He has prepared for them at great cost to Himself, but worldly interests look to them of greater importance than the heavenly treasure. They are invited to take part in things of eternal value; but their farms, their cattle, and their home interests seem of so much greater importance than obedience to the heavenly invitation that they overpower every divine attraction, and these earthly things are made the excuse for their disobedience to the heavenly command, "Come; for all things are now ready." These brethren are blindly following the example of those represented in the parable. They look at their worldly possessions, and say: No, Lord, I cannot follow Thee; "I pray Thee have me excused."

The very blessings which God has given to these men to prove them, to see if they will render "unto God the things that are God's," they use as an excuse that they cannot obey the claims of truth. They have grasped their earthly treasure in their arms and say, "I must take care of these things; I must not neglect the things of this life; these things are mine." Thus the hearts of these men have become as unimpressible as the beaten highway. They close the door of their hearts to the heavenly messenger, who says, "Come; for all things are now ready," and throw it open, inviting the entrance of the world's burden and business cares, and Jesus knocks in vain for admittance.

Their hearts are so overgrown with thorns and with the cares of this life that heavenly things can find no place in them. Jesus invites the weary and heavy-laden with promises of rest if they will come to Him. He invites them to exchange the galling yoke of selfishness and covetousness, which makes them slaves to mammon, for His yoke, which He declares is easy, and His burden, which is light. He says: "Learn of Me; for I am meek and lowly in heart: and ye shall find rest unto your souls." He would have them lay aside the heavy burdens of worldly care and perplexity, and take His yoke, which is self-denial and sacrifice for others. This burden will prove to be light. Those who refuse to accept the relief which Christ offers them, and continue to wear the galling yoke of selfishness, tasking their souls to the utmost in plans to accumulate money for selfish gratification, have not experienced the peace and rest found in bearing the yoke of Christ and lifting the burdens of self-denial and disinterested benevolence which Christ has borne in their behalf.

When the love of the world takes possession of the heart and becomes a ruling passion, there is no room left for adoration to God; for the higher powers of the mind submit to the slavery of mammon, and cannot retain thoughts of God and of heaven. The mind loses its remembrance of God and is narrowed and dwarfed to the accumulation of money.

Because of selfishness and love of the world, these men have been passing on with less and less sense of the magnitude of the work for these last days. They have not educated their minds to make a business of serving God. They have not an experience in that direction. Their property has absorbed their affections and eclipsed the magnitude of the plan of salvation. While they are improving and enlarging their worldly plans, they see no necessity for the enlargement and extension of the work of God. They invest their means in temporal but not in eternal things. Their hearts are ambitious for more means. God has made them depositaries of His law, that they might let the light so graciously given them shine forth to others. But they have so increased their cares and anxieties that they have no time to bless others with their influence, to converse with their neighbors, to pray with and for them, and to seek to bring them to the knowledge of the truth.

These men are responsible for the good they might do, but from which they excuse themselves because of worldly cares and burdens, which engross their minds and absorb their affections. Souls for whom Christ died might be saved by their personal effort and godly example. Precious souls are perishing for the light which God has given to men to be reflected upon the pathway of others. But the precious light is hid under a bushel, and it gives no light to those who are in the house.

Every man is a steward of God. To each the Master has

committed His means, but man claims that means as his own. Christ says: "Occupy till I come." A time is coming when Christ will require His own with usury. He will say to each of His stewards: "Give an account of thy stewardship." Those who have hid their Lord's money in a napkin in the earth, instead of putting it out to the exchangers, and those who have squandered their Lord's money by expending it for needless things, instead of putting it out to usury by investing it in His cause, will not receive approval from the Master, but decided condemnation. The unprofitable servant in the parable brought back the one talent to God, and said: "I knew thee that thou art an hard man, reaping where thou hast not sown, and gathering where thou hast not strewed: and I was afraid, and went and hid thy talent in the earth: lo, there thou hast that is thine." His Lord takes up his words: "Thou wicked and slothful servant, thou knewest that I reap where I sowed not, and gather where I have not strewed; thou oughtest therefore to have put my money to the exchangers, and then at my coming I should have received mine own with usury."

This unprofitable servant was not ignorant of God's plans, but he set himself firmly to thwart the purpose of God, charging Him with unfairness in requiring improvement upon the talents entrusted to him. This very complaint and murmuring is made by a large class of wealthy men professing to believe the truth. Like the unfaithful servant they are afraid that the increase of the talent that God has lent them will be called for to advance the spread of truth; therefore they tie it up by investing it in earthly treasures and burying it in the world, thus making it so fast that they have nothing, or next to nothing, to invest in the cause of God. They have buried it, fearing that God would call for some of the principal or increase. When, at the demand of their Lord, they bring the amount given them, they come with ungrateful excuses for not having put the means lent them by God out to the exchangers, by investing it in His cause to carry on His work.

He who embezzles his Lord's goods not only loses the talent lent him of God, but loses eternal life. Of him it is said: "Cast ye the unprofitable servant into outer darkness." The faithful servant, who invests his money in the cause of God to save souls, employs his means to the glory of God and will receive the commendation of the Master: "Well done, thou good and faithful servant . . . enter thou into the joy of thy Lord." What will be this joy of our Lord? It will be the joy of seeing souls saved in the kingdom of glory. "Who for the joy that was set before Him endured the cross, despising the shame, and is set down at the right hand of the throne of God."

The idea of stewardship should have a practical bearing upon all the people of God. The parable of the talents, rightly understood, will bar out covetousness, which God calls idolatry. Practical benevolence will give spiritual life to thousands of nominal professors of the truth who now mourn over their darkness. It will transform them from selfish, covetous worshipers of mammon to earnest, faithful co-workers with Christ in the salvation of sinners.

The foundation of the plan of salvation was laid in *sacrifice*. Jesus left the royal courts and became poor, that we through His poverty might be made rich. All who share this salvation, purchased for them at such an infinite sacrifice by the Son of God, will follow the example of the true Pattern. Christ was the chief Cornerstone, and we must build upon this Foundation. Each must have a spirit of self-denial and self-sacrifice. The life of Christ upon earth was unselfish; it was marked with humiliation and sacrifice. And shall men, partakers of the great salvation which Jesus came from heaven to bring them, refuse to follow their Lord and to share in His self-denial and sacrifice? Says Christ: "I am the Vine, ye are the branches." "Every branch in Me that beareth not fruit He taketh away: and every branch that beareth fruit, He purgeth it, that it may bring forth more fruit." The very vital principle, the sap which flows through the vine, nourishes the branches, that they may flourish and bear fruit.

Is the servant greater than his Lord? Shall the world's Redeemer practice self-denial and sacrifice on our account, and the members of Christ's body practice self-indulgence? Self-denial is an essential condition of discipleship.

"Then said Jesus unto His disciples, If any man will come after Me, let him deny himself, and take up his cross, and follow Me." I lead the way in the path of self-denial. I require nothing of you, My followers, but that of which I, your Lord, give you an example in My own life.

The Saviour of the world conquered Satan in the wilderness of temptation. He overcame to show man how he may overcome. He announced in the synagogue of Nazareth. "The Spirit of the Lord is upon Me, because He hath anointed Me to preach the gospel to the poor; He hath sent Me to heal the brokenhearted, to preach deliverance to the captives, and recovering of sight to the blind, to set at liberty them that are bruised, to preach the acceptable year of the Lord."

The great work which Jesus announced that He came to do was entrusted to His followers upon the earth. Christ, as our head, leads out in the great work of salvation and bids us follow His example. He has given us a world-wide message. This truth must be extended to all nations, tongues, and people. Satan's power was to be contested, and he was to be overcome by Christ and also by His followers. An extensive war was to be maintained against the powers of darkness. And in order to do this work successfully, means were required. God does not propose to send means direct from heaven, but He gives into the hands of His followers talents of means to use for the very purpose of sustaining this warfare.

He has given His people a plan for raising sums sufficient to make the enterprise self-sustaining. God's plan in the tithing system is beautiful in its simplicity and equality. All may take hold of it in faith and courage, for it is divine in its origin. In it are combined simplicity and utility, and it does not require depth of learning to understand and execute it. All may feel that they can act a part in carrying forward the precious work of salvation. Every man, woman, and youth may become a treasurer for the Lord and may be an agent to meet the demands upon the treasury. Says the apostle: "Let every one of you lay by him in store, as God hath prospered him."

Great objects are accomplished by this system. If one and all would accept it, each would be made a vigilant and faithful treasurer for God, and there would be no want of means with which to carry forward the great work of sounding the last message of warning to the world. The treasury will be full if all adopt this system, and the contributors will not be left the poorer. Through every investment made they will become more wedded to the cause of present truth. They will be "laying up in store for themselves a good foundation against the time to come, that they may lay hold on eternal life."

As the persevering, systematic workers see that the tendency of their benevolent efforts is to nourish love to God and their fellow men, and that their personal efforts are extending their sphere of usefulness, they will realize that it is a great blessing to be co-workers with Christ. The Christian church, as a general thing, are disowning the claims of God upon them to give alms of the things which they possess to support the warfare against the moral darkness which is flooding the world. Never can the work of God advance as it should until the followers of Christ become active, zealous workers.

Every individual in the church should feel that the truth which he professes is a reality, and all should be disinterested workers. Some rich men feel like murmuring because the work of God is extending and there is a demand for money. They say that there is no end to the calls for means. One object after another is continually arising, demanding help. To such we would say that we hope the cause of God will so extend that there will be greater occasion, and more frequent and urgent calls, for supplies from the treasury to prosecute the work.

If the plan of systematic benevolence were adopted by every individual and fully carried out, there would be a constant supply in the treasury. The income would flow in like a steady stream constantly supplied by overflowing springs of benevolence. Almsgiving is a part of gospel religion. Does not the consideration of the infinite price paid for our redemption leave upon us solemn obligations pecuniarily, as well as lay claim upon all our powers to be devoted to the work of the Master?

We shall have a debt to settle with the Master by and by, when He shall say: "Give an account of thy stewardship." If men prefer to set aside the claims of God and to grasp and selfishly retain all that He gives them, He will hold His peace at present and continue frequently to test them by increasing His bounties by letting His blessings flow on, and these men may pass on receiving honor of men and without censure in the church; but by and by He will say: "Give an account of thy stewardship." Says Christ: "Inasmuch as ye did it not to one of the least of these, ye did it not to Me." "Ye are not your own, for ye are bought with a price," and are under obligation to glorify God with your means as well as in your body and in your spirit, which are His. "Ye are bought with a *price*," not "with corruptible things, as silver and gold," "but with the precious blood of Christ." He asks a return of the gifts that He has entrusted to us, to aid in the salvation of souls. He has given His blood; He asks our silver. It is through His poverty that we are made rich; and will we refuse to give back to Him His own gifts?

God is not dependent upon man for the support of His cause. He could have sent means direct from heaven to supply His treasury, if His providence had seen that this was best for man. He might have devised means whereby angels would have been sent to publish the truth to the world without the agency of men. He might have written the truth upon the heavens, and let that declare to the world His requirements in living characters. God is not dependent upon any man's gold or silver. He says: "Every beast of the forest is Mine, and the cattle upon a thousand hills." "If I were hungry, I would not tell thee: for the world is Mine, and the fullness thereof." Whatever necessity there is for our agency in the advancement of the cause of God, He has purposely arranged for our good. He has honored us by making us co-workers with Him. He has ordained that there should be a necessity for the co-operation of men, that they may keep in exercise their benevolence.

God has in His wise providence placed the poor always with us, that while we should witness the various forms of want and suffering in the world, we should be tested and proved, and brought into positions to develop Christian character. He has placed the poor among us to call out from us Christian sympathy and love.

Sinners, who are perishing for lack of knowledge, must be left in ignorance and darkness unless men carry to them the light of truth. God will not send angels from heaven to do the work which He has left for man to do. He has given all a work to do, for the very reason that He might prove them and that they might reveal their true character. Christ places the poor among us as His representatives. "I was anhungered," He says, "and ye gave Me no meat: I was thirsty, and ye gave Me no drink." Christ identifies Himself with suffering humanity in the persons of the suffering children of men. He makes their necessities His own and takes to His bosom their woes.

The moral darkness of a ruined world pleads to Christian men and women to put forth individual effort, to give of their means and of their influence, that they may be assimilated to the image of Him who, though He possessed infinite riches, yet for our sakes became poor. The Spirit of God cannot abide with those to whom He has sent the message of His truth but who need to be urged before they can have any sense of their duty to be co-workers with Christ. The apostle enforces the duty of giving from higher grounds than merely human sympathy because the feelings are moved. He enforces the principle that we should labor unselfishly with an eye single to the glory of God.

Christians are required by the Scriptures to enter upon a

plan of active benevolence which will keep in constant exercise an interest in the salvation of their fellow men. The moral law enjoined the observance of the Sabbath, which was not a burden except when that law was transgressed and they were bound by the penalties involved in breaking it. The tithing system was no burden to those who did not depart from the plan. The system enjoined upon the Hebrews has not been repealed or relaxed by the One who originated it. Instead of being of no force now, it was to be more fully carried out and more extended, as salvation through Christ alone should be more fully brought to light in the Christian age.

Jesus made known to the lawyer that the condition of his having eternal life was to carry out in his life the special requirements of the law, which consisted in his loving God with all his heart, and soul, and mind, and strength, and his neighbor as himself. When the typical sacrifices ceased at the death of Christ, the original law, engraved in tables of stone, stood immutable, holding its claims upon man in all ages. And in the Christian age the duty of man was not limited, but more especially defined and simply expressed.

The gospel, extending and widening, required greater provisions to sustain the warfare after the death of Christ, and this made the law of almsgiving a more urgent necessity than under the Hebrew government. Now God requires, not less, but greater gifts than at any other period of the world. The principle laid down by Christ is that the gifts and offerings should be in proportion to the light and blessings enjoyed. He has said: "For unto whomsoever much is given, of him shall be much required."

The blessings of the Christian Age were responded to by the first disciples in works of charity and benevolence. The outpouring of the Spirit of God, after Christ left His disciples and ascended to heaven, led to self-denial and self-sacrifice for the salvation of others. When the poor saints at Jerusalem were in distress, Paul wrote to the Gentile Christians in regard to works of benevolence, and said: "Therefore, as ye abound in everything, in faith, and utterance, and knowledge, and in all diligence, and in your love to us, see that ye abound in this grace also." Here benevolence is placed by the side of faith, love, and Christian diligence. Those who think that they can be good Christians and close their ears and hearts to the calls of God for their liberalities, are in a fearful deception. There are those who abound in professions of great love for the truth, and, so far as words are concerned, have an interest to see the truth advance, but who do nothing for its advancement. The faith of such is dead, not being made perfect by works. The Lord never made such a mistake as to convert a soul and leave it under the power of covetousness.

The tithing system reaches back beyond the days of Moses. Men were required to offer to God gifts for religious purposes before the definite system was given to Moses, even as far back as the days of Adam. In complying with God's requirements, they were to manifest in offerings their appreciation of His mercies and blessings to them. This was continued through successive generations, and was carried out by Abraham, who gave tithes to Melchizedek, the priest of the most high God. The same principle existed in the days of Job. Jacob, when at Bethel, an exile and penniless wanderer, lay down at night, solitary and alone, with a rock for his pillow, and there promised the Lord: "Of all that Thou shalt give me I will surely give the tenth unto Thee." God does not compel men to give. All that they give must be voluntary. He will not have His treasury replenished with unwilling offerings.

The Lord designed to bring man into close relationship with Himself and into sympathy and love with his fellow men by placing upon him responsibilities in deeds that would counteract selfishness and strengthen his love for God and man. The plan of system in benevolence God designed for the good of man, who is inclined to be selfish and to close his heart to generous deeds. The Lord requires gifts to be made at stated times, being so arranged that giving will become habit and benevolence be felt to be a Christian duty. The heart, opened by one gift, is not to have time to become selfishly cold and to close before the next is bestowed. The stream is to be continually flowing, thus keeping open the channel by acts of benevolence.

As to the amount required, God has specified one tenth of the increase. This is left to the conscience and benevolence of men, whose judgment in this tithing system should have free play. And while it is left free to the conscience, a plan has been laid out definite enough for all. No compulsion is required.

God called for men in the Mosaic dispensation to give the tenth of all their increase. He committed to their trust the things of this life, talents to be improved and returned to Him. He has required a tenth, and this He claims as the very least that man should return to Him. He says: I give you nine tenths, while I require one tenth; that is Mine. When men withhold the one tenth, they rob God. Sin offerings, peace offerings, and thank offerings were also required in addition to the tenth of the increase.

All that is withheld of that which God claims, the tenth of the increase, is recorded in the books of heaven against the withholders, as robbery. Such defraud their Creator; and when this sin of neglect is brought before them, it is not enough for them to change their course and begin to work from that time upon the right principle. This will not correct the figures made in the heavenly record for embezzling the property committed to them in trust to be returned to the Lender. Repentance for unfaithful dealing with God, and for base ingratitude, is required.

"Will a man rob God? Yet ye have robbed Me. But ye say, Wherein have we robbed Thee? In tithes and offerings. Ye are cursed with a curse: for ye have robbed Me, even this whole nation. Bring ye all the tithes into the storehouse, that there may be meat in Mine house, and prove Me now herewith, saith the Lord of hosts, if I will not open you the windows of heaven, and pour you out a blessing, that there shall not be room enough to receive it." A promise is here given that, if all the tithes are brought into the storehouse, a blessing from God will be poured upon the obedient.

"And I will rebuke the devourer for your sakes, and he shall not destroy the fruits of your ground; neither shall your vine cast her fruit before the time in the field, saith the Lord of hosts. And all nations shall call you blessed: for ye shall be a delightsome land, saith the Lord of hosts." If all who profess the truth will come up to the claims of God in giving the tenth, which God says is His, the treasury will be abundantly supplied with means to carry forward the great work for the salvation of man.

God gives man nine tenths, while He claims one tenth for sacred purposes, as He has given man six days for his own work and has reserved and set apart the seventh day to Himself. For, like the Sabbath, a tenth of the increase is sacred; God has reserved it for Himself. He will carry forward His work upon the earth with the increase of the means that He has entrusted to man.

God required of His ancient people three yearly gatherings. "Three times in a year shall all thy males appear before the Lord thy God in the place which He shall choose; in the Feast of Unleavened Bread, and in the Feast of Weeks, and in the Feast of Tabernacles: and they shall not appear before the Lord empty: every man shall give as he is able, according to the blessing of the Lord thy God which He hath given thee." No less than one third of their income was devoted to sacred and religious purposes.

Whenever God's people, in any period of the world, have cheerfully and willingly carried out His plan in systematic benevolence and in gifts and offerings, they have realized the standing promise that prosperity should attend all their labors just in proportion as they obeyed His requirements. When they acknowledged the claims of God and complied with His requirements, honoring Him with their substance, their barns were filled with plenty. But when they robbed God in tithes and in offerings they were made to realize that they were not only robbing Him but themselves, for He limited His blessings to them just in proportion as they limited their offerings to Him.

Some will pronounce this one of the rigorous laws binding upon the Hebrews. But this was not a burden to the willing heart that loved God. It was only when their selfish natures were strengthened by withholding that men lost sight of eternal considerations and valued their earthly treasures above souls. There are even more urgent necessities upon the Israel of God in these last days than were upon ancient Israel. There is a great and important work to be accomplished in a very short time. God never designed that the law of the tithing system should be of no account among His people; but, instead of this, He designed that the spirit of sacrifice should widen and deepen for the closing work.

Systematic benevolence should not be made systematic compulsion. It is freewill offerings that are acceptable to God. True Christian benevolence springs from the principle of grateful love. Love to Christ cannot exist without corresponding love to those whom He came into the world to redeem. Love to Christ must be the ruling principle of the being, controlling all the emotions and directing all the energies. Redeeming love should awaken all the tender affection and self-sacrificing devotion that can possibly exist in the heart of man. When this is the case, no heart-stirring appeals will be needed to break through their selfishness and awaken their dormant sympathies, to call forth benevolent offerings for the precious cause of truth.

Jesus has purchased us at an infinite sacrifice. All our capabilities and our influence are indeed our Saviour's, and should be dedicated to His service. By doing this we show our gratitude that we have been ransomed from the slavery of sin by the precious blood of Christ. Our Saviour is ever working for us. He has ascended on high and pleads in behalf of the purchase of His blood. He pleads before His Father the agonies of the crucifixion. He raises His wounded hands and intercedes for His church, that they may be kept from falling under temptation.

If our perceptions could be quickened to take in this wonderful work of our Saviour for our salvation, love, deep and ardent, would burn in our hearts. Our apathy and cold indifference would then alarm us. Entire devotion and benevolence, prompted by grateful love, will impart to the smallest offering, the willing sacrifice, a divine fragrance, making the gift of priceless value. But, after willingly yielding to our Redeemer all that we can bestow, be it ever so valuable to us, if we view our debt of gratitude to God as it really is, all that we may have offered will seem to us very insufficient and meager. But angels take these offerings, which to us seem poor, and present them as a fragrant offering before the throne, and they are accepted.

We do not, as followers of Christ, realize our true position. We do not have correct views of our responsibilities as hired servants of Christ. He has advanced us the wages in His suffering life and spilled blood, to bind us in willing servitude to Himself. All the good things we have are a loan from our Saviour. He has made us stewards. Our smallest offerings, our humblest services, presented in faith and love, may be consecrated gifts to win souls to the service of the Master and to promote His glory. The interest and prosperity of Christ's kingdom should be paramount to every other consideration. Those who make their pleasure and selfish interest the chief objects of their lives are not faithful stewards.

Those who deny self to do others good, and who devote themselves and all they have to Christ's service, will realize the happiness which the selfish man seeks for in vain. Said our Saviour: "Whosoever he be of you that forsaketh not all that he hath, he cannot be My disciple." Charity "seeketh not her own." This is the fruit of that disinterested love and benevolence which characterized the life of Christ. The law of God in our hearts will bring our own interests in subordination to high and eternal considerations. We are enjoined by Christ to seek first the kingdom of God and His righteousness. This is our first and highest duty. Our Master expressly warned His servants not to lay up treasures upon the earth; for in so doing their hearts would be upon earthly rather than heavenly things. Here is where many poor souls have made shipwreck of faith. They have gone directly contrary to the express injunction of our Lord, and have allowed the love of money to become the ruling passion of their lives. They are intemperate in their efforts to acquire means. They are as much intoxicated with their insane desire for riches as is the inebriate with his liquor.

Christians forget that they are servants of the Master; that they themselves, their time, and all that they have belong to Him. Many are tempted, and the majority are overcome, by the delusive inducements which Satan presents to invest their money where it will yield them the greatest profit in dollars and cents. There are but few who consider the binding claims that God has upon them to make it their first business to meet the necessities of His cause and let their own desires be served last. There are but few who invest in God's cause in proportion to their means. Many have fastened their money in property which they must sell before they can invest it in the cause of God and thus put it to a practical use. They make this an excuse for doing but little in their Redeemer's cause. They have as effectually buried their money in the earth as had the man in the parable. They rob God of the tenth, which He claims as His own, and in robbing Him they rob themselves of the heavenly treasure.

The plan of systematic benevolence does not press heavily upon any one man. "Now concerning the collection for the saints as I have given order to the churches of Galatia, even so do ye. Upon the first day of the week let every one of you lay by him in store, as God hath prospered him, that there be no gatherings when I come." The poor are not excluded from the privilege of giving. They, as well as the wealthy, may act a part in this work. The lesson that Christ gave in regard to the widow's two mites shows us that the smallest willing offerings of the poor, if given from a heart of love, are as acceptable as the largest donations of the rich.

In the balances of the sanctuary the gifts of the poor, made from love to Christ, are not estimated according to the amount given, but according to the love which prompts the sacrifice. The promises of Jesus will as surely be realized by the liberal poor man, who has but little to offer, but who gives that little freely, as by the wealthy man who gives of his abundance. The poor man makes a sacrifice of his little, which he really feels. He really denies himself of some things that he needs for his own comfort, while the wealthy man gives of his abundance, and feels no want, denies himself nothing that he really needs. Therefore there is a sacredness in the poor man's offering that is not found in the rich man's gift, for the rich give of their abundance. God's providence has arranged the entire plan of systematic benevolence for the benefit of man. His providence never stands still. If God's servants follow His opening providence, all will be active workers.

Those who withhold from the treasury of God and hoard their means for their children, endanger the spiritual interest of their children. They place their property, which is a stumbling block to themselves, in the pathway of their children, that they may stumble over it to perdition. Many are making a great mistake in regard to the things of this life. They economize, withholding from themselves and others the good they might receive from a right use of the means which God has lent them, and become selfish and avaricious. They neglect their spiritual interests and become dwarfs in religious growth, all for the sake of accumulating wealth which they cannot use. They leave their property to their children, and nine times out of ten it is even a greater curse to their heirs than it has been to themselves. Children, relying upon the property of their parents, often fail to make a success of this life, and generally utterly fail to secure the life to come. The very best legacy which parents can leave their children is a knowledge of useful labor and the example of a life characterized by disinterested benevolence. By such a life they show the true value of money, that it is only to be appreciated for the good that it will accomplish in relieving their own wants and the necessities of others, and in advancing the cause of God.

Some are willing to give according to what they have, and feel that God has no further claims upon them, because they have not a great amount of means. They have no income that they can spare from the necessities of their families. But there are many of this class who might ask themselves the question: Am I giving according to what I might have had? God designed that their powers of body and mind should be put to use. Some have not improved to the best account the ability that God has given them. Labor is apportioned to man. It was connected with the curse, because made necessary by sin. The physical, mental, and moral well-being of man makes a life of useful labor necessary. "Be . . . not slothful in business," is the injunction of the inspired apostle Paul.

No person, whether rich or poor, can glorify God by a life of indolence. All the capital that many poor men have is time and physical strength, and this is frequently wasted in love of ease and in careless indolence so that they have nothing to bring to their Lord in tithes and in offerings. If Christian men lack wisdom to labor to the best account and to make a judicious appropriation of their physical and mental powers, they should have meekness and lowliness of mind to receive advice and counsel of their brethren, that their better judgment may supply their own deficiencies. Many poor men who are now content to do nothing for the good of their fellow men and for the advancement of the cause of God might do much if they would. They are as accountable to God for their capital of physical strength as is the rich man for his capital of money.

Some who ought to put means into the treasury of God will be receivers from it. There are those who are now poor who might improve their condition by a judicious use of their time, by avoiding patent rights, and by restraining their inclination to engage in speculations in order to obtain means in some easier way than by patient, persevering labor. If those who have not made life a success were willing to be instructed, they could train themselves to habits of self-denial and strict economy, and have the satisfaction of being distributors, rather than receivers, of charity. There are many slothful servants. If they would do what it is in their power to do they would experience so great a blessing in helping others that they would indeed realize that "it is more blessed to give than to receive."

Rightly directed benevolence draws upon the mental and moral energies of men, and excites them to most healthful action in blessing the needy and in advancing the cause of God. If those who have means should realize that they are accountable to God for every dollar that they expend, their supposed wants would be much less. If conscience were alive, she would testify of needless appropriations to the gratification of appetite, of pride, vanity, and love of amusements, and would report the squandering of the Lord's money, which should have been devoted to His cause. Those who waste their Lord's goods will by and by have to give an account of their course to the Master.

If professed Christians would use less of their wealth in adorning the body and in beautifying their own houses, and would consume less in extravagant, health-destroying luxuries upon their tables, they could place much larger sums in the treasury of God. They would thus imitate their Redeemer, who left heaven, His riches, and His glory, and for our sakes became poor, that we might have eternal riches. If we are too poor to faithfully render to God the tithes and offerings that He requires, we are certainly too poor to dress expensively and to eat luxuriously; for we thus waste our Lord's money in hurtful indulgences to please and glorify ourselves. We should inquire diligently of ourselves: What treasure have we secured in the kingdom of God? Are we rich toward God?

Jesus gave His disciples a lesson upon covetousness. "And He spake a parable unto them, saying, The ground of a certain rich man brought forth plentifully: and he thought within himself, saying, What shall I do, because I have no room where to bestow my fruits? And he said, This will I do: I will pull down my barns, and build greater; and there will I bestow all my fruits and my goods. And I will say to my soul, Soul, thou hast much goods laid up for many years; take thine ease, eat, drink, and be merry. But God said unto him, Thou fool, this night thy soul shall be required of thee: then whose shall those things be which thou hast provided? So is he that layeth up treasure for himself, and is not rich toward God."

The length and happiness of life does not consist in the amount of our earthly possessions. This foolish rich man in his supreme selfishness had laid up for himself treasures that he could not use. He had lived only for himself. He had overreached in trade, had made sharp bargains, and had not exercised mercy or the love of God. He had robbed the fatherless and widow, and defrauded his fellow men, to add to his increasing stock of worldly possessions. He might have laid up his treasure in heaven in bags that wax not old; but through his covetousness he lost both worlds. Those who humbly use to the glory of God the means that He has entrusted to them will receive their treasure by and by from the Master's hand with the benediction: "Well done, good and faithful servant: . . . enter thou into the joy of thy Lord."

When we consider the infinite sacrifice made for the salvation of men we are lost in amazement. When selfishness clamors for the victory in the hearts of men, and they are tempted to withhold their due proportion in any good work, they should strengthen their principles of right by the thought that He who was rich in heaven's priceless treasure turned away from it all and became poor. He had not where to lay His head. And all this sacrifice was in our behalf, that we might have eternal riches.

Christ set His own feet in the path of self-denial and sacrifice which all His disciples must travel if they would be exalted with Him at last. He took to His own heart the sorrows which man must suffer. The minds of worldly men frequently become gross. They can see only earthly things, which eclipse the glory and value of heavenly things. Men will compass land and sea for earthly gain, and endure privation and suffering to obtain their object, yet will turn away from heaven's attractions and not regard eternal riches. Men who are in comparative poverty are usually the ones who do the most to sustain the cause of God. They are generous with their little. They have strengthened their generous impulses by continual liberalities. When their expenditures pressed close upon the income, their passion for earthly riches had no room or chance to strengthen.

But many, when they begin to gather earthly riches, commence to calculate how long it will be before they can be in possession of a certain sum. In their anxiety to amass wealth for themselves they fail to become rich toward God. Their benevolence does not keep pace with their accumulation. As their passion for riches increases, their affections are bound up with their treasure. The increase of their property strengthens the eager desire for more, until some consider that their giving to the Lord a tenth is a severe and unjust tax. Inspiration has said: "If riches increase, set not your heart upon them." Many have said: "If I were as rich as such a one, I would multiply my gifts to the treasury of God. I would do nothing else with my wealth but use it for the advancement of the cause of God." God has tested some of these by giving them riches, but with the riches came the fiercer temptation, and their benevolence was far less than in the days of their poverty. A grasping desire for greater riches absorbed their minds and hearts, and they committed idolatry.

He who presents to men infinite riches and an eternal life of blessedness in His kingdom as the reward of faithful obedience, will not accept a divided heart. We are living amid the perils of the last days, where there is everything to divert the mind and allure the affections from God. Our duty will only be discerned and appreciated when viewed in the light which shines from the life of Christ. As the sun rises in the east and passes toward the west, filling the world with light, so the true follower of Christ will be a light unto the world. He will go out into the world as a bright and shining light, that those who are in darkness may be lightened and warmed by the rays shining forth from him. Christ says of His followers: "Ye are the light of the world. A city that is set on an hill cannot be hid."

Our great Exemplar was self-denying, and shall the course of His professed followers be in such marked contrast to His? The Saviour gave all for a perishing world, not withholding even Himself. The church of God are asleep. They are enfeebled by inaction. Voices come to us from every part of the world, "Come over and help us;" but there is no answering movement. There is a feeble effort now and then; a few show that they would be co-workers with their Master; but such are frequently left to toil almost alone. There is but one missionary from our people in all the wide field in foreign countries.

The truth is mighty, but it is not carried into practice. It is not sufficient to lay money alone upon the altar. God calls for men, volunteers, to carry the truth to other nations and tongues and people. It is not our numbers nor our wealth that will give us a signal victory; but it is devotion to the work, moral courage, ardent love for souls, and untiring, unflagging zeal.

There are many who have looked upon the Jewish nation as a people to be pitied because they were constantly taxed for the support of their religion; but God, who created man and provided him with all the blessings he enjoys, knew what was for his best good. And through His blessing He made their nine tenths worth more to them than the entire amount without His blessing. If any, through selfishness, robbed God or brought to Him an offering not perfect, disaster and loss were sure to follow them. God reads the motives of the heart. He is acquainted with the purposes of men and will mete out to them in His own good time as they have merited.

The special system of tithing was founded upon a principle which is as enduring as the law of God. This system of tithing was a blessing to the Jews, else God would not have given it them. So also will it be a blessing to those who carry it out to the end of time. Our heavenly Father did not originate the plan of systematic benevolence to enrich Himself, but to be a great blessing to man. He saw that this system of beneficence was just what man needed.

Those churches who are the most systematic and liberal in sustaining the cause of God are the most prosperous spiritually. True liberality in the follower of Christ identifies his interest with that of his Master. In God's dealing with the Jews and His people to the end of time, He requires systematic benevolence proportionate to their income. The plan of salvation was laid by the infinite sacrifice of the Son of God. The light of the gospel shining from the cross of Christ rebukes selfishness and encourages liberality and benevolence. It is not to be a lamented fact that there are increasing calls to give. God in His providence is calling His people out from their limited sphere of action to enter upon greater enterprises. Unlimited effort is demanded at this time when moral darkness is covering the world. Worldliness and covetousness are eating out the vitals of God's people. They should understand that it is His mercy which multiplies the demands for their means. The angel of God places benevolent acts close beside prayer. He said to Cornelius: "Thy prayers and thine alms are come up for a memorial before God."

In the teachings of Christ He said: "If therefore ye have not been faithful in the unrighteous mammon, who will commit to your trust the true riches?" The spiritual health and prosperity of the church is dependent in a great degree upon her systematic benevolence. It is like the lifeblood which must flow through the whole being, vitalizing every member of the body. It increases love for the souls of our fellow men; for by self-denial and self-sacrifice we are brought into a closer relation to Christ, who for our sakes became poor. The more we invest in the cause of God to aid in the salvation of souls, the closer to our hearts will they be brought. Were our numbers half as large, and all of these devoted workers, we should have a power that would make the world tremble. To the active workers Christ has addressed these words:

"Lo, I am with you alway, even unto the end of the world."

We shall meet opposition arising from selfish motives and from bigotry and prejudice; yet, with undaunted courage and living faith, we should sow beside all waters. The agents of Satan are formidable; we shall meet them and must combat them. Our labors are not to be confined to our own country. The field is the world; the harvest is ripe. The command given by Christ to the disciples just before He ascended was: "Go ye into all the world, and preach the gospel to every creature."

We feel pained beyond measure to see some of our ministers hovering about the churches, apparently putting forth some little effort, but having next to nothing to show for their labors. The field is the world. Let them go out into the unbelieving world and labor to convert souls to the truth. We refer our brethren and sisters to the example of Abraham going up to Mount Moriah to offer his only son at the command of God. Here was obedience and sacrifice. Moses was in kingly courts, and a prospective crown was before him. But he turned away from the tempting bribe, and "refused to be called the son of Pharaoh's daughter; choosing rather to suffer affliction with the people of God, than to enjoy the pleasures of sin for a season; esteeming the reproach of Christ greater riches than the treasures in Egypt."

The apostles counted not their lives dear unto themselves, rejoicing that they were counted worthy to suffer shame for the name of Christ. Paul and Silas suffered the loss of all things. They suffered scourging, and were in no gentle manner thrown upon the cold floor of a dungeon in a most painful position, their feet elevated and fastened in the stocks. Did repinings and complaints then reach the ear of the jailer? Oh, no! From the inner prison, voices broke the silence of midnight with songs of joy and praise to God. These disciples were cheered by a deep and earnest love for the cause of their Redeemer, for which they suffered.

As the truth of God fills our hearts, absorbs our affections, and controls our lives, we also will count it joy to suffer for the truth's sake. No prison walls, no martyr's stake, can then daunt or hinder us in the great work.

Come, O my soul, to Calvary.

Mark the humble life of the Son of God. He was "a man of sorrows, and acquainted with grief." Behold His ignominy, His agony in Gethsemane, and learn what self-denial is. Are we suffering want? so was Christ, the Majesty of heaven. But His poverty was for our sakes. Are we ranked among the rich? so was He. But He consented for our sakes to become poor, that we through His poverty might be made rich. In Christ we have self-denial exemplified. His sacrifice consisted not merely in leaving the royal courts of heaven, in being tried by wicked men as a criminal and pronounced guilty, and in being delivered up to die as a malefactor, but in bearing the weight of the sins of the world. The life of Christ rebukes our indifference and coldness. We are near the close of time, when Satan has come down, having great wrath, knowing that his time is short. He is working with all deceivableness of unrighteousness in them that perish. The warfare has been left in our hands by our great Leader for us to carry forward with vigor. We are not doing a twentieth part of what we might do if we were awake. The work is retarded by love of ease and a lack of the self-denying spirit of which our Saviour has given us an example in His life.

Co-workers with Christ, men who feel the need of extended effort, are wanted. The work of our presses should not be lessened, but doubled. Schools should be established in different places to educate our youth preparatory to their laboring to advance the truth.

Already a great deal of time has been wasted, and angels bear to heaven the record of our neglects. Our sleepy and unconsecrated condition has lost to us precious opportunities which God has sent us in the persons of those who were qualified to help us in our present need. Oh, how much we need our Hannah More to aid us at this time in reaching other nations! Her extensive knowledge of missionary fields would give us access to those of other tongues whom we cannot now approach. God brought this gift among us to meet our present emergency; but we prized not the gift, and He took her from us. She is at rest from her labors, but her self-denying works follow her. It is to be deplored that our missionary work should be retarded for the want of knowledge how to gain access to the different nations and localities in the great harvest field.

We feel anguish of spirit because some gifts are lost to us that we might now have if we had only been awake. Laborers have been kept back from the whitening harvest. It becomes the people of God to humble their hearts before Him, and in the deepest humiliation to pray the Lord to pardon our apathy and selfish indulgence, and to blot out the shameful record of duties neglected and privileges unimproved. In contemplation of the cross of Calvary the true Christian will abandon the thought of restricting his offerings to that which costs him nothing and will hear in trumpet tones:

> Go, labor in My vineyard;
> There's resting by and by.

When Jesus was about to ascend on high, He pointed to the harvest fields and said to His followers: "Go ye into all the world, and preach the gospel." "Freely ye have received, freely give." Shall we deny self that the wasting harvest may be gathered?

God calls for talents of influence and of means. Shall we refuse to obey? Our heavenly Father bestows gifts and solicits a portion back, that He may test us whether we are worthy to have the gift of everlasting life.

SYSTEMATIC BENEVOLENCE

Should all whom God has prospered with earth's riches carry out His plan by faithfully giving a tenth of all their increase, and should they not withhold their trespass offerings and their thank offerings, the treasury would be constantly replenished. The simplicity of the plan of systematic benevolence does not detract from its merits, but extols the wisdom of God in its arrangement. Everything bearing the divine stamp unites simplicity with utility. If systematic benevolence were universally adopted according to God's plan, and the tithing system carried out as faithfully by the wealthy as it is by the poorer classes, there would be no need of repeated and urgent calls for means at our large religious gatherings. There has been a neglect in the churches of keeping up the plan of systematic benevolence, and the result has been an impoverished treasury and a backslidden church.

"Will a man rob God? Yet ye have robbed Me. But ye say, Wherein have we robbed Thee? In tithes and offerings. Ye are cursed with a curse: for ye have robbed Me, even this whole nation. Bring ye all the tithes into the storehouse, that there may be meat in Mine house, and prove Me now herewith, saith the Lord of hosts, if I will not open you the windows of heaven, and pour you out a blessing, that there shall not be room enough to receive it. And I will rebuke the devourer for your sakes, and he shall not destroy the fruits of your ground; neither shall your vine cast her fruit before the time in the field, saith the Lord of hosts. And all nations shall call you blessed: for ye shall be a delightsome land, saith the Lord of hosts."

God has been robbed in tithes and offerings. It is a fearful thing to be guilty of withholding from the treasury or of robbing God. Ministers who preach the word at our large gatherings feel the sinfulness of neglecting to render to God the things that are His. They know that God will not bless His people while they are disregarding His plan of benevolence. They seek to arouse the people to their duty by pointed, practical discourses, showing the danger and sinfulness of selfishness and covetousness. Conviction fastens upon minds, and the icy chill of selfishness is broken. And when the call is made for donations to the cause of God, some, under the stirring influence of the meetings, are aroused to give who otherwise would do nothing. As far as this class is concerned, good results have been realized. But under pressing calls many feel the deepest who have not had their hearts frozen up with selfishness. They have conscientiously kept their means flowing out to advance the cause of God. Their whole being is stirred by the earnest appeals made, and the very ones respond who may have given all that their circumstances in life would justify.

But these liberal, wholehearted believers, prompted by a zealous love for the cause and a desire to act promptly, judge themselves capable of doing more than God requires them to do, for their usefulness is crippled in other directions. These willing ones sometimes pledge to raise money when they know not from what source it is coming, and some are placed in distressing circumstances to meet their pledges. Some are obliged to sell their produce at great disadvantage, and some have actually suffered for the conveniences and necessities of life in order to meet their pledges.

There was a time at the commencement of our work when such sacrifice would have been justified, when God would have blessed all who thus ventured out to do for His cause. The friends of truth were few and their means very limited. But the work has been widening and strengthening until there is means enough in the hands of believers to amply sustain the work in all its departments without embarrassing any, if all would bear their proportional part. The cause of God need not be crippled in the slightest degree. The precious truth has been made so plain that many have taken hold of it who have in their hands means which God has entrusted to them to use in advancing the interests of the truth. If these men of means do their duty, there need not be a pressure brought upon the poorer brethren.

We are in a world of plenty. If the gifts and offerings were proportionate to the means which each has received of God, there would be no need of urgent calls for means at our large gatherings. I am fully convinced that it is not the best plan to bring a pressure upon the point of means at our camp meetings. Men and women who love the cause of God as they do their lives will pledge upon these occasions, when their families must suffer for the very means that they have promised to give to advance the cause. Our God is not a taskmaster and does not require the poor man to give means to the cause that belongs to his family and that should be used to keep them in comfort and above pinching want.

The calls for means at our large camp meetings have hitherto been attended with apparently good results so far as the wealthy are concerned. But we fear the result of a continued effort to thus replenish the treasury. We fear that there will be a reaction. Greater effort should be put forth by responsible men in the different churches to have all follow the plan of God's arrangement. If systematic benevolence is carried out, the urgent calls at the camp meetings for means for various enterprises will not be necessary.

God has devised a plan by which all may give as He has prospered them, and which will make giving a habit without waiting for special calls. Those who can do this, but will not because of their selfishness, are robbing their Creator, who has bestowed upon them means to invest in His cause to advance its interests. Until all shall carry out the plan of systematic benevolence, there will be a failure in coming up to the apostolic rule. Those who minister in word and doctrine should be men of discrimination. They should, while they make general appeals, become acquainted with the ability of those who respond to their appeals, and should not allow the poor to pay large pledges. After a man has once consecrated a certain sum to the Lord, he feels that it is sacred, consecrated to a holy use. This is true, and therefore our preaching brethren should be well informed of whom they accept pledges.

Each member of the different families in our churches who believes the truth may act a part in its advancement by cheerfully adopting systematic benevolence. "Let every one of you lay by him in store [by himself at home], . . . that there be no gatherings when I come." The burden of urging and pressing individuals to give of their means was not designed to be the work of God's ministers. The responsibility should rest upon every individual who enjoys the belief of the truth. "Let every one of you lay by him in store, as God hath prospered him." Every member of the family, from the oldest down to the youngest, may take part in this work of benevolence.

The offerings of little children may be acceptable and pleasing to God. In accordance with the spirit that prompts the gifts will be the value of the offering. The poor, by following the rule of the apostle and laying by a small sum every week, help to swell the treasury, and their gifts are wholly acceptable to God; for they make just as great, and even greater, sacrifices than their more wealthy brethren. The plan of systematic benevolence will prove a safeguard to every family against temptations to spend means for needless things, and especially will it prove a blessing to the rich by guarding them from indulging in extravagances.

Every week the demands of God upon each family are brought to mind by each of its members fully carrying out the plan; and as they have denied themselves some superfluity in order to have means to put into the treasury, lessons of value in self-denial for the glory of God have been impressed upon the heart. Once a week each is brought face to face with the doings of the past week—the income that he might have had if he had been economical and the means that he does not have because of indulgence. His conscience is reined up, as it were, before God, and either commends or accuses him. He learns that if he retains peace of mind and the favor of God he must eat and drink and dress to His glory.

Systematic and liberal giving in accordance with the plan keeps the channel of the heart open. We place ourselves in connection with God, that He may use us as channels through which His gifts may flow to others. The poor will not complain of systematic benevolence, for it touches them lightly. They are not neglected and passed by, but are favored with acting a part in being co-workers with Christ, and will receive the blessing of God as well as the wealthy. In the very process of laying aside the littles as they can spare them they are denying self and cultivating liberality of heart. They are educating themselves to good works, and are as effectually meeting the design of God in the plan of systematic benevolence as are the more wealthy who give of their abundance.

In the days of the apostles, men went everywhere preaching the word. New churches were raised up. Their love and zeal for Christ led them to acts of great denial and sacrifice. Many of these Gentile churches were very poor, yet the apostle declares that their deep poverty abounded to the riches of their liberality. Their gifts were extended beyond their ability to give. Men periled their lives and suffered the loss of all things for the truth's sake.

The apostle suggests the first day of the week as a proper time to review the course of Providence and the prosperity experienced, and in the fear of God, with true gratitude of heart for the blessings He has bestowed, to decide how much, according to His own devised plan, shall be rendered back to Him.

God designs that the exercise of benevolence shall be purely voluntary, not having recourse even to eloquent appeals to excite sympathy. "God loveth a cheerful giver." He is not pleased to have His treasury replenished with forced supplies. The loyal hearts of His people, rejoicing in the saving truth for this time, will, through love and gratitude to Him for this precious light, be earnest and anxious to aid with their means in sending the truth to others. The very best manner in which to give expression to our love for our Redeemer is to make offerings to bring souls to the knowledge of the truth. The plan of redemption was entirely voluntary on the part of our Redeemer, and it is the purpose of Christ that all our benevolence should be freewill offerings.

INDIVIDUAL INDEPENDENCE

Dear Brother A: My mind is exercised in regard to your case. I have written you some things which have been shown me in regard to your past, present, and future course. I feel anxious for you because I have seen your dangers. Your former experience in spiritualism exposes you to temptations and severe conflicts. When once the mind has been yielded to the direct control of the enemy through evil angels, that person should be very distrustful of impressions and feelings which would lead him on an independent track, away from the church of Christ. The first step that such a one would take independently of the church should be regarded as a device of the enemy to deceive and destroy. God has made His church a channel of light, and through it He communicates His purposes and His will. He does not give one an experience independent of the church. He does not give one man a knowledge of His will for the entire church, while the church, Christ's body, is left in darkness.

Brother A, you need to watch with the greatest care how you build. There is a storm coming which will test your hope to the utmost. You should dig deep and lay your foundation sure. "Therefore whosoever heareth these sayings of Mine, and doeth them, I will liken him unto a wise man, which built his house upon a rock: and the rain descended, and the floods came, and the winds blew, and beat upon that house; and it fell not: for it was founded upon a rock." Steadily the builder places one stone upon another until the structure rises stone upon stone. The gospel builder frequently carries on his work in tears and amid trials, storms of persecution, bitter opposition, and unjust reproach; but he feels deeply in earnest, for he is building for eternity. Be careful, Brother A, that your foundation is solid rock, that you are riveted to it, Christ being that Rock.

You have a strong, set will, a very independent spirit, which you feel that you must preserve at all hazards. And you have carried this same spirit into your religious experience and life. You have not always been in harmony with the work of God as carried on by your American brethren. You have not seen as they see nor been in union with their manner of proceeding. You have had very little acquaintance with the work in its different departments. You have not felt very anxious to become acquainted with the various branches of the work. You have looked with suspicion and distrust upon the work, and upon God's chosen leaders to carry it forward. You have been more ready to question and surmise and be jealous of those upon whom God has laid the heavier responsibilities of His work, than to investigate and to so connect yourself with the cause of God as to become acquainted with its workings and advancement.

God saw that you were not fitted to be a shepherd, a minister of righteousness to proclaim the truth to others, until you should be a thoroughly transformed man. He permitted you to pass through real trials and feel privation and want, that you might know how to exercise pity and sympathy, and tender love for the unfortunate and oppressed, and for those borne down with want and passing through trial and affliction.

While you prayed in your affliction for peace in Christ, a cloud of darkness seemed to blacken across your mind. The rest and peace did not come as you expected. At times your faith seemed to be tested to the utmost. As you looked back to your past life, you saw sorrow and disappointment; as you viewed the future, all was uncertainty. The divine Hand led you wondrously to bring you to the cross and to teach you that God was indeed a rewarder of those who diligently seek Him. Those who ask aright will receive. He that seeketh in faith shall find. The experience gained in the furnace of trial and affliction is worth more than all the inconvenience and painful experience it costs.

The prayers that you offered in your loneliness, in your weariness and trial, God answered, not always according to your expectations, but for your good. You did not have clear and correct views of your brethren, neither did you see yourself in a correct light. But, in the providence of God, He has been at work to answer the prayers you have offered in your distress, in a way to save you and glorify His own name. In your ignorance of yourself you asked for things which were not best for you. God heard your prayers of sincerity, but the blessing granted was something very different from your expectations. God designed, in His providence, to place you more directly in connection with His church, that your confidence might be less in yourself and greater in others whom He is leading out to advance His work.

God hears every sincere prayer. He would place you in connection with His work that He might bring you more directly to the light. And unless you should seal your vision against evidence and light you would be persuaded that if you were more distrustful of yourself and less distrustful of your brethren you would be more prosperous in God. It is God who has led you through strait places. He had a purpose in this, that tribulation might work in you patience, and patience experience, and experience hope. He permitted trials to come upon you, that, through them, you might experience the peaceable fruits of righteousness.

Peter denied the Man of Sorrows in His acquaintance with grief in the hour of His humiliation. But he afterward repented and was reconverted. He had true contrition of soul and gave himself afresh to his Saviour. With blinding tears he makes his way to the solitudes of the Garden of Gethsemane and there prostrates himself where he saw his Saviour's prostrate form when the bloody sweat was forced from His pores by His great agony. Peter remembers with remorse that he was asleep when Jesus prayed during those fearful hours. His proud heart breaks, and penitential tears moisten the sods so recently stained with the bloody sweat drops of God's dear Son. He left that garden a converted man. He was ready then to pity the tempted. He was humbled and could sympathize with the weak and erring. He could caution and warn the presumptuous, and was fully fitted to strengthen his brethren.

God led you through affliction and trials that you might

have more perfect trust and confidence in Him, and that you might think less of your own judgment. You can bear adversity better than prosperity. The all-seeing eye of Jehovah detected in you much dross that you considered gold and too valuable to throw away. The enemy's power over you had at times been direct and very strong. The delusions of spiritualism had entangled your faith, perverted your judgment, and confused your experience. God in His providence would try you, to purify you, as the sons of Levi, that you might offer to Him an offering in righteousness.

Self is mingled too much with all your labors. Your will must be molded by God's will, or you will fall into grievous temptations. I saw that when you labor in God, putting self out of sight, you will realize a strength from Him which will give you access to hearts. Angels of God will work with your efforts when you are humble and little in your own eyes. But when you think you know more than those whom God has been leading for years, and whom He has been instructing in the truth and fitting for the extension of His work, you are self-exalted and will fall into temptations.

You need to cultivate kindness and tenderness. You need to be pitiful and courteous. Your labors savor too much of severity and an exacting, dictatorial, overbearing spirit. You are not always kindly considerate of the feelings of others, and you create trials and dissatisfaction needlessly. More love in your labors, and more kindly sympathy, would give you access to hearts and would win souls to Christ and the truth.

You are constantly inclined to individual independence. You do not realize that independence is a poor thing when it leads you to have too much confidence in yourself and to trust to your own judgment rather than to respect the counsel and highly estimate the judgment of your brethren, especially of those in the offices which God has appointed for the saving of His people. God has invested His church with special authority and power which no one can be justified in disregarding and despising, for in so doing he despises the voice of God.

It is not safe for you to trust to impressions and feelings. It has been your misfortune to come under the power of that satanic delusion, spiritualism. This pall of death has covered you, and your imagination and nerves have been under the control of demons; and when you become self-confident and do not cling with unwavering confidence to God you are in positive danger. You may, and frequently do, let down the bars and invite the enemy in, and he controls your thoughts and actions, while you are really deceived and flatter yourself that you are in favor with God.

Satan has tried to prevent you from having confidence in your American brethren. You have regarded them and their moves and experience with suspicion, when they are the very ones who could help you and would be a blessing to you. It will be Satan's studied effort to separate you from those who are as channels of light, through whom God has communicated His will and through whom He has wrought in building up and extending His work. Your views and your feelings and experience are altogether too narrow, and your labors are of the same character.

In order to be a blessing to your people, you need to improve in many things. You should cultivate courtesy and cherish a tender sympathy for all. You should have the crowning grace of God, which is love. You criticize too much and are not so forbearing as you must be if you would win souls. You could have much more influence if you were less formal and rigid, and were actuated more by the Holy Spirit. Your fear of being led by men is too great. God uses men as His instruments and will use them as long as the world shall stand.

The angels who fell were anxious to become independent of God. They were very beautiful, very glorious, but dependent on God for their happiness and for the light and intelligence they enjoyed. They fell from their high estate through insubordination. Christ and His church are inseparable. To neglect or despise those whom God has appointed to lead out and to bear the responsibilities connected with His work and with the advancement and spread of the truth is to reject the means which God has ordained for the help, encouragement, and strength of His people. To pass these by and think your light must come through no other channel than directly from God places you in a position where you are liable to deception and to be overthrown.

God has placed you in connection with His appointed helps in His church that you may be aided by them. Your former connection with spiritualism makes your danger greater than it otherwise would be, because your judgment, wisdom, and discrimination have been perverted. You cannot of yourself always tell or discern the spirits; for Satan is very wily. God has placed you in connection with His church that they may help you.

You are sometimes too formal, cold, and unsympathizing. You must meet the people where they are, and not place yourself too far above them and require too much of them. You need to be all softened and subdued by the Spirit of God while you preach to the people. You should educate yourself as to the best manner of laboring to secure the desired end. Your labor must be characterized by the love of Jesus abounding in your heart, softening your words, molding your temperament, and elevating your soul.

You frequently talk too long when you do not have the vitalizing influence of the Spirit of heaven. You weary those who hear you. Many make a mistake in their preaching in not stopping while the interest is up. They go on speechifying until the interest that had risen in the minds of the hearers dies out and the people are really wearied with words of no special weight or interest. Stop before you get there. Stop when you have nothing of special importance to say. Do not go on with dry words that only excite prejudice and do not soften the heart. You want to be so united to Christ that your words will melt and burn their way to the soul. Mere prosy talk is insufficient for this time. Arguments are good, but there may be too much of the argumentative and too little of the spirit and life of God.

Without the special power of God to work with your efforts, your spirit subdued and humbled in God, your heart softened, your words flowing from a heart of love, your labors will be wearing to yourself and not productive of blessed results. There is a point which the minister of Christ reaches, beyond which human knowledge and skill are powerless. We are struggling with giant errors, and evils which we are impotent to remedy or to arouse the people to see and understand, for we cannot change the heart. We cannot quicken the soul to discern the sinfulness of sin and to feel the need of a Saviour. But if our labors bear the impress of the Spirit of God, if a higher, a divine power attends our efforts to sow the gospel seed, we shall see fruits of our labor to the glory of God. He alone can water the seed sown.

Thus with you, Brother A. You must not get in too great a hurry and expect too much of darkened minds. You must cherish humble hope that God will graciously impart the mysterious, quickening influence of His Spirit, by which alone your labors will not be in vain in the Lord. You need to cling to God by living faith, every moment realizing your dangers and your weakness, and constantly seeking that strength and power which God alone can give. Try the best you may, of yourself you can do nothing.

You need to educate yourself, that you may have wisdom to deal with minds. You should with some have compassion, making a difference, while others you may save with fear, pulling them out of the fire. Our heavenly Father frequently leaves us in uncertainty in regard to our efforts. We are to sow beside all waters, not knowing which shall prosper, this or that. We may stimulate our faith and energy from the Source of our strength, and lean with full and entire dependence upon Him.

Brother A, you need to work with the utmost diligence to control self and develop a character in harmony with the principles of the word of God. You need to educate and train yourself in order to become a successful shepherd. You need to cultivate a good temper—kindly, cheerful, buoyant, generous, pitiful, courteous, compassionate traits of character. You should overcome a morose, bigoted, narrow, faultfinding, overbearing spirit. If you are connected with the work of God you need to battle with yourself vigorously and form your character after the divine Model.

Without constant effort on your part some development, under the influence of a corrupt mind, will appear and block up your way, which hindrance you will be inclined to charge to some other than the true cause. You need self-discipline. Our piety should not appear sour, cold, and morose; but lovable and teachable. A censorious spirit will hedge up your way and close hearts against you. If not humbly dependent on God, you will frequently close your own path with obstacles and charge the same to the course of others.

You need to stand guard over yourself, that you do not teach the truth or perform duties in a bigoted spirit that will excite prejudice. You need to study how you may show yourself approved unto God, a workman that needeth not to be ashamed. Inquire of yourself what your natural disposition is, what character you have developed. It should be your study, as well as that of every minister of Christ, to exercise the greatest watchfulness that you do not cherish habits of action, or mental and moral tendencies, which you would not wish to see appear among those whom you bring out upon the truth.

Ministers of Christ are enjoined to be examples to the flock of God. The influence of a minister can do much toward molding the character of his people. If the minister is indolent, if he is not pure in heart and life, and if he is sharp, critical, and faultfinding, selfish, independent, and lacking self-control, he will have these same unpleasant elements in a large degree to meet and deal with among his people, and it is hard work to set things in order where wrong influences have made confusion. What is seen in their minister will make a great difference in regard to the development of Christian virtue in the people. If his life is a combination of excellences, those whom he brings to the knowledge of the truth through his labors will, to a great degree, if they truly love God, reflect his example and influence, for he is a representative of Christ. Thus the minister should feel his responsibility to adorn the doctrine of God our Saviour in all things.

The highest efforts of the gospel minister should be to devote all his talents to the work of saving souls; then he will be successful. Wise and watchful discipline is necessary for everyone who names the name of Christ; but in a much higher sense is it essential for a gospel minister, who is a representative of Christ. Our Saviour awed men by His purity and elevated morality, while His love and gentle benignity inspired them with enthusiasm. The poorest and humblest were not afraid to approach Him; even little children were attracted to Him. They loved to climb upon His lap and to kiss that pensive face, benignant with love. This loving tenderness you need. You should cultivate love. Expressions of sympathy and acts of courtesy and respect for others would not detract from your dignity one particle, but would open to you many hearts that are now closed against you.

Christ was just what every minister should strive to be. We should learn to imitate His character and combine strict justice, purity, integrity, love, and noble generosity. A pleasant face in which love is reflected, with kind and courteous manners, will do more, aside from pulpit efforts, than labor in the desk can do without these. It becomes us to cultivate a deference to other people's judgment, when, to a greater or less extent, we are absolutely dependent upon them. We should cultivate true Christian courtesy and tender sympathy, even for the roughest, hardest cases of humanity. Jesus came from the pure courts of heaven to save just such. You close your heart too readily to many who have apparently no interest in the message you bear, but who are still subjects of grace and precious in the sight of the Lord. "He that winneth souls is wise." Paul became all things to all men if by any means he might save some. You must be in a similar position. You must bend from your independence. You lack humbleness of mind. You need the softening influence of the grace of

God upon your heart, that you may not irritate, but melt your way to the hearts of men, although these hearts may be affected by prejudice.

The cause of God is in great need of earnest men, men who abound in zeal, hope, faith, and courage. It is not self-willed men who can meet the demands for this time, but men who are in earnest. We have too many sensitive ministers who are feeble in experience, deficient in the Christian graces, lacking in consecration, and are easily discouraged; who are earnest to gratify their own wills and are persevering in their efforts to accomplish their own selfish purposes. Such men will not fill the demands for this time. We need men in these last days who are ever awake. Minutemen are wanted who are sincere in their love for the truth and willing to labor at a sacrifice if they can advance the cause of God and save precious souls. Men are wanted in this work who will not murmur or complain at hardships or trials, knowing that this is a part of the legacy that Jesus has left them. They should be willing to go without the camp and suffer reproach and bear burdens as good soldiers of Christ. They will bear the cross of Christ without complaint, without murmuring or fretfulness, and will be patient in tribulation.

The solemn, testing truth for these last days is committed to us, and we should make it a reality. Brother A, you should avoid making yourself a criterion. Avoid, I entreat you, appealing to your own sympathies. All that we can suffer, and all that we may ever be called to suffer, for the truth's sake will seem too small to be compared with what our Saviour endured for us sinners. You need not expect always to be correctly judged or correctly represented. Christ says that in the world we shall have tribulation, but in Him we shall have peace.

You have cultivated a combative spirit. When your track is crossed, you immediately throw yourself into a defensive position; and, although you may be among your brethren who love the truth and have given their lives to the cause of God, you will justify yourself, while you criticize them and become jealous of their words and suspicious of their motives, and thus lose great blessings that it is your privilege to gain through the experience of your brethren.

DISCUSSIONS TO BE AVOIDED

You have loved to debate the truth and loved discussions; but these contests have been unfavorable to your forming a harmonious Christian character, for in this is a favorable opportunity for the exhibition of the very traits of character that you must overcome if you ever enter heaven. Discussions cannot always be avoided. In some cases the circumstances are such that of the two evils the choice must be made of the least, which is discussion. But whenever they can be avoided, they should be, for the result is seldom honoring to God.

People who love to see opponents combat, may clamor for discussion. Others, who have a desire to hear the evidences on both sides, may urge discussion in all honesty of motive, but whenever discussions can be avoided, they should be. They generally strengthen combativeness and weaken that pure love and sacred sympathy which should ever exist in the hearts of Christians although they may differ in opinions.

Discussions in this age of the world are not real evidences of earnest desire on the part of the people to investigate the truth, but come through the love of novelty and the excitement which generally attends discussions. God is seldom glorified or the truth advanced in these combats. Truth is too solemn, too momentous in its results, to make it a small matter whether it is received or rejected. To discuss truth for the sake of showing opponents the skill of the combatants is ever poor policy, for it does but very little to advance the truth.

Opponents to the truth will show skill in misstating their opponent. They will make the most solemn, sacred truths the subject of ridicule. They will generally sport and deride precious, sacred truth and place it in so false a light before the people that minds that are darkened by error and polluted by sin do not discern the motives and objects of these designing men in thus covering up and falsifying precious and important truth. Because of the men who engage in them, there are but few discussions that it is possible to conduct upon right principles. Sharp thrusts are too frequently given by both parties, personalities are indulged in, and frequently both parties descend to sarcasm and witticism. The love of souls is lost in the greater desire for the mastery. Prejudice, deep and bitter, is often the result of discussions.

I have beheld angels grieved as the most precious jewels of truth have been brought before men utterly incapable of appreciating the evidences in favor of the truth. Their entire being was at war with the principles of truth; their natures were at enmity with it. Their object in discussing was not that they might get hold of the evidences of the truth themselves or that the people might have a fair understanding of our true position, but that they might confuse the understanding by placing the truth in a perverted light before the people. There are men who have educated themselves as combatants. It is their policy to misstate an opponent and to cover up clear arguments with dishonest quibbles. They have devoted their God-given powers to this dishonest work, for there is nothing in their hearts in harmony with the pure principles of truth. They seize any argument they can get with which to tear down the advocates of truth, when they themselves do not believe the things they urge against them. They bolster themselves up in their chosen position, irrespective of justice and truth. They do not consider that before them is the judgment, and that then their ill-gotten triumph, with all its disastrous results, will appear in its true character. Error, with all its deceptive policies, its windings and twistings and turnings to change the truth into a lie, will then appear in all its deformity. No victory will stand in the day of God, except that which truth, pure, elevated, sacred truth, shall win to the glory of God.

Angels weep to see the precious truth of heavenly origin cast before swine, to be seized by them and trampled with the mire and dirt. Cast not "your pearls before swine, lest they trample them under their feet, and turn again and rend you." These are the words of the world's Redeemer.

God's ministers should not count the opportunity of engaging in discussion a great privilege. All points of our faith are not to be borne to the front and presented before the prejudiced crowds. Jesus spoke before the Pharisees and Sadducees in parables, hiding the clearness of truth under symbols and figures because they would make a wrong use of the truths He presented before them; but to His disciples He spoke plainly. We should learn from Christ's method of teaching and be careful not to cut off the ears of the people by presenting truths which, not being fully explained, they are in no way prepared to receive.

The truths that we hold in common should be dwelt upon first and the confidence of the hearers obtained; then, as the people can be brought along, we can advance slowly with the matter presented. Great wisdom is needed to present unpopular truth before a prejudiced people in the most cautious manner, that access may be gained to their hearts. Discussions place before the people, who are unenlightened in regard to our position and who are ignorant of Bible truth, a set of arguments skillfully gotten up and carefully arranged to cover over the clear points of truth. Some men have made it their business to cover up plain statements of facts in the word of God by their deceptive theories, which they make plausible to those who have not investigated for themselves.

These agents of Satan are hard to meet, and it is difficult to have patience with them. But calmness, patience, and self-control are elements which every minister of Christ should cultivate. The combatants of the truth have educated themselves for intellectual battle. They are prepared to present on the surface sophistry and assertions as the word of God. They confuse unsuspecting minds and place the truth in obscurity, while pleasing fables are presented to the people in the place of pure Bible truth.

Many choose darkness rather than light because their

deeds are evil. But there are those who, if the truth could have been presented in a different manner, under different circumstances, giving them a fair chance to weigh the arguments for themselves and to compare scripture with scripture, would have been charmed by its clearness and would have taken hold upon it.

It has been very indiscreet for our ministers to publish to the world the wily sophistry of error, furnished by designing men to cover up and make of none effect the solemn, sacred truth of Jehovah. These crafty men who lie in wait to deceive the unwary give their strength of intellect to perverting the word of God. The inexperienced and unsuspecting are deceived to their ruin. It has been a great error to publish to all the arguments wherewith opponents battle the truth of God, for in so doing minds of every class are furnished with arguments which many of them had never thought of. Someone must render an account for this unwise generalship.

Arguments against the sacred truth, subtle in their influence, affect minds that are not well informed in regard to the strength of the truth. The moral sensibilities of the community at large are blunted by familiarity with sin. Selfishness, dishonesty, and the varied sins which prevail in this degenerate age have blunted the senses to eternal things so that God's truth is not discerned. In giving publicity to the erroneous arguments of our opponents, truth and error are placed upon a level in their minds, when, if they could have the truth before them in its clearness long enough to see and realize its sacredness and importance, they would be convinced of the strong arguments in its favor and would then be prepared to meet the arguments urged by opposers.

Those who are seeking to know the truth and to understand the will of God, who are faithful to the light and zealous in the performance of their daily duties, will surely know of the doctrine, for they will be guided into all truth. God does not promise, by the masterly acts of His providence, to irresistibly bring men to the knowledge of His truth, when they do not seek for truth and have no desire to know the truth. Men have the power to quench the Spirit of God; the power of choosing is left with them. They are allowed freedom of action. They may be obedient through the name and grace of our Redeemer, or they may be disobedient, and realize the consequences. Man is responsible for receiving or rejecting sacred and eternal truth. The Spirit of God is continually convicting, and souls are deciding for or against the truth. The deportment, the words, the actions, of the minister of Christ may balance a soul for or against the truth. How important that every act of the life be such that it need not be repented of. Especially is this important among the ambassadors of Christ, who are acting in the place of Christ.

THE AUTHORITY OF THE CHURCH

The world's Redeemer has invested great power with His church. He states the rules to be applied in cases of trial with its members. After He has given explicit directions as to the course to be pursued, He says: "Verily I say unto you, Whatsoever ye shall bind on earth shall be bound in heaven: and whatsoever [in church discipline] ye shall loose on earth shall be loosed in heaven." Thus even the heavenly authority ratifies the discipline of the church in regard to its members when the Bible rule has been followed.

The word of God does not give license for one man to set up his judgment in opposition to the judgment of the church, neither is he allowed to urge his opinions against the opinions of the church. If there were no church discipline and government, the church would go to fragments; it could not hold together as a body. There have ever been individuals of independent minds who have claimed that they were right, that God had especially taught, impressed, and led them. Each has a theory of his own, views peculiar to himself, and each claims that his views are in accordance with the word of God. Each one has a different theory and faith, yet each claims special light from God. These draw away from the body, and each one is a separate church of himself. All these cannot be right, yet they all claim to be led of the Lord. The word of Inspiration is not Yea and Nay, but Yea and Amen in Christ Jesus.

Our Saviour follows His lessons of instruction with a promise that if two or three should be united in asking anything of God it should be given them. Christ here shows that there must be union with others, even in our desires for a given object. Great importance is attached to the united prayer, the union of purpose. God hears the prayers of individuals, but on this occasion Jesus was giving especial and important lessons that were to have a special bearing upon His newly organized church on the earth. There must be an agreement in the things which they desire and for which they pray. It was not merely the thoughts and exercises of one mind, liable to deception; but the petition was to be the earnest desire of several minds centered on the same point.

In the wonderful conversion of Paul we see the miraculous power of God. A brightness above the glory of the midday sun shone round about him. Jesus, whose name of all others he most hated and despised, revealed Himself to Paul for the purpose of arresting his mad yet honest career, that He might make this most unpromising instrument a chosen vessel to bear the gospel to the Gentiles. He had conscientiously done many things contrary to the name of Jesus of Nazareth. In his zeal he was a persevering, earnest persecutor of the church of Christ. His convictions of his duty to exterminate this alarming doctrine, which was prevailing everywhere, that Jesus was the Prince of life were deep and strong.

Paul verily believed that faith in Jesus made of none effect the law of God, the religious service of sacrificial offerings, and the rite of circumcision, which had in all past ages received the full sanction of God. But the miraculous revelation of Christ brings light into the darkened chambers of his mind. The Jesus of Nazareth whom he is arrayed against is indeed the Redeemer of the world.

Paul sees his mistaken zeal and cries out: "Lord, what

wilt Thou have me to do?" Jesus did not then and there tell him, as He might have done, the work that He had assigned him. Paul must receive instruction in the Christian faith and move understandingly. Christ sends him to the very disciples whom he had been so bitterly persecuting, to learn of them. The light of heavenly illumination had taken away Paul's eyesight; but Jesus, the Great Healer of the blind, does not restore it. He answers the question of Paul in these words: "Arise, and go into the city, and it shall be told thee what thou must do." Jesus could not only have healed Paul of his blindness, but He could have forgiven his sins and told him his duty by marking out his future course. From Christ all power and mercies were to flow; but He did not give Paul an experience, in his conversion to truth, independent of His church recently organized upon the earth.

The marvelous light given Paul upon that occasion astonished and confounded him. He was wholly subdued. This part of the work man could not do for Paul, but there was a work still to be accomplished which the servants of Christ could do. Jesus directs him to His agents in the church for a further knowledge of duty. Thus He gives authority and sanction to His organized church. Christ had done the work of revelation and conviction, and now Paul was in a condition to learn of those whom God had ordained to teach the truth. Christ directs Paul to His chosen servants, thus placing him in connection with His church.

The very men whom Paul was purposing to destroy were to be his instructors in the very religion that he had despised and persecuted. He passed three days without food or sight, making his way to the men whom, in his blind zeal, he was purposing to destroy. Here Jesus places Paul in connection with His representatives upon the earth. The Lord gave Ananias a vision to go up to a certain house in Damascus and call for Saul of Tarsus; "for, behold, he prayeth."

After Saul was directed to go to Damascus, he was led by

the men who accompanied him to help him bring the disciples bound to Jerusalem to be tried and put to death. Saul tarried with Judas at Damascus, devoting the time to fasting and prayer. Here the faith of Saul was tested. Three days he was in darkness of mind in regard to what was required of him, and three days he was without sight. He had been directed to go to Damascus, for it should there be told him what he should do. He is in uncertainty, and he cries earnestly to God. An angel is sent to Ananias, directing him to go to a certain house where Saul is praying to be instructed in what he is to do next. Saul's pride is gone. A little before he was self-confident, thinking he was engaged in a good work for which he should receive a reward; but all is now changed. He is bowed down and humbled to the dust in penitence and shame, and his supplications are fervent for pardon. Said the Lord, through His angel, to Ananias: "Behold, he prayeth." The angel informed the servant of God that he had revealed to Saul in vision a man named Ananias coming in and putting his hand on him that he might receive his sight. Ananias can scarcely credit the words of the angel, and repeats what he has heard of Saul's bitter persecution of the saints at Jerusalem. But the command to Ananias is imperative: "Go thy way: for he is a chosen vessel unto Me, to bear My name before the Gentiles, and kings, and the children of Israel."

Ananias was obedient to the direction of the angel. He laid his hands upon the man who so recently was exercised with a spirit of the deepest hatred, breathing out threatenings against all who believed on the name of Christ. Ananias said to Saul: "Brother Saul, the Lord, even Jesus, that appeared unto thee in the way as thou camest, hath sent me, that thou mightest receive thy sight, and be filled with the Holy Ghost. And immediately there fell from his eyes as it had been scales: and he received sight forthwith, and arose, and was baptized."

Jesus might have done all this work for Paul directly, but

this was not His plan. Paul had something to do in the line of confession to the men whose destruction he had premeditated, and God had a responsible work for the men to do whom He had ordained to act in His stead. Paul was to take those steps necessary in conversion. He was required to unite himself to the very people whom he had persecuted for their religion. Christ here gives all His people an example of the manner of His working for the salvation of men. The Son of God identified Himself with the office and authority of His organized church. His blessings were to come through the agencies that He has ordained, thus connecting man with the channel through which His blessings come. Paul's being strictly conscientious in his work of persecuting the saints does not make him guiltless when the knowledge of his cruel work is impressed upon him by the Spirit of God. He is to become a learner of the disciples.

He learns that Jesus, whom in his blindness he considered an impostor, is indeed the author and foundation of all the religion of God's chosen people from Adam's day, and the finisher of the faith, now so clear to his enlightened vision. He saw Christ as the vindicator of truth, the fulfiller of all prophecies. Christ had been regarded as making of none effect the law of God; but when his spiritual vision was touched by the finger of God, he learned of the disciples that Christ was the originator and the foundation of the entire Jewish system of sacrifices, that in the death of Christ type met antitype, and that Christ came into the world for the express purpose of vindicating His Father's law.

In the light of the law, Paul sees himself a sinner. That very law which he thought he had been keeping so zealously he finds he has been transgressing. He repents and dies to sin, becomes obedient to the claims of God's law, and has faith in Christ as his Saviour, is baptized, and preaches Jesus as earnestly and zealously as he once condemned Him. In the conversion of Paul are given us important principles which we should ever bear in mind. The Redeemer of the world does not sanction experience and exercise in religious matters independent of His organized and acknowledged church, where He has a church.

Many have the idea that they are responsible to Christ alone for their light and experience, independent of His acknowledged followers in the world. But this is condemned by Jesus in His teachings and in the examples, the facts, which He has given for our instruction. Here was Paul, one whom Christ was to fit for a most important work, one who was to be a chosen vessel unto Him, brought directly into the presence of Christ; yet He does not teach him the lessons of truth. He arrests his course and convicts him; and when he asks, "What wilt Thou have me to do?" the Saviour does not tell him directly, but places him in connection with His church. They will tell thee what thou must do. Jesus is the sinner's friend, His heart is ever open, ever touched with human woe; He has all power, both in heaven and upon earth; but He respects the means which He has ordained for the enlightenment and salvation of men. He directs Saul to the church, thus acknowledging the power that He has invested in it as a channel of light to the world. It is Christ's organized body upon the earth, and respect is required to be paid to His ordinances. In the case of Saul, Ananias represents Christ, and he also represents Christ's ministers upon the earth who are appointed to act in Christ's stead.

Saul was a learned teacher in Israel; but while he is under the influence of blind error and prejudice, Christ reveals Himself to him, and then places him in communication with His church, who are the light of the world. They are to instruct this educated, popular orator, in the Christian religion. In Christ's stead Ananias touches his eyes that they may receive sight; in Christ's stead he lays his hands upon him, prays in Christ's name, and Saul receives the Holy Ghost. All is done in the name and authority of Christ. Christ is the fountain. The church is the channel of communication. Those who boast of personal independence need to be brought into closer relation to Christ by connection with His church upon the earth.

Brother A, God loves you and desires to save you and bring you into working order. If you will be humble and teachable, and will be molded by His Spirit, He will be your strength, your righteousness, and your exceeding great reward. You may accomplish much for your brethren if you will hide in God and let His Spirit soften your spirit. You have a hard class to meet. They are filled with bitter prejudice, but no more so than was Saul. God can work mightily for your brethren if you do not allow yourself to get in the way and hedge up your own path. Let melting love, pity, and tenderness dwell in your heart while you labor. You may break down the iron walls of prejudice if you only cling to Christ and are ready to be counseled by your more experienced brethren.

You must not, as God's servant, be too easily discouraged by difficulties or by the fiercest opposition. Go forth, not in your own name, but in the might and power of Israel's God. Endure hardness as a good soldier of the cross of Christ. Jesus endured the contradiction of sinners against Himself. Consider the life of Christ and take courage, and press on in faith, courage, and hope.

UNITY IN THE CHURCH

In my last vision I was shown the introduction of the truth, and the progress of the cause of God, upon the Pacific Coast. I saw that good work had been wrought for many in California, but that there were many who professed the truth who were not ready to take hold of the work of God at the right time and to move as the opening providence of God indicates their duty. A great work may be done on this coast in bringing souls to the knowledge of the truth if there is united action.

If all who have influence felt the necessity of co-operation and would seek to answer the prayer of Christ, that they may be one as He is one with the Father, the cause of present truth would be a power upon this coast. But the people of

God are asleep, and do not see the wants of the cause for this time. They do not feel the importance of concentrated action. Satan is ever seeking to divide the faith and hearts of God's people. He well knows that union is their strength, and division their weakness. It is important and essential that all of Christ's followers understand Satan's devices and with a united front meet his attacks and vanquish him. They need to make continual efforts to press together even if it be at some sacrifice to themselves.

The people of God, with various temperaments and organizations, are brought together in church capacity. The truth of God, received into the heart, will do its work of refining, elevating, and sanctifying the life and overcoming the peculiar views and prejudices of each. All should labor to come as near to one another as possible. All who love God and keep His commandments in truth will have influence with unbelievers and will win souls to Christ, to swell the glad songs of triumph and victory before the great white throne. Selfishness will be overcome, and overflowing love for Christ will be manifested in the burden they feel to save souls for whom He died.

I was shown many families who are not living as Jesus would have them; they have a work to do at home before they can make advancement in the divine life. I was shown the case of Brother B and was pointed back to the time when he first accepted the truth. It then had a transforming influence upon his life. Self was in a measure lost in the interest he felt for the truth. He sought to show his faith by his works, and his personal interests were made secondary. He loved the work of the Lord and cheerfully sought to advance the interest of His cause; the Lord accepted his efforts to serve Him, and the hand of the Lord prospered him.

I was shown that Brother B displeased God and brought great darkness upon himself when he set up his judgment in opposition to that of his brethren in regard to the true way to observe the Sabbath. Brother B's interest was at stake, and he refused to see the correct bearing of the question under consideration. He never would have taken the course he did when he returned from the East, if he had been in the light. I was then carried to another point in his history and saw him journeying. While among unbelievers he did not let his light so shine before men that they by seeing his good works would glorify our Father which is in heaven. He was forgetful of God and of his duty to rightly represent his Saviour in every place and upon all occasions.

Brother B is especially weak upon some points; he loves praise and flattery; he loves pleasure and distinction. He exalted himself and talked much and prayed little, and God left him to his own weakness; for he did not bear fruit to the glory of God. On that journey he had an opportunity to do a great amount of good, but he did not realize that he was accountable to God for his talents and that as a steward of God he would be called to an account whether he had used his ability to please himself or to glorify God. If Brother B had felt the power of the love of Christ in his own heart, he would have felt an interest for the salvation of those with whom he was brought in contact, that he might speak to them words which would cause them to reflect in regard to their eternal interest.

He had an opportunity to sow the seed of truth, but he did not improve it as he should. He should have carried his religion with him while among his relatives. His holy profession and the truth of God should have blended with all his thoughts, feelings, words, and actions. Christ commands His followers to walk in the light. Walking means moving onward, exerting ourselves, exercising our ability, being actively engaged. Unless we exercise ourselves in the good work to which our Saviour has called us, and feel the importance of personal effort in this work, we shall have a sickly, stunted religion. We gain new victories by our experience in working. We gain activity and strength by walking in the light, that we may have energy to run in the way of God's commandments. We may gain an increase of strength at every step we advance heavenward. God will bless His people only when they try to be a blessing to others. Our graces are matured and developed by exercise.

I was shown that while Brother B was at Battle Creek he was weak in moral power. He had not been seeking to cling to God and preserve his soul in purity of thought and action, and he was left to follow his own mind and to receive impressions that were detrimental to his spiritual interest. He met those who perverted the truth and was led by them to believe things that were untrue; and as he had opened the door to the enemy and received him as an angel of light, he was readily overcome by temptation.

He became wickedly prejudiced and was suspicious of the very ones in whom God would have him have confidence. He saw things in a perverted light, and the meetings, which should have been to him a great source of strength, were an injury. This was as Satan would have it, that Brother B might lose confidence in the men whom God had appointed to lead out in this work. He became at variance with them and with the heart of the work. He was like a vessel at sea without an anchor or a rudder. If he could not have confidence in those at the head of the work he would have confidence in no one.

Brother B has but little reverence or respect for his brethren; he thinks that his judgment and his knowledge and abilities are superior to theirs; therefore he will not receive anything from them, nor trust to their judgment, nor seek to counsel with them, unless he can lead and teach them. He will act according to his own judgment, irrespective of his brethren's feelings, their griefs, or entreaties. When he separated his confidence from the heart of the work, Satan knew that, unless this confidence could be restored, he was sure of him. Brother B's eternal interest depends upon his accepting and respecting the helps and governments which God has been pleased to place in the church. If he follows a course of his own choosing he will eventually find out that he has been altogether upon a wrong track and that he has deceived himself to his ruin. He will take first one turn, then another, and yet after all miss the true and only path which leads to heaven.

There are thousands who are traveling the road of darkness and error, the broad road which leads to death, who flatter themselves that they are in the path to happiness and heaven; but they will never find the one nor reach the other. Brother B needs the helps that God has placed in the church, for he cannot constitute a church of himself, and yet his course shows that he would be satisfied to be a complete church, subject to none. Brother B long since lost his consecration to God; he did not guard the avenue of his soul against the suggestions of Satan. I saw that angels of God were writing his words and actions. He was going further and further from the light of heaven. When the grace of God does not especially control you, Brother B, you are a hard man to connect with. You have great self-confidence and firmness, which are felt in your family and in the church. You have but little reverence and respect for anyone. You do not possess the grace of humility.

Brother B returned to this coast in great darkness; he had lost his love for the truth and his love for God. His natural feelings controlled him, and he was proud. He loved himself, and he loved money better than he loved the truth and his Redeemer. I was shown that his course after he returned to the coast was a dishonor to the Christian name. I saw him joining hands with the gay lovers of pleasure. He grieved his brethren and wounded his Saviour and put Him to open shame before unbelievers. I saw that from this time he did not take pleasure in the service of God or in the advancement of the truth. He seemed to possess a zeal to search the Scriptures and different authors, not that he might become established upon important points of present truth which the providence of God had furnished him through men of His choice, but to find a new position and to advance new views in opposition to the established faith of the body. His researches were not made for the glory of God, but to promote self.

When Brother B once takes a position on the wrong side, it is not according to his nature to see his error and confess his wrong, but to fight it out to the last, whatever may be the consequences. This spirit is ruinous to the church and ruinous in his family. He needs to soften his heart and let in tenderness, humility, and love. He needs benevolence and noble generosity. In short, he needs to be thoroughly converted, to be a new man in Christ Jesus. Then his influence in the church will be all right and he will be just the help they need. He will have the respect and love of his family and will command his household after him. Duty and love like twin sisters, will be his helps in the management of his children.

I saw that Sister B had much to grieve over in the course that her husband had pursued toward her; that her life had been very sad, when he was able to make it happy. She seemed to be dispirited and to keenly feel that she was neglected and unloved by her husband. In his absence she at times felt nearly distracted and became jealous and distrustful in regard to him. Satan was present with his temptations, and she looked upon some things in an exaggerated light. All this might have been saved had Brother B preserved his consecration to God. I was carried on still further and saw that he was walking in unbelief and darkness while he was flattering himself that he alone had the true light. The further he separated from God the less love did he have for his brethren and for the truth.

I was shown Brother B questioning one after another of the points of our faith which have brought us out from the world and made us a separate and distinct people, looking for the blessed hope and the glorious appearing of our Lord and Saviour Jesus Christ. His unbelief and darkness have not moved the main pillars of our faith. The truth of God is not made of none effect by him. It remains the truth still, but he has had some influence upon the minds of his brethren. The reports of lying lips in regard to my husband and me, which he brought from the East, had an influence to create suspicions and doubts in the minds of others. Those unacquainted with us could not stand in our defense. The church in _____, I saw, might have numbered three times as many as it now does, and might have had tenfold greater strength, had not Brother B played himself into the hands of the enemy. In his blind unbelief he has done all that he could to discourage and scatter the believers in the truth. In his blindness he has not realized that his course was grievous in the sight of God. The discouragement and darkness which he has caused have made the labors of Brother C doubly hard, for his influence has not only been felt by the church in _____, but by other churches.

Brother B has strengthened unbelief and an opposing influence which Brother C has had to meet. I saw that we would meet the same and that it would take time to eradicate the old root of bitterness whereby many have been defiled; that there is a time to speak and a time to keep silent; that when God should lay upon us the burden to speak we should not hesitate, whether men would hear or whether they would forbear; and that we should press the matter through if it left some outside the church and outside the truth. God has a great and important work for somebody to do in _____, and at the right time it will be done, and truth will triumph.

Those of our brethren who had not obtained an experience for themselves in present truth could not answer the arguments of Brother B, and although they could not receive the views advocated by him, they were more or less affected by his talk and reasoning. Some have felt no spirit of freedom when they met for worship. They were afraid upon the Sabbath to speak out their real feelings and faith, expecting that he would criticize what they would say. There has been death in the meetings and but little freedom.

Brother B desires that others should look up to him as a man who can explain the Scriptures, but I was shown that he is deceived and does not understand them. He has started upon a wrong track in seeking to get up a new faith, an original theory of faith. He would uproot and misplace those waymarks which show us our correct bearings, that we are near the close of this earth's history. He may flatter himself that he is being led of the Lord, but it is surely another spirit.

Unless he changes his course entirely, and is willing to be led and to learn, he will be left to follow his own ways and make entire shipwreck of faith.

Some have been so blinded by their own unbelief that they could not discern the spirit of Brother B. They might have been helped by him if he had been standing in the counsel of God. He could have led them to the light instead of increasing their confusion of faith and their perplexities. But he has been a stumbling block, a blind leader of the blind. Had he made straight paths for his feet, the lame would not have been turned out of the way, but would have been healed. He has refused to walk in the light of truth which God has given His people, and those who would walk in the light he has hindered.

He feels that it is an honor to suggest doubts and unbelief in regard to the established faith of God's commandment-keeping people. The truth that he once rejoiced in is now darkness to him, and, unless he changes his course, he will fall back into a mixture of the views of the different denominations, but will agree in the whole with none of them; he will be a distinct church of himself, but not under the control of the great Head of the church. By bringing his views in opposition to the faith of the body, he is disheartening and discouraging the church. He sees that if the body of Sabbathkeepers have the truth he is in darkness, and this he cannot admit. The truth condemns him, and instead of seeking to bring his soul into harmony with it, surrendering to its claims and dying to self, he is seeking a position where he will not be under condemnation.

I was shown that if he continues in his present course, blinded to his real condition, he will be glad after a while to find some pretext for giving up the Sabbath. Satan is surely leading him, as he has led many others, away from the body in a course of deception and error. How much safer for Brother B to bring his soul into harmony with the truth than to misinterpret Scripture to bring it into harmony with his ideas and actions. If he would bring his actions into harmony with the principles of God's law he has a task on his hands of which he has scarcely dreamed. The carnal heart is at enmity with God. It is not subject to the law of God, neither indeed can be.

The insinuations and open speeches of those who are our enemies in Battle Creek were received by Brother B while on his journey East, and he returned with bitter and wicked feelings in his heart against those at the heart of the work and especially against me and my work. He had no good reason for the feelings he cherished and the views he expressed in regard to my labors and testimonies. The unbelief and prejudice which had corrupted his own soul he sought to instill into the minds of others. He did this with considerable effect. At first, many were influenced by his sophistry and darkness, for he can make assertions and draw inferences as though he were handling positive facts. He knows how to press matters and is of ready speech. His words had influence with some who were unconsecrated and who wished to have it just as he represented in regard to our work and our calling. He had influence and excited prejudice in the minds of some whom we could have helped, had he not closed our way so that we could not gain access to them. Of this class were Brother and Sister D.

In this Brother B may see the fruits of his course, and there are others who were influenced in the same way, with the same results, so far as their faith and confidence in the truth are concerned. As soon as Brother B or any others decide that the men who have had the most to do in bringing the cause of present truth up to its present condition are not led of God, but are scheming and designing men, deceiving the people, then the course for them to pursue in order to be consistent is to renounce the entire work as a delusion, a fraud. In order to be consistent, they must throw all overboard. This Brother B has almost imperceptibly to himself been doing, and this others have done. He will at some future time, if not now, review his work with different feelings than he now has. He will see the work which he has been doing during the past few years as God sees it, and will not view it with the satisfaction he now feels. When he sees the miserable work in which he has been engaged for a few years past, his proud boasting of wisdom and superior knowledge will have an end, and he will repent in bitterness of soul, for the blood of souls is on his garments.

If Brother B had wanted to view things correctly and had felt the possibility of being deceived, he would have come to Brother and Sister White with the reports injurious to their reputation and would have given them an opportunity to speak for themselves. The reports which he brought away across the plains to the Pacific Coast bear false witness, thus breaking the law of God. He will one day meet the hard speeches, as well as the deceptive sophistry instigated by Satan, which he has instilled into minds to injure the influence of my husband and myself. This matter lies not between Brother B and me, but between him and God.

God has given us our work, and if He has given us a message to bear to His people, those who would hinder us in the work and weaken the faith of the people in its truth and verity are not fighting against the instrument, but against God, and they must answer to Him for the result of their words and actions. All who have spiritual discernment may judge of the tree by its fruits. Brother B stands forth as one enlightened by God to undeceive the people in regard to our work and mission. All may see, if they will, the fruit growing upon this tree. Brother B, is it to eternal life, or is it to death?

After Brother B received from Battle Creek this special knowledge, which led him to take a course to belittle our work and mission, he felt at liberty to join with the unbelieving in the dissipation of pleasure, and by his levity of conduct he brought reproach upon the cause of Christ and great suffering upon his wife. Was he so blinded that he had no conviction that he was seeking to tear down what God was building up? Had he no thoughts that he might be fighting against God? The work which he has been doing angels have recorded in heaven, and he will have to answer for it when every work shall be brought into judgment to bear the inspection of the infinite God. In his blindness Brother B has been lifting his puny arm to fight against God while flattering his deceived soul that he was doing God service. Every man's work is to be tried by the fire of the last day, and only gold, silver, and precious stones will stand the test.

God will not be trifled with. He may bear long with men, but He will visit their transgressions and render to every man as his works have been. Although men may talk boastingly and pride themselves upon their wisdom, one breath from the lips of God can bring their honor and glorying to the dust. I was shown that Brother B will be inexcusable in the day of God, when every case is weighed in the balances of the sanctuary. He knows better than to do as he has done. He has had sufficient evidence to determine the character of the work which God has committed to us. The fruits of this work are before him, which he can see and understand if he will.

Brother B's self-confidence is most wonderful, and is a fearful snare to him. If he does not overcome this dangerous trait in his character, it will prove his ruin. He is in his natural element when he is battling and controverting points of doctrine; he will question and quibble and be at variance with his brethren until Satan so controls his mind that he really thinks that he has the truth and his brethren are in error. He does not stand in the light and has not the blessing of God, for it constitutes a part of his religion to oppose the settled points of God's commandment-keeping people. Are all these deceived? and is Brother B the only man to whom God has given correct truth? Is not God just as willing to give His devoted, self-sacrificing servants a correct understanding of the Scriptures as to give it to Brother B for them?

Does Brother B try his course by this simple test: "Does this light and knowledge that I have found, and which places me at variance with my brethren, draw me more closely to Christ? does it make my Saviour more precious to me and make my character more closely resemble His?" It is a natural, but not a pleasing, trait in our characters to be keen in our perceptions, and tenacious in our remembrance, of the faults and failings of others.

Brother B does not try to be in union with his brethren; his self-confidence has led him to feel no special necessity for union. He feels that their minds have been cast in a mold inferior to his own and that to receive their opinions and counsel as worthy of attention would be a great condescension. This self-confidence has shut him away from the love and sympathy of his brethren and from union with them. He feels that he is too wise and experienced to need the precautions which are indispensable to many. He has so high an opinion of his own abilities and such a reliance upon his own attainments that he believes himself prepared for any emergency. Said the heavenly angels, pointing to Brother B: "Let him that thinketh he standeth take heed lest he fall." Self-confidence leads to neglect of watchfulness and of humble, penitential prayer. There are outward temptations to be shunned and inward foes and perplexities to be overcome, for Satan adapts his temptations to the different characters and temperaments of individuals.

The church of Christ is in constant peril. Satan is seeking to destroy the people of God, and one man's mind, one man's judgment, is not sufficient to be trusted. Christ would have His followers brought together in church capacity, observing order, having rules and discipline, and all subject one to another, esteeming others better than themselves. Union and confidence are essential to the prosperity of the church. If each member of the church feels at liberty to move independently of the others, taking his own peculiar course, how can the church be in any safety in the hour of danger and peril? The prosperity and very existence of a church depend upon the prompt, united action and mutual confidence of its members. When, at a critical time, one sounds the alarm of danger, there is need of prompt and active work, without stopping to question and canvass the whole subject from end to end, thus letting the enemy gain every advantage by delay, when united action might save many souls from perdition.

God wants His people to be united in the closest bonds of Christian fellowship; confidence in our brethren is essential to the prosperity of the church; union of action is important in a religious crisis. One imprudent step, one careless action, may plunge the church into difficulties and trials from which it may not recover for years. One member of the church filled with unbelief may give an advantage to the great foe that will affect the prosperity of the entire church, and many souls may be lost as the result. Jesus would have His followers subject one to another; then God can use them as instruments to save one another; for one may not discern the dangers which another's eye is quick to perceive; but if the undiscerning will in confidence obey the warning, they may be saved great perplexities and trials.

As Jesus was about to leave His disciples, He prayed for them in a most touching, solemn manner that they all might be one "as Thou, Father, art in Me, and I in Thee, that they also may be one in Us: that the world may believe that Thou hast sent Me. And the glory which Thou gavest Me I have given them; that they may be one, even as We are one: I in them, and Thou in Me, that they may be made perfect in one; and that the world may know that Thou hast sent Me, and hast loved them, as Thou hast loved Me." The apostle Paul in his first epistle to the Corinthians exhorts them to unity: "Now I beseech you, brethren, by the name of our Lord Jesus Christ, that ye all speak the same thing, and that there be no divisions among you; but that ye be perfectly joined together in the same mind and in the same judgment."

God is leading a people out from the world upon the exalted platform of eternal truth, the commandments of God and the faith of Jesus. He will discipline and fit up His people. They will not be at variance, one believing one thing, and another having faith and views entirely opposite, each moving independently of the body. Through the diversity of the gifts and governments that He has placed in the church, they will all come to the unity of the faith. If one man takes his views of Bible truth without regard to the opinions of his brethren, and justifies his course, alleging that he has a right to his own peculiar views, and then presses them upon others, how can he be fulfilling the prayer of Christ? And if another and still another arises, each asserting his right to believe and talk what he pleases without reference to the faith of the body, where will be that harmony which existed between Christ and His Father, and which Christ prayed might exist among His brethren?

God is leading out a people and establishing them upon the one great platform of faith, the commandments of God and the testimony of Jesus. He has given His people a straight chain of Bible truth, clear and connected. This truth is of heavenly origin and has been searched for as for hidden treasure. It has been dug out through careful searching of the Scriptures and through much prayer.

Brother B is doubting point after point of our faith. If he is right in his new theories, the body of Sabbathkeepers is wrong. Shall the established faith in the strong points of our position, which has led us out from the world and united us a distinct and peculiar people, be given up as erroneous? Shall we receive the faith of this one man, with the evidences he gives us of the fruits of his religious character? Or will Brother B yield his judgment and opinions, and come to the body? If he had not blinded his soul by receiving prejudice, and by cherishing wicked opposition to the work of God, he would not have been left to such darkness and deception.

He is a ready talker and will persistently urge his opinions and will not yield to the weight of evidence against him. It is cruel for him to stand in the way of the prosperity of the church, as he has done. The world is large; he has all the privileges that he can ask of going out among unbelievers and converting them to his theories; and when he can present a well-organized body that he has been the means of converting from sin to righteousness, then, and not before, should he press his peculiar views upon the church of God, which is pained and disheartened with his darkness and error. He has no right to build upon another man's foundation his wood, hay, and stubble to be consumed by the fires of the last day.

I was shown that the only safe position for Brother B is to sit at the feet of Jesus and learn the way of life more perfectly. His doctrine shall drop as the rain, and His speech shall distill as the dew, upon the heart of the humble and teachable. Brother B must obtain a teachable disposition. He is not to sit as a judge, but as a learner; not to cavil, but to believe; not to question and find fault and oppose, but to listen. Pride must give way to humility, and prejudice must be exchanged for candor, or the gracious words of Christ will be in vain to him. My brother, you may reason with your blind judgment and unsanctified mind until the day of God and not advance a step toward heaven; you may debate and investigate and search learned authors, and even the Scriptures, and yet grow more and more self-deceived, and become darker and darker, as did the Jews in reference to Christ. What was their fault? They rejected the light which God had already given them and were seeking for some new light by which they might so interpret the Scriptures as to sustain their actions.

You are doing the same; you pass over the light that God has seen fit to give you in the publications upon present truth and in His word, and are seeking doctrines of your own, theories which cannot be sustained by the word of God. When you become as a little child, willing to be led, and when your understanding is sanctified and your will and prejudices surrendered, such a light will be shed abroad in your heart as will illumine the Scriptures and show you present truth in its beautiful harmony. It will appear like a golden chain, link joined to link in a perfect whole. "Except ye be converted and become as little children, ye shall not enter into the kingdom of heaven." "Learn of Me," says Christ; "for I am meek and lowly in heart: and ye shall find rest unto your souls."

If you have indeed entered the school of Christ, He expects you to manifest in your character and deportment the lowliness which is so beautifully exemplified in His character. Christ will not undertake to teach the self-righteous, self-conceited, and self-willed. If such come to Him with the inquiry, What is truth? He gives them no answer. It is only the meek that He will guide in judgment; the meek will He teach His way. Solomon was naturally endowed with good judgment and large reasoning powers, but he acknowledged himself before God as a little child. He sought for wisdom from God with humility, and he sought not in vain. If you really search for the truth with the right motive you will come with the body, for they have the truth. If you are searching the Scriptures and different authors that you may find doctrines which will coincide with your own preconceived opinions, and if you have already settled your faith, then you will be boastful, self-confident, and unyielding.

SELF-CONFIDENCE A SNARE

Brother B, with your present self-willed, stubborn spirit, you will go further and further from the truth; and unless you are converted you will prove to be a great hindrance to the cause of God in any place where you have any influence. You are persistent to carry your points. Your self-sufficient spirit must be yielded before you can see anything clearly. You have led your wife to think that you knew the truth better than any of our ministers; you have taken the key of knowledge into your own hands, so far as she is concerned, and have kept her in darkness. God has given His church men of judgment, experience, and faith. They know the way of truth and salvation, for they have searched for it in agony of spirit because of the opposition they had to meet from men who turned the truth of God into a lie; and the benefit of the labor of these faithful servants of God is given to the world.

There are very few who realize the exalted nature of the work of God in comparison with the temporal business cares of life. Jesus, the heavenly Teacher, has given us lessons of instruction through His disciples. When He sent out the twelve, He instructed them that into whatever city or town they should enter they must inquire who in it was worthy of their attention and visits; and if a suitable place was found where the people would esteem the blessing sent them,—the privilege of entertaining the messengers of Christ,—there they were to abide and there let their peace rest until they left that city. They were not instructed to visit any and every house indiscriminately, urging their presence upon the people whether they were welcome or not; but if they were not welcomed, if their peace could not rest in the house, they were to leave it and seek a house where the members were worthy and where their spirit could rest.

When the messengers of Christ who go forth to teach the truth to others are rejected and their words find no place in the heart, Christ is rejected and His word despised in the messengers of truth whom He has chosen and sent. This has just as full an application in this age of the world as it had when Christ gave the instruction to His chosen messengers.

When Christ was upon the earth, there were men who had no respect or reverence for God's messengers and no more regard for their warning than for their own judgment; also in this age of the world there are those who do not respect the testimony of God's chosen servants so highly as their own opinions. Such cannot be benefited by the labors of God's servants, and time should not be lost in degrading the work of God to meet such minds. Christ said to the servants whom He sent forth: "He that heareth you heareth Me; and he that despiseth you despiseth Me; and he that despiseth Me despiseth Him that sent Me."

Christ gives power to the voice of the church. "Verily I say unto you, Whatsoever ye shall bind on earth shall be bound in heaven: and whatsoever ye shall loose on earth shall be loosed in heaven." No such thing is countenanced as one man's starting out upon his own individual responsibility and advocating what views he chooses, irrespective of the judgment of the church. God has bestowed the highest power under heaven upon His church. It is the voice of God in His united people in church capacity which is to be respected.

God has given to His church men who have an experience, those who have fasted and wept and prayed, even through the entire night, for the Lord to open the Scriptures to their minds. In humility these men have given the world the benefit of their mature experience. Is this light of heaven, or of men? Is it of any value, or is it worthless? Brother B is doing a work in disseminating erroneous views of Bible truth that he will one day wish to undo; but it will be in vain. He may repent, he may yet be saved as by fire; but, oh, how much precious time will have been lost that never can be redeemed! How much seed has he sown that has borne only briers and thorns! How many souls have been lost that might have been saved had he tried as earnestly to let the true light shine as he has to scatter his darkness! What might he not have done had he been consecrated, sanctified through the truth! Brother B feels too self-sufficient, too rich and increased with goods, to see his need of anything. The True Witness pointed to him and said: "Unless ye become converted as a little child, ye cannot see the kingdom of heaven." The light of truth so carefully brought out in books and papers he does not respect; but he exalts his own judgment above the most precious light, and this light will rise up in the judgment to condemn him.

I saw that he would question the men upon whom God has seen fit to lay the responsibility of His work. He would exalt his own opinions and views above the light which God had given through them, and would boast of his knowledge; and he would be an accuser of his brethren, not excepting the ambassadors of Christ. All this overbearing influence to belittle the judgment of the servants of God and to accuse them of weaknesses and errors, exalting his own opinions above theirs, if not repented of, will be found written against him in the books, which he will see with shame in the day of God.

God will hold up His servants, will preserve His favored ones; but woe unto him who would make of none effect the words of Christ's ambassadors, who receive the word from the mouth of God to speak to the people and who would tell the people that the sword is coming and warn them to prepare for the great day of God. Brother B will find that it is no light or trivial work in which he has been engaged; it is a work which will roll back upon his soul with crushing weight. He has brought his spirit in opposition to God. He has a hard work before him. Said Christ: "It must needs be that offenses come; but woe to that man by whom the offense cometh."

Brother B, the course that you have been pursuing was shown me three years ago. I saw that you were wrong in almost every action, and yet you tried to gauge the truth to your actions instead of gauging them to the truth. You were not a light to the people of God, but a terrible burden. You will not lift when there is lifting to be done, and you discourage others from union of action. You are ever finding fault and talking of your brethren, and while you have been questioning the course of others, a rank growth of poisonous weeds has flourished and taken deep root in your own heart. These roots of bitterness springing up have defiled many and will defile many more unless you see them and root them out.

I was shown that a harsh, pharisaical spirit would grow upon Brother B and control him unless he sees the terrible defects in his character and obtains grace from God to correct the evil. Before he embraced the truth, his hand seemed to be against everyone; his combative spirit would strengthen at any provocation, and his self-esteem would be injured; he was a hard man, getting into and making trouble. The truth of God wrought a reformation in him. God accepted him, and His hand held him up. But since Brother B has lost the spirit of consecration, his old, turbulent spirit, at variance with others, has been strengthening and seeking to gain the mastery. When he dies to self and humbles his proud heart before God he will find how weak is his strength; he will feel the need of heavenly succor and will cry: "Unclean, unclean, before Thee, O God." All his proud boasting in self will have an end.

Life in this stormy world, where moral darkness triumphs over truth and virtue, will be to the Christian a continual conflict. He will find that he must keep the armor on, for he will have to fight against forces that never tire and foes that never sleep. We shall find ourselves beset with countless temptations, and we must find strength in Christ to overcome them or be overcome by them and lose our souls. We have a great and solemn work to do, and how terrible will be our loss if we fail. If the work which our Master has left us be found undone, we cannot have a second probation granted us. It must remain undone forever.

I was shown the life of Brother B in his family. Angels wept as they viewed his course at home, as they viewed the unloved wife, who receives no respect from him whose duty it is to love and cherish her as his own body, even as Christ has loved and cherished the church. He takes pains to make her defects apparent and to exalt his own wisdom and judgment and to make her feel her inferiority in company and alone. Notwithstanding she is illiterate, her spirit is far more acceptable to God than the spirit of her husband. God looks upon Sister B with feelings of the deepest pity. She lives out the principles of truth, as far as she has light, much better than her husband. She will not be answerable for the light and knowledge that her husband has had but which she has not had. He could be a light and comfort and blessing to her, but his influence is used in a wrong way. He reads to her what he pleases, that which will give strength to his views and his ideas, while he keeps back essential light which he does not want her to hear.

He does not respect his wife, and he allows his children to show her disrespect. Like Eli's sons, these children are left to come up. They are not restrained, and all this neglect will by and by rebound upon himself. That which Brother B is now sowing he will most assuredly reap. Sister B, in many respects, is nearer the kingdom of heaven than her husband. These unruly, disobedient children, that are not educated to self-control, will plant thorns in the hearts of their parents that they cannot prevent; and then in the judgment God will call the parents to account for bringing children into the world and letting them come up untrained, unloving, and unloved. These children cannot be saved in the kingdom of heaven without a great change in their characters.

Brother B seeks to have his wife believe as he believes, and he would have her think that all he does is right and that he knows more than any of the ministers and is wise above all men. I was shown that in his boasted wisdom he is dealing with the bodies of his children as he is with the soul of his wife. He has been following a course according to his own wisdom, which is ruining the health of his child. He flatters himself that the poison which he has introduced into her system keeps her alive. What a mistake! He should reason how much better she might have been had he let her alone and not abused nature. This child can never have a sound constitution, for her bones and the current of blood in her veins have been poisoned. The shattered constitutions of his children and their aches and distressing pains will cry out against his boasted wisdom, which is folly.

But what is more deplorable than all the rest is that he has, as it were, left the door to perdition wide open for his children to enter and be lost. The natures of his children will have to be changed, their characters transformed and made over new, or there can be no hope for them. Can angels look lovingly upon your family, Brother B? Can they delight to dwell in your house? The building is good, but the house does not make the happiness within. Those who live within the walls make it a heaven or a hell. You do not respect the mother of your children. You permit in them disobedience and disrespect.

You may say: "Why does Sister White come to me with this? I have no faith in the visions." I knew this before I attempted to write, but I feel that the time has come for me to set these things before you. I must tell you the truth, for I expect to meet in the judgment what I have here imperfectly written. I have waited, hoping that I might say something that would reach your heart and soften it for the very words I have here written. But I have lost all hope in that direction, for you are fortified with an armor as impenetrable as steel. You will not accept of anything that does not meet your mind. I was shown that it would have been better for the cause of present truth if you had never embraced the Sabbath. Your conscience is not a very sensitive one; you are blinded by the enemy.

I have given up all hope of doing anything for the church in _____ while you are a stumbling block to them. You once loved the truth, and had you followed on in the pathway of truth and holiness you would now have been an ambassador for Christ. You will have a fearful account to give in the great day of God for your talents which have been unimproved. You had good abilities. God lent these talents to you for you to put to good account, but you have abused these gifts. Had you used the ability that God had given you, on the right side, you would have done much in winning souls to Christ, and you would see in the kingdom of heaven souls saved through your instrumentality. But you have scattered abroad instead of gathering with Christ. Your brethren have been discouraged from trying to rise and advance, because you, like an opposing body, counteract the good they would do.

The heart of God never yearned toward His earthly children with deeper love and more compassionate tenderness than now. There never was a time when God was ready and waiting to do more for His people than now. And He will instruct and save all who choose to be saved in His appointed way. Those who are spiritual can discern spiritual things and see tokens of the presence and work of God everywhere. Satan, by his skillful and wicked strategy, led our first parents from the Garden of Eden—from their innocence and purity into sin and unspeakable wretchedness. He has not ceased to destroy; all the forces which he can command are diligently employed by him in these last days to compass the ruin of souls. He seizes every artifice that he can use to deceive, perplex, and confuse the people of God.

He has used you as his agent to scatter darkness and confusion, and he finds that you work admirably in his hands. You are the very instrument that he can handle with good effect to hurt, discourage, and tear down. You are not zealous to put your shoulder under the load with the people of God; but when they would move, you throw yourself as an additional load to prevent them from doing what they might do in advancing in the right direction. Satan is at work with those who keep the commandments of God and have the faith of Jesus. The most bitter hatred exists within him against all who are loyal to God and who obey His commandments. He sleeps not; he does not abate his vigilance for one moment. Would that God's professed followers were half as wise, diligent, and persevering in the work of God as Satan is in his work.

Had you, Brother B, followed on when you first set your hand to the plow, and not looked back, you would now have been a messenger of light to bear the truth to those in darkness. But God could not use you to His glory until you should learn to counsel with your brethren and not to think you knew all that was worth knowing. Satan has succeeded in keeping you from doing good. You did run well for a season, but Satan's temptations overcame you. You loved to be first and to be flattered. You loved the power which money gives. Satan understands the weakness of men. He has the knowledge which he has accumulated for ages and is an experienced hand at his work. His cunning and devices are well matured, and are too often successful because God's people are not as wise as serpents.

Satan frequently appears as an angel of light, arrayed in the livery of heaven; he assumes friendly airs, manifesting great sanctity of character and high regard for his victims, the souls whom he means to deceive and destroy. Perils lie in the path which he invites souls to travel, but he succeeds in concealing these and presents the attractions only. The great Captain of our salvation has conquered in our behalf, that through Him we might conquer, if we would, in our own behalf. But Christ saves none against their choice; He compels none to obedience. He made the infinite sacrifice that they might overcome in His name and His righteousness be imputed unto them.

But in order to be saved you must accept the yoke of Christ and lay off the yoke which you have fashioned for your neck. The victory that Jesus gained in the wilderness is a pledge to you of the victory that you may gain through His name. Your only hope and salvation is in overcoming as Christ overcame. The wrath of God now hangs over you. You love the attractions of the world above the heavenly treasure. The lust of the eye and the pride of life have separated you from God. Your confidence in your own poor, weak, faulty self must be broken. You must feel your weakness before you will drop, with your burden, into the hands of God. The soul that trusts fully and entirely in God will never be confounded.

God would not have us consult our own convenience in obeying Him. Christ pleased not Himself when He was a man among men. He was a man of sorrows and acquainted with grief. The Majesty of heaven had not where to lay His head, no place that He could claim as His own. He became poor for our sakes, that through Him we might be rich indeed. Let us not talk of sacrifice, for we know not what it is to sacrifice for the truth. As yet we have scarcely lifted the cross for Christ's dear sake. Let us not seek for a way which is easier than the path our Redeemer has traveled before us. How incompetent are you, with all your boasted wisdom, to guide yourself! How liable are you to follow the dictates of a deceived conscience, to run in the way of error, and drag others with you!

Your natural temperament is such that submission and obedience to God's requirements are very hard. Your unbounded self-confidence, your prejudices, and your feelings easily lead you to choose a wrong path. Christ will be to you an infallible guide if you will choose Him before your own blind judgment. In your business you have not had an eye single to the glory of God. You have had many perplexities and many difficulties to encounter, and if you had trusted to the True Counselor instead of to your own judgment, you would ever have been guided out of your perplexities in your business transactions.

You have an important work before you which you can never do without the special help of God. You are capable of securing the companionship of angels and of being an heir of God, a joint heir with Jesus Christ; and for you to labor to confine the range of hope and desire within the narrow compass of your own convenience would be a lifelong mistake. It is a terrible mistake to live only for this world. You look back and feel the condemnation of your own wrong course, and seek to justify yourself by finding fault with others. Whatever course others may pursue, or however wrong they may be, their errors will never cover one of your mistakes; and in the day of final reckoning you will not dare to plead this before God as a palliation for your neglect of duty.

God proposes to accept you as His child and make you a member of the royal family, a child of the heavenly King, upon conditions that you come out from the world and be separate and touch not the unclean thing. The Monarch of heaven would have you possess and enjoy all that can ennoble, expand, and exalt your being and fit you to dwell with Him forever, your existence measuring with the life of God. What a prospect is the life which is to come! What charms it possesses! How broad and deep and measureless is the love of God manifested to man! No words can describe this love; it surpasses all thought and imagination, but it is a reality that you may learn by experience; you may rejoice in it with joy unspeakable and full of glory.

With such a prospect before you, how can you narrow your mind to the compass of worldly thoughts and to the range of worldly occupations, seeking gain and yielding one point after another of present truth. Truth, principle, and conscience are desirable for you to retain. The favor of God is better than houses of silver and of gold. The deepest joy of the heart comes from the deepest humiliation. Trust and submission to God work out strength and nobleness of character. Tears are not in every case evidences of weakness. In order for you to build up a character which is symmetrical in the sight of a pure and holy God you must begin at the foundation. The heart must be broken before God, and true repentance for sin must be shown, till you meet the demands of truth and duty. Then you will have true respect for yourself and true confidence in God. You will have tenderness of feeling. All that braggadocio spirit will be gone. In the place of harshness will be great tenderness blended with firmness of purpose to stand for the truth at all events. You will then see much in the world and in your own heart to make you weep.

TRUE REFINEMENT IN THE MINISTRY

Brother E: I have designed to write to you for some time past, but have not found an opportunity to do so until now. While speaking to the people last Sabbath, I felt so clearly impressed with your case that I could with difficulty refrain from calling your name in public. I will now unburden my mind by writing to you. In my last vision I was shown the deficiencies of those who profess to labor in word and doctrine. I saw that you had not been improving your abilities, but had been growing less and less efficient to teach the truth. You need a thorough conversion. You have a strong, set will, even to stubbornness. You might now have been fitted for the solemn work of bearing the message of truth to others had you been less self-confident and more humble and meek in spirit.

You do not love close application nor the taxation of continued effort. You have not been a persevering student of the word of God, neither have you been a zealous worker in the cause of God. Your life has been far from representing the life of Christ. You are not discriminating. You are not a wise, judicious worker. You do not study to win souls to Christ, as every minister of Christ should. You have a set track, a standard of your own, to which you wish to bring the people; but you fail to do this because they will not accept your standard. You are bigoted and frequently carry things to extremes and thereby seriously hurt the cause of God and turn souls from the truth instead of winning them to it.

I was shown that you had spoiled several good openings by your injudicious manner of laboring, and what shall I say to you in regard to this matter? Souls have been lost through your lack of wisdom in presenting the truth and your failure to adorn your calling as a gospel minister by courtesy, kindness, and long-suffering. True Christian politeness should characterize all the actions of a minister of Christ. Oh, how poorly have you represented our pitiful, compassionate Redeemer, whose life was the embodiment of goodness and true purity. You have turned souls from the truth by a harsh, censorious, overbearing spirit. Your words have not been in the gentleness of Christ, but in the spirit of E. Your nature is naturally coarse and unrefined, and because you have never felt the necessity of true refinement and Christian politeness, your life has not been as elevated as it might have been.

You have remained in the rut of habit. Your education and training have not been correct, and therefore your efforts should have been the more earnest to improve, to reform, and make decided and thorough changes. Unless you realize a decided and thorough conversion in almost every respect you are entirely unfitted to preach the truth, and unless you can have a proper and becoming elevation of character, manners, and address, you will do more harm than you can do good. You have not done much in advancing the truth, for you have lingered about the churches too much, when you could do them no good, but only injury. Your ways and manners need refining and sanctifying. You should no longer mar the work of God by your deficiencies, since you have shown no decided improvement in becoming a workman in the cause of God.

It is impossible for you to bring others up to any higher standard than that to which you yourself attain. If you do not advance, how can you lead the church of God forward to a higher standard of piety and holiness? All such ministers as you have been for several years are more of a curse than a blessing to the cause of God, and the fewer we have of them the more prosperous will be the cause of present truth.

You are not elevated in your ideas, or aspiring in your labors. You are content to be commonplace and to make a cheap minister. You do not aspire to perfection of Christian character and to that position in the work that Christ requires every one of His chosen ministers to attain. No one professing to bear the truth to others is fitted for the responsible work unless he is making advancement in knowledge and in consecration to the work, and is improving his manners and temper, and growing in true wisdom from day to day. Close communion with God is necessary for every man who would guide souls into the truth. It should ever be borne in mind by those who take upon themselves the burden of guiding souls out of nature's darkness into the marvelous light that they themselves must be advancing in the light, else how can they lead others? If they are walking in darkness themselves, it is a most fearful responsibility which they assume in pretending to teach others the way.

You have engaged in labor in places where you were not competent to do justice to the work which you undertook. You did not labor judiciously. You sought to make up for your lack of real knowledge by censuring other denominations, running down others, and making hard and bitter criticisms upon their course and condition. Had your heart been all aglow with the spirit of truth, had you been sanctified to God and walking in the light as Christ is in the light, you would have moved in wisdom and would have had enough ways and means at your command to maintain an interest without going out of your way and aside from your specific work to rail out against others who profess to be Christians.

Unbelievers have been disgusted; they think that Seventh-day Adventists have been fairly represented by you, and they decide that it is enough and that they want no more of such doctrines. Our faith is unpopular at best and is in wide contrast to the faith and practices of other denominations. In order to reach those who are in the darkness of error and false theories, we must approach them with the utmost caution and with the greatest wisdom, agreeing with them on every point that we can conscientiously.

All consideration should be shown for those in error and all just credit given them for honesty. We should come as near the people as possible, and then the light and truth which we have may benefit them. But Brother E, like many of our ministers, commences a warfare at once against the errors that others cherish; he thus raises their combativeness and their set wills, and this holds them encased in an armor of selfish prejudice which no amount of evidence can remove.

Who but yourself will be responsible for the souls that you have turned away from the truth by your unsanctified labors? Who can break down the walls of prejudice which your injudicious labor has built up? I know of no greater sin against God than for men to engage in the ministry who labor in self and not in Christ. They are looked up to as the representatives of Christ, when they do not represent His spirit in any of their labors. They do not see or realize the dangers attending the efforts made by unconsecrated, unconverted men. They move on like blind men, deficient in almost everything and yet self-confident and self-sufficient, themselves walking in darkness and stumbling at every step. They are bodies of darkness.

Brother E, you have narrow ideas, and your labor has a tendency to lower rather than to elevate the truth. This is not because you have no ability. You could have made a good workman, but you are too indolent to make the effort necessary to attain the object. You would rather come down in a harsh and overbearing manner upon those who differ with you than to take the trouble to elevate the tone of your labor. You take positions, and then when they are questioned you are not humble enough to yield your notions though they are shown to be wrong; but you stand up in your independence and firmly hold to your ideas when concession on your part is essential and is required of you as a duty. You have stubbornly and unyieldingly held to your own judgment and opinions to the sacrifice of souls.

Brother E, your set positions and your strong, determined will to carry out your points at all hazards were felt and deplored by your wife, and her health suffered in consequence. You were not gentle and tender to this sensitive child of God; your strong spirit overbore her more gentle disposition. She grieved over many things. You could have made her life happier had you tried; but you sought to have her see things as you saw them, and, instead of trying to assimilate yourself to her refined temperament, you tried to mold her to your coarser nature and your extreme ideas. She was warped in her nature and could not act out herself. She withered like a plant transplanted to an uncongenial soil.

You should not seek to mold minds and characters after your pattern, but should allow your own character to be molded after the divine Pattern. If this world were composed of men like yourself in character and temperament, woe would be to it. As like would meet like whichever way you might turn, you would be disgusted with your associates, the exact patterns of yourself, and would wish to be out of the world.

You boast and glory in yourself. But, oh, how improper is this for any man, even if he have the finest qualities of mind and the most extended influence! Men of fine qualities have the greatest influence because they do not know their worth and how much good they do accomplish in the world. But it is all out of place for men of your stamp of character to be lifted up and boastful in self.

In your labors you frequently start out well; you raise an interest, and conviction rests upon minds that the arguments used cannot be controverted; but just at the time when souls are balancing in favor of the truth, self appears so plainly, is so prominent, that all which might have been gained, had Jesus shone forth in your words and deportment, is lost.

You lack the very graces which are essential to win souls to Christ and the truth. You can argue well; but you have not an experimental knowledge of the divine will, and for want of a religious experience yourself you are unable to lead others to the Fountain of living waters. Your own soul is not in communion with God, but is in darkness; and nothing can supply the deficiency realized by souls groping their way in the dark, except the light of truth. Unless you are thoroughly converted, your efforts to convert others might as well cease now as for you to labor longer, mangling and perverting the religious standard by your narrow and bigoted ideas. You have not an experimental knowledge of the divine will; your own righteousness seems to you to be of value, when it is valueless. You need to be transformed before you can be of use in the cause of God. When you are converted then you can labor to acceptance.

You do not possess the religion of Christ. You must soften your heart and die to self, and Christ must live in you; then you will walk in the light as He is in the light, and you will leave a bright track heavenward to lighten the pathway of others. You have felt too well satisfied with yourself. You should educate yourself and overcome your bigoted and fault-finding spirit. You need to keep the body under and bring it into subjection, lest, after you have preached to others, you yourself should be a castaway.

You take small views of matters, pick at straws, find fault, and question the course of others, when you might far better be overcoming the defects in your own character and life, working from a Christian standpoint, seeking light from God, and preparing to unite with pure angels in the kingdom of heaven. As you are, you would mar all heaven. You are uncultivated, unrefined, and unsanctified. There is no place in heaven for such a character as you now possess.

If you will take hold of the work earnestly and, without making any apology for sin, will condemn sin in the flesh and reach up in faith and hope for divine grace and right judgment, you may overcome those deficiencies in your character which disqualify you for laboring in the cause of God. You have not advanced or improved for many years. You are further today from the standard of Christian perfection, from possessing the qualifications which should be found in the minister of the gospel, than you were a few months after you had received the truth.

God is displeased with those who are not intelligent in regard to the Christian religion and yet are trying to lead others. You are correctly represented by the man who sought to pull out a mote from his brother's eye when a beam was in his own eye. First set your own heart in order, and reform your own character; obtain a connection with God, and gain a daily Christian experience; then you may bear a burden for souls who are out of Christ.

There are but few of the brethren who have taken more time to read different authors than you have, and yet you are very deficient in the qualifications necessary for a minister teaching the truth. You fail to quote, or even read, the Scriptures correctly. This should not be. You have not advanced in mental culture and have not secured a growth of grace in the soul which would shine out in your words and deportment. You have not felt the necessity of reaching up for higher and holier attainments.

Chasing through books superficially clogs the mind and causes you to become a mental dyspeptic. You cannot digest and use one half that you read. If you should read with the one object in view to improve the mind, and should read only as much as the mind can comprehend and digest, and would patiently persevere in such a course of reading, good results would be accomplished. You, as well as other ministers, need to attend school and to commence like a child to master the first branches of knowledge. You can neither read, spell, nor pronounce correctly, and yet there are but few who have had less taxation and less burdens of responsibility to bear than yourself.

The position of our ministers calls for health of body and discipline of mind. Good sound sense, strong nerves, and a cheerful temper will recommend the gospel minister anywhere. These should be sought for and perseveringly cultivated.

Your life thus far has been unprofitable. You have some very good ideas, but the Spirit of God does not dwell in your heart. You are not quickened by His power, and you have not genuine faith, hope, and love. The Spirit of Christ dwelling in you will enable you to take of the things of God and reveal them to others. You can be of no benefit to the cause of God till the work of a faithful minister of Christ is more exalted in your mind. You want a purpose in your life to do good, as did Jesus. The self-denial and love which you manifest in this work will tell upon the lives and characters of others.

You should get rid of your cold, frozen formality as soon as possible. You need to cultivate feelings of tenderness and friendliness in your everyday life. You should exhibit true courtesy and Christian politeness. The heart that really loves Jesus loves those for whom He died. Just as truly as the needle points to the pole, so will the true follower of Christ, with a spirit of earnest labor, seek to save souls for whom Christ has given His life. Working for the salvation of sinners will keep the love of Christ warm in the heart and will give that love a proper growth and development. Without a correct knowledge of the divine will there will be a lack of harmonious development in the Christian character.

I beseech you, my brother, to become acquainted with God. "The steps of a good man are ordered by the Lord." Ministering angels mark every step of our progress. But your will is not surrendered to God; your thoughts are not holy.

You go on, stumbling along in darkness, not knowing where to place your feet. The Lord reveals His will to those who are earnest and anxious to be guided. The reason for your inefficiency is that you have given up the idea of knowing and doing the will of God, therefore you do not know anything positively. Though blind yourself, you attempt to lead the blind.

Oh, in what a position are you and many other ministers! Having forsaken God, the Fountain of living waters, you and they have hewn out to yourselves broken cisterns that can hold no water. I entreat of you to be alarmed and turn to the Lord with that deep and earnest repentance which will secure to you His forgiveness and the enduring strength of His might, that you may indeed be filled with all the fullness of God. He frowns upon your course, for you have been as a stumbling block to souls. You have depended on your own works and righteousness for success, and have not a knowledge of the divine will.

May the Lord reveal to you your true character and let you see your real deficiencies. When you are enlightened by the Spirit of God to understand this you will have such a sense of your sinful neglect and unimproved life as will strike terror to your soul and cause you sorrow that will lead to repentance that needeth not to be repented of.

NUMBER TWENTY-FIVE

TESTIMONY FOR THE CHURCH

IMPORTANCE OF THE WORK

January 3, 1875, I was shown many things relative to the great and important interests at Battle Creek in the work of the Publishing Association, the school, and the Health Institute. If these institutions were properly conducted, they would greatly advance the cause of God in the spread of the truth and in the salvation of souls. We are living amid the perils of the last days. Consecration to God can alone fit any of us to act a part in the solemn and important closing work for this time. There are but few wholly unselfish men to fill responsible positions, few who have given themselves unreservedly to God to hear His voice and study His glory. There are but few who would, if required, give their lives to advance the cause of God. Yet it is just such devotion as this that God claims.

Men are deceived in thinking they are serving God when they are serving themselves and making the interest of the cause and work of God a secondary matter. Their hearts are not consecrated. The Lord takes no pleasure in the services of this class. From time to time, as the cause has progressed, He has in His providence designated men to fill positions at Battle Creek. These men could have filled important positions if they had consecrated themselves to God and devoted their energies to His work. These men of God's selection needed the very discipline that a devotion to His work would give them. He would honor them by connecting them with Himself and giving them His Holy Spirit to qualify them for the responsibilities they were called to bear. They could not gain that breadth of experience and knowledge of the divine will unless they were in positions to bear burdens and responsibilities.

None should be deceived in thinking that in connecting themselves with the work of God in Battle Creek they will have less care, less hard labor, and fewer trials. Satan is most active where the most is being done to advance the truth and to save souls. He understands human nature, and he will not let these men alone if there is any prospect of their becoming more like Christ and more useful workers in the cause of God. Satan lays his plans to press his temptations upon the very men whom God has signified that He would accept to act a part in connection with His work. It is Satan's study to know how he can best war against and defeat the purposes of God. He is acquainted with the weak as well as the strong points in the characters of men. And in a subtle manner he works with all deceivableness of unrighteousness to thwart the purposes of God by assailing the weak points in their characters; and when this is done, the way is prepared for him to attack and overcome the stronger points. He gains control of the mind and blinds the understanding. He lends men who are bewildered and overcome by his devices to self-confidence and self-sufficiency at the very time when they are the weakest in moral power. They become self-deceived and think they are in good spiritual condition.

The enemy will seize everything possible to use in his favor and to destroy souls. Testimonies have been borne in favor of individuals occupying important positions. They commence well to lift the burdens and act their part in connection with the work of God. But Satan pursues them with his temptations, and they are finally overcome. As others look upon their wrong course, Satan suggests to their minds that there must be a mistake in the testimonies given for these persons, else these men would not have proved themselves unworthy to bear a part in the work of God.

This is just as Satan designed it should be. He would

throw doubt in regard to the light that God has given. These men might have withstood the temptations of Satan had they been watchful and guarded, feeling their own insufficiency, and trusting in the name and strength of Jesus to stand faithful to duty. But it should be borne in mind that conditions have ever been connected with the encouragement given these men, that if they would maintain an unselfish spirit, if they would feel their weakness and would rely upon God, not trusting in their own wisdom and judgment, but making Him their strength, they could be a great blessing in His cause and work. But Satan has come in with his temptations and has triumphed almost every time. He has so arranged circumstances as to assail the weak points in the characters of these men, and they have been overcome. How shamefully they have injured the cause of God! How fully they have separated themselves from Him by following their own corrupt hearts, their own souls may answer! But the day of God will reveal the true cause for all our disappointments in man. God is not at fault. He gave them encouraging promises upon conditions, but they did not comply with these conditions. They trusted to their own strength and fell under temptation.

That which can be said of men under certain circumstances cannot be said of them under other circumstances. Men are weak in moral power and so supremely selfish, so self-sufficient and so easily puffed up with vain conceit, that God cannot work in connection with them, and they are left to move like blind men and to manifest so great weakness and folly that many are astonished that such individuals should ever have been accepted and acknowledged as worthy of having any connection with God's work. This is just what Satan designed. This was his object from the time he first specially tempted them to reproach the cause of God and to cast reflections upon the *Testimonies*. Had they remained where their influence would not have been specially felt upon the cause of God, Satan would not have beset them so fiercely; for he could not have accomplished his purpose by using them as his instruments to do a special work.

In the advancement of the work of God that which may be said in truth of individuals at one time may not correctly be said of them at another time. The reason of this is that one month they may have stood in innocency, living up to the best light they had, while the month following was none too short for them to be overcome by Satan's devices and, through self-confidence, to fall into grievous sins and become unfitted for the work of God.

Minds are so subject to change through the subtle temptations of Satan that it is not the best policy for my husband or myself to take the responsibility of even stating our opinions of the qualifications of persons to fill different positions, because we are made responsible for the course that such individuals pursue. Notwithstanding, if they had maintained the humility and firm trust in God which they possessed when recommended to take responsibilities they might have been the very persons for the place. These persons change, yet are not sensible of the change in themselves. They fall under temptation, are led away from their steadfastness, and sever their connection with God. They are then controlled by the enemy and do and say things which dishonor God and reproach His cause. Then Satan exults to see our brethren and sisters looking upon us with doubt because we have given these persons encouragement and influence.

THE STATE OF THE WORLD

I was shown the state of the world, that it is fast filling up its cup of iniquity. Violence and crime of every description are filling our world, and Satan is using every means to make crime and debasing vice popular. The youth who walk the streets are surrounded with handbills and notices of crime and sin, presented in some novel or to be acted at some theater. Their minds are educated into familiarity with sin.

The course pursued by the base and vile is kept before them in the periodicals of the day, and everything which can excite curiosity and arouse the animal passions is brought before them in thrilling and exciting stories.

The literature that proceeds from corrupted intellects poisons the minds of thousands in our world. Sin does not appear exceeding sinful. They hear and read so much of debasing crime and vileness that the once tender conscience which would have recoiled with horror becomes so blunted that it can dwell upon the low and vile sayings and actions of men with greedy interest.

"As it was in the days of Noe, so shall it be also in the days of the Son of man." God will have a people zealous of good works, standing firm amid the pollutions of this degenerate age. There will be a people who hold so fast to the divine strength that they will be proof against every temptation. Evil communications in flaming handbills may seek to speak to their senses and corrupt their minds; yet they will be so united to God and angels that they will be as those who see not and hear not. They have a work to do which no one can do for them, which is to fight the good fight of faith, and lay hold on eternal life. They will not be self-confident and self-sufficient. Knowing their weakness, they will unite their ignorance to Christ's wisdom, their weakness to His strength.

The youth may have principles so firm that the most powerful temptations of Satan will not draw them away from their allegiance. Samuel was a child surrounded by the most corrupting influences. He saw and heard things that grieved his soul. The sons of Eli, who ministered in holy office, were controlled by Satan. These men polluted the whole atmosphere which surrounded them. Men and women were daily fascinated with sin and wrong, yet Samuel walked untainted. His robes of character were spotless. He did not fellowship, or have the least delight in, the sins which filled all Israel with fearful reports. Samuel loved God; he kept his soul in such close connection with heaven that an angel was sent to talk with him in reference to the sins of Eli's sons, which were corrupting Israel.

Appetite and passion are overcoming thousands of Christ's professed followers. Their senses become so blunted on account of familiarity with sin that they do not abhor it, but view it as attractive. The end of all things is at hand. God will not much longer bear with the crimes and debasing iniquity of the children of men. Their crimes have indeed reached unto the heavens and will soon be answered by the fearful plagues of God upon the earth. They will drink the cup of God's wrath unmixed with mercy.

I have seen that there is danger that even the professed children of God will be corrupted. Licentiousness is binding men and women as captives. They seem to be infatuated and powerless to resist and overcome upon the point of appetite and passion. In God there is power; in Him there is strength. If they will take hold upon it, the life-giving power of Jesus will stimulate everyone who has named the name of Christ. Dangers and perils surround us; and we are only safe when we feel our weakness and cling with the grasp of faith to our mighty Deliverer. It is a fearful time in which we live. We cannot cease watchfulness and prayer for a moment. Our helpless souls must rely on Jesus, our compassionate Redeemer.

I was shown the greatness and importance of the work before us. But few realize the true state of things. All who are asleep, and who cannot realize any necessity for vigilance and alarm, will be overcome. Young men are arising to engage in the work of God, some of whom have scarcely any sense of the sacredness and responsibility of the work. They have but little experience in exercising faith and in earnest soul hunger for the Spirit of God, which ever brings returns. Some men of good capabilities, who might fill important positions, do not know what spirit they are of. They run in a jovial mood as naturally as water flows downhill. They talk nonsense, and sport with young girls, while almost daily listening to the most solemn, soul-stirring truths. These men have a religion of the head, but their hearts are not sanctified by the truths they hear. Such can never lead others to the Fountain of living waters until they have drunk of the stream themselves.

It is no time now for lightness, vanity, or trifling. The scenes of this earth's history are soon to close. Minds that have been left to loose thought need change. Says the apostle Peter: "Gird up the loins of your mind, be sober, and hope to the end for the grace that is to be brought unto you at the revelation of Jesus Christ; as obedient children, not fashioning yourselves according to the former lusts in your ignorance: but as He which hath called you is holy, so be ye holy in all manner of conversation; because it is written, Be ye holy; for I am holy."

Loose thoughts must be gathered up and centered on God. The very thoughts should be in obedience to the will of God. Praise should not be given or expected; for this will have a tendency to foster self-confidence rather than to increase humility, to corrupt rather than to purify. Men who are really qualified and who feel that they have a part to act in connection with the work of God will feel pressed beneath the sense of the sacredness of the work, as a cart beneath sheaves. Now is the time to make the most earnest efforts to overcome the natural feelings of the carnal heart.

THE STATE OF THE CHURCH

There is great necessity for a reformation among the people of God. The present state of the church leads to the inquiry: Is this a correct representation of Him who gave His life for us? Are these the followers of Christ and the brethren of those who counted not their lives dear unto themselves? Those who come up to the Bible standard, the Bible description of Christ's followers, will be found rare indeed. Having forsaken God, the Fountain of living waters, they have hewn them out cisterns, "broken cisterns, that can hold no water."

Said the angel: "Lack of love and faith are the great sins of which God's people are now guilty." Lack of faith leads to carelessness and to love of self and the world. Those who separate themselves from God and fall under temptation indulge in gross vices, for the carnal heart leads to great wickedness. And this state of things is found among many of God's professed people. While they are professedly serving God they are to all intents and purposes corrupting their ways before Him. Appetite and passion are indulged by many, notwithstanding the clear light of truth points out the danger and lifts its warning voice: Beware, restrain, deny. "The wages of sin is death." Although the example of those who have made shipwreck of faith stands as a beacon to warn others from pursuing the same course, yet many rush madly on. Satan has control of their minds and seems to have power over their bodies.

Oh, how many flatter themselves that they have goodness and righteousness, when the true light of God reveals that all their lives they have only lived to please themselves! Their whole conduct is abhorred of God. How many are alive without the law! In their gross darkness they view themselves with complacency; but let the law of God be revealed to their consciences, as it was to Paul, and they would see that they are sold under sin and must die to the carnal mind. Self must be slain.

How sad and fearful the mistakes that many are making! They are building on the sand, but flatter themselves that they are riveted to the eternal Rock. Many who profess godliness are rushing on as recklessly, and are as insensible of their danger, as though there were no future judgment. A fearful retribution awaits them, and yet they are controlled by impulse and gross passion; they are filling out a dark life record for the judgment. I lift my voice of warning to all who name the name of Christ to depart from all iniquity. Purify your souls by obeying the truth. Cleanse yourselves from all filthiness of the flesh and spirit, perfecting holiness in the fear of God. You to whom this applies know what I mean.

Even you who have corrupted your ways before the Lord, partaken of the iniquity that abounds, and blackened your souls with sin, Jesus still invites you to turn from your course, take hold of His strength, and find in Him that peace, power, and grace that will make you more than conquerors in His name.

The corruptions of this degenerate age have stained many souls who have been professedly serving God. But even now it is not too late for wrongs to be righted and for the blood of a crucified and risen Saviour to atone in your behalf if you repent and feel your need of pardon. We need now to watch and pray as never before, lest we fall under the power of temptation and leave the example of a life that is a miserable wreck. We must not, as a people, become careless and look upon sin with indifference. The camp needs purging. All who name the name of Christ need to watch and pray and guard the avenues of the soul; for Satan is at work to corrupt and destroy if the least advantage is given him.

My brethren, God calls upon you as His followers to walk in the light. You need to be alarmed. Sin is among us, and it is not seen to be exceedingly sinful. The senses of many are benumbed by the indulgence of appetite and by familiarity with sin. We need to advance nearer heaven. We may grow in grace and in the knowledge of the truth. Walking in the light, running in the way of God's commandments, does not give the idea that we can stand still and do nothing. We must be advancing.

In self-love, self-exaltation, and pride there is great weakness; but in humility there is great strength. Our true dignity is not maintained when we think most of ourselves, but when God is in all our thoughts and our hearts are all aglow with love to our Redeemer and love to our fellow men. Simplicity of character and lowliness of heart will give happiness, while self-conceit will bring discontent, repining, and continual disappointment. It is learning to think less of ourselves and more of making others happy that will bring to us divine strength.

In our separation from God, in our pride and darkness, we are constantly seeking to elevate ourselves, and we forget that lowliness of mind is power. Our Saviour's power was not in a strong array of sharp words that would pierce through the very soul; it was His gentleness and His plain, unassuming manners that made Him a conqueror of hearts. Pride and self-importance, when compared with lowliness and humility, are indeed weakness. We are invited to learn of Him who was meek and lowly of heart; then we shall experience that rest and peace so much to be desired.

LOVE OF THE WORLD

The temptation that was presented by Satan to our Saviour upon the exceeding high mountain is one of the leading temptations which humanity must meet. The kingdoms of the world in their glory were offered to Christ by Satan as a gift upon condition that Christ would yield to him the honor due to a superior. Our Saviour felt the strength of this temptation, but He met it in our behalf and conquered. He would not have been tested upon this point if man were not to be tried with the same temptation. In His resistance, He gave us an example of the course that we should pursue when Satan should come to us individually to lead us from our integrity.

No man can be a follower of Christ and yet place his affections upon the things of the world. John in his first epistle writes: "Love not the world, neither the things that are in the world. If any man love the world, the love of the Father is not in him." Our Redeemer, who met this temptation of Satan in its fullest power, is acquainted with man's danger of yielding to the temptation to love the world.

Christ identified Himself with humanity by bearing the test upon this point and overcoming in man's behalf. He has guarded with warnings those very points where Satan would best succeed in his temptations to man. He knew that Satan would gain the victory over man unless he was especially guarded upon the points of appetite and the love of worldly riches and honor. He says: "Lay not up for yourselves treasures upon earth, where moth and rust doth corrupt, and where thieves break through and steal: but lay up for yourselves treasures in heaven, where neither moth nor rust doth corrupt, and where thieves do not break through nor steal: for where your treasure is, there will your heart be also." "No man can serve two masters: for either he will hate the one, and love the other; or else he will hold to the one, and despise the other. Ye cannot serve God and mammon."

Here Christ has brought before us two masters, God and the world, and has plainly presented the fact that it is simply impossible for us to serve both. If our interest in, and love for, this world predominate, we shall not appreciate the things, which, above all others, are worthy of our attention. The love of the world will exclude the love of God and make our highest interests subordinate to worldly considerations. Thus God will not hold so exalted a place in our affections and devotions as do the things of the world.

Our works will show the exact extent to which earthly treasures have our affections. The greatest care, anxiety, and labor are devoted to worldly interests, while eternal considerations are made secondary. Here Satan receives of man that homage which he claimed of Christ but failed to obtain. It is the selfish love of the world which corrupts the faith of the professed followers of Christ and makes them weak in moral power. The more they love their earthly riches, the further they depart from God, and the less do they partake of His divine nature that would give them a sense of the corrupting influences in the world and the dangers to which they are exposed.

In Satan's temptations it is his purpose to make the world very attractive. Through love of riches and worldly honor he has a bewitching power to gain the affections of even the professed Christian world. A large class of professedly Christian men will make any sacrifice to gain riches, and the better they succeed in their object the less love they have for precious truth and the less interest for its advancement. They lose their love for God and act like insane men. The more they are prospered in securing riches the poorer they feel because they have no more, and the less will they invest in the cause of God.

The works of those men who have an insane love for riches show that it is not possible for them to serve two masters, God and mammon. Money is their god. They yield homage to its power. They serve the world to all intents and purposes. Their honor, which is their birthright, is sacrificed for worldly gain. This ruling power controls their minds, and they will violate the law of God to serve personal interests, to increase their earthly treasure.

Many may profess the religion of Christ who love not and heed not the letter or principles of Christ's teachings. They give the best of their strength to worldly pursuits and bow down to mammon. It is alarming that so many are deceived by Satan and their imaginations excited by their brilliant prospects of worldly gain. They become infatuated with the prospect of perfect happiness if they can gain their object in acquiring honor and wealth in the world. Satan tempts them with the alluring bribe, "All this will I give thee," all this power, all this wealth, with which you may do a great amount of good. But when the object for which they have labored is gained, they do not have that connection with the self-denying Redeemer which would make them partakers of the divine nature. They hold to their earthly treasures and despise the self-denial and self-sacrifice required for Christ. They have no desire to part with the dear earthly treasures upon which their hearts are set. They have exchanged masters; they have accepted mammon in the place of Christ. Mammon is their god, and mammon they serve.

Satan has secured to himself the worship of these deceived souls through their love of riches. The change has been so imperceptibly made, and Satan's power is so deceptive, so wily, that they are conformed to the world and perceive not that they have parted with Christ and are no longer His servants except in name.

Satan deals with men more guardedly than he dealt with Christ in the wilderness of temptation, for he is admonished that he there lost his case. He is a conquered foe. He does not come to man directly and demand homage by outward worship. He simply asks men to place their affections upon the good things of this world. If he succeeds in engaging the mind and affections, the heavenly attractions are eclipsed. All he wants of man is for him to fall under the deceitful power of his temptations, to love the world, to love rank and positions, to love money, and to place his affections upon earthly treasures. If he secures this, he gains all that he asked of Christ.

The example of Christ shows us that our only hope of victory is in continual resistance of Satan's attacks. He who triumphed over the adversary of souls in the conflict of temptation understands Satan's power over the race and has conquered him in our behalf. As an overcomer He has given us the advantage of His victory, that in our efforts to resist the temptations of Satan we may unite our weakness to His strength, our worthlessness to His merits. And, sustained by His enduring might under strong temptation, we may resist in His all-powerful name and overcome as He overcame.

It was through inexpressible suffering that our Redeemer placed redemption within our reach. In this world He was unhonored and unknown that through His wonderful condescension and humiliation He might exalt man to receive heavenly honors and immortal joys in His kingly courts. Will fallen man murmur because heaven can be obtained only by conflict, self-abasement, and toil?

The inquiry of many a proud heart is: Why need I go in humiliation and penitence before I can have the assurance of my acceptance with God, and attain the immortal reward? Why is not the path to heaven less difficult and more pleasant and attractive? We refer all these doubting, murmuring ones to our great Exemplar while suffering under the load of man's guilt and enduring the keenest pangs of hunger. He was sinless, and more than this, He was the prince of heaven; but in man's behalf He became sin for the race. "He was wounded for our transgressions, He was bruised for our iniquities: the chastisement of our peace was upon Him; and with His stripes we are healed."

Christ sacrificed everything for man in order to make it possible for him to gain heaven. Now it is for fallen man to show what he will sacrifice on his own account for Christ's sake, that he may win immortal glory. Those who have any just sense of the magnitude of salvation and of its cost will never murmur that their sowing must be in tears and that conflict and self-denial are the Christian's portion in this life. The conditions of salvation for man are ordained of God. Self-abasement and cross bearing are the provisions made by which the repenting sinner is to find comfort and peace. The thought that Jesus submitted to humiliation and sacrifice that man will never be called to endure, should hush every murmuring voice. The sweetest joy comes to man through his sincere repentance toward God because of the transgression of His law, and faith in Christ as the sinner's Redeemer and Advocate.

Men labor at great cost to secure the treasures of this life. They suffer toil and endure hardships and privations to gain some worldly advantage. Why should the sinner be less willing to endure, to suffer, and to sacrifice in order to secure an imperishable treasure, a life that runs parallel with the life of God, a crown of immortal glory that fadeth not away? The infinite treasures of heaven, the inheritance which passes all estimate in value, which is an eternal weight of glory, must be obtained by us at any cost. We should not murmur at self-denial, for the Lord of life and glory endured it before us. Suffering and deprivation we should not avoid, for the Majesty of heaven accepted these in behalf of sinners. Sacrifice of ease and convenience should not cause one thought of repining, because the world's Redeemer accepted all these in our behalf. Making the largest estimate of all our self-denials, privations, and sacrifices, it costs us far less in every respect than it did the prince of life. Any sacrifice that we may make sinks into insignificance when compared with that which Christ made in our behalf.

PRESUMPTION

There are those who have a reckless spirit, which they term courage and bravery. They needlessly place themselves in scenes of danger and peril, thus exposing themselves to temptations out of which it would require a miracle of God to bring them unharmed and untainted. Satan's temptation to the Saviour of the world to cast Himself from the pinnacle of the temple was firmly met and resisted. Satan quoted a promise of God as security that Christ might with safety do this on the strength of the promise. Christ met the temptation with scripture: "It is written, . . . Thou shalt not tempt the Lord thy God." The only safe course for Christians is to repulse the enemy with God's word. Satan urges men into places where God does not require them to go, and presents scripture to justify his suggestions.

God's precious promises are not given to strengthen man in a presumptuous course or for him to rely upon when he rushes needlessly into danger. The Lord requires us to move with a humble dependence upon His providence. "It is not in man that walketh to direct his steps." In God is our prosperity and our life. Nothing can be done prosperously without the permission and blessing of God. He can set His hand to prosper and bless, or He can turn His hand against us. "Commit thy way unto the Lord; trust also in Him; and He shall bring it to pass." We are required, as children of God, to maintain a consistent Christian character. We should exercise prudence, caution, and humility, and walk circumspectly toward them that are without. Yet we are not in any case to surrender principle.

Our only safety is in giving no place to the devil, for his

suggestions and purposes are ever to injure us and hinder us from relying upon God. He transforms himself into an angel of purity that he may, through his specious temptations, introduce his devices in such a manner that we may not discern his wiles. The more we yield, the more powerful will be his deceptions over us. It is unsafe to enter into controversy or to parley with him. For every advantage that we give the enemy he will claim more. Our only safety is in rejecting firmly the first approach to presumption. God has, through the merits of Christ, given us sufficient grace to withstand Satan and be more than conquerors. Resistance is success. "Resist the devil, and he will flee from you." Resistance must be firm and steadfast. We lose all we gain if we resist today only to yield tomorrow.

The sin of this age is disregard of God's express commands. The power of influence in a wrong direction is very great. Eve had all that her wants required. There was nothing lacking to make her happy, but intemperate appetite desired the fruit of the only tree that God had withheld. She had no need of the fruit of the tree of knowledge, but she permitted her appetite and curiosity to control her reason. She was perfectly happy in her Eden home by her husband's side; but, like restless modern Eves, she was flattered that there was a higher sphere than that which God had assigned her. But in attempting to climb higher than her original position, she fell far below it. This will most assuredly be the result with the Eves of the present generation if they neglect to cheerfully take up their daily life duties in accordance with God's plan.

There is a work for women that is even more important and elevating than the duties of the king upon his throne. They may mold the minds of their children and shape their characters so that they may be useful in this world and that they may become sons and daughters of God. Their time should be considered too valuable to be passed in the ballroom or in needless labor. There is enough necessary and important labor in this world of need and suffering without wasting precious moments for ornamentation or display. Daughters of the heavenly King, members of the royal family, will feel a burden of responsibility to attain to a higher life, that they may be brought into close connection with heaven and work in unison with the Redeemer of the world. Those who are engaged in this work will not be satisfied with the fashions and follies which absorb the mind and affections of women in these last days. If they are indeed the daughters of God they will be partakers of the divine nature. They will be stirred with deepest pity, as was their divine Redeemer, as they see the corrupting influences in society. They will be in sympathy with Christ, and in their sphere, as they have ability and opportunity, will work to save perishing souls as Christ worked in His exalted sphere for the benefit of man.

A neglect on the part of woman to follow God's plan in her creation, an effort to reach for important positions which He has not qualified her to fill, leaves vacant the position that she could fill to acceptance. In getting out of her sphere, she loses true womanly dignity and nobility. When God created Eve, He designed that she should possess neither inferiority nor superiority to the man, but that in all things she should be his equal. The holy pair were to have no interest independent of each other; and yet each had an individuality in thinking and acting. But after Eve's sin, as she was first in the transgression, the Lord told her that Adam should rule over her. She was to be in subjection to her husband, and this was a part of the curse. In many cases the curse has made the lot of woman very grievous and her life a burden. The superiority which God has given man he has abused in many respects by exercising arbitrary power. Infinite wisdom devised the plan of redemption, which places the race on a second probation by giving them another trial.

Satan uses men as his agents to lead to presumption those who love God; especially is this the case with those who are deluded by spiritualism. Spiritualists generally do not accept Christ as the Son of God, and through their infidelity they lead many souls to presumptuous sins. They even claim superiority over Christ as did Satan in contesting with the Prince of life. Spiritualists whose souls are dyed with sins of a revolting character, and whose consciences are seared, dare to take the name of the spotless Son of God in their polluted lips and blasphemously unite His most exalted name with the vileness which marks their own polluted natures.

Men who bring in these damnable heresies will dare those who teach the word of God to enter into controversy with them, and some who teach the truth have not had the courage to withstand a challenge from this class, who are marked characters in the word of God. Some of our ministers have not had the moral courage to say to these men: God has warned us in His word in regard to you. He has given us a faithful description of your character and of the heresies which you hold. Some of our ministers, rather than give this class any occasion to triumph or to charge them with cowardice, have met them in open discussion. But in discussing with spiritualists they do not meet man merely, but Satan and his angels. They place themselves in communication with the powers of darkness and encourage evil angels about them.

Spiritualists desire to give publicity to their heresies; and ministers who advocate Bible truth help them to do this when they consent to engage in discussion with them. They improve their opportunities to get their heresies before the people, and in every discussion with them some will be deceived. The very best course for us to pursue is to avoid them.

POWER OF APPETITE

One of the strongest temptations that man has to meet is upon the point of appetite. Between the mind and the body there is a mysterious and wonderful relation. They react upon each other. To keep the body in a healthy condition to develop its strength, that every part of the living machinery may act harmoniously, should be the first study of our life. To neglect the body is to neglect the mind. It cannot be to the glory of God for His children to have sickly bodies or dwarfed minds. To indulge the taste at the expense of health is a wicked abuse of the senses. Those who engage in any species of intemperance, either in eating or drinking, waste their physical energies and weaken moral power. They will feel the retribution which follows the transgression of physical law.

The Redeemer of the world knew that the indulgence of appetite would bring physical debility, and so deaden the perceptive organs that sacred and eternal things would not be discerned. Christ knew that the world was given up to gluttony and that this indulgence would pervert the moral powers. If the indulgence of appetite was so strong upon the race that, in order to break its power, the divine Son of God, in behalf of man, was required to fast nearly six weeks, what a work is before the Christian in order that he may overcome even as Christ overcame! The strength of the temptation to indulge perverted appetite can be measured only by the inexpressible anguish of Christ in that long fast in the wilderness.

Christ knew that in order to successfully carry forward the plan of salvation He must commence the work of redeeming man just where the ruin began. Adam fell by the indulgence of appetite. In order to impress upon man his obligations to obey the law of God, Christ began His work of redemption by reforming the physical habits of man. The declension in virtue and the degeneracy of the race are chiefly attributable to the indulgence of perverted appetite.

There is a solemn responsibility upon all, especially upon ministers who teach the truth to overcome upon the point of appetite. Their usefulness would be much greater if they had control of their appetites and passions, and their mental and moral powers would be stronger if they combined physical labor with mental exertion. With strictly temperate habits and with mental and physical labor combined, they could accomplish a far greater amount of labor and preserve clearness of mind. If they would pursue such a course, their thoughts and words would flow more freely, their religious exercises would be more energized, and the impressions made upon their hearers would be more marked.

Intemperance in eating, even of food of the right quality will have a prostrating influence upon the system and will blunt the keener and holier emotions. Strict temperance in eating and drinking is highly essential for the healthy preservation and vigorous exercise of all the functions of the body. Strictly temperate habits, combined with exercise of the muscles as well as of the mind, will preserve both mental and physical vigor, and give power of endurance to those engaged in the ministry, to editors, and to all others whose habits are sedentary. As a people, with all our profession of health reform, we eat too much. Indulgence of appetite is the greatest cause of physical and mental debility, and lies at the foundation of the feebleness which is apparent everywhere.

Intemperance commences at our tables in the use of unhealthful food. After a time, through continued indulgence, the digestive organs become weakened, and the food taken does not satisfy the appetite. Unhealthy conditions are established, and there is a craving for more stimulating food. Tea, coffee, and flesh meats produce an immediate effect. Under the influence of these poisons the nervous system is excited, and, in some cases, for the time being, the intellect seems to be invigorated and the imagination to be more vivid. Because these stimulants produce for the time being such agreeable results, many conclude that they really need them and continue their use. But there is always a reaction. The nervous system, having been unduly excited, borrowed power for present use from its future resources of strength. All this temporary invigoration of the system is followed by depression. In proportion as these stimulants temporarily invigorate the system will be the letting down of the power of the excited organs after the stimulus has lost its force. The appetite is educated to crave something stronger which will have a tendency to keep up and increase the agreeable excitement, until indulgence becomes habit, and there is a continual craving for stronger stimulus, as tobacco, wines, and liquors. The more the appetite is indulged, the more frequent will be its demands and the more difficult of control. The more debilitated the system becomes and the less able to do without unnatural stimulus the more the passion for these things increases, until the will is overborne and there seems to be no power to deny the unnatural craving for these indulgences.

The only safe course is to touch not, taste not, handle not, tea, coffee, wines, tobacco, opium, and alcoholic drinks. The necessity for the men of this generation to call to their aid the power of the will, strengthened by the grace of God in order to withstand the temptations of Satan and resist the least indulgence of perverted appetite is twice as great as it was several generations ago. But the present generation have less power of self-control than had those who lived then. Those who have indulged the appetite for these stimulants have transmitted their depraved appetites and passions to their children, and greater moral power is required to resist intemperance in all its forms. The only perfectly safe course to pursue is to stand firmly on the side of temperance and not venture in the path of danger.

The great end for which Christ endured that long fast in the wilderness was to teach us the necessity of self-denial and temperance. This work should commence at our tables and should be strictly carried out in all the concerns of life. The Redeemer of the world came from heaven to help man in his weakness, that, in the power which Jesus came to bring him, he might become strong to overcome appetite and passion, and might be victor on every point.

Many parents educate the tastes of their children and form their appetites. They indulge them in eating flesh meats and in drinking tea and coffee. The highly seasoned flesh meats and the tea and coffee, which some mothers encourage their children to use, prepare the way for them to crave stronger stimulants, as tobacco. The use of tobacco encourages the appetite for liquor, and the use of tobacco and liquor invariably lessens nerve power.

If the moral sensibilities of Christians were aroused upon the subject of temperance in *all things,* they could, by their example, commencing at their tables, help those who are weak in self-control, who are almost powerless to resist the cravings of appetite. If we could realize that the habits we form in this life will affect our eternal interests, that our eternal destiny depends upon strictly temperate habits, we would work to the point of strict temperance in eating and drinking. By our example and personal effort we may be the means of saving many souls from the degradation of intemperance, crime, and death. Our sisters can do much in the great work for the salvation of others by spreading their tables with only healthful, nourishing food. They may employ their precious time in educating the tastes and appetites of their children, in forming habits of temperance in all things, and in encouraging self-denial and benevolence for the good of others.

Notwithstanding the example that Christ gave us in the wilderness of temptation by denying appetite and overcoming its power, there are many Christian mothers who by their example and by the education which they are giving their children are preparing them to become gluttons and winebibbers. Children are frequently indulged in eating what they choose and when they choose, without reference to health. There are many children who are educated gourmands from their babyhood. Through indulgence of appetite they are made dyspeptics at an early age. Self-indulgence and intemperance in eating grow with their growth and strengthen with their strength. Mental and physical vigor are sacrificed through the indulgence of parents. A taste is formed for certain articles of food from which they can receive no benefit, but only injury; and as the system is taxed, the constitution becomes debilitated.

Ministers, teachers, and students do not become as intelligent as they should in regard to the necessity of physical exercise in the open air. They neglect this duty, which is most essential for the preservation of health. They closely apply their minds to books and eat the allowance of a laboring man. Under such habits some grow corpulent, because the system is clogged. Others become lean, feeble, and weak because their vital powers are exhausted in throwing off the excess of food; the liver becomes burdened and unable to throw off the impurities in the blood, and sickness is the result. If physical exercise were combined with mental exertion, the blood would be quickened in its circulation, the action of the heart would be more perfect, impure matter would be thrown off, and new life and vigor would be experienced in every part of the body.

When the minds of ministers, school teachers, and students are continually excited by study, and the body is allowed to be inactive, the nerves of emotion are taxed, while the nerves of motion are inactive. The wear being all upon the mental organs, they become overworked and enfeebled, while the muscles lose their vigor for want of employment. There is no inclination to exercise the muscles by engaging in physical labor because exertion seems to be irksome.

Ministers of Christ, professing to be His representatives, should follow His example, and above all others should form habits of strictest temperance. They should keep the life and example of Christ before the people by their own lives of self-denial, self-sacrifice, and active benevolence. Christ overcame appetite in man's behalf, and in His stead they are to set others an example worthy of imitation. Those who do not feel the necessity of engaging in the work of overcoming upon the point of appetite will fail to secure precious victories which they might have gained and will become slaves to appetite and lust, which are filling the cup of iniquity of those who dwell upon the earth.

Men who are engaged in giving the last message of warning to the world, a message which is to decide the destiny of souls, should make a practical application in their own lives of the truths they preach to others. They should be examples to the people in their eating, in their drinking, and in their chaste conversation and deportment. Gluttony, indulgence of the baser passions, and grievous sins are hidden under the garb of sanctity by many professed representatives of Christ throughout our world. There are men of excellent natural ability whose labor does not accomplish half what it might if they were temperate in all things. Indulgence of appetite and passion beclouds the mind, lessens physical strength, and weakens moral power. Their thoughts are not clear. Their words are not spoken in power, are not vitalized by the Spirit of God so as to reach the hearts of the hearers.

As our first parents lost Eden through the indulgence of appetite, our only hope of regaining Eden is through the firm denial of appetite and passion. Abstemiousness in diet and control of all the passions will preserve the intellect and give mental and moral vigor, enabling men to bring all their propensities under the control of the higher powers and to discern between right and wrong, the sacred and the common. All who have a true sense of the sacrifice made by Christ in leaving His home in heaven to come to this world that He might by His own life show man how to resist temptation will cheerfully deny self and choose to be partakers with Christ of His sufferings.

The fear of the Lord is the beginning of wisdom. Those who overcome as Christ overcame will need to constantly guard themselves against the temptations of Satan. The appetite and passions should be restricted and under the control of enlightened conscience, that the intellect may lie unimpaired, the perceptive powers clear, so that the workings of Satan and his snares may not be interpreted to be the providence of God. Many desire the final reward and victory which are to be given to overcomers, but are not willing to endure toil, privation, and denial of self, as did their Redeemer. It is only through obedience and continual effort that we shall overcome as Christ overcame.

The controlling power of appetite will prove the ruin of thousands, when, if they had conquered on this point, they would have had moral power to gain the victory over every other temptation of Satan. But those who are slaves to appetite will fail in perfecting Christian character. The continual transgression of man for six thousand years has brought sickness, pain, and death as its fruits. And as we near the close of time, Satan's temptation to indulge appetite will be more powerful and more difficult to overcome.

LEADERSHIP

Brother A, your experience in reference to leadership two years ago was for your own benefit and was highly essential to you. You had very marked, decided views in regard to individual independence and right to private judgment. These views you carry to extremes. You reason that you must have light and evidence for yourself in reference to your duty.

I have been shown that no man's judgment should be surrendered to the judgment of any one man. But when the judgment of the General Conference, which is the highest authority that God has upon the earth, is exercised, private independence and private judgment must not be maintained, but be surrendered. Your error was in persistently maintaining your private judgment of your duty against the voice of the highest authority the Lord has upon the earth. After you had taken your own time, and after the work had been much hindered by your delay, you came to Battle Creek in answer to the repeated and urgent calls of the General Conference. You firmly maintained that you had done right in following your own convictions of duty. You considered it a virtue in you to persistently maintain your position of independence. You did not seem to have a true sense of the power that God has given to His church in the voice of the General Conference. You thought that in responding to the call made to you by the General Conference you were submitting to the judgment and mind of one man. You accordingly manifested an independence, a set, willful spirit, which was all wrong.

God gave you a precious experience at that time which was of value to you, and which has greatly increased your success as a minister of Christ. Your proud, unyielding will was subdued. You had a genuine conversion. This led to reflection and to your position upon leadership. Your principles in regard to leadership are right, but you do not make the right application of them. If you should let the power in the church, the voice and judgment of the General Conference, stand in the place you have given my husband, there could then be no fault found with your position. But you greatly err in giving to one man's mind and judgment that authority and influence which God has invested in His church in the judgment and voice of the General Conference.

When this power which God has placed in the church is accredited to one man, and he is invested with the authority to be judgment for other minds, then the true Bible order is changed. Satan's efforts upon such a man's mind will be most subtle and sometimes overpowering, because through this mind he thinks he can affect many others. Your position on leadership is correct, if you give to the highest organized authority in the church what you have given to one man. God never designed that His work should bear the stamp of one man's mind and one man's judgment.

The great reason why Brethren B and C are at this time deficient in the experience they should now have is because they have not been self-reliant. They have shunned responsibilities because in assuming them their deficiencies would be brought to the light. They have been too willing to have my husband lead out and bear responsibilities, and have allowed him to be mind and judgment for them. These brethren are weak where they should be strong. They have not dared to follow their own independent judgment, lest they should make mistakes and be blamed for it, while they have stood ready to be tempted and to make my husband responsible if they thought they could see mistakes in his course. They have not lifted the burdens with him. They have referred continually to my husband, making him bear the responsibilities which they should have shared with him, until they are weak in those qualifications wherein they should be strong. They are weak in moral power when they might be giants, qualified to stand as pillars in the cause of God.

These brethren have not self-reliance, or confidence that God will indeed lead them if they follow the light He has given them. God never intended that strong, independent men of superior intellect should cling to others for support as the ivy clings to the oak. All the difficulties, the backsets, the hardships, and the disappointments which God's servants will meet in active labor will only strengthen them in the formation of correct characters. By putting their own energies of mind to use, the obstacles they meet will prove to them positive blessings. They will gain mental and spiritual muscle to be used upon important occasions with the very best results. They will learn self-reliance and will gain confidence in their own experience that God is really leading and guiding them. And as they meet peril and have real anguish of spirit they are obliged to meditate and are made to feel the necessity of prayer in their effort to move understandingly and work to advantage in the cause of God; they find that conflict and perplexity call for the exercise of faith and trust in God, and for that firmness which develops power. Necessities are constantly arising for new ways and means to meet emergencies. Faculties are called into use that would lie dormant were it not for these pressing necessities in the work of God. This gives a varied experience so that there will be no use for men of one idea and those who are only half developed.

Men of might and power in this cause, whom God will use to His glory, are those who have been opposed, baffled, and thwarted in their plans. Brethren B and C might have turned their own failures into important victories; but, instead of this, they have shunned the responsibilities which would make liability to mistakes possible. These precious brethren have failed to gain that education which is strengthened by experience and which reading and study and all the advantages otherwise gained will never give them.

You, Brother A, have had strength to bear some responsibilities. God has accepted your energetic labors and blessed your efforts. You have made some mistakes, but because of some failures you should in nowise misjudge your capabilities nor distrust the strength that you may find in God. You have not been willing and ready to assume responsibilities. You are naturally inclined to shun them and to choose an easier position, to write and exercise the mind where no special, vital interests are involved. You make a mistake in relying upon my husband to tell you what to do. This is not the work God has given my husband. You should search out what is to be done and lift the disagreeable burdens yourself. God will bless you in so doing. You must bear burdens in connection with the work of God according to your best judgment. But you must be guarded, lest your judgment shall be influenced by the opinions of others. If it is apparent that you have made mistakes, it is your privilege to turn these failures into victories by avoiding the same in the future. By being told what to do you will never gain the experience necessary for any important position.

The same is applicable to all who are standing in the different positions of trust in the various offices at Battle Creek. They are not to be coaxed and petted and helped at every turn, for this will not make men competent for important positions. It is obstacles that make men strong. It is not helps, but difficulties, conflicts, rebuffs, that make men of moral sinew. Too much ease and avoiding responsibility have made weaklings and dwarfs of those who ought to be responsible men of moral power and strong spiritual muscle.

Men who ought to be as true in every emergency as the needle to the pole, have become inefficient by their efforts to shield themselves from censure and by evading responsibilities for fear of failure. Men of giant intellect are babes in discipline because they are cowardly in regard to taking and bearing the burdens they should. They are neglecting to become efficient. They have too long trusted one man to plan for them and to do the thinking which they are highly capable of doing themselves in the interest of the cause of God. Mental deficiencies meet us at every point. Men who are content to let others plan and do their thinking for them are not fully developed. If they were left to plan for themselves they would be found judicious, close-calculating men. But when brought into connection with God's cause, it is entirely another thing to them; they lose this faculty almost altogether. They are content to remain as incompetent and inefficient as though others must do the planning and much of the thinking for them. Some men appear to be utterly unable to hew out a path for themselves. Must they ever rely upon others to do their planning and their studying, and to be mind and judgment for them? God is ashamed of such soldiers. He is not honored by their having any part to act in His work while they are mere machines.

Independent men of earnest endeavor are needed, not men as impressible as putty. Those who want their work made ready to their hand, who desire a fixed amount to do and a fixed salary, and who wish to prove an exact fit without the trouble of adaptation or training, are not the men whom God calls to work in His cause. A man who cannot adapt his abilities to almost any place if necessity requires is not the man for this time. Men whom God will connect with His work are not limp and fiberless, without muscle or moral force of character. It is only by continued and persevering labor that men can be disciplined to bear a part in the work of God. These men should not become discouraged if circumstances and surrounding are the most unfavorable. They should not give up their purpose as a complete failure until they are convinced beyond a doubt that they cannot do much for the honor of God and the good of souls.

There are men who flatter themselves that they might do something great and good if they were only circumstanced differently, while they make no use of the faculties they already have by working in the positions where Providence has placed them. Man can make his circumstances, but circumstances should never make the man. Man should seize circumstances as his instruments with which to work. He should master circumstances, but should never allow circumstances to master him. Individual independence and individual power are the qualities now needed. Individual character need not be sacrificed, but it should be modulated, refined, elevated.

I have been shown that it is my husband's duty to lay off the responsibilities which others would be glad to have him bear because it excuses them from many difficulties. My husband's ready judgment and clear discernment, which have been gained through training and exercise, have led him to take on many burdens which others should have borne.

Brother A, you are too slow. You should cultivate opposite qualities. The cause of God demands men who can see quickly and act instantaneously at the right time and with power. If you wait to measure every difficulty and balance every perplexity you meet you will do but little. You will have obstacles and difficulties to encounter at every turn, and you must with firm purpose decide to conquer them, or they will conquer you.

Sometimes various ways and purposes, different modes of operation in connection with the work of God, are about evenly balanced in the mind; but it is at this very point that the nicest discrimination is necessary. And if anything is accomplished to the purpose it must be done at the golden moment. The slightest inclination of the weight in the balance should be seen and should determine the matter at once. Long delays tire the angels. It is even more excusable to make a wrong decision sometimes than to be continually in a wavering position, to be hesitating, sometimes inclined in one direction, then in another. More perplexity and wretchedness result from thus hesitating and doubting than from sometimes moving too hastily.

I have been shown that the most signal victories and the most fearful defeats have been on the turn of minutes. God requires promptness of action. Delays, doubtings, hesitation, and indecision frequently give the enemy every advantage. My brother, you need to reform. The timing of things may tell much in favor of truth. Victories are frequently lost through delays. There will be crises in this cause. Prompt and decisive action at the right time will gain glorious triumphs, while delay and neglect will result in great failures and positive dishonor to God. Rapid movements at the critical moment often disarm the enemy, and he is disappointed and vanquished, for he had expected time to lay plans and work by artifice.

God wants men connected with His work in Battle Creek whose judgment is at hand, whose minds, when it is necessary, will act like the lightnings. The greatest promptness is positively necessary in the hour of peril and danger. Every plan may be well laid to accomplish certain results, and yet a delay of a very short time may leave things to assume an entirely different shape, and the great objects which might have been gained are lost through lack of quick foresight and prompt dispatch. Much may be done in training the mind to overcome indolence. There are times when caution and great deliberation are necessary; rashness would be folly. But even here, much has been lost by too great hesitancy. Caution, up to a certain point, is required; but hesitancy and policy on particular occasions have been more disastrous than would have been a failure through rashness.

My brother, you need to cultivate promptness. Away with your hesitating manner. You are slow and neglect to seize the work and accomplish it. You must get out of this narrow manner of labor, for it is of the wrong order. When unbelief takes hold of your soul, your labor is of such a hesitating, halting, balancing kind that you accomplish nothing yourself and hinder others from doing. You have just enough interest to see difficulties and start doubts, but have not the interest or courage to overcome the difficulties or dispel the doubts. At such times you need to surrender to God. You need force of character and less stubbornness and set willfulness. This slowness, this sluggishness of action, is one of the greatest defects in your character and stands in the way of your usefulness.

Your slowness of decision in connection with the cause and work of God is sometimes painful. It is not at all necessary. Prompt and decisive action may accomplish great results. You are generally willing to work when you feel just like it, ready to do when you can see clearly what is to be done; but you fail to be that benefit to the cause that you might be if you were prompt and decisive at the critical moment, and would overcome the habit of hesitation and delay which has marked your character and which has greatly retarded the work of God. This defect, unless overcome, will prove, in instances of great crises, disastrous to the cause and fatal to your own soul. Punctuality and decisive action at the right time must be acquired, for you have not these qualities. In the warfare and battles of nations there is often more gained by good management in prompt action than in earnest, dead encounter with the enemy.

The ability to do business with dispatch, and yet do it thoroughly, is a great acquisition. My brother, you have really felt that your cautious, hesitating course was commendable, rather a virtue than a wrong. But from what the Lord has shown me in this matter, these sluggish movements on your part have greatly hindered the work of God and caused many things to be left undone which in justice ought to have been done with promptness. It will be difficult now for you to make the changes in your character which God requires you to make, because it was difficult for you to be punctual and prompt of action in youth. When the character is formed, the habits fixed, and the mental and moral faculties have become firm, it is most difficult to unlearn wrong habits, to be prompt in action. You should realize the value of time. You are not excusable for leaving the most important, though unpleasant work, hoping to get rid of doing it altogether, or thinking that it will become less unpleasant, while you occupy your time upon pleasant matters not really taxing. You should first do the work which must be done and which involves the vital interests of the cause, and only take up the less important matters after the more essential are accomplished. Punctuality and decision in the work and cause of God are highly essential. Delays are virtually defeats. Minutes are golden and should be improved to the very best account. Earthly relations and personal interests should ever be secondary. Never should the cause of God be left to suffer, in a single particular, because of our earthly friends or dearest relatives.

"And He said to another, Follow Me. But he said, Lord, suffer me first to go and bury my father. Jesus said unto him, Let the dead bury their dead: but go thou and preach the kingdom of God. And another also said, Lord, I will follow Thee; but let me first go bid them farewell, which are at home at my house. And Jesus said unto him, No man, having put his hand to the plow, and looking back, is fit for the kingdom of God."

No earthly ties, no earthly considerations, should weigh one moment in the scale against duty to the cause and work of God. Jesus severed His connection from everything to save a lost world, and He requires of us a full and entire consecration. There are sacrifices to be made for the interests of God's cause. The sacrifice of feeling is the most keen that is required of us; yet after all it is a small sacrifice. You have plenty of friends, and if the feelings are only sanctified, you need not feel that you are making a very great sacrifice. You do not leave your wife among heathen. You are not called to tread the burning African desert or to face prisons and encounter trial at every step. Be careful how you appeal to your sympathies and let human feelings and personal considerations mingle with your efforts and labors for the cause of God. He demands unselfish and willing service. You can render this and yet do all your duties to your family; but hold this as a secondary matter.

My husband and myself have made mistakes in consenting to take responsibilities that others should carry. In the commencement of this work a man was needed to propose, to execute with determination, and to lead out, battling with error and surmounting obstacles. My husband bore the heaviest burden and met the most determined opposition. But when we became a fully organized body, and several men were chosen to act in responsible positions, then it was the proper time for my husband to cease to act longer as one man to stand under the responsibilities and carry the heavy burdens. This labor devolved on more than one. Here is where the mistake has been made by his brethren in urging him, and by himself in consenting, to stand under the burdens and responsibilities that he had borne alone for years. He should have laid down these burdens years ago, and they should have been divided with other men chosen to act in behalf of the people. Satan would be pleased to have one man's mind and one man's judgment control the minds and judgment of those who believe the present truth.

My husband has frequently been left almost alone to see and feel the wants of the cause of God and to act promptly. His leading brethren were not deficient in intellect, but they lacked a willing mind to stand in the position which my husband has occupied. They have inconsistently allowed a paralytic to bear the burdens and responsibilities of this work, which no one of them alone could endure with their strong nerves and firm muscles. He has sometimes used apparent severity and has spoken so as to give offense. When he has seen others who might have shared his burdens avoiding responsibilities, it has grieved him to the heart, and he has spoken impulsively. He has not been placed in this unreasonable position by the Lord, but by his brethren. His life has been but little better than a species of slavery. The constant trial, the harassing care, the exhausting brainwork, have not been valued by his brethren. He has led an unenjoyable life, and he has increased his unhappiness by complaining of his brother ministers who neglected to do what they might have done. Nature has been outraged time and again. While his brethren have found fault with him for doing so much, they have not come up to take their share of the responsibility, but have been too willing to make him responsible for everything. You came nobly up to bear responsibilities when there were no others who would lift them. If his brethren in the ministry had cultivated a willingness to lift the burdens they should have borne, my husband would not have seen and done so much work which needed to be done and which he thought must not be neglected.

God has not suffered the life of my husband to end ingloriously. He has sustained him. But the man who performs double labor, who crowds the work of two years into one, is burning his candle at both ends. There is yet a work for my husband to do which he should have done years ago. He should now have less of the strife, perplexity, and responsibility of life, and be ripening, softening, and elevating for his last change. He should now husband his strength. He should not allow the responsibilities of the cause to rest upon him so heavily, but should stand free, where the prejudices and suspicions of his brethren will not disturb his peace.

God has permitted the precious light of truth to shine upon His word and illuminate the mind of my husband. He may reflect the rays of light from the presence of Jesus upon others by his preaching and writing. But while serving tables, doing business in connection with the cause, he has been deprived, to a great degree, of the privilege of using his pen and of preaching to the people.

He has felt that he was called of God to stand in defense of the truth, and to reprove, sometimes severely, those who were not doing justice to the work. The pressure of care and the affliction of disease have often thrown him into discouragement, and he has sometimes viewed matters in an exaggerated light. His brethren have taken advantage of his words, and of his prompt manners, which have been in marked contrast with their tardy labor and narrow plans of operation. They have accredited to my husband motives and feelings which were not his due. The wide contrast between themselves and him seemed like a gulf; but this might easily have been bridged, had these men of intellect put their undivided interests and whole hearts into the work of building up and advancing the precious cause of God.

We might exert a constant influence in this place, at the head of the work, which would advance the prosperity of our institutions. But the course of others who do not do what they might, who are subject to temptation, and who, if their track is crossed, would reflect upon our most earnest efforts for the prosperity of God's cause, compels us to seek an asylum elsewhere where we may work to better advantage with less danger of being crushed under burdens. God has given us great freedom and power with His people at Battle Creek. When we came to this place last summer, our work commenced in earnest, and it has continued ever since. One perplexity and difficulty has followed closely upon another, calling forth taxing labor to set things right.

When the Lord showed that Brother D might be the man for the place, if he remained humble and relied upon His strength, He did not make a blunder and select the wrong man. For a time Brother D had a true interest and acted as a father at the Health Institute. But he became self-exalted, self-sufficient. He pursued a wrong course. He yielded to temptation. The excuses which the directors have made for their neglect of duty are all wrong. Their shifting responsibilities upon Brother and Sister White is marked against them. They simply neglected their duty because it was unpleasant.

I saw that help was needed upon the Pacific Coast. But God would not have us take the responsibilities or bear the perplexities which belong to others. We may stand as counselors and help them with our influence and our judgment. We may do much if we will not be induced to get under the load and bear the weight which others should bear, and which it is important for them to bear in order to gain a necessary experience. We have important matter to write out which the people greatly need. We have precious light on Bible truth which we should speak to the people.

I was shown that God did not design that my husband should bear the burdens he has borne for the last five months.

The working part in connection with the cause has been left to fall upon him. This has brought perplexity, weariness, and nervous debility, which have resulted in discouragement and depression. From the commencement of the cause there has been a lack of harmonious action on the part of his brethren. His brethren in the ministry have loved freedom. They have not borne the responsibilities which they might, and have failed to gain the experience which they might have had to enable them to stand in the most responsible positions relative to the vital interests of the cause of God at the present time. They have excused their neglect to bear responsibilities on the ground that they feared being reflected upon afterward.

The religion we profess is colored by our natural dispositions and temperaments; therefore it is of the highest importance that the weak points in our character be strengthened by exercise and that the strong, unfavorable points be weakened by working in an opposite direction and by strengthening opposite qualities. But some brethren have not done what they might and should have done, and which would have given my husband sufficient encouragement and help to continue to bear some responsibilities at the head of the work. His fellow laborers did not move independently, looking to God for light and for duty for themselves; they did not follow in His opening providence and consult together upon plans of operation and unite in their plans and manner of labor.

Since coming to Michigan last summer, the Lord has especially blessed the labors of my husband. He has been sustained in a most remarkable manner to do work that so much needed to be done. Had those associated with him been awake to see and understand the wants of the cause of God at our last Michigan camp meeting, the many things not done might have been accomplished. There was a failure to meet the wants of the occasion. Had Brother A stood cheerful in God, walking in the light, ready to see what was to be done, and executing the work with dispatch, we should now be months advanced in our work, and we might long ago have been working to establish the press upon the Pacific Coast.

God cannot be glorified by our falling into singular gloom and then remaining under the cloud. The light does shine, although we may not realize its blessing; but if we make all diligence to press to the light, and if we move ahead just as though the light did shine, we shall soon pass out of the darkness and find light all around us.

At our last camp meeting the angels of God in a special manner came with their power to lighten, to heal, and to bless both my husband and Brother Waggoner. A precious victory was there gained which should never lose its influence. I have been shown that God had in a most marked manner given my husband tokens of His love and care, and also of His sustaining grace. He has regarded his zeal and devotion to His cause and work. This should ever lead to humility and gratitude on the part of my husband.

God wants minutemen. He will have men who, when important decisions are to be made, are as true as the needle to the pole; men whose special and personal interests are swallowed up, as were our Saviour's, in the one great general interest for the salvation of souls. Satan plays upon the human mind wherever a chance has been left for him to do so; and he seizes upon the very time and place where he can do the most service to himself and the greatest injury to the cause of God. A neglect to do what we might do, and what God requires us to do in His cause, is a sin which cannot be palliated with excuses of circumstances or conditions, for Jesus has made provision for all in every emergency.

My brother, in doing the work of God you will be placed in a variety of circumstances which will require self-possession and self-control, but which will qualify you to adapt yourself to circumstances and the peculiarities of the situation. Then you can act yourself unembarrassed. You should not place too low an estimate upon your ability to act your part in the various callings of practical life. Where you are aware of deficiencies, go to work at once to remedy those defects. Do not trust to others to supply your deficiencies, while you go on indifferently, as though it were a matter of course that your peculiar organization must ever remain so. Apply yourself earnestly to cure these defects, that you may be perfect in Christ Jesus, wanting in nothing.

If you form too high an opinion of yourself, you will think that your labors are of more real consequence than they are, and you will plead individual independence which borders on arrogance. If you go to the other extreme and form too low an opinion of yourself, you will feel inferior and will leave an impression of inferiority which will greatly limit the influence that you might have for good. You should avoid either extreme. Feeling should not control you; circumstances should not affect you. You may form a correct estimate of yourself, one which will prove a safeguard from both extremes. You may be dignified without vain self-confidence; you may be condescending and yielding without sacrificing self-respect or individual independence, and your life may be of great influence with those in the higher as well as the lower walks of life.

Brother A, your danger now is of being affected by reports. Your labors are decidedly practical, close, and cutting. You rein up the people to very close tests and requirements. This is necessary at times; but your labors are getting to be too much of this character, and will lose their force unless mingled with more of the softening, encouraging grace of the Spirit of God. You allow the words of your relatives and special friends to influence your propositions and affect your decisions. You credit them too readily and incorporate their views into your own ideas and are too often led astray. You need to be guarded. The families in _____ which are so closely related have had an influence. Your judgment, your feelings, your views, influence them, and, in turn, they influence you; and a strong current will be set flowing in a wrong direction unless you are all humble and thoroughly consecrated to God. All the elements of these family connections are naturally independent and conscientious, and, unless especially balanced and controlled by the Spirit of God, are inclined to extremes.

Never, never be influenced by reports. Never let your conduct be influenced by your dearest relatives. The time has come when the greatest wisdom needs to be exercised in reference to the cause and work of God. Judgment is needed to know when to speak and when to keep silent. Hunger for sympathy frequently leads to imprudence of a grave character in opening the feelings to others. Your appearance frequently claims sympathy when it would be better for you if you did not receive it. It is an important duty for all to become familiar with the tenor of their conduct from day to day and the motives which prompt their actions. They need to become acquainted with the particular motives which prompt particular actions. Every action of their lives is judged, not by the external appearance, but from the motive which dictated the action.

All should guard the senses, lest Satan gain victory over them; for these are the avenues to the soul. We may be as severe as we like in disciplining ourselves, but we must be very cautious not to push souls to desperation. Some feel that Brother White is altogether too severe in speaking in a decided manner to individuals, in reproving what he thinks is wrong in them. He may be in danger of not being so careful in his manner of reproving as to give no occasion for reflection; but some of those who complain of his manner of reproving use the most cutting, reproving, condemnatory language, too indiscriminating to be spoken to a congregation, and they feel that they have relieved their souls and done a good work. But the angels of God do not always approve such labor. If Brother White makes one individual feel that he is not doing right, if he is too severe toward that one and needs to be taught to modify his manners, to soften his spirit, how much more necessary for his ministering brethren to feel the inconsistency of making a large congregation suffer from cutting reproofs and strong denunciations, when the really innocent must suffer with the guilty.

It is worse, far worse, to give expression to the feelings in a large gathering, firing at anyone and everyone, than to go to the individuals who may have done wrong and personally reprove them. The offensiveness of this severe, overbearing, denunciatory talk in a large gathering is of as much more grave a character in the sight of God than giving personal, individual reproof as the numbers are greater and the censure more general. It is ever easier to give expression to the feelings before a congregation, because there are many present, than to go to the erring and, face to face with them, openly, frankly, plainly state their wrong course. But bringing into the house of God strong feelings against individuals and making all the innocent as well as the guilty suffer, is a manner of labor which God does not sanction and which does harm rather than good. It has too often been the case that criticizing and denunciatory discourses have been given before a congregation. These do not encourage a spirit of love in the brethren. They do not tend to make them spiritually minded and lead them to holiness and heaven, but a spirit of bitterness is aroused in hearts. These very strong sermons that cut a man all to pieces are sometimes positively necessary to arouse, alarm, and convict. But unless they bear the especial marks of being dictated by the Spirit of God they do far more injury than they can do good.

I was shown that my husband's course has not been perfect. He has erred sometimes in murmuring and in giving too severe reproof. But from what I have seen, he has not been so greatly at fault in this respect as many have supposed and as I have sometimes feared. Job was not understood by his friends. He flings back upon them their reproaches. He shows them that if they are defending God by avowing their faith in Him and their consciousness of sin, he has a more deep and thorough knowledge of it than they ever had. "Miserable comforters are ye all," is the answer he makes to their criticisms and censures. "I also," says Job, "could speak as ye do: if your soul were in my soul's stead, I could heap up words against you, and shake mine head at you." But he declares that he would not do this. "I," he says, "would strengthen you with my mouth, and the moving of my lips should assuage your grief."

Brethren and sisters who are well meaning, but who have narrow conceptions and look only at externals, may attempt to help matters of which they have no real knowledge. Their limited experience cannot fathom the feelings of a soul who has been urged out by the Spirit of God, who has felt to the depths that earnest and inexpressible love and interest for the cause of God and for souls that they have never experienced, and who has borne burdens in the cause of God that they have never lifted.

Some shortsighted, short-experienced friends cannot, with their narrow vision, appreciate the feelings of one who has been in close harmony with the soul of Christ in connection with the salvation of others. His motives are misunderstood and his actions misconstrued by those who would be his friends, until, like Job, he sends forth the earnest prayer: Save me from my friends. God takes the case of Job in hand Himself. His patience has been severely taxed; but when God speaks, all his pettish feelings are changed. The self-justification which he felt was necessary to withstand the condemnation of his friends is not necessary toward God. He never misjudges; He never errs. Says the Lord to Job, "Gird up now thy loins like a man;" and Job no sooner hears the divine voice than his soul is bowed down with a sense of his sinfulness, and he says before God, "I abhor myself, and repent in dust and ashes."

When God has spoken, my husband has hearkened to His voice; but to bear the condemnation and reflection of his friends who do not seem to discriminate has been a great trial. When his brethren shall have stood under the same circumstances, and borne the responsibilities that he has borne with as little encouragement and help as he has had, then they may be able to understand how to sustain, how to comfort, how to bless, without torturing his feelings by reflections and censures which he in no way deserves.

CALLS FOR MEANS

I was shown that there have been unhappy results from making urgent calls for means at our camp meetings. This matter has been pressed too hard. Many men of means would not have done anything had not their hearts been softened and melted under the influence of the testimonies borne to them. But the poor have been deeply affected and, in the sincerity of their souls, have pledged means which they had a heart to give, but which they were unable to pay. In most instances urgent calls for means have left a wrong impression upon some minds. Some have thought that money was the burden of our message. Many have gone to their homes blessed because they had donated to the cause of God. But there are better methods of raising means, by freewill offerings, than by urgent calls at our large gatherings. If all come up to the plan of systematic benevolence, and if our tract and missionary workers are faithful in their department of the work, the treasury will be well supplied without these urgent calls at our large gatherings.

But there has been a great neglect of duty. Many have withheld means which God claims as His, and in so doing they have committed robbery toward God. Their selfish hearts have not given the tenth of all their increase, which God claims. Neither have they come up to the yearly gatherings with their freewill offerings, their thank offerings, and their trespass offerings. Many have come before the Lord empty-handed. "Will a man rob God? Yet ye have robbed Me. But ye say, Wherein have we robbed Thee? In tithes and offerings. Ye are cursed with a curse: for ye have robbed Me, even this whole nation. Bring ye all the tithes into the storehouse, that there may be meat in Mine house, and prove Me now herewith, saith the Lord of hosts, if I will not open you the windows of heaven, and pour you out a blessing, that there shall not be room enough to receive it."

Sin will rest upon us as a people if we do not make most

earnest efforts to ascertain those who have donated to the different enterprises who are too poor to give anything. All that they, in the liberality of their souls, have given should be returned to them with an additional gift to relieve their necessities. The raising of money has been carried to extremes. It has left a bad impression on many minds. Making urgent calls is not the best plan of raising means. There has been manifested an indifference to investigate the cases of the poor and make returns to them, that they should not suffer for the necessaries of life. A neglect of our duty in this respect, of becoming acquainted with the necessities of the needy and of relieving their pressing wants by returning means which has been given to advance the cause of God, would be on our part a neglect of our Saviour in the persons of His saints.

DUTY TO THE UNFORTUNATE

I have been shown some things in reference to our duty to the unfortunate which I feel it my duty to write at this time.

I saw that it is in the providence of God that widows and orphans, the blind, the deaf, the lame, and persons afflicted in a variety of ways, have been placed in close Christian relationship to His church; it is to prove His people and develop their true character. Angels of God are watching to see how we treat these persons who need our sympathy, love, and disinterested benevolence. This is God's test of our character. If we have the true religion of the Bible we shall feel that a debt of love, kindness, and interest is due to Christ in behalf of His brethren; and we can do no less than to show our gratitude for His immeasurable love to us while we were sinners unworthy of His grace, by having a deep interest and unselfish love for those who are our brethren and who are less fortunate than ourselves.

The two great principles of the law of God are supreme

love to God and unselfish love to our neighbor. The first four commandments and the last six hang upon, or grow out of, these two principles. Christ explained to the lawyer who his neighbor was in the illustration of the man who was traveling from Jerusalem to Jericho and who fell among thieves and was robbed and beaten and left half dead. The priest and the Levite saw this man suffering, but their hearts did not respond to his wants. They avoided him by passing by on the other side. The Samaritan came that way, and when he saw the stranger's need of help he did not question whether he was a relative or was of his country or creed, but he went to work to help the sufferer because there was work which needed to be done. He relieved him as best he could, put him upon his own beast, and carried him to an inn and made provision for his wants at his own expense. This Samaritan, said Christ, was neighbor to him who fell among thieves. The Levite and the priest represent a class in the church who manifest an indifference to the very ones who need their sympathy and help. This class, notwithstanding their position in the church, are commandment breakers. The Samaritan represents a class who are true helpers with Christ and who are imitating His example in doing good.

Those who have pity for the unfortunate, the blind, the lame, the afflicted, the widows, the orphans, and the needy, Christ represents as commandment keepers, who shall have eternal life. There is in _____ a great lack of personal religion and of a sense of individual obligation to feel for others' woes and to work with disinterested benevolence for the prosperity of the unfortunate and afflicted. Some have no experience in these duties. They have all their lives been like the Levite and the priest, who passed by on the other side. There is a work for the church to do, which, if left undone, will bring darkness upon them. The church as a whole and individually should bring their motives under faithful examination and compare their lives with the life and teachings of the only correct Pattern. Christ regards all acts of mercy, benevolence, and thoughtful consideration for the unfortunate, the blind, the lame, the sick, the widow, and the orphan as done to Himself; and these works are preserved in the heavenly records and will be rewarded. On the other hand, a record will be written in the book against those who manifest the indifference of the priest and the Levite to the unfortunate, and those who take any advantage of the misfortunes of others and increase their affliction in order to selfishly advantage themselves. God will surely repay every act of injustice and every manifestation of careless indifference to and neglect of the afflicted among us. Everyone will finally be rewarded as his works have been.

I was shown in regard to Brother E that he has not been dealt justly with by his brethren. Brethren F, G, and others pursued a course toward him which was displeasing to God. Brother F had no special interest in Brother E, only so far as he thought he could advantage himself through him. I was shown that some looked upon Brother E as being penurious and dishonest. God is displeased with this judgment. Brother E would have had no trouble and would have had means to abundantly sustain himself had it not been for the selfish course of his brethren who had eyesight and property, and who worked against him by seeking to turn his abilities to their own selfish interest. Those who take advantage of the hard study of a blind man and seek to benefit themselves with his inventions, commit robbery and are virtually commandment breakers.

There are some in the church who profess to be keeping the law of Jehovah, but who are transgressors of that law. There are men who do not discern their own defects. They possess a selfish, penurious spirit and blind their own eyes to their sin of covetousness, which the Bible defines as idolatry. Men of this character may have been esteemed by their brethren as most exemplary Christians; but the eye of God reads the heart and discerns the motives. He sees that which man cannot see in the thoughts and character. In His providence He brings these persons into positions which will in time reveal the defects in their character, that if they wish to see and correct them they can do so. There are some who have all their lives studied their own interest and been swallowed up in their own selfish plans and who have been anxious to advantage themselves without much thought whether others would be distressed or perplexed by any plans or actions of theirs. Selfish interest overbears mercy and the love of God. The Lord sometimes permits this class to go on in their selfish course in spiritual blindness until their defects are apparent to all who have spiritual discernment and they evidence by their works that they are not genuine Christians.

Men who have property and a measure of health, and who enjoy the inestimable blessing of sight, have every advantage over a blind man. Many ways are open to them in their business career that are closed to a man who has lost his sight. Persons enjoying the use of all their faculties should not look to their own selfish interest and deprive a blind brother of one iota of his opportunity to gain means. Brother E is a poor man. He is a feeble man; he is also a blind man. He has had an earnest desire to help himself, and, although living under a weight of discouraging infirmities, his affliction has not dried up the generous impulses of his soul. In his limited circumstances he has had a heart to do and has done more in the sight of God for those who were in need of help than many of his brethren who are blessed with sight and who have a good property. Brother E has a capital in his business calculation and inventive faculty. He has worked earnestly with high hopes of inventing a business by which he might support himself and not be dependent upon his brethren.

I wish that we might all see as God sees. I wish all could realize how God looks upon those men who profess to be followers of Christ, who have the blessing of sight and the advantage of means in their favor, and who yet envy the little prosperity enjoyed by a poor blind man and would benefit themselves, increase their stock of means, at the disadvantage of their afflicted brother. This is regarded of God as the most criminal selfishness and robbery, and is an aggravating sin, which He will surely punish. God never forgets. He does not look upon these things with human eyes and with cold, unfeeling human judgment. He views things, not from the worldling's standpoint, but from the standpoint of mercy, pity, and infinite love.

Brother H tried to help Brother E, but not with unselfish motives. At first his pity was excited. He saw that Brother E needed help. But soon he lost his interest, and selfish feelings gathered strength, until the course of his brethren resulted in Brother E's being disadvantaged rather than benefited. These things have greatly discouraged Brother E and have had a tendency to shake his confidence in his brethren. They have resulted in involving him in debts which he could not pay. As he has realized the selfish feelings exercised toward him by some of his brethren, it has grieved him and sometimes stirred him. His feelings at times have been almost uncontrollable as he has realized his helpless condition, without sight, without means, without health, and with some of his brethren working against him. This has added greatly to his affliction and told fearfully upon his health.

I was shown that Brother E has some good qualities of mind which would be better appreciated if he had greater power of self-control and would not become excited. Every exhibition of impatience and fretfulness tells against him, and is made the most of by some who are guilty of much more grievous sins in the sight of God. Brother E's principles are good. He has integrity. He is not a dishonest man. He would not knowingly defraud any man. But he has faults and sins which must be overcome. He, as well as other men, has to deal with human nature. He is too often impatient and is sometimes overbearing. He should cherish a more kindly, courteous spirit and should cultivate gratitude of heart toward those who have felt an interest in his case. Naturally he has an impetuous temper when suddenly aroused or unreasonably provoked. But, notwithstanding this, he has a heart to do right, and he feels sincere repentance toward God when he reflects upon his wrongs.

If he sees his brethren inclined to do him justice he will

be generous to forgive and humble enough to desire peace, even if he has to make great sacrifices to obtain it. But he is easily excited; he is of a nervous temperament. He has need of the subduing influence of the Spirit of God. If those who are ready to censure him would consider their own wrongs and kindly overlook his faults as generously as they should, they would manifest the spirit of Christ. Brother E has a work to do to overcome. His words and deportment to others should be gentle, kind, and pleasant. He should strictly guard against everything which savors of a dictatorial spirit or of overbearing manners or words.

While God is a friend to the blind and the unfortunate, He does not excuse their sins. He requires them to overcome and to perfect Christian character in the name of Jesus, who overcame in their behalf. But Jesus pities our weakness, and He is ready to give strength to bear up in trial and to resist the temptations of Satan, if we will cast our burden upon Him. Angels are sent to minister to the children of God who are physically blind. Angels guard their steps and save them from a thousand dangers, which, unknown to them, beset their path. But His Spirit will not attend them unless they cherish a spirit of kindness and seek earnestly to have control over their natures and to bring their passions and every power into submission to God. They must cultivate a spirit of love and control their words and actions.

I was shown that God requires His people to be far more pitiful and considerate of the unfortunate than they are. "Pure religion and undefiled before God and the Father is this, To visit the fatherless and widows in their affliction, and to keep himself unspotted from the world." Here genuine religion is defined. God requires that the same consideration which should be given to the widow and fatherless be given to the blind and to those suffering under the affliction of other physical infirmities. Disinterested benevolence is very rare in this age of the world.

I was shown, in Brother E's case, that those who would in any way deal unjustly with him and discourage him in his efforts to help himself, or who, coveting the poor blind man's prosperity, would advantage themselves to his disadvantage, will bring upon themselves the curse of God, who is the blind man's friend. Special injunctions were given to the children of Israel in reference to the blind: "Thou shalt not defraud thy neighbor, neither rob him: the wages of him that is hired shall not abide with thee all night until the morning. Thou shalt not curse the deaf, nor put a stumbling block before the blind, but shalt fear thy God; I am the Lord. Ye shall do no unrighteousness in judgment; thou shalt not respect the person of the poor, nor honor the person of the mighty; but in righteousness shalt thou judge thy neighbor." "Cursed be he that removeth his neighbor's landmark. And all the people shall say, Amen. Cursed be he that maketh the blind to wander out of the way. And all the people shall say, Amen. Cursed be he that perverteth the judgment of the stranger, fatherless, and widow. And all the people shall say, Amen."

It is strange that professed Christian men should disregard the plain, positive teachings of the word of God and feel no compunctions of conscience. God places upon them the responsibility of caring for the unfortunate, the blind, the lame, the widow, and the fatherless; but many make no effort to regard it. In order to save such, God frequently brings them under the rod of affliction and places them in positions similar to those occupied by the persons who were in need of their help and sympathy, but who did not receive it at their hands.

God will hold the church at _____ responsible, as a body, for the wrong course of its members. If a selfish and unsympathizing spirit is allowed to exist in any of its members toward the unfortunate, the widow, the orphan, the blind, the lame, or those who are sick in body or mind, He will hide His face from His people until they do their duty and remove the wrong from among them. If any professing the name of Christ so far misrepresent their Saviour as to be unmindful of their duty to the afflicted, or if they in any way seek to advantage themselves to the injury of the unfortunate and thus rob them of means, the Lord holds the church accountable for the sin of its members until they have done all they can to remedy the existing evil. He will not hearken to the prayer of His people while the orphan, the fatherless, the lame, the blind, and the sick are neglected among them.

There is more meant by "being on the Lord's side" than merely saying so in meeting. The Lord's side is ever the side of mercy, pity, and sympathy for the suffering, as will be seen by the example given us in the life of Jesus. We are required to imitate His example. But there are some who are not on the Lord's side in regard to these things; they are on the side of the enemy. In giving to His hearers an illustration of this subject, Jesus said:

"Inasmuch as ye have done it unto one of the least of these My brethren, ye have done it unto Me. Then shall He say also unto them on the left hand, Depart from Me, ye cursed, into everlasting fire, prepared for the devil and his angels: for I was anhungered, and ye gave Me no meat: I was thirsty, and ye gave Me no drink: I was a stranger, and ye took Me not in: naked, and ye clothed Me not: sick, and in prison, and ye visited Me not. Then shall they also answer Him, saying, Lord, when saw we Thee anhungered, or athirst, or a stranger, or naked, or sick, or in prison, and did not minister unto Thee? Then shall He answer them, saying, Verily I say unto you, Inasmuch as ye did it not to one of the least of these, ye did it not to Me. And these shall go away into everlasting punishment: but the righteous into life eternal."

Here in His sermon Christ identifies Himself with suffering humanity and plainly impresses upon us all that indifference or injustice done to the least of His saints is done to Him. Here is the Lord's side, and whoever will be on the Lord's side, let him come over with us. The dear Saviour is wounded when we wound one of His humble saints.

Righteous Job moans because of his afflictions and pleads his own cause when unjustly accused by one of his comforters. He says: "I was eyes to the blind, and feet was I to the lame. I was a father to the poor: and the cause which I knew not I searched out. And I brake the jaws of the wicked, and plucked the spoil out of his teeth."

The sin of one man discomfited the entire army of Israel. A wrong course pursued by one toward his brother will turn the light of God from His people until the wrong is searched out and the cause of the oppressed is vindicated. God requires His people to be tender in their feelings and discriminations, while their hearts should be enlarged, their feelings should be broad and deep not narrow, selfish, and penurious. Noble sympathy, largeness of soul, and disinterested benevolence are needed. Then can the church triumph in God. But just as long as the church suffer selfishness to dry up kindly sympathy and tender, thoughtful love and interest for their brethren, every virtue will be corroded. Isaiah's fast should be studied and close self-examination made with a spirit to discern whether there is in them the principles which God's people are required to possess in order that they may receive the rich blessings promised.

God requires that His people should not allow the poor and afflicted to be oppressed. If they break every yoke and release the oppressed, and are unselfish and kindly considerate of the needy, then shall the blessings promised be theirs. If there are those in the church who would cause the blind to stumble, they should be brought to justice: for God has made us guardians of the blind, the afflicted, the widows, and the fatherless. The stumbling block referred to in the word of God does not mean a block of wood placed before the feet of the blind to cause him to stumble, but it means much more than this. It means any course that may be pursued to injure the influence of their blind brother, to work against his interest, or to hinder his prosperity.

A brother who is blind and poor and diseased, and who is making every exertion to help himself that he may not be dependent, should be encouraged by his brethren in every way possible. But those who profess to be his brethren who have the use of all their faculties, who are not dependent, but who so far forget their duty to the blind as to perplex and distress and hedge up his way, are doing a work which will require repentance and restoration before God will accept their prayers. And the church of God who have permitted their unfortunate brother to be wronged will be guilty of sin until they do all in their power to have the wrong righted.

All are doubtless familiar with Achan's case. It is recorded in sacred history for all generations, but more especially for those upon whom the ends of the world are come. Joshua lay moaning upon his face before God because the people were obliged to make a disgraceful retreat before their enemies. The Lord bade Joshua arise: "Get thee up; wherefore liest thou thus upon thy face?" Have I humbled without cause by removing My presence from thee? Does God forsake His people without a cause? No; He tells Joshua that there is a work for him to do before his prayer can be answered. "Israel hath sinned, and they have also transgressed My covenant which I commanded them: for they have even taken of the accursed thing, and have also stolen, and dissembled also." He declares: "Neither will I be with you any more, except ye destroy the accursed from among you."

Here in this example we have some idea of the responsibility resting upon the church and the work that God requires them to do in order to have His presence. It is a sin in any church not to search for the cause of their darkness and of the afflictions which have been in the midst of them. The church in _____ cannot be a living, prosperous church until they are more awake to the wrongs among them, which hinder the blessing of God from coming upon them. The church should not suffer their brethren in affliction to be wronged. These are the very ones that should awaken the sympathy of all hearts and call into exercise noble, benevolent feelings from all the followers of Christ. The true disciples of Christ will work in harmony with Him and, following His example, will help those who need help. Brother E's blindness is a terrible affliction, and all should seek to be eyes for the blind and thus make him feel his loss as little as possible. There are some who improve their eyes by watching opportunities to work for their own advantage to get gain, but God may bring confusion upon them in a manner they do not expect.

If God in His mercy has given the blind man inventive faculties that he can use for his own good, God forbid that anyone should grudge him this privilege and rob him of the benefits he might derive from God's gift to him. The blind man has disadvantages to meet on every side in the loss of his sight. That heart in which pity and sympathy are not excited at seeing a blind man groping his way in a world clothed to him in darkness, is hard indeed and must be softened by the grace of God. Not a face can the blind man look upon and there read kindly sympathy and true benevolence. He cannot look upon the beauties of nature and trace the finger of God in His created works. Their cheering gladness does not speak to him to comfort and to bless when despondency broods over him. How quickly would he exchange his blindness and every temporal blessing for the blessing of sight. But he is shut up to a world of darkness, and his God-given rights have been trampled upon that others might get gain.

MAN'S DUTY TO HIS FELLOW MEN

I have been shown some things in regard to Brother I's family which have pressed upon my mind so strongly since I have been in this place that I venture to write them out. I have been shown, Brother I, that there exists in your family an element of selfishness which clings to you like the leprosy. This selfishness must be seen and overcome, for it is a grievous sin in the sight of God. As a family you have so long consulted your own wishes, your own pleasure and convenience, that you do not feel that others have claims upon you.

Your thoughts, plans, and efforts are for yourselves. You live for self; you do not cultivate disinterested benevolence, which, if exercised, would increase and strengthen until it would be your delight to live for others' good. You would feel that you had an object in life, a purpose that would bring you returns of greater value than money. You need to have a more special interest for humanity, and in so doing you would bring your souls into closer connection with Christ and would be so imbued with His Spirit and would cleave to Him with so firm a tenacity that nothing could separate you from His love.

Christ is the living Vine; and if you are branches of that Vine, the life nourishment which flows through it will nourish you, that you will not be barren or unfruitful. You have, as a family and as individuals, professedly connected yourselves with the service of Christ; and yet you are weighed in the balances of the sanctuary and found wanting. All of you need to have an entire transformation before you can do those things which unselfish, devoted Christians should do. Nothing but a thorough conversion can give you a correct sense of your defects of character. You all have the spirit and love of the world to a great extent. Says the apostle John: "If any man love the world, the love of the Father is not in him." Your selfish spirit narrows and dwarfs your minds to your own interests. You need pure and undefiled religion. The simplicity of the truth will lead you to feel a sympathy for other's woes. There are those who need your sympathy and love. To exercise these traits of character is a part of the lifework which Christ has given us all to do.

God will not excuse you for not taking up the cross and practicing self-denial in doing good to others with unselfish motives. If you will take the trouble to make the self-denial required of Christians, you may, by the grace of God, be qualified to win souls to Christ. God has claims upon you to which you have never responded. There are many all around us who hunger for sympathy and love. But, like many others, you have been nearly destitute of that humble love which naturally flows out in pity and sympathy for the destitute, the suffering and the needy. The human countenance itself is a mirror of the soul, read by others, and having a telling influence upon them for good or evil. God does not call upon any of us to watch our brethren and to repent of their sins. He has left us a work to do, and He calls upon us to do it resolutely, in His fear with an eye single to His glory.

Everyone, whether he is faithful or otherwise, must give to God an account of himself, not of others. Seeing faults in other professors and condemning their course will not excuse or offset one error of ours. We should not make others our criterion nor excuse anything in our course because others have done wrong. God has given us consciences for ourselves. Great principles have been laid down in His word, which are sufficient to guide us in our Christian walk and general deportment. You, my dear friends, as a family, have not kept the principles of the law of God. You have never felt the burden of the duty devolving upon man to his fellow men.

"And, behold, a certain lawyer stood up, and tempted Him, saying, Master, what shall I do to inherit eternal life? He said unto him, What is written in the law? how readest thou? And he answering said, Thou shalt love the Lord thy God with all thy heart, and with all thy soul, and with all thy strength, and with all thy mind; and thy neighbor as thyself. And He said unto him, Thou hast answered right: this do and thou shalt live. But he, willing to justify himself, said unto Jesus, And who is my neighbor? And Jesus answering said,

"A certain man went down from Jerusalem to Jericho, and fell among thieves, which stripped him of his raiment, and wounded him, and departed, leaving him half dead. And by chance there came down a certain priest that way: and when he saw him, he passed by on the other side. And likewise a Levite, when he was at the place, came and looked on him, and passed by on the other side. But a certain Samaritan, as he journeyed, came where he was: and when he saw him, he had compassion on him, and went to him, and bound up his wounds, pouring in oil and wine, and set him on his own beast, and brought him to an inn, and took care of him. And on the morrow when he departed, he took out two pence, and gave them to the host, and said unto him, Take care of him; and whatsoever thou spendest more, when I come again, I will repay thee. Which now of these three, thinkest thou, was neighbor unto him that fell among the thieves? And he said, He that showed mercy on him. Then said Jesus unto him, Go, and do thou likewise."

Here the conditions of inheriting eternal life are plainly stated by our Saviour in the most simple manner. The man who was wounded and robbed represents those who are subjects of our interest, sympathy, and charity. If we neglect the cases of the needy and the unfortunate that are brought under our notice, no matter who they may be, we have no assurance of eternal life; for we do not answer the claims that God has upon us. We are not compassionate and pitiful to humanity, because they may not be kith or kin to us. You have been found transgressors of the second great commandment, upon which the last six commandments depend. Whosoever offendeth in one point, is guilty of all. Those who do not open their hearts to the wants and sufferings of humanity will not open their hearts to the claims of God as stated in the first four precepts of the Decalogue. Idols claim the heart and affections, and God is not honored and does not reign supreme.

You have, as a family, made a sad failure. You are not, in the strictest sense, commandment keepers. You may be quite exact in some things, yet neglect the weightier matters—judgment, mercy, and the love of God. Although the customs of the world are no criterion for us, yet I have been shown that the pitying sympathy and the benevolence of the world for the unfortunate in many cases shame the professed followers of Christ. Many manifest indifference toward those whom God has thrown among them for the purpose of testing and proving them, and developing what is in their hearts. God reads. He marks every act of selfishness, every act of indifference toward the afflicted, the widows, and the fatherless; and He writes against their names: "Guilty, wanting, lawbreakers." We shall be rewarded as our works have been. Any neglect of duty to the needy and to the afflicted is a neglect of duty to Christ in the person of His saints.

When the cases of all come in review before God, the question, What did they profess? will not be asked, but, What have they done? Have they been doers of the word? Have they lived for themselves, or have they been exercised in works of benevolence, in deeds of kindness and love, preferring others before themselves, and denying themselves that they might bless others? If the record shows that this has been their life, that their characters have been marked with tenderness, self-denial, and benevolence, they will receive the blessed assurance and benediction from Christ: "Well done." "Come, ye blessed of My Father, inherit the kingdom prepared for you from the foundation of the world." Christ has been grieved and wounded by your marked selfish love and your indifference to the woes and needs of others.

Many times our efforts for others may be disregarded and apparently lost. But this should be no excuse for us to become weary in well-doing. How often has Jesus come to find fruit upon the plants of His care and found nothing but leaves. We may be disappointed as to the result of our best efforts, but this should not lead us to be indifferent to others' woes and to do nothing. "Curse ye Meroz, said the angel of the Lord, curse ye bitterly the inhabitants thereof; because they came not to the help of the Lord, to the help of the Lord against the mighty." How often is Christ disappointed in those who profess to be His children! He has given them unmistakable evidences of His love. He became poor, that through His poverty we might be made rich. He died for us that we might not perish, but have eternal life. What if Christ had refused to bear our iniquity because He was rejected by many and because so few appreciated His love and the infinite blessings He came to bring them? We need to encourage patient, painstaking efforts. Courage is now wanted, not lazy despondency and fretful murmuring. We are in this world to do work for the Master and not to study our inclination and pleasure, to serve and glorify ourselves. Why, then, should we be inactive and discouraged because we do not see the immediate results we desire?

Our work is to toil in the vineyard of the Lord, not merely for ourselves, but for the good of others. Our influence is a blessing or a curse to others. We are here to form perfect characters for heaven. We have something to do besides repining and murmuring at God's providences, and writing bitter things against ourselves. Our adversary will not allow us to rest. If we are indeed God's children we shall be harassed and sorely beset, and we need not expect that Satan or those under his influence will treat us well. But there are angels who excel in strength who will be with us in all our conflicts if we will only be faithful. Christ conquered Satan in our behalf in the wilderness of temptation. He is mightier than Satan, and He will shortly bruise him under our feet.

You have, as a family and as individuals, excused yourselves from earnest, active service in your Master's cause. You have been too indolent and have left others to carry many of the heavier burdens which you could and should have borne. Your spiritual strength and blessing will be proportionate to the labor of love and the good works which you perform. The injunction of the apostle Paul is: "Bear ye one another's burdens, and so fulfill the law of Christ." Keeping the commandments of God requires of us good works, self-denial, self-sacrifice, and devotion for the good of others; not that our good works alone can save us, but that we surely cannot be saved without good works. After we have done all that we are capable of doing, we are then to say: We have done no more than our duty, and at best are unprofitable servants, unworthy of the smallest favor from God. Christ must be our righteousness and the crown of our rejoicing.

Self-righteousness and carnal security have closed you about as a wall. As a family you possess a spirit of independence and pride. This element separates you from God. It is a fault, a defect which must be seen and overcome. It is almost impossible for you to see your errors and wrongs. You have too good an opinion of yourselves, and it is difficult for you to see and remove by confession the mistakes in your lives. You are inclined to justify and defend your course in almost everything, whether it be right or wrong. While it is not too late for wrongs to be righted, bring your hearts near to Jesus by humiliation and prayer, and seek to know yourselves. You must be lost unless you arouse yourselves and work with Christ. You encase yourselves in a cold, unfeeling, unsympathizing armor. There is but little life and warmth in your association with others. You live for yourselves, not for Christ. You are careless and indifferent to the needs and conditions of others less fortunate than yourselves. All around you there are those who have soul hunger and who long for love expressed in words and deeds. Friendly sympathy and real feelings of tender interest for others would bring to your souls blessings that you have never yet experienced and would bring you into close relation to our Redeemer, whose advent to the world was for the purpose of doing good and whose life we are to copy. What are you doing for Christ? "Strive to enter in at the strait gate: for many, I say unto you, will seek to enter in, and shall not be able."

LOVE AND SYMPATHY AT HOME

There are many in our world who are starving for the love and sympathy which should be given them. Many men love their wives, but are too selfish to manifest it. They have a false dignity and pride and will not show their love by words and deeds. There are many men who never know how starved is the heart of the wife for words of tender appreciation and affection. They bury their loved ones from their sight and murmur at the providence of God that has deprived them of their companions, when, could they look into the inner life of those companions, they would see that their own course was the cause of their premature death. The religion of Christ will lead us to be kind and courteous and not so tenacious of our opinions. We should die to self and esteem others better than ourselves.

God's word is our standard, but how far have His professed people departed from it! Our religious faith must be not only theoretical, but practical. Pure and undefiled religion will not allow us to trample upon the rights of the least of God's creatures, much less of the members of His body and the members of our own family. God is love, and whoso dwelleth in Him dwelleth in love. The influence of worldly selfishness, which is carried about by some like a cloud, chilling the very atmosphere that others breathe, causes sickness of soul and frequently chills to death.

It will be a great cross for you to cultivate pure, unselfish love and disinterested benevolence. To yield your opinions and ideas, to give up your judgment, and to follow the counsel of others will be a great cross to you. The several members of your family now have families of their own. But the same spirit which existed to a greater or less extent in their father's home is carried to their own firesides and is felt by those outside of their family circles. They lack sweet simplicity, Christlike tenderness, and unselfish love. They have a work to do to overcome these selfish traits of character in order to be fruitful branches of the True Vine. Said Christ: "Herein is My Father glorified, that ye bear much fruit." You need to bring Jesus near to you, to have Him in your homes and in your hearts. You should not only have a knowledge of what is right, but should practice it from right motives, having an eye single to the glory of God. You may be helps, if you will comply with the conditions given in the word of God.

The religion of Christ is something more than talk. The righteousness of Christ consists in right actions and good works from pure, unselfish motives. Outside righteousness, while the inward adorning is wanting, will be of no avail. "This then is the message which we have heard of Him, and declare unto you, that God is light, and in Him is no darkness at all. If we say that we have fellowship with Him, and walk in darkness, we lie, and do not the truth: but if we walk in the light, as He is in the light, we have fellowship one with another, and the blood of Jesus Christ His Son cleanseth us from all sin." If we have not the light and love of God we are not His children. If we gather not with Christ we scatter abroad. We all have an influence, and that influence is telling upon the destiny of others for their present and future good or for their eternal loss.

J and K both lack sympathy and love for those outside of their own families. They are in danger of watching to see defects in others while greater evils exist undiscerned in themselves. If these dear souls ever enter heaven, they must die to self and obtain an experience in well-doing. They have lessons to learn in the school of Christ in order to perfect Christian characters and have a oneness with Christ. Said Christ to His disciples: "Except ye be converted, and become as little children, ye shall not enter into the kingdom of heaven." He explained His meaning to them. He did not wish them to become children in understanding, but in malice. Little children do not manifest feelings of superiority and aristocracy. They are simple and natural in their appearance. Christ would have His followers cultivate unaffected manners, that their whole bearing may be humble and Christlike. He has made it our duty to live for others good. He came from the royal courts of heaven to this world to show how great an interest He had in man, and the infinite price paid for the redemption of man shows that man is of so great value that Christ could sacrifice His riches and honor in the royal courts to lift him from the degradation of sin.

If the Majesty of heaven could do so much to show His love for man, what ought not men to be willing to do to help one another out of the pit of darkness and suffering! Said Christ, "Love one another, as I have loved you;" not with a greater love; for "greater love hath no man than this, that a man lay down his life for his friends." Our love is frequently selfish, for we confine it to prescribed limits. When we come into close union and fellowship with Christ, our love and sympathy and our works of benevolence will reach down deeper and will widen and strengthen with exercise. The love and interest of Christ's followers must be as broad as the world. Those who live merely for "me and mine" will fail of heaven. God calls upon you as a family to cultivate love, to become less sensitive in regard to yourselves and more sensitive to the griefs and trials of others. This selfish spirit that you have cherished all your lives is correctly represented by the priest and the Levite who passed by the unfortunate on the other side. They saw that he needed help, but purposely avoided him.

Each one of you needs to awake and face square about to get out of the cart rut of selfishness. Improve the short, probationary time given you by working with your might to redeem the failures of your past life. God has placed you in a world of suffering to prove you, to see if you will be found worthy of the gift of eternal life. There are those all around you who have woes, who need words of sympathy, love, and tenderness, and our humble, pitying prayers. Some are suffering under the iron hand of poverty, some with disease, and others with heartaches, despondency, and gloom. Like Job, you should be eyes to the blind and feet to the lame, and you should inquire into the cause which you know not and search it out with the object in view to relieve their necessities and help just where they most need help.

L needs to cultivate love for his wife, love that will find expression in words and deeds. He should cultivate tender affection. His wife has a sensitive, clinging nature and needs to be cherished. Every word of tenderness, every word of appreciation and affectionate encouragement, will be remembered by her and will reflect back in blessings upon her husband. His unsympathizing nature needs to be brought into close contact with Christ, that that stiffness and cold reserve may be subdued and softened by divine love. It will not be weakness or a sacrifice of manhood and dignity to give his wife expressions of tenderness and sympathy in words and acts; and let it not end with the family circle, but extend to those outside the family. L has a work to do for himself that no one can do for him. He may grow strong in the Lord by bearing burdens in His cause. His affection and love should be centered upon Christ and heavenly things, and he should be forming a character for everlasting life.

Dear K has very limited ideas of what constitutes a Christian. She has freed herself from burdens which Christ has borne for her. She is not willing to bear His cross and has not exercised to the best account the ability, the talents, given her of God. She has not grown strong in moral fortitude and courage, nor felt the weight of individual responsibility. She has not loved to bear reproach for Christ's sake, considering the promise: "If ye be reproached for the name of Christ, happy are ye; for the Spirit of glory and of God resteth upon you." "If we suffer, we shall also reign with Him." The Master has a work for each to do. None can be idle, none can be careless and selfish, and yet perfect Christian character. He wants all of your family to unclose their hearts to the benign influence of His love and grace, that their compassion for others may overflow the boundaries of self and the enclosures of family walls, as did the Samaritan's to the poor, suffering stranger who was neglected and left to die by the priest and the Levite. I was shown that there are many who need our sympathy and advice; and when we consider that we can pass through this world but once, that we can never return to repair the errors and mistakes we have made, how important that we go through it as we ought!

Some time ago I was shown the case of J. Her errors and wrongs were faithfully portrayed before her; but in the last view given me I saw that the wrongs still existed, that she was cold and unsympathizing with her husband's children. Correction and reproof are not given by her for grave offenses merely, but for trivial matters that should be passed by unnoticed. Constant faultfinding is wrong, and the Spirit of

Christ cannot abide in the heart where it exists. She is disposed to pass over the good in her children without a word of approval, but is ever ready to bear down with censure if any wrong is seen. This ever discourages children and leads to habits of heedlessness. It stirs up the evil in the heart and causes it to cast up mire and dirt. In children who are habitually censured there will be a spirit of "I don't care," and evil passions will frequently be manifested regardless of consequences.

Whenever the mother can speak a word of commendation for the good conduct of her children, she should do so. She should encourage them by words of approval and looks of love. These will be as sunshine to the heart of a child and will lead to the cultivation of self-respect and pride of character. Sister J should cultivate love and sympathy. She should manifest tender affection for the motherless children under her care. This would be a blessing to these children of God's love and would be reflected back upon her in affection and love.

Children have sensitive, loving natures. They are easily pleased and easily made unhappy. By gentle discipline in loving words and acts, mothers may bind their children to their hearts. To manifest severity and to be exacting with children are great mistakes. Uniform firmness and unimpassioned control are necessary to the discipline of every family. Say what you mean calmly, move with consideration, and carry out what you say without deviation.

It will pay to manifest affection in your association with your children. Do not repel them by lack of sympathy in their childish sports, joys, and griefs. Never let a frown gather upon your brow or a harsh word escape your lips. God writes all these words in His book of records. Harsh words sour the temper and wound the hearts of children, and in some cases these wounds are difficult to heal. Children are sensitive to the least injustice, and some become discouraged under it and will neither heed the loud, angry voice of command nor care for threatenings of punishment. Rebellion is too frequently established in the hearts of children through the wrong discipline of the parents, when if a proper course had been taken, the children would have formed good and harmonious characters. A mother who does not have perfect control of herself is unfit to have the management of children.

Brother M is molded by the positive temperament of his wife. He has become in a degree selfish like her. His mind is almost completely occupied by "me and mine," to the exclusion of other things of infinitely more importance. He does not take his position in his family as father of his flock and, unprejudiced and uninfluenced, pursue a uniform course with his children. His wife is not, and without a transformation never can be, a true mother to his motherless children. Brother M, as a father to his children, has not stood in the position that God would have him. These motherless children are God's little ones, precious in His sight. Naturally Brother M has a tender, refined, loving, generous, sensitive nature, while his wife is exactly the opposite. Instead of his molding and softening the character of his wife, she is transforming him.

He thinks that in order to have peace he must let things pass which trouble his mind. He has learned that submission and the yielding of her opinion are not to be expected. She will rule; she will carry out her ideas at any cost. Unless they are both in earnest in their efforts to reform, they will not obtain eternal life. They have had light, but have neglected to follow it. Selfish love of the world has blinded their perceptions and hardened their hearts. J needs to see that unless she lays aside her selfishness, and overcomes her will and her temper, she cannot have heaven. She would mar all heaven with these elements in her character. I warn Sister J to repent. I call upon her in the name of my Master to arouse quickly from her stupid indifference, to heed the counsel of the True Witness, and zealously repent; for she is imperiling her soul.

God is merciful. He will now accept the offering of a broken heart and a contrite spirit. Will Sister J excuse herself as did the Levite and the priest, for not seeing and feeling others' woes, and pass by on the other side? God holds her accountable for neglect of duty in not exercising sympathy and tenderness for the unfortunate. She does not keep the commandments of God which plainly show her duty to her neighbor. Said Christ to the lawyer: "This do, and thou shalt live." Thus a neglect of duty to our neighbor will result in our loss of eternal life.

FAMILY EXCLUSIVENESS

K, poor child, like many others, has a work to do that she has never dreamed of. She has backslidden from God. Her thoughts are too much upon herself, and she seeks to please the world, not by disinterested love for souls and by seeking to turn them to Christ, but by her lack of spirituality, and her conformity to the world in spirit and works. She should die to self and obtain an experience in well-doing. She is cold and unsympathizing. She needs to have all this icy, unapproachable spirit subdued, melted away by the sunshine of Christ's love. She is very much shut up to herself. God saw that she was a poor dwarfed plant, bearing no fruit, nothing but leaves. Her thoughts were almost exclusively occupied with "me and mine." In mercy He has been pruning this plant of His love, lopping off the branches, that the roots might strike down deeper. He has been seeking to draw this child to Himself. Her religious life has been almost entirely without fruit. She is accountable for the talent God has given her. She may be useful, she may be a co-worker with Christ if she will break down the wall of selfishness which has shut her away from God's light and love.

There are many who need our sympathy and advice, but not that advice which implies superiority in the giver and inferiority in the receiver. K needs the softening, melting love of God in her heart. The looks and tones of the voice should be modulated by thoughtful consideration and tender, respectful love. Every look and every tone of voice that implies, "I am superior," chills the atmosphere of her presence and is more like an icicle than a ray of light that gives warmth. My sister, your influence is positive. You mold those with whom you associate, or else you cannot agree with them. You have not the least thought of being molded yourself by the better influence of others and of yielding your judgment and your opinions to them. You will reason for your way and justify your ideas and your course. If you do not convince others you will recur again and again to the same point. This trait in your character will be a valuable one if sanctified to God and controlled by His Holy Spirit, but if not, it will prove a curse to you and a curse to others. Assertions and advice which savor of a dictatorial spirit are not good fruit. You need the softening, melting love of Christ in your heart, which will be reflected in all your acts toward your family and to all who are brought under your influence.

I fear, greatly fear, that J will fail of heaven. She loves the world and the things of the world so well that she has no love to spare for Jesus. She is so incrusted in selfishness that the illuminating light from heaven cannot penetrate the cold, dark walls of self-love and self-esteem which she has been building up for a lifetime. Love is the key to open hearts, but the precious plant of love has not been cherished. J has so long blinded her eyes to her selfishness that she can not now discern it. She has had so little experimental religion that in heart she is of the world, and I fear that this world is all the heaven she will ever have. Her influence over her husband is not good. He is swayed by it and does not see the necessity of being fortified by the grace of God to stand for the right with true moral courage. Not only does she fail to realize and do the work that God requires of her, but she exerts an overpowering influence to hold her husband and tie his hands. And she has succeeded to a great extent. He is blinded.

Brother M should consider that God has claims upon him which are above every earthly relationship. He needs the eyesalve, the white raiment, and the gold, that he may have a symmetrical character and an abundant entrance into the kingdom of God. Nothing short of an entire conversion can ever open the soul of his wife to see her errors and to confess her wrongs. She has great changes to make, which she has not made because she did not realize her true condition and could not see the necessity of reform. So far from being willing to learn of the heavenly Teacher, who was meek and lowly of heart, she considers meekness servility; and a becoming spirit, lowliness of mind to esteem others better than herself, she regards as degrading and humiliating.

J has a positive, imperious, proud, self-willed spirit. She does not see anything particularly desirable in a meek and quiet spirit that she should covet it. This valuable ornament possesses so little value for her that she cannot consent to wear it. She has, too frequently, a spirit of resentment which is as opposite to the Spirit of God as the east is to the west. True gentleness is a gem of great value in the sight of God. A meek and quiet spirit will not be ever looking out for happiness for itself, but will seek for self-forgetfulness and find sweet content and true satisfaction in making others happy.

In the providence of God, Sister N has been separated from her father's family. Although, with others, she shares the characteristics of the family association, bearing grave responsibilities has led her out of herself; and has given her an interest in others' woes. She has, in a measure, opened her heart in sympathy and love for God's family, taking an interest in others. The work and cause of God have engaged her attention. She has felt, in some degree, that poor fallen mortals are one great brotherhood. She has had to educate herself to think for others, do for others, and forget self; and yet she has not cultivated as thoroughly as she should the interest, sympathy, and affection for others that are necessary for the followers of Christ. She needs to have greater sympathy and less tense, rigid justice. As she has given her interest and time to the great subject of health reform she has reached out beyond self. As she has done this she has been blessed. The more she does for others' good, the more she sees to do and the more she feels inclined to do.

Her work for others frequently brings her where the exercise of faith is necessary to bring her through hard and trying positions. But answers to earnest prayers are realized, and faith, love, and confidence in God are strengthened. Through oft repeated perplexities and trials, experience is obtained. God is molding the heart into something more like Himself. And yet self clamors constantly for the victory. Sister N needs to cultivate more tenderness and thoughtful care in her daily connection with others. She needs to study to subdue self. If she is indeed a Christian she will feel that she must devote the best part, and if need be the whole, of her life to unselfish, patient toil and thus show her love for the Master. Without this experience she would fall far short of perfection of Christian character.

Sister N has taken some advance steps, and the family feel that she has left them, and this is a crucifixion to them. They do not feel that she now has the same interest and affections and objects in life as themselves. They feel that they can no longer enjoy, as formerly, the society of their sister. They feel that she is to blame, that she has changed, and that her sympathy is no longer one with theirs. The reason for this lack of assimilation of feeling is that Sister N has been advancing in feeling for others' woes, while they have been slothful servants, not doing the work God has given them to do on earth. Consequently they have been retrograding. The family have selfishly shut up their interest and affection to themselves and the love of the world.

N has been a worker in a good cause. The health reform has been to her a subject of great importance, for her experience has shown her its necessity. Her father's family have not seen the necessity of health reform. They have not seen the part that it acts in the closing work of these last days, because they have not been inclined to see. They have dropped into the cart rut of custom, and it is a difficult work to make the effort required to get out. They would rather be let alone. It is a terrible thing to rust from inaction. But this family will surely be weighed in the balances and found wanting unless they begin at once to do something. "Now if any man have not the Spirit of Christ, he is none of His." This is close language. Who can stand the test? The word of God is to us a daguerreotype of the mind of God and of Christ, also of man fallen, and of man renewed after the image of Christ, possessing the divine mind. We may compare our thoughts, feelings, and intentions with the picture of Christ. We have no relationship with Him unless we are willing to work the works of Christ.

Christ came to do His Father's will. Are we following in His steps? All who have named the name of Christ should be constantly seeking for a more intimate acquaintance with Him, that they may walk even as He walked, and do the works of Christ. We should appropriate the lessons of His life to our lives. Christ "gave Himself for us, that He might redeem us from all iniquity, and purify unto Himself a peculiar people, zealous of good works." "Hereby perceive we the love of God, because He laid down His life for us: and we ought to lay down our lives for the brethren." Here is the work of self-denial upon which we must enter with cheerfulness, in imitation of the example of our Redeemer. The Christian's life must be one of conflict and of sacrifice. The path of duty should be followed, not the path of inclination and choice.

When the family of Brother I see the work before them, and do the work God has left them to do, they will not be so widely separated from Brother and Sister O and Sister N, and those who are working in union with the Master. It may take time to attain perfect submission to God's will, but we can never stop short of it and be fitted for heaven. True religion will lead its possessor on to perfection. Your thoughts, your words, and your actions, as well as your appetites and passions, must be brought into subjection to the will of God. You must bear fruit unto holiness. Then you will be led to defend the poor, the fatherless, the motherless, and the afflicted. You will do justice to the widow and will relieve the needy. You will deal justly, love mercy, and walk humbly before God.

We must let Christ into our hearts and homes if we would walk in the light. Home should be made all that the word implies. It should be a little heaven upon earth, a place where the affections are cultivated instead of being studiously repressed. Our happiness depends upon this cultivation of love, sympathy, and true courtesy to one another. The reason there are so many hardhearted men and women in our world is that true affection has been regarded as weakness and has been discouraged and repressed. The better part of the nature of persons of this class was perverted and dwarfed in childhood, and unless rays of divine light can melt away their coldness and hardhearted selfishness, the happiness of such is buried forever. If we would have tender hearts, such as Jesus had when He was upon the earth, and sanctified sympathy, such as the angels have for sinful mortals, we must cultivate the sympathies of childhood, which are simplicity itself. Then we shall be refined, elevated, and directed by heavenly principles.

A cultivated intellect is a great treasure; but without the softening influence of sympathy and sanctified love, it is not of the highest value. We should have words and deeds of tender consideration for others. We can manifest a thousand little attentions in friendly words and pleasant looks, which will be reflected upon us again. Thoughtless Christians manifest by their neglect of others that they are not in union with Christ. It is impossible to be in union with Christ and yet be unkind to others and forgetful of their rights. Many long intensely for friendly sympathy. God has given each of us an identity of our own, which cannot be merged in that of another; but our individual characteristics will be much less prominent if we are indeed Christ's and His will is ours. Our lives should be consecrated to the good and happiness of others, as was our Saviour's. We should be self-forgetful, ever looking out for opportunities, even in little things, to show gratitude for the favors we have received of others, and watching for opportunities to cheer others and lighten and relieve their sorrows and burdens by acts of tender kindness and little deeds of love. These thoughtful courtesies, that, commencing in our families, extend outside the family circle, help make up the sum of life's happiness; and the neglect of these little things makes up the sum of life's bitterness and sorrow.

It is the work that we do or do not do that tells with tremendous power upon our lives and destinies. God requires us to improve every opportunity for usefulness that is offered us. Neglect to do this is perilous to our spiritual growth. We have a great work to do. Let us not pass in idleness the precious hours that God has given us in which to perfect characters for heaven. We must not be inactive or slothful in this work, for we have not a moment to spend without a purpose or object. God will help us to overcome our wrongs if we will pray and believe on Him. We can be more than conquerors through Him who has loved us. When the short life in this world is ended, and we see as we are seen and know as we are known, how short in duration and how small will the things of this world appear to us in comparison with the glory of the better world. Christ would never have left the royal courts and taken humanity, and become sin for the race, had He not seen that man might, with His help, become infinitely happy and obtain durable riches and a life that would run parallel with the life of God. He knew that without His help sinful man could not attain these things.

We should have a spirit of progress. We must guard continually against being fixed in our views, feelings, and actions. The work of God is onward. Reforms must be carried on, and we must take hold and help move on the car of reform. Energy, tempered with patience and ambition, and balanced by wisdom, is now needed by every Christian. The work of saving souls is yet left to us, the disciples of Christ. Not one of us is excused. Many have become dwarfed and stunted in their Christian life because of inaction. We should employ our time diligently while in this world. How earnestly should we improve every opportunity of doing good, of bringing others to a knowledge of the truth! Our motto should ever be, "Onward, higher," surely, steadily onward to duty and to victory.

I have been shown in regard to the individuals mentioned that God loves them and would save them if they would be saved in His appointed way. "And He shall sit as a refiner and purifier of silver: and He shall purify the sons of Levi, and purge them as gold and silver, that they may offer unto the Lord an offering in righteousness. Then shall the offering of Judah and Jerusalem be pleasant unto the Lord, as in the days of old, and as in former years." This is the process, the refining, purifying process, which is to be carried on by the Lord of hosts. The work is most trying to the soul, but it is only through this process that the rubbish and defiling impurities can be removed. Our trials are all necessary to bring us close to our heavenly Father, in obedience to His will, that we may offer to the Lord an offering in righteousness. To each whose name is here mentioned, God has given capabilities, talents to improve. You each need a new and living experience in the divine life in order to do the will of God. No amount of past experience will suffice for the present nor strengthen us to overcome the difficulties in our path. We must have new grace and fresh strength daily in order to be victorious.

We are seldom, in all respects, placed in the same circumstances twice. Abraham, Moses, Elijah, Daniel, and many others were all sorely tried, but not in the same way. Everyone has his individual tests and trials in the drama of life, but the very same trials seldom come twice. Each has his own experience, peculiar in its character and circumstances, to accomplish a certain work. God has a work, a purpose, in the life of each of us. Every act, however small, has its place in our life experience. We must have the continual light and experience that come from God. We all need these, and God is more than willing that we should have them if we will take them. He has not closed the windows of heaven to your prayers, but you have felt satisfied to pass on without the divine help you so much need.

How little you know the bearing of your daily acts upon the history of others. You may think that what you do or say is of little consequence, when the most important results for good or evil are the consequence of our words and actions. The words and actions looked upon as so small and unimportant are links in the long chain of human events. You have not felt the need of God's manifesting His will to us in all the acts of our daily life. With our first parents the desire for a single gratification of appetite opened the floodgate of woe and sin upon the world. Would that you, my dear sisters, might feel that every step you take may have a lasting and controlling influence upon your own lives and the characters of others. Oh, how much need, then, of communion with God! What need of divine grace to direct every step and show us how to perfect Christian characters!

Christians will have new scenes and new trials to pass through where past experience cannot be a sufficient guide. We have greater need to learn of the divine Teacher now than at any other period of our lives. And the more experience we gain, the nearer we draw toward the pure light of heaven, the more shall we discern in ourselves that needs reforming. We may all do a good work in blessing others if we will seek counsel of God and follow on in obedience and faith. The path of the just is progressive, from strength to strength, from grace to grace, and from glory to glory. The divine illumination will increase more and more, corresponding with our onward movements, qualifying us to meet the responsibilities and emergencies before us.

When trials press you, when despondency and dark unbelief control your thoughts, when selfishness molds your actions, you do not see your need of God and of a deep and thorough knowledge of His will. You know not the will of God, neither can you know it while you live for self. You rely upon your good intentions and resolutions, and the principal sum of life is composed of resolutions made and resolutions broken. What you all need is to die to self, cease clinging to self, and surrender to God. Gladly would I comfort you if I could. Gladly would I praise your good qualities, good purposes, and good acts; but God was not pleased to show me these. He presented before me the hindrances to your gaining the noble, elevated character of holiness needful for you to have that you may not lose the heavenly rest and immortal glory He would have you attain. Look away from yourselves to Jesus. He is all and in all. The merits of the blood of a crucified and risen Saviour will avail to cleanse from the least and greatest sin. In trusting faith commit the keeping of your souls to God as unto a faithful Creator. Be not continually in fear and apprehension that God will leave you. He never will unless you depart from Him. Christ will come in and dwell with you if you will open the door of your hearts to Him. There may be perfect harmony between you and the Father and His Son if you will die to self and live unto God.

How few are aware that they have darling idols, that they have cherished sins! God sees these sins to which you may be blinded, and He works with His pruning knife to strike deep and separate these cherished sins from you. You all want to choose for yourselves the process of purification. How hard it is for you to submit to the crucifixion of self; but when the work is all submitted to God, to Him who knows our weakness and our sinfulness, He takes the very best way to bring about the desired results. It was through constant conflict and simple faith that Enoch walked with God. You may all do the same. You may be thoroughly converted and transformed, and be indeed children of God, enjoying not only the knowledge of His will, but, by your example, leading others in the same path of humble obedience and consecration. Real godliness is diffusive and communicative. The psalmist says: "I have not hid Thy righteousness within my heart; I have declared Thy faithfulness and Thy salvation: I have not concealed Thy loving-kindness and Thy truth from the great congregation." Wherever the love of God is, there is always a desire to express it.

May God help you all to make earnest efforts to gain everlasting life and to lead others in the path of holiness.

THE SIN OF COVETOUSNESS

Dear Brother P: I would make one more effort to warn you to be in earnest to gain the kingdom. Warning after warning has been given you, which you have not heeded. But, oh, if you would even now repent of your past wrong course and turn to the Lord, it might not be too late for wrongs to be righted. All the powers of your mind have been devoted to money getting. You have worshiped money. It has been your god. The rod of God is hanging over you. His judgments may overtake you at any moment and you go down to the grave unready, your garments spotted and stained with the corruptions of the world. What is your record in heaven? Every dollar that you have accumulated has been like an extra link in the chain that fastens you to this poor world. Your passion to get gain has been continually strengthening. The burden of your thoughts has been how you could obtain more means. You have had a fearful experience, which should be a warning to those who allow the love of the world to take possession of their souls. You have become mammon's slave. What will you say when the Master shall demand of you an account of your stewardship? You have allowed the love of money getting to become the ruling passion of your life. You are as much intoxicated with the love of money as is the inebriate with his liquor.

Jesus has pleaded that the unfruitful tree might be spared a little longer; and I make one more plea for you to put forth no faint effort, but a most earnest one, for the kingdom. Rescue yourself from the snare of Satan before the word, "He is joined to idols, let him alone," shall be spoken in regard to you in heaven. All money lovers, like yourself, will one day cry in bitter anguish: "Oh, the deceitfulness of riches! I have sold my soul for money." Your only hope now is to make no feeble move, but to turn square about. Resolutely call to your aid the will power that you have so long exercised in the wrong direction, and now work in the opposite direction. This is the only way for you to overcome covetousness.

God has opened ways in which covetousness can be overcome—by performing benevolent deeds. By your life you are saying that you esteem the treasures of the world more highly than immortal riches. You are saying: "Farewell, heaven; farewell, immortal life; I have chosen this world." You are bartering away the pearl of great price for present gain. While thus admonished of God, while in His providence He has, as it were, already placed your feet in the dark river, will you, dare you, cultivate your money-loving propensities? Will you, as the last act of a misspent life, overreach and retain that which is another's just due? Will you reason yourself into the belief that you are doing justice to your brother? Will you add another act of scheming and overreaching to those already written against you in the records above? Shall the blow of God's retributive judgment fall upon you and you be called without warning to pass through the dark waters?

Our Saviour frequently and earnestly rebuked the sin of covetousness. "And He said unto them, Take heed, and beware of covetousness: for a man's life consisteth not in the abundance of the things which he possesseth. And He spake a parable unto them, saying, The ground of a certain rich man brought forth plentifully: and he thought within himself, saying, What shall I do, because I have no room where to bestow my fruits? And he said, This will I do: I will pull down my barns, and build greater; and there will I bestow all my fruits and my goods. And I will say to my soul, Soul, thou hast much goods laid up for many years; take thine ease, eat, drink, and be merry. But God said unto him, Thou fool, this night thy soul shall be required of thee: then whose shall those things be, which thou hast provided? So is he that layeth up treasure for himself, and is not rich toward God."

God has made a law for His people that a tenth of all the increase shall be His. I have given you, says God, nine tenths; I ask one tenth of all the increase. That one tenth the rich man had withheld from God. If he had not done this, if he had loved God supremely instead of loving and serving himself, he would not have accumulated so great treasures that there would be lack of room to bestow them. Had he bestowed his goods upon his needy brethren to supply their necessities, there would have been no need of tearing down and building greater barns. But he had disregarded the principles of the law of God. He had not loved the Lord with all his heart and his neighbor as himself. Had he used his wealth as a bounty lent him of God with which to do good he would have laid up treasure in heaven and been rich in good works.

The length and usefulness of life do not consist in the amount of our earthly possessions. Those who use their wealth in doing good will see no necessity for large accumulations in this world; for the treasure which is used to advance the cause of God and which is given to the needy in Christ's name is given to Christ, and He lays it up for us in the bank of heaven in bags which wax not old. He who does this is rich toward God, and his heart will be where his treasures are secured. He who humbly uses what God has given for the honor of the Giver, freely giving as he has received, may feel the peace and assurance in all his business that God's hand is over him for good, and he himself will bear the impress of God, having the Father's smile.

Many have pitied the lot of the Israel of God in being compelled to give systematically, besides making liberal offerings yearly. An all-wise God knew best what system of benevolence would be in accordance with His providence, and has given His people directions in regard to it. It has ever proved that nine tenths are worth more to them than ten tenths. Those who have thought to increase their gains by withholding from God, or by bringing Him an inferior offering,—the lame, the blind, or the diseased,—have been sure to suffer loss.

Providence, though unseen, is ever at work in the affairs of men. God's hand can prosper or withhold, and He frequently withholds from one while He seems to prosper another. All this is to test and prove men and to reveal the heart. He lets misfortune overtake one brother while He prospers others to see if those whom He favors have His fear before their eyes and will perform the duty enjoined upon them in His word to love their neighbor as themselves and to help their poorer brother from a love to do good. Acts of generosity and benevolence were designed by God to keep the hearts of the children of men tender and sympathetic, and to encourage in them an interest and affection for one another in imitation of the Master, who for our sakes became poor, that we through His poverty might be made rich. The law of tithing was founded upon an enduring principle and was designed to be a blessing to man.

The system of benevolence was arranged to prevent that great evil, covetousness. Christ saw that in the prosecution of business the love of riches would be the greatest cause of rooting true godliness out of the heart. He saw that the love of money would freeze deep and hard into men's souls, stopping the flow of generous impulses and closing their senses to the wants of the suffering and the afflicted. "Take heed," was His oft-repeated warning, "and beware of covetousness." "Ye cannot serve God and mammon." The oft-repeated and striking warnings of our Redeemer are in marked contrast with the actions of His professed followers who evidence in their lives so great eagerness to be rich and who show that the words of Christ are lost upon them. Covetousness is one of the most common and popular sins of the last days, and has a paralyzing influence upon the soul.

Brother P, the desire for wealth has been the central idea of your mind. This one passion for money getting has deadened every high and noble consideration, and has made you indifferent to the needs and interests of others. You have made yourself nearly as unimpressible as a piece of iron. Your gold and your silver are cankered, and have become an eating canker to the soul. Had your benevolence grown with your riches, you would have regarded money as a means by which you could do good. Our Redeemer, who knew man's danger in regard to covetousness, has provided a safeguard against this dreadful evil. He has arranged the plan of salvation so that it begins and ends in benevolence. Christ offered Himself, an infinite sacrifice. This, in and of itself, bears directly against covetousness and exalts benevolence.

Constant, self-denying benevolence is God's remedy for the cankering sins of selfishness and covetousness. God has arranged systematic benevolence to sustain His cause and relieve the necessities of the suffering and needy. He has ordained that giving should become a habit, that it may counteract the dangerous and deceitful sin of covetousness. Continual giving starves covetousness to death. Systematic benevolence is designed in the order of God to tear away treasures from the covetous as fast as they are gained and to consecrate them to the Lord, to whom they belong.

This system is so arranged that men may give something from their wages every day and lay by for their Lord a portion of the profits of every investment. The constant practice of God's plan of systematic benevolence weakens covetousness and strengthens benevolence. If riches increase, men, even those professing godliness, set their hearts upon them; and the more they have, the less they give to the treasury of the Lord. Thus riches make men selfish, and hoarding feeds covetousness; and these evils strengthen by active exercise. God knows our danger and has hedged us about with means to prevent our own ruin. He requires the constant exercise of benevolence, that the force of habit in good works may break the force of habit in an opposite direction.

God requires an appropriation of means for benevolent objects every week, that in the frequent exercise of this good quality the heart may be kept open like a flowing stream and not allowed to close up. By exercise, benevolence constantly enlarges and strengthens, until it becomes a principle and reigns in the soul. It is highly dangerous to spirituality to allow selfishness and covetousness the least room in the heart.

The word of God has much to say in regard to sacrificing. Riches are from the Lord and belong to Him. "Both riches and honor come of Thee." "The silver is Mine, and the gold is Mine, saith the Lord of hosts." "For every beast of the forest is Mine, and the cattle upon a thousand hills." "The earth is the Lord's, and the fullness thereof; the world, and they that dwell therein." It is the Lord thy God that giveth thee power to get wealth.

Riches are in themselves transient and unsatisfying. We are warned not to trust in uncertain riches. "Riches certainly make themselves wings; they fly away." "Lay not up for yourselves treasures upon earth, where moth and rust doth corrupt, and where thieves break through and steal."

Riches bring no relief in man's greatest distress. "Riches profit not in the day of wrath." "Neither their silver nor their gold shall be able to deliver them in the day of the Lord's wrath." "Because there is wrath, beware lest He take thee away with His stroke: then a great ransom cannot deliver thee." This warning, my brother, is appropriate in your case.

What provision, Brother P, have you made for eternal life? Have you a good foundation against the time to come, that will secure to yourself eternal joys? Oh, may God arouse you! May you, my dear brother, now, just now, commence to work in earnest to get some of your gain and riches into the treasury of God. Not a dollar of it is yours. All is God's, and you have claimed for your own that which God has lent you to devote to good works. Your time is very short. Work with all your might. By repentance you may now find pardon. You must loosen your grasp of earthly possessions and fasten your affections upon God. You must be a converted man. Agonize with God. Do not be content to perish forever, but make an effort for salvation before it shall be everlastingly too late.

It is not now too late for wrongs to be righted. Show your repentance for past wrongs by redeeming the time. Where you have wronged anyone, make restitution as it comes to your mind. This is your only hope of the pardoning love of God. It will be like taking out the right eye or cutting off the right arm, but there is no other way for you. You have made efforts repeatedly, but have failed because you have loved money, some of which has not been very honestly gained. You would not try to redeem the past by restitution. When you begin to do this, there will be hope for you. If during the few remaining days of your life you choose to go on as you have done, your case will be hopeless; you will lose both worlds; you will see the saints of God glorified in the heavenly city and yourself thrust out; you will have no part in that precious life which was purchased for you at an infinite cost, but which you valued so little as to sell it for earthly riches.

Now there is a little time left you. Will you work? Will you repent? Or will you die all unready, worshiping money, glorying in your riches, and forgetting God and heaven? No faint struggle or feeble efforts will wean your affections from the world. Jesus will help you. In every earnest effort you make, He will be near you and bless your endeavors. You must make earnest efforts or you will be lost. I warn you not to delay one moment, but commence just now. You have long disgraced the Christian name by your covetousness and small dealing. Now you may honor it by working in an opposite direction and by letting all see that there is a power in the truth of God to transform human nature. You may, in the strength of God, save your soul if you will.

You have a work to do which you should begin at once. Satan will stand by your side, as he did by the side of Christ in the wilderness of temptation, to overcome you with reasonings, to pervert your judgment, and to paralyze your sense of right and equity. If you do justice in one instance, you must not wait for Satan to overpower your good impulses by his reasoning. You have so long been controlled by selfishness and covetousness that you cannot trust yourself. I do not want you to lose heaven. I have been shown the selfish acts of your life, your close scheming and figuring, your bartering, and the advantage which you have taken of your brethren and fellow men. God has every instance written in the book. Will you pray to Him to enlighten your mind to see where you have overreached, and then will you repent and redeem the past?

Brother P, may God help you before it is too late.

INDUSTRY IN THE MINISTRY

I have been shown that there is danger of our young ministers entering the field and engaging in the work of teaching the truth to others when they are not fitted for the sacred work of God. They have no just sense of the sacredness of the work for this time. They feel a desire to be connected with the work, but they fail to bear the burdens lying directly in the pathway of duty. They do that which costs them but little taxation and inconvenience, and neglect to put their whole souls into the work.

Some are too indolent to make a success of life in business matters and are deficient in the experience necessary to make them good Christians in a private capacity; yet they feel competent to engage in the work which is of all others the most difficult, that of dealing with minds and trying to convert souls from error to the truth. The hearts of some of these ministers are not sanctified by the truth. All such are merely stumbling blocks to sinners and are standing in the way of real laborers. It will take more stern labor to educate them to right ideas, that they may not injure the cause of God, than to do the work. God cannot be glorified or His cause advanced by unconsecrated workmen who are entirely deficient in the qualifications necessary to make a gospel minister. Some young ministers who go forth to labor for others need themselves to be thoroughly converted to the genuine religion of the Bible.

I was shown the case of Brother R of _____, which in many respects represents the cases of others. I was shown that Brother R is no real advantage to the cause of God and never can be unless he has a thorough conversion. He has many defects in his character which he must see before he can be accepted of God as a laborer in His vineyard. The word of God is sacred. In the first place, Brother R has not met with that change of heart which transforms the man and is called conversion. He has a religion of the head, but he needs the work of the grace of God upon the heart to be carried out in the life before he can understandingly point others to the Lamb of God who taketh away the sins of the world. The work for this time is altogether too solemn and too important to be handled with unclean hands and impure hearts.

Brother R has a very unhappy temperament. This makes trouble for himself and for his best friends. He is naturally jealous, suspicious, and faultfinding. Those most closely connected with him will feel this most deeply. He has much self-love and large self-esteem, and if he is not especially regarded and made an object of attention he feels as though someone were to blame. The fault exists in himself. He loves to have his vanity flattered. He is suspicious of the motives of others and shows in these feelings a very narrow, selfish mind. He thinks that he sees much to question, to find fault with, and to censure in the plan of others' labors, when the real evil exists in his own unhumbled, unconsecrated heart. Self, in him, must die, and he must learn of Jesus, who is meek and lowly of heart, or he will fail of perfecting Christian character and of gaining heaven at last.

Brother R has made a failure in his manner of seeking to teach the truth to others. His spirit is not winning. Self is mixed with all his efforts. He is quite particular about the externals, so far as his apparel is concerned, as though this would designate him as a minister of Christ; but he has neglected the inward adornment of the soul. He has not felt the necessity of seeking for a beautiful, harmonious character, resembling the character of Christ, the correct pattern. The meekness and humility which characterized the life of Jesus would win hearts and give him access to souls; but when Brother R speaks in his own spirit, the people see so much self exhibited, and so little of the spirit of humility, that their hearts are not touched, but grow hard and cold under his preaching, because it lacks the divine unction.

The self-confident, self-exalted spirit of Brother R must be put away, and he must see that he is sinful and in need of continual grace and power from God to press through the moral darkness of this degenerate age and reach souls who need to be saved. He has put on upon the outside the dignity of a gospel minister, while he has not felt that a real experience in the mystery of godliness and a knowledge of the divine will were essential to making a success of presenting the truth.

Brother R is too cold and unsympathizing. He does not come directly to hearts by the Christian simplicity, tenderness, and love which characterized the life of Christ. In this respect it is essential that every man who labors for the salvation of souls should imitate the pattern given him in the life of Christ. If men fail to educate themselves to become workers in the vineyard of the Lord, they might better be spared than not. It would be poor policy to support from the treasury of God those who really mar and injure His work, and who are constantly lowering the standard of Christianity.

In order for a man to become a successful minister, something more than book knowledge is essential. The laborer for souls needs integrity, intelligence, industry, energy, and tact. All these are highly essential for the success of a minister of Christ. No man with these qualifications can be inferior, but will have commanding influence. Unless the laborer in God's cause can gain the confidence of those for whom he is laboring, he can do but little good. The worker in the Lord's vineyard must daily derive strength from above to resist wrong and to maintain uprightness through the varied trials of life, and his soul must be brought into harmony with his Redeemer. He can be a co-worker with Jesus, working as He worked, loving as He loved, and possessing, like Him, moral power to stand the strongest tests of character.

Brother R should cultivate simplicity. He should lay aside his false dignity and let the Spirit of God come in and sanctify, elevate, purify, and ennoble his life. Then he can bear the burden for souls which a true gospel minister must feel when presenting a message of solemn warning to those in peril, who must perish in their darkness unless they accept the light of truth. This dignity borrowed from his Redeemer will adorn with divine grace, for by it he is brought into close union with Jesus Christ.

I was carried forward in the life of Brother R, and then carried back to review the result of his labors, while he was attempting to teach others the truth. I saw that some few would listen, and, as far as the head is concerned, might be convinced; but Brother R has not an experimental, daily, living knowledge of the grace of God and His saving power, and he cannot convey to others what he does not himself possess. He has not the experience of a truly converted man. How, then, can God make him a blessing to sinners? He is blind himself, while striving to lead the blind.

I was shown that his work has spoiled good fields for others. Some men who were truly consecrated to God and who felt the burden of the work might have done good and brought souls into the truth in places where he has made attempts without success, but after his superficial work the golden opportunity was gone. The minds that might have been convinced, and the hearts that might have been softened, have been hardened and prejudiced under his efforts.

I looked to see what souls of value were holding on to the truth as the result of his labors. I watched closely to see what watchcare he had had for souls, to strengthen and encourage them, a labor which should ever accompany the ministry of the word. I could not see one who would not have been in a far better condition had he not received the first impressions of the truth from him. It is about impossible for a stream to rise higher than its fountainhead. The man who bears the truth to sinners stands in a fearfully responsible position. Either he will convert souls to Christ or his efforts will balance them in the wrong direction.

I have been shown that Brother R is an indolent man. He loves his pleasure and his ease. He does not love physical labor, neither does he love close application of the mind to the study of the word. He wants to take things lazily. He will go to a place and attempt to introduce the truth there, when his heart is not in it. He feels no weight of the work, no real burden for souls. He has not the love of souls at heart. He lets his inclinations divert him from the work, suffers his feelings to control him, and leaves the work and goes back to his family. He has not an experience in self-denial, in sacrificing his ease and his inclinations. He labors too much with respect to wages. He does not apply himself closely to his work, but merely touches it here and there without perseverance or earnestness, and so makes a success of nothing. God frowns upon all such professed workers. They are unfaithful in everything. Their consciences are not sensitive and tender.

To introduce the truth into places and then lack courage, energy, and tact to carry the matter through is a great error, for the work is left without that thorough and persevering effort being made which is positively essential in these places. If matters go hard, if opposition arises, he makes a cowardly retreat instead of fleeing to God with fasting and praying and weeping, and by faith clinging to the Source of light and power and strength until the clouds break away and the darkness disperses. Faith grows strong by coming in conflict with doubts and opposing influences. The experience gained in these trials is of more value than the most costly jewels.

The result of your labors, Brother R, should make you ashamed. God cannot accept them. It would be better for the cause of God if you would cease preaching, and take up a work which involves less responsibility. It would be better for you to go to work with your hands. Humble your heart before God; be faithful in temporal matters; and when you show that you are faithful in the smaller responsibilities, God may commit to you higher trusts. "He that is faithful in that which is least is faithful also in much: and he that is unjust in the least is unjust also in much." You need a deeper experience in religious things. I advise you to go to work with your hands and earnestly plead with God for an experience for yourself. Cling to Jesus and never, never dare to assume the responsibilities of a gospel minister until you are a converted man and have a meek and peaceable spirit. You need to tarry away from the work of God till you are endowed with power from on high. No man can make a success of saving souls unless Christ works with his efforts and self is put out of sight.

A minister of Christ should be thoroughly furnished unto all good works. You have made a miserable failure. You must show in your family that kindly consideration, that tenderness, love, gentleness, noble forbearance, and true courtesy, that is becoming to the head of a family, before you can make a success of winning souls to Christ. If you have not wisdom to manage the small number with whom you are closely united, how can you make a success of managing a larger company, who are not especially interested in yourself? Your wife needs to be truly and thoroughly converted to God. Neither of you are in a condition to correctly represent our faith. You both need a thorough conversion.

Retirement from the work of God at present is best for you. Brother R, you have neither perseverance nor moral backbone. You are very deficient in those traits of character which are necessary for the work of God at this time. You have not received that education in practical life that is necessary for you in order to make a success as a practical minister of Christ. Your education has been deficient in many respects. Your parents have not read your character, nor trained you to overcome its defects to the end that you might develop a symmetrical character, and possess firmness, self-denial, self-control, humility, and moral power. You know very little of practical life or of perseverance under difficulties. You have a strong desire to controvert others' ideas and to press forward your own. This is the result of your feelings of self-sufficiency and of following your own inclinations in youth.

You do not see yourself and your errors. You are not willing to be a learner, but have a great desire to teach. You form opinions of your own and cling to your peculiar ideas with a persistency that is wearying. You are anxious to carry your points, and in your eyes your ideas are of greater importance than the experienced judgment of men of moral worth who have been proved in this cause. You have been flattered with the idea that you had ability that would be prized and make you a valuable man; but these qualities have not been tested and proved. You have a one-sided education. You have no inclination or love for the homely, daily duties of life. Your indolence would be sufficient to disqualify you for the work of the ministry were there no other reasons why you should not engage in it. The cause does not need preachers so much as workers. Of all the vocations of life, there is none that requires such earnest, faithful, persevering, self-sacrificing workers as the cause of God in these last days.

The enterprise of obtaining eternal life is above every other consideration. God wants no laggards in His cause. The work of warning sinners to flee from the wrath to come requires earnest men who feel the burden of souls and who will not be ready to avail themselves of every excuse to avoid burdens or to leave the work. Little discouragements, as unpleasant weather or imaginary infirmities, seem sufficient to Brother R to excuse him from making exertion. He will even appeal to his sympathies, and when duties arise that he does not feel inclined to perform, when his indolence clamors for indulgence, he frequently makes the excuse that he is sick, when there is no reason why he should be sick, unless through indolent habits and indulgence of appetite his entire system has become clogged by inaction. He may have good health if he will strictly observe the laws of life and health, and carry out the light upon health reform in all his habits.

Brother R is not the man for the work in these last days unless he entirely reforms. God does not call for ministers who are too indolent to engage in physical labor, to bear the testing message of warning to the world. He wants workers in His cause. Real, earnest, self-denying workers will accomplish something.

Brother R, your teaching the truth to others has been an entire mistake. If God calls a man, He will not make so great a blunder as to take one of so little experience in practical life and spiritual things as you have had. You have ability to talk, as far as that is concerned, but God's cause requires men of consecration and energy. These traits you may cultivate, you may gain them if you will. By perseveringly cultivating the opposite traits of those wherein you now fail, you may learn to overcome those deficiencies in your character which have increased from your youth. To merely go out and speak to the people now and then is not working for God. There is no real work in it.

Those who labor for God have but just begun the work when they have given a discourse in the desk. After this comes the real labor, the visiting from house to house, conversing with members of families, praying with them, and coming close in sympathy to those whom we wish to benefit. It will not detract from the dignity of a minister of Christ to be awake to see and realize the temporal burdens and cares of the families he visits, and to be useful, seeking to relieve them where he can by engaging in physical labor. In this way he can have a power of influence to disarm opposition and break down prejudice, that he would fail to have if he were in every other respect fully efficient as a minister of Christ.

Our young ministers have not the burden of writing that the older and more experienced ones have. They have not a multiplicity of responsibilities which tax the mind and wear upon the man. But it is these very burdens of care that perfect Christian experience, give moral power, and make strong, efficient men of those engaged in the work of God. Avoiding burdens and disagreeable responsibilities will never make our ministers strong men that can be depended upon in a religious crisis. Many of our young ministers are as weak as babes in the work of God. And some who have been engaged in the work of teaching the truth for years are not yet able workmen, who need not be ashamed. They have not grown strong in experience by being called out by opposing influences. They have excused themselves from that exercise which would strengthen the moral muscles, giving spiritual power. But this is the very experience they need in order to attain to the full stature of men in Christ Jesus. They gain no spiritual power by shirking duties and responsibilities, and giving up to indolence and selfish love of ease and pleasure.

Brother R is not lacking in ability to clothe his ideas in words, but he is lacking in spirituality and true heart holiness. He has not drunk deeply himself at the fountain of truth. Had he improved his golden moments in studying the work of God he might now have been an able workman, but he is too indolent to make close application of the mind and to learn for himself the reasons of our hope. He is content to take material which other minds and other pens have labored to produce, and to use their thoughts, which are prepared to his hand, without effort or exertion of mind, careful thought, or prayerful meditation himself.

Brother R does not love close application either in the study of the Scriptures or in physical labor. He prefers an easier way, and as yet knows nothing experimentally of the burden of the work of God. It is easier for him to repeat the thoughts of others than to diligently search for the truth himself. It is only by personal effort, close application of the mind, and thorough devotion to the work that men become competent for the ministry.

Says Christ: "Ye are the salt of the earth: but if the salt have lost his savor, wherewith shall it be salted?" The savor of the salt is divine grace. All the efforts made to advance the truth are of but little value unless the Spirit of God accompanies them. You have made child's play of teaching the truth. Your mind has been on your own ease and pleasure, following your inclination. You and your wife have no real sense of the sacredness of the work of God. You both think more of pleasing your fancies and studying to gratify your desires for ease and enjoyment than of engaging in the stern duties of life, especially the responsibilities connected with the work of warning the world of the coming judgment.

You have seen Brother S weighed down with burdens and wearied with physical labor; but you have had so great a love for your ease and such a desire to maintain your own importance that you have held yourself aloof, excusing yourself from engaging in the duties which someone was obliged to perform. You have passed days in easy indolence without benefiting anyone, and then your conscience could permit you without compunction to bring in time mostly spent in indolence and to receive pay from God's treasury.

You have shown by your course that you had not a high sense of sacred things. You have robbed God, and you should now seek to make thorough work of repentance. Do not attempt to teach others. When you are converted, then you may be able to strengthen your brethren, but God has no use for men of your stamp of character in His vineyard. When you get this stamp off, and bear the impress of the divine, then you may work for the cause of God. You have almost everything to learn and but a short time in which to learn these lessons. God help you to work earnestly and to the point. I have written much more upon general principles, but cannot find time to give it to you at present.

PARENTS AS REFORMERS

January 3, 1875, I was shown that none of us realize the perils that attend us at every step. We have a vigilant foe, and yet we are not awake and in earnest in our efforts to resist the temptations of Satan and to overcome his devices.

God has permitted the light of health reform to shine upon us in these last days, that by walking in the light we may escape many dangers to which we will be exposed. Satan's temptations are powerful upon the human family to lead them to indulge appetite, gratify inclination, and live a life of heedless folly. He presents attractions in a life of personal enjoyment, and in seeking to gratify the animal instinct. Licentiousness prevails to an alarming extent and is ruining constitutions for life, and not only this, but the moral powers are sacrificed. Intemperate indulgences are reducing the vital energies of both body and mind. They place the one that is overcome upon the enemy's ground, where Satan can tempt, annoy, and finally control the will at pleasure.

Those who have been overcome on the point of appetite and are using tobacco freely are debasing their mental and moral powers and bringing them into servitude to the animal. And when the appetite for spirituous liquor is indulged, the man voluntarily places to his lips the draft which debases below the level of the brute him who was made in the image of God. Reason is paralyzed, the intellect is benumbed, the animal passions are excited, and then follow crimes of the most debasing character. If men would become temperate in all things, if they would touch not, taste not, handle not, spirituous liquors and narcotics, reason would hold the reigns of government in her hands and control the animal appetites and passions. In this fast age the less exciting the food the better. Temperance in all things and firm denial of appetite is the only path of safety.

Satan comes to man, as he came to Christ, with his overpowering temptations to indulge appetite. He well knows his power to overcome man upon this point. He overcame Adam and Eve in Eden upon appetite, and they lost their blissful home. What accumulated misery and crime have filled our world in consequence of the fall of Adam. Entire cities have been blotted from the face of the earth because of the debasing crimes and revolting iniquity that made them a blot upon the universe. Indulgence of appetite was the foundation of all their sins. Through appetite, Satan controlled the mind and being. Thousands who might have lived, have prematurely passed into their graves, physical, mental, and moral wrecks. They had good powers, but they sacrificed all to indulgence of appetite which led them to lay the reins upon the neck of lust. Our world is a vast hospital. Vicious habits are increasing.

It is unpleasant, if not dangerous, to remain in a railroad car or in a crowded room that is not thoroughly ventilated, where the atmosphere is impregnated with the properties of liquor and tobacco. The occupants give evidence by the breath and emanations from the body that the system is filled with the poison of liquor and tobacco. Tobacco using is a habit which frequently affects the nervous system in a more powerful manner than does the use of alcohol. It binds the victim in stronger bands of slavery than does the intoxicating cup; the habit is more difficult to overcome. Body and mind are, in many cases, more thoroughly intoxicated with the use of tobacco than with spirituous liquors, for it is a more subtle poison.

Intemperance is increasing everywhere, notwithstanding the earnest efforts made during the past year* to stay its progress. I was shown that the giant power of intemperance will not be controlled by any such efforts as have been made. The work of temperance must begin in our families, at our tables. Mothers have an important work to do that they may give to the world, through correct discipline and education, children who will be capable of filling almost any position, and who can also honor and enjoy the duties of domestic life.

The work of the mother is very important and sacred. She should teach her children from the cradle to practice habits of self-denial and self-control. If her time is mostly occupied with the follies of this degenerate age, if dress and parties engage her precious time, her children fail to receive that education which it is essential they should have in order that they may form correct characters. The anxiety of the Christian

---

*This *Testimony* was first published in 1875.

mother should not be in regard to the external merely, but that her children may have healthy constitutions and good morals.

Many mothers who deplore the intemperance which exists everywhere do not look deep enough to see the cause. They are daily preparing a variety of dishes and highly seasoned food which tempt the appetite and encourage overeating. The tables of our American people are generally prepared in a manner to make drunkards. Appetite is the ruling principle with a large class. Whoever will indulge appetite in eating too often, and food not of a healthful quality, is weakening his power to resist the clamors of appetite and passion in other respects in proportion as he has strengthened the propensity to incorrect habits of eating. Mothers need to be impressed with their obligation to God and to the world to furnish society with children having well-developed characters. Men and women who come upon the stage of action with firm principles will be fitted to stand unsullied amid the moral pollutions of this corrupt age. It is the duty of mothers to improve their golden opportunities to correctly educate their children for usefulness and duty. Their time belongs to their children in a special sense. Precious time should not be devoted to needless work upon garments for display, but should be spent in patiently instructing and carefully teaching their children the necessity of self-denial and self-control.

The tables of many professed Christian women are daily set with a variety of dishes which irritate the stomach and produce a feverish condition of the system. Flesh meats constitute the principal article of food upon the tables of some families, until their blood is filled with cancerous and scrofulous humors. Their bodies are composed of what they eat. But when suffering and disease come upon them, it is considered an affliction of Providence.

We repeat: Intemperance commences at our tables. The appetite is indulged until its indulgence becomes second nature. By the use of tea and coffee an appetite is formed for tobacco, and this encourages the appetite for liquors.

Many parents, to avoid the task of patiently educating their children to habits of self-denial and teaching them how to make a right use of all the blessings of God, indulge them in eating and drinking whenever they please. Appetite and selfish indulgence, unless positively restrained, grow with the growth and strengthen with the strength. When these children commence life for themselves and take their place in society, they are powerless to resist temptation. Moral impurity and gross iniquity abound everywhere. The temptation to indulge taste and to gratify inclination has not lessened with the increase of years, and youth in general are governed by impulse and are slaves to appetite. In the glutton, the tobacco devotee, the winebibber, and the inebriate we see the evil results of defective education.

When we hear the sad lamentations of Christian men and women over the terrible evils of intemperance, the questions at once arise in the mind: Who have educated the youth and given them their stamp of character? Who have fostered in them the appetites they have acquired? Who have neglected the most solemn responsibility of molding their minds and forming their characters for usefulness in this life, and for the society of the heavenly angels in the next? A large class of the human beings we everywhere meet are a living curse to the world. They live for no other purpose than to indulge appetite and passion, and to corrupt soul and body by dissolute habits. This is a terrible rebuke to mothers who are the votaries of fashion, who have lived for dress and show, who have neglected to beautify their own minds and to form their own characters after the divine Pattern, and who have also neglected the sacred trust committed to them, to bring their children up in the nurture and admonition of the Lord.

I saw that Satan, through his temptations, is instituting ever-changing fashions and attractive parties and amusements, that mothers may be led to devote their God-given probationary time to frivolous matters so that they can have but little opportunity to educate and properly train their children. Our youth want mothers who will teach them from their very cradles to control passion, to deny appetite, and to overcome selfishness. They need line upon line and precept upon precept, here a little and there a little.

Direction was given to the Hebrews how to train their children to avoid the idolatry and wickedness of the heathen nations: "Therefore shall ye lay up these My words in your heart and in your soul, and bind them for a sign upon your hand, that they may be as frontlets between your eyes. And ye shall teach them your children, speaking of them when thou sittest in thine house, and when thou walkest by the way, when thou liest down, and when thou risest up."

We have an earnest desire that woman shall fill the position which God originally designed, as her husband's equal. We so much need mothers who are mothers not merely in name, but in every sense that the word implies. We may safely say that the dignity and importance of woman's mission and distinctive duties are of a more sacred and holy character than the duties of man.

There are speculations as to woman's rights and duties in regard to voting. Many are in no way disciplined to understand the bearing of important questions. They have lived lives of present gratification because it was the fashion. Women who might develop good intellects and have true moral worth are now mere slaves to fashion. They have not breadth of thought nor cultivated intellect. They can talk understandingly of the latest fashion, the styles of dress, this or that party or delightful ball. Such women are not prepared to intelligently take a prominent position in political matters. They are mere creatures of fashion and circumstance. Let this order of things be changed. Let woman realize the sacredness of her work and, in the strength and fear of God, take up her life mission. Let her educate her children for usefulness in this world and for a fitness for the better world.

We address Christian mothers. We entreat that you feel your responsibility as mothers and that you live not to please yourselves, but to glorify God. Christ pleased not Himself, but took upon Him the form of a servant. He left the royal courts and condescended to clothe His divinity with humanity, that by His condescension and His example of self-sacrifice He might teach us how we may become elevated to the position of sons and daughters of the royal family, children of the heavenly King. But what are the conditions of these sacred, elevated blessings? "Come out from among them, and be ye separate, saith the Lord, and touch not the unclean thing; and I will receive you, and will be a Father unto you, and ye shall be My sons and daughters, saith the Lord Almighty."

Christ humbled Himself from the highest authority, from the position of one equal with God, to the lowest place, that of a servant. His home was in Nazareth, which was proverbial for its wickedness. His parents were among the lowly poor. His trade was that of a carpenter, and He labored with His hands to do His part in sustaining the family. For thirty years He was subject to His parents. Here the life of Christ points us to our duty to be diligent in labor and to provide for and to train the weak and the ignorant. In His lessons of instruction to His disciples Jesus taught them that His kingdom was not a worldly kingdom, where all were striving for the highest position.

Woman is to fill a more sacred and elevated position in the family than the king upon his throne. Her great work is to make her life a living example which she would wish her children to copy. By precept as well as example she is to store their minds with useful knowledge and lead them to self-sacrificing labor for the good of others. The great stimulus to the toiling, burdened mother should be that every child who is trained aright, and who has the inward adorning, the ornament of a meek and quiet spirit, will have a fitness for heaven and will shine in the courts of the Lord.

How few see anything attractive in the true humility of Christ! His humility did not consist in a low estimate of His own character and qualifications, but in His humbling

Himself to fallen humanity in order to raise them up with Him to a higher life. Worldlings try to exalt themselves to the position of those above them or to become superior to them. But Jesus, the Son of God, humbled Himself to elevate man, and the true follower of Christ will seek to meet men where they are in order to elevate them.

Will mothers of this generation feel the sacredness of their mission and not try to vie with their wealthy neighbors in appearances, but seek to excel them in faithfully performing the work of instructing their children for the better life? If children and youth were trained and educated to habits of self-denial and self-control, if they were taught that they eat to live instead of living to eat, there would be less disease and less moral corruption. There would be little necessity for temperance crusades, which amount to so little, if in the youth who form and fashion society, right principles in regard to temperance could be implanted. They would then have moral worth and moral integrity to resist, in the strength of Jesus, the pollutions of these last days.

It is a most difficult matter to unlearn the habits which have been indulged through life and have educated the appetite. The demon of intemperance is not easily conquered. It is of giant strength and hard to overcome. But let parents begin a crusade against intemperance at their own firesides, in their own families, in the principles they teach their children to follow from their very infancy, and they may hope for success. It will pay you, mothers, to use the precious hours which are given you of God in forming, developing, and training the characters of your children, and in teaching them to strictly adhere to the principles of temperance in eating and drinking.

Parents may have transmitted to their children tendencies to appetite and passion, which will make more difficult the work of educating and training these children to be strictly temperate and to have pure and virtuous habits. If the appetite for unhealthy food and for stimulants and narcotics has been transmitted to them as a legacy from their parents, what a fearfully solemn responsibility rests upon the parents to counteract the evil tendencies which they have given to their children! How earnestly and diligently should the parents work to do their duty, in faith and hope, to their unfortunate offspring!

Parents should make it their first business to understand the laws of life and health, that nothing shall be done by them in the preparation of food, or through any other habits, which will develop wrong tendencies in their children. How carefully should mothers study to prepare their tables with the most simple, healthful food, that the digestive organs may not be weakened, the nervous forces unbalanced, and the instruction which they should give their children counteracted by the food placed before them. This food either weakens or strengthens the organs of the stomach and has much to do in controlling the physical and moral health of the children, who are God's blood-bought property. What a sacred trust is committed to parents to guard the physical and moral constitutions of their children so that the nervous system may be well balanced and the soul not be endangered. Those who indulge the appetite of their children, and do not control their passions, will see the terrible mistake they have made, in the tobacco-loving, liquor-drinking slave, whose senses are benumbed and whose lips utter falsehoods and profanity.

When parents and children meet at the final reckoning, what a scene will be presented! Thousands of children who have been slaves to appetite and debasing vice, whose lives are moral wrecks, will stand face to face with the parents who made them what they are. Who but the parents must bear this fearful responsibility? Did the Lord make these youth corrupt? Oh, no! He made them in His image, a little lower than the angels. Who, then, has done the fearful work of forming the life character? Who changed their characters so that they do not bear the impress of God, and must be forever separated from His presence as too impure to have any place with the pure angels in a holy heaven? Were the sins of the parents transmitted to the children in perverted appetites and passions? And was the work completed by the pleasure-loving mother in neglecting to properly train them according to the pattern given her? All these mothers will pass in review before God just as surely as they exist. Satan is ready to do his work and to present temptations which they have no will or moral power to resist.

Our people are constantly retrograding upon health reform. Satan sees that he cannot have such a controlling power over them as he could if appetite were indulged. Under the influence of unhealthful food the conscience becomes stupefied, the mind becomes darkened, and its susceptibility to impressions is blunted. But because violated conscience is benumbed and becomes insensible, the guilt of the transgressor is not lessened.

Satan is corrupting minds and destroying souls through his subtle temptations. Will our people see and feel the sin of indulging perverted appetite? Will they discard tea, coffee, flesh meats, and all stimulating food, and devote the means expended for these hurtful indulgences to spreading the truth? These stimulants do only harm, and yet we see that a large number of those who profess to be Christians are using tobacco. These very men will deplore the evil of intemperance, and while speaking against the use of liquors will eject the juice of tobacco. While a healthy state of mind depends upon the normal condition of the vital forces, what care should be exercised that neither stimulants nor narcotics be used.

Tobacco is a slow, insidious poison, and its effects are more difficult to cleanse from the system than those of liquor. What power can the tobacco devotee have to stay the progress of intemperance? There must be a revolution in our world upon the subject of tobacco before the ax is laid at the root of the tree. We press the subject still closer. Tea and coffee are fostering the appetite which is developing for stronger stimulants, as tobacco and liquor. And we come still closer home, to the daily meals, the tables spread in Christian households. Is temperance practiced in all things? Are the reforms which are essential to health and happiness carried out there? Every true Christian will have control of his appetite and passions. Unless he is free from the bondage and slavery of appetite he cannot be a true, obedient servant of Christ. It is the indulgence of appetite and passion which makes the truth of none effect upon the heart. It is impossible for the spirit and power of the truth to sanctify a man, soul, body, and spirit, when he is controlled by appetite and passion.

"CANNOT COME DOWN"

"I am doing a great work," says Nehemiah, "so that I cannot come down: why should the work cease, whilst I leave it, and come down to you?"

I was shown, January 3, 1875,* that God's people should not for one moment relax their watchfulness or their vigilance. Satan is upon our track. He is determined to overcome God's commandment-keeping people with his temptations. If we give no place to him, but resist his devices, steadfast in the faith, we shall have strength to depart from all iniquity. Those who keep the commandments of God will be a power in the land if they live up to their light and privileges. They may be patterns of piety, holy in heart and in conversation. We shall not have ease, that we may cease watchfulness and prayer. As the time draws near for Christ to be revealed in the clouds

---

*It is a pleasure here to state relative to the gracious manifestation of the Holy Spirit to Mrs. White on the eve of January 3, 1875, that she had been sick with severe influenza, and confined to her room and bed for one week, till the physicians at the Health Institute had become anxious in her case. In this condition she followed the directions given in the fifth chapter of the Epistle of James, and after a great stretch of faith like the man in the gospel who stretched forth his withered hand, she reached the point of deliverance from pain and sickness, and was soon in vision which lasted ten minutes. She then dressed for meeting, walked to the church, and spoke to the crowded assembly twenty minutes, and walked home. Since that time she has written very much and has spoken to the people with freedom. She is now preparing for the long journey to the Pacific Coast.   J. W., *in first edition*

of heaven, Satan's temptations will be brought to bear with greater power upon those who keep God's commandments, for he knows that his time is short.

The work of Satan will be carried on through agents. Ministers who hate the law of God will employ any means to lead souls from their loyalty to God. Our bitterest foes will be among the first-day Adventists. Their hearts are fully determined to make war against those who keep the commandments of God and have the faith of Jesus. This class feel that it is a virtue to talk, write, and act out the most bitter hatred against us. We need not look for fair dealing or for justice at their hands. Many of them are inspired by Satan with insane madness against those who are keeping the commandments of God. We shall be maligned and misrepresented; all our motives and actions will be misjudged, and our characters will be attacked. The wrath of the dragon will be manifested in this manner. But I saw that we should not be in the least discouraged. Our strength is in Jesus, our Advocate. If in humility we trust in God and hold fast to His promises, He will give us grace and heavenly wisdom to withstand all the wiles of Satan and to come off victors.

In my recent view I saw that it will not increase our influence, or bring us into favor with God, to retaliate or come down from our great work to their level in meeting their slanders. There are those who will resort to any species of deception and gross falsehood to gain their object and deceive souls, and to cast stigma upon the law of God and those who love to obey it. They will repeat the most inconsistent and vile falsehoods, over and over, until they make themselves believe that they are truth. These are the strongest arguments they have to use against the Sabbath of the fourth commandment. We should not allow our feelings to control us and divert us from the work of warning the world.

The case of Nehemiah was presented before me. He was engaged in building the walls of Jerusalem, and the enemies of God were determined that the walls should not be built. "But it came to pass, that when Sanballat, and Tobiah, and the

Arabians, and the Ammonites, and the Ashdodites, heard that the walls of Jerusalem were made up, and that the breaches began to be stopped, then they were very wroth, and conspired all of them together to come and to fight against Jerusalem, and to hinder it."

In this case a spirit of hatred and opposition to the Hebrews formed the bond of union and created a mutual sympathy among different bodies of men who might otherwise have warred with one another. This well illustrates what we frequently witness in our day in the existing union of men of different denominations to oppose present truth, men whose only bond seems to be that which is dragonic in its nature, manifesting bitterness and hatred against the remnant who keep the commandments of God. This is especially seen in the first-day, no-day, and all-days-alike Adventists, who seem to be famous for hating and slandering one another, when they can spare time from their efforts to misrepresent, slander, and in every way abuse Seventh-day Adventists.

"Nevertheless we made our prayer unto our God, and set a watch against them day and night, because of them." We are in constant danger of becoming self-sufficient, relying upon our own wisdom, and not making God our strength. Nothing disturbs Satan so much as our knowledge of his devices. If we feel our dangers we shall feel the need of prayer, as did Nehemiah, and like him we shall obtain that sure defense that will give us security in peril. If we are careless and indifferent, we shall surely be overcome by Satan's devices. We must be vigilant. While, like Nehemiah, we resort to prayer, taking all our perplexities and burdens to God, we should not feel that we have nothing to do. We are to watch as well as pray. We should watch the work of our adversaries, lest they gain advantage in deceiving souls. We should, in the wisdom of Christ, make efforts to defeat their purposes, while, at the same time, we do not suffer them to call us from our great work. Truth is stronger than error. Righteousness will prevail over wrong.

The Lord's people are seeking to heal the breach which has been made in the law of God. "And they that shall be of thee shall build the old waste places: thou shalt raise up the foundations of many generations; and thou shalt be called, The repairer of the breach, The restorer of paths to dwell in. If thou turn away thy foot from the Sabbath, from doing thy pleasure on My holy day; and call the Sabbath a delight, the holy of the Lord, honorable; and shalt honor Him, not doing thine own ways, nor finding thine own pleasure, nor speaking thine own words: then shalt thou delight thyself in the Lord; and I will cause thee to ride upon the high places of the earth, and feed thee with the heritage of Jacob thy father: for the mouth of the Lord hath spoken it."

This disturbs the enemies of our faith, and every means is employed to hinder us in our work. And yet the broken-down wall is going steadily up. The world is being warned, and many are turning away from trampling under their feet the Sabbath of Jehovah. God is in this work, and man cannot stop it. Angels of God are working with the efforts of His faithful servants, and the work steadily advances. We shall meet with opposition of every description, as did the builders of the walls of Jerusalem; but if we watch and pray and work, as they did, God will fight our battles for us and give us precious victories.

Nehemiah "clave to the Lord, and departed not from following Him, but kept His commandments, which the Lord commanded Moses. And the Lord was with him." Messengers were sent repeatedly, soliciting a conference with Nehemiah; but he refused to meet them. Bold threats were made of what they proposed to do, and messengers were sent to harangue the people engaged in the work of building. These presented flattering inducements and promised the builders freedom from restraint, and wonderful privileges, if they would unite their interest with them and cease their work of building.

But the people were commanded not to engage in controversy with their enemies and to answer them not a word, that no advantage of words might be given them. Threatenings and ridicule were resorted to. They said: "Even that which they build, if a fox go up, he shall even break down their stone wall." Sanballat "was wroth, and took great indignation, and mocked the Jews." Nehemiah prayed: "Hear, O our God; for we are despised: and turn their reproach upon their own head."

"And I sent messengers unto them, saying, I am doing a great work, so that I cannot come down: why should the work cease, whilst I leave it, and come down to you? Yet they sent unto me four times after this sort; and I answered them after the same manner. Then sent Sanballat his servant unto me in like manner the fifth time with an open letter in his hand."

We shall receive the most fierce opposition from the Adventists who oppose the law of God. But, like the builders of the walls of Jerusalem, we should not be diverted and hindered from our work by reports, by messengers desiring discussion or controversy, or by intimidating threats, the publication of falsehoods, or any of the devices that Satan may instigate. Our answer should be: We are engaged in a great work, and we cannot come down. We shall sometimes be perplexed to know what course we should pursue to preserve the honor of the cause of God and to vindicate His truth.

The course of Nehemiah should have a strong bearing upon our minds as to the manner of meeting this kind of opponents. We should take all these things to the Lord in prayer, as Nehemiah made his supplication to God, while his own spirit was humbled. He clung to God with unwavering faith. This is the course that we should pursue. Time is too precious to be devoted by the servants of God to vindicating their character, blackened by those who hate the Sabbath of the Lord. We should move forward with unwavering confidence, believing that God will give His truth great and precious victories. In humility, meekness, and purity of life, relying upon Jesus, we should carry a convincing power with us that we have the truth.

We do not understand as is our privilege, the faith and

confidence that we may have in God, and the great blessings which faith will give us. An important work is before us. We are to obtain a moral fitness for heaven. Our words and our example are to tell upon the world. Angels of God are actively engaged in ministering to the children of God. Precious promises are upon record on condition of our obedience to God's requirements. Heaven is full of the richest of blessings, all waiting to be communicated to us. If we feel our need, and come to God in sincerity and in earnest faith, we shall be brought into close connection with heaven and shall be channels of light to the world.

The warning needs to be often sounded: "Be sober, be vigilant; because your adversary the devil, as a roaring lion, walketh about, seeking whom he may devour."

DATES OF FIRST PUBLICATION

The *Testimonies for the Church* in this volume were first published in Battle Creek, appearing in the following years: No. 21, 1872; No. 22, 1872; No. 23, 1873; No. 24, 1875; No. 25, 1875.

SCRIPTURAL INDEX

Genesis
2:16	50
3:4	72
5:5, 8	138
11:28	138
22:12	368
28:22	393
42:36	67

Exodus
20:2-6	296
20:3	340
20:12	232
23:20, 21	340
24:7	297
24:10	297, 343
32:1	340
32:4	296, 300
32:21-24	298
32:26	279
32:26-29	301
32:30-35	303

Leviticus
19:13-15	517

Numbers
16:3	345
16:5-11, 13, 14	347
16:16-18	348
16:19-30	349
16:24	354
16:34	357
16:36-38	350
16:41	351, 357
16:42-50	362
16:45	357
20:10	302
22:12	73

Deuteronomy
3:26	319
9:24	319
11:18, 19	565
16:16, 17	395
27:17-19	517

Joshua
6:18, 26	264
7:10-12	264, 520
7:12, 13	267
7:19-25	268

Judges
5:23	525

1 Samuel
15:22	57
15:23	357
17:45, 47	219

1 Kings
16:30-33	262
16:34	273
17:1	273
18:1	277
18:8, 11, 14	277
18:17, 18	278
18:21	280
18:22-26	281
18:26	282
18:27-29	282
18:30-39	283
18:39, 40	285
18:41	286
18:44	286
18:45, 46	287
19:3-9	289
19:4	290
19:5, 7, 9-14	291

2 Kings
18:6, 7	573

1 Chronicles
16:22	94
29:12	549

Nehemiah
4:1, 3, 4	574
4:7, 8	571
4:9	572
6:3	570
6:3-5	574

Job
3:3	262
16:2, 4, 5	508
29:15-17	518
36:18	549
38:3	509
42:6	509

Psalms
8:3 4	377
8:9; 9:1	377
24:1	549
37:5	482
37:23	466
40:10	543
50:10	390, 549
50:12	390
62:10	403
66:18	249
81:11, 12	73
105:15	94
126:5, 6	234

Proverbs
3:23	108
4:18	64
4:18, 19	377
10:9	108
11:4	549
11:30	422
16:32	183
22:6	131
23:5	549

Ecclesiastes
8:11	72
9:18	125
11:6	209

Isaiah
52:11	60
53:3	407
53:5	481
58:12-14	573

Jeremiah
2:13	474
10:23	482
17:9	253

Ezekiel
9	267
9:4	266, 267
9:5, 6	267
33:8, 9	195
44:23, 24	195

Joel
2:17	234

Zephaniah
1:12, 14-18	271
1:18	549

SCRIPTURAL INDEX

Haggai
2:8 549

Malachi
3:3, 4 541
3:8-10 .... 394, 510
3:8-12 409
3:11, 12 395
4:5, 6 62

Matthew
4:7 482
4:19 383
5:5 334
5:13 .... 248, 559
5:14 248
5:14-16 40
5:14, 16 .... 376, 404
5:20 193
6:19 549
6:19-21 478
6:24 .... 478, 547
6:28, 29 375
6:33 144
7:1-4 93
7:6 426
7:23 84
7:24, 25 414
9:2 .... 168, 169
9:5 169
10:8 408
11:28-30 335
11:29 .... 384, 448
12:30 328
13:27-30 113
16:24 .... 81, 388
18:3 .... 448, 529
18:7 452
18:18 .... 428, 450
20:22 48
20:28 229
22:21 384
24:37-39 163
24:48 255
25:21 .... 119, 145, 387
25:23 .... 247, 327, 402
25:24-27 386
25:26 145
25:30 387
25:34 525
25:34-46 174
25:35, 36 186
25:40-46 518
25:41 84
25:42 391
25:45 390
28:20 406

Mark
2:5 169

2:17 49
8:36, 37 250
16:15 .... 406, 408

Luke
3:4 279
4:18, 19 388
9:59-62 500
10:16 450
10:25-37 523
10:28 534
12:15 547
12:15-21 545
12:16-21 401
12:19-21 154
12:45 255
12:48 392
13:24 527
13:27 84
14:16-21 383
14:17-19 384
14:33 397
15:6 99
15:7 .... 99, 381
15:9, 10 100
15:21 102
15:29, 30, 32 103
16:2 .... 386, 390
16:10 556
16:11 405
16:13 547
17:12-19 179
17:26 472
17:28-30 163
18:37 32
19:10 49
19:13 386

John
4:14 84
4:29 217
5:30 107
5:39 81
11:9, 10 108
12:26 56
13:16 229
15:2, 5 387
15:7 209
15:8 528
15:12 .... 248, 529
16:13 529
16:33 115
17:20-23 361
17:21-23 446

Acts
9:6 .... 430, 433
9:11 .... 430 431
9:15, 17, 18 431

10:4 405
20:35 401

Romans
6:16-18 82
6:23 .... 365, 475
8:9 538
12:1 .... 83, 162
12:2 .... 157, 163
12:9, 10 361
12:10, 11 400
12:10-13 224
15:1-3 229

1 Corinthians
1:10 446
3:16,17 372
6:19,20 .... 43, 372, 390
10:9-11 353
10:12 445
10:31 84
13:5 397
15:31 221
15:33 125
16:1, 2 398
16:2 .... 389, 411, 412

2 Corinthians
4:5, 6 31
4:17,18 .... 98, 115
6:14-18 373
6:17 126
6:17, 18 566
6:17, 18; 7:1 245
8:7 392
9:7 413
10:5 83
11:9, 10 319

Galatians
5:22-26 236
6:2 526

Ephesians
3:17-19 213
5:21 361

Philippians
2:1-5 360
2:7 229
4:13 45

1 Thessalonians
5:22 239

1 Timothy
6:19 389

2 Timothy
1:8 67
2:12 531
4:2 .... 359, 360

Titus
2:11-14 52
2:14 538
2:15 359

Hebrews
10:32, 33 319
11:24-26 406
12:2 387
13:13 49

James
1:27 516
4:7 483

1 Peter
1:13-16 474
1:18, 19 390
2:9 201
2:11 51
3:3,4 .... 154, 376
4:14 531
5:5 360
5:8 575
5:8, 9 374

1 John
1:5-7 528
2:9 60
2:15 .... 477, 522

3:10 59
3:16 538
4:20, 21 60

Jude
9 220
22, 23 .... 108, 270

Revelation
2:2, 9, 13, 19 256
3:1, 8, 15 256
3:14-17 252
3:15 259
3:15-19 42
3:17 255
3:18 21 257
3:19 .... 256, 258, 259
3:20, 21 260
12:12 374

GENERAL INDEX

AARON, experiences and death of 293-303, 340
Ability, unsanctified 22
Abraham, faith of, tested in sacrifice of Isaac 368, 369
Abstemiousness, reward of 491
Abstinence from stimulants and narcotics our only safety 488
Achan, sin of 239, 264-272, 520
Activity, lack of, lessens resistance to disease 157
Adam, employment of 77, 153, 235
  given rule over Eve 483, 484
  not deceived by serpent 72
  sin of, by disobedience in one small thing 324, 542
    through transgression of God's law 72, 139, 161
  temptation of 139, 161, 372
  vital force of 138, 139
Adaptability, lack of, unfits workers 496
Advancement, steady, necessary 476
Adventists, first-day, opposition of 36-38, 571-575
Advice, manner of giving 534, 535
Affection, God calls for 364, 365
Affliction, purpose in 28
Aged, duty of, regarding wills 116, 117, 129, 130
Agony of Christ on way to Calvary 369
Agriculture in connection with schools 153, 155
Ahab, and Elijah 273-278
  apostasy of, unparalleled 276, 277
  establishes Baal worship 262, 263
Aim, higher than worldly gain 522
  necessity of having 540
Almsgiving a part of gospel religion 390
Amusements, harmful, dancing 172
  desire for, increased when brain is overworked 155
  desire for, increases by indulgence 222
  money squandered for 401
  Satan ever instituting 564
  squandering time in 222, 223
  world absorbed in 366, 367
  profitable, for children 137, 138
  for students 137, 138, 142
  test for 222, 223
  regulation of, necessary 137, 142
  See also Pleasure.
Anecdotes, trifling, told by ministers 233
Angel of light, Satan assumes form of 456
Angels, fallen, one third lost high estate 115
  See also Spiritualism.
  good, anguish of, in witnessing Christ's humiliation 369
  bring messages of mercy 64
  choose words for us to speak 363, 364
  destroying, brought down walls of Jericho 264
  excel in strength 280
  have sanctified sympathy for sinful mortals 539
  influence our actions to better course 363, 364
  labor untiringly for man in Christian warfare 575
  move on hearts of other nationalities 202
  present our offerings before God's throne 397

Angels, good— *continued*
  preserve us from unseen dangers 373
  record influence exerted, words, deportment 363
  repel temptation 526
  unite with human agencies in soul-saving work 381, 382
Animals have not reason 132
Antediluvians, intemperance of 162, 163
Apostasy in time of Ahab 273-286
Appetite, Christians not to please 239
  Christ's victory over 486, 489-491, 561
  conquer, lest temptation to indulge increase 491, 492
  control of, example of John Baptist 61, 62
    increases usefulness of ministers 486
    learned in childhood 567, 568
  denial of, Eden regained through 491, 492
  firm, only safety 561
  depraved, transmitted to offspring 140
  gratification of, led to destruction of Sodom and Gomorrah 162
  indulgence of, Adam fell by 486
    among antediluvians 162, 163
    at expense of right principles 485-487
    by Aaron's sons 295
    by ministers 486
    by parents and children 141, 488, 489, 562-568
    cause of disease and sickness 63, 140, 141, 171, 178
    cause of ruin of thousands 491, 492
    continued weakens digestive organs 487
    Eden lost through 491, 542
    enfeebles moral powers 164, 486, 490, 491
    for stimulants, influence of 487, 488
    for tobacco 561
    makes sin appear less sinful 164, 569
    makes truth of no effect 570
    makes us enemies of God 62, 63
    physical decline of race result of 139, 140, 486, 567, 568
    Satan controls mind and body through 562
    strengthens animal propensities 164, 563
  natural, preserves health and prolongs life 63
  of Israelites 339
  overcome through Christ's power 488
  power of will in control of 488
  Satan knew the liability of temptation through 478, 561
  solemn responsibility to overcome 486
  to be kept under control of reason and conscience 491, 492, 561
  unnatural, beware, restrain, deny 63, 475
    indulged, lowers brain power 51
  See also Diet; Eating; Food.
Applause, danger of 185
Approbation, love of 52, 225
Argument, ministers obscuring truth with 34-39
  not appropriate for spiritual food 228

Arguments, plain, pointed, do good 39
Ark in earthly sanctuary carried by priests only 345
Artificials, wearing of, for display 376
Associates, choice of, by youth 126
Association, degrading, influence upon youth 124-126
  worldly, corrupts morals 39
Atmosphere vitiated by evil companions 125
Audience, low spirits of minister when small 322
Avenues to soul, guard well 324, 476, 507

BAAL, power of, tested 274, 275, 279-286
  worship of among the Israelites 263
Babylon, ancient, gluttony and drunkenness in 162
Backsliding, sin of 365, 366
Balaam, solemn prayer of, nullified by covetous life 73
Bank, God's cause a never-failing 90
Baptism, temptations after 365, 366
Barrenness of soul caused by self-love 330, 331
Baths, benefits of frequent 69-71
Battle and march, Christian life is a 253
Battle Creek, calling workers to 57, 492
  contrasted with, Capernaum 200, 201
    the Jews 200
  difficulties at, taxing 503
  moving to 97
  neglect of health and dress reforms at 171
  responsibilities at 170, 197-201
  youth of, unconverted 199
Battle Creek church, trials in 104-111, 186-188
Battle Creek College, location of 197
Beauty, God the lover of 376
Beneficence, a blessing to man 405
  to others benefits us 382
Benevolence, example of Paul in 392, 393
  excites to healthful action 401, 405
  keeps heart open like flowing stream 393, 394, 412, 548
  makes one Christlike 382, 383, 547
  not increased by riches 403
  of Seventh-day Adventists 49
  overcomes covetousness 545, 547, 548
  plan of salvation begins and ends in 548
  sustains cause, relieves suffering and needy 548
  systematic, according as God has prospered 405
    brings prosperity in proportion 395
    corrects covetousness, avarice, selfishness, idolatry 547, 548
    counteracts selfishness 393
    example of Israelites in 546
    exercise of, is to be purely voluntary 413
    liberally sustains preachers and cause 389, 390, 510, 548
    not to be made systematic compulsion 396
    originated with God 405, 546
    plan of, is pleasing to God 412, 413
    spirituality of church largely dependent on 405

Benevolence— *continued*
  too rarely found 516
  world's, often shames that of Christian 524
  See also Giving; Liberality; Offerings; Sacrifice.
Benevolent acts close beside prayer 405
Bible study, benefits of 374
  daily, by workers in institutions 194
  necessary to witnessing to unbelievers 331, 334
Blessings, beneficence brings double 382
  of stewardship 387
Blind, angels minister to 516
  duty toward 511
  required to perfect Christian character 516
  taking advantage of, in business 513
Blindness, spiritual, Aaron's 300
  reason for 255
    rejection of testimonies cause of 266, 267
Blood, circulation of, improved by bathing 70, 71
Body, and mind, relation between 485, 486
  brain controls vital action of 69
  composed of what we eat 563
  duty regarding, care for and appreciate 63
  not our own 62-64
Book of life, Lamb's, contains names of repentant sinners 372
  Moses asks to be blotted from 303, 304
Books of record in heaven, search for names of youth in 370
  words and acts recorded in 312, 363, 364, 532
Brain, capital of body 69, 136
  overtaxation of, creates desire for exciting amusements 155
  overworked 149, 157
  system vitalized from, to resist disease 157
  See also Faculties; Intellect; Mental powers; Mind.
Brain power weakened by intemperance 50
Breadmaking, knowledge of, essential to health of family 156
Brotherhood, children of God are one 52
  humanity is one great 209
Burden bearers efficient and willing are few indeed 16
Burden for souls, minister's first qualification 557
Burdens, bearing, which others should bear 176, 177
  church should bear its own 10, 11
  disagreeable, expecting others to bear 495, 496
  heavy, sharing 9-17
  ministers who avoid 9-17, 558-560
  of Elder James White too many 9-17
  result of bearing too many 127
Business, ability to dispatch 499
  dishonesty in 246, 249, 250
  leaving, unsettled until death 117
  not to neglect study of 153
  perplexities of, cast upon God 458
  practical knowledge of 142
Butter, better to dispense with 19-21

CAKES, rich 21
Calf, golden 296-301, 340-342
California, cause in 504

Camp meetings, calls for means at 409-411, 510, 511
Cares, worldly, buried in 112, 381-385
Cause of God calls for more than means 57
   extension of, continual 210
   sustained largely by those in comparative poverty 403
   weakness of ministers brings reproach upon 241, 242
   See also Work of God.
Caution, loss through extreme 497-500
Censure, frequent, weakens faith, courage, self-confidence 92, 93
   of children without encouragement 532
Character, acquaintance with weak and strong points of, necessary 322
   and dispositions of Christians like Master's 58
   children's, built on sliding sand 143
   considered of less importance than dress 564
   defects in, disqualify for responsibilities 22
      God reveals, through varied circumstances 513, 514
      if not overcome, prevent place with Christ 305
      lack of reverence and due respect for others 305
      lack of spirituality and devotion 24
      strong, uncontrolled by Spirit, become curse 535
      to be corrected before too hardened 304
   deformed by, cherishing any sin 112
      improper education 22, 23, 26
      self-indulgence 30, 31
      superficial early training and education 143, 144
   developed by, difficulties, backsets, hardships, disappointments 494
      diversity of temporal blessings shared 391, 511, 547
      faithfulness in small matters 22
      home training 143-145
      strengthening weak points in 25, 26, 504-506
      useful and well-directed exercise 151
   development of, in youth 376
      family communities not best for 55
      now for future 331
      parents responsible for children's 144, 145
      required of blind 516
      symmetrical through eyesalve, white raiment, gold 535, 536
   distinguishes God's people 58
   God is weighing our 370
   good, traits of, stability, firmness, self-denial, self-control 143, 144, 535
   may deny God in 332
   models of, are liable to errors and mistakes 55
   perfection of, depends on grace and strength found in God 188
      slaves to appetite will fail in 491, 492
   tests of, helpless and poor persons 511
      little things 22
   See also Perfection; Sanctification.
Cheese objectionable 136
Children, amusement and work for, in useful labor 147-150

Children— *continued*
  open air necessary for proper development 137, 138
  are at no time in life excused from honoring parents 230-232, 294, 368
  characteristics of, are easily pleased and easily made unhappy 532
    are what parents' example and discipline make them 144
    love of change 147, 148
    sensitive, loving natures 532
    unaffected and natural are most attractive 529
  discipline of, neglect of, by Aaron resulted in sons' death 294, 295
    prosperity, order, harmony of church and nation depend on 294
  education of, not like training dumb animals 132
  gratification of appetite a cruel kindness to 141
  harmed by, being allowed to follow inclination instead of duty 26
    being left to think and act independently of parents 133
    close confinement to books and school 135-138, 142, 143, 148-150, 153, 155
    demoralizing associates in boarding schools 148, 149
    destroying will and individuality of 132-134
    indulgence of appetite 136, 141, 488, 489
    lack of employment and steadfast purpose 148, 149
    petting and indulgence 143, 295
    transferring means to unfaithful 121-123, 127, 129, 130
    transmitting evil tendencies and diseases 567
    unwise management and stern compulsion 134
  home training of, in eating to live, not living to eat 567
    in education of appetites 562, 567
    in expecting and overcoming temptations, difficulties, dangers 144
    in self-control, self-denial 143, 562, 563, 567
    in self-denial and giving to missions 412
    to respect experienced judgment 133
  See also Home training.
  improperly disciplined, are deficient in moral energy and individual responsibility 132
    are slaves to appetite 564
    at home rebel against school and church discipline 294
    become a living curse to world and self 564
    become moral wrecks 568
    become powerless to resist temptation 364
    become selfish, exacting, disobedient, unthankful, unholy 141
    bring dishonor and bitterness to parents 141
    entire lifetime of many, proves a failure 148
    have weak and impulsive characters 364
    unfitted for usefulness to society 26
  in babyhood, greatest attention to be given to physical constitution of 143
    parents should be only teachers of 137, 143

influence of elder sister upon 337
ingratitude in 149
needs of, discipline of minds 25, 26
  proper education 142
  words and looks of encouragement and sympathy 148
  properly disciplined, habits and principles of, are defense against temptation 144, 567
  have well-developed characters 363
  mean less disease and moral corruption 567
  thousands of, die because of parents' and teachers' ignorance 136, 137
See also Parents.
Christ Jesus, youth and early manhood of, perfect example for all 566
Christ Jesus, second year of public ministry of, parable of rich fool 545
  parable of wheat and tares 113-116
  teaches from boat, parable of sower and seed 111-113
Christ Jesus, third year of public ministry of, parable of great supper 383
  parables of lost sheep, coin, son 99-104
Christ Jesus, last Passover week of, parable of five talents 386, 387
Christ Jesus, offices, titles, and appellations of, Angel 339, 342
  Cornerstone 387
  Example 371
  Friend of sinners 433
  Leader 339, 356
  Man of Sorrows, 416
  Pattern 387
Christ Jesus, as man, visage marred with sorrow and anguish 380
  came to make men happy 540
  condescension of 190, 208
  characteristics of 164
  divinity and humanity united 566
  on Mount Sinai 343
  our pattern in sufferings and privations 107
  picture of, in word, we to be compared with 538
  resisted continually Satan's attacks 480
Christian experience, a battle and march daily 253
Christians, control of passion requisite in 570
  true, always cheerful and confident 377
See also Church; Church Members.
Church, authority of, heaven ratifies 428, 433
  individual judgment subject to 492, 493
  voice of God 417
  channel between God and man 414
  highest power under heaven bestowed upon 450, 451
  Laodicean message applicable to now 259, 260
  members to be soul winners 61
  order necessary in 445
  purging, urgent need of 476, 477
  relatives in, dwarf development 53-56
  reproof necessary to 359
  responsibilities of, to care for widows, orphans 517

Church— *continued*
  to reprove sin in members 265-270
  to save perishing sinners 381
  shortcomings and failures of, backsliding into worldliness 474-477
    indolence and spiritual sloth 95
    lack of love and faith 186-188
  trials, cause of 104-111
    danger of acting prematurely in 113-116
    proper procedure in 428
    unity in 445
    dependent on home discipline 294
    testimonies to maintain 361
  See also People of God.
Circumstances, ascribing lack of success to 496, 497
  masters of, how to become 47, 505
  seldom twice alike 541
Cleansing, great need of, in church 476
Clothing, debilitating effect of too much 74
  See also Dress.
Combativeness, ministers not to be lovers of 215
  See also Debate.
Commandment keepers, Satan's power will increase against 571
  those who are compassionate to ready are 512
  See also Sabbathkeepers.
Compassion, for afflicted and needy 524
  physicians to exercise Christlike 179
  See also Sympathy.
Concentration upon one idea taxes mind 34, 35

Condiments, children permitted to eat 136
Confession, delaying, until too late 270-272, 354-356
  vindicating cause of God 271
  See also Repentance.
Confidence and cheerfulness mark true Christian 377
Confinement, close, in school injurious 135-138
Conformity to world gaining ground 51
  See also World, harmony with.
Conscience, enlightened, appetite under control of 491
Consecration, entire, what is involved in 301
Constitution, value of a sound physical 151
Conversation, corrupt, results of 125
  frivolous, ministers engaging in, 228, 233, 238, 473, 474
  jesting and joking, by young 222
    denying Lord by 332
  parents to set example in 246
  self the theme of 235
  vain and empty 189
  See also Words.
Conversion, transformation through 552
Cooking, requires intelligence and experience 158
  to be taught to students 156
Co-operation called for 16
Corruption, moral, indulgence of appetite increases 567, 568
  of youth in schools 148, 149
Counsel, too exalted to receive 305
  with brethren by workers 66
  young ministers should take, of pioneers 317
  See also Judgment, individual.

Countenance a mirror 523
Courtesy, and kindness 323
　true happiness depends upon 539
　See also Kindness.
Courtship, among those in institutions 191
　sentimental, to be avoided 45
　See also Marriage; Sentimentalism.
Covenant, old, tables broken 298
Covetousness, how to get free from 545
　in the church 127, 130
　is idolatry 130, 201, 387, 513
　love of Christ crowded out by 382-384
　many sink into darkness because of 269
　of Achan 264, 268
　starved by continual giving 548
　warning against 393
Cowardice is not fighting foe but sharing spoils 316
Co-workers, discouragement caused by disloyalty of 17, 18
Crime, judgments of God because of 561
Crisis, promptness in meeting 497-500, 505
Criterion, man not to be 523
Criticism among church members 92, 523
　cold, no help to needy souls 186
　of, colaborers 552
　leading men 89, 92, 94, 261, 262, 292, 293, 312-325
Crocheting in relation to domestic work 151
Cross of Christ, beholding, leads to self-sacrifice 382
　God's love for man revealed by 369
Cross bearing our portion 481
Crowns, stars in, represent souls saved 95

Culture, measured by intellect and moral worth 154
　mental, how obtained 159
　importance of 26, 32, 33, 144-148
　mental and physical, to be combined 157
　See also Education; Refinement.
Custom, sacrificing health of children for 136

DALLYING on Satan's ground 483
Dancing at popular health institutions 172
Darkness, spiritual, how overcome 505
　terrible, blinding people to God's judgments 276
Daughters, elder assist in educating younger 337
　husbands of, to be confided in 130
　indulged, warning to 329-338
　should obtain knowledge of useful labor 150, 151
　spending precious hours in sleep 152
David slays Goliath 218, 219
Daydreaming 329-338
Debate, love of, unfits ministers 216
Debating, ministers unreliable 217
　young ministers show passion for 212, 213, 220, 424, 485
　See also Discussions.
Debt on, institutions, avoided 175
　Health Institute 173
Deception, concerning, Christian experience 253, 259
　God's guidance 446, 447
　God's people liable to fall into 353
　power of, illustrated by Korah 351

Deceptions, Satan disturbed at our knowledge of 572
Decision, lack of, to stand on side of right or wrong 272
Decision and promptness in workers 499
Deeds, not profession, count in end 525
Degeneracy, of race 138-141
    indulgence of appetite chiefly responsible for 486-488
    rapid, unbalanced education cause of 153
    transmitted as a legacy 567
Delays, are virtually defeats 500
    long, tire angels 497
Denial of Christ, how accomplished 332
Denominations, union among, growing sentiment in favor of 572
Dependence, Elijah's lack of 288-292
    ministers', out of pulpit 27
Depravity, cause of, in lack of home training 563, 564
Despondency, assails those impelled to do special work 293
    caused by, lack of appreciation 292
        living for self 542
        overwork 502
        reviewing past failures 60
    Elder James White erred in giving way to 261, 262, 292, 293
    leading to inactivity, not wanted 526
Destiny, eternal, now being decided 363
Development, harmonious, of physical, mental, and spiritual 33-35
    unbalanced, consequences of 33-35

Diet, abstemious, gives mental and moral vigor 491
    erroneous, great variety at one meal 563
    Israelites, murmurings of, over fleshless 171, 172
    liquid, not strengthening 74
    of children relating to health 136
    prepared to educate drunkards 563
    reform in, moderate better than extreme 21
    See also Appetite; Eating; Food; Indulgence.
Diet and exercise 489-492
Digestion promoted by bathing 70, 71
Dignity, human, recognized by Christ 527, 531
    of labor to be recognized 156-159
    should appear in home management 287, 288
    valueless without godliness 553
Discernment blunted through wrong course 242
Discipleship, self-denial essential condition of 388
Discipline 132, 133
    family, Aaron's lack of 294, 295
    extremes in 106
    See also Rules.
Discontent with surroundings and circumstances 334, 335
Discourses, injured by apologies and preliminaries 235
    of Christ, examples for speakers 214, 215
    on practical subjects 228, 237, 257
    should, close while interest is greatest 419
    not be merely theoretical 257, 313-315

See also Preaching; Sermons.

Discrimination perverted through influence of companion 105

Discussions, advocates of truth not to seek 213-220, 424-427
  avoid, whenever possible 424
  danger in holding 570-575
  detrimental to spirituality 215
  effect of 212-221
  not to engage in at sanitariums 166, 167
  with spiritualists always to be avoided 485
  See also Debating.

Disease, avoided if light were followed 171, 172
  man has withstood, six thousand years 138, 139
  mind and will an aid in combating 157, 158
  of mind and heart prevails everywhere 182-184
  responsibility for, in creating perverted appetite 63
  walking as cure for 78
  See also Sickness.

Domestic duties, unhappiness caused by ignorance of 156
  no employment more important than 158

Doubts, occasion for, not removed 255
  pious, cautiously dropped 259

Dress, and parties are time robbers 562-565
  display of, betrays vanity and weakness 376
    ceases when burden for souls is felt 370
    in wearing artificials, gold, pearls, costly array 366, 367, 376
    in wearing feathers on hats 379
    Jesus' caution against 375
    neglecting inward adorning through 29, 30
    physical, mental, moral health sacrificed for 136
    wasting time in 144, 145, 189
    whole heart and mind absorbed in love of 360
  proper, has grace, beauty, appropriateness, and simplicity 375, 376
  reform, physical and moral purpose of 171
  self-denial in, a part of our Christian duty 366
  See also Clothing.

Dressmaking, knowledge of, essential for girls 156

Drinks, alcoholic, touch not, taste not, handle not 488

Drought, Elijah prays for 263

Drugs, poison the bones and the blood 454

Dunces, educated 152, 159

Duty, deal only with present 333
  how determined 72-74
  lack of sense of personal, toward Lord's poor 512
  our first, obedience to God's laws, including health laws 164
  to fellow men 521-527
  to reprove sin 265-269
  to unfortunate 511-521
  twin sisters of, kindness, love 108, 195

Duties, practical, children to be educated in 150
  results of ignorance of 152
  smallest, fit for greater trusts 330, 331
  unpleasant, shifting of, upon others 503

Dyspeptics, children made, at early age 489
  heart sickness makes many 184

EASE evil fruit of for children 232
Eating, and drinking, excess in, sign of Christ's coming 164
    knowledge must be gained in healthful 164
    we to be examples in 490, 491
  improper, between meals, 136, 139, 489, 564
  takes heavy toll of children 136
  too frequent 563
  See also Appetite; Diet; Food; Indulgence.
Economy, habits of, to be cultivated 119
  in personal expenditure 401
  lack of, because of defective education 30
Editors, importance of temperance and physical exercise for 487
Education, children in great need of proper, to be useful 142
  choose practical, if it must be one-sided 156
  Christian teacher interested in student's physical, mental, moral, and spiritual 135
  defective, general intemperance and depravity testify of 564
  for gospel service 160
  health not to be sacrificed to obtain 150
  in domestic duties 147, 150
  mistakes in, close confinement to books and school 135-138, 153, 155
    concentrating upon many studies and letting soul languish 223-224
    dealing with abstract and theoretical only 221
    sending children to school while too young 137, 142, 143
    students having too much leisure time 148-150
  most advantageous if knowledge of labor and science is combined 152-159
  object of true, not to be lost sight of 223, 224
    fitting for service of God and our fellow men 407
    to enable use of God-given powers to God's glory 160
  of children affects entire business career and religious experience 131, 148
    not like training of dumb animals 132
    physical, mental, moral, and religious, must have attention 132
  of youth, daily, systematic labor a part of 158, 159
    early, demands greatest attention to physical constitution 143
    early, generally shapes character for life 131, 135
    in sciences and preservation of health 141, 142
    mostly a failure because not properly balanced 153
    to call forth high and noble powers of mind 131
  one-sided, unfits minister 557
  street, acquired through indolence 151
  true higher, disciplines mind and develops its powers 160
    is harmonious development of physical, mental, spiritual powers 131, 132
  See also Culture; Refinement; Schools.

Efficiency, men of, needed in God's work 495, 496
  result of self-denial 490, 491
Effort, faithful, results of 173-176
  rewards for 78
  Jesus, helps in every earnest 550
  persevering, eternal life is worth 338
Efforts, earnest, or be lost 240, 550
  souls saved through 247
Eleazar successor of Aaron 293
Electric power of brain vitalizes system 157
Electricity a vital power 138, 139
Elijah, history of 261-263, 273-296
  spirit and power of 62
Employment, Adam needed 153, 235
  for exercise of muscles 159
  safeguards against evil habits 151, 158, 159
  sedentary, sought by many 158
  See also Labor, physical.
Enemies of Nehemiah 570-574
Enmity, law of God occasion of, toward Sabbathkeepers 573-575
Enoch, faith of, not without constant conflict 543
Erring, duty toward 93-111, 113-115, 186-188, 229
  unwise sympathy for the 258, 267, 313, 325, 328, 329, 341, 342, 350
Error, how to deal with 37
Eve, position of, lowered after Fall 483, 484
Evidence, faith based on, not perfect knowledge 258
Evidences, neglect of, has fatal results to rebellious Israelites 356
Evilspeaking, denying Lord by 332
Exaltation, young ministers to guard against 320
Example, Christ's, for success in soul winning 233
  in, continual resistance of Satan's attacks 480
  manual labor 566
Excess in eating, drinking, and dressing a sign of end 163, 164
Excitability of temperament 515, 516
Excitement, almost uncontrollable desire for 155
Exclusiveness, family 521, 534-536
Exercise, improves circulation 490
  in domestic duties promotes health 75-77
  lack of, evil results of 76, 78, 138, 158, 490
  makes action of heart more perfect 490
  mind acquires strength and knowledge by 77
  most essential for preservation of health 489, 490
  needed by, children and youth 137, 138
    feeble and indolent out of doors 78
    invalids 76
    ministers 211, 309, 310, 489, 490
    students 137, 138, 142, 148-160, 489, 490
    teachers 489, 490
    those of sedentary and literary habits 157, 490
    young men in active labor 151
    young women and girls in household work 151, 152, 158

Exercise— *continued*
- of, mind and muscle to be proportionate 77, 78, 138, 310
- will needed by imaginary sick 76
- outdoor, is best 78
- promotes health 158
- should be systematized to strengthen debilitated organs 76
- to be combined with mental 490
- variety of, calls into use all body muscles 78
- walking, most beneficial 75, 76, 78
- *See also* Labor, physical; Work, physical.

Experience, education strengthened by 494
- false, many remain invalids through relying upon 69
- ministers failed to obtain, designed of God to strengthen 14
- necessity of health reform shown by 537
- obtained through perplexities and trials 537
- personal, feasibility of referring to 318
- unreliable if influenced by faulty imagination 67-69
- varied, saves from one-sidedness 494

Exposure, unwise, brought sickness 19

Extension, constant, of gospel work 210
- *See also* Third angels message.

Extravagance in dress, are we guilty of? 366

Extremes, in health reform, harm of, to others 20
- some ever ready to go to 315
- to be avoided 106, 506

Eyeservants 192

Ezekiel describes the sealing work 266, 267

FACULTIES, accountable to God for 32
- all should be well developed 26, 34, 132
- mental, dormant from lack of use 32
- *See also* Brain; Intellect; Mental powers; Mind.

Faith, a golden treasure greatly wanting among God's people 255
- Elijah grasps promises of heaven by 274, 275, 286, 287
- Enoch by faith walked with God 543
- and love, lack of, great sin 475
- hold fast to, in perplexities 537
- hope, love, great moral powers of soul 187
- physicians to be men of 178
- source of 258
- trials develop strong 67, 505
- works combined with 526

Faithfulness, in little things fits for greater 22, 46
- of Abraham in surrendering son 368

Falsehood, dies under silent contempt 37
- of enemies, how to meet 570-575

Familiarity with sin, results of 476

Families, of ministers 556
- self-caring 521

Family community dwarfs mental and spiritual strength 55, 56

Family, exclusiveness 534-544
- selfishness 521
- *See also* Home.

Fanaticism, in Maine 313
  strenuous labors to get away from 315
Fancywork, doing, rather than healthful physical labor 151
Fashion, Christian women not satisfied with 484
  health and lives of children sacrificed to 136
  many Sabbathkeepers wedded to 51
  Satan invents, to cause mothers to neglect children 564
Father, humiliated prodigal felt need of 101
  See also Home; Husband; Parents.
Fathers and mothers needed in Israel 198
Faultfinding, by parents in home 531, 532
  recorded by angel along with defects of faultfinder 312
  Spirit cannot abide in heart with 531, 532
  with, aged workers displeases God 320, 321
    Brother and Sister White and leaders 312, 313
Faults, in character, important to correct 104
  pointing to others', to divert attention from own 312
Feathers on hats 379
Feelings, dwelling upon 108
  God requires tender, toward afflicted 519
  not a safe guide 68-79, 112, 506
Fellow men, duty toward 521-544
Fidelity tested by God 29
Firmness, for truth and right 302, 303, 327
  men of, needed in God's work 496
  not hardheartedness 315
  See also Steadfastness.
Flattery, danger of, to children 143
  harmful to students 224-226
  Korah won people by 345, 349
  ruins ministers 185, 186, 236, 552
  true friendship void of 226
Flesh food, clamor of Israelites for 171, 172
  injures physical health 136
  irritates and excites nerves 487
  positive testimony against 21
Food, beneficial, simple, healthful 568
  bountiful variety of, given to man 50
  good, bodies built up from 563
  harmful, animal 563
    develops habits of intemperance 563, 568, 569
    poor quality does not give vigor 74, 563
    stimulating 487, 488
    too much liquid 74
  largely controls physical and moral health 568
  original, for man 50
  preparation of, mothers to study 568
  results of improper 563
  See also Appetite; Diet; Eating; Indulgence.
Force, need for stimulation by Jesus' life-giving 47
Foresight, men of quick, needed 498
Forgetfulness, a sin 12
  need of, in regard to failures of past 97, 98
Forgiveness, lingers for Hebrews 356
  spirit of, prerequisite to being forgiven 95
  taught in Lord's Prayer 95
French, publications in 211

Friendship true void of flattery 226
  with conscientious persons 24
  with world, dangers of 41-43
Furnace, fiery 47

GAIN, deviating from strict integrity for 249
  love of, a ruling passion in last days 382
General Conference, authority of 492, 493
Gentleness a gem of great value 536
Girls, household labor a safeguard for 152
  vain and proud 29
Giving, a blessing in 381
  beyond their ability 410
  calls for, increasing 389
  continual, starves covetousness to death 548
  co-operating with God by 390, 391
  systematic, to keep hearts tender 393, 412, 546-548
  weekly 548
  See also Benevolence; Liberality; Offerings; Sacrifice.
Glory, immortal, reward of obedient 365
  of redeemed terrifies sinful men 355
Godliness, real, is diffusive and communicative 543
Gold, wearing of 366, 376
Goliath 218, 219
Grace, growing in 541, 542
  prayer for daily supply of 333
Gratitude of healed leper 179, 180
Guardians, responsibility of 131
Guidance, deception regarding source of 440, 441

HABITS, corrupt, acquired at school 148, 149
  determine present and future destinies 489
  formation of right, difficult for children because of transmitted tendencies 567
  formed in youth are seldom essentially changed 143
  lifelong, are difficult to overcome 567
  of, self-indulgence formed in childhood 563, 564
    temperance to be cultivated 489, 490
  right physical, make education possible without sacrifice of health 138
  strictly temperate, combined with exercise preserve vigor 486, 487
    eternal destiny depends upon 489
  wrong physical, Christ began His work by reforming 486
Hand compared to health reform 62
Happiness, looking upon, as sin is not genuine religion 334
  marred by, being wrapped up in own interests 330, 331
    brooding over unhappy experiences 330, 331
    looking for some great work to do 79
  meekness makes its own songs of 335
  not found in selfishly searching for greater work 330, 331, 337
  obtained by, cheerful performance of daily tasks 330
    faithfulness in little things 79-81
    humble cross bearing 329, 330
    properly treating God-given light 363

simplicity of character and lowliness of heart 476
studying to make others happy 79
true meekness 81, 335
unselfish ministry to others 330, 539
useful work 77
See also Joy.
Hardships, endured by Jesus every day 372
experience in, worth more than lands or gold 318
Healing, by Christ, of lepers 179, 180
of paralytics 168, 169
gives opportunity to redeem past 28
Health, abuse of, by ministers in overeating 310
is a terrible sin 150
affected by condition of mind 67-69, 184
efficiency of labor depends on worker's 13
good bread is essential to 156
greatest treasure of mortals 150
heaven is all 172
impaired through, close confinement at school 137, 138
indulgence of appetite 486
lack of physical exercise 150, 151
remaining too much indoors 150
sinful indulgences 165
laws of, disregard of, invites disease 164
included in laws of God 165
of body and mind, education to be obtained without sacrificing 137, 138
religion of Bible is not detrimental to 172

of ministers, ordinarily need not fail 309
preservation of, by knowing how to eat, drink, and dress 164
parents and teachers to seek, of children 136
physical exercise in open air is essential to 489, 490
required by God 13
should be taught to students 141, 142
principles, wisdom in teaching of 20, 21
prompted by, frequent bathing 70, 71
uniting physical with mental labor 157
useful physical labor 78, 155, 158
reform, angel Gabriel gave discourse on 62
disregarded, leads to disregard of other duties and to guilt before God 51, 62, 63
God's love and pity cause light to shine on 161
hand compared to 62
neglect of, by Battle Creek church 171
our churches retrograding on 50, 569
stir public mind on 62
that we may escape many dangers 561
to aid in preparation for Christ's coming 161-165
to aid in sanctification 570
to be kept prominent from religious standpoint 168, 170
to be progressive 20, 21
to show sin of violating laws of being 161
restoration by outdoor life and useful exercise 78

Health Institute at Battle Creek, donations and investments for 173
   financial embarrassment of 173-175
   great object of, to teach how to live 165-170
   physicians and helpers at 175-184
   promise of prosperity for 175
   religious discussions to be avoided at 166, 167
Health Reformer, aided Health Institute 175, 176
   extreme views urged in 19, 20
Heart sickness, effect of, on physical health 184
Heaven, all health 172
   divine love makes words and works savor of 65
   home on earth symbol of 539
   laying up treasure in 120
   preparation for, inward adorning of meek and quiet spirit 566
   pure, elevated character 526
   put means into bank of 83
Hereditary tendencies make training more difficult 567
Heredity, disease, suffering, and mortality through 140, 141
Hesitancy more dangerous than haste 497, 498
High Priest in heaven typified by Moses 357, 358
History of the Sabbath, undue delay in publishing 38, 39
Holy Spirit, fighting, by opposing testimony 200, 201
   influence of, the best restorative 172
Home, made happy by, cheerfulness, courtesy, love 539
   faithfulness in home duties 79-81
   seeking happiness of others 79
   marred by, needless repining and unhappy discontent 222, 330
   not expressing love and sympathy 527-529
   parents' being irritable and faultfinding 531-533
   women's unconcern regarding responsibilities of 330, 331
   symbolic of heaven 539
   temperance principles to be carried out in 562, 563, 569, 570
   training, importance of 141
   youths' highest duty is to make, happy 80, 222
   See also Children, home training of.
Honesty in business, lack of 246, 249, 250
Hospitality, Christian duty 308
House-to-house work more important than preaching 558, 559
Housework, advantage and safeguard for girls 152, 153
   no employment more important than 158
Humanity, more interest needed for 522
Humiliation of Christ 371-380
Humility, acquired by, confessing our faults 211
   remembering how we appear in sight of God and others 211
   example of, Christ in coming to earth 566, 567
   Elijah 287, 288
   God desires individual seeking for 527
   lack of, grows with increase of success 305

strength of God's children is in 307, 476
  to be cultivated by workers 106, 107, 307
  See also Meekness.
Humility and simplicity, getting above 307
Hundred and forty-four thousand feel wrongs in church 266
Husband, duty of, to counsel with wife 244
  God's word gives preference to judgment of 484
  mistakes of, in assuming arbitrary authority 106, 245
    in placing too implicit confidence in wife's judgment 105, 106
  See also Fathers; Home; Parents; Wife.

IDEA, some ministers are men of one 34, 35
Idleness, indulged daughters love and enjoy 151
  See also Inactivity; Indolence.
Idolatry among, inhabitants of Jericho 264
  professed Christians 543
Idols, few aware of having darling 543
Ignorance, humility and spirituality not increased by 160
  no excuse now for transgression of physical law 162
  results in, death of children 136
    disease 178
Imagination, influence of, on health 152
  power of 67-79
Imbeciles, no record of, in Genesis 138
Impatience, causes parents to lose control of children 532, 533
  struggle of blind man with 515
Impurities of body, liver cleanses blood of 490
  physical exercise aids throwing off of 490
Inactivity, and indolence unfit for real life 152
  curse of Meroz pronounced upon 525
  greatest curse that ever came upon youth 151
  poverty a blessing if it saves from 151
Income of Israelites, not less than a third devoted to God 395
Indecision, loss through 497-500
  of Israel in Elijah's days 280, 281
Independence, proper, men of, are needed 496, 497
  selfish, in relation to General Conference 492
    Korah's and Israelites' contention for 346, 347, 360
    rebels at reproof and exhortation 360
Indifference in time of crisis a crime 281
Individuality, need not be sacrificed 360
  of children to be preserved 132
Indolence unfits for real life 152
  See also Idleness; Inactivity.
Indolent young men frequently obtain street education 151
Indulgence, of appetite, Eden lost through 491
  makes Satan's control easier 569
  temptations for, grow more powerful near close of time 492
  leads to violation of Ten Commandments 51

Indulgence— *continued*
  parental, makes children selfish, corrupt, inefficient 46, 151
  See also Appetite; Eating; Diet; Food; Self-Indulgence.
Industries to be taught in our schools 153
Infants affected by sins of parents 140
Influence, accountability for 363
  every step of our course leaves some 542
  exerted for good or evil 526
  of, Aaron on side of wrong 299
    countenance 523
    elder members of family 337
    laborers decides destiny of souls 60
    students upon one another 362-367
    those who lack principle 24
  possessed by all 248, 529
  recorded in books of heaven 363, 364
  unconscious 246, 363, 364
Institutions, deportment of workers in 191, 192
Instruction to be varied 131
Insult to God when His appointed instrumentalities are despised 355
Integrity, habits of, acquired by faithfulness in little things 22-25
Intellect, continual study weakens 137, 142, 143
  cultivated, a great treasure 539
  enfeebled by improper eating 136 sound body required for sound 152
  strengthened by Bible study 374
  See also Brain; Mind; Mental powers.
Intemperance, our tables the foundation of 563
  caused by wrong habits of eating 487-489, 568
  in eating and drinking, beclouds and enfeebles mind 310, 311
  cause of inefficiency 491
  effects of 50, 51, 487
  source of degeneracy 486
  in study 490, 491
  sign of end 163
  wastes energy and weakens moral power 486
  See also Temperance.
Intercession, Moses held back arm of vengeance by 358
Interest, religious, allowed to sink 231
  killed by denunciatory spirit 247
  moderate and gradual, better 218
  selfish, in professed Christians 514
Invalids, many made, by overstudy and indoor life 149, 150
Investigation, habits of, to be encouraged 142
Iowa, 109-111
Irritants in diet, effect of 563
Isaac a symbol of Christ 369
Israel, Christ leader of 339, 342
  murmurings of 296, 339-357
  why forbidden to mingle with other nations 263

JERICHO, destruction of 264, 269
  wealth and wickedness of 264
Jerusalem, men with slaughter weapons go through 266, 267
  rebuilding walls of, lesson from 570-575
Jesting and joking by young 222
Jewelry, wearing of 366, 367

Jews, astonishment and reproach to world 200
Jezebel, character of 262
  destroys prophets of God 276
  Elijah flees from 261
  prophets of 274, 275, 279
Job, affliction of, lesson in 262
  benevolence of, to friends 530
  integrity of 311
  justifies himself before reprover 518
John the Baptist, lessons from life of 61-63
Joseph and Mary, simple occupation of 372
Joshua, grief of, in view of Israel's sin 264
  zealous to search out sin 267, 268
Joy of Christ, over souls 387
  over returned prodigal 104
  See also Happiness.
Joy of the Lord 387
Judgment, executive, souls will condemn unfaithful minister in 243
  test in 518
  individual, correct ideas of 360
  of God, why visited upon men 350-352
Justice in small matters important 25

KINDNESS, and duty twin sisters 108
  in care of sick 170
  See also Courtesy.
Knowledge of books not most essential 553
Korah, Dathan, Abiram, experience of, a warning 353, 362
  honors bestowed on 343
  insidious methods of 344, 345
  rebellion of 339-362

LABOR, evangelistic, in new fields 218
  just begun when souls are convicted of truth 228
Labor, aid to purity 151
  benefits of, to all 142, 152
  to young 223
  blessing of 155
  Christ's example in 566
  excess of, harmful 157
  for students 150, 151, 156, 159
  not degrading 156-159
  physical and mental, to be combined 152-159, 235, 486
  See also Employment; Exercise;
  Work, physical.
Laborers, evangelistic, in new fields, increase in knowledge 48
Lady, false ideas regarding what constitutes a 152
Languages help in missionary work 204
Laodicean message, addressed to believers, in carnal security 42, 252, 259
  in honest self-deception 253-257
  applies to God's people at this time 252
  to cause a shaking followed by loud cry 259
Law, of God, causes enmity between God's people and world 573-575
  crucified like Christ 214
  hated by Satan's agents 571
  mirror 116
  tables of, broken by Moses 298, 301, 341
  of being, as much sin to violate, as to break Ten Commandments 161

Law— *continued*
- one may enjoy fruit, grain, vegetables, without violence to 50
- perverted appetite prepares for violation of 63
- of health and life, first business of parents to understand 568
- of nature, making plain, accompanies work of third angel's message 161
- obedience to, all our enjoyment traced to 161
- obedience to, God requires 63
- violation of, all our suffering may be traced to 161
- violation of, impossible without violation of law of God 51, 161
- *See also* Natural law.
- physical, children not educated to conform to 141
- violation of, invites disease, suffering, debility, death 139

Leader, Aaron's deficiency as 296
- of Israel, Christ, the invisible 356

Leaders, bad, partial 23, 24
- Satan's plan to drive, from duty 343
- wrong attitude toward, despising and rejecting 355
- distrust and suspicion of 343

Leadership, of Israel by Moses 300
- right and wrong ideas concerning 492-505

Legacy, a knowledge of useful labor the best 399

Lepers, cleansing of, lessons from 179, 180

Lessons for young children from book of nature only 137

Levite and priest, significance of 512

Levites had no part in worshiping golden calf 345

Liberality, blessings attending 381-383
- occasional, not sufficient 393, 394, 412, 413, 548
- *See also* Benevolence; Giving; Offerings; Sacrifice.

Licentiousness, among professed believers 475
- in worldly schools 149
- makes many captives 473
- special sin of the age 561

Life, artificial, in our age as in Christ's 144
- continual conflict to Christian 453
- daily, acts of self-denial make blessing 539, 540
- eternal, reward of obedient 365
- length of decline in after Flood, from indulgence 138-140
- practical, children spoiled for 143
- present, preparation for life above 540
- sacrificed for education 149

Light, and darkness, no union of 248
- spiritual, acceptance of, gives experience of inestimable value 64, 65
- darkness from rejection of 65
- Israel incurred great guilt by rejecting 171, 172
- on health reform rejected brings guilt and sickness 171, 172
- our duty to improve, as prophets did 65
- rejection of today greater sin than that of Sodom and Gomorrah 380

Lightness, this is no time for 474

Liquor, snuff, spices 21, 136, 488, 489
　spirituous 561, 562
Liver, burdened by overeating 490
Livery of heaven, Satan arrayed in 456
Logical reasoning scarce 142, 143
Love, all need 530
　broad as the world 530
　daily cultivate precious plant of 530, 532, 535, 539
　effects of, as sunshine to heart of child 532
　　binds children to hearts of parents 532
　　brings nearer to standard of perfect holiness 188
　　illuminates countenance and subdues voice 534
　express in home by deed and word 539, 540
　for brethren 186, 187, 529, 530
　lacking 95, 187
　for children, parents to manifest 131, 531, 532
　for God, purest and most elevated, manifested in soul winning 187
　for Jesus, service for Him is proof of 537
　God is 528
　golden chain binding believers together and to God 187
　increased by exercise 527
　is key that opens hearts 535
　lack of, for destitute, suffering, needy 522-524
　　in home 527-534
　　makes minister's labor unproductive of good 187
　of Christ winning, softening, melting 535
　　revealed in character makes us lights of world 538
　of God, infinite, 369
　　demonstrated to Abraham 368, 369
　　selfishness separates from 534
　　softening, melting 534
　　subdues and softens stiffness and cold reserve 530
　of world, blinds perceptions and hardens heart 533
　　family shut up to itself and 537
　　Satan tempted Christ and tempts followers with 377, 378
　　so great there is none to spare for Jesus 535
　　takes entire control of being 544
　twin sister of duty 195
　unselfish, knows no limit of service 530
　whoso dwells in God dwells in 528

MAGNET points north, so claims of religion point to God 45
Mammon in exchange for God 479
Manna food provided for Israel 340
Manners, abruptness in 242
Manufacturing establishments connected with schools 153-155
Marcus Lichtenstein directed by God to Battle Creek 205, 206
Marriage, early, not to be encouraged 44
　religion to dictate and guide in 47
　with unbelievers 262
Means, accountable to God for 82, 117, 118
　God is not dependent upon man for 390

Means— *continued*
　large amount of surplus, among us 173, 208
　misuse of, delaying right disposal of until death 116, 117
　　expending in display and self-indulgence 83, 401
　　withholding from cause 208
　no end to calls for 389
　now is the time to use, for God 209
　proper use of, building up God's kingdom 117, 120, 208
　　giving for benevolent objects each week 548
　　putting into bank of heaven 83
　　sustaining institutions 173
　urgent calls for, at camp meetings 510, 511
　wrong ways of securing, pressing individuals 249
　　unfair dealing 249, 250
　See also Money; Property; Riches; Wealth.
Meat, apparent need for 20
Meditation and prayer, take time for 336
Meekness, description of 335
　of Moses 297
　spirit of, inestimable jewel 367
　opposite of discontent 334
　See also Humility.
Meekness and quietness a gem of high value 536
Meetings, small attendance at, should not discourage minister 322
Melchizedek, Abraham gives tithes to 393
Men of lofty integrity and justice in small matters 25
Mental power to be improved 157, 158
Mental powers, overtaxation of 149, 490
　See also Brain; Faculties; Intellect; Mind.
Mental suffering of sick 168
Mental work, diet for those engaged in 490
　nerves of emotion taxed by continual 490
Mercy, divine, slighted, by rebellious Israel 355
Meribah 301, 302
Message, grievous sin of rejecting 380
Mince pies, stomach no place for 21
Mind, and body, dealing with diseased, is nice work 184
　　intimate relation between 485, 486
　　reaction of, one on other, most mothers know nothing of 136
　　sickly and dwarfed, not to God's glory 486
　benefited by, being trained by daily tests 22
　　developing all the faculties 152, 153, 155
　　discipline, education, training 22
　　mild treatment and sympathy when discouraged 184
　　peace and happiness 169
　　relief of bodily pain 169
　　uniting labor with study 152, 153, 309, 310
　carnal, sinners must die to 475
　control of, by Satan through appetite 562
　diseased, physicians should know how to minister to 168, 169
　God would have His people be of same 360
　great deal of humanity's diseases have foundation in 184

misused by indulgence of appetite and passion 491
must have action 153
office of, allies finite to Infinite 136
  reacts on health of body 170
  sickness cured through 169, 184
susceptible of high cultivation 147
true independence of, differs from rashness 104, 105
See also Brain; Faculties; Intellect; Mental powers.

Minds, balancing, in right direction, a most important work 146
dealing with, danger of misjudging and erring in 104
  much study and earnest prayer needed for 146
  nicest of all work 104, 269
  youthful 131
duty of mothers to cultivate their 147
not to be purposeless, but accomplish good 147
of children, parents to take time to discipline 146-148
physician, associated with all classes of 184
  wanted who can minister to 168
Satan controls, not fully consecrated to God 300, 475

Ministers, called to be, Christ's representatives 422
  colaborers with God 31
  learners 557
  living epistles 31, 66
  shepherds 228, 229
  watchmen 242
counsel with brethren 66, 305
dangers and mistakes of, accepting hospitality without benefiting homes 232, 233, 308, 309
being wrongly influenced by reports and relatives 506, 507
carelessness in use of vocal organs 311
confining labor mostly to one locality 61
defying and provoking discussions 36-38, 212-221, 424-427
engaging in interests separate from soul winning 242
leaving interests unfinished 228, 231
publishing opponent's arguments 427
trusting to strength of prepared arguments alone 219, 220
using sensational methods 227
working merely for wages 555
disqualifications of, acting from impulse, passion, prejudice 237, 241-243
becoming too easily discouraged 322
cold and unsympathizing 187, 553
deficient in faith, hope, love 187
false dignity 287, 288, 309, 554
frivolity, trifling, jesting, joking 228, 233, 238, 241
guided by inclination rather than duty 243
having divided interests 242
indolence and pride 210, 256, 552, 553, 555, 557
indulging appetite 486-490
lacking experimental religion 553, 554

Ministers— *continued*
    lacking zeal, energy, perseverance 555
    losing courage when congregations are small 322, 323
    love of debate and controversy 212-217, 220
    ruling imperiously over flock 228
    selfishness 229, 232
    self-sufficiency, self-importance, self-confidence, independence 240, 417-419
    sharp, critical, exacting 238, 239, 323, 507
    shirking pastoral responsibilities outside of pulpit 240
    shunning burdens, responsibilities, care, privation 13, 14, 557
    studying own interests, convenience, pleasure 240, 555
    unconsecrated 243
  education of, one-sided 556, 557
  example of in Christian simplicity, tenderness, love 553
    in meeting opponents 220
    in self-denial 490
    in temperance 490
  needs of, close connection with God 323
    physical exercise 211, 309, 310, 489, 490
    realization of sacredness of calling 228
  pioneer, hardships of 256
  qualifications of, bearing message with fearlessness 195, 196, 229, 265-271, 302, 359, 507
    calm contemplation, thought, devotion 217
    capable of adapting teachings to people's needs 228
    converted 233, 556
    dealing justly, loving mercy, walking humbly before God 187
    faithful in home duties and relations 556
    holding natural appetites and passions in restraint 486
    integrity, intelligence, industry, energy, tact 553
    intelligent on, and living out health reform 311
    kind, considerate, courteous, sympathetic 417
    self-reliance and confidence in God 493, 494
    simplicity 554
    thoroughly furnished unto all good works 556
  to exemplify Christ by benevolence 490
  unconverted, hindrance to church and unbelieving neighbors 58
    preaching of, lacks spirituality 31, 32
    souls will condemn, in judgment 243
    spoil good fields for other workers 554
  wives of, destroying husbands' influence and usefulness 105, 106, 109
  work of, defend the truth 38, 213, 217, 220, 221, 424-427
    in dealing with church difficulties 104-111
    in house-to-house work 210, 232-234, 558
    in new fields 66, 203, 210, 406
    present truth to people 36, 257
    reveal Saviour to world 32
  young, careful lest they become exalted 320

Ministry, industry in 551-560
Miracles, at Meribah 301, 302
  giving of manna 340
  of Elijah on Mount Carmel 279-286
Missionary, only one, in all foreign countries (written in 1875) 404
  work requires full consecration 202-210
Mistakes, in premature moves in gospel work 110, 114
  turn into victories 495
Money, god of some professed Christians 544
  investment of, for high objects yields permanent enjoyment 208, 386
  love of, a snare 126, 127, 130
    leads to dishonesty 249, 250
    root of all evil 121, 122, 244
  worshiping of 544
  See also Means; Property; Riches; Wealth.
Monomania, cause of 33, 34
Moral perceptions to be aroused 142
Moses, accusations against 89, 90, 342, 345, 351, 355-357
  breaks tables of stone 298, 300, 301, 341
  compassion of, for Israel 352, 357, 358
  countenance of, reflects divine glory 354, 355
  failure of, in time of weakness 301, 302
  meekness of 319
  on Mount Sinai 296, 340, 341
  pleads for Israel 297, 298, 303, 304, 340, 341
  prayers of 297, 303, 304, 357, 358
  prostrates himself before God at time of rebellion 357
  rebellion against, by Korah and others, 339, 345-357
  renewing of tables a pledge to 354, 355
  self-denial of 89, 90, 406
  sorely tried 541
  typifies Christ 358
  vindicates his course 319
Mothers, and fathers in Israel, need of 198
  in every sense of word are needed 565
  influence of, seen in judgment 141, 568, 569
  injure daughters by not sharing burdens with them 152
  position of, more elevated than king's 565, 566
  responsibility of, consider children's characters of greatest consequence 562, 563, 566, 567
    educate children for usefulness 562, 563, 565, 566
    learn physical laws 568
    live to glorify God 565, 566
    plan amusement and work for children 152
    study simple but nutritious diet 568
    teach children temperance, self-denial, self-control 562-569
  rewarded, children will shine in heavenly courts 566
    in physical well-being and moral character of children 562, 563
  Satan leads, to devote time to frivolous matters 564
  to cultivate love for beautiful 137
  work of, sacred and important 562, 565, 567
  wrong course of, being slaves to fashionable dress 563

Mothers— *continued*
  encouraging intemperance 563
  encouraging self-indulgence, in children 141
  lacking interest in health matters 136
  loving children with idolatrous love 141
  neglecting children 562, 564, 568, 569
  remaining ignorant regarding duties 156
  seeking excitement of world 146, 147, 564
Motherhood, story reading detrimental to 152
Motives, all should carefully examine 512
  God weighs in balance of sanctuary 370
  men to be judged by 507
  selfish 191
  unselfish, service from 522, 528
Motto of Christian worker 541
Movement cure 76, 78
Murmuring, against leading brethren 312-315
  no time for 526
  of Israelites 342, 343
  over fleshless diet 171
  temptations to, in our day 358
Murmurings, against burden bearers 85, 87
  of inexperienced workers 321
Muscles, becoming weak 149
  well-regulated labor brings into exercise all 151
Music not to take place of practical subjects 156

NADAB AND ABIHU, dishonor sacred office 295
  on Mount Sinai 297
Names of believers graven on Christ's palms 251
Narcotics, abstinence from 569
Nations, unsettled state of, sign of end 202
Natural law, accountable beings can understand 161
  beauty of, appreciation of 335
  has tongue, speaks of God 333, 377
  leads soul to God 377
  true experience in harmony with 71
  See also Laws of nature.
Nature, human, characteristics of 361
  lessonbook for young children 137
  lessons from 333, 375
  reveals glory, power, wisdom, of God 377
Nature study by parents with children 137
Nature's path broad enough for Christian 63
Nazareth, people of, proverbial for wickedness 566
Needy, God tests us by sending, among us 524
  laying up treasures by aiding 249, 250
  See also Poor.
Neglect, of work for pleasure 26-28
  pharisaical, of youth 197
Nehemiah our example in meeting falsehoods 570-575
Neighbor, who is our? 512
Neighbors, duty to labor for 198, 385
Nerves, functions of 69, 70
  enfeebled, desire excitement 155
  of emotion taxed, of motion inactive 490

Nervous system, borrowing for present use from future resources of 487
 controlled by brain 69, 70
 effect of stimulants on 487
 undermined by use of tobacco 562
Nervousness in children, work and nature study will help 137, 138
Neutrality, in crisis a grievous crime 281, 282
 position of, impossible in God's service 327, 328
New York, cause in 48-53
Noah, intemperance in day of 162, 163
Nonprofessors, no excuse for 364-366
Novels and love stories, dwarf the intellect 152
 young ladies read, and lead useless lives 151, 152
 See also Reading.
Nurses and helpers to have sympathy and patience 182, 183

OBEDIENCE, results of, happiness, joy, health 161
 to natural law a necessary part of preparation for Christ's coming 161
Occupation of Adam and Eve 153
Offering, small, how made valuable 397
Offerings, Israel's, at yearly assemblies 546
 freewill 396, 413
 See also Benevolence; Giving; Liberality; Sacrifice; Tithes and offerings.
One-idea men 34
Opinions, personal stubbornness in maintaining 244
Opium, touch not, taste not, handle not 488

Opponents, avoid discussions with 424-428
 repeating false statements of 427
 unreasonable, how to treat 36-38, 427
 See also Debating; Discussions.
Opportunities, for service, golden, in speaking and acting at proper time 110
 in enlightening those needing present truth 541
 of Christian homes in giving cheer and help 539, 540
 neglected, imperil spiritual growth 540
Opposition, meeting, drives to God 256
 strengthens workers 495, 555
Organism, human, each organ of, has its work to do 310
Ornaments, all to deny themselves of needless 366
Ornamentation, called to account for hours spent in needless 189
Orphans, care of 511-513, 539
Overcomers, reward of 247
Overcoming, as Christ overcame 457, 491
 Christ our pattern in 380
 on appetite 490
 See also Victory.
Overeating, affects functions of mind 310, 311
 educated gourmands from babyhood through indulgence in 489
 evils of 489, 490
Overreaching in business 545
Overstudy, children injured by 137
 health lost through 149, 150, 155, 157, 490
Overwork, cause of discouragement 502, 504

Overwork— *continued*
  physical, and nonuse of brain results in feeble intellect 156-158
  physicians to guard against 182
  warning against 9-18, 128, 129, 178

PACIFIC COAST, establishment of press upon 504
Parables and parabolic sayings of Christ, beam and mote 465
  blind leading blind, 467, 554
  foolish rich man 545
  great supper 383
  lost sheep, silver 99, 100
  pearls before swine 425, 426
  prodigal son 100-104
  seed growing secretly 111-113
  strait gate and narrow way 527
  talents 385-387
  tares 113
  well of water springing up 84, 322, 381
Paralytic, healing of 168, 169
Parents, aged, children's duty to care for 230-232
  and teachers, duty of, to become acquainted with physical organism 136
    erroneous idea of, that continual study strengthens intellect 143
    harmful results of severe training by 132-134
    ignorance of, causes death of thousands of children 136, 137
    to have learned self-control, patience, forbearance, gentleness, love 131
    to instruct, cultivate, polish, refine children 142, 143
  best legacy of 399
  disqualifications of, dignified, cold, unsympathetic, lack of self-control 531-533
  evil tendencies and diseases of, transmitted to children 140, 567, 568
  examples of unfaithful, Aaron in indulging his sons 294, 295
  improper discipline by, arbitrary, which destroys children's will and individuality 132-134
    with continual censure and harsh words 531, 532
  mistakes of, allowing children to follow inclination instead of duty 26, 147, 148
    allowing children to grow up in ignorance 145
    allowing children to spend time in idleness 151
    indulging children's and own appetites 136, 141, 488, 489, 563, 564, 567, 568
    leaving children to think and act independently 133
    misspending time 144-146
    petting and indulging children 26, 143, 295, 367
    setting wrong example before children 246, 249
    teaching children intemperance 488, 489, 563
    too early and closely confining children to study 135-138, 142, 143, 148-150, 153, 155
    transferring means to unbelieving children 116-130
    treating trifling misdemeanors as grave sins 531
  neglect of aged, forfeits blessing of God 232
  proper discipline by, with commendation and encouragement 147, 148, 532

with self-control, prayer, patience, kindness 131, 132
with wisdom, calmness, firmness, determination 532
qualifications of, cultivating their minds 144, 145, 147
hearts in obedience to will of Christ 144
knowledge of laws of life and health 568
manifesting affection in associations with children 532
preserving simplicity in eating and dressing 144
responsibilities of, for salvation of children 146, 147
in teaching Sabbath school lesson to children 189
to develop children's mental powers 26
to develop strong character in children 144, 145
to educate children for practical life 25, 26, 145, 147
to make proper disposal of property and means 121-123
to see that children have firm constitutions 151
to study and teach health principles 136, 139-147, 568
should be honored by children 230-232, 294, 368
to teach children, at home until age of eight or ten 137
knowledge and love of nature 137
perseverance 147, 148
self-denial and self-control 132, 143, 144, 562, 567
that they eat to live, not live to eat 567
to control passion, deny appetite, overcome selfishness 564, 565
to expect and nobly overcome temptation and difficulties 143, 144
to have part in domestic duties 150-157
to respect and reverence parental authority 294
to respect experienced judgment and rightful authority 133
to take their exercise in doing something useful 148, 149
unfaithfulness of, accounts for children's rebellion against school and church discipline 294
brings dishonor and bitterness 141
consequences of, reach to children's children 528
results in children's and own eternal loss 145
to work in harmony with Sabbath school teachers 189
will stand face to face in judgment with children 568
See also Children; Family; Home; Husband; Wife.
Paris, Maine, murmuring in 313
Partiality is offensive to God 24
Parties and amusements, Satan ever instituting 564, 565
Parties and dress are time robbers 562-565
Passions, control of, brings mental and moral vigor 491
duty to control 183, 570
Pastor, duties of, in visiting 233
Pastries and rich foods, children permitted to eat 136
Path of the just is progressive 542
Patience, and sympathy in physicians 179, 180
Elijah's lesson in 290

Patience— *continued*
  in physicians and helpers 182-184
  need of, in teaching health reform 20, 21
  trial of, in humble work 81
  See also Self-control.
Patients at sanitariums, adapt prayers and testimonies to 166, 167
  all classes of characters and conditions 178
  appreciation of even one in twenty 180
  benefited by confidence in physicians and nurses 184
  harmed by offending words of physicians 181, 182
  lack of gratitude in 180, 181
  of our own faith frequently most difficult to manage 180, 181
  See also Sanitariums; Sick.
Patriarchs, longevity of 138-140
Pattern, Christ our perfect 58
Paul, conversion of 429, 430
  directed to church for knowledge regarding duty 430-433
  toils and trials of 406
People of God, angels are engaged in ministering to 575
  liability of being deceived 353
  true witness reveals condition of 254
  See also Church.
Perception, organs of, benumbed by intemperance 50, 51
Perfection of character a lifelong work 325, 326
  See also Character; Sanctification.
Persecution, preparation to meet 112
Perseverance, heaven not obtained without 338
  minister must not lack 556, 557
  need of, in God's work 496
  to teach young 147, 148
Peter denied the Man of Sorrows 416
Physical powers, inactive, the mental are overtaxed 148-150
  men who have good, should think as well as act 158
  neglect to strengthen 137
Physician, Christ as the all-healing 184
Physicians, dangers of, gathering unnecessary responsibilities 176, 177
  injuring health by too close confinement to professional work 182
  disqualifications of, harshness and abruptness 170
  duties of, to preserve strength 177, 178, 182
  may be powerful, agents for good in world 169
  need of, being freed from unnecessary burdens 177, 178
  necessary conveniences in health institutions 169
  qualifications of, calm, kind, cheerful, courteous to all under all circumstances 182, 183
  discernment, patience, kindness, love 184
  faith and spirituality 178
  firmness mingled with respectful courtesy 170
  knowing how to minister to diseased minds 169
  responsibilities of, as spiritual fathers 168
  tried by things that annoy, perplex, and try patience 182

work of, includes healing of body and mind 184
point patients to Christ 184
Physiology, little interest taken in 136
parents and teachers to understand 136, 140, 141, 568
Pillar of fire was a living memorial before Israel 340
Pioneers, hardships gave experience to 317
labors and sacrifices of 256, 317-320, 326, 327
Plague, Israelites smitten with 352
Plagues, seven last 473
Pleasure, desire for, allures from duty 24, 25
love of, cause of souls' perishing 198
lovers of, more than peace of Christ 370
dwarfed intellect of 377, 378
guilty of aggravating sins 366
sinful, denying Lord by 332
See also Amusements.
Poor, care for, a test of Christian character 547
Christ identified Himself with 173, 174
defending, and fatherless 538, 539
giving to, a blessing 381-383
worthy, duty toward 173, 511-521
sick among, to receive help 173
See also Needy; Unfortunates.
Popularity, danger of seeking 204, 296, 303, 340
Pork, forbidden as food 136
Position, dissatisfaction with 344
Possessions, offerings required in proportion to 405
See also Property.
Poverty at times a blessing 151
Power, moral, enfeebled by wrong habits 51
Powers of mind and body proportionately taxed 142, 143, 149-159, 490
Prayer, angels record 363
answer your own, as far as possible 378
benevolent acts are placed close beside 405
conditions of answer to, repentance and restoration 519, 520
examples of, Christ, entire night frequently 379
Elijah, for drought and then rain 263, 286
pioneers of message, nights of agonizing 326
for additional light on known duties 72-74
God hears every sincere 416
importance of, to young in meeting temptations 363, 364, 370
marked by angels 363, 364
meetings at sanitariums, character of 167
ministers of Christ to live life of 241
neglect of, those guilty of, sure to go astray 364
secret, importance of, to students 224, 225
kept from unconscious wrong through 363, 364
selfish as Balaam's 73
sincere, brings in touch with mind of Infinite 323
unceasing watchfulness and humble, only safety for young 374
united, great importance attached to 429
Preaching may be fluent, without melting heart 31
See also Discourses; Sermons.

Prejudice, against truth caused by abrupt manners 242
　danger of cultivating, against co-workers 306
Present, deal only with, not future 333
Presumption, Christ tested upon 372
　of Korah, Dathan, Abiram 344
　reject firmly first approach to 482-485
Prevarication, sin of 332
Price, infinite, paid for human family 372
Pride, feelings arise when anything touches 314
　of appearance 335
Pride and self-esteem in workers 552, 553
Principle, exercising, in small transactions a test of character 22
　youth, to be taught to act from 143, 144
　some are laughed out of 51
Privation, value of, to young ministers 318
Probation, night of, for Israelites after death of Korah 356
Prodigal, parable of 100-104
Profession, deeds count more than 525
Progress, Christians to make constant 331
Promises of God not for man in a presumptuous course 482
Promptness, importance of, in crisis 497-500, 505
　See also Punctuality.
Property, belonging to God, bequeathed to children 116-130
　sacrifice of, for cause 389
　See also Means; Money; Possessions; Riches; Wealth.
Prophecy, study of, in school 160

Prophets, of Baal, at Carmel 280-285
　slain by Elijah 286, 288
　slain by Jezebel 276
Prosperity, ascribed to favor of idols 263
　dangers in 479
　fruit of consecrated effort 175
　Lord sometimes tests His people with 307, 547
　withdrawn because of neglect of the afflicted 517
　why removed 307
Publications, denominational, foreign, to be multiplied 204, 205, 211
Publishing houses, duty of, toward apprentices in 194
　selection of help for 193, 194
　workers in, unfaithfulness in 190
Publishing work, increase of, predicted 90-92
Punctuality and decisive action at right time 499
　See also Promptness.

RACE, human, physical decline of 139, 486-488
Reading, effects of harmful, blunts conscience 472
　makes sin appear less repulsive 472
　time for reflection not to be occupied in 15
　unprofitable, exciting love stories and novels 151, 152
　storybooks 81
　See also Novels.
Reasoners, close, are few 142
Rebellion, of Korah, Dathan, and Abiram 339-358
　steps in, jealousy and envy 346
Redemption, cost of 371
　plan of, made plain to Abraham 369

magnitude of, eclipsed by covetousness 385
man's co-operation in, for his own good 390, 391
sacrifice is foundation of 387
work of, began where Adam failed 486
Refinement, natural, not artificial 375
See also Culture.
Refining process 541, 543
Reflection to be encouraged 142
Reform, caution needed in introducing 20, 21
duty to aid in carrying forward 540
Reforms, greater interest in, would increase influence of church tenfold 171
Reformers, better one step short than one step beyond 21
parents as 562-567
we are 159
Relatives in the church 53-56
Relatives and home, leaving, to work for God 500
Relaxation necessary 182
Religion, Christian, effect of, on character 374
claims of 45
conducive to health 172
definition of 516
ennobling, purifying 377
points to God as magnet to north 45
Remarks, light, trivial, spoil interest 247
Remuneration, suitable 178
Repentance, opportunity for, to followers of Korah 351, 352
See also Confession.
Reports, never to be influenced by 506
Reproof, always hurts human nature 329

cutting, of congregation, making innocent suffer with guilty 507, 508
despisers of, in Israel 358-362
despising straight testimony of 272
disagreeable duty of giving 328
manner of giving 55, 92, 93, 359
necessary to prevent demoralization in church 359
Satan would prevent 261
to children, without encouragement 532
through testimonies, duty to give 314
from God through humble instrument 257
resentment against 312
result of despising 230, 231
unwise sympathy encourages rebellion and annuls 313, 328, 359
Resentfulness, spirit of 536
Resistance to Satan's attacks, Christ's continual 480
is success 483
Resolutions, making 542, 543
Respiration promoted by frequent bathing 70
Responsibility, fearful, of a soul winner 555
of parents toward children 145
shunning 9, 13, 14, 95, 234, 240, 558-560
Responsibilities, benefit of bearing 493-495, 499
lead out of self and give interest in others' woes 536
Rest for young, how to arrange 223
Restitution, duty to make, for dishonesty 550
Results in work for souls 248

Review and Herald publishing house, laborers in 190-195
   selection of 90
   unbelieving 191
   unfaithfulness in 86, 87
Reward of, faithfulness 88
  physicians for efforts to help sick 180
  soul winning 247
Ribbon of blue 171
Rich, fear of, that spread of truth might demand money 386
Rich man, parable of 154, 545
Riches, curse to youth deprived of practical education 150
  danger in love of 112, 113
  deceitfulness of, how to get free from 545
  love of, unfits men to love God 478
  object of 117, 154, 546, 548, 549
  safe bank for 90, 249, 250, 546
  unreliable nature of 549
  See also Means; Money; Property; Wealth.
Riding, benefit of 75
Right, hard to wait for vindication of 327
  lack of decision to stand for 272
Rights, individual, of members of family, trampling on 528
Righteousness of Christ consists in right actions from pure, unselfish motives 528
Risk, workers called to run 316
Robbery of God limits God's blessings proportionately 395
Romance, reading of, unfits for real life 152
Rules, children under iron 132
  regulating hours for study 138
  See also Discipline.

SABBATHKEEPERS, conformity of, to world 51
  See also Commandment keepers.
Sabbath reform, opposers of 570-575
Sabbath school, members to attend public worship 188, 189
  power of grace, needful in the 188
  study of, lesson in home 189
Sacrifice, complete, of all for Christ 45
  everything worth gaining secured by 255
  foundation of plan of salvation 387
  of feelings required of us 500
  spirit of, call for, to win heavenly treasure 381, 481
    in pioneers of cause 256, 317-320, 326, 327
    in sanitarium workers in early days 173-175
  See also Benevolence; Giving; Liberality; Offerings; Self-denial.
Saints, glory of, a terror to wicked 355
Salt, free use of 21
  symbolic meaning of 559
Salvation, working out our own 549
Samaritan, parable of 512, 513, 523, 524
Samaritan woman, conversation of Christ with 217, 218, 322
Sanctification not work of a moment 325
  See also Character; Perfection.
Sanitarium, managers, high calling and influence of 174
  workers, early experiences of 175

need change from strenuous work 182
need necessary conveniences 169, 170
need reasonable wages 175-178
need religious principle 166, 167

Sanitariums, amusements and entertainments at 172
assignment of stockholders in 173, 176
dangers of, imitating popular institutions 166
losing sight of object 169
debts of 174-176
economy in operating 169, 175
jealousy of, of other health institutions 184, 185
no lack of helpers in 177, 178, 182
not established to obtain money 169
parlor talks at 181-184
patients at, peculiar beliefs not to be urged upon 166, 167
religion not detrimental to 172
physicians in, qualifications of 78, 79, 167, 168, 170, 178, 181-184
to exercise sympathy and patience 178-180, 184
to preserve strength 177
prayer meetings at, character of 166, 167
purpose of, disseminate light and advance reform 165, 167, 170
heal diseased mind, soul, body 168, 169, 184

Sabbathkeepers not to be special burden to 180
See also Patients; Sick.

Sarcasm, places on enemy's ground 220
use of, by preachers 212, 216

Sarepta, Elijah's visit to 274, 288

Satan, agencies of, ministers who have rejected truth 571
as prince of world, disturbed most by our knowledge of his devices 572
seat of, in wicked cities 110
conquered foe since the cross 480
devices, snares, wiles of, appears as angel of light 456, 483
discouragement 343
doubts regarding testimonies 255
perplexes and discourages God's workers 343, 344
worldly entanglements, error, superstition 479, 480
driven from heaven with third of angels 115
instills discontent and spreads disaffection among angels 328
most active where most is done to save souls 469
origin, history of, strife between loyal angels and sympathizers of 328
power of, bounds set to, through Christ 283
can pervert, judgment, sight, hearing 351
controls unconverted minds 328
increases in effectiveness, 570, 571
over minds, increased hundredfold 328
safety from, by being constantly on guard 572
in continual resistance 480
in firm rejection to first approach of 482, 483
unsafe to enter into controversy or to parley with 483
See also Wiles of Satan.

Saviour a conqueror of hearts 477
School age of children 137, 143
Schools, establishment of, on right plans, would prevent many unbalanced minds 153
    industries and manual training in, agricultural and manufacturing establishments for 153, 155
        cooking and dressmaking 156
        household labor 153
    physical labor in, promotes health of students 159
    See also Education.
Schoolroom, ill-formed seats in 143
    improperly ventilated 135, 143
    little children's, should be in open air, amid nature 137
School of Christ, ceasing to learn in, selling birthright 223
Seal of God received by those who feel deeply regarding sin 266, 267
Sealing time, wrongs felt deeply in 266, 267
Second advent, faith in, waning 255, 256
    message of, now going to world 388
    signs of, as in Noah's and Lot's day 163, 164
Seed of truth planted too deep 35
Self, entire subjection of, lacking 29
    mixed with efforts of some ministers 552
    theme of conversation 235
    warfare against, greatest battle 106
Self-confidence, warning against 305-309
Self-control, cultivated by many who do not profess love of God 336
    Eden redesigned through 491
    greatest conquest 182, 183
    help those weak in, by example 489
    in teachers 135
    parents to possess 131, 132
    physicians' need of 182, 183
    power of will in gaining 488
    to be taught children 562
    See also Patience.
Self-deception, condition of many 475
    great danger of, history of Israelites presents, 361
    Laodiceans honest in 252, 253
    of, Israel as to position of Moses 347
    Korah 349
Self-denial, Christian's portion in this life 481
    efficiency through 490, 491
    essential condition of discipleship 388
    required 522
    See also Sacrifice.
Self-examination, duty of, to become familiar with motives 507
    reveals weak points in character 321, 322
Self-forgetfulness, virtue of 539, 540
Self-importance must be overcome 65, 66, 244
Self-indulgence, habits of, formed in childhood 489, 564
    prevalence of, in world 563, 564
    See also Indulgence.
Selfishness, constant danger of cherishing 308, 309
    incrusted in 535
    vanishes in proportion to love of Christian heart 382-384
Self-knowledge, need of 321, 322

Self-love causes barrenness of soul 329-338
Self-reliance, duty to cultivate 493-496
  to be encouraged 123
Self-sufficiency ruinous 244
Sensation, ministers building upon 227
Senses are avenues of the soul 507
Sensibilities, how to preserve 50, 51
Sensitiveness to be unselfish 530
Sentimentalism, denying Jesus by 332
  fruit of novel reading 152
Separation from church not to be premature 114
Sermons, on practical subjects make work of tenfold value 237, 238
  of Christ, furnish discourses always appropriate 214, 215
    little known by argumentative preachers 216
  See also Discourses; Preaching.
Service, intelligent, best glorifies Christ 160
Seventh-day Adventists, benevolence of 49
Severity, in reproof, necessary 301-303
  undue, of ministers 108
Sewing, teachers of 155, 156
  women ignorant of 156
Sheep, lost, finding of, causes joy, not murmuring and censure 99
Shepherd, when the sheep bear burdens of 234
Sick, attendants of, sure reward awaits 512, 513
  benefited by, prayer for 184, 185
  true religion 172
  harmed by stubbornness 67-79
  mental suffering of 168
  See also Patients; Sanitariums.
Sickness, result of, disregarding light 171, 172
  imprudent exposure 19
  transgression 164
  See also Disease.
Sifting, example of Korah 347
Signs betokening last days 164
Sight-seeing for pleasure 26, 27
Silver, lost piece of 99
Simplicity, and humility, getting above, 306, 307
  instead of false dignity for ministers 554
  nature a lesson on 375
  of character will give happiness 476, 477
Sin, calling, by right name a disagreeable duty 328
  duty to reprove 265-269
  familiarity with, mind educated to 471, 472, 476
  God hates 272
  humility in view of, to be sought 265-267, 357, 358
  instances of, covetousness 544-551
    forgetfulness 12
    murmuring against God 302
    rejecting present truth greater than of Sodom 380
  See also Reproof.
Sins, cherishing of, unawares 543
  church responsible for individual 265-270
Skin, breathes 74
  thorough cleansing of 70, 71
Sleep, hours of, to be regulated 152
  loss of, sin when caused by selfish plans 242
  spending precious hours in 152
Snares of Satan, Christ's followers must understand 435
  God's servants not awake to 196

Snares of Satan— *continued*
  interpreted to be providence of God 491
  more subtle now than in temptations of Christ 480
  special, for commandment keepers and remnant church 456
  See also Satan, devices, snares, wiles of.
Snuff, use of 21
Sodom, drunkenness in 163
Soldiers, faithful, without cowardice 316
Soul, guard avenues of, against Satan 324, 476, 507
  moral powers of, faith, hope, love 187
  winners, apostles as 27
  thorough conversion of 64
Sower, gospel 111-113
Spices, diet to be free from 21, 136, 488, 563, 564
Spiritualism, influence of, debases, Christ and Bible 484, 485
  power of 40
  satanic delusion 418
  views of, concerning Christ 484, 485
  See also Angels, fallen.
Spiritualists, danger of discussion with 485
Spirituality, lack of, in preaching 31
  physicians to be men of 178
  zeal encouraged instead of 217
Standard, God's word is our 528
Steadfastness cultivated by habits of fidelity 22
  See also Firmness.
Step toward heaven 379
Stewards of God, all are 385
  to discharge duty regarding means before death 117
Stimulants, effects of 487, 488, 569
Stomach harmfully affected by eating irregularly and between meals 136
Straying, duty of Christians toward 99
  See also Erring.
Strength, physical, accountability for 164, 165, 177, 182
  poor man's capital 400
  value of 150
  spiritual, in proportion to love and good works 526
Stubbornness of Israelites in spite of their sin 357
Students, amusements of, should harmonize with physical law 142
  danger of, becoming, engrossed with study 224
  being exposed to manifold temptations in associations 148, 149, 155
  exciting amusements 155
  in being flattered 224-226
  in neglecting home duties 221-224
  health of 149, 150
  influence of 155
  physical labor for 137, 138, 142, 148-160, 489, 490
  prayer a necessity for 224, 225
Study, and exercise to correspond 137, 138
  and labor for students 148, 149
  continual, for children 137, 142, 143, 155
  excessive, destroys health 149, 150
  leads to moral weakness 155
  unfits for usefulness 153, 224
  needed to deal with youth 146
Subjection necessary among Christ's followers 360
Submission, in judgment, Paul teaches 360

Isaac an example of 368
perfect, takes time 538
Subordination, angels in 325
Success, in sanitariums 175, 176
  indolence robs some workers of 551-560
Suffering, caused by transgression of natural laws 161
  Christ lived to save others from 54
  greatest proof of God's love 369
  of Christ 18, 371, 372
Sufficiency in Christ alone 543
Sugar, moderate amount of 21
Superficiality, age of 143
Supper, parable of 383
Supplication, Moses prevailed in 298
  of Christ for man 379
Surrender, unconditional, of heart and affections 45
Swine, flesh of, forbidden as food 136
Sympathy, duty to cultivate 532
  for, Aaron 341, 342
    Korah, Dathan, Abiram 345, 350
  those who commit wrong 267
  undeserving 114, 229
  friendly, brings blessings 527
  needed by, patients 182, 183
  poor and afflicted 519
  souls around us 527, 531
  of, Job for friends 530
  worldlings shames Christians 524
  sanctified, such as angels have for mortals 539
Satan found, in heaven 328
selfish desire for 239, 507
sharers of sin by 354, 359
simplicity of truth leads to 522
to be manifested, among brethren 560
  by sanitarium helpers 182, 183
unsanctified, not prompted by God 313
unwise, carries out purpose of Satan 328
  destroys souls 329
  encourages rebellion against God 258
encourages wrongs 325, 507
See also Compassion.

TABERNACLE, glory of God upon 349, 352, 357
  transportation of 345
Talent, how to develop 56, 57
Talents, accountability for improvement of 534
  parable of 386, 387
  result of nonimprovement of 128
Tares and wheat commingled 113-115
Taste, educate, to habits of temperance 489
  God provided palatable food for 50
Tatting in relation to domestic work 151
Tea and coffee, bear clear testimony against 21
  create appetite for tobacco and liquor 488, 563, 569
  stimulating effect of 487
  touch not, taste not, handle not 488
Teachers, danger of mistaken discipline by 133, 134
  disqualifications of, unapproachable, harsh, censorious 134
  habits and principles of, more important than literary qualifications 135
  need knowledge of physiology and health laws 136, 141, 142
    physical exercise in open air 489, 490

Teachers— *continued*
  privilege of, molding minds and characters of youth 135
  qualifications of, calm, kind, manifesting forbearance 131
    companionship with students in play, joys, sorrows, work 134, 135
    firmness of character 135
    having equal interest in pupils' physical, mental, moral, spiritual education 135
    love for pupils manifested in looks, words, acts 135
    perfect self-control 131, 135
  to teach, cooking and sewing 156
    different branches of study and labor 155, 156
  work of, give attention to physical, mental, moral influences 132
    give special attention to cultivation of weaker faculties 132
    teach children to make right use of blessings 564
Temperament, and disposition, relation of, to religion 504
  calmness of, in physicians 183
Temperance, absolute, only safety 488
  begins in, habits of family 488, 562
    home 568
  Christ endured long fast to teach 486, 488, 489
  examples of strict, ministers to be 490
  in all things 62, 63, 561
  lessons in, from John the Baptist 61-64
  principles to be implanted in youth 567
  saving souls by example of 489
  strict, essential for health 487
  woman's influence regarding 141
  work, importance of mothers in 562-570
  workers, tobacco users as 569
  See also Intemperance.
Temple, body as a 63
Temptation, avoid running into 45, 144
  Christ conquered, in our behalf 372, 526
  increases unless appetite is conquered 491, 492
  invited by, careless words and deportment 378
    idle moments 148
    needless exposure to it 482, 483
    worldly association 111
  no divine aid against invited 47
  pleasure parties a source of 564
  power of, measured by Christ's anguish in wilderness 486
  resistance to, a duty 378
  answer own prayer by 378
    by repulsing enemy with word 482
    continual, only hope of victory 480
  safeguards against, cultivate a steady uniform, unwavering energy 46
    guard avenues of soul 324
    prayer 364
    watchfulness and prayer 373
  to indulge appetite, Adam fell through 139
    race enfeebled through succumbing to 139
  strength of 486
Temptations, beset all God's true children 526
  of Christ in the wilderness 372, 374, 380

overcome in our behalf, 372, 477, 478, 526
upon love of the world 477, 478
upon three great leading allurements 372
Tempted, dealing with 265, 266
Tenderness, in helpers at sanitarium 170
most effectual in child training 532
spirit of, indispensable in work for souls 108
Test, final, prepared by God for all 230, 231
Testimonies, acceptance of, opens door of heart to Saviour 257
despisers of, left in blindness 257-260
expressions of doubt of, lie cause of vanity 313
hatred of, because cherished sins are reproved 266, 314
brings blindness 266
motive, object, influence of 314, 324, 361
must live in church 269
object of, to bring unity to church 361
of reproof from God, not man 257
origin of, Spirit of God has spoken 314
plain, raised question, "Who told Sister White?" 314
rejection of 255
revealed by Spirit of God 314
straight, must be revived and will cause separation 324, 361
to question, is to insult Spirit of God 314, 315
unbelief in, shuts away light 255
why given 254, 356, 358-361
youth should read 362
Textbooks, nature's treasures as 137
Theory of message, dwelling too much upon 214-220
Thinkers, logical, are few 142
Third angel's message, extent of 236, 388
relation of health reform to 161
Thought, minds given to loose, must change 474
Thoughts, brought into captivity and subjection to Christ 83, 336, 538
dwelling on self bring unhappiness 330-335
God has full knowledge of all 82
not to dwell on, of self, or unhappy experience 330-335
pure, when in captivity to Christ 83
should be in obedience to God's will 474
to dwell on God 476
vain, responsibility to God for indulgence of 82
Time, accountability for 146
redeeming, in making wrongs right 550
shortness of, education to be gained in view of 158, 159
solemnity of present 53
use of, in Review office 24
wasted in, gloomy musings 337
pleasure seeking 378
wasted, is waste of intellect 146
youth accountable for 222
Times, perilous, we are in 53
Tithe, Abraham paid, to Melchizedek 393
paying not to be made compulsory 396
required by God 394

Tithe— *continued*
  robbery of, is recorded in heaven 394
Tithes and offerings, blessing attending payment of 381-383, 395, 404
  faithfulness in, would fill treasury 389, 390, 408, 409
  robbing God in 269, 394, 409, 510, 546
  unfaithfulness in, withholds blessing 409
  See also Offerings.
Tithing system, beautiful in simplicity and equality 388, 409
  blessing to man 405
  founded upon a principle as enduring as God's law 404
  not now repealed but extended 392
  of divine origin 388
  reaches back beyond days of Moses 393
Tobacco, and liquor, positive testimony against 21
  appetite for, created by use of tea and coffee 488, 563, 569
  slavery of 562
  is more subtle poison than liquor 562, 569
  revolution regarding, necessary for temperance cause 569
  touch not, taste not, handle not 488, 561
  unpleasant and dangerous to remain amid fumes of 562
  using, binds victims in stronger slavery than liquor 562
  by professed Christians 569
  creates appetite for liquor 488, 489, 563
  debases mental and moral powers 561
Trade, dishonesty in 249, 250

Trades, schools to teach 153, 155, 156
Transformation, entire, needed 522
Transgression, ignorance no excuse for 162
  one small, destroyed allegiance of first parents 324
Translators, young ladies might qualify as 204
Treasure, earthly, affection upon 250
  cannot be follower of Christ with affection upon 478
  ever planning to increase 385
  zeal for 208
  heavenly, sacrifice called for to win 481
  laid up in heaven 546
  by aiding needy 249, 250
Treasury of God, everyone may have part in filling 389, 412
  filled by systematic benevolence fully carried out 389, 390, 409
  forced replenishing of, displeasing to God 413
  impoverished by neglect in payment of tithe and pledges 409
Trials, benefits of, develop character for heaven 115
  develop Christian graces 416
  develop strength to do and to suffer 67
  discipline and refine 115, 541
  brooding over 332, 335
  cause of, family communities 55, 56
  inactivity 235, 236
  necessary to bring us to God 541
  personal, magnifying 240

repeated until victory is won 542
Trifling, angels grieved by 191, 192
    conscience blunted by 225
    lowers standard 27
    this is no time for 474
Trouble, borrowing 332
    imaginary 335
    taxing effect of 503
Trust in God, Elijah's lack of 290
Truth, accepted, bears fruit in righteousness 59
    advancement of, hindered by unintelligent conversation 331
    boasting of, yet denying in works 210, 211
    clearer when backed by a few strong proofs 36
    extension of, must be world wide 181
    how to be presented 331, 334
    obscured by detailed argument 35
    sowing seed of, with care, anxiety, self-denial 210
Twentieth part of what we might do 407

UNBELIEF, danger of cherishing 225, 226, 258, 259, 343, 344
    God will not remove all occasion for 255, 258
    gradually gains power over mind 313
    of Hebrews in requiring golden calf 340
Unbelievers, conversation with, while unprepared 331-334
    friendship with, dangers in 39, 40, 245
    neglecting 198
Unfaithfulness of colaborers, result of 17

Unfortunates, duty toward 511-527
    God tests by sending, among us 524
    taking advantage of 513-520
    See also Poor.
Unhappiness, ignorance of life's duties a cause of 156
    See also Happiness, marred.
Usefulness brings healthful pleasure 151

VENTILATION, danger from lack of 143, 562
    necessity of in schoolrooms 135-138, 143
Vermont, cause in 116-130
Vice, among youth in schools 148, 149, 155
    debasing, parents will face children concerning 568
    increase of, result of indulgence of appetite 486
Victory, frequently lost through delay 498
    gained through, continual resistance against Satan's attacks 480
    merits of Christ 338
    working 436
    of Christ is pledge of ours 457
    See also Overcoming.
Victories, God will give His truth 574
Views, gathering up, detrimental to God's ministers 312
Vigor, mental and moral, through control of passions 491
Vindication, impatience does not hasten 327
Vine, Christ the living 522
Visiting homes more important than preaching 558, 559
Vital force, God endows man with 138, 139

Vitality increased by mental activity 157
Voice, duty to cultivate 311
  love to be expressed in 534

WALKING benefits of 75-78
  in light, meaning of 436
Warfare, Christian life a constant 253
  some will not venture in Christian 316
Watchfulness, and prayer constant 473
  necessity of continual 570, 572
Wealth, curse, when depriving youth of practical education 150
  fear that spreading of truth might demand 356
  See also Property; Riches.
Wheat and tares 113-116
White, Elder James, warned concerning preservation of health, October 25, 1869 9-15
  characteristics, clear foresight, judgment 95
    self-sacrificing for cause 85, 87
    zeal and devotion to God's cause 505
  difficulties and hardships of, bearing responsibilities shunned by others 9-13, 16-18, 95, 493, 500-504
    censure and injustice from brethren 85, 89, 96, 509
    discouragement due to pressure of care and affliction 261, 502, 504
    lack of time for study, meditation, prayer 85
  help and encouragement for, angels brought power to lighten, heal, bless 505
    especially qualified of God for specific work 89
    remarkable evidences of God's care, love, power 292, 505
  mistakes of, complaining of brother minister's neglect of duty 501
    consenting to carry burdens which others should have borne 500, 501
    giving way to despondency and distrust of God 96-98, 292
    speaking impulsively and with severity 86, 501, 508
  responsibilities and labors of, as counselor 15, 317, 503
    bearing pointed testimony 261, 502
    carrying burden of early leadership alone 500, 501
    in connection with publishing work 16, 17, 19, 20, 96
White, Elder and Mrs. James, difficulties and hardships of, prejudice, false reports, opposition 258-261, 305, 311-315
  Satan's special plans to destroy usefulness of 11
  struggles with poverty 317, 318
  labors of, at campmeetings 16-18
    bearing plain reproof and counsel to God's people 258-262, 292, 314, 315
    entirely for cause 319
    for Health Institute 174-176
    in health reform work 16
White, Ellen G., discouragement of, because messages were unheeded 292
  broadening of missionary work, receives vision regarding, December 10, 1871 202-209

White, Ellen G.— *continued*
  education, writes on proper 131-160
  gives reproof and counsel to young minister and wife, August 12, 1873 304-329
  receives vision concerning expansion of work, January 3, 1875 570
  responsibilities and labors of, in reproving wrongs of God's people 314, 315
Widows, duty to 511-527
Wife, ignorance of, of domestic duties 156
  individuality of, to be respected 245
  influence of, husband swayed by 533, 535
    unconsecrated, upon husband 109
  See also Husband; Marriage.
Wiles of Satan, servants of God not awake to 196
  See also Satan, devices of.
Will, of child, to be guided, not forced or broken 133
  passions are to be controlled by 183
  power, resolutely call, to aid 545
  strengthened by God's grace 488
Willfullness, spirit of 534-536
Wills, duty, in regard to making 116-127, 129, 130
Wine, fermented, use of 488, 564
  by Aaron's sons 295
Woman, lot of, embittered by man's abuse of God-given supremacy 484
  position of, designed by God as husband's equal 484
    God-given, left vacant by reaching for other positions 484
    more sacred than of king on throne 483, 566
    since the Fall, in subjection to man 484
  women, work of, educate children for this world and next 483, 565
    in home, most sacred and elevated 79, 80
    in temperance cause 141, 488, 489, 562
    sacredness of 565
    set worthy example for children 566
Women's rights, movement of 565
Word of God daguerreotype of God and man 538
Words, apples of gold in pictures of silver 109
  of commendation and approval by mothers 532
Work, of God, calls for men of lofty integrity 25
  delayed, if all fallacies are investigated 38
  See also Cause of God.
  physical, mistaken ideas regarding dignity of 156-159
  and mental, combined 148-160
  See also Exercise; Labor, physical.
Workers, failures and mistakes of, conversation, light, trifling, nonsensical 473, 474
  forwardness in reproving those of experience 320, 321
  overworking mentally and and physically 490
    self-confidence 320, 321
    starting work without completing 555

Workers— *continued*
- in new fields, to prove themselves 64, 66
  - commence efforts in, not in churches 203
  - praise not to be expected by 474
  - promise to, of Eden regained through self-denial 491
  - qualifications of, burden for souls 557
    - consecration, energy, moral integrity, and strong purpose 23, 558
    - willingness to leave friends and relatives 500
- Working classes, mistakes of 157, 158
- Workmen, afflictions, temptations, trials, are God's 115
- World, harmony with, makes us enemies of God 63
  - vast hospital 562
- Worldliness, warning regarding 41
- Worldlings, friendship with, danger of 42, 43
- Worthies, three 47
- Writings as medium of uplift to others 96, 97
- Wrongs, church responsible for individual 265, 270
  - unpleasant burden to reprove 314
  - unsanctified sympathy makes one sharer of 325, 359

YOUNG, men and women, accountable to God for light received 363
- God wants affections, obedience, devotion of 364, 365
- spiritual weakness of many, deplorable 379
- to learn other languages 204
- men, counsel to 221-227
  - dangerous and helpful amusement for 222, 223
  - duty of, to be burden bearers, 202, 203
  - not to commence efforts in churches 203, 204
  - responsible for privileges enjoyed 222
  - trades to be learned by 156
  - training of, for ministry 160
  - training of, for service 159, 160
- women, as translators 204
  - neglecting essentials of practical life 150
  - simple, plain dress for, recommendation of 376
Youth, appeal to 362-380
- dangers of, at school, association with many 197
- disregard of warning testimonies 362-364, 378
- following inclination rather than duty 199, 221, 373, 379
- frivolity, jesting, and laughing 222
- ignorance and neglect of duties 373
- improper association 42, 43, 125
- in gaining education 224, 225
- indulgence, flattery, indolence, warp character 148, 149, 226, 364
- lack of stability 379
- light regard for solemn responsibilities 370
- love of approbation 225
- love of dress and display 364, 366, 367, 370, 376, 379
- love of pleasure 364, 366, 378
- moral pollution 149
- neglecting Bible study and prayer 364

perverted ideas concerning religion 374, 375
Satan binds eyes, diverts from God 125, 222, 223, 374, 379
self-gratification 370, 371
Ellen G. White contemplated condition of, with sadness 366, 367
exhorted to, arise, shake off indifference and stupor 380
  awake to need of divine strength 373
  compare life with Master's 371-380
  elevate thoughts and words above world 371
  excel in seeking for inward adornment 367, 376, 377
  feed on God's word 374
  place affections on Christ and heaven 362
  resist temptation 378
  watch, pray 374
faculties of, if properly cultivated, qualify for trust 367
guilt of, proportionate to light and privileges 365, 366
habits grow with growth of 143
have no true sense of danger 373, 374
highest duty of, in home 80
if watchful and prayerful, God will keep safe 373
influence of, on other's minds and characters 363, 364
  directed by angels if sincerely prayerful 363, 364
  exerted, is recorded in heaven 363
  in home 80
  might be elevating 367
  mighty if character is right 199
is sowing time 363
labors for, by church at headquarters 198, 199
may be workers if they will 370
must sacrifice to obtain eternal life 371
now decide and shape own destinies 363
opportunity of, now to form character for heaven 376
responsibilities of, for opportunities to influence for right 378
  for testimonies of warning and counsel 362, 363
  severity in 133
  to do all possible to save fellow mortals 370
  to help one another to be faithful 379
  to include all faculties 223, 224
  to lighten home cares 79-81
training of, in self-denial and self-control will meet faithful record kept 363, 364, 370

ZEAL, false, of ministers failing to cultivate spirituality 217